Series V, No. 44

Department of Economic and Social Affairs

Statistics Division

T5-AWJ-463

World Statistics Pocketbook 2020 edition

Containing data available
as of 30 June 2020

United Nations, New York, 2020

The **Department of Economic and Social Affairs** of the United Nations is a vital interface between global policies in the economic, social and environmental spheres and national action. The Department works in three main interlinked areas: (i) it compiles, generates and analyses a wide range of economic, social and environmental data and information on which United Nations Member States draw to review common problems and to take stock of policy options; (ii) it facilitates the negotiations of Member States in many intergovernmental bodies on joint courses of action to address ongoing or emerging global challenges; and (iii) it advises interested Governments on the ways and means of translating policy frameworks developed in United Nations conferences and summits into programmes at the country level and, through technical assistance, helps build national capacities.

Note

The designations employed and the presentation of the material in the present publication do not imply the expression of any opinion whatsoever on the part of the United Nations concerning the legal status of any country or of its authorities, or the delimitations of its frontiers. The term "country" as used in this report also refers, as appropriate, to territories or areas. The designations of country groups are intended solely for statistical or analytical convenience and do not necessarily express a judgement about the stage reached by a particular country, territory or area in the development process. Mention of the names of firms and commercial products does not imply endorsement by the United Nations. The symbols of United Nations documents are composed of capital letters and numbers.

The term "country" as used in the text of this publication also refers, as appropriate, to territories or areas.

Visit the United Nations World Wide Web site on the Internet:
For the Department of Economic and Social Affairs,
    http://www.un.org/esa/desa/
For statistics and statistical publications,
    http://unstats.un.org/unsd/
For UN publications, https://shop.un.org/

ST/ESA/STAT/SER.V/44
United Nations Publication
Sales No. E.20.XVII.11
ISBN: **978-92-1-259149-0**
eISBN: **978-92-1-005063-0**
Print ISSN: **2411-8915**
eISSN: **2411-894X**

JX
1977
.A2
2020

All queries on rights and licenses, including subsidiary rights, should be addressed to United Nations Publications Customer Service, PO Box 960, Herndon, VA 20172, USA, e-mail: order@un.org, web: https://shop.un.org/

Contents

World, Regional and Country profiles

10,2020

Contents (*continued*)

Contents (*continued*)

Explanatory notes

The following symbols and abbreviations have been used in the *World Statistics Pocketbook*:

.	A point is used to indicate decimals.
...	Data are not available or not applicable.
~0.0	Not zero, but less than half of the unit employed.
–~0.0	Not zero, but negative and less than half of the unit employed.
%	Percentage
000	Thousands
Assist.	Assistance
Bol. Rep.	Bolivarian Republic
CIF	Cost, Insurance and Freight
CO_2	Carbon dioxide
const.	Constant
CPI	Consumer price index
Dem. Rep.	Democratic Republic
est.	Estimate
F	Females
FOB	Free on board
GDP	Gross domestic product
GNI	Gross national income
GVA	Gross value added
ISIC	International Standard Industrial Classification
ISO	International Organization for Standardization
Km^2	Square kilometres
M	Males
nes	Not elsewhere specified
pop.	Population
Rep.	Republic
SAR	Special Administrative Region
UN	United Nations
UNHCR	Office of the UN High Commissioner for Refugees
United Kingdom	United Kingdom of Great Britain and Northern Ireland
United States	United States of America
UNSD	United Nations Statistics Division
US$/USD	United States dollars

The metric system of weights and measures has been employed in the *World Statistics Pocketbook*.

The *World Statistics Pocketbook* is an annual compilation of key economic, social and environmental indicators, presented in one-page profiles. This edition includes profiles for the 30 world geographical regions and 232 countries or areas. Prepared by the United Nations Statistics Division of the Department of Economic and Social Affairs, it responds to General Assembly resolution 2626 (XXV), in which the Secretary-General is requested to supply basic national data that will increase international public awareness of countries' development efforts.

The indicators shown are selected from the wealth of international statistical information compiled regularly by the Statistics Division and the Population Division of the United Nations, the statistical services of the United Nations specialized agencies and other international organizations and institutions. Special recognition is gratefully given for their assistance in continually providing data.

Organization of the Pocketbook

The profiles are presented first with the world and its geographical regions and sub-regions, based on the M49 regional classification[1], and then countries and areas alphabetically according to their names in English. Each profile is organised into 5 sections, where relevant and/or available:

- *General information:* includes data on surface area, population and population density, sex ratio of the population, capital city and its population, national currency and its exchange rate to the US dollar, location by geographical region and the date of admission to the United Nations.

- *Economic indicators:* includes data on national accounts Gross domestic product (GDP), GDP per capita, GDP growth rate, Gross Value Added (GVA) share by industry, employment share by industry, unemployment rate, labour force participation rate, consumer price index, agricultural production index, the value of total exports, imports and the trade balance and balance of payments.

- *Major trading partners:* shows a country's main trading partners

- *Social indicators:* includes data on population (growth rates, including for the urban population), total fertility rate, life expectancy at birth, population age distribution, international migrant stock, refugees, infant mortality rate, health (expenditure and physicians), education (expenditure and gross enrolment ratios), intentional homicide rate and seats held by women in the National Parliament.

- *Environmental and infrastructure indicators:* includes data on internet users, Research & Development expenditure, threatened species, forested area, CO_2 emission estimates, energy production and energy

---

[1] See UNSD website: https://unstats.un.org/unsd/methodology/m49/

supply per capita, tourist/visitor arrivals, important sites for terrestrial biodiversity protected, population using safely managed water sources and sanitation facilities and Official Development Assitance received or disbursed.

The complete set of indicators, listed by category and in the order in which they appear in the profiles, is shown before the country profile section (see page ix). Not all indicators are shown for each country or area due to different degrees of data availability.

The technical notes section, which follows the country profile pages, contains brief descriptions of the concepts and methodologies used in the compilation of the indicators as well as information on the statistical sources for the indicators. Readers interested in longer time-series data or more detailed descriptions of the concepts or methodologies should consult the primary sources of the data and the references listed in the section following the technical notes.

For brevity the Pocketbook omits specific information on the source or methodology for individual data points, and when a data point is estimated no distinction is made between whether the estimation was done by the international or national organization. See the technical notes section for the primary source which may provide this information.

Time period

This issue of the *World Statistics Pocketbook* presents data for the economic, social, environmental and infrastructure sections for three reference years - 2010, 2015 and 2020 - when available or the most recent data previous to these years, back to 2000. These instances are footnoted in each profile. For the general information and major trading partners sections the reference year is 2020 and 2019 respectively, unless otherwise footnoted.

Acknowledgement

The *World Statistics Pocketbook* is prepared annually by the Statistical Services Branch of the Statistics Division, Department of Economic and Social Affairs of the United Nations Secretariat. The programme manager is Matthias Reister and Anuradha Chimata is the editor; David Carter, Mohamed Nabassoua, and Zin Lin provided production assistance; Joshua Kneidl provided IT support. Comments on this publication are welcome and may be sent by e-mail to statistics@un.org.

Profile information and indicator list*

General information

Region
Population (000)
Population density (per km^2)
Capital city
Capital city population (000)
UN membership date
Surface area (km^2)
Sex ratio (males per 100 females)
National currency
Exchange rate (per US$)

Economic indicators

GDP: Gross domestic product (million current US$)
GDP growth rate (annual %, constant 2015 prices)
GDP per capita (current US$)
Economy: Agriculture, industry and services and other activity (% of GVA)
Employment in agriculture, industry and services & other sectors (% of employed)
Unemployment rate (% of labour force)
Labour force participation rate (% of female/male population)
CPI: Consumer Price Index (2010=100)
Agricultural production index (2004-2006=100)
International trade: Exports, imports and balance (million current US$)
Balance of payments, current account (million current US$)

Major trading partners (% of exports and imports)

Social indicators

Population growth rate (average annual %)
Urban population (% of total population)
Urban population growth rate (average annual %)
Fertility rate, total (live births per woman)
Life expectancy at birth (females/males, years)
Population age distribution (0-14/60+ years old, %)
International migrant stock (000/% of total population)
Refugees and others of concern to the UNHCR (000)
Infant mortality rate (per 1 000 live births)
Health: Current expenditure (% of GDP)
Health: Physicians (per 1 000 population)
Education: Government expenditure (% of GDP)
Education: Primary, Secondary and Tertiary gross enrolment ratio (females/males per 100 population)
Intentional homicide rate (per 100 000 population)
Seats held by women in the National Parliament (% of total seats)

Environmental and infrastructure indicators

Individuals using the Internet (per 100 inhabitants)
Research & Development expenditure (% of GDP)
Threatened species (number)
Forested area (% of land area)
CO_2 emission estimates (million tons/tons per capita)
Energy production, primary (Petajoules)
Energy supply per capita (Gigajoules)
Tourist/visitor arrivals at national borders (000)
Important sites for terrestrial biodiversity protected (%)
Population using safely managed drinking water sources (urban/rural, %)
Population using safely managed sanitation facilities (urban/rural, %)
Net Official Development Assistance disbursed (% of GNI of donor)
Net Official Development Assistance received (% of GNI of recipient)

The complete set of information and indicators listed here may not be shown for each country or area depending upon data availability. The technical notes provide a brief description of each information item and indicator.

**World, Regional and
Country /Area profiles**

World

Population (000, 2020)	7 794 799	Surface area (km2)	136 162 000 [a]
Pop. density (per km2, 2020)	59.9	Sex ratio (m per 100 f)	101.7

Economic indicators	2010	2015	2020
GDP: Gross domestic product (million current US$)	66 231 829	74 882 648	85 693 322 [b]
GDP growth rate (annual %, const. 2015 prices)	4.4	3.0	3.1 [b]
GDP per capita (current US$)	9 522.7	10 149.4	11 232.2 [b]
Employment in agriculture (% of employed) [c]	33.0	28.9	26.5
Employment in industry (% of employed) [c]	22.6	23.2	23.1
Employment in services & other sectors (% employed) [c]	44.4	48.0	50.4
Unemployment rate (% of labour force) [c]	5.9	5.6	5.4
Labour force participation rate (female/male pop. %) [c]	48.8 / 76.1	47.7 / 75.0	47.0 / 74.0
Agricultural production index (2004-2006=100)	113	126	127 [d]
International trade: exports (million current US$)	15 102 218	16 361 680	18 723 356 [e]
International trade: imports (million current US$)	15 275 115	16 465 359	18 964 357 [e]
International trade: balance (million current US$)	- 172 897	- 103 679	- 241 001 [e]

Social indicators	2010	2015	2020
Population growth rate (average annual %) [f]	1.2	1.2	1.1
Urban population (% of total population)	51.7	53.9	55.7 [e]
Urban population growth rate (average annual %) [f]	2.2	2.0	...
Fertility rate, total (live births per woman) [f]	2.6	2.5	2.5
Life expectancy at birth (females/males, years) [f]	71.3 / 66.7	73.3 / 68.5	74.7 / 69.9
Population age distribution (0-14/60+ years old, %)	27.0 / 11.0	26.2 / 12.2	25.4 / 13.5
International migrant stock (000/% of total pop.)	220 781.9 / 3.2	248 861.3 / 3.4	271 642.1 / 3.5 [e]
Refugees and others of concern to the UNHCR (000)	...	57 959.7	79 391.4 [e]
Infant mortality rate (per 1 000 live births) [f]	41.0	33.9	29.3
Education: Primary gross enrol. ratio (f/m per 100 pop.)	101.8 / 104.4	102.5 / 102.5	104.1 / 103.8 [c,b]
Education: Secondary gross enrol. ratio (f/m per 100 pop.)	69.8 / 72.2	74.9 / 75.9	75.1 / 76.0 [c,b]
Education: Tertiary gross enrol. ratio (f/m per 100 pop.)	30.7 / 28.5	38.9 / 34.8	40.6 / 35.6 [c,b]
Intentional homicide rate (per 100 000 pop.)	6.0	5.9	5.8 [b]
Seats held by women in the National Parliament (%)	19.0	22.3	24.9 [g]

Environment and infrastructure indicators	2010	2015	2020
Individuals using the Internet (per 100 inhabitants)	28.7	41.5	51.4 [b]
Research & Development expenditure (% of GDP)	1.6	1.7	1.7 [a]
Forested area (% of land area)	30.9	30.8	30.8 [a]
Energy production, primary (Petajoules)	530 934	570 508	581 665 [a]
Energy supply per capita (Gigajoules)	74	75	75 [a]
Important sites for terrestrial biodiversity protected (%)	40.9	43.1	43.7 [e]
Pop. using safely managed drinking water (urban/rural, %)	85.9 / 45.8	85.4 / 51.0	85.1 / 53.0 [a]
Pop. using safely managed sanitation (urban/rural %)	41.3 / 32.5	45.4 / 39.6	47.0 / 42.5 [a]
Net Official Development Assist. received (% of GNI) [h]	0.68	0.58	0.59 [b]

a 2017. **b** 2018. **c** Estimate. **d** 2016. **e** 2019. **f** Data refers to a 5-year period preceding the reference year. **g** Data are as at 1 January of reporting year. **h** Including regional aid disbursements in addition to the disbursements made to individual countries and areas.

Africa

Region	World	Population (000, 2020)	1 340 598
Surface area (km2)	30 311 000ᵃ	Pop. density (per km2, 2020)	45.2
Sex ratio (m per 100 f)	99.9		

Economic indicators	2010	2015	2020
GDP: Gross domestic product (million current US$)	1 968 455	2 306 279	2 365 243ᵇ
GDP growth rate (annual %, const. 2015 prices)	5.6	2.6	3.2ᵇ
GDP per capita (current US$)	1 896.8	1 953.1	1 856.2ᵇ
Employment in agriculture (% of employed)ᶜ	53.4	50.4	48.7
Employment in industry (% of employed)ᶜ	12.2	13.0	13.3
Employment in services & other sectors (% of employed)ᶜ	34.3	36.7	38.1
Unemployment rate (% of labour force)ᶜ	6.5	6.6	6.8
Labour force participation rate (female/male pop. %)ᶜ	54.8 / 74.6	54.0 / 72.8	54.4 / 72.0
Agricultural production index (2004-2006=100)	117	131	130ᵈ
International trade: exports (million current US$)	496 594	403 742	457 061ᵉ
International trade: imports (million current US$)	468 435	548 215	578 284ᵉ
International trade: balance (million current US$)	28 159	- 144 473	- 121 223ᵉ

Social indicators	2010	2015	2020
Population growth rate (average annual %)ᶠ	2.5	2.6	2.5
Urban population (% of total population)	38.9	41.2	43.0ᵉ
Urban population growth rate (average annual %)ᶠ	3.6	3.7	...
Fertility rate, total (live births per woman)ᶠ	4.9	4.7	4.4
Life expectancy at birth (females/males, years)ᶠ	58.3 / 55.2	61.9 / 58.6	64.4 / 60.9
Population age distribution (0-14/60+ years old, %)	41.5 / 5.1	41.1 / 5.3	40.3 / 5.5
International migrant stock (000/% of total pop.)	17 804.2 / 1.7	23 476.3 / 2.0	26 529.3 / 2.0ᵉ
Refugees and others of concern to the UNHCR (000)	...	17 067.3	30 073.8ᵉ
Infant mortality rate (per 1 000 live births)ᶠ	67.7	55.9	47.5
Intentional homicide rate (per 100 000 pop.)	12.7	12.8	12.9ᵇ

Environment and infrastructure indicators	2010	2015	2020
Forested area (% of land area)	21.5	21.0	21.0ᵃ
Energy production, primary (Petajoules)	47 153	44 265	45 629ᵃ
Energy supply per capita (Gigajoules)	27	26	26ᵃ
Net Official Development Assist. received (% of GNI)ᵍ	2.55	2.21	2.44ᵇ

a 2017. b 2018. c Estimate. d 2016. e 2019. f Data refers to a 5-year period preceding the reference year. g Including regional aid disbursements in addition to the disbursements made to individual countries and areas.

Northern Africa

Region	Africa	Population (000, 2020)	246 232
Surface area (km2)	7 880 000[a]	Pop. density (per km2, 2020)	31.7
Sex ratio (m per 100 f)	101.0		

Economic indicators	2010	2015	2020
GDP: Gross domestic product (million current US$)	648 727	729 675	666 216[b]
GDP growth rate (annual %, const. 2015 prices)	4.7	1.8	3.6[b]
GDP per capita (current US$)	3 204.2	3 267.2	2 814.3[b]
Employment in agriculture (% of employed)[c]	29.2	26.7	24.8
Employment in industry (% of employed)[c]	24.5	24.6	25.6
Employment in services & other sectors (% employed)[c]	46.3	48.7	49.6
Unemployment rate (% of labour force)[c]	10.6	13.1	11.9
Labour force participation rate (female/male pop. %)[c]	22.8 / 73.1	22.6 / 71.0	22.2 / 69.3
Agricultural production index (2004-2006=100)	112	119	118[d]
International trade: exports (million current US$)	165 544	108 845	114 636[e]
International trade: imports (million current US$)	181 147	205 559	212 061[e]
International trade: balance (million current US$)	- 15 603	- 96 714	- 97 425[e]

Social indicators	2010	2015	2020
Population growth rate (average annual %)[f]	1.7	2.0	1.9
Urban population (% of total population)	50.5	51.4	52.2[e]
Urban population growth rate (average annual %)[f]	2.1	2.3	...
Fertility rate, total (live births per woman)[f]	3.1	3.3	3.3
Life expectancy at birth (females/males, years)[f]	71.7 / 67.9	73.0 / 69.4	74.2 / 70.4
Population age distribution (0-14/60+ years old, %)	32.1 / 7.4	32.4 / 8.0	32.7 / 8.8
International migrant stock (000/% of total pop.)[g]	1 948.3 / 1.0	2 138.9 / 1.0	2 955.8 / 1.2[e]
Infant mortality rate (per 1 000 live births)[f]	31.7	26.6	23.0
Education: Primary gross enrol. ratio (f/m per 100 pop.)	95.5 / 100.8	98.0 / 101.5[c]	100.1 / 102.7[b]
Education: Secondary gross enrol. ratio (f/m per 100 pop.)	70.3 / 72.0	78.2 / 78.6[c]	81.2 / 81.2[c,b]
Education: Tertiary gross enrol. ratio (f/m per 100 pop.)	28.2 / 26.2	33.1 / 30.1	37.7 / 32.2[c,b]
Seats held by women in the National Parliament (%)	13.2	24.6	20.1[h]

Environment and infrastructure indicators	2010	2015	2020
Individuals using the Internet (per 100 inhabitants)	24.6	38.8	44.1[b]
Research & Development expenditure (% of GDP)	0.5	0.6	0.6[a]
Forested area (% of land area)	4.4	3.4	3.4[a]
Important sites for terrestrial biodiversity protected (%)	22.0	34.5	34.9[e]
Pop. using safely managed sanitation (urban/rural %)	35.7 / ...	38.4 / ...	39.3 / ...[a]
Net Official Development Assist. received (% of GNI)[g,i]	0.46	0.79	0.85[d]

a 2017. **b** 2018. **c** Estimate. **d** 2016. **e** 2019. **f** Data refers to a 5-year period preceding the reference year. **g** Excluding Sudan. **h** Data are as at 1 January of reporting year. **i** Including regional aid disbursements in addition to the disbursements made to individual countries and areas.

Sub-Saharan Africa

Region	Africa	Population (000, 2020)	1 094 366
Surface area (km2)	22 431 000[a,b]	Pop. density (per km2, 2020)	50.0
Sex ratio (m per 100 f)	99.6		

Economic indicators	2010	2015	2020
GDP: Gross domestic product (million current US$)	1 319 729	1 576 604	1 699 027[c]
GDP growth rate (annual %, const. 2015 prices)	6.1	3.0	3.0[c]
GDP per capita (current US$)	1 579.9	1 646.6	1 637.6[c]
Employment in agriculture (% of employed)[d]	58.1	54.5	52.6
Employment in industry (% of employed)[d]	9.9	10.9	11.2
Employment in services & other sectors (% employed)[d]	32.1	34.5	36.2
Unemployment rate (% of labour force)[d]	5.7	5.4	5.9
Labour force participation rate (female/male pop. %)[d]	64.1 / 75.0	62.7 / 73.3	62.7 / 72.6
International trade: exports (million current US$)	331 050	294 897	342 425[e]
International trade: imports (million current US$)	287 288	342 656	366 222[e]
International trade: balance (million current US$)	43 762	- 47 759	- 23 798[e]

Social indicators	2010	2015	2020
Population growth rate (average annual %)[f]	2.7	2.7	2.6
Urban population (% of total population)	36.1	38.8	40.9[e]
Urban population growth rate (average annual %)[f]	4.1	4.1	...
Fertility rate, total (live births per woman)[f]	5.4	5.1	4.7
Life expectancy at birth (females/males, years)[f]	55.5 / 52.6	59.5 / 56.2	62.3 / 58.8
Population age distribution (0-14/60+ years old, %)	43.8 / 4.6	43.2 / 4.6	42.1 / 4.8
International migrant stock (000/% of total pop.)	15 855.9 / 1.9	21 337.3 / 2.2	23 573.5 / 2.2[e]
Infant mortality rate (per 1 000 live births)	73.5	61.0	51.5
Education: Primary gross enrol. ratio (f/m per 100 pop.)	94.6 / 102.2	96.8 / 101.0	96.5 / 100.7[d,c]
Education: Secondary gross enrol. ratio (f/m per 100 pop.)	35.7 / 43.5	40.5 / 46.9	40.5 / 46.0[d,c]
Education: Tertiary gross enrol. ratio (f/m per 100 pop.)	6.1 / 9.0	7.4 / 10.3[d]	7.7 / 10.5[d,c]
Seats held by women in the National Parliament (%)	18.4	22.6	24.3[g]

Environment and infrastructure indicators	2010	2015	2020
Individuals using the Internet (per 100 inhabitants)	6.5	20.5	26.0[c]
Research & Development expenditure (% of GDP)	0.4	0.4	0.4[b]
Forested area (% of land area)	28.3	28.0	28.0[b]
Important sites for terrestrial biodiversity protected (%)	39.2	40.5	41.0[e]
Pop. using safely managed drinking water (urban/rural, %)	46.0 / 8.9	48.7 / 10.7	50.0 / 11.6[b]
Pop. using safely managed sanitation (urban/rural %)	19.1 / 16.1	19.6 / 17.0	19.8 / 17.5[b]
Net Official Development Assist. received (% of GNI)[h,i]	3.38	2.66	2.90[c]

a Calculated by the UN Statistics Division. b 2017. c 2018. d Estimate. e 2019. f Data refers to a 5-year period preceding the reference year. g Data are as at 1 January of reporting year. h Including regional aid disbursements in addition to the disbursements made to individual countries and areas. i Including Sudan.

Eastern Africa

Region	Sub-Saharan Africa	Population (000, 2020)	445 406
Surface area (km2)	7 005 000 [a]	Pop. density (per km2, 2020)	66.8
Sex ratio (m per 100 f)	98.5		

Economic indicators	2010	2015	2020
GDP: Gross domestic product (million current US$)	217 860	321 979	393 669 [b]
GDP growth rate (annual %, const. 2015 prices)	7.9	5.9	6.0 [b]
GDP per capita (current US$)	644.0	828.6	934.1 [b]
Employment in agriculture (% of employed) [c]	69.7	66.2	63.7
Employment in industry (% of employed) [c]	7.4	8.1	8.7
Employment in services & other sectors (% employed) [c]	22.9	25.6	27.6
Unemployment rate (% of labour force) [c]	4.0	3.3	3.2
Labour force participation rate (female/male pop. %) [c]	73.3 / 83.6	72.7 / 82.9	72.9 / 82.0
Agricultural production index (2004-2006=100)	124	145	140 [d]
International trade: exports (million current US$)	31 652	40 728	42 498 [e]
International trade: imports (million current US$)	62 688	94 004	90 934 [e]
International trade: balance (million current US$)	- 31 036	- 53 276	- 48 436 [e]

Social indicators	2010	2015	2020
Population growth rate (average annual %) [f]	2.8	2.8	2.7
Urban population (% of total population)	24.4	26.6	28.5 [e]
Urban population growth rate (average annual %) [f]	4.4	4.6	...
Fertility rate, total (live births per woman) [f]	5.4	4.9	4.4
Life expectancy at birth (females/males, years) [f]	57.7 / 54.4	62.9 / 59.0	66.2 / 62.1
Population age distribution (0-14/60+ years old, %)	44.9 / 4.3	43.6 / 4.4	41.8 / 4.6
International migrant stock (000/% of total pop.)	4 757.9 / 1.4	6 716.5 / 1.7	7 908.2 / 1.8 [e]
Infant mortality rate (per 1 000 live births) [f]	62.6	50.4	42.0
Seats held by women in the National Parliament (%)	21.6	27.2	30.9 [g]

Environment and infrastructure indicators	2010	2015	2020
Individuals using the Internet (per 100 inhabitants)	4.5	14.5	17.6 [b]
Forested area (% of land area)	32.4	32.6	32.6 [a]
Pop. using safely managed drinking water (urban/rural, %)	45.6 / 5.8	50.8 / 7.9	53.2 / 8.9 [a]

a 2017. **b** 2018. **c** Estimate. **d** 2016. **e** 2019. **f** Data refers to a 5-year period preceding the reference year. **g** Data are as at 1 January of reporting year.

Middle Africa

Region	Sub-Saharan Africa	Population (000, 2020)	179 595
Surface area (km2)	6 613 000[a]	Pop. density (per km2, 2020)	27.6
Sex ratio (m per 100 f)	99.6		

Economic indicators	2010	2015	2020
GDP: Gross domestic product (million current US$)	189 046	237 287	250 276[b]
GDP growth rate (annual %, const. 2015 prices)	5.0	1.4	1.0[b]
GDP per capita (current US$)	1 436.3	1 538.8	1 479.9[b]
Unemployment rate (% of labour force)[c]	5.4	5.0	4.8
Labour force participation rate (female/male pop. %)[c]	66.8 / 73.8	65.6 / 72.8	65.3 / 72.2
Agricultural production index (2004-2006=100)	132	143	150[d]
International trade: exports (million current US$)	90 717	70 050	67 001[e]
International trade: imports (million current US$)	43 623	56 177	39 026[e]
International trade: balance (million current US$)	47 094	13 873	27 975[e]

Social indicators	2010	2015	2020
Population growth rate (average annual %)[f]	3.2	3.2	3.0
Urban population (% of total population)	45.2	47.9	50.1[e]
Urban population growth rate (average annual %)[f]	4.4	4.3	...
Fertility rate, total (live births per woman)[f]	6.2	5.9	5.5
Life expectancy at birth (females/males, years)[f]	55.4 / 52.4	58.6 / 55.4	61.1 / 57.7
Population age distribution (0-14/60+ years old, %)	45.8 / 4.4	45.8 / 4.3	45.0 / 4.4
International migrant stock (000/% of total pop.)	2 430.3 / 1.8	3 494.4 / 2.3	3 785.3 / 2.2[e]
Infant mortality rate (per 1 000 live births)[f]	87.7	74.1	64.0
Seats held by women in the National Parliament (%)	13.5	18.1	17.6[g]

Environment and infrastructure indicators	2010	2015	2020
Individuals using the Internet (per 100 inhabitants)	2.1	8.7	13.9[b]
Forested area (% of land area)	47.2	46.7	46.7[a]

a 2017. **b** 2018. **c** Estimate. **d** 2016. **e** 2019. **f** Data refers to a 5-year period preceding the reference year. **g** Data are as at 1 January of reporting year.

Southern Africa

Region	Sub-Saharan Africa
Surface area (km2)	2 675 000[a]
Sex ratio (m per 100 f)	96.9

Population (000, 2020)	67 504
Pop. density (per km2, 2020)	25.5

Economic indicators	2010	2015	2020
GDP: Gross domestic product (million current US$)	406 242	350 025	408 569[b]
GDP growth rate (annual %, const. 2015 prices)	3.3	1.2	0.9[b]
GDP per capita (current US$)	6 958.2	5 557.3	6 215.0[b]
Employment in agriculture (% of employed)[c]	6.9	7.3	6.6
Employment in industry (% of employed)[c]	24.5	24.1	23.0
Employment in services & other sectors (% employed)[c]	68.6	68.6	70.4
Unemployment rate (% of labour force)[c]	24.5	24.7	27.5
Labour force participation rate (female/male pop. %)[c]	46.0 / 61.2	49.7 / 63.4	50.7 / 63.5
Agricultural production index (2004-2006=100)	116	120	115[d]
International trade: exports (million current US$)	95 232	93 648	103 238[e]
International trade: imports (million current US$)	97 723	104 173	105 685[e]
International trade: balance (million current US$)	- 2 491	- 10 525	- 2 447[e]

Social indicators	2010	2015	2020
Population growth rate (average annual %)[f]	1.3	1.5	1.4
Urban population (% of total population)	59.4	62.1	64.1[e]
Urban population growth rate (average annual %)[f]	2.1	2.3	...
Fertility rate, total (live births per woman)[f]	2.7	2.6	2.5
Life expectancy at birth (females/males, years)[f]	56.5 / 51.6	63.6 / 57.2	66.8 / 59.9
Population age distribution (0-14/60+ years old, %)	30.5 / 7.0	30.1 / 7.7	29.5 / 8.3
International migrant stock (000/% of total pop.)	2 352.3 / 4.0	4 060.5 / 6.4	4 481.7 / 6.7[e]
Infant mortality rate (per 1 000 live births)[f]	49.5	35.0	29.4
Seats held by women in the National Parliament (%)	33.4	33.4	35.6[g]

Environment and infrastructure indicators	2010	2015	2020
Individuals using the Internet (per 100 inhabitants)	22.0	49.1	54.9[b]
Forested area (% of land area)	10.7	10.4	10.4[a]
Pop. using safely managed drinking water (urban/rural, %)	87.2 / ...	83.4 / ...	81.9 / ...[a]

a 2017. **b** 2018. **c** Estimate. **d** 2016. **e** 2019. **f** Data refers to a 5-year period preceding the reference year. **g** Data are as at 1 January of reporting year.

Western Africa

Region	Sub-Saharan Africa	Population (000, 2020)	401 861 [a]
Surface area (km2)	6 138 000 [b]	Pop. density (per km2, 2020)	66.3
Sex ratio (m per 100 f)	101.4 [a]		

Economic indicators	2010	2015	2020
GDP: Gross domestic product (million current US$)	506 581	667 313	646 513 [c]
GDP growth rate (annual %, const. 2015 prices)	7.5	3.0	3.2 [c]
GDP per capita (current US$)	1 649.9	1 897.3	1 696.0 [c]
Employment in agriculture (% of employed) [d]	48.2	42.6	39.9
Employment in industry (% of employed) [d]	11.2	13.3	13.9
Employment in services & other sectors (% employed) [d]	40.6	44.2	46.2
Unemployment rate (% of labour force) [d]	4.4	4.6	6.0
Labour force participation rate (female/male pop. %) [d]	57.1 / 69.5	53.1 / 65.2	52.5 / 64.3
Agricultural production index (2004-2006=100)	113	130	131 [e]
International trade: exports (million current US$)	113 448	90 470	129 687 [f]
International trade: imports (million current US$)	83 254	88 302	130 577 [f]
International trade: balance (million current US$)	30 194	2 168	- 889 [f]

Social indicators	2010	2015	2020
Population growth rate (average annual %) [g]	2.7	2.7	2.7
Urban population (% of total population)	41.1	44.5	47.0 [f]
Urban population growth rate (average annual %) [g]	4.4	4.3	...
Fertility rate, total (live births per woman) [a,g]	5.7	5.5	5.2
Life expectancy at birth (females/males, years) [a,g]	53.5 / 51.6	56.0 / 54.1	58.4 / 56.3
Population age distribution (0-14/60+ years old, %) [a]	44.2 / 4.5	44.0 / 4.5	43.1 / 4.6
International migrant stock (000/% of total pop.)	6 315.4 / 2.1	7 065.9 / 2.0	7 398.4 / 1.9 [f]
Infant mortality rate (per 1 000 live births) [a,g]	81.2	68.5	57.3
Seats held by women in the National Parliament (%)	11.6	14.5	14.8 [h]

Environment and infrastructure indicators	2010	2015	2020
Individuals using the Internet (per 100 inhabitants)	7.7	27.2	35.8 [c]
Forested area (% of land area)	11.6	11.1	11.1 [b]
Pop. using safely managed drinking water (urban/rural, %)	33.3 / 12.4	33.5 / 14.5	33.6 / 15.4 [b]
Pop. using safely managed sanitation (urban/rural %)	21.2 / 16.3	21.8 / 16.8	21.9 / 17.0 [b]

a Including Saint Helena. b 2017. c 2018. d Estimate. e 2016. f 2019. g Data refers to a 5-year period preceding the reference year. h Data are as at 1 January of reporting year.

Americas

Region	World	Population (000, 2020)	1 022 832 [a]
Surface area (km2)	42 322 000 [a,b]	Pop. density (per km2, 2020)	24.2 [a]
Sex ratio (m per 100 f)	97.2 [a]		

Economic indicators	2010	2015	2020
GDP: Gross domestic product (million current US$)	21 963 119	25 283 842	27 867 704 [c]
GDP growth rate (annual %, const. 2015 prices)	3.3	2.1	2.3 [c]
GDP per capita (current US$)	23 529.7	25 806.6	27 721.7 [c]
Employment in agriculture (% of employed) [d]	10.0	9.1	9.0
Employment in industry (% of employed) [d]	20.9	20.9	20.0
Employment in services & other sectors (% employed) [d]	69.1	70.0	71.0
Unemployment rate (% of labour force) [d]	7.9	6.2	6.6
Labour force participation rate (female/male pop. %) [d]	53.6 / 74.8	53.1 / 73.9	53.6 / 73.4
Agricultural production index (2004-2006=100)	111	122	124 [e]
International trade: exports (million current US$)	2 551 125	2 827 588	3 134 354 [f]
International trade: imports (million current US$)	3 230 657	3 739 612	4 076 214 [f]
International trade: balance (million current US$)	- 679 532	- 912 024	- 941 860 [f]

Social indicators	2010	2015	2020
Population age distribution (0-14/60+ years old, %) [a]	24.8 / 13.1	23.2 / 14.8	21.8 / 16.6
Intentional homicide rate (per 100 000 pop.)	15.8	16.0	15.9 [c]

Environment and infrastructure indicators	2010	2015	2020
Forested area (% of land area)	41.4	41.2	41.2 [b]
Net Official Development Assist. received (% of GNI) [g]	0.19	0.21	0.23 [c]

a Calculated by the UN Statistics Division. b 2017. c 2018. d Estimate. e 2016. f 2019. g Including regional aid disbursements in addition to the disbursements made to individual countries and areas.

Northern America

Region	Americas	Population (000, 2020)	368 870[a]
Surface area (km2)	21 776 000[b]	Pop. density (per km2, 2020)	19.8
Sex ratio (m per 100 f)	98.0[a]		

Economic indicators	2010	2015	2020
GDP: Gross domestic product (million current US$)	16 617 674	19 789 297	22 302 188[c]
GDP growth rate (annual %, const. 2015 prices)	2.6	2.7	2.8[c]
GDP per capita (current US$)	48 408.4	55 428.3	61 220.9[c]
Employment in agriculture (% of employed)[d]	1.5	1.5	1.3
Employment in industry (% of employed)[d]	19.7	19.9	19.7
Employment in services & other sectors (% employed)[d]	78.8	78.7	79.0
Unemployment rate (% of labour force)[d]	9.5	5.5	4.0
Labour force participation rate (female/male pop. %)[d]	58.0 / 70.1	56.4 / 68.6	56.4 / 68.0
Agricultural production index (2004-2006=100)	106	112	116[e]
International trade: exports (million current US$)	1 665 220	1 911 491	2 092 331[f]
International trade: imports (million current US$)	2 362 932	2 736 654	3 026 538[f]
International trade: balance (million current US$)	- 697 713	- 825 163	- 934 208[f]

Social indicators	2010	2015	2020
Population growth rate (average annual %)[g]	1.0	0.8	0.7
Urban population (% of total population)	80.8	81.6	82.4[f]
Urban population growth rate (average annual %)[g]	1.1	1.0	...
Fertility rate, total (live births per woman)[a,g]	2.0	1.8	1.8
Life expectancy at birth (females/males, years)[a,g]	80.9 / 75.9	81.6 / 76.8	81.6 / 76.7
Population age distribution (0-14/60+ years old, %)[a]	19.8 / 18.5	18.9 / 20.7	18.1 / 23.1
International migrant stock (000/% of total pop.)	50 970.9 / 14.8	55 633.4 / 15.6	58 647.8 / 16.0[f]
Refugees and others of concern to the UNHCR (000)	...	655.4	1 233.1[f]
Infant mortality rate (per 1 000 live births)[a,g]	6.7	5.8	5.7
Education: Primary gross enrol. ratio (f/m per 100 pop.)	99.7 / 100.6	100.5 / 100.5	101.5 / 102.0[d,c]
Education: Secondary gross enrol. ratio (f/m per 100 pop.)	95.9 / 95.1	99.3 / 98.3	100.0 / 100.4[d,c]
Education: Tertiary gross enrol. ratio (f/m per 100 pop.)	104.8 / 75.2	99.9 / 73.8	99.8 / 73.4[d,c]
Intentional homicide rate (per 100 000 pop.)	4.5	4.6	4.6[c]
Seats held by women in the National Parliament (%)	19.0	21.8	25.9[h]

Environment and infrastructure indicators	2010	2015	2020
Individuals using the Internet (per 100 inhabitants)	72.5	76.1	89.2[c]
Research & Development expenditure (% of GDP)	2.7	2.6	2.7[b]
Forested area (% of land area)	35.4	35.5	35.5[b]
Important sites for terrestrial biodiversity protected (%)	39.6	40.9	41.4[f]
Pop. using safely managed drinking water (urban/rural, %)	99.6 / ...	99.6 / ...	99.6 / ...[b]
Pop. using safely managed sanitation (urban/rural %)	90.1 / ...	90.2 / ...	90.2 / ...[b]

a Including Bermuda, Greenland, and Saint Pierre and Miquelon. b 2017. c 2018. d Estimate. e 2016. f 2019. g Data refers to a 5-year period preceding the reference year. h Data are as at 1 January of reporting year.

Latin America & the Caribbean

Region	Americas	Population (000, 2020)	653 962
Surface area (km2)	20 546 000[a]	Pop. density (per km2, 2020)	32.5
Sex ratio (m per 100 f)	96.8		

Economic indicators	2010	2015	2020
GDP: Gross domestic product (million current US$)	5 345 445	5 494 545	5 565 516[b]
GDP growth rate (annual %, const. 2015 prices)	5.9	0.1	0.5[b]
GDP per capita (current US$)	9 057.9	8 823.5	8 682.9[b]
Employment in agriculture (% of employed)[c]	15.4	13.9	13.7
Employment in industry (% of employed)[c]	21.6	21.6	20.3
Employment in services & other sectors (% employed)[c]	63.0	64.6	66.1
Unemployment rate (% of labour force)[c]	7.0	6.7	8.1
Labour force participation rate (female/male pop. %)[c]	50.8 / 77.9	51.1 / 77.2	52.0 / 76.6
International trade: exports (million current US$)	885 906	916 097	1 042 023[d]
International trade: imports (million current US$)	867 725	1 002 958	1 049 676[d]
International trade: balance (million current US$)	18 181	- 86 861	- 7 653[d]

Social indicators	2010	2015	2020
Population growth rate (average annual %)[e]	1.2	1.1	0.9
Urban population (% of total population)	78.6	79.9	80.9[d]
Urban population growth rate (average annual %)[e]	1.6	1.5	...
Fertility rate, total (live births per woman)[e]	2.3	2.1	2.0
Life expectancy at birth (females/males, years)[e]	76.8 / 70.2	77.7 / 71.2	78.5 / 72.0
Population age distribution (0-14/60+ years old, %)	27.7 / 10.0	25.6 / 11.4	23.9 / 13.0
International migrant stock (000/% of total pop.)	8 262.4 / 1.4	9 441.7 / 1.5	11 673.3 / 1.8[d]
Refugees and others of concern to the UNHCR (000)	...	7 071.2	13 430.4[d]
Infant mortality rate (per 1 000 live births)[e]	20.2	17.1	15.5
Education: Primary gross enrol. ratio (f/m per 100 pop.)	113.1 / 116.7	107.9 / 110.1	108.2 / 110.3[c,b]
Education: Secondary gross enrol. ratio (f/m per 100 pop.)	92.9 / 85.8	97.1 / 92.0	97.9 / 94.0[c,b]
Education: Tertiary gross enrol. ratio (f/m per 100 pop.)	46.5 / 36.1	55.2 / 42.7	58.6 / 45.1[c,b]
Seats held by women in the National Parliament (%)	22.7	27.4	32.1[f]

Environment and infrastructure indicators	2010	2015	2020
Individuals using the Internet (per 100 inhabitants)	34.7	54.6	66.3[b]
Research & Development expenditure (% of GDP)	0.7	0.7	0.7[a]
Forested area (% of land area)	47.0	46.5	46.5[a]
Important sites for terrestrial biodiversity protected (%)	34.9	36.9	38.0[d]
Pop. using safely managed drinking water (urban/rural, %)	82.3 / 39.0	82.3 / 41.0	82.3 / 41.7[a]
Pop. using safely managed sanitation (urban/rural %)	25.0 / ...	33.6 / ...	37.0 / ...[a]

a 2017. **b** 2018. **c** Estimate. **d** 2019. **e** Data refers to a 5-year period preceding the reference year. **f** Data are as at 1 January of reporting year.

Caribbean

Region	Latin America & Caribbean	Population (000, 2020)	43 532
Surface area (km2)	234 000[a]	Pop. density (per km2, 2020)	192.6
Sex ratio (m per 100 f)	97.5[b]		

Economic indicators	2010	2015	2020
GDP: Gross domestic product (million current US$)	290 518	344 059	371 468[c]
GDP growth rate (annual %, const. 2015 prices)	1.7	2.5	1.0[c]
GDP per capita (current US$)	7 219.1	8 257.1	8 800.3[c]
Employment in agriculture (% of employed)[d]	18.3	17.1	16.0
Employment in industry (% of employed)[d]	15.5	15.3	15.3
Employment in services & other sectors (% employed)[d]	66.2	67.6	68.7
Unemployment rate (% of labour force)[d]	8.5	8.5	7.3
Labour force participation rate (female/male pop. %)[d]	47.1 / 69.7	49.2 / 70.1	50.0 / 70.2
Agricultural production index (2004-2006=100)	105	119	121[e]
International trade: exports (million current US$)	24 874	26 475	27 958[f]
International trade: imports (million current US$)	53 245	58 007	51 914[f]
International trade: balance (million current US$)	- 28 371	- 31 533	- 23 956[f]

Social indicators	2010	2015	2020
Population growth rate (average annual %)[g]	0.7	0.7	0.4
Urban population (% of total population)	67.8	70.0	71.8[f]
Urban population growth rate (average annual %)[g]	1.5	1.4	...
Fertility rate, total (live births per woman)[b,g]	2.4	2.3	2.2
Life expectancy at birth (females/males, years)[b,g]	73.4 / 68.4	74.2 / 69.1	75.1 / 70.0
Population age distribution (0-14/60+ years old, %)[b]	26.5 / 12.0	25.1 / 13.3	23.9 / 14.9
International migrant stock (000/% of total pop.)	1 326.9 / 3.2	1 489.9 / 3.5	1 524.8 / 3.5[f]
Infant mortality rate (per 1 000 live births)[b,g]	34.8	33.2	30.7
Intentional homicide rate (per 100 000 pop.)	17.0	14.4	12.1[c]
Seats held by women in the National Parliament (%)	29.4	33.1	36.7[h]

Environment and infrastructure indicators	2010	2015	2020
Individuals using the Internet (per 100 inhabitants)	23.7	39.6	58.7[c]
Forested area (% of land area)	29.8	32.2	32.2[a]

a 2017. **b** Including Anguilla, Bonaire, Sint Eustatius and Saba, British Virgin Islands, Cayman Islands, Dominica, Montserrat, Saint Kitts and Nevis, Sint Maarten (Dutch part) and Turks and Caicos Islands. **c** 2018. **d** Estimate. **e** 2016. **f** 2019. **g** Data refers to a 5-year period preceding the reference year. **h** Data are as at 1 January of reporting year.

Central America

Region	Latin America & Caribbean	Population (000, 2020)	179 670
Surface area (km2)	2 480 000 [a]	Pop. density (per km2, 2020)	73.3
Sex ratio (m per 100 f)	96.1		

Economic indicators	2010	2015	2020
GDP: Gross domestic product (million current US$)	1 210 271	1 402 101	1 492 059 [b]
GDP growth rate (annual %, const. 2015 prices)	4.9	3.4	2.1 [b]
GDP per capita (current US$)	7 679.8	8 298.9	8 503.1 [b]
Employment in agriculture (% of employed) [c]	17.5	16.7	16.0
Employment in industry (% of employed) [c]	23.3	23.7	24.2
Employment in services & other sectors (% employed) [c]	59.2	59.6	59.8
Unemployment rate (% of labour force) [c]	5.2	4.4	4.1
Labour force participation rate (female/male pop. %) [c]	43.4 / 80.2	44.2 / 79.8	44.9 / 79.6
Agricultural production index (2004-2006=100)	110	123	128 [d]
International trade: exports (million current US$)	336 529	426 846	510 072 [e]
International trade: imports (million current US$)	366 171	464 286	547 594 [e]
International trade: balance (million current US$)	- 29 642	- 37 441	- 37 523 [e]

Social indicators	2010	2015	2020
Population growth rate (average annual %) [f]	1.5	1.4	1.2
Urban population (% of total population)	72.1	73.7	75.0 [e]
Urban population growth rate (average annual %) [f]	2.1	1.9	...
Fertility rate, total (live births per woman) [f]	2.5	2.4	2.2
Life expectancy at birth (females/males, years) [f]	77.3 / 71.5	77.6 / 71.6	77.8 / 72.0
Population age distribution (0-14/60+ years old, %)	30.9 / 8.4	28.8 / 9.5	26.9 / 10.7
International migrant stock (000/% of total pop.)	1 749.9 / 1.1	1 878.9 / 1.1	1 927.7 / 1.1 [e]
Infant mortality rate (per 1 000 live births) [f]	19.5	16.9	14.6
Intentional homicide rate (per 100 000 pop.)	27.8	23.1	28.1 [b]
Seats held by women in the National Parliament (%)	21.6	30.1	36.9 [g]

Environment and infrastructure indicators	2010	2015	2020
Forested area (% of land area)	35.7	35.2	35.2 [a]
Pop. using safely managed drinking water (urban/rural, %)	... / 39.0	... / 40.9	... / 41.6 [a]
Pop. using safely managed sanitation (urban/rural %)	29.2 / ...	39.6 / ...	44.0 / ... [a]

a 2017. b 2018. c Estimate. d 2016. e 2019. f Data refers to a 5-year period preceding the reference year. g Data are as at 1 January of reporting year.

South America

Region	Latin America & Caribbean	Population (000, 2020)	430 760
Surface area (km2)	17 832 000[a]	Pop. density (per km2, 2020)	24.7
Sex ratio (m per 100 f)	97.0[b]		

Economic indicators	2010	2015	2020
GDP: Gross domestic product (million current US$)	3 844 656	3 748 385	3 701 989[c]
GDP growth rate (annual %, const. 2015 prices)	6.6	- 1.3	- 0.2[c]
GDP per capita (current US$)	9 800.1	9 095.8	8 745.7[c]
Employment in agriculture (% of employed)[d]	14.4	12.5	12.5
Employment in industry (% of employed)[d]	21.5	21.3	19.2
Employment in services & other sectors (% employed)[d]	64.1	66.1	68.3
Unemployment rate (% of labour force)[d]	7.4	7.4	9.7
Labour force participation rate (female/male pop. %)[d]	53.9 / 77.9	54.0 / 76.9	55.0 / 76.1
Agricultural production index (2004-2006=100)	118	135	132[e]
International trade: exports (million current US$)	524 502	462 776	503 993[f]
International trade: imports (million current US$)	448 308	480 665	450 167[f]
International trade: balance (million current US$)	76 194	- 17 888	53 826[f]

Social indicators	2010	2015	2020
Population growth rate (average annual %)[g]	1.1	1.0	0.9
Urban population (% of total population)	82.4	83.5	84.4[f]
Urban population growth rate (average annual %)[g]	1.5	1.3	...
Fertility rate, total (live births per woman)[b,g]	2.1	2.0	1.9
Life expectancy at birth (females/males, years)[b,g]	76.9 / 69.9	78.1 / 71.3	79.1 / 72.2
Population age distribution (0-14/60+ years old, %)[b]	26.5 / 10.4	24.4 / 11.9	22.6 / 13.7
International migrant stock (000/% of total pop.)	5 185.6 / 1.3	6 072.9 / 1.5	8 220.8 / 1.9[f]
Infant mortality rate (per 1 000 live births)[b,g]	18.9	15.4	14.2
Intentional homicide rate (per 100 000 pop.)	20.8	23.1	21.0[c]
Seats held by women in the National Parliament (%)	19.2	22.2	26.5[h]

Environment and infrastructure indicators	2010	2015	2020
Forested area (% of land area)	48.8	48.2	48.2[a]
Energy production, primary (Petajoules)	29 335	31 960	31 442[a]
Energy supply per capita (Gigajoules)	56	58	57[a]
Pop. using safely managed drinking water (urban/rural, %)	86.7 / 38.8	86.9 / 41.1	86.9 / 41.8[a]
Pop. using safely managed sanitation (urban/rural %)	24.6 / ...	33.1 / ...	36.5 / ...[a]
Net Official Development Assist. received (% of GNI)[i]	0.07	0.13	0.15[c]

a 2017. b Including Falkland Islands (Malvinas). c 2018. d Estimate. e 2016. f 2019. g Data refers to a 5-year period preceding the reference year. h Data are as at 1 January of reporting year. i Including regional aid disbursements in addition to the disbursements made to individual countries and areas.

Region	World	Population (000, 2020)	4 641 055
Surface area (km2)	31 915 000[a]	Pop. density (per km2, 2020)	149.6
Sex ratio (m per 100 f)	104.7		

Economic indicators	2010	2015	2020
GDP: Gross domestic product (million current US$)	20 957 643	26 659 277	31 839 880[b]
GDP growth rate (annual %, const. 2015 prices)	7.7	4.8	4.5[b]
GDP per capita (current US$)	4 979.0	6 013.8	6 982.1[b]
Agricultural production index (2004-2006=100)	118	134	135[c]
International trade: exports (million current US$)	5 896 164	6 831 778	7 707 847[d]
International trade: imports (million current US$)	5 459 724	6 214 435	7 174 349[d]
International trade: balance (million current US$)	436 440	617 343	533 498[d]

Social indicators	2010	2015	2020
Population growth rate (average annual %)[e]	1.1	1.0	0.9
Urban population (% of total population)	44.8	48.0	50.5[d]
Urban population growth rate (average annual %)[e]	2.8	2.4	...
Fertility rate, total (live births per woman)[e]	2.3	2.2	2.2
Life expectancy at birth (females/males, years)[e]	72.0 / 68.2	74.0 / 69.8	75.5 / 71.2
Population age distribution (0-14/60+ years old, %)	25.9 / 10.0	24.6 / 11.5	23.5 / 13.1
International migrant stock (000/% of total pop.)	65 938.7 / 1.6	77 231.8 / 1.7	83 559.2 / 1.8[d]
Refugees and others of concern to the UNHCR (000)	...	28 420.7	28 369.9[d]
Infant mortality rate (per 1 000 live births)[e]	37.1	29.5	24.9
Intentional homicide rate (per 100 000 pop.)	2.7	2.3	2.1[b]
Seats held by women in the National Parliament (%)	16.8	17.8	19.5[f]

Environment and infrastructure indicators	2010	2015	2020
Individuals using the Internet (per 100 inhabitants)	22.6	35.7	47.3[b]
Forested area (% of land area)	19.0	19.1	19.1[a]
Energy production, primary (Petajoules)	236 089	261 124	268 302[a]
Energy supply per capita (Gigajoules)	56	61	62[a]
Pop. using safely managed drinking water (urban/rural, %)	86.1 / 50.4	85.9 / 57.1	85.8 / 59.8[a]
Pop. using safely managed sanitation (urban/rural %)	33.7 / 32.0	40.1 / 41.8	42.7 / 46.0[a]
Net Official Development Assist. received (% of GNI)[g]	0.33	0.24	0.24[b]

a 2017. b 2018. c 2016. d 2019. e Data refers to a 5-year period preceding the reference year. f Data are as at 1 January of reporting year. g Including regional aid disbursements in addition to the disbursements made to individual countries and areas.

Central Asia

Region	Asia	Population (000, 2020)	74 339
Surface area (km2)	4 103 000[a,b]	Pop. density (per km2, 2020)	18.9
Sex ratio (m per 100 f)	98.1		

Economic indicators	2010	2015	2020
GDP: Gross domestic product (million current US$)	227 976	316 820	286 205[c]
GDP growth rate (annual %, const. 2015 prices)	7.5	3.5	4.7[c]
GDP per capita (current US$)	3 629.9	4 626.5	3 972.2[c]
Employment in agriculture (% of employed)[d]	31.2	25.4	22.0
Employment in industry (% of employed)[d]	23.4	25.3	26.9
Employment in services & other sectors (% employed)[d]	45.3	49.3	51.1
Unemployment rate (% of labour force)[d]	6.1	5.7	5.9
Labour force participation rate (female/male pop. %)[d]	53.2 / 73.6	53.3 / 74.4	51.8 / 74.2
Agricultural production index (2004-2006=100)	115	143	145[e]
International trade: exports (million current US$)	74 961	64 827	81 196[f]
International trade: imports (million current US$)	40 985	53 082	71 667[f]
International trade: balance (million current US$)	33 976	11 746	9 529[f]

Social indicators	2010	2015	2020
Population growth rate (average annual %)[g]	1.4	1.7	1.6
Urban population (% of total population)	48.0	48.1	48.2[f]
Urban population growth rate (average annual %)[g]	1.9	1.7	...
Fertility rate, total (live births per woman)[g]	2.7	2.8	2.8
Life expectancy at birth (females/males, years)[g]	71.5 / 63.5	72.9 / 66.1	74.7 / 68.5
Population age distribution (0-14/60+ years old, %)	28.7 / 7.0	29.3 / 7.6	30.5 / 8.9
International migrant stock (000/% of total pop.)	5 264.9 / 8.4	5 392.8 / 7.9	5 543.4 / 7.6[f]
Infant mortality rate (per 1 000 live births)[g]	36.6	26.4	20.6
Intentional homicide rate (per 100 000 pop.)	5.6	3.0	2.7[c]
Seats held by women in the National Parliament (%)	20.0	21.8	25.4[h]

Environment and infrastructure indicators	2010	2015	2020
Individuals using the Internet (per 100 inhabitants)	18.4	43.7	51.3[c]
Research & Development expenditure (% of GDP)	0.2	0.2	0.2[b]
Forested area (% of land area)	3.0	3.0	3.0[b]
Important sites for terrestrial biodiversity protected (%)	12.1	12.2	12.6[f]
Pop. using safely managed drinking water (urban/rural, %)	87.6 / 41.6	89.8 / 49.9	90.4 / 52.9[b]
Pop. using safely managed sanitation (urban/rural %)	49.0 / ...	49.0 / ...	49.0 / ...[b]

a Calculated by the UN Statistics Division. b 2017. c 2018. d Estimate. e 2016. f 2019. g Data refers to a 5-year period preceding the reference year. h Data are as at 1 January of reporting year.

Eastern Asia

Region	Asia	Population (000, 2020)	1 678 090
Surface area (km2)	11 799 000[a]	Pop. density (per km2, 2020)	145.2
Sex ratio (m per 100 f)	104.0		

Economic indicators	2010	2015	2020
GDP: Gross domestic product (million current US$)	13 653 535	17 788 106	21 355 820[b]
GDP growth rate (annual %, const. 2015 prices)	8.1	4.8	4.7[b]
GDP per capita (current US$)	8 508.3	10 813.1	12 816.0[b]
Employment in agriculture (% of employed)[c]	33.2	26.1	22.6
Employment in industry (% of employed)[c]	28.2	28.5	27.5
Employment in services & other sectors (% employed)[c]	38.6	45.4	49.8
Unemployment rate (% of labour force)[c]	4.5	4.5	4.2
Labour force participation rate (female/male pop. %)[c]	62.0 / 77.5	61.0 / 76.3	59.0 / 74.5
Agricultural production index (2004-2006=100)	118	134	136[d]
International trade: exports (million current US$)	3 219 271	3 942 643	4 284 884[e]
International trade: imports (million current US$)	2 967 424	3 317 929	3 894 237[e]
International trade: balance (million current US$)	251 847	624 714	390 648[e]

Social indicators	2010	2015	2020
Population growth rate (average annual %)[f]	0.5	0.5	0.4
Urban population (% of total population)	54.4	59.8	63.9[e]
Urban population growth rate (average annual %)[f]	2.9	2.4	...
Fertility rate, total (live births per woman)[f]	1.6	1.6	1.7
Life expectancy at birth (females/males, years)[f]	77.2 / 72.7	78.9 / 73.9	80.4 / 75.3
Population age distribution (0-14/60+ years old, %)	18.2 / 13.8	17.5 / 16.5	17.1 / 18.9
International migrant stock (000/% of total pop.)	7 062.5 / 0.4	7 636.4 / 0.5	8 105.8 / 0.5[e]
Infant mortality rate (per 1 000 live births)[f]	16.9	11.5	9.3
Education: Primary gross enrol. ratio (f/m per 100 pop.)	98.4 / 100.0	96.7 / 96.4	101.3 / 100.2[b]
Education: Secondary gross enrol. ratio (f/m per 100 pop.)	89.1 / 89.3	86.5 / 84.6	86.3 / 84.8[b]
Education: Tertiary gross enrol. ratio (f/m per 100 pop.)	27.9 / 27.8	51.5 / 45.7	55.4 / 47.8[b]
Intentional homicide rate (per 100 000 pop.)	0.9	0.6	0.5[b]
Seats held by women in the National Parliament (%)	18.7	20.4	21.6[g]

Environment and infrastructure indicators	2010	2015	2020
Individuals using the Internet (per 100 inhabitants)	39.5	54.4	59.1[b]
Research & Development expenditure (% of GDP)	2.2	2.4	2.5[a]
Forested area (% of land area)	21.7	22.2	22.2[a]
Important sites for terrestrial biodiversity protected (%)	24.0	25.7	26.2[e]
Pop. using safely managed drinking water (urban/rural, %)	93.8 / ...	93.5 / ...	93.3 / ...[a]
Pop. using safely managed sanitation (urban/rural %)	59.3 / 38.0	72.5 / 50.3	78.2 / 56.2[a]

a 2017. **b** 2018. **c** Estimate. **d** 2016. **e** 2019. **f** Data refers to a 5-year period preceding the reference year. **g** Data are as at 1 January of reporting year.

South-eastern Asia

Region	Asia	Population (000, 2020)	668 620
Surface area (km2)	4 495 000 [a]	Pop. density (per km2, 2020)	154.0
Sex ratio (m per 100 f)	99.8		

Economic indicators	2010	2015	2020
GDP: Gross domestic product (million current US$)	1 980 866	2 466 781	2 974 090 [b]
GDP growth rate (annual %, const. 2015 prices)	7.9	4.7	5.0 [b]
GDP per capita (current US$)	3 318.3	3 888.9	4 538.5 [b]
Employment in agriculture (% of employed) [c]	40.5	35.2	29.8
Employment in industry (% of employed) [c]	19.2	21.3	22.9
Employment in services & other sectors (% employed) [c]	40.3	43.5	47.3
Unemployment rate (% of labour force) [c]	3.2	2.9	3.1
Labour force participation rate (female/male pop. %) [c]	56.5 / 81.1	56.2 / 80.5	56.0 / 79.3
Agricultural production index (2004-2006=100)	120	134	133 [d]
International trade: exports (million current US$)	1 054 178	1 172 850	1 409 910 [e]
International trade: imports (million current US$)	953 410	1 100 730	1 373 529 [e]
International trade: balance (million current US$)	100 767	72 119	36 381 [e]

Social indicators	2010	2015	2020
Population growth rate (average annual %) [f]	1.2	1.2	1.1
Urban population (% of total population)	44.3	47.2	49.4 [e]
Urban population growth rate (average annual %) [f]	2.7	2.5	...
Fertility rate, total (live births per woman) [f]	2.4	2.3	2.2
Life expectancy at birth (females/males, years) [f]	72.5 / 66.8	74.3 / 68.2	75.5 / 69.5
Population age distribution (0-14/60+ years old, %)	27.9 / 8.1	26.5 / 9.4	25.2 / 11.1
International migrant stock (000/% of total pop.)	8 685.6 / 1.5	10 237.7 / 1.6	10 190.9 / 1.5 [e]
Infant mortality rate (per 1 000 live births) [f]	28.6	24.0	19.5
Education: Primary gross enrol. ratio (f/m per 100 pop.)	107.1 / 106.8	106.1 / 108.9	105.6 / 108.2 [c,b]
Education: Secondary gross enrol. ratio (f/m per 100 pop.)	71.3 / 70.5	80.9 / 80.7	83.5 / 81.4 [c,b]
Education: Tertiary gross enrol. ratio (f/m per 100 pop.)	27.7 / 26.0	35.7 / 30.3	37.8 / 30.6 [c,b]
Intentional homicide rate (per 100 000 pop.)	2.8	2.7	2.2 [b]
Seats held by women in the National Parliament (%)	19.3	17.8	20.4 [g]

Environment and infrastructure indicators	2010	2015	2020
Individuals using the Internet (per 100 inhabitants)	18.8	31.9	48.2 [b]
Research & Development expenditure (% of GDP)	0.7	0.9	1.0 [a]
Forested area (% of land area)	49.4	48.6	47.8 [a]
Important sites for terrestrial biodiversity protected (%)	30.7	34.2	35.6 [e]

a 2017. b 2018. c Estimate. d 2016. e 2019. f Data refers to a 5-year period preceding the reference year. g Data are as at 1 January of reporting year.

Southern Asia

Region	Asia	Population (000, 2020)	1 940 370
Surface area (km2)	6 688 000 [a,b]	Pop. density (per km2, 2020)	303.2
Sex ratio (m per 100 f)	106.5		

Economic indicators	2010	2015	2020
GDP: Gross domestic product (million current US$)	2 542 992	3 129 879	3 949 688 [c]
GDP growth rate (annual %, const. 2015 prices)	7.1	6.2	5.1 [c]
GDP per capita (current US$)	1 484.9	1 712.3	2 083.4 [c]
Employment in agriculture (% of employed) [d]	49.4	44.3	40.0
Employment in industry (% of employed) [d]	21.5	23.7	25.5
Employment in services & other sectors (% employed) [d]	29.1	32.1	34.5
Unemployment rate (% of labour force)	5.2	5.4	5.4
Labour force participation rate (female/male pop. %) [d]	26.0 / 80.2	23.7 / 78.1	23.1 / 76.9
Agricultural production index (2004-2006=100)	120	137	139 [e]
International trade: exports (million current US$)	354 892	394 653	413 627 [f]
International trade: imports (million current US$)	497 340	560 507	650 524 [f]
International trade: balance (million current US$)	- 142 448	- 165 854	- 236 897 [f]

Social indicators	2010	2015	2020
Population growth rate (average annual %) [g]	1.5	1.3	1.2
Urban population (% of total population)	32.5	34.5	36.2 [f]
Urban population growth rate (average annual %) [g]	2.6	2.5	...
Fertility rate, total (live births per woman) [g]	2.9	2.5	2.4
Life expectancy at birth (females/males, years) [g]	66.9 / 64.9	69.2 / 66.8	70.7 / 68.1
Population age distribution (0-14/60+ years old, %)	31.7 / 7.5	29.5 / 8.4	27.5 / 9.5
International migrant stock (000/% of total pop.)	14 311.4 / 0.8	14 051.0 / 0.8	14 083.6 / 0.7 [f]
Infant mortality rate (per 1 000 live births) [g]	51.7	42.4	35.9
Education: Primary gross enrol. ratio (f/m per 100 pop.)	105.8 / 105.9	109.9 / 103.6	114.8 / 106.8 [d,c]
Education: Secondary gross enrol. ratio (f/m per 100 pop.)	57.1 / 61.1	68.9 / 69.0	69.9 / 69.7 [d,c]
Education: Tertiary gross enrol. ratio (f/m per 100 pop.)	15.0 / 19.3	24.1 / 25.2	25.8 / 25.7 [c]
Intentional homicide rate (per 100 000 pop.)	4.0	3.5	3.1 [c]
Seats held by women in the National Parliament (%)	18.2	17.6	17.3 [h]

Environment and infrastructure indicators	2010	2015	2020
Individuals using the Internet (per 100 inhabitants)	7.6	17.5	33.5 [c]
Research & Development expenditure (% of GDP)	0.7	0.6	0.6 [b]
Forested area (% of land area)	14.6	14.7	14.7 [b]
Important sites for terrestrial biodiversity protected (%)	25.7	28.1	28.1 [f]
Pop. using safely managed drinking water (urban/rural, %)	60.7 / 47.1	59.1 / 56.2	58.5 / 59.9 [b]
Pop. using safely managed sanitation (urban/rural %)	... / 24.3	... / 34.4	... / 38.7 [b]

a Calculated by the UN Statistics Division. b 2017. c 2018. d Estimate. e 2016. f 2019. g Data refers to a 5-year period preceding the reference year. h Data are as at 1 January of reporting year.

Western Asia

Region	Asia	Population (000, 2020)	279 637
Surface area (km2)	4 831 000[a]	Pop. density (per km2, 2020)	58.2
Sex ratio (m per 100 f)	110.0		

Economic indicators	2010	2015	2020
GDP: Gross domestic product (million current US$)	2 552 273	2 957 691	3 274 077[b]
GDP growth rate (annual %, const. 2015 prices)	5.7	3.8	2.2[b]
GDP per capita (current US$)	10 994.4	11 493.1	12 094.7[b]
Employment in agriculture (% of employed)[c,d]	10.8	10.6	9.0
Employment in industry (% of employed)[c,d]	27.2	26.2	25.8
Employment in services & other sectors (% employed)[c,d]	62.0	63.2	65.1
Unemployment rate (% of labour force)[c,d]	7.2	7.4	8.0
Labour force participation rate (female/male pop. %)[c,d]	16.9 / 76.0	18.6 / 77.6	18.0 / 77.7
Agricultural production index (2004-2006=100)	106	115	117[e]
International trade: exports (million current US$)	919 156	976 785	1 165 271[f]
International trade: imports (million current US$)	749 249	953 678	898 246[f]
International trade: balance (million current US$)	169 907	23 107	267 025[f]

Social indicators	2010	2015	2020
Population growth rate (average annual %)[g]	2.5	2.1	1.6
Urban population (% of total population)	68.2	70.4	72.0[f]
Urban population growth rate (average annual %)[g]	3.2	2.7	...
Fertility rate, total (live births per woman)[g]	3.0	2.9	2.7
Life expectancy at birth (females/males, years)[g]	75.2 / 69.6	76.3 / 70.8	77.2 / 72.1
Population age distribution (0-14/60+ years old, %)	31.1 / 7.3	29.3 / 7.9	28.1 / 8.8
International migrant stock (000/% of total pop.)	30 614.3 / 13.2	39 913.9 / 15.5	45 635.5 / 16.6[f]
Infant mortality rate (per 1 000 live births)[g]	23.4	20.5	18.0
Education: Primary gross enrol. ratio (f/m per 100 pop.)	98.1 / 105.5	98.1 / 104.5[d]	93.5 / 99.5[d,b]
Education: Secondary gross enrol. ratio (f/m per 100 pop.)	72.2 / 80.0	79.0 / 86.7[d]	80.1 / 88.6[d,b]
Education: Tertiary gross enrol. ratio (f/m per 100 pop.)	34.0 / 36.2	50.0 / 51.7	55.5 / 57.1[d,b]
Intentional homicide rate (per 100 000 pop.)	3.8	3.5	3.4[b]
Seats held by women in the National Parliament (%)	9.3	12.8	15.6[h]

Environment and infrastructure indicators	2010	2015	2020
Individuals using the Internet (per 100 inhabitants)	32.7	56.5	67.6[b]
Research & Development expenditure (% of GDP)	0.5	0.6	0.6[a]
Forested area (% of land area)	4.0	4.1	4.1[a]
Important sites for terrestrial biodiversity protected (%)	15.2	16.6	17.0[f]
Pop. using safely managed sanitation (urban/rural %)	60.9 / ...	63.4 / ...	64.0 / ...[a]
Net Official Development Assist. received (% of GNI)[i,j]	1.21	1.99	7.51[b]

a 2017. b 2018. c Data excludes Armenia, Azerbaijan, Cyprus, Georgia, Israel and Turkey. d Estimate. e 2016. f 2019. g Data refers to a 5-year period preceding the reference year. h Data are as at 1 January of reporting year. i Excluding Armenia, Azerbaijan, Cyprus, Georgia and Turkey. Includes Iran (Islamic Rep. of). j Including regional aid disbursements in addition to the disbursements made to individual countries and areas.

Region	World	Population (000, 2020)	747 636
Surface area (km2)	23 049 000 [a]	Pop. density (per km2, 2020)	33.8
Sex ratio (m per 100 f)	93.4		

Economic indicators

	2010	2015	2020
GDP: Gross domestic product (million current US$)	19 860 115	19 160 796	21 908 725 [b]
GDP growth rate (annual %, const. 2015 prices)	2.3	1.9	2.0 [b]
GDP per capita (current US$)	26 904.9	25 723.6	29 278.7 [b]
Agricultural production index (2004-2006=100)	100	109	110 [c]
International trade: exports (million current US$)	5 904 975	6 063 469	7 100 768 [d]
International trade: imports (million current US$)	5 868 691	5 711 583	6 852 851 [d]
International trade: balance (million current US$)	36 284	351 886	247 918 [d]

Social indicators

	2010	2015	2020
Population growth rate (average annual %) [e]	0.2	0.2	0.1
Urban population (% of total population)	72.9	73.9	74.7 [d]
Urban population growth rate (average annual %) [e]	0.5	0.3	...
Fertility rate, total (live births per woman) [e]	1.6	1.6	1.6
Life expectancy at birth (females/males, years) [e]	79.3 / 71.3	80.7 / 73.6	81.6 / 74.9
Population age distribution (0-14/60+ years old, %)	15.5 / 22.0	15.8 / 23.8	16.1 / 25.7
International migrant stock (000/% of total pop.)	70 678.0 / 9.6	75 008.2 / 10.1	82 304.5 / 11.0 [d]
Refugees and others of concern to the UNHCR (000)	...	4 673.8	6 141.3 [d]
Infant mortality rate (per 1 000 live births) [e]	6.4	5.3	4.2
Education: Primary gross enrol. ratio (f/m per 100 pop.)	101.6 / 102.1	100.7 / 100.5	100.9 / 101.1 [f,b]
Education: Secondary gross enrol. ratio (f/m per 100 pop.)	100.5 / 101.2	106.5 / 106.9	106.7 / 107.4 [f,b]
Education: Tertiary gross enrol. ratio (f/m per 100 pop.)	76.8 / 59.7	76.8 / 62.5	79.0 / 64.5 [f,b]
Intentional homicide rate (per 100 000 pop.)	3.5	3.5	2.8 [b]
Seats held by women in the National Parliament (%)	23.2	26.7	31.4 [g]

Environment and infrastructure indicators

	2010	2015	2020
Individuals using the Internet (per 100 inhabitants)	61.3	74.3	82.0 [b]
Research & Development expenditure (% of GDP)	1.7	1.8	1.9 [a]
Forested area (% of land area)	45.8	45.9	45.9 [a]
Energy production, primary (Petajoules)	102 627	101 198	104 101 [a]
Energy supply per capita (Gigajoules)	152	141	144 [a]
Important sites for terrestrial biodiversity protected (%)	63.0	65.2	65.6 [d]
Pop. using safely managed sanitation (urban/rural %)	77.9 / 50.1	80.3 / 52.4	81.1 / 53.3 [a]
Net Official Development Assist. received (% of GNI) [h,i]	0.53	0.62	0.61 [b]

a 2017. **b** 2018. **c** 2016. **d** 2019. **e** Data refers to a 5-year period preceding the reference year. **f** Estimate. **g** Data are as at 1 January of reporting year. **h** Including regional aid disbursements in addition to the disbursements made to individual countries and areas. **i** Including Turkey and Cyprus.

Eastern Europe

Region	Europe	Population (000, 2020)	293 013
Surface area (km2)	18 814 000 [a]	Pop. density (per km2, 2020)	16.2
Sex ratio (m per 100 f)	88.8		

Economic indicators	2010	2015	2020
GDP: Gross domestic product (million current US$)	2 864 772	2 627 186	3 262 795 [b]
GDP growth rate (annual %, const. 2015 prices)	3.3	--0.0	3.2 [b]
GDP per capita (current US$)	9 715.3	8 924.1	11 105.9 [b]
Employment in agriculture (% of employed) [c]	11.7	9.8	8.4
Employment in industry (% of employed) [c]	28.6	28.1	28.2
Employment in services & other sectors (% employed) [c]	59.7	62.0	63.4
Unemployment rate (% of labour force) [c]	8.0	6.6	4.7
Labour force participation rate (female/male pop. %) [c]	52.0 / 66.7	52.0 / 67.7	51.3 / 67.0
Agricultural production index (2004-2006=100)	99	119	127 [d]
International trade: exports (million current US$)	994 605	1 023 967	1 286 023 [e]
International trade: imports (million current US$)	868 649	847 926	1 120 392 [e]
International trade: balance (million current US$)	125 955	176 042	165 631 [e]

Social indicators	2010	2015	2020
Population growth rate (average annual %) [f]	- 0.2	--0.0	- 0.1
Urban population (% of total population)	68.9	69.3	69.8 [e]
Urban population growth rate (average annual %) [f]	- 0.1	--0.0	...
Fertility rate, total (live births per woman) [f]	1.4	1.6	1.7
Life expectancy at birth (females/males, years) [f]	75.1 / 64.1	77.1 / 67.2	78.4 / 69.0
Population age distribution (0-14/60+ years old, %)	14.9 / 19.3	16.0 / 21.4	17.0 / 23.7
International migrant stock (000/% of total pop.)	19 110.7 / 6.5	19 841.5 / 6.7	20 278.7 / 6.9 [e]
Infant mortality rate (per 1 000 live births) [f]	9.8	7.6	5.5
Intentional homicide rate (per 100 000 pop.)	6.9	7.1	5.5 [b]
Seats held by women in the National Parliament (%)	15.2	16.9	22.4 [g]

Environment and infrastructure indicators	2010	2015	2020
Forested area (% of land area)	47.6	47.7	47.7 [a]
Pop. using safely managed sanitation (urban/rural %)	56.1 / ...	59.9 / ...	61.4 / ... [a]

a 2017. **b** 2018. **c** Estimate. **d** 2016. **e** 2019. **f** Data refers to a 5-year period preceding the reference year. **g** Data are as at 1 January of reporting year.

Northern Europe

Region	Europe	Population (000, 2020)	106 261
Surface area (km2)	1 810 000ᵃ	Pop. density (per km2, 2020)	62.4
Sex ratio (m per 100 f)	97.6ᵇ		

Economic indicators	2010	2015	2020
GDP: Gross domestic product (million current US$)	4 286 874	4 755 722	5 005 288ᶜ
GDP growth rate (annual %, const. 2015 prices)	2.3	3.6	2.1ᶜ
GDP per capita (current US$)	42 823.4	46 072.6	47 699.4ᶜ
Employment in agriculture (% of employed)ᵈ	2.2	2.1	1.7
Employment in industry (% of employed)ᵈ	19.8	19.3	18.5
Employment in services & other sectors (% employed)ᵈ	78.0	78.7	79.8
Labour force participation rate (female/male pop. %)ᵈ	56.3 / 68.1	57.1 / 67.8	57.9 / 67.6
Agricultural production index (2004-2006=100)	101	110	106ᵉ
International trade: exports (million current US$)	1 045 978	1 045 828	1 157 774ᶠ
International trade: imports (million current US$)	1 122 240	1 132 508	1 289 321ᶠ
International trade: balance (million current US$)	- 76 262	- 86 680	- 131 546ᶠ

Social indicators	2010	2015	2020
Population growth rate (average annual %)ᵍ	0.8	0.6	0.5
Urban population (% of total population)	80.1	81.4	82.4ᶠ
Urban population growth rate (average annual %)ᵍ	1.1	0.9	...
Fertility rate, total (live births per woman)ᵇ,ᵍ	1.8	1.8	1.7
Life expectancy at birth (females/males, years)ᵇ,ᵍ	81.6 / 76.6	82.6 / 78.3	83.1 / 78.9
Population age distribution (0-14/60+ years old, %)ᵇ	17.4 / 22.6	17.5 / 23.6	17.5 / 24.8
International migrant stock (000/% of total pop.)	11 344.8 / 11.3	13 269.4 / 12.8	15 094.9 / 14.3ᶠ
Infant mortality rate (per 1 000 live births)ᵇ,ᵍ	4.4	3.7	3.3
Intentional homicide rate (per 100 000 pop.)	1.4	1.2	1.3ᶜ
Seats held by women in the National Parliament (%)	29.6	30.4	36.4ʰ

Environment and infrastructure indicators	2010	2015	2020
Forested area (% of land area)	43.8	44.0	44.0ᵃ
Pop. using safely managed sanitation (urban/rural %)	95.6 / 71.1	96.4 / 72.2	96.5 / 72.4ᵃ

a 2017. b Including the Faroe Islands and the Isle of Man. c 2018. d Estimate. e 2016. f 2019. g Data refers to a 5-year period preceding the reference year. h Data are as at 1 January of reporting year.

Southern Europe

Region	Europe	Population (000, 2020)	152 215
Surface area (km2)	1 317 000[a]	Pop. density (per km2, 2020)	117.5
Sex ratio (m per 100 f)	95.5[b]		

Economic indicators	2010	2015	2020
GDP: Gross domestic product (million current US$)	4 302 127	3 619 794	4 209 516[c]
GDP growth rate (annual %, const. 2015 prices)	0.7	1.9	1.6[c]
GDP per capita (current US$)	28 121.9	23 654.1	27 584.7[c]
Employment in agriculture (% of employed)[d]	7.6	6.9	6.1
Employment in industry (% of employed)[d]	25.8	23.5	23.4
Employment in services & other sectors (% employed)[d]	66.6	69.6	70.5
Unemployment rate (% of labour force)[d]	14.3	17.2	11.3
Labour force participation rate (female/male pop. %)[d]	44.7 / 62.7	45.6 / 61.4	45.9 / 60.9
Agricultural production index (2004-2006=100)	100	98	99[e]
International trade: exports (million current US$)	830 354	886 303	1 070 693[f]
International trade: imports (million current US$)	1 039 442	925 085	1 134 330[f]
International trade: balance (million current US$)	- 209 088	- 38 782	- 63 637[f]

Social indicators	2010	2015	2020
Population growth rate (average annual %)[g]	0.4	~0.0	- 0.1
Urban population (% of total population)	69.2	70.6	71.8[f]
Urban population growth rate (average annual %)[g]	0.9	0.2	...
Fertility rate, total (live births per woman)[b,g]	1.5	1.4	1.4
Life expectancy at birth (females/males, years)[b,g]	82.9 / 77.1	83.8 / 78.5	84.5 / 79.5
Population age distribution (0-14/60+ years old, %)[b]	14.9 / 24.0	14.5 / 25.8	13.9 / 27.9
International migrant stock (000/% of total pop.)	16 206.1 / 10.6	15 815.4 / 10.3	16 503.6 / 10.8[f]
Infant mortality rate (per 1 000 live births)[b,g]	4.3	3.6	3.1
Intentional homicide rate (per 100 000 pop.)	1.2	0.9	0.7[c]
Seats held by women in the National Parliament (%)	23.0	30.0	33.3[h]

Environment and infrastructure indicators	2010	2015	2020
Forested area (% of land area)	34.8	35.2	35.2[a]
Pop. using safely managed sanitation (urban/rural %)	82.6 / 63.2	84.7 / 65.1	85.2 / 65.4[a]

a 2017. **b** Including Andorra, Gibraltar, Holy See, and San Marino. **c** 2018. **d** Estimate. **e** 2016. **f** 2019. **g** Data refers to a 5-year period preceding the reference year. **h** Data are as at 1 January of reporting year.

Region	Europe	Population (000, 2020)	196 146
Surface area (km2)	1 108 000[a]	Pop. density (per km2, 2020)	180.8
Sex ratio (m per 100 f)	96.6[b]		

Economic indicators	2010	2015	2020
GDP: Gross domestic product (million current US$)	8 406 342	8 158 094	9 431 125[c]
GDP growth rate (annual %, const. 2015 prices)	2.9	1.5	1.8[c]
GDP per capita (current US$)	44 197.5	42 002.8	47 884.7[c]
Employment in agriculture (% of employed)[d]	2.4	2.1	1.8
Employment in industry (% of employed)[d]	24.7	23.6	22.9
Employment in services & other sectors (% employed)[d]	72.9	74.2	75.3
Unemployment rate (% of labour force)[d]	7.2	6.9	5.0
Labour force participation rate (female/male pop. %)[d]	52.6 / 65.4	53.5 / 64.6	53.9 / 64.3
Agricultural production index (2004-2006=100)	102	106	103[e]
International trade: exports (million current US$)	3 034 038	3 107 370	3 586 278[f]
International trade: imports (million current US$)	2 838 360	2 806 064	3 308 808[f]
International trade: balance (million current US$)	195 679	301 306	277 470[f]

Social indicators	2010	2015	2020
Population growth rate (average annual %)[g]	0.2	0.4	0.4
Urban population (% of total population)	78.5	79.4	80.0[f]
Urban population growth rate (average annual %)[g]	0.6	0.6	...
Fertility rate, total (live births per woman)[b,g]	1.6	1.7	1.7
Life expectancy at birth (females/males, years)[b,g]	83.0 / 77.3	83.7 / 78.4	84.2 / 79.2
Population age distribution (0-14/60+ years old, %)[b]	15.9 / 24.3	15.6 / 25.8	15.6 / 27.4
International migrant stock (000/% of total pop.)	24 016.4 / 12.8	26 081.8 / 13.6	30 427.3 / 15.6[f]
Infant mortality rate (per 1 000 live births)[b,g]	3.8	3.4	3.1
Intentional homicide rate (per 100 000 pop.)	1.1	1.1	1.0[c]
Seats held by women in the National Parliament (%)	28.4	32.0	35.8[h]

Environment and infrastructure indicators	2010	2015	2020
Forested area (% of land area)	31.4	32.0	32.0[a]
Pop. using safely managed sanitation (urban/rural %)	97.8 / 85.7	98.4 / 85.9	98.4 / 85.9[a]

a 2017. **b** Including Liechtenstein and Monaco. **c** 2018. **d** Estimate. **e** 2016. **f** 2019. **g** Data refers to a 5-year period preceding the reference year. **h** Data are as at 1 January of reporting year.

Oceania

Region	World	Population (000, 2020)	42 678
Surface area (km2)	8 564 000[a]	Pop. density (per km2, 2020)	5.0
Sex ratio (m per 100 f)	100.2		

Economic indicators	2010	2015	2020
GDP: Gross domestic product (million current US$)	1 482 497	1 472 455	1 711 770[b]
GDP growth rate (annual %, const. 2015 prices)	2.4	3.1	2.0[b]
GDP per capita (current US$)	40 518.5	37 211.2	41 469.2[b]
Unemployment rate (% of labour force)[c]	5.0	5.5	4.8
Labour force participation rate (female/male pop. %)[c]	56.9 / 69.1	57.2 / 67.8	57.8 / 67.2
Agricultural production index (2004-2006=100)	98	111	109[d]
International trade: exports (million current US$)	253 360	235 103	323 326[e]
International trade: imports (million current US$)	247 608	251 514	282 660[e]
International trade: balance (million current US$)	5 752	- 16 410	40 666[e]

Social indicators	2010	2015	2020
Population growth rate (average annual %)[f]	1.8	1.6	1.4
Urban population (% of total population)	68.1	68.1	68.2[e]
Urban population growth rate (average annual %)[f]	1.8	1.5	...
Fertility rate, total (live births per woman)[f]	2.5	2.4	2.4
Life expectancy at birth (females/males, years)[f]	78.4 / 74.1	79.4 / 75.4	80.5 / 76.5
Population age distribution (0-14/60+ years old, %)	24.1 / 15.2	23.7 / 16.2	23.6 / 17.5
International migrant stock (000/% of total pop.)	7 127.7 / 19.3	8 069.9 / 20.2	8 927.9 / 21.2[e]
Refugees and others of concern to the UNHCR (000)	...	71.3	143.0[e]
Infant mortality rate (per 1 000 live births)[f]	23.1	20.5	18.0
Education: Primary gross enrol. ratio (f/m per 100 pop.)	96.4 / 99.4	101.8 / 104.9	101.7 / 104.6[c,b]
Education: Secondary gross enrol. ratio (f/m per 100 pop.)	107.1 / 114.7[c]	104.1 / 117.6	102.0 / 113.8[c,b]
Education: Tertiary gross enrol. ratio (f/m per 100 pop.)	82.4 / 61.0[c]	90.5 / 63.6	86.1 / 61.0[c,b]
Intentional homicide rate (per 100 000 pop.)	3.0	2.9	2.9[b]
Seats held by women in the National Parliament (%)	13.2	13.2	16.6[g]

Environment and infrastructure indicators	2010	2015	2020
Individuals using the Internet (per 100 inhabitants)	57.3	65.7	68.2[a]
Forested area (% of land area)	20.3	20.4	20.4[a]
Energy production, primary (Petajoules)	14 530	17 039	17 969[a]
Energy supply per capita (Gigajoules)	178	167	163[a]
Important sites for terrestrial biodiversity protected (%)	29.7	33.2	33.7[e]
Pop. using safely managed drinking water (urban/rural, %)	95.3 / ...	96.1 / ...	96.1 / ...[a]
Pop. using safely managed sanitation (urban/rural, %)	61.6 / 22.8	65.4 / 23.4	66.7 / 23.5[a]
Net Official Development Assist. received (% of GNI)[h]	9.56	6.35	6.98[b]

a 2017. b 2018. c Estimate. d 2016. e 2019. f Data refers to a 5-year period preceding the reference year. g Data are as at 1 January of reporting year. h Including regional aid disbursements in addition to the disbursements made to individual countries and areas.

Australia and New Zealand

Region	Oceania	Population (000, 2020)	30 322
Surface area (km2)	8 012 000 [a]	Pop. density (per km2, 2020)	3.8
Sex ratio (m per 100 f)	98.8		

Economic indicators	2010	2015	2020
GDP: Gross domestic product (million current US$)	1 446 047	1 426 321	1 661 791 [b]
GDP growth rate (annual %, const. 2015 prices)	2.3	3.0	2.1 [b]
GDP per capita (current US$)	54 516.9	49 963.9	56 063.4 [b]
Agricultural production index (2004-2006=100)	97	111	108 [c]
International trade: exports (million current US$)	243 502	222 149	305 917 [d]
International trade: imports (million current US$)	232 319	236 642	263 753 [d]
International trade: balance (million current US$)	11 183	- 14 493	42 164 [d]

Social indicators	2010	2015	2020
Population growth rate (average annual %) [e]	1.7	1.5	1.2
Urban population (% of total population)	85.3	85.8	86.2 [d]
Urban population growth rate (average annual %) [e]	1.8	1.5	...
Fertility rate, total (live births per woman) [e]	2.0	1.9	1.8
Life expectancy at birth (females/males, years) [e]	83.5 / 79.0	84.2 / 80.2	85.0 / 81.1
Population age distribution (0-14/60+ years old, %)	19.3 / 18.8	19.1 / 20.2	19.3 / 21.8
International migrant stock (000/% of total pop.)	6 830.4 / 25.8	7 769.5 / 27.2	8 618.0 / 28.7 [d]
Infant mortality rate (per 1 000 live births) [e]	4.5	3.7	3.2
Intentional homicide rate (per 100 000 pop.)	1.0	1.0	0.9 [b]
Seats held by women in the National Parliament (%)	30.1	28.8	35.1 [f]

Environment and infrastructure indicators	2010	2015	2020
Individuals using the Internet (per 100 inhabitants)	76.7	85.2	86.9 [b]
Research & Development expenditure (% of GDP)	2.2	1.8	1.8 [a]
Forested area (% of land area)	16.8	17.0	17.0 [a]
Important sites for terrestrial biodiversity protected (%)	46.5	52.5	53.0 [d]
Pop. using safely managed drinking water (urban/rural, %)	95.7 / ...	96.5 / ...	96.5 / ... [a]

a 2017. **b** 2018. **c** 2016. **d** 2019. **e** Data refers to a 5-year period preceding the reference year. **f** Data are as at 1 January of reporting year.

Melanesia

Region	Oceania	Population (000, 2020)	11 123
Surface area (km2)	541 000[a]	Pop. density (per km2, 2020)	21.0
Sex ratio (m per 100 f)	104.0		

Economic indicators	2010	2015	2020
GDP: Gross domestic product (million current US$)	28 167	38 235	40 948[b]
GDP growth rate (annual %, const. 2015 prices)	8.2	4.9	1.0[b]
GDP per capita (current US$)	3 065.6	3 777.5	3 821.4[b]
Agricultural production index (2004-2006=100)	110	118	119[c]
International trade: exports (million current US$)	8 112	10 998	15 271[d]
International trade: imports (million current US$)	9 665	7 968	9 368[d]
International trade: balance (million current US$)	- 1 553	3 030	5 903[d]

Social indicators	2010	2015	2020
Population growth rate (average annual %)[e]	2.2	1.9	1.9
Urban population (% of total population)	19.0	19.2	19.5[d]
Urban population growth rate (average annual %)[e]	2.3	2.2	...
Fertility rate, total (live births per woman)[e]	3.9	3.7	3.5
Life expectancy at birth (females/males, years)[e]	64.2 / 61.4	65.5 / 62.7	66.8 / 64.1
Population age distribution (0-14/60+ years old, %)	37.2 / 5.7	36.1 / 5.9	34.7 / 6.5
International migrant stock (000/% of total pop.)	110.7 / 1.2	119.3 / 1.2	123.6 / 1.1[d]
Infant mortality rate (per 1 000 live births)[e]	48.4	43.1	37.5
Seats held by women in the National Parliament (%)	1.4	4.2	4.9[f]

Environment and infrastructure indicators	2010	2015	2020
Forested area (% of land area)	71.9	71.8	71.8[a]

a 2017. b 2018. c 2016. d 2019. e Data refers to a 5-year period preceding the reference year. f Data are as at 1 January of reporting year.

Micronesia

Region	Oceania	Population (000, 2020)	549
Surface area (km2)	3 000 [a]	Pop. density (per km2, 2020)	173.2
Sex ratio (m per 100 f)	102.1 [b]		

Economic indicators	2010	2015	2020
GDP: Gross domestic product (million current US$)	864	1 050	1 185 [c]
GDP growth rate (annual %, const. 2015 prices)	2.5	5.8	1.2 [c]
GDP per capita (current US$)	2 977.7	3 440.5	3 755.4 [c]
Agricultural production index (2004-2006=100)	79	82	76 [d]
International trade: exports (million current US$)	1 508	1 737	1 949 [e]
International trade: imports (million current US$)	3 292	4 627	6 536 [e]
International trade: balance (million current US$)	- 1 783	- 2 891	- 4 587 [e]

Social indicators	2010	2015	2020
Population growth rate (average annual %) [f]	0.2	0.8	1.0
Urban population (% of total population)	66.6	67.9	69.0 [e]
Urban population growth rate (average annual %) [f]	0.2	1.0	...
Fertility rate, total (live births per woman) [b,f]	3.1	3.0	2.9
Life expectancy at birth (females/males, years) [b,f]	73.2 / 68.2	74.7 / 69.1	76.3 / 70.2
Population age distribution (0-14/60+ years old, %) [b]	32.1 / 7.4	30.5 / 9.0	29.3 / 10.9
International migrant stock (000/% of total pop.)	115.0 / 22.8	113.5 / 21.7	118.0 / 21.7 [e]
Infant mortality rate (per 1 000 live births) [b,f]	30.6	28.7	25.0
Seats held by women in the National Parliament (%)	2.4	4.7	7.0 [g]

Environment and infrastructure indicators	2010	2015	2020
Forested area (% of land area)	58.2	58.0	58.0 [a]
Pop. using safely managed drinking water (urban/rural, %)	87.3 / ...	89.0 / ...	89.5 / ... [a]
Net Official Development Assist. received (% of GNI) [h]	20.77	21.70	24.76 [c]

a 2017. **b** Including Marshall Islands, Nauru, Northern Mariana Islands and Palau. **c** 2018. **d** 2016. **e** 2019. **f** Data refers to a 5-year period preceding the reference year. **g** Data are as at 1 January of reporting year. **h** Including regional aid disbursements in addition to the disbursements made to individual countries and areas.

Polynesia

Region	Oceania	Population (000, 2020)	684[a]
Surface area (km2)	8 000[b]	Pop. density (per km2, 2020)	84.5[a]
Sex ratio (m per 100 f)	102.9[c]		

Economic indicators	2010	2015	2020
GDP: Gross domestic product (million current US$)	7 419	6 848	7 846[d]
GDP growth rate (annual %, const. 2015 prices)	- 1.7	2.3	2.3[d]
GDP per capita (current US$)	12 675.1	11 488.3	12 947.1[d]
Agricultural production index (2004-2006=100)	111	118	117[e]
International trade: exports (million current US$)	238	219	189[f]
International trade: imports (million current US$)	2 333	2 277	3 004[f]
International trade: balance (million current US$)	- 2 095	- 2 058	- 2 815[f]

Social indicators	2010	2015	2020
Population growth rate (average annual %)[c,g]	0.3	0.3	0.5
Urban population (% of total population)	44.3	44.5	44.4[f]
Urban population growth rate (average annual %)[g]	0.9	0.6	...
Fertility rate, total (live births per woman)[c,g]	3.2	2.9	2.8
Life expectancy at birth (females/males, years)[c,g]	74.9 / 70.4	75.9 / 71.6	76.9 / 72.7
Population age distribution (0-14/60+ years old, %)[c]	32.0 / 8.4	30.9 / 9.6	29.2 / 11.2
International migrant stock (000/% of total pop.)[c]	71.6 / 10.9	67.6 / 10.1	68.4 / 10.1[f]
Infant mortality rate (per 1 000 live births)[c,g]	14.7	13.2	12.0
Seats held by women in the National Parliament (%)	5.2	4.4	8.6[h]

Environment and infrastructure indicators	2010	2015	2020
Forested area (% of land area)	48.8	48.7	48.7[b]
Pop. using safely managed sanitation (urban/rural %)	... / 46.5	... / 46.5	... / 46.2[b]

a Including Pitcairn. b 2017. c Including American Samoa, Cook Islands, Niue, Pitcairn, Tokelau, Tuvalu, and Wallis and Futuna Islands. d 2018. e 2016. f 2019. g Data refers to a 5-year period preceding the reference year. h Data are as at 1 January of reporting year.

Afghanistan

Region	Southern Asia	UN membership date	19 November 1946
Population (000, 2020)	38 928	Surface area (km2)	652 864[a]
Pop. density (per km2, 2020)	59.6	Sex ratio (m per 100 f)	105.4
Capital city	Kabul	National currency	Afghani (AFN)
Capital city pop. (000, 2020)	4 114.0[b]	Exchange rate (per US$)	78.4[b]

Economic indicators	2010	2015	2020
GDP: Gross domestic product (million current US$)	16 078	20 608	20 514[c]
GDP growth rate (annual %, const. 2015 prices)	3.2	- 1.8	- 1.7[c]
GDP per capita (current US$)	550.9	598.8	551.9[c]
Economy: Agriculture (% of Gross Value Added)	28.8	22.7	21.4[c]
Economy: Industry (% of Gross Value Added)	21.3	22.7	24.5[c]
Economy: Services and other activity (% of GVA)	49.8	54.7	54.1[c]
Employment in agriculture (% of employed)[d]	54.7	47.1	42.4
Employment in industry (% of employed)[d]	14.4	17.0	18.3
Employment in services & other sectors (% employed)[d]	30.9	35.8	39.4
Unemployment rate (% of labour force)[d]	11.5	11.4	11.2
Labour force participation rate (female/male pop. %)[d]	14.9 / 78.4	18.8 / 76.2	21.8 / 74.6
CPI: Consumer Price Index (2010=100)	100	133	146[a]
Agricultural production index (2004-2006=100)	116	120	125[e]
International trade: exports (million current US$)	388	571	1 038[d,b]
International trade: imports (million current US$)	5 154	7 723	8 370[d,b]
International trade: balance (million current US$)	- 4 766	- 7 151	- 7 332[d,b]
Balance of payments, current account (million US$)	- 578	- 4 193	- 3 799[b]

Major trading partners						2019
Export partners (% of exports)[d]	Pakistan	42.9	India	40.6	China	3.2
Import partners (% of imports)[d]	Iran	17.1	China	15.7	Pakistan	14.7

Social indicators	2010	2015	2020
Population growth rate (average annual %)[f]	2.6	3.3	2.5
Urban population (% of total population)	23.7	24.8	25.8[b]
Urban population growth rate (average annual %)[f]	3.7	4.0	...
Fertility rate, total (live births per woman)[f]	6.5	5.4	4.6
Life expectancy at birth (females/males, years)[f]	61.0 / 58.3	63.8 / 60.9	65.8 / 62.8
Population age distribution (0-14/60+ years old, %)	48.2 / 3.9	44.9 / 4.0	41.8 / 4.2
International migrant stock (000/% of total pop.)	102.2 / 0.4	489.7 / 1.4	149.8 / 0.4[b]
Refugees and others of concern to the UNHCR (000)	1 200.0[g]	1 421.4	2 826.4[b]
Infant mortality rate (per 1 000 live births)[f]	72.2	60.1	51.7
Health: Current expenditure (% of GDP)	8.6	10.1	11.8[a]
Health: Physicians (per 1 000 pop.)	0.2	0.3	0.3[e]
Education: Government expenditure (% of GDP)	3.5	3.3	4.1[d,a]
Education: Primary gross enrol. ratio (f/m per 100 pop.)	80.6 / 118.6	83.5 / 122.7	82.9 / 124.2[c]
Education: Secondary gross enrol. ratio (f/m per 100 pop.)	33.3 / 66.9	36.8 / 65.9	40.0 / 70.1[c]
Education: Tertiary gross enrol. ratio (f/m per 100 pop.)	1.4 / 6.0[h]	3.5 / 12.6[i]	4.9 / 14.2[c]
Intentional homicide rate (per 100 000 pop.)	3.4	9.8	6.7[c]
Seats held by women in the National Parliament (%)	27.3	27.7	27.0[j]

Environment and infrastructure indicators	2010	2015	2020
Individuals using the Internet (per 100 inhabitants)	4.0[d]	8.3[d]	13.5[k,a]
Threatened species (number)	34	38	40
Forested area (% of land area)[d]	2.1	2.1	2.1[a]
Energy production, primary (Petajoules)	41	60	82[a]
Energy supply per capita (Gigajoules)	5	4	3[a]
Important sites for terrestrial biodiversity protected (%)	5.7	5.7	5.7[b]
Net Official Development Assist. received (% of GNI)	39.25	21.28	19.46[c]

a 2017. b 2019. c 2018. d Estimate. e 2016. f Data refers to a 5-year period preceding the reference year. g Data as at the end of December. h 2009. i 2014. j Data are as at 1 January of reporting year. k Population aged 18 years and over.

Albania

Region	Southern Europe	UN membership date	14 December 1955
Population (000, 2020)	2 878	Surface area (km2)	28 748[a]
Pop. density (per km2, 2020)	105.0	Sex ratio (m per 100 f)	103.7
Capital city	Tirana	National currency	Lek (ALL)
Capital city pop. (000, 2020)	484.6[b]	Exchange rate (per US$)	108.6[b]

Economic indicators

	2010	2015	2020
GDP: Gross domestic product (million current US$)	11 927	11 387	15 059[c]
GDP growth rate (annual %, const. 2015 prices)	3.7	2.2	4.1[c]
GDP per capita (current US$)	4 045.7	3 939.4	5 223.8[c]
Economy: Agriculture (% of Gross Value Added)[d]	20.7	22.5	21.0[c]
Economy: Industry (% of Gross Value Added)[d,e]	28.7	24.8	24.3[c]
Economy: Services and other activity (% of GVA)[d,f,g]	50.7	52.7	54.7[c]
Employment in agriculture (% of employed)	42.1	41.4	36.1[h]
Employment in industry (% of employed)	20.6	18.6	20.2[h]
Employment in services & other sectors (% employed)	37.3	40.0	43.7[h]
Unemployment rate (% of labour force)[h]	14.1	17.1	12.8
Labour force participation rate (female/male pop. %)[h]	45.8 / 62.9	46.1 / 63.8	46.6 / 64.4
CPI: Consumer Price Index (2010=100)[i]	100	111	119[b]
Agricultural production index (2004-2006=100)	119	139	143[i]
International trade: exports (million current US$)[k]	1 550	1 930	2 720[h,b]
International trade: imports (million current US$)[k]	4 603	4 320	5 908[h,b]
International trade: balance (million current US$)[k]	- 3 053	- 2 391	- 3 189[h,b]
Balance of payments, current account (million US$)	- 1 356	- 980	- 1 165[b]

Major trading partners

						2019
Export partners (% of exports)[h]	Italy	48.0	Serbia	11.3	Spain	7.8
Import partners (% of imports)[h]	Italy	27.3	Turkey	8.4	China	8.4

Social indicators

	2010	2015	2020
Population growth rate (average annual %)[l]	- 0.9	- 0.4	- 0.1
Urban population (% of total population)	52.2	57.4	61.2[b]
Urban population growth rate (average annual %)[l]	1.3	1.8	...
Fertility rate, total (live births per woman)[l]	1.6	1.7	1.6
Life expectancy at birth (females/males, years)[l]	78.5 / 73.2	80.0 / 75.2	80.1 / 76.7
Population age distribution (0-14/60+ years old, %)	22.5 / 15.0	18.7 / 17.9	17.2 / 21.2
International migrant stock (000/% of total pop.)	52.8 / 1.8	52.0 / 1.8	49.2 / 1.7[b]
Refugees and others of concern to the UNHCR (000)	0.1[m]	8.1	4.3[n,b]
Infant mortality rate (per 1 000 live births)[l]	16.8	9.2	8.0
Health: Physicians (per 1 000 pop.)	1.2	1.3[o]	1.2[i]
Education: Government expenditure (% of GDP)	3.3[p]	3.4	4.0[i]
Education: Primary gross enrol. ratio (f/m per 100 pop.)	93.8 / 93.2	107.3 / 104.0	109.1 / 105.2[c]
Education: Secondary gross enrol. ratio (f/m per 100 pop.)	88.4 / 87.9	95.1 / 99.5	95.7 / 95.2[c]
Education: Tertiary gross enrol. ratio (f/m per 100 pop.)	51.6 / 38.0	73.5 / 51.6	67.6 / 43.0[c]
Intentional homicide rate (per 100 000 pop.)	4.3	2.2	2.3[c]
Seats held by women in the National Parliament (%)	16.4	20.7	29.5[q]

Environment and infrastructure indicators

	2010	2015	2020
Individuals using the Internet (per 100 inhabitants)	45.0	63.3[h]	71.8[h,a]
Research & Development expenditure (% of GDP)	0.2[r,s]	...	...
Threatened species (number)	100	112	142
Forested area (% of land area)[h]	28.3	28.2	28.2[a]
CO2 emission estimates (million tons/tons per capita)	3.9 / 1.3	3.8 / 1.3	4.3 / 1.5[a]
Energy production, primary (Petajoules)	69	87	69[a]
Energy supply per capita (Gigajoules)	31	31	34[a]
Tourist/visitor arrivals at national borders (000)[t]	2 191	3 784	5 340[c]
Important sites for terrestrial biodiversity protected (%)	47.2	55.9	57.2[b]
Pop. using safely managed sanitation (urban/rural %)	40.0 / 37.2	40.2 / 39.4	40.2 / 39.4[a]
Net Official Development Assist. received (% of GNI)	3.09	2.91	2.29[c]

a 2017. b 2019. c 2018. d Data classified according to ISIC Rev. 4. e Excludes publishing activities. Includes irrigation and canals. f Excludes repair of personal and household goods. g Excludes computer and related activities and radio/TV activities. h Estimate. i Calculated by the UN Statistics Division from national indices. j 2016. k In 2014, the reported share of non-standard HS codes was relatively high. l Data refers to a 5-year period preceding the reference year. m Data as at the end of December. n The statelessness figure refers to a survey conducted in late 2017. o 2013. p 2007. q Data are as at 1 January of reporting year. r Partial data. s 2008. t Excluding nationals residing abroad.

Algeria

Region	Northern Africa	
Population (000, 2020)	43 851	
Pop. density (per km2, 2020)	18.4	
Capital city	Algiers	
Capital city pop. (000, 2020)	2 729.3[b,c]	

UN membership date	08 October 1962
Surface area (km2)	2 381 741[a]
Sex ratio (m per 100 f)	102.1
National currency	Algerian Dinar (DZD)
Exchange rate (per US$)	119.2[c]

Economic indicators

	2010	2015	2020
GDP: Gross domestic product (million current US$)	161 207	165 979	173 757[d]
GDP growth rate (annual %, const. 2015 prices)	3.6	3.7	1.4[d]
GDP per capita (current US$)	4 480.8	4 177.9	4 114.7[d]
Economy: Agriculture (% of Gross Value Added)	8.6	12.1	12.4[d]
Economy: Industry (% of Gross Value Added)	51.4	37.3	41.0[d]
Economy: Services and other activity (% of GVA)	40.0	50.6	46.6[d]
Employment in agriculture (% of employed)[e]	11.9	10.3	9.7
Employment in industry (% of employed)[e]	30.1	31.0	30.7
Employment in services & other sectors (% employed)[e]	58.0	58.7	59.6
Unemployment rate (% of labour force)[e]	10.0	11.2	11.5
Labour force participation rate (female/male pop. %)[e]	14.4 / 70.0	15.2 / 67.4	14.6 / 67.0
CPI: Consumer Price Index (2010=100)[f]	100	127	151[g,c]
Agricultural production index (2004-2006=100)	130	151	151[h]
International trade: exports (million current US$)	57 051	34 796	34 571[e,c]
International trade: imports (million current US$)	41 000	51 803	45 140[e,c]
International trade: balance (million current US$)	16 051	- 17 007	- 10 569[e,c]
Balance of payments, current account (million US$)	12 220	- 27 038	- 22 059[a]

Major trading partners

							2019
Export partners (% of exports)[e]	Italy	16.0	France	12.6	Spain	11.7
Import partners (% of imports)[e]	China	18.1	France	9.3	Italy	8.2

Social indicators

	2010	2015	2020
Population growth rate (average annual %)[i]	1.6	2.0	2.0
Urban population (% of total population)	67.5	70.8	73.2[c]
Urban population growth rate (average annual %)[i]	2.8	2.9	...
Fertility rate, total (live births per woman)[i]	2.7	3.0	3.0
Life expectancy at birth (females/males, years)[i]	75.4 / 73.0	76.7 / 74.4	77.8 / 75.4
Population age distribution (0-14/60+ years old, %)	27.3 / 7.8	28.7 / 8.9	30.8 / 9.9
International migrant stock (000/% of total pop.)[j]	217.0 / 0.6	239.5 / 0.6	249.1 / 0.6[c]
Refugees and others of concern to the UNHCR (000)	94.4[k]	100.0	99.5[c]
Infant mortality rate (per 1 000 live births)[i]	29.4	24.9	21.2
Health: Current expenditure (% of GDP)	5.1	7.0	6.4[a]
Health: Physicians (per 1 000 pop.)	1.2[l]	...	1.7[d]
Education: Government expenditure (% of GDP)	4.3[m]	...	...
Education: Primary gross enrol. ratio (f/m per 100 pop.)	111.5 / 119.0	113.0 / 118.7	107.3 / 112.4[d]
Education: Secondary gross enrol. ratio (f/m per 100 pop.)	98.7 / 95.2	101.5 / 97.8[n]	... / ...
Education: Tertiary gross enrol. ratio (f/m per 100 pop.)	35.4 / 24.5	45.0 / 28.8	64.4 / 38.8[d]
Intentional homicide rate (per 100 000 pop.)	0.7	1.4	...
Seats held by women in the National Parliament (%)	7.7	31.6	25.8[o]

Environment and infrastructure indicators

	2010	2015	2020
Individuals using the Internet (per 100 inhabitants)	12.5	38.2[e]	49.0[d]
Research & Development expenditure (% of GDP)	0.1[p,q]	...	0.5[r,a]
Threatened species (number)	105	114	155
Forested area (% of land area)	0.8	0.8	0.8[e,a]
CO2 emission estimates (million tons/tons per capita)	95.5 / 2.6	130.4 / 3.3	130.5 / 3.2[a]
Energy production, primary (Petajoules)	6 200	5 883	6 285[a]
Energy supply per capita (Gigajoules)	45	56	55[a]
Tourist/visitor arrivals at national borders (000)[s]	2 070	1 710	2 657[d]
Important sites for terrestrial biodiversity protected (%)	16.6	16.6	16.6[c]
Pop. using safely managed sanitation (urban/rural %)	17.0 / 20.3	16.5 / 20.8	16.5 / 20.8[a]
Net Official Development Assist. received (% of GNI)	0.13	0.04	0.08[d]

2017. **b** Refers to the Governorate of Grand Algiers. **c** 2019. **d** 2018. **e** Estimate. **f** Algiers **g** Calculated by the UN Statistics Division from national indices. **h** 2016. **i** Data refers to a 5-year period preceding the reference year. **j** Including refugees. **k** Data as at the end of December. **l** 2007. **m** 2008. **n** 2011. **o** Data are as at 1 January of reporting year. **p** Partial data. **q** 2005. **r** Break in the time series. **s** Including nationals residing abroad.

American Samoa

Region	Polynesia	Population (000, 2020)	56
Surface area (km2)	199[a]	Pop. density (per km2, 2020)	279.0
Sex ratio (m per 100 f)	103.6[b,c]	Capital city	Pago Pago
National currency	US Dollar (USD)	Capital city pop. (000, 2020)	48.5[d]

Economic indicators	2010	2015	2020
Employment in agriculture (% of employed)	3.0[b,e,f]	...	...
Employment in industry (% of employed)	23.2[b,e,f]	...	...
Employment in services & other sectors (% employed)	73.8[b,e,f]	...	...
Unemployment rate (% of labour force)	9.2[b,f]	...	...
Agricultural production index (2004-2006=100)	110	115	116[c]

Social indicators	2010	2015	2020
Population growth rate (average annual %)	- 1.2[g]	---0.0[g]	0.1
Urban population (% of total population)	87.6	87.2	87.1[h]
Urban population growth rate (average annual %)[g]	- 1.3	- 0.1	...
Fertility rate, total (live births per woman)	...	2.6[i]	...
Life expectancy at birth (females/males, years)	76.2 / 68.5[j]	77.8 / 71.1[k]	... / ...
Population age distribution (0-14/60+ years old, %)	35.0 / 6.7[l,m]	... / ...	33.3 / 9.0[b,c]
International migrant stock (000/% of total pop.)	23.6 / 42.0	23.5 / 42.1	23.5 / 42.6[h]
Infant mortality rate (per 1 000 live births)	...	9.6[n,o]	...
Intentional homicide rate (per 100 000 pop.)	8.9	7.2	5.4[c]

Environment and infrastructure indicators	2010	2015	2020
Research & Development expenditure (% of GDP)	0.4[p,j]	...	...
Threatened species (number)	79	90	99
Forested area (% of land area)[q]	88.6	87.7	87.7[a]
Tourist/visitor arrivals at national borders (000)	23	20	20[d]
Important sites for terrestrial biodiversity protected (%)	71.1	71.1	71.1[h]

a 2017. b Break in the time series. c 2016. d 2018. e Data classified according to ISIC Rev. 3. f Population aged 16 years and over. g Data refers to a 5-year period preceding the reference year. h 2019. i 2013. j 2006. k 2011. l De jure population. m Including armed forces stationed in the area. n Data refers to a 2-year period up to and including the reference year. o 2012. p Partial data. q Estimate.

Andorra

Region	Southern Europe		UN membership date	28 July 1993	
Population (000, 2020)	77		Surface area (km2)	468 [a]	
Pop. density (per km2, 2020)	164.2		Sex ratio (m per 100 f)	102.3 [b,c,d]	
Capital city	Andorra la Vella		National currency	Euro (EUR)	
Capital city pop. (000, 2020)	22.6 [e]		Exchange rate (per US$)	0.9 [f]	

Economic indicators

	2010	2015	2020
GDP: Gross domestic product (million current US$)	3 355	2 812	3 238 [e]
GDP growth rate (annual %, const. 2015 prices)	- 5.4	0.8	1.6 [e]
GDP per capita (current US$)	39 734.0	36 041.3	42 051.6 [e]
Economy: Agriculture (% of Gross Value Added) [g]	0.5	0.5	0.5 [e]
Economy: Industry (% of Gross Value Added) [g,h]	14.6	10.8	11.0 [e]
Economy: Services and other activity (% of GVA) [g,i,j]	84.8	88.6	88.5 [e]
CPI: Consumer Price Index (2010=100) [k]	100	103	106 [f]
International trade: exports (million current US$)	92	90	124 [l,f]
International trade: imports (million current US$)	1 541	1 294	1 538 [l,f]
International trade: balance (million current US$)	- 1 448	- 1 204	- 1 414 [l,f]

Major trading partners 2019

Export partners (% of exports) [l]	Spain	61.7	France	18.3	Norway	3.7
Import partners (% of imports) [l]	Spain	64.2	France	13.2	China	3.6

Social indicators

	2010	2015	2020
Population growth rate (average annual %)	1.4 [m]	- 1.6 [m]	- 0.2
Urban population (% of total population)	88.8	88.3	88.0 [f]
Urban population growth rate (average annual %) [m]	1.0	- 1.7	...
Fertility rate, total (live births per woman)	1.2	1.2 [n]	...
Population age distribution (0-14/60+ years old, %)	14.0 / 18.6 [c,b]	... / ...	14.4 / 19.0 [c,b,d]
International migrant stock (000/% of total pop.) [o]	52.1 / 61.6	42.3 / 54.2	45.1 / 58.5 [f]
Health: Current expenditure (% of GDP)	9.4	10.3	10.3 [a]
Health: Physicians (per 1 000 pop.)	3.1 [p]	3.3	...
Education: Government expenditure (% of GDP)	3.1	3.3	3.2 [a]
Intentional homicide rate (per 100 000 pop.)	0.0	0.0	...
Seats held by women in the National Parliament (%)	35.7	50.0	46.4 [q]

Environment and infrastructure indicators

	2010	2015	2020
Individuals using the Internet (per 100 inhabitants)	81.0	96.9 [l]	91.6 [a]
Threatened species (number)	8	11	15
Forested area (% of land area) [l]	34.0	34.0	34.0 [a]
Energy production, primary (Petajoules)	1	1	1 [l,a]
Energy supply per capita (Gigajoules)	114	113	117 [a]
Tourist/visitor arrivals at national borders (000)	1 808 [r]	2 663 [r]	3 042 [e]
Important sites for terrestrial biodiversity protected (%)	17.9	26.1	26.1 [f]
Pop. using safely managed sanitation (urban/rural %)	86.5 / 86.5	100.0 / 100.0	100.0 / 100.0 [a]

a 2017. **b** De jure population. **c** Population statistics are compiled from registers. **d** 2016. **e** 2018. **f** 2019. **g** Data classified according to ISIC Rev. 4. **h** Excludes publishing activities. Includes irrigation and canals. **i** Excludes repair of personal and household goods. **j** Excludes computer and related activities and radio/TV activities. **k** Calculated by the UN Statistics Division from national indices. **l** Estimate. **m** Data refers to a 5-year period preceding the reference year. **n** 2012. **o** Refers to foreign citizens. **p** 2009. **q** Data are as at 1 January of reporting year. **r** Break in the time series.

Angola

Region	Middle Africa	UN membership date	01 December 1976
Population (000, 2020)	32 866	Surface area (km2)	1 246 700[a]
Pop. density (per km2, 2020)	26.4	Sex ratio (m per 100 f)	97.9
Capital city	Luanda	National currency	Kwanza (AOA)
Capital city pop. (000, 2020)	8 044.7[b,c]	Exchange rate (per US$)	482.2[c]

Economic indicators

	2010	2015	2020
GDP: Gross domestic product (million current US$)	83 799	116 194	105 902[d]
GDP growth rate (annual %, const. 2015 prices)	4.9	0.9	- 1.2[d]
GDP per capita (current US$)	3 587.9	4 167.0	3 437.3[d]
Economy: Agriculture (% of Gross Value Added)	6.2	9.1	9.7[d]
Economy: Industry (% of Gross Value Added)	52.1	42.1	42.5[d]
Economy: Services and other activity (% of GVA)	41.7	48.8	47.8[d]
Employment in agriculture (% of employed)[e]	48.9	50.6	50.2
Employment in industry (% of employed)[e]	7.8	8.6	8.1
Employment in services & other sectors (% employed)[e]	43.3	40.8	41.7
Unemployment rate (% of labour force)[e]	9.4	7.3	6.8
Labour force participation rate (female/male pop. %)[e]	75.8 / 78.9	76.1 / 79.1	76.1 / 78.8
CPI: Consumer Price Index (2010=100)[e,f]	100	161	337[d]
Agricultural production index (2004-2006=100)	167	181	192[g]
International trade: exports (million current US$)	52 612	33 925	50 822[e,c]
International trade: imports (million current US$)	18 143	21 549	21 340[e,c]
International trade: balance (million current US$)	34 469	12 376	29 482[e,c]
Balance of payments, current account (million US$)	7 506	- 10 273	5 137[c]

Major trading partners

						2019
Export partners (% of exports)[e]	China	58.2	India	9.0	United States	3.5
Import partners (% of imports)[e]	China	14.5	Portugal	13.6	Singapore	9.6

Social indicators

	2010	2015	2020
Population growth rate (average annual %)[h]	3.7	3.5	3.3
Urban population (% of total population)	59.8	63.4	66.2[c]
Urban population growth rate (average annual %)[h]	4.9	4.7	...
Fertility rate, total (live births per woman)[h]	6.4	6.0	5.6
Life expectancy at birth (females/males, years)[h]	55.3 / 50.3	60.5 / 55.2	63.4 / 57.8
Population age distribution (0-14/60+ years old, %)	47.0 / 3.8	47.1 / 3.6	46.4 / 3.7
International migrant stock (000/% of total pop.)[i]	332.1 / 1.4	632.2 / 2.3	669.5 / 2.1[c]
Refugees and others of concern to the UNHCR (000)	19.4[j]	45.7[j]	70.1[c]
Infant mortality rate (per 1 000 live births)[h]	104.2	78.2	61.5
Health: Current expenditure (% of GDP)	2.7	2.6	2.8[a]
Health: Physicians (per 1 000 pop.)	0.1[k]	...	0.2[a]
Education: Government expenditure (% of GDP)	3.4	...	...
Education: Primary gross enrol. ratio (f/m per 100 pop.)	94.1 / 117.7	105.9 / 121.1	... / ...
Education: Secondary gross enrol. ratio (f/m per 100 pop.)	21.3 / 31.3	20.7 / 32.3[l]	39.7 / 61.8[g]
Education: Tertiary gross enrol. ratio (f/m per 100 pop.)	... / ...	7.4 / 9.4	8.5 / 10.2[g]
Intentional homicide rate (per 100 000 pop.)	...	4.8[m]	...
Seats held by women in the National Parliament (%)	38.6	36.8	30.0[n]

Environment and infrastructure indicators

	2010	2015	2020
Individuals using the Internet (per 100 inhabitants)[e]	2.8	12.4	14.3[a]
Research & Development expenditure (% of GDP)	...	...	~0.0[o,p,q,g]
Threatened species (number)	117	130	171
Forested area (% of land area)	46.9	46.4	46.4[e,a]
CO2 emission estimates (million tons/tons per capita)	15.2 / 0.6	21.5 / 0.8	18.0 / 0.6[a]
Energy production, primary (Petajoules)	4 016	4 089	3 820[a]
Energy supply per capita (Gigajoules)	20	20	21[a]
Tourist/visitor arrivals at national borders (000)	425	592	218[d]
Important sites for terrestrial biodiversity protected (%)	28.1	28.1	28.1[c]
Net Official Development Assist. received (% of GNI)	0.31	0.35	0.16[d]

a 2017. **b** Refers to the urban population of the province of Luanda. **c** 2019. **d** 2018. **e** Estimate. **f** Luanda **g** 2016. **h** Data refers to a 5-year period preceding the reference year. **i** Including refugees. **j** Data as at the end of December. **k** 2009. **l** 2011. **m** 2012. **n** Data are as at 1 January of reporting year. **o** Excluding business enterprise. **p** Excluding private non-profit. **q** Partial data.

Anguilla

Region	Caribbean	Population (000, 2020)	15
Surface area (km2)	91 [a]	Pop. density (per km2, 2020)	169.8
Sex ratio (m per 100 f)	97.6 [b,c]	Capital city	The Valley
National currency	E. Caribbean Dollar (XCD) [d]	Capital city pop. (000, 2020)	1.4 [e]
Exchange rate (per US$)	2.7 [f]		

Economic indicators

	2010	2015	2020
GDP: Gross domestic product (million current US$)	268	331	293 [e]
GDP growth rate (annual %, const. 2015 prices)	- 4.5	3.1	- 5.0 [e]
GDP per capita (current US$)	19 938.3	23 148.3	19 890.7 [e]
Economy: Agriculture (% of Gross Value Added)	2.0	2.3	3.5 [e]
Economy: Industry (% of Gross Value Added)	15.8	15.3	14.6 [e]
Economy: Services and other activity (% of GVA)	82.2	82.4	81.9 [e]
CPI: Consumer Price Index (2010=100)	0 [g]	105	106 [a]
International trade: exports (million current US$) [h]	12	11	12 [f]
International trade: imports (million current US$) [h]	149	204	283 [f]
International trade: balance (million current US$) [h]	- 137	- 193	- 270 [f]
Balance of payments, current account (million US$)	- 51	- 89	- 136 [e]

Major trading partners

						2019
Export partners (% of exports) [h]	Chile	55.4	Malta	26.6	United States	5.3
Import partners (% of imports) [h]	United States	49.5	Chile	39.2	Japan	2.1

Social indicators

	2010	2015	2020
Population growth rate (average annual %)	1.7 [i]	1.2 [i]	0.9
Urban population (% of total population)	100.0	100.0	100.0 [f]
Urban population growth rate (average annual %) [i]	1.7	1.2	...
Fertility rate, total (live births per woman)	2.0 [j]	...	...
Population age distribution (0-14/60+ years old, %)	... / ...	23.3 / 7.6 [b,c,k]	... / ...
International migrant stock (000/% of total pop.)	5.1 / 38.0	5.5 / 38.3	5.7 / 38.2 [f]
Refugees and others of concern to the UNHCR (000)	...	...	~0.0 [e]
Education: Government expenditure (% of GDP)	2.8 [l]	...	...
Education: Primary gross enrol. ratio (f/m per 100 pop.)	118.9 / 124.4	119.0 / 124.2 [c]	... / ...
Education: Secondary gross enrol. ratio (f/m per 100 pop.)	111.0 / 112.1	114.3 / 114.2 [c]	... / ...
Education: Tertiary gross enrol. ratio (f/m per 100 pop.)	7.6 / 1.6 [l]	... / ...	... / ...
Intentional homicide rate (per 100 000 pop.)	0.0	28.3 [m]	...

Environment and infrastructure indicators

	2010	2015	2020
Individuals using the Internet (per 100 inhabitants) [h]	49.6	76.0	81.6 [n]
Threatened species (number)	33	51	60
Forested area (% of land area) [h]	61.1	61.1	61.1 [a]
Energy production, primary (Petajoules) [h]	0	0	0 [a]
Energy supply per capita (Gigajoules) [h]	155	151	136 [a]
Tourist/visitor arrivals at national borders (000) [o]	62	73	55 [e]
Important sites for terrestrial biodiversity protected (%)	6.7	6.7	6.8 [f]

a 2017. **b** Provisional data. **c** 2011. **d** East Caribbean Dollar. **e** 2018. **f** 2019. **g** Break in the time series. **h** Estimate. **i** Data refers to a 5-year period preceding the reference year. **j** 2006. **k** Population aged 65 years and over. **l** 2008. **m** 2014. **n** 2016. **o** Excluding nationals residing abroad.

Antigua and Barbuda

Region	Caribbean	UN membership date	11 November 1981
Population (000, 2020)	98	Surface area (km2)	442[a]
Pop. density (per km2, 2020)	222.6	Sex ratio (m per 100 f)	93.3
Capital city	Saint John's	National currency	E. Caribbean Dollar (XCD)[b]
Capital city pop. (000, 2020)	20.8[c]	Exchange rate (per US$)	2.7[d]

Economic indicators

	2010	2015	2020
GDP: Gross domestic product (million current US$)	1 149	1 337	1 611[c]
GDP growth rate (annual %, const. 2015 prices)	- 7.8	3.8	7.4[c]
GDP per capita (current US$)	13 049.3	14 286.1	16 727.0[c]
Economy: Agriculture (% of Gross Value Added)	1.8	1.8	2.0[c]
Economy: Industry (% of Gross Value Added)	18.3	18.7	23.8[c]
Economy: Services and other activity (% of GVA)	79.9	79.5	74.2[c]
Employment in agriculture (% of employed)	2.8[e,f]	...	...
Employment in industry (% of employed)	15.6[e,f]	...	...
Employment in services & other sectors (% employed)	81.6[e,f]	...	...
CPI: Consumer Price Index (2010=100)	100	110	114[c]
Agricultural production index (2004-2006=100)	73	71	70[g]
International trade: exports (million current US$)	35	26	37[d]
International trade: imports (million current US$)	501	465	568[d]
International trade: balance (million current US$)	- 466	- 439	- 531[d]
Balance of payments, current account (million US$)	- 167	29	- 113[c]

Major trading partners   2019

Export partners (% of exports)	United Arab Emirates	52.7	United States	9.8	Netherlands	7.6
Import partners (% of imports)	United States	48.2	China	7.4	Japan	4.4

Social indicators

	2010	2015	2020
Population growth rate (average annual %)[h]	1.6	1.2	0.9
Urban population (% of total population)	26.2	25.0	24.5[d]
Urban population growth rate (average annual %)[h]	- 1.0	0.1	...
Fertility rate, total (live births per woman)[h]	2.0	2.0	2.0
Life expectancy at birth (females/males, years)[h]	76.8 / 74.1	77.4 / 74.8	77.9 / 75.7
Population age distribution (0-14/60+ years old, %)	24.3 / 10.7	22.6 / 12.1	21.9 / 14.1
International migrant stock (000/% of total pop.)	26.4 / 30.0	28.1 / 30.0	29.2 / 30.1[d]
Refugees and others of concern to the UNHCR (000)	...	~0.0	0.2[d]
Infant mortality rate (per 1 000 live births)[h]	9.0	6.8	5.2
Health: Current expenditure (% of GDP)[i]	5.2	4.7	4.5[a]
Health: Physicians (per 1 000 pop.)	0.5[f]	...	3.0[a]
Education: Government expenditure (% of GDP)	2.5[j]	...	...
Education: Primary gross enrol. ratio (f/m per 100 pop.)	107.3 / 117.2	103.2 / 106.8	104.6 / 105.4[c]
Education: Secondary gross enrol. ratio (f/m per 100 pop.)	115.7 / 109.9	109.3 / 107.1	109.1 / 113.3[c]
Education: Tertiary gross enrol. ratio (f/m per 100 pop.)	24.2 / 9.0	34.3 / 15.3[k]	... / ...
Intentional homicide rate (per 100 000 pop.)	6.8	11.1[k]	...
Seats held by women in the National Parliament (%)	10.5	11.1	11.1[l]

Environment and infrastructure indicators

	2010	2015	2020
Individuals using the Internet (per 100 inhabitants)	47.0[m]	70.0[m]	76.0[a]
Threatened species (number)	38	53	61
Forested area (% of land area)[m]	22.3	22.3	22.3[a]
Energy production, primary (Petajoules)	...	0	0[a]
Energy supply per capita (Gigajoules)[m]	69	69	69[a]
Tourist/visitor arrivals at national borders (000)[n,o]	230	250	269[c]
Important sites for terrestrial biodiversity protected (%)	8.2	8.2	8.2[d]
Net Official Development Assist. received (% of GNI)	1.75	0.12	1.10[c]

a 2017. **b** East Caribbean Dollar. **c** 2018. **d** 2019. **e** Data classified according to ISIC Rev. 3. **f** 2008. **g** 2016. **h** Data refers to a 5-year period preceding the reference year. **i** Data revision. **j** 2009. **k** 2012. **l** Data are as at 1 January of reporting year. **m** Estimate. **n** Excluding nationals residing abroad. **o** Arrivals by air.

Argentina

Region	South America	UN membership date	24 October 1945
Population (000, 2020)	45 196	Surface area (km2)	2 780 400[a]
Pop. density (per km2, 2020)	16.5	Sex ratio (m per 100 f)	95.3
Capital city	Buenos Aires	National currency	Argentine Peso (ARS)
Capital city pop. (000, 2020)	15 057.3[b,c]	Exchange rate (per US$)	59.8[c]

Economic indicators

	2010	2015	2020
GDP: Gross domestic product (million current US$)	426 487	644 903	518 475[d]
GDP growth rate (annual %, const. 2015 prices)	10.1	2.7	- 2.5[d]
GDP per capita (current US$)	10 428.6	14 971.5	11 687.6[d]
Economy: Agriculture (% of Gross Value Added)	8.5	6.1	7.2[d]
Economy: Industry (% of Gross Value Added)	30.1	27.5	27.2[d]
Economy: Services and other activity (% of GVA)	61.4	66.3	65.6[d]
Employment in agriculture (% of employed)	1.3	0.3[e]	0.1[e]
Employment in industry (% of employed)	23.3	23.7[e]	21.0[e]
Employment in services & other sectors (% employed)	75.4	76.1[e]	78.9[e]
Unemployment rate (% of labour force)[e]	7.7	7.8	10.4
Labour force participation rate (female/male pop. %)[e]	48.0 / 74.0	48.0 / 73.0	50.6 / 72.6
CPI: Consumer Price Index (2010=100)	...	...	233[f,c]
Agricultural production index (2004-2006=100)	112	131	131[g]
International trade: exports (million current US$)	68 174	56 784	65 114[c]
International trade: imports (million current US$)	56 792	60 203	49 125[c]
International trade: balance (million current US$)	11 382	- 3 419	15 989[c]
Balance of payments, current account (million US$)	- 1 623	- 17 622	- 3 462[c]

Major trading partners

							2019
Export partners (% of exports)	Brazil	15.9	China	10.5	United States	6.3	
Import partners (% of imports)	Brazil	20.5	China	18.8	United States	12.8	

Social indicators

	2010	2015	2020
Population growth rate (average annual %)[h]	1.0	1.0	1.0
Urban population (% of total population)	90.8	91.5	92.0[c]
Urban population growth rate (average annual %)[h]	1.2	1.2	...
Fertility rate, total (live births per woman)[h]	2.4	2.3	2.3
Life expectancy at birth (females/males, years)[h]	78.2 / 71.4	79.0 / 72.2	79.8 / 73.0
Population age distribution (0-14/60+ years old, %)	26.0 / 14.2	25.2 / 14.9	24.4 / 15.5
International migrant stock (000/% of total pop.)	1 806.0 / 4.4	2 086.3 / 4.8	2 212.9 / 4.9[c]
Refugees and others of concern to the UNHCR (000)	4.2[i]	4.4	165.6[c]
Infant mortality rate (per 1 000 live births)[h]	14.2	12.1	10.2
Health: Current expenditure (% of GDP)	8.6	8.8	9.1[a]
Health: Physicians (per 1 000 pop.)	...	3.9[j]	4.0[a]
Education: Government expenditure (% of GDP)	5.0	5.8	5.5[a]
Education: Primary gross enrol. ratio (f/m per 100 pop.)	116.2 / 117.7	111.2 / 111.4	109.6 / 109.9[a]
Education: Secondary gross enrol. ratio (f/m per 100 pop.)	104.2 / 95.0	110.2 / 103.8	111.0 / 106.5[a]
Education: Tertiary gross enrol. ratio (f/m per 100 pop.)	87.8 / 58.9	104.5 / 64.1	112.8 / 67.8[a]
Intentional homicide rate (per 100 000 pop.)	5.8	6.6	5.3[d]
Seats held by women in the National Parliament (%)	38.5	36.2	40.9[k]

Environment and infrastructure indicators

	2010	2015	2020
Individuals using the Internet (per 100 inhabitants)	45.0[e]	68.0	74.3[a]
Research & Development expenditure (% of GDP)	0.6	0.6	0.5[a]
Threatened species (number)	213	243	285
Forested area (% of land area)[e]	10.4	9.9	9.9[a]
CO2 emission estimates (million tons/tons per capita)	173.8 / 4.2	190.4 / 4.4	183.4 / 4.1[a]
Energy production, primary (Petajoules)	3 343	3 072	3 035[a]
Energy supply per capita (Gigajoules)	80	79	76[a]
Tourist/visitor arrivals at national borders (000)	6 800[l]	6 816	6 942[d]
Important sites for terrestrial biodiversity protected (%)	29.5	30.7	31.8[c]
Net Official Development Assist. received (% of GNI)	0.03	0.00	0.02[d]

a 2017. b Refers to Gran Buenos Aires. c 2019. d 2018. e Estimate. f Index base: December 2016=100. g 2016. h Data refers to a 5-year period preceding the reference year. i Data as at the end of December. j 2013. k Data are as at 1 January of reporting year. l Break in the time series.

Armenia

Region	Western Asia	UN membership date	02 March 1992
Population (000, 2020)	2 963	Surface area (km2)	29 743[a]
Pop. density (per km2, 2020)	104.1	Sex ratio (m per 100 f)	88.8
Capital city	Yerevan	National currency	Armenian Dram (AMD)
Capital city pop. (000, 2020)	1 083.3[b]	Exchange rate (per US$)	479.7[b]

Economic indicators

	2010	2015	2020
GDP: Gross domestic product (million current US$)	9 875	10 553	12 433[c]
GDP growth rate (annual %, const. 2015 prices)	2.2	3.2	5.2[c]
GDP per capita (current US$)	3 432.1	3 607.3	4 212.1[c]
Economy: Agriculture (% of Gross Value Added)[d]	17.8	18.9	15.0[c]
Economy: Industry (% of Gross Value Added)[d]	34.7	28.2	27.4[c]
Economy: Services and other activity (% of GVA)[d,e,f]	47.4	52.9	57.6[c]
Employment in agriculture (% of employed)	38.6	35.3	28.9[g]
Employment in industry (% of employed)	17.4	15.9	17.5[g]
Employment in services & other sectors (% employed)	44.0	48.8	53.6[g]
Unemployment rate (% of labour force)[g]	19.0	18.3	16.6
Labour force participation rate (female/male pop. %)[g]	47.2 / 67.8	49.0 / 66.8	47.0 / 65.8
CPI: Consumer Price Index (2010=100)[g]	100[h]	125	129[b]
Agricultural production index (2004-2006=100)	96	140	127[i]
International trade: exports (million current US$)	1 011	1 483	2 612[b]
International trade: imports (million current US$)	3 782	3 257	5 053[b]
International trade: balance (million current US$)	- 2 770	- 1 774	- 2 441[b]
Balance of payments, current account (million US$)	- 1 261	- 287	- 1 118[b]

Major trading partners

						2019
Export partners (% of exports)	Russian Federation	27.2	Switzerland	17.5	Bulgaria	7.9
Import partners (% of imports)	Russian Federation	29.2	China	14.7	Iran	6.4

Social indicators

	2010	2015	2020
Population growth rate (average annual %)[j]	- 0.7	0.3	0.3
Urban population (% of total population)	63.4	63.1	63.2[b]
Urban population growth rate (average annual %)[j]	- 0.9	0.2	...
Fertility rate, total (live births per woman)[j]	1.7	1.7	1.8
Life expectancy at birth (females/males, years)[j]	75.8 / 69.4	77.0 / 70.6	78.3 / 71.1
Population age distribution (0-14/60+ years old, %)	19.5 / 14.8	20.1 / 15.8	20.8 / 18.5
International migrant stock (000/% of total pop.)[k]	211.1 / 7.3	191.2 / 6.5	190.2 / 6.4[b]
Refugees and others of concern to the UNHCR (000)	85.8[l]	16.0	19.0[b]
Infant mortality rate (per 1 000 live births)[j]	21.0	13.2	10.8
Health: Current expenditure (% of GDP)	9.2	10.1	10.4[a]
Health: Physicians (per 1 000 pop.)	2.8	2.9	4.4[a]
Education: Government expenditure (% of GDP)	3.2	2.8	2.7[a]
Education: Primary gross enrol. ratio (f/m per 100 pop.)	100.7 / 97.7	95.8 / 94.3	92.7 / 92.7[c]
Education: Secondary gross enrol. ratio (f/m per 100 pop.)	103.7 / 105.6	88.3 / 84.0	84.8 / 81.7[c]
Education: Tertiary gross enrol. ratio (f/m per 100 pop.)	58.0 / 47.6	50.5 / 42.4	62.6 / 47.1[c]
Intentional homicide rate (per 100 000 pop.)	1.9	2.6	1.7[c]
Seats held by women in the National Parliament (%)	9.2	10.7	23.5[m]

Environment and infrastructure indicators

	2010	2015	2020
Individuals using the Internet (per 100 inhabitants)	25.0[g]	59.1[g]	64.7[a]
Research & Development expenditure (% of GDP)	0.2[n]	0.2[o,p]	0.2[o,p,c]
Threatened species (number)	36	111	119
Forested area (% of land area)	11.6	11.7[g]	11.7[g,a]
CO2 emission estimates (million tons/tons per capita)	4.0 / 1.4	4.7 / 1.6	5.2 / 1.8[a]
Energy production, primary (Petajoules)	52	45	45[a]
Energy supply per capita (Gigajoules)	41[g]	44	47[a]
Tourist/visitor arrivals at national borders (000)	684	1 192	1 652[c]
Important sites for terrestrial biodiversity protected (%)	21.6	21.6	21.6[b]
Pop. using safely managed sanitation (urban/rural %)	45.5 / ...	45.5 / ...	45.3 / ...[a]
Net Official Development Assist. received (% of GNI)	3.30	3.16	1.12[c]

a 2017. b 2019. c 2018. d Data classified according to ISIC Rev. 4. e Excludes repair of personal and household goods. f Excludes computer and related activities and radio/TV activities. g Estimate. h Break in the time series. i 2016. j Data refers to a 5-year period preceding the reference year. k Including refugees. l Data as at the end of December. m Data are as at 1 January of reporting year. n Partial data. o Excluding private non-profit. p Excluding business enterprise.

Aruba

Region	Caribbean	Population (000, 2020)	107
Surface area (km2)	180[a]	Pop. density (per km2, 2020)	593.1
Sex ratio (m per 100 f)	90.2	Capital city	Oranjestad
National currency	Aruban Florin (AWG)	Capital city pop. (000, 2020)	29.9[b]
Exchange rate (per US$)	1.8[c]		

Economic indicators

	2010	2015	2020
GDP: Gross domestic product (million current US$)	2 502	2 920	3 203[b]
GDP growth rate (annual %, const. 2015 prices)	- 3.3	5.7	0.9[b]
GDP per capita (current US$)	24 607.3	27 980.4	30 262.5[b]
Economy: Agriculture (% of Gross Value Added)[d]	0.0	0.0	0.0[b]
Economy: Industry (% of Gross Value Added)[e]	12.0	13.7	13.7[b]
Economy: Services and other activity (% of GVA)[f,g]	88.0	86.3	86.2[b]
Employment in agriculture (% of employed)[h,i]	0.6[j]	0.6[k]	...
Employment in industry (% of employed)[h,i]	14.5[j]	14.0[k]	...
Employment in services & other sectors (% employed)[h,i]	84.4[j]	85.1[k]	...
Unemployment rate (% of labour force)	10.6[h,i]	...	...
Labour force participation rate (female/male pop. %)	59.5 / 68.9[h,j,l]	58.8 / 69.6[h,k]	... / ...
CPI: Consumer Price Index (2010=100)[m]	100	103	110[c]
International trade: exports (million current US$)	125	80	84[n,c]
International trade: imports (million current US$)	1 071	1 165	1 353[n,c]
International trade: balance (million current US$)	- 947	- 1 085	- 1 270[n,c]
Balance of payments, current account (million US$)	- 460	111	- 3[b]

Major trading partners

						2019
Export partners (% of exports)[n]	Areas nes[o]	52.2	Colombia	21.0	United States	17.9
Import partners (% of imports)[n]	United States	54.0	Areas nes[o]	23.5	Netherlands	10.9

Social indicators

	2010	2015	2020
Population growth rate (average annual %)[p]	0.3	0.5	0.5
Urban population (% of total population)	43.1	43.1	43.5[c]
Urban population growth rate (average annual %)[p]	- 0.5	0.5	...
Fertility rate, total (live births per woman)[p]	1.8	1.8	1.9
Life expectancy at birth (females/males, years)[p]	77.1 / 72.2	77.8 / 72.9	78.4 / 73.6
Population age distribution (0-14/60+ years old, %)	20.9 / 15.5	18.7 / 18.4	17.4 / 21.8
International migrant stock (000/% of total pop.)	34.3 / 33.8	36.1 / 34.6	36.5 / 34.4[c]
Refugees and others of concern to the UNHCR (000)	~0.0[q]	~0.0	16.0[c]
Infant mortality rate (per 1 000 live births)[p]	16.2	14.8	13.6
Education: Government expenditure (% of GDP)	6.9	6.5	6.2[r]
Education: Primary gross enrol. ratio (f/m per 100 pop.)	113.0 / 114.5	115.2 / 118.9[s]	... / ...
Education: Secondary gross enrol. ratio (f/m per 100 pop.)	98.3 / 93.5	112.1 / 110.2[t]	... / ...
Education: Tertiary gross enrol. ratio (f/m per 100 pop.)	43.9 / 31.1	21.4 / 9.4	20.7 / 10.7[r]
Intentional homicide rate (per 100 000 pop.)	3.9	1.9[s]	...

Environment and infrastructure indicators

	2010	2015	2020
Individuals using the Internet (per 100 inhabitants)[n]	62.0	88.7	97.2[a]
Threatened species (number)	22	29	44
Forested area (% of land area)[n]	2.3	2.3	2.3[a]
Energy production, primary (Petajoules)[n]	5	1	1[a]
Energy supply per capita (Gigajoules)[n]	550	122	123[a]
Tourist/visitor arrivals at national borders (000)[u]	824	1 225	1 082[b]
Important sites for terrestrial biodiversity protected (%)	37.1	37.1	37.1[c]

a 2017. b 2018. c 2019. d Including mining and quarrying. e Excludes publishing activities. Includes irrigation and canals. f Excludes repair of personal and household goods. g Excludes computer and related activities and radio/TV activities. h Break in the time series. i Data classified according to ISIC Rev. 3. j Population aged 14 years and over. k 2011. l Resident population (de jure). m Calculated by the UN Statistics Division from national indices. n Estimate. o Areas not elsewhere specified. p Data refers to a 5-year period preceding the reference year. q Data as at the end of December. r 2016. s 2014. t 2012. u Arrivals by air.

Australia

Region	Oceania	UN membership date	01 November 1945
Population (000, 2020)	25 500[a]	Surface area (km2)	7 692 060[b,c]
Pop. density (per km2, 2020)	3.3[a]	Sex ratio (m per 100 f)	99.2[a]
Capital city	Canberra	National currency	Australian Dollar (AUD)
Capital city pop. (000, 2020)	452.5[d,e]	Exchange rate (per US$)	1.4[e]

Economic indicators

	2010	2015	2020
GDP: Gross domestic product (million current US$)	1 299 463	1 248 854	1 453 871[f]
GDP growth rate (annual %, const. 2015 prices)	2.5	2.8	2.0[f]
GDP per capita (current US$)	58 654.1	52 182.3	58 392.7[f]
Economy: Agriculture (% of Gross Value Added)[g]	2.4	2.6	2.8[f]
Economy: Industry (% of Gross Value Added)[g,h]	28.3	24.0	25.0[f]
Economy: Services and other activity (% of GVA)[g,i,j]	69.3	73.4	72.3[f]
Employment in agriculture (% of employed)	3.2	2.6	2.5[k]
Employment in industry (% of employed)	21.0	19.4	19.8[k]
Employment in services & other sectors (% employed)	75.8	78.0	77.7[k]
Unemployment rate (% of labour force)[k]	5.2	6.0	5.3
Labour force participation rate (female/male pop. %)[k]	58.8 / 72.5	59.2 / 71.2	60.2 / 70.6
CPI: Consumer Price Index (2010=100)[m,n]	100[l]	112	120[e]
Agricultural production index (2004-2006=100)	95	108	104[o]
International trade: exports (million current US$)[p]	212 109	187 792	266 377[e]
International trade: imports (million current US$)[p]	201 703	200 114	221 481[e]
International trade: balance (million current US$)[p]	10 405	- 12 322	44 896[e]
Balance of payments, current account (million US$)	- 44 714	- 56 959	7 122[e]

Major trading partners

						2019
Export partners (% of exports)	China	38.7	Japan	14.8	Rep. of Korea	6.6
Import partners (% of imports)	China	25.7	United States	11.8	Japan	7.0

Social indicators

	2010	2015	2020
Population growth rate (average annual %)[a,q]	1.9	1.5	1.3
Urban population (% of total population)[a]	85.2	85.7	86.1[e]
Urban population growth rate (average annual %)[a,q]	1.9	1.6	...
Fertility rate, total (live births per woman)[a,q]	2.0	1.9	1.8
Life expectancy at birth (females/males, years)[a,q]	83.8 / 79.2	84.4 / 80.3	85.2 / 81.2
Population age distribution (0-14/60+ years old, %)[a]	19.0 / 18.8	18.9 / 20.2	19.3 / 21.8
International migrant stock (000/% of total pop.)[a]	5 883.0 / 26.6	6 729.7 / 28.1	7 549.3 / 30.0[e]
Refugees and others of concern to the UNHCR (000)	25.6[r]	58.4	129.2[s,e]
Infant mortality rate (per 1 000 live births)[a,q]	4.4	3.6	3.1
Health: Current expenditure (% of GDP)[k]	8.4	9.3	9.2[c]
Health: Physicians (per 1 000 pop.)	3.3	3.5	3.7[c]
Education: Government expenditure (% of GDP)	5.6	5.3	5.3[o]
Education: Primary gross enrol. ratio (f/m per 100 pop.)	105.5 / 105.7	101.6 / 101.6	100.3 / 100.3[c]
Education: Secondary gross enrol. ratio (f/m per 100 pop.)	... / ...	145.9 / 167.9	141.2 / 159.0[c]
Education: Tertiary gross enrol. ratio (f/m per 100 pop.)	... / ...	141.0 / 97.6	133.3 / 93.8[c]
Intentional homicide rate (per 100 000 pop.)	1.0	1.0	0.9[f]
Seats held by women in the National Parliament (%)	27.3	26.7	30.5[t]

Environment and infrastructure indicators

	2010	2015	2020
Individuals using the Internet (per 100 inhabitants)	76.0[k]	84.6[u]	86.5[u,v,c]
Research & Development expenditure (% of GDP)[k]	2.4	1.9	1.9[c]
Threatened species (number)	853[w]	909[w]	1 308
Forested area (% of land area)	16.0	16.2	16.2[k,c]
CO2 emission estimates (million tons/tons per capita)[w]	383.6 / 17.4	373.8 / 15.7	384.6 / 15.6[c]
Energy production, primary (Petajoules)[w]	13 646	16 014	16 963[c]
Energy supply per capita (Gigajoules)[w]	246	224	219[c]
Tourist/visitor arrivals at national borders (000)[x]	5 790	7 449	9 246[f]
Important sites for terrestrial biodiversity protected (%)	46.8	55.0	55.7[e]
Pop. using safely managed drinking water (urban/rural, %)	98.6 / ...	98.8 / ...	98.8 / ...[c]
Net Official Development Assist. disbursed (% of GNI)[y]	0.32	0.29	0.23[c]

a Including Christmas Island, Cocos (Keeling) Islands and Norfolk Island. **b** Including Norfolk Island. **c** 2017. **d** Refers to Significant Urban Areas as of 2001. **e** 2019. **f** 2018. **g** Data classified according to ISIC Rev. 4. **h** Excludes publishing activities. Includes irrigation and canals. **i** Excludes repair of personal and household goods. **j** Excludes computer and related activities and radio/TV activities. **k** Estimate. **l** Break in the time series. **m** Calculated by the UN Statistics Division from national indices. **n** Weighted average of index values computed for the 8 capital cities. **o** 2016. **p** Imports FOB. **q** Data refers to a 5-year period preceding the reference year. **r** Data as at the end of December. **s** Asylum-seekers based on number of applications for protection visas. **t** Data are as at 1 January of reporting year. **u** Population aged 15 years and over. **v** Accessed the internet for personal use in a typical week. **w** Excluding overseas territories. **x** Excluding nationals residing abroad and crew members. **y** Development Assistance Committee member (OECD).

Austria

Region	Western Europe	UN membership date	14 December 1955
Population (000, 2020)	9 006	Surface area (km2)	83 871 [a]
Pop. density (per km2, 2020)	109.3	Sex ratio (m per 100 f)	97.2
Capital city	Vienna	National currency	Euro (EUR)
Capital city pop. (000, 2020)	1 915.3 [b]	Exchange rate (per US$)	0.9 [b]

Economic indicators

	2010	2015	2020
GDP: Gross domestic product (million current US$)	391 893	381 818	455 508 [c]
GDP growth rate (annual %, const. 2015 prices)	1.8	1.0	2.4 [c]
GDP per capita (current US$)	46 598.7	43 995.0	51 230.3 [c]
Economy: Agriculture (% of Gross Value Added) [d]	1.4	1.3	1.3 [c]
Economy: Industry (% of Gross Value Added) [d,e]	28.7	28.2	28.8 [c]
Economy: Services and other activity (% of GVA) [d,f,g]	69.9	70.5	69.9 [c]
Employment in agriculture (% of employed)	5.2	4.5	3.5 [h]
Employment in industry (% of employed)	24.9	25.8	25.0 [h]
Employment in services & other sectors (% employed)	69.9	69.7	71.5 [h]
Unemployment rate (% of labour force) [h]	4.8	5.7	4.8
Labour force participation rate (female/male pop. %) [h]	53.5 / 66.9	54.5 / 66.0	55.0 / 66.4
CPI: Consumer Price Index (2010=100)	100	111	118 [b]
Agricultural production index (2004-2006=100)	98	98	100 [i]
International trade: exports (million current US$)	144 882	145 276	171 532 [b]
International trade: imports (million current US$)	150 593	147 928	176 596 [b]
International trade: balance (million current US$)	- 5 711	- 2 652	- 5 064 [b]
Balance of payments, current account (million US$)	11 472	6 634	11 714 [b]

Major trading partners

						2019
Export partners (% of exports)	Germany	29.2	United States	6.6	Italy	6.3
Import partners (% of imports)	Germany	34.7	Italy	6.6	China	6.2

Social indicators

	2010	2015	2020
Population growth rate (average annual %) [j]	0.4	0.6	0.7
Urban population (% of total population)	57.4	57.7	58.5 [b]
Urban population growth rate (average annual %) [j]	- 0.1	0.7	...
Fertility rate, total (live births per woman) [j]	1.4	1.4	1.5
Life expectancy at birth (females/males, years) [j]	82.8 / 77.3	83.5 / 78.4	83.8 / 78.9
Population age distribution (0-14/60+ years old, %)	14.7 / 23.3	14.1 / 24.3	14.4 / 25.7
International migrant stock (000/% of total pop.)	1 276.0 / 15.2	1 492.4 / 17.2	1 779.9 / 19.9 [b]
Refugees and others of concern to the UNHCR (000)	68.7 [k]	92.2 [l]	163.7 [b]
Infant mortality rate (per 1 000 live births) [j]	3.8	3.3	3.2
Health: Current expenditure (% of GDP) [h]	10.2	10.4	10.4 [a]
Health: Physicians (per 1 000 pop.)	4.8	5.1	5.2 [a]
Education: Government expenditure (% of GDP)	5.7	5.5	5.5 [i]
Education: Primary gross enrol. ratio (f/m per 100 pop.)	99.1 / 100.4	101.5 / 102.4	103.0 / 103.2 [a]
Education: Secondary gross enrol. ratio (f/m per 100 pop.)	96.8 / 100.7	98.5 / 102.1	98.3 / 102.5 [a]
Education: Tertiary gross enrol. ratio (f/m per 100 pop.)	... / ...	88.0 / 73.8	92.5 / 78.1 [a]
Intentional homicide rate (per 100 000 pop.)	0.7	0.5	1.0 [c]
Seats held by women in the National Parliament (%)	27.9	30.6	39.3 [m]

Environment and infrastructure indicators

	2010	2015	2020
Individuals using the Internet (per 100 inhabitants)	75.2 [n]	83.9 [n]	87.5 [c]
Research & Development expenditure (% of GDP)	2.7 [h]	3.0	3.2 [o,c]
Threatened species (number)	82	106	185
Forested area (% of land area)	46.7	46.9 [h]	46.9 [h,a]
CO2 emission estimates (million tons/tons per capita)	68.6 / 8.2	62.2 / 7.2	64.9 / 7.4 [a]
Energy production, primary (Petajoules)	483	497	507 [a]
Energy supply per capita (Gigajoules)	168	157	161 [a]
Tourist/visitor arrivals at national borders (000) [p]	22 004	26 728	30 816 [c]
Important sites for terrestrial biodiversity protected (%)	66.3	67.3	67.3 [b]
Pop. using safely managed sanitation (urban/rural %)	100.0 / 92.3	100.0 / 92.3	100.0 / 92.3 [a]
Net Official Development Assist. disbursed (% of GNI) [q]	0.32	0.35	0.30 [a]

2017. **b** 2019. **c** 2018. **d** Data classified according to ISIC Rev. 4. **e** Excludes publishing activities. Includes irrigation and canals. **f** Excludes computer and related activities and radio/TV activities. **g** Excludes repair of personal and household goods. **h** Estimate. **i** 2016. **j** Data refers to a 5-year period preceding the reference year. **k** Data as at the end of December. **l** Data relates to the end of 2014. **m** Data are as at 1 January of reporting year. **n** Population aged 16 to 74 years. **o** Provisional data. **p** Only paid accommodation; excluding stays at friends and relatives and second homes. **q** Development Assistance Committee member (OECD).

Azerbaijan

Region	Western Asia	UN membership date	02 March 1992
Population (000, 2020)	10 139[a]	Surface area (km2)	86 600[b]
Pop. density (per km2, 2020)	122.7[a]	Sex ratio (m per 100 f)	99.8[a]
Capital city	Baku	National currency	Azerbaijan manat (AZN)
Capital city pop. (000, 2020)	2 313.1[c,d]	Exchange rate (per US$)	1.7[d]

Economic indicators

	2010	2015	2020
GDP: Gross domestic product (million current US$)	52 906	53 076	46 939[e]
GDP growth rate (annual %, const. 2015 prices)	4.8	1.1	1.4[e]
GDP per capita (current US$)	5 857.3	5 515.7	4 717.7[e]
Economy: Agriculture (% of Gross Value Added)[f]	5.9	6.8	5.7[e]
Economy: Industry (% of Gross Value Added)[f,g]	64.1	49.3	56.6[e]
Economy: Services and other activity (% of GVA)[f,h,i]	30.0	43.9	37.7[e]
Employment in agriculture (% of employed)	38.2	36.4	35.5[j]
Employment in industry (% of employed)	13.7	14.1	15.0[j]
Employment in services & other sectors (% employed)	48.0	49.6	49.5[j]
Unemployment rate (% of labour force)[j]	5.6	5.0	6.0
Labour force participation rate (female/male pop. %)[j]	60.2 / 67.5	62.5 / 68.7	63.1 / 69.2
CPI: Consumer Price Index (2010=100)	100	118	157[j]
Agricultural production index (2004-2006=100)	117	139	141[k]
International trade: exports (million current US$)	21 278	12 646	19 636[d]
International trade: imports (million current US$)	6 597	9 214	13 649[d]
International trade: balance (million current US$)	14 682	3 432	5 986[d]
Balance of payments, current account (million US$)	15 040	- 222	4 365[d]

Major trading partners

						2019
Export partners (% of exports)	Italy	28.7	Turkey	14.6	Israel	6.8
Import partners (% of imports)	Russian Federation	16.8	Turkey	12.1	China	10.5

Social indicators

	2010	2015	2020
Population growth rate (average annual %)[a,l]	1.1	1.3	1.0
Urban population (% of total population)[a]	53.4	54.7	56.0[d]
Urban population growth rate (average annual %)[a,l]	1.5	1.7	...
Fertility rate, total (live births per woman)[a,l]	1.8	2.1	2.1
Life expectancy at birth (females/males, years)[a,l]	73.4 / 66.9	74.6 / 68.6	75.3 / 70.3
Population age distribution (0-14/60+ years old, %)[a]	22.8 / 8.1	22.9 / 9.3	23.5 / 11.6
International migrant stock (000/% of total pop.)[a,m]	276.9 / 3.1	264.2 / 2.7	253.9 / 2.5[d]
Refugees and others of concern to the UNHCR (000)	596.9[n]	628.1	625.2[d]
Infant mortality rate (per 1 000 live births)[a,l]	40.7	31.4	20.8
Health: Current expenditure (% of GDP)[o]	4.8	6.7	6.7[b]
Health: Physicians (per 1 000 pop.)	3.7	3.4[p]	...
Education: Government expenditure (% of GDP)	2.8	3.0	2.5[b]
Education: Primary gross enrol. ratio (f/m per 100 pop.)[j]	93.2 / 94.2	105.6 / 107.4	100.0 / 99.5[e]
Education: Secondary gross enrol. ratio (f/m per 100 pop.)	... / ...	... / ...	94.5 / 94.4[j,e]
Education: Tertiary gross enrol. ratio (f/m per 100 pop.)[j]	19.2 / 19.4	27.5 / 23.6	29.7 / 25.9[e]
Intentional homicide rate (per 100 000 pop.)	2.3	2.3	2.2[e]
Seats held by women in the National Parliament (%)	11.4	15.6	16.8[q]

Environment and infrastructure indicators

	2010	2015	2020
Individuals using the Internet (per 100 inhabitants)	46.0[r]	77.0[r]	79.8[e]
Research & Development expenditure (% of GDP)	0.2	0.2	0.2[e]
Threatened species (number)	45	92	102
Forested area (% of land area)[j]	12.2	13.8	13.8[b]
CO2 emission estimates (million tons/tons per capita)	23.5 / 2.6	30.8 / 3.2	30.8 / 3.1[b]
Energy production, primary (Petajoules)	2 759	2 474	2 308[b]
Energy supply per capita (Gigajoules)	54	63	61[b]
Tourist/visitor arrivals at national borders (000)	1 280	1 922	2 633[e]
Important sites for terrestrial biodiversity protected (%)	36.6	36.6	36.6[d]
Pop. using safely managed sanitation (urban/rural, %)	84.8 / ...	92.4 / ...	92.2 / ...[b]
Net Official Development Assist. disbursed (% of GNI)	...	0.02	0.05[b]
Net Official Development Assist. received (% of GNI)	0.32	0.14	0.20[e]

a Including Nagorno-Karabakh. b 2017. c Including communities under the authority of the Town Council. d 2019. e 2018. f Data classified according to ISIC Rev. 4. g Excludes publishing activities. Includes irrigation and canals. h Excludes repair of personal and household goods. i Excludes computer and related activities and radio/TV activities. j Estimate. k 2016. l Data refers to a 5-year period preceding the reference year. m Including refugees. n Data as at the end of December. o Data revision. p 2014. q Data are as at 1 January of reporting year. r Population aged 7 years and over.

Bahamas

Region	Caribbean	UN membership date	18 September 1973
Population (000, 2020)	393	Surface area (km2)	13 940[a]
Pop. density (per km2, 2020)	39.3	Sex ratio (m per 100 f)	94.5
Capital city	Nassau	National currency	Bahamian Dollar (BSD)
Capital city pop. (000, 2020)	279.7[b]	Exchange rate (per US$)	1.0[c]

Economic indicators

	2010	2015	2020
GDP: Gross domestic product (million current US$)	10 096	11 752	12 424[b]
GDP growth rate (annual %, const. 2015 prices)	1.5	0.6	1.6[b]
GDP per capita (current US$)	28 443.5	31 406.0	32 218.1[b]
Economy: Agriculture (% of Gross Value Added)[d]	1.2	0.9	1.0[b]
Economy: Industry (% of Gross Value Added)[d,e]	12.3	13.1	14.8[b]
Economy: Services and other activity (% of GVA)[d,f,g]	86.6	86.0	84.2[b]
Employment in agriculture (% of employed)[h]	2.8	2.4	2.1
Employment in industry (% of employed)[h]	16.1	14.7	14.0
Employment in services & other sectors (% employed)[h]	81.1	82.9	83.9
Unemployment rate (% of labour force)[h]	14.8	12.0	11.3
Labour force participation rate (female/male pop. %)[h]	68.1 / 81.6	68.4 / 81.7	68.0 / 81.5
CPI: Consumer Price Index (2010=100)[h]	100	110	113[b]
Agricultural production index (2004-2006=100)	123	130	131[h]
International trade: exports (million current US$)	620	443	494[h,c]
International trade: imports (million current US$)	2 862	3 161	4 087[h,c]
International trade: balance (million current US$)	- 2 242	- 2 719	- 3 593[h,c]
Balance of payments, current account (million current US$)	- 814	- 1 203	- 1 505[b]

Major trading partners

						2019
Export partners (% of exports)[h]	United States	27.6	Poland	26.7	Germany	7.2
Import partners (% of imports)[h]	United States	29.2	Rep. of Korea	24.6	Japan	11.3

Social indicators

	2010	2015	2020
Population growth rate (average annual %)[j]	1.8	1.1	1.0
Urban population (% of total population)	82.4	82.7	83.1[c]
Urban population growth rate (average annual %)[j]	1.9	1.5	...
Fertility rate, total (live births per woman)[j]	1.9	1.8	1.8
Life expectancy at birth (females/males, years)[j]	74.6 / 69.3	74.8 / 70.1	75.9 / 71.5
Population age distribution (0-14/60+ years old, %)	26.9 / 9.0	24.0 / 10.2	21.6 / 12.2
International migrant stock (000/% of total pop.)	54.7 / 15.4	59.3 / 15.8	63.0 / 16.2[c]
Refugees and others of concern to the UNHCR (000)	~0.0[k]	0.1	~0.0[c]
Infant mortality rate (per 1 000 live births)[j]	11.3	8.0	5.9
Health: Current expenditure (% of GDP)	5.9	5.7	5.8[l,a]
Health: Physicians (per 1 000 pop.)	2.8[m]	2.3[n]	2.0[a]
Education: Primary gross enrol. ratio (f/m per 100 pop.)	88.0 / 89.9	85.1 / 87.4	81.2 / 81.6[b]
Education: Secondary gross enrol. ratio (f/m per 100 pop.)	91.2 / 87.6	66.7 / 66.1	71.6 / 67.3[b]
Intentional homicide rate (per 100 000 pop.)	26.5	39.0	32.0[a]
Seats held by women in the National Parliament (%)	12.2	13.2	12.8[o]

Environment and infrastructure indicators

	2010	2015	2020
Individuals using the Internet (per 100 inhabitants)[h]	43.0	78.0	85.0[a]
Threatened species (number)	62	81	96
Forested area (% of land area)[h]	51.4	51.4	51.4[a]
Energy production, primary (Petajoules)	0	0	0[a]
Energy supply per capita (Gigajoules)	96	76[h]	72[a]
Tourist/visitor arrivals at national borders (000)	1 370	1 502	1 633[b]
Important sites for terrestrial biodiversity protected (%)	12.4	29.2	29.2[c]

2017. **b** 2018. **c** 2019. **d** Data classified according to ISIC Rev. 4. **e** Excludes publishing activities. Includes irrigation and canals. **f** Excludes computer and related activities and radio/TV activities. **g** Excludes repair of personal and household goods. **h** Estimate. **i** 2016. **j** Data refers to a 5-year period preceding the reference year. **k** Data as at the end of December. **l** Break in the time series. **m** 2008. **n** 2011. **o** Data are as at 1 January of reporting year.

Bahrain

Region	Western Asia	UN membership date	21 September 1971
Population (000, 2020)	1 702	Surface area (km2)	771[a]
Pop. density (per km2, 2020)	2 238.9	Sex ratio (m per 100 f)	183.1
Capital city	Manama	National currency	Bahraini Dinar (BHD)
Capital city pop. (000, 2020)	600.4[b,c]	Exchange rate (per US$)	0.4[c]

Economic indicators

	2010	2015	2020
GDP: Gross domestic product (million current US$)	25 713	31 126	37 876[d]
GDP growth rate (annual %, const. 2015 prices)	4.3	2.9	2.5[d]
GDP per capita (current US$)	20 722.1	22 688.9	24 133.5[d]
Economy: Agriculture (% of Gross Value Added)[e]	0.3	0.3	0.3[d]
Economy: Industry (% of Gross Value Added)[e]	45.5	40.7	43.7[d]
Economy: Services and other activity (% of GVA)[e]	54.2	59.0	56.0[d]
Employment in agriculture (% of employed)	1.1	1.1	1.0[f]
Employment in industry (% of employed)	35.7	35.2	35.1[f]
Employment in services & other sectors (% employed)	63.2	63.8	64.0[f]
Unemployment rate (% of labour force)[f]	1.1	1.1	0.8
Labour force participation rate (female/male pop. %)[f]	43.8 / 87.4	43.8 / 87.0	45.0 / 87.2
CPI: Consumer Price Index (2010=100)[g]	100	111	119[c]
Agricultural production index (2004-2006=100)	118	199	198[h]
International trade: exports (million current US$)	16 059	13 882	14 355[f,c]
International trade: imports (million current US$)	16 002	16 390	18 680[f,c]
International trade: balance (million current US$)	58	- 2 508	- 4 325[f,c]
Balance of payments, current account (million current US$)	770	- 752	- 2 435[d]

Major trading partners

							2019
Export partners (% of exports)[f]	Areas nes[i]	48.1	Saudi Arabia	13.3	United Arab Emirates	6.1	
Import partners (% of imports)[f]	Saudi Arabia	33.1	China	9.1	United Arab Emirates	6.4	

Social indicators

	2010	2015	2020
Population growth rate (average annual %)[j]	6.7	2.0	4.3
Urban population (% of total population)	88.6	89.0	89.4[c]
Urban population growth rate (average annual %)[j]	6.7	2.1	...
Fertility rate, total (live births per woman)[j]	2.2	2.1	2.0
Life expectancy at birth (females/males, years)[j]	76.7 / 74.9	77.5 / 75.6	78.2 / 76.2
Population age distribution (0-14/60+ years old, %)	20.3 / 3.5	20.8 / 4.1	18.3 / 5.3
International migrant stock (000/% of total pop.)[k]	657.9 / 53.0	704.1 / 51.3	741.2 / 45.2[c]
Refugees and others of concern to the UNHCR (000)	0.2[l]	0.4	0.3[c]
Infant mortality rate (per 1 000 live births)[j]	7.9	6.9	6.0
Health: Current expenditure (% of GDP)	3.8	5.0	4.7[a]
Health: Physicians (per 1 000 pop.)	0.9	0.9	...
Education: Government expenditure (% of GDP)	2.5[m]	2.7	2.3[a]
Education: Primary gross enrol. ratio (f/m per 100 pop.)	101.0 / 96.1[n]	101.7 / 100.7	98.8 / 100.0[d]
Education: Secondary gross enrol. ratio (f/m per 100 pop.)	93.5 / 92.2	101.8 / 102.5	101.7 / 95.8[d]
Education: Tertiary gross enrol. ratio (f/m per 100 pop.)	38.3 / 12.2[n]	59.3 / 30.9	67.8 / 37.0[d]
Intentional homicide rate (per 100 000 pop.)	0.9	0.5[o]	...
Seats held by women in the National Parliament (%)	2.5	7.5	15.0[p]

Environment and infrastructure indicators

	2010	2015	2020
Individuals using the Internet (per 100 inhabitants)	55.0	93.5[q]	98.6[d]
Research & Development expenditure (% of GDP)	...	0.1[o]	...
Threatened species (number)	32	32	47
Forested area (% of land area)[f]	0.7	0.8	0.8[a]
CO2 emission estimates (million tons/tons per capita)	25.6 / 20.6	30.1 / 21.9	29.8 / 20.0[a]
Energy production, primary (Petajoules)	849	957	942[a]
Energy supply per capita (Gigajoules)	413	423	389[a]
Tourist/visitor arrivals at national borders (000)[r]	11 952	9 670[s]	12 045[d]
Important sites for terrestrial biodiversity protected (%)	0.0	0.0	0.0[c]

a 2017. **b** Refers to the urban area of the municipality of Al-Manamah. **c** 2019. **d** 2018. **e** At producers' prices. **f** Estimate. **g** Calculated by the UN Statistics Division from national indices. **h** 2016. **i** Areas not elsewhere specified. Data refers to a 5-year period preceding the reference year. **k** Refers to foreign citizens. **l** Data as at the end of December. **m** 2008. **n** 2006. **o** 2014. **p** Data are as at 1 January of reporting year. **q** Population aged 15 years and over. **r** Excluding nationals residing abroad. **s** Break in the time series.

Bangladesh

Region	Southern Asia	UN membership date	17 September 1974
Population (000, 2020)	164 689	Surface area (km2)	147 570[a]
Pop. density (per km2, 2020)	1 265.2	Sex ratio (m per 100 f)	102.2
Capital city	Dhaka	National currency	Taka (BDT)
Capital city pop. (000, 2020)	20 283.6[b,c]	Exchange rate (per US$)	84.9[c]

Economic indicators

	2010	2015	2020
GDP: Gross domestic product (million current US$)	114 508	194 466	269 628[d]
GDP growth rate (annual %, const. 2015 prices)	5.6	6.6	7.9[d]
GDP per capita (current US$)	775.9	1 244.5	1 670.8[d]
Economy: Agriculture (% of Gross Value Added)	17.8	15.3	13.8[d]
Economy: Industry (% of Gross Value Added)	26.1	27.8	30.2[d]
Economy: Services and other activity (% of GVA)	56.0	57.0	56.0[d]
Employment in agriculture (% of employed)	47.3	43.5[e]	37.7[e]
Employment in industry (% of employed)	17.6	19.9[e]	21.6[e]
Employment in services & other sectors (% employed)	35.1	36.6[e]	40.6[e]
Unemployment rate (% of labour force)[e]	3.4	4.4	4.2
Labour force participation rate (female/male pop. %)[e]	29.8 / 83.2	32.4 / 80.4	36.4 / 81.3
CPI: Consumer Price Index (2010=100)[f]	100	145	180[c]
Agricultural production index (2004-2006=100)	128	141	149[g]
International trade: exports (million current US$)	19 231	31 734	34 186[e,c]
International trade: imports (million current US$)	30 504	48 059	66 060[e,c]
International trade: balance (million current US$)	- 11 273	- 16 325	- 31 874[e,c]
Balance of payments, current account (million US$)	2 109	2 580	- 3 087[c]

Major trading partners

							2019
Export partners (% of exports)[e]	United States	14.9	Germany	14.4	United Kingdom	8.4
Import partners (% of imports)[e]	China	30.5	India	14.2	Singapore	5.3

Social indicators

	2010	2015	2020
Population growth rate (average annual %)[h]	1.2	1.1	1.1
Urban population (% of total population)	30.5	34.3	37.4[c]
Urban population growth rate (average annual %)[h]	3.7	3.5	...
Fertility rate, total (live births per woman)[h]	2.5	2.2	2.1
Life expectancy at birth (females/males, years)[h]	70.0 / 67.8	72.4 / 69.4	74.1 / 70.5
Population age distribution (0-14/60+ years old, %)	32.0 / 7.0	29.3 / 7.2	26.8 / 8.0
International migrant stock (000/% of total pop.)[i]	1 345.5 / 0.9	1 422.8 / 0.9	2 185.6 / 1.3[c]
Refugees and others of concern to the UNHCR (000)	229.3[j]	233.0	911.8[k,c]
Infant mortality rate (per 1 000 live births)[h]	43.3	33.2	26.8
Health: Current expenditure (% of GDP)[l]	2.5	2.5	2.3[a]
Health: Physicians (per 1 000 pop.)	0.4	0.5	0.6[d]
Education: Government expenditure (% of GDP)	1.9[m]	2.0[e,n]	2.0[d]
Education: Primary gross enrol. ratio (f/m per 100 pop.)	109.3 / 102.8[e]	... / ...	120.8 / 112.4[d]
Education: Secondary gross enrol. ratio (f/m per 100 pop.)	54.7 / 48.7	69.7 / 61.8	78.3 / 67.4[d]
Education: Tertiary gross enrol. ratio (f/m per 100 pop.)	8.1 / 13.5[m]	11.7 / 15.9[o]	17.0 / 24.0[d]
Intentional homicide rate (per 100 000 pop.)	2.7	2.6	2.4[d]
Seats held by women in the National Parliament (%)	18.6	20.0	20.9[p]

Environment and infrastructure indicators

	2010	2015	2020
Individuals using the Internet (per 100 inhabitants)	3.7[e]	14.4[e]	15.0[q,a]
Threatened species (number)	122	137	165
Forested area (% of land area)[e]	11.1	11.0	11.0[a]
CO2 emission estimates (million tons/tons per capita)[l]	49.9 / 0.3	70.9 / 0.4	78.3 / 0.5[a]
Energy production, primary (Petajoules)	1 304	1 509	1 605[a]
Energy supply per capita (Gigajoules)	10	11	12[a]
Tourist/visitor arrivals at national borders (000)	303	643	1 026[a]
Important sites for terrestrial biodiversity protected (%)	43.6	43.7	43.7[c]
Pop. using safely managed drinking water (urban/rural, %)	44.6 / 60.6	44.6 / 61.2	44.6 / 61.5[a]
Pop. using safely managed sanitation (urban/rural %)	... / 24.1	... / 30.0	... / 32.3[a]
Net Official Development Assist. received (% of GNI)	1.06	1.25	1.06[a]

a 2017. b Mega city. c 2019. d 2018. e Estimate. f Calculated by the UN Statistics Division from national indices. g 2016. h Data refers to a 5-year period preceding the reference year. i Including refugees. j Data as at the end of December. k Includes 911,660 people with dual status as both refugees and stateless persons. l Data refer to fiscal years beginning 1 July. m 2009. n 2013. o 2014. p Data are as at 1 January of reporting year. q Population aged 18 years and over.

Barbados

Region	Caribbean	UN membership date	09 December 1966
Population (000, 2020)	287	Surface area (km2)	431 [a]
Pop. density (per km2, 2020)	668.3	Sex ratio (m per 100 f)	93.8
Capital city	Bridgetown	National currency	Barbados Dollar (BBD)
Capital city pop. (000, 2020)	89.2 [b]	Exchange rate (per US$)	2.0 [c]

Economic indicators	2010	2015	2020
GDP: Gross domestic product (million current US$)	4 530	4 715	5 087 [b]
GDP growth rate (annual %, const. 2015 prices)	- 2.3	2.4	- 0.4 [b]
GDP per capita (current US$)	16 056.1	16 525.1	17 745.9 [b]
Economy: Agriculture (% of Gross Value Added)	1.5	1.5	1.5 [b]
Economy: Industry (% of Gross Value Added)	15.8	15.4	14.9 [b]
Economy: Services and other activity (% of GVA)	82.7	83.1	83.6 [b]
Employment in agriculture (% of employed)	2.8	2.9	2.6 [d]
Employment in industry (% of employed)	18.8	19.4	18.9 [d]
Employment in services & other sectors (% employed)	78.4	77.8	78.5 [d]
Unemployment rate (% of labour force) [d]	10.7	11.4	10.9
Labour force participation rate (female/male pop. %) [d]	62.9 / 72.4	61.6 / 69.5	61.4 / 68.7
CPI: Consumer Price Index (2010=100)	100 [e,f]	168 [g,h]	192 [g,h,c]
Agricultural production index (2004-2006=100)	91	85	85 [i]
International trade: exports (million current US$)	314	483	462 [d,c]
International trade: imports (million current US$)	1 196	1 618	1 618 [d,c]
International trade: balance (million current US$)	- 883	- 1 135	- 1 157 [d,c]
Balance of payments, current account (million US$)	- 272	- 99	- 453 [i]

Major trading partners						2019
Export partners (% of exports) [d]	Areas nes [j]	23.8	United States	22.7	Trinidad and Tobago	6.9
Import partners (% of imports) [d]	United States	39.5	Trinidad and Tobago	17.9	China	5.9

Social indicators	2010	2015	2020
Population growth rate (average annual %) [k]	0.4	0.2	0.1
Urban population (% of total population)	31.9	31.2	31.2 [c]
Urban population growth rate (average annual %) [k]	- 0.2	- 0.1	...
Fertility rate, total (live births per woman) [k]	1.8	1.6	1.6
Life expectancy at birth (females/males, years) [k]	79.6 / 76.5	80.0 / 77.1	80.4 / 77.6
Population age distribution (0-14/60+ years old, %)	19.7 / 18.1	18.3 / 20.3	16.8 / 23.2
International migrant stock (000/% of total pop.)	32.8 / 11.6	34.5 / 12.1	34.8 / 12.1 [c]
Refugees and others of concern to the UNHCR (000)	...	~0.0	~0.0 [c]
Infant mortality rate (per 1 000 live births) [k]	12.6	11.5	10.0
Health: Current expenditure (% of GDP)	6.8	7.0	6.8 [a]
Health: Physicians (per 1 000 pop.)	...	...	2.5 [a]
Education: Government expenditure (% of GDP)	6.0	6.2 [i]	4.7 [a]
Education: Primary gross enrol. ratio (f/m per 100 pop.)	100.4 / 98.8 [d]	95.6 / 96.2	97.5 / 101.2 [b]
Education: Secondary gross enrol. ratio (f/m per 100 pop.)	102.1 / 101.7 [d]	109.5 / 105.7	105.8 / 101.8 [b]
Education: Tertiary gross enrol. ratio (f/m per 100 pop.)	95.8 / 43.9	90.6 / 40.3 [m]	... / ...
Intentional homicide rate (per 100 000 pop.)	11.0	10.9	9.8 [b]
Seats held by women in the National Parliament (%)	10.0	16.7	20.0 [n]

Environment and infrastructure indicators	2010	2015	2020
Individuals using the Internet (per 100 inhabitants) [d]	65.1	76.1	81.8 [a]
Threatened species (number)	36	51	62
Forested area (% of land area)	14.7	14.7	14.7 [d,a]
Energy production, primary (Petajoules)	4	3	2 [a]
Energy supply per capita (Gigajoules)	72	59	55 [a]
Tourist/visitor arrivals at national borders (000)	532	592	680 [b]
Important sites for terrestrial biodiversity protected (%)	0.2	0.2	0.2 [c]
Net Official Development Assist. received (% of GNI)	0.35	...	...

a 2017. b 2018. c 2019. d Estimate. e Calculated by the UN Statistics Division from national indices. f Metropolitan Lima. g Data refer to the Retail Price Index. h Index base: July 2001=100. i 2016. j Areas not elsewhere specified. k Data refers to a 5-year period preceding the reference year. l 2014. m 2011. n Data are as at 1 January of reporting year.

Belarus

Region	Eastern Europe	UN membership date	24 October 1945
Population (000, 2020)	9 449	Surface area (km2)	207 600[a]
Pop. density (per km2, 2020)	46.6	Sex ratio (m per 100 f)	87.1
Capital city	Minsk	National currency	Belarusian Ruble (BYN)
Capital city pop. (000, 2020)	2 016.7[b,c]	Exchange rate (per US$)	2.1[c]

Economic indicators

	2010	2015	2020
GDP: Gross domestic product (million current US$)	57 232	56 455	59 662[d]
GDP growth rate (annual %, const. 2015 prices)	7.8	- 3.8	3.0[d]
GDP per capita (current US$)	6 075.2	5 980.7	6 311.7[d]
Economy: Agriculture (% of Gross Value Added)[e]	10.1	7.2	7.5[d]
Economy: Industry (% of Gross Value Added)[e,f]	40.3	37.7	36.8[d]
Economy: Services and other activity (% of GVA)[e,g,h]	49.5	55.1	55.7[d]
Employment in agriculture (% of employed)	11.0[i]	9.7	10.8[i]
Employment in industry (% of employed)	32.2[i]	31.1	30.2[i]
Employment in services & other sectors (% employed)	56.8[i]	59.2	59.0[i]
Unemployment rate (% of labour force)[i]	6.1	5.9	4.6
Labour force participation rate (female/male pop. %)[i]	57.5 / 69.6	58.6 / 71.0	57.3 / 71.3
CPI: Consumer Price Index (2010=100)	100[i]	387	508[c]
Agricultural production index (2004-2006=100)	117	121	120[j]
International trade: exports (million current US$)	25 283	26 660	32 764[i,c]
International trade: imports (million current US$)	34 884	30 291	39 317[i,c]
International trade: balance (million current US$)	- 9 601	- 3 631	- 6 553[i,c]
Balance of payments, current account (million US$)	- 8 280	- 1 831	- 1 166[c]

Major trading partners

						2019
Export partners (% of exports)[i]	Russian Federation	38.2	Ukraine	12.0	United Kingdom	9.1
Import partners (% of imports)[i]	Russian Federation	58.4	China	7.8	Germany	4.7

Social indicators

	2010	2015	2020
Population growth rate (average annual %)[k]	- 0.3	~0.0	~0.0
Urban population (% of total population)	74.7	77.2	79.0[c]
Urban population growth rate (average annual %)[k]	0.3	0.7	...
Fertility rate, total (live births per woman)[k]	1.4	1.6	1.7
Life expectancy at birth (females/males, years)[k]	75.2 / 63.6	78.0 / 66.8	79.3 / 69.3
Population age distribution (0-14/60+ years old, %)	14.9 / 19.1	16.3 / 20.4	17.2 / 22.6
International migrant stock (000/% of total pop.)	1 090.4 / 11.6	1 082.9 / 11.5	1 069.4 / 11.3[c]
Refugees and others of concern to the UNHCR (000)	8.4[l]	7.9	8.6[c]
Infant mortality rate (per 1 000 live births)[k]	6.3	3.4	3.0
Health: Current expenditure (% of GDP)	5.7	6.1	5.9[m,a]
Health: Physicians (per 1 000 pop.)	3.2	5.2	...
Education: Government expenditure (% of GDP)	5.1	4.8	4.8[a]
Education: Primary gross enrol. ratio (f/m per 100 pop.)	104.3 / 104.5	99.2 / 99.1	100.4 / 100.6[d]
Education: Secondary gross enrol. ratio (f/m per 100 pop.)	106.4 / 109.9	104.6 / 106.3	101.7 / 103.1[d]
Education: Tertiary gross enrol. ratio (f/m per 100 pop.)	94.6 / 65.4[i]	102.6 / 77.2	95.1 / 80.2[d]
Intentional homicide rate (per 100 000 pop.)	4.3	3.5	2.4[d]
Seats held by women in the National Parliament (%)	31.8	27.3	40.0[n]

Environment and infrastructure indicators

	2010	2015	2020
Individuals using the Internet (per 100 inhabitants)	31.8[o]	62.2[p]	79.1[d]
Research & Development expenditure (% of GDP)	0.7[q]	0.5[q]	0.6[d]
Threatened species (number)	16	21	30
Forested area (% of land area)	42.1	42.5	42.5[i,a]
CO2 emission estimates (million tons/tons per capita)	59.5 / 6.3	52.6 / 5.5	54.1 / 5.7[a]
Energy production, primary (Petajoules)	167	163	180[a]
Energy supply per capita (Gigajoules)	122	112	114[a]
Tourist/visitor arrivals at national borders (000)	119[r]	4 386[r,s]	11 502[t,d]
Important sites for terrestrial biodiversity protected (%)	37.2	47.1	47.1[c]
Pop. using safely managed sanitation (urban/rural %)	85.8 / 84.7	82.6 / 77.8	81.7 / 76.4[a]
Net Official Development Assist. received (% of GNI)	0.24	0.19	0.21[d]

a 2017. b Including communities under the authority of the Town Council. c 2019. d 2018. e Data classified according to ISIC Rev. 4. f Excludes publishing activities. Includes irrigation and canals. g Excludes repair of personal and household goods. h Excludes computer and related activities and radio/TV activities. i Estimate. j 2016. k Data refers to a 5-year period preceding the reference year. l Data as at the end of December. m Data revision. n Data are as at 1 January of reporting year. o Population aged 16 years and over. p Users in the last 12 months. q Data have been converted from the former national currency using the appropriate conversion rate. r Excludes the Belarusian-Russian border segment. s Break in the time series. t Includes estimation of the Belarusian-Russian border segment.

Belgium

Region	Western Europe	UN membership date	27 December 1945
Population (000, 2020)	11 590	Surface area (km2)	30 528 [a]
Pop. density (per km2, 2020)	382.7	Sex ratio (m per 100 f)	98.3
Capital city	Brussels	National currency	Euro (EUR)
Capital city pop. (000, 2020)	2 065.3 [b,c]	Exchange rate (per US$)	0.9 [c]

Economic indicators	2010	2015	2020
GDP: Gross domestic product (million current US$)	480 952	462 150	543 026 [d]
GDP growth rate (annual %, const. 2015 prices)	2.9	2.0	1.5 [d]
GDP per capita (current US$)	43 967.7	40 941.9	47 293.0 [d]
Economy: Agriculture (% of Gross Value Added) [e]	0.9	0.8	0.6 [d]
Economy: Industry (% of Gross Value Added) [e,f]	23.4	22.0	21.4 [d]
Economy: Services and other activity (% of GVA) [e,g,h]	75.7	77.3	78.0 [d]
Employment in agriculture (% of employed)	1.4	1.2	0.9 [i]
Employment in industry (% of employed)	23.4	21.4	20.6 [i]
Employment in services & other sectors (% employed)	75.3	77.4	78.4 [i]
Unemployment rate (% of labour force) [i]	8.3	8.5	5.7
Labour force participation rate (female/male pop. %) [i]	47.5 / 60.8	48.0 / 59.1	48.5 / 58.4
CPI: Consumer Price Index (2010=100)	100 [j]	109 [j]	117 [c]
Agricultural production index (2004-2006=100)	100	106	101 [k]
International trade: exports (million current US$)	407 596	397 739	445 214 [c]
International trade: imports (million current US$)	391 256	371 025	426 489 [c]
International trade: balance (million current US$)	16 340	26 714	18 725 [c]
Balance of payments, current account (million US$)	7 338	6 363	- 6 512 [c]

Major trading partners						2019
Export partners (% of exports)	Germany	17.9	France	14.1	Netherlands	12.1
Import partners (% of imports)	Netherlands	17.4	Germany	13.2	France	9.7

Social indicators	2010	2015	2020
Population growth rate (average annual %) [l]	0.7	0.6	0.5
Urban population (% of total population)	97.7	97.9	98.0 [c]
Urban population growth rate (average annual %) [l]	0.8	0.7	...
Fertility rate, total (live births per woman) [l]	1.8	1.8	1.7
Life expectancy at birth (females/males, years) [l]	82.3 / 76.8	83.0 / 78.0	83.7 / 79.0
Population age distribution (0-14/60+ years old, %)	16.9 / 23.2	17.0 / 24.0	17.0 / 25.6
International migrant stock (000/% of total pop.)	1 503.8 / 13.7	1 783.5 / 15.8	1 981.9 / 17.2 [c]
Refugees and others of concern to the UNHCR (000)	36.9 [m]	45.8	83.5 [c]
Infant mortality rate (per 1 000 live births) [l]	3.8	3.5	2.8
Health: Current expenditure (% of GDP) [i]	10.0	10.3	10.3 [a]
Health: Physicians (per 1 000 pop.)	2.9	3.0	3.1 [a]
Education: Government expenditure (% of GDP)	6.4	6.5	6.5 [k]
Education: Primary gross enrol. ratio (f/m per 100 pop.)	101.8 / 102.0	103.1 / 103.2	104.0 / 103.9 [a]
Education: Secondary gross enrol. ratio (f/m per 100 pop.)	167.3 / 146.9	174.7 / 153.6	167.8 / 149.7 [a]
Education: Tertiary gross enrol. ratio (f/m per 100 pop.)	75.9 / 60.0	84.7 / 64.8	90.5 / 69.3 [a]
Intentional homicide rate (per 100 000 pop.)	1.7	2.0	1.7 [a]
Seats held by women in the National Parliament (%)	38.0	39.3	40.7 [n]

Environment and infrastructure indicators	2010	2015	2020
Individuals using the Internet (per 100 inhabitants)	75.0	85.1 [o,p]	88.7 [d]
Research & Development expenditure (% of GDP)	2.1	2.5	2.8 [q,d]
Threatened species (number)	27	30	66
Forested area (% of land area)	22.5	22.6 [i]	22.6 [i,a]
CO2 emission estimates (million tons/tons per capita)	103.9 / 9.5	92.8 / 8.3	90.4 / 8.0 [a]
Energy production, primary (Petajoules)	646	445	626 [a]
Energy supply per capita (Gigajoules)	228	194	201 [a]
Tourist/visitor arrivals at national borders (000)	7 186	8 355 [r]	9 119 [d]
Important sites for terrestrial biodiversity protected (%)	80.3	83.7	84.2 [c]
Net Official Development Assist. disbursed (% of GNI) [s]	0.64	0.42	0.45 [a]

a 2017. b Refers to the population of Brussels-Capital Region and "communes" of the agglomeration and suburbs. c 2019. d 2018. e Data classified according to ISIC Rev. 4. f Excludes publishing activities. Includes irrigation and canals. g Excludes repair of personal and household goods. h Excludes computer and related activities and radio/TV activities. i Estimate. j Calculated by the UN Statistics Division from national indices. k 2016. l Data refers to a 5-year period preceding the reference year. m Data as at the end of December. n Data are as at 1 January of reporting year. o Users in the last 3 months. p Population aged 16 to 74 years. q Provisional data. r Break in the time series. s Development Assistance Committee member (OECD).

Belize

Region	Central America	UN membership date	25 September 1981
Population (000, 2020)	398	Surface area (km2)	22 966[a]
Pop. density (per km2, 2020)	17.4	Sex ratio (m per 100 f)	98.9
Capital city	Belmopan	National currency	Belize Dollar (BZD)
Capital city pop. (000, 2020)	23.0[b]	Exchange rate (per US$)	2.0[c]

Economic indicators

	2010	2015	2020
GDP: Gross domestic product (million current US$)	1 377	1 724	1 871[b]
GDP growth rate (annual %, const. 2015 prices)	3.0	2.8	2.1[b]
GDP per capita (current US$)	4 270.8	4 775.9	4 884.7[b]
Economy: Agriculture (% of Gross Value Added)	12.8	14.7	11.0[b]
Economy: Industry (% of Gross Value Added)	21.0	16.3	13.7[b]
Economy: Services and other activity (% of GVA)	66.2	69.0	75.3[b]
Employment in agriculture (% of employed)	18.9[d]	18.1	16.6[d]
Employment in industry (% of employed)	16.5[d]	15.4	15.7[d]
Employment in services & other sectors (% employed)	64.5[d]	66.5	67.7[d]
Unemployment rate (% of labour force)[d]	8.5	7.6	6.4
Labour force participation rate (female/male pop. %)[d]	46.4 / 80.4	48.4 / 80.0	50.2 / 80.6
CPI: Consumer Price Index (2010=100)[e]	100	104	106[c]
Agricultural production index (2004-2006=100)	97	102	97[f]
International trade: exports (million current US$)	282	314	245[c]
International trade: imports (million current US$)	700	996	986[c]
International trade: balance (million current US$)	- 418	- 682	- 741[c]
Balance of payments, current account (million current US$)	- 46	- 175	- 155[b]

Major trading partners

						2019
Export partners (% of exports)	United Kingdom	33.5	United States	25.4	Ireland	6.4
Import partners (% of imports)	United States	44.2	China	13.6	Mexico	10.9

Social indicators

	2010	2015	2020
Population growth rate (average annual %)[g]	2.6	2.3	1.9
Urban population (% of total population)	45.2	45.4	45.9[c]
Urban population growth rate (average annual %)[g]	2.5	2.3	...
Fertility rate, total (live births per woman)[g]	2.8	2.6	2.3
Life expectancy at birth (females/males, years)[g]	73.6 / 68.0	76.0 / 71.1	77.6 / 71.4
Population age distribution (0-14/60+ years old, %)	35.6 / 6.0	32.1 / 6.6	29.2 / 7.6
International migrant stock (000/% of total pop.)[h]	46.4 / 14.4	54.7 / 15.1	60.0 / 15.4[c]
Refugees and others of concern to the UNHCR (000)	0.2[i]	0.1	6.5[c]
Infant mortality rate (per 1 000 live births)[g]	17.3	15.0	12.8
Health: Current expenditure (% of GDP)	5.8	5.9	5.6[a]
Health: Physicians (per 1 000 pop.)	0.8[j]	0.6[k]	1.1[a]
Education: Government expenditure (% of GDP)	6.6	6.8	7.4[a]
Education: Primary gross enrol. ratio (f/m per 100 pop.)	110.3 / 114.8	110.2 / 115.5	108.7 / 114.6[b]
Education: Secondary gross enrol. ratio (f/m per 100 pop.)	78.2 / 72.4	81.7 / 79.6	87.1 / 83.7[b]
Education: Tertiary gross enrol. ratio (f/m per 100 pop.)	26.9 / 16.8	28.7 / 17.8	30.5 / 18.8[a]
Intentional homicide rate (per 100 000 pop.)	40.0	33.0	37.8[a]
Seats held by women in the National Parliament (%)	0.0	3.1	9.4[l]

Environment and infrastructure indicators

	2010	2015	2020
Individuals using the Internet (per 100 inhabitants)	28.2[m]	41.6[d]	47.1[d,a]
Threatened species (number)	92	117	143
Forested area (% of land area)[d]	61.0	59.9	59.9[a]
Energy production, primary (Petajoules)	14	9	9[a]
Energy supply per capita (Gigajoules)	40	44	43[a]
Tourist/visitor arrivals at national borders (000)	242	341	489[b]
Important sites for terrestrial biodiversity protected (%)	39.3	41.5	41.5[c]
Net Official Development Assist. received (% of GNI)	1.92	1.70	1.88[b]

a 2017. b 2018. c 2019. d Estimate. e Calculated by the UN Statistics Division from national indices. f 2016. g Data refers to a 5-year period preceding the reference year. h Including refugees. i Data as at the end of December. j 2009. k 2014. l Data are as at 1 January of reporting year. m Population aged 5 years and over.

Benin

Region	Western Africa	UN membership date	20 September 1960
Population (000, 2020)	12 123	Surface area (km2)	114 763[a]
Pop. density (per km2, 2020)	107.5	Sex ratio (m per 100 f)	99.8
Capital city	Porto-Novo[b]	National currency	CFA Franc, BCEAO (XOF)[c]
Capital city pop. (000, 2020)	285.3[d]	Exchange rate (per US$)	583.9[e]

Economic indicators	2010	2015	2020
GDP: Gross domestic product (million current US$)	6 970	8 454	10 412[d]
GDP growth rate (annual %, const. 2015 prices)	2.1	6.5	6.5[d]
GDP per capita (current US$)	757.7	799.4	906.5[d]
Economy: Agriculture (% of Gross Value Added)	25.4	22.7	24.5[d]
Economy: Industry (% of Gross Value Added)	24.7	24.4	23.4[d]
Economy: Services and other activity (% of GVA)	49.9	52.9	52.0[d]
Employment in agriculture (% of employed)[f]	44.0	41.2	38.0
Employment in industry (% of employed)[f]	18.7	18.6	19.1
Employment in services & other sectors (% employed)[f]	37.3	40.2	42.9
Unemployment rate (% of labour force)[f]	1.0	2.6	2.0
Labour force participation rate (female/male pop. %)[f]	69.2 / 73.0	68.4 / 73.3	69.0 / 73.0
CPI: Consumer Price Index (2010=100)[f,g]	100	110	110[d]
Agricultural production index (2004-2006=100)	118	147	153[h]
International trade: exports (million current US$)	534	626	1 706[f,e]
International trade: imports (million current US$)	2 134	2 475	3 967[f,e]
International trade: balance (million current US$)	- 1 600	- 1 849	- 2 261[f,e]
Balance of payments, current account (million US$)	- 531	- 679	- 649[d]

Major trading partners						2019
Export partners (% of exports)[f]	Bangladesh	22.7	India	18.3	Viet Nam	10.0
Import partners (% of imports)[f]	Thailand	14.0	India	12.1	Togo	9.3

Social indicators	2010	2015	2020
Population growth rate (average annual %)[i]	2.8	2.8	2.7
Urban population (% of total population)	43.1	45.7	47.9[e]
Urban population growth rate (average annual %)[i]	4.1	4.0	...
Fertility rate, total (live births per woman)[i]	5.5	5.2	4.9
Life expectancy at birth (females/males, years)[i]	60.0 / 57.1	61.4 / 58.5	62.8 / 59.8
Population age distribution (0-14/60+ years old, %)	43.8 / 4.9	43.0 / 5.0	41.9 / 5.1
International migrant stock (000/% of total pop.)[j,k]	309.1 / 3.4	366.3 / 3.5	390.1 / 3.3[e]
Refugees and others of concern to the UNHCR (000)	7.3[l]	0.6	1.6[e]
Infant mortality rate (per 1 000 live births)[i]	74.5	67.7	61.1
Health: Current expenditure (% of GDP)	4.1	4.0	3.7[a]
Health: Physicians (per 1 000 pop.)	0.1	0.2[m]	0.1[d]
Education: Government expenditure (% of GDP)	5.0	4.4	4.0[f,h]
Education: Primary gross enrol. ratio (f/m per 100 pop.)	113.2 / 126.9	127.6 / 137.2	118.0 / 125.8[d]
Education: Secondary gross enrol. ratio (f/m per 100 pop.)	... / ...	48.9 / 68.5	50.7 / 67.1[h]
Education: Tertiary gross enrol. ratio (f/m per 100 pop.)	7.2 / 20.3	7.7 / 19.3	7.5 / 17.0[a]
Intentional homicide rate (per 100 000 pop.)	...	...	1.1[a]
Seats held by women in the National Parliament (%)	10.8	8.4	7.2[n]

Environment and infrastructure indicators	2010	2015	2020
Individuals using the Internet (per 100 inhabitants)	3.1	11.3[f]	20.0[o,a]
Threatened species (number)	62	74	106
Forested area (% of land area)[f]	40.4	38.2	38.2[a]
CO2 emission estimates (million tons/tons per capita)	4.6 / 0.5	5.3 / 0.5	6.8 / 0.6[a]
Energy production, primary (Petajoules)	86	114	114[a]
Energy supply per capita (Gigajoules)	17	18	19[a]
Tourist/visitor arrivals at national borders (000)	199	255	295[d]
Important sites for terrestrial biodiversity protected (%)	66.7	66.7	66.7[e]
Net Official Development Assist. received (% of GNI)	9.96	5.31	5.58[d]

a 2017. b Porto-Novo is the constitutional capital and Cotonou is the economic capital. c African Financial Community (CFA) Franc, Central Bank of West African States (BCEAO). d 2018. e 2019. f Estimate. g For Cotonou only. h 2016. i Data refers to a 5-year period preceding the reference year. j Refers to foreign citizens. k Including refugees. l Data as at the end of December. m 2013. n Data are as at 1 January of reporting year. o Population aged 18 years and over.

Bermuda

Region	Northern America	Population (000, 2020)	61
Surface area (km2)	53[a]	Pop. density (per km2, 2020)	1 212.8
Sex ratio (m per 100 f)	91.4[b,c,a]	Capital city	Hamilton
National currency	Bermudian Dollar (BMD)	Capital city pop. (000, 2020)	10.1[d]
Exchange rate (per US$)	1.0[e]		

Economic indicators	2010	2015	2020
GDP: Gross domestic product (million current US$)	5 853	5 891	6 351[d]
GDP growth rate (annual %, const. 2015 prices)	- 2.5	0.4	- 0.4[d]
GDP per capita (current US$)	89 510.1	92 487.0	101 207.9[d]
Economy: Agriculture (% of Gross Value Added)	0.7	0.7	0.7[d]
Economy: Industry (% of Gross Value Added)[f]	7.1	5.5	5.6[d]
Economy: Services and other activity (% of GVA)	92.2	93.9	93.7[d]
Employment in agriculture (% of employed)[g,h,i]	1.4	1.6[j,k]	...
Employment in industry (% of employed)[g,h,i]	12.9	10.3[j,k]	...
Employment in services & other sectors (% employed)[g,h,i]	85.7	87.6[j,k]	...
Unemployment rate (% of labour force)[i]	4.5[g,l]	6.7[j,k]	...
Labour force participation rate (female/male pop. %)	81.0 / 87.0[i]	72.6 / 80.0[i,j,m]	... / ...
CPI: Consumer Price Index (2010=100)	...	148[n,o]	...
Agricultural production index (2004-2006=100)	109	113	112[p]
International trade: exports (million current US$)	15[q]	9	23[q,e]
International trade: imports (million current US$)	970	929	1 204[q,e]
International trade: balance (million current US$)	- 955	- 920	- 1 181[q,e]
Balance of payments, current account (million US$)	696	943	958[d]

Major trading partners							2019
Export partners (% of exports)[q]	United States	62.6	Areas nes[r]	18.4	United Kingdom	6.2	
Import partners (% of imports)[q]	United States	69.4	Canada	9.1	United Kingdom	3.5	

Social indicators	2010	2015	2020
Population growth rate (average annual %)	- 0.4[s]	- 0.6[s]	- 0.4
Urban population (% of total population)	100.0	100.0	100.0[e]
Urban population growth rate (average annual %)[s]	- 0.4	- 0.6	...
Fertility rate, total (live births per woman)	1.7	1.4	1.5[p]
Life expectancy at birth (females/males, years)	82.3 / 76.9	84.9 / 77.3	85.1 / 77.5[p]
Population age distribution (0-14/60+ years old, %)[b]	17.4 / 18.7	15.3 / 23.4[c]	14.8 / 24.9[c,a]
International migrant stock (000/% of total pop.)	18.9 / 28.9	19.1 / 30.0	19.3 / 30.9[e]
Education: Government expenditure (% of GDP)	2.6	1.7	1.5[a]
Education: Primary gross enrol. ratio (f/m per 100 pop.)	101.2 / 93.8[t]	100.2 / 102.1	... / ...
Education: Secondary gross enrol. ratio (f/m per 100 pop.)	83.7 / 71.2	81.5 / 72.6	... / ...
Education: Tertiary gross enrol. ratio (f/m per 100 pop.)	41.4 / 20.1	35.3 / 15.3	22.9 / 15.3[d]
Intentional homicide rate (per 100 000 pop.)	10.9	6.5	8.1[a]

Environment and infrastructure indicators	2010	2015	2020
Individuals using the Internet (per 100 inhabitants)[q]	84.2	98.3	98.4[a]
Research & Development expenditure (% of GDP)[u]	0.2	0.2	0.3[d]
Threatened species (number)	50	64	80
Forested area (% of land area)[q]	18.5	18.5	18.5[a]
Energy production, primary (Petajoules)[q]	1	1	1[a]
Energy supply per capita (Gigajoules)	138[q]	130	151[a]
Tourist/visitor arrivals at national borders (000)[v,w]	232	220	282[d]
Important sites for terrestrial biodiversity protected (%)	52.0	52.0	52.0[e]

a 2017. b De jure population. c Data refer to projections based on the 2010 Population Census. d 2018. e 2019. f Excluding mining and quarrying. g Break in the time series. h Data classified according to ISIC Rev. 3. i Population aged 16 years and over. j Excluding the institutional population. k 2013. l 2009. m 2012. n Base: 2000=100. o 2014. p 2016. q Estimate. r Areas not elsewhere specified. s Data refers to a 5-year period preceding the reference year. t 2006. u Overestimated or based on overestimated data. v Excluding nationals residing abroad. w Arrivals by air.

Bhutan

Region	Southern Asia	UN membership date	21 September 1971
Population (000, 2020)	772	Surface area (km2)	38 394 [a]
Pop. density (per km2, 2020)	20.2	Sex ratio (m per 100 f)	113.4
Capital city	Thimphu	National currency	Ngultrum (BTN)
Capital city pop. (000, 2020)	203.3 [b]	Exchange rate (per US$)	71.3 [c]

Economic indicators

	2010	2015	2020
GDP: Gross domestic product (million current US$)	1 585	2 060	2 658 [b]
GDP growth rate (annual %, const. 2015 prices)	11.7	6.6	5.8 [b]
GDP per capita (current US$)	2 312.8	2 829.9	3 523.8 [b]
Economy: Agriculture (% of Gross Value Added)	17.5	17.5	17.7 [b]
Economy: Industry (% of Gross Value Added)	44.6	43.2	43.1 [b]
Economy: Services and other activity (% of GVA)	37.9	39.3	39.2 [b]
Employment in agriculture (% of employed)	59.6	58.0	54.6 [d]
Employment in industry (% of employed)	6.6	9.7	11.1 [d]
Employment in services & other sectors (% employed)	33.8	32.4	34.3 [d]
Unemployment rate (% of labour force) [d]	3.3	2.4	2.4
Labour force participation rate (female/male pop. %) [d]	63.5 / 72.5	58.2 / 72.6	59.0 / 73.8
CPI: Consumer Price Index (2010=100)	100	146	167 [c]
Agricultural production index (2004-2006=100)	95	99	102 [e]
International trade: exports (million current US$)	413	549 [d]	659 [d,c]
International trade: imports (million current US$)	854	1 062 [d]	1 049 [d,c]
International trade: balance (million current US$)	- 440	- 512 [d]	- 390 [d,c]
Balance of payments, current account (million US$)	- 323	- 548	- 564 [c]

Major trading partners

						2019
Export partners (% of exports) [d]	India	92.3	Italy	2.1	Nepal	1.4
Import partners (% of imports) [d]	India	84.3	Thailand	5.0	France	2.3

Social indicators

	2010	2015	2020
Population growth rate (average annual %) [f]	1.1	1.2	1.2
Urban population (% of total population)	34.8	38.7	41.6 [c]
Urban population growth rate (average annual %) [f]	4.4	3.7	...
Fertility rate, total (live births per woman) [f]	2.6	2.1	2.0
Life expectancy at birth (females/males, years) [f]	67.3 / 66.8	69.6 / 69.2	71.6 / 71.0
Population age distribution (0-14/60+ years old, %)	31.2 / 7.5	27.4 / 8.1	24.9 / 9.0
International migrant stock (000/% of total pop.)	48.4 / 7.1	51.1 / 7.0	53.3 / 7.0 [c]
Infant mortality rate (per 1 000 live births) [f]	39.5	30.5	24.1
Health: Current expenditure (% of GDP) [g,h]	3.5	3.7	3.2 [a]
Health: Physicians (per 1 000 pop.)	0.3 [i]	0.3	0.4 [b]
Education: Government expenditure (% of GDP)	4.0	7.4	6.6 [b]
Education: Primary gross enrol. ratio (f/m per 100 pop.)	109.4 / 107.0	104.8 / 103.7	100.2 / 100.1 [b]
Education: Secondary gross enrol. ratio (f/m per 100 pop.)	64.7 / 62.5	86.8 / 81.3	95.7 / 84.7 [d,b]
Education: Tertiary gross enrol. ratio (f/m per 100 pop.)	5.5 / 8.8	9.4 / 12.2 [j]	15.5 / 15.6 [b]
Intentional homicide rate (per 100 000 pop.)	2.3	1.6	1.2 [b]
Seats held by women in the National Parliament (%)	8.5	8.5	14.9 [k]

Environment and infrastructure indicators

	2010	2015	2020
Individuals using the Internet (per 100 inhabitants) [d]	13.6	39.8	48.1 [a]
Threatened species (number)	59	71	101
Forested area (% of land area)	71.0	72.3	72.2 [d,a]
Energy production, primary (Petajoules)	73	77	79 [a]
Energy supply per capita (Gigajoules)	78	81	83 [a]
Tourist/visitor arrivals at national borders (000)	41 [l,m]	155	274 [b]
Important sites for terrestrial biodiversity protected (%)	45.8	47.3	47.3 [c]
Pop. using safely managed drinking water (urban/rural, %)	48.8 / 25.5	48.9 / 27.4	48.9 / 27.6 [a]
Net Official Development Assist. received (% of GNI)	6.50	5.07	4.52 [b]

a 2017. b 2018. c 2019. d Estimate. e 2016. f Data refers to a 5-year period preceding the reference year. g Data revision. h Data refer to fiscal years beginning 1 July. i 2008. j 2013. k Data are as at 1 January of reporting year. l Including regional high end tourists. m Break in the time series.

Bolivia (Plurinational State of)

Region	South America	UN membership date	14 November 1945
Population (000, 2020)	11 673	Surface area (km2)	1 098 581 [a,b]
Pop. density (per km2, 2020)	10.8	Sex ratio (m per 100 f)	100.7
Capital city	Sucre [c]	National currency	Boliviano (BOB)
Capital city pop. (000, 2020)	277.9 [d]	Exchange rate (per US$)	6.9 [e]

Economic indicators	2010	2015	2020
GDP: Gross domestic product (million current US$)	19 650	33 000	40 288 [d]
GDP growth rate (annual %, const. 2015 prices)	4.1	4.9	4.2 [d]
GDP per capita (current US$)	1 955.5	3 036.0	3 548.6 [d]
Economy: Agriculture (% of Gross Value Added)	12.4	12.6	13.2 [d]
Economy: Industry (% of Gross Value Added)	35.8	31.0	30.2 [d]
Economy: Services and other activity (% of GVA)	51.8	56.5	56.5 [d]
Employment in agriculture (% of employed)	30.0 [f]	27.8	30.4 [f]
Employment in industry (% of employed)	20.7 [f]	22.5	19.4 [f]
Employment in services & other sectors (% employed)	49.3 [f]	49.6	50.3 [f]
Unemployment rate (% of labour force) [f]	2.6	3.1	3.4
Labour force participation rate (female/male pop. %) [f]	62.0 / 82.1	54.4 / 79.7	63.0 / 80.4
CPI: Consumer Price Index (2010=100) [g]	100	134	148 [e]
Agricultural production index (2004-2006=100)	120	148	147 [h]
International trade: exports (million current US$)	7 051	8 923	8 988 [f,e]
International trade: imports (million current US$)	5 604	9 843	9 783 [f,e]
International trade: balance (million current US$)	1 448	- 920	- 795 [f,e]
Balance of payments, current account (million US$)	874	- 1 936	- 1 362 [e]

Major trading partners						2019
Export partners (% of exports) [f]	Brazil	19.0	Argentina	16.0	India	8.0
Import partners (% of imports) [f]	China	20.7	Brazil	16.1	Argentina	11.6

Social indicators	2010	2015	2020
Population growth rate (average annual %) [i]	1.7	1.6	1.4
Urban population (% of total population)	66.4	68.4	69.8 [e]
Urban population growth rate (average annual %) [i]	2.4	2.1	...
Fertility rate, total (live births per woman) [i]	3.4	3.0	2.8
Life expectancy at birth (females/males, years) [i]	69.0 / 64.4	71.9 / 66.7	74.0 / 68.3
Population age distribution (0-14/60+ years old, %)	34.5 / 8.8	32.4 / 9.5	30.2 / 10.4
International migrant stock (000/% of total pop.)	122.8 / 1.2	143.0 / 1.3	156.1 / 1.4 [e]
Refugees and others of concern to the UNHCR (000)	0.7 [i]	0.8	0.9 [k,e]
Infant mortality rate (per 1 000 live births) [i]	42.1	32.4	29.7
Health: Current expenditure (% of GDP)	5.5	6.6	6.4 [b]
Health: Physicians (per 1 000 pop.)	0.4	0.5 [l]	1.6 [h]
Education: Government expenditure (% of GDP)	7.6	7.3 [m]	...
Education: Primary gross enrol. ratio (f/m per 100 pop.)	104.2 / 104.8	94.9 / 96.9	97.6 / 98.6 [d]
Education: Secondary gross enrol. ratio (f/m per 100 pop.)	88.5 / 88.9	90.7 / 92.0	88.8 / 90.7 [d]
Intentional homicide rate (per 100 000 pop.)	12.7	6.2	6.2 [h]
Seats held by women in the National Parliament (%)	22.3	53.1	53.1 [n,o]

Environment and infrastructure indicators	2010	2015	2020
Individuals using the Internet (per 100 inhabitants)	22.4 [f]	35.6 [f]	44.3 [d]
Research & Development expenditure (% of GDP)	0.2 [p,q]	...	...
Threatened species (number)	163	216	296
Forested area (% of land area) [f]	51.9	50.6	50.6 [b]
CO2 emission estimates (million tons/tons per capita)	13.6 / 1.4	18.1 / 1.7	21.9 / 2.0 [b]
Energy production, primary (Petajoules)	658	954	878 [b]
Energy supply per capita (Gigajoules)	26	32	34 [b]
Tourist/visitor arrivals at national borders (000)	679	882	1 142 [d]
Important sites for terrestrial biodiversity protected (%)	48.3	48.3	48.3 [e]
Pop. using safely managed sanitation (urban/rural %)	20.2 / ...	23.4 / ...	24.7 / ... [b]
Net Official Development Assist. received (% of GNI)	2.98	2.48	1.86 [d]

Data updated according to "Superintendencia Agraria". Interior waters correspond to natural or artificial bodies of water or snow. **b** 2017. **c** La Paz is the seat of government and Sucre is the constitutional capital. **d** 2018. **e** 2019. **f** Estimate. **g** Calculated by the UN Statistics Division from national indices. **h** 2016. **i** Data refers to a 5-year period preceding the reference year. **j** Data as at the end of December. **k** All data relate to end of 2018. **l** 2011. **m** 2014. **n** Data are as at 1 January of reporting year. **o** The statistics refer to the situation before the 2019 election, which itself was invalidated. Fresh elections are expected in May 2020. **p** Break in the time series. **q** 2009.

Bonaire, Sint Eustatius and Saba

Region	Caribbean	Population (000, 2020)	26
Pop. density (per km2, 2020)	79.9	Capital city	Kralendijk
National currency	US Dollar (USD)	Capital city pop. (000, 2020)	11.3 a,b

Social indicators	2010	2015	2020
Population growth rate (average annual %)	7.5 c	3.2 c	1.3
Urban population (% of total population)	74.7	74.8	75.0 d
Urban population growth rate (average annual %) c	7.5	3.2	...
International migrant stock (000/% of total pop.)	11.4 / 54.7	13.0 / 52.9	15.5 / 59.6 d
Refugees and others of concern to the UNHCR (000)	~0.0 e,f	...	...

Environment and infrastructure indicators	2010	2015	2020
Threatened species (number)	...	55	67
Energy production, primary (Petajoules)	...	0	0 g
Energy supply per capita (Gigajoules) h	...	214	214 g
Important sites for terrestrial biodiversity protected (%)	39.3	39.3	39.3 d

a Refers to the island of Bonaire. b 2018. c Data refers to a 5-year period preceding the reference year. d 2019. e Bonaire only. f Data as at the end of December. g 2017. h Estimate.

Bosnia and Herzegovina

Region	Southern Europe	UN membership date	22 May 1992
Population (000, 2020)	3 281	Surface area (km2)	51 209[a]
Pop. density (per km2, 2020)	64.3	Sex ratio (m per 100 f)	96.0
Capital city	Sarajevo	National currency	Convertible Mark (BAM)
Capital city pop. (000, 2020)	342.7[b,c]	Exchange rate (per US$)	1.7[c]

Economic indicators

	2010	2015	2020
GDP: Gross domestic product (million current US$)	17 176	16 212	19 782[d]
GDP growth rate (annual %, const. 2015 prices)	0.9	3.1	2.6[d]
GDP per capita (current US$)	4 635.4	4 727.3	5 951.4[d]
Economy: Agriculture (% of Gross Value Added)[e]	8.0	7.3	7.0[d]
Economy: Industry (% of Gross Value Added)[e,f]	26.4	26.5	27.7[d]
Economy: Services and other activity (% of GVA)[e,g,h]	65.6	66.2	65.3[d]
Employment in agriculture (% of employed)	19.7	17.5[i]	15.1[i]
Employment in industry (% of employed)	30.9	30.6[i]	32.3[i]
Employment in services & other sectors (% employed)	49.4	51.9[i]	52.6[i]
Unemployment rate (% of labour force)[i]	27.3	27.7	18.4
Labour force participation rate (female/male pop. %)[i]	34.3 / 58.2	36.2 / 58.2	35.2 / 57.7
CPI: Consumer Price Index (2010=100)	100	104	105[c]
Agricultural production index (2004-2006=100)	107	105	118[i]
International trade: exports (million current US$)	4 803	5 099	6 578[c]
International trade: imports (million current US$)	9 223	8 994	11 159[c]
International trade: balance (million current US$)	- 4 420	- 3 895	- 4 581[c]
Balance of payments, current account (million US$)	- 1 031	- 822	- 710[c]

Major trading partners

						2019
Export partners (% of exports)	Germany	14.6	Croatia	12.2	Serbia	11.4
Import partners (% of imports)	Germany	12.0	Italy	12.0	Serbia	11.1

Social indicators

	2010	2015	2020
Population growth rate (average annual %)[k]	- 0.3	- 1.5	- 0.9
Urban population (% of total population)	45.6	47.2	48.6[c]
Urban population growth rate (average annual %)[k]	0.4	- 0.3	...
Fertility rate, total (live births per woman)[k]	1.3	1.3	1.3
Life expectancy at birth (females/males, years)[k]	78.1 / 72.9	78.9 / 74.0	79.6 / 74.6
Population age distribution (0-14/60+ years old, %)	15.7 / 19.3	15.2 / 21.5	14.5 / 25.3
International migrant stock (000/% of total pop.)[i,j]	38.8 / 1.0	38.6 / 1.1	35.7 / 1.1[c]
Refugees and others of concern to the UNHCR (000)	179.0[m]	143.9	151.7[c]
Infant mortality rate (per 1 000 live births)[k]	9.0	6.9	6.0
Health: Current expenditure (% of GDP)	9.0	9.3	8.9[a]
Health: Physicians (per 1 000 pop.)	1.8	2.2	...
Intentional homicide rate (per 100 000 pop.)	1.5	1.7	1.2[d]
Seats held by women in the National Parliament (%)	19.0	21.4	21.4[n]

Environment and infrastructure indicators

	2010	2015	2020
Individuals using the Internet (per 100 inhabitants)	42.8[i]	52.6[i]	70.1[d]
Research & Development expenditure (% of GDP)	−0.0[o,p]	0.2	0.2[d]
Threatened species (number)	67	85	104
Forested area (% of land area)[i]	42.7	42.7	42.7[a]
CO2 emission estimates (million tons/tons per capita)	20.5 / 5.5	19.3 / 5.5	22.3 / 6.4[a]
Energy production, primary (Petajoules)	182	173	194[a]
Energy supply per capita (Gigajoules)	72	71	79[a]
Tourist/visitor arrivals at national borders (000)	365	678	1 053[d]
Important sites for terrestrial biodiversity protected (%)	18.2	18.2	18.2[c]
Pop. using safely managed sanitation (urban/rural %)	8.6 / ...	10.3 / ...	11.3 / ...[a]
Net Official Development Assist. received (% of GNI)	2.93	2.18	1.80[d]

a 2017. b Refers to the municipalities of Stari Grad Sarajevo, Centar Sarajevo, Novo Sarajevo, Novi Grad Sarajevo and Ilidza. c 2019. d 2018. e Data classified according to ISIC Rev. 4. f Excludes publishing activities. Includes irrigation and canals. g Excludes repair of personal and household goods. h Excludes computer and related activities and radio/TV activities. i Estimate. j 2016. k Data refers to a 5-year period preceding the reference year. l Including refugees. m Data as at the end of December. n Data are as at 1 January of reporting year. o Partial data. p 2009.

Botswana

Region	Southern Africa	
Population (000, 2020)	2 352	
Pop. density (per km2, 2020)	4.1	
Capital city	Gaborone	
Capital city pop. (000, 2020)	269.3[b]	

UN membership date	17 October 1966
Surface area (km2)	582 000[a]
Sex ratio (m per 100 f)	93.9
National currency	Pula (BWP)
Exchange rate (per US$)	10.6[c]

Economic indicators

	2010	2015	2020
GDP: Gross domestic product (million current US$)	12 787	14 421	18 615[b]
GDP growth rate (annual %, const. 2015 prices)	8.6	- 1.7	4.5[b]
GDP per capita (current US$)	6 434.8	6 799.9	8 258.2[b]
Economy: Agriculture (% of Gross Value Added)	2.8	2.4	2.2[b]
Economy: Industry (% of Gross Value Added)	35.7	33.2	32.3[b]
Economy: Services and other activity (% of GVA)	61.6	64.4	65.5[b]
Employment in agriculture (% of employed)[d]	24.6	22.3	20.4
Employment in industry (% of employed)[d]	18.2	18.3	18.1
Employment in services & other sectors (% employed)[d]	57.1	59.5	61.5
Unemployment rate (% of labour force)[d]	17.9	17.8	18.7
Labour force participation rate (female/male pop. %)[d]	53.8 / 66.9	64.9 / 77.7	65.5 / 77.0
CPI: Consumer Price Index (2010=100)[e]	100	133	150[c]
Agricultural production index (2004-2006=100)	125	116	120[f]
International trade: exports (million current US$)	4 693	6 330	5 238[c]
International trade: imports (million current US$)	5 657	8 048	6 559[c]
International trade: balance (million current US$)	- 964	- 1 718	- 1 320[c]
Balance of payments, current account (million US$)	- 804	318	345[b]

Major trading partners
							2019
Export partners (% of exports)	India	21.6	Belgium	19.6	United Arab Emirates	18.2
Import partners (% of imports)	South Africa	57.9	Namibia	7.9	Canada	6.9

Social indicators

	2010	2015	2020
Population growth rate (average annual %)[g]	2.0	1.3	2.1
Urban population (% of total population)	62.4	67.2	70.2[c]
Urban population growth rate (average annual %)[g]	3.8	3.3	...
Fertility rate, total (live births per woman)[g]	3.0	3.0	2.9
Life expectancy at birth (females/males, years)[g]	58.1 / 53.6	67.0 / 61.8	71.9 / 66.0
Population age distribution (0-14/60+ years old, %)	35.0 / 5.3	34.9 / 6.2	33.4 / 7.0
International migrant stock (000/% of total pop.)	94.6 / 4.8	103.3 / 4.9	110.6 / 4.8[c]
Refugees and others of concern to the UNHCR (000)	3.3[h]	2.4	2.3[c]
Infant mortality rate (per 1 000 live births)[g]	44.2	35.5	30.2
Health: Current expenditure (% of GDP)	6.2	5.7	6.1[a]
Health: Physicians (per 1 000 pop.)	0.4	0.4[i]	0.5[f]
Education: Government expenditure (% of GDP)	9.6[i]	...	...
Education: Primary gross enrol. ratio (f/m per 100 pop.)	106.6 / 109.8[i]	102.1 / 104.4	... / ...
Education: Secondary gross enrol. ratio (f/m per 100 pop.)	83.5 / 76.4[k]	... / ...	... / ...
Education: Tertiary gross enrol. ratio (f/m per 100 pop.)	9.7 / 12.1[l]	34.6 / 25.8	29.2 / 20.5[a]
Intentional homicide rate (per 100 000 pop.)	15.2	...	...
Seats held by women in the National Parliament (%)	7.9	9.5	10.8[m]

Environment and infrastructure indicators

	2010	2015	2020
Individuals using the Internet (per 100 inhabitants)	6.0	37.3[d]	47.0[n,a]
Research & Development expenditure (% of GDP)	0.5[o]	0.5[p]	...
Threatened species (number)	18	24	33
Forested area (% of land area)[d]	20.0	19.1	19.1[a]
CO2 emission estimates (million tons/tons per capita)	3.3 / 1.6	7.1 / 3.2	7.7 / 3.4[a]
Energy production, primary (Petajoules)	30	56	59[a]
Energy supply per capita (Gigajoules)	37	36	43[a]
Tourist/visitor arrivals at national borders (000)	1 973	1 528	1 623[a]
Important sites for terrestrial biodiversity protected (%)	51.1	51.1	51.1[c]
Pop. using safely managed drinking water (urban/rural, %)	83.7 / ...	83.4 / ...	83.2 / ...[a]
Net Official Development Assist. received (% of GNI)	1.26	0.46	0.48[b]

a 2017. b 2018. c 2019. d Estimate. e Calculated by the UN Statistics Division from national indices. f 2016. g Data refers to a 5-year period preceding the reference year. h Data as at the end of December. i 2012. j 2009. k 2008. l 2006. m Data are as at 1 January of reporting year. n Population aged 18 years and over. o 2005. p 2013.

Brazil

Region	South America	UN membership date	24 October 1945
Population (000, 2020)	212 559	Surface area (km2)	8 515 767 [a]
Pop. density (per km2, 2020)	25.4	Sex ratio (m per 100 f)	96.6
Capital city	Brasilia	National currency	Brazilian Real (BRL)
Capital city pop. (000, 2020)	4 559.0 [b,c]	Exchange rate (per US$)	4.0 [c]

Economic indicators

	2010	2015	2020
GDP: Gross domestic product (million current US$)	2 208 838	1 802 212	1 868 613 [d]
GDP growth rate (annual %, const. 2015 prices)	7.5	- 3.5	1.1 [d]
GDP per capita (current US$)	11 286.1	8 814.0	8 920.7 [d]
Economy: Agriculture (% of Gross Value Added) [e]	4.8	5.0	5.1 [d]
Economy: Industry (% of Gross Value Added) [e,f]	27.4	22.5	21.6 [d]
Economy: Services and other activity (% of GVA) [e,g,h]	67.8	72.5	73.3 [d]
Employment in agriculture (% of employed)	12.6 [i]	10.2	9.1 [i]
Employment in industry (% of employed)	22.5 [i]	22.2	19.6 [i]
Employment in services & other sectors (% employed)	64.8 [i]	67.6	71.3 [i]
Unemployment rate (% of labour force) [i]	7.7	8.4	12.0
Labour force participation rate (female/male pop. %) [i]	53.5 / 76.5	53.3 / 75.3	54.0 / 73.9
CPI: Consumer Price Index (2010=100) [i]	100	138	167 [c]
Agricultural production index (2004-2006=100)	122	139	136 [k]
International trade: exports (million current US$) [l]	201 915	191 127	225 383 [c]
International trade: imports (million current US$) [l]	181 768	171 446	177 348 [c]
International trade: balance (million current US$) [l]	20 147	19 681	48 036 [c]
Balance of payments, current account (million US$)	- 79 014	- 54 472	- 49 452 [c]

Major trading partners

							2019
Export partners (% of exports)	China	28.1	United States	13.2	Netherlands	4.5
Import partners (% of imports)	China	19.9	United States	17.2	Argentina	6.0

Social indicators

	2010	2015	2020
Population growth rate (average annual %) [m]	1.0	0.9	0.8
Urban population (% of total population)	84.3	85.8	86.8 [c]
Urban population growth rate (average annual %) [m]	1.4	1.2	...
Fertility rate, total (live births per woman) [m]	1.9	1.8	1.7
Life expectancy at birth (females/males, years) [m]	76.6 / 69.1	78.0 / 70.7	79.3 / 71.9
Population age distribution (0-14/60+ years old, %)	24.8 / 10.2	22.4 / 12.0	20.7 / 14.0
International migrant stock (000/% of total pop.)	592.6 / 0.3	716.6 / 0.4	807.0 / 0.4 [c]
Refugees and others of concern to the UNHCR (000)	5.2 [n]	66.0	271.6 [c]
Infant mortality rate (per 1 000 live births) [m]	20.3	15.8	13.0
Health: Current expenditure (% of GDP)	7.9	8.9	9.5 [a]
Health: Physicians (per 1 000 pop.)	1.8	1.9 [o]	2.2 [d]
Education: Government expenditure (% of GDP)	5.6	6.2	...
Education: Primary gross enrol. ratio (f/m per 100 pop.) [i]	128.2 / 133.9 [p]	110.4 / 115.1	113.4 / 117.4 [a]
Education: Secondary gross enrol. ratio (f/m per 100 pop.) [i]	102.1 / 91.5 [p]	102.9 / 97.4	102.4 / 99.3 [a]
Education: Tertiary gross enrol. ratio (f/m per 100 pop.) [i]	42.2 / 31.9 [p]	58.5 / 43.7	59.4 / 43.5 [a]
Intentional homicide rate (per 100 000 pop.)	22.1	28.6	27.4 [d]
Seats held by women in the National Parliament (%)	8.8	9.0	14.6 [q]

Environment and infrastructure indicators

	2010	2015	2020
Individuals using the Internet (per 100 inhabitants)	40.6 [r,s]	58.3	70.4 [d]
Research & Development expenditure (% of GDP)	1.2	1.3	1.3 [a]
Threatened species (number)	773	966	1 078
Forested area (% of land area) [i]	59.6	59.0	59.0 [a]
CO2 emission estimates (million tons/tons per capita)	372.0 / 1.9	453.6 / 2.2	427.6 / 2.0 [a]
Energy production, primary (Petajoules)	10 127	11 969	13 066 [a]
Energy supply per capita (Gigajoules)	56	62	62 [a]
Tourist/visitor arrivals at national borders (000) [t]	5 161	6 306	6 621 [d]
Important sites for terrestrial biodiversity protected (%)	42.0	42.5	42.8 [c]
Pop. using safely managed drinking water (urban/rural, %)	91.8 / ...	92.2 / ...	92.3 / ... [a]
Pop. using safely managed sanitation (urban/rural, %)	36.5 / ...	47.0 / ...	51.6 / ... [a]
Net Official Development Assist. received (% of GNI)	0.02	0.06	0.02 [d]

2017. **b** Refers to the "Região Integrada de Desenvolvimento do Distrito Federal e Entorno". **c** 2019. **d** 2018. **e** Data classified according to ISIC Rev. 4. **f** Excludes publishing activities. Includes irrigation and canals. **g** Excludes computer and related activities and radio/TV activities. **h** Excludes repair of personal and household goods. **i** Estimate. **j** Calculated by the UN Statistics Division from national indices. **k** 2016. **l** Imports FOB. **m** Data refers to a year period preceding the reference year. **n** Data as at the end of December. **o** 2013. **p** 2009. **q** Data are as at 1 January of reporting year. **r** Population aged 10 years and over. **s** Users in the last 3 months. **t** Including nationals residing abroad.

British Virgin Islands

Region	Caribbean	Population (000, 2020)	33
Surface area (km2)	151 [a]	Pop. density (per km2, 2020)	217.6
Sex ratio (m per 100 f)	97.1 [b]	Capital city	Road Town
National currency	US Dollar (USD)	Capital city pop. (000, 2020)	15.1 [c]

Economic indicators	2010	2015	2020
GDP: Gross domestic product (million current US$)	1 021	1 174	1 446 [c]
GDP growth rate (annual %, const. 2015 prices)	- 0.1	0.8	3.1 [c]
GDP per capita (current US$)	36 732.2	40 283.1	48 511.3 [c]
Economy: Agriculture (% of Gross Value Added) [d]	0.1	0.1	0.1 [c]
Economy: Industry (% of Gross Value Added) [d,e]	4.8	6.7	7.0 [c]
Economy: Services and other activity (% of GVA) [d,f,g]	95.0	93.1	92.9 [c]
Employment in agriculture (% of employed)	0.5 [h]	...	...
Employment in industry (% of employed)	11.1 [h]	...	...
Employment in services & other sectors (% employed)	87.4 [h]	...	...
Agricultural production index (2004-2006=100)	102	103	103 [i]
International trade: exports (million current US$) [j]	~0	~0	0 [k]
International trade: imports (million current US$) [j]	313	430	538 [k]
International trade: balance (million current US$) [j]	- 313	- 430	- 538 [k]

Major trading partners						2019
Export partners (% of exports) [j]	Indonesia	14.6	India	13.2	United States	8.6
Import partners (% of imports) [j]	United States	50.4	Areas nes [l]	32.8	Russian Federation	2.4

Social indicators	2010	2015	2020
Population growth rate (average annual %)	3.2 [m]	2.0 [m]	1.6
Urban population (% of total population)	44.8	46.6	48.1 [k]
Urban population growth rate (average annual %) [m]	4.0	2.8	...
Population age distribution (0-14/60+ years old, %)	22.3 / 9.7	... / ...	... / ...
International migrant stock (000/% of total pop.)	17.1 / 61.4	19.1 / 65.6	20.8 / 69.2 [k]
Refugees and others of concern to the UNHCR (000)	~0.0 [n]	...	~0.0 [k]
Education: Government expenditure (% of GDP)	4.4	6.3	3.2 [a]
Education: Primary gross enrol. ratio (f/m per 100 pop.)	108.7 / 109.6 [o]	114.5 / 122.3	125.9 / 131.5 [a]
Education: Secondary gross enrol. ratio (f/m per 100 pop.)	109.1 / 107.1	96.9 / 89.3	107.1 / 96.3 [a]
Education: Tertiary gross enrol. ratio (f/m per 100 pop.)	89.6 / 56.2 [o]	54.2 / 30.2	20.9 / 11.7 [c]
Intentional homicide rate (per 100 000 pop.)	8.3 [p]	...	...

Environment and infrastructure indicators	2010	2015	2020
Individuals using the Internet (per 100 inhabitants)	37.0	37.6 [q]	77.7 [a]
Threatened species (number)	43	61	88
Forested area (% of land area) [j]	24.3	24.1	24.1 [a]
Energy production, primary (Petajoules)	0	0	0 [a]
Energy supply per capita (Gigajoules) [j]	103	99	77 [a]
Tourist/visitor arrivals at national borders (000)	330	393	192 [c]
Important sites for terrestrial biodiversity protected (%)	10.5	10.5	10.5 [k]

a 2017. b 2010. c 2018. d Data classified according to ISIC Rev. 4. e Excludes publishing activities. Includes irrigation and canals. f Excludes computer and related activities and radio/TV activities. g Excludes repair of personal and household goods. h Data classified according to ISIC Rev. 3. i 2016. j Estimate. k 2019. l Areas not elsewhere specified. m Data refers to a 5-year period preceding the reference year. n Data as at the end of December. o 2009. p 2006. q 2012.

Brunei Darussalam

Region	South-eastern Asia	UN membership date	21 September 1984
Population (000, 2020)	438	Surface area (km2)	5 765[a]
Pop. density (per km2, 2020)	83.0	Sex ratio (m per 100 f)	107.8
Capital city	Bandar Seri Begawan	National currency	Brunei Dollar (BND)
Capital city pop. (000, 2020)	40.8[b]	Exchange rate (per US$)	1.3[c]

Economic indicators

	2010	2015	2020
GDP: Gross domestic product (million current US$)	13 707	12 930	13 567[b]
GDP growth rate (annual %, const. 2015 prices)	2.6	- 0.4	0.1[b]
GDP per capita (current US$)	35 268.9	31 164.3	31 627.2[b]
Economy: Agriculture (% of Gross Value Added)[d]	0.7	1.1	1.0[b]
Economy: Industry (% of Gross Value Added)[d,e]	67.4	60.2	62.2[b]
Economy: Services and other activity (% of GVA)[d,f,g]	31.9	38.7	36.7[b]
Employment in agriculture (% of employed)[h]	0.7	0.7	1.3
Employment in industry (% of employed)[h]	19.3	17.8	15.8
Employment in services & other sectors (% employed)[h]	80.0	81.5	82.8
Unemployment rate (% of labour force)[h]	6.7	7.9	9.0
Labour force participation rate (female/male pop. %)[h]	57.0 / 75.3	58.0 / 73.1	57.6 / 70.7
CPI: Consumer Price Index (2010=100)	100	100	99[c]
Agricultural production index (2004-2006=100)	139	170	169[i]
International trade: exports (million current US$)	8 908	6 353	7 039[c]
International trade: imports (million current US$)	2 539	3 229	5 103[c]
International trade: balance (million current US$)	6 369	3 124	1 936[c]
Balance of payments, current account (million US$)	5 016	2 157	894[c]

Major trading partners

						2019
Export partners (% of exports)	Japan	31.4	Singapore	13.7	Australia	10.2
Import partners (% of imports)	China	13.2	Singapore	12.5	Malaysia	11.9

Social indicators

	2010	2015	2020
Population growth rate (average annual %)[j]	1.2	1.3	1.1
Urban population (% of total population)	75.0	76.7	77.9[c]
Urban population growth rate (average annual %)[j]	1.7	1.9	...
Fertility rate, total (live births per woman)[j]	1.9	2.0	1.8
Life expectancy at birth (females/males, years)[j]	75.5 / 73.4	76.2 / 73.8	76.9 / 74.5
Population age distribution (0-14/60+ years old, %)	26.0 / 5.4	24.1 / 7.0	22.3 / 9.5
International migrant stock (000/% of total pop.)	100.6 / 25.9	102.7 / 24.8	110.6 / 25.5[c]
Refugees and others of concern to the UNHCR (000)	21.0[k]	20.5	20.9[c]
Infant mortality rate (per 1 000 live births)[j]	9.3	8.8	7.9
Health: Current expenditure (% of GDP)[l]	2.3	2.4	2.4[a]
Health: Physicians (per 1 000 pop.)	1.4	1.8	1.6[a]
Education: Government expenditure (% of GDP)	2.0	3.4[m]	4.4[i]
Education: Primary gross enrol. ratio (f/m per 100 pop.)	106.3 / 106.8	105.3 / 105.7	103.6 / 102.7[b]
Education: Secondary gross enrol. ratio (f/m per 100 pop.)	99.5 / 98.9	97.5 / 95.5	94.6 / 92.4[b]
Education: Tertiary gross enrol. ratio (f/m per 100 pop.)	20.4 / 10.9	39.9 / 23.4	38.7 / 24.8[b]
Intentional homicide rate (per 100 000 pop.)	0.3	0.5[n]	...
Seats held by women in the National Parliament (%)	...	...	9.1[o]

Environment and infrastructure indicators

	2010	2015	2020
Individuals using the Internet (per 100 inhabitants)[h]	53.0	71.2	94.9[a]
Research & Development expenditure (% of GDP)	...	...	0.3[p,q,b]
Threatened species (number)	170	189	275
Forested area (% of land area)[h]	72.1	72.1	72.1[a]
CO2 emission estimates (million tons/tons per capita)	6.9 / 17.6	6.0 / 14.3	6.7 / 15.6[a]
Energy production, primary (Petajoules)	775	673	652[a]
Energy supply per capita (Gigajoules)	349	273	356[a]
Tourist/visitor arrivals at national borders (000)[r]	214	218	278[b]
Important sites for terrestrial biodiversity protected (%)	41.7	41.7	41.7[c]

a 2017. b 2018. c 2019. d Data classified according to ISIC Rev. 4. e Excludes publishing activities. Includes irrigation and canals. f Excludes repair of personal and household goods. g Excludes computer and related activities and radio/TV activities. h Estimate. i 2016. j Data refers to a 5-year period preceding the reference year. k Data as at the end of December. l Data refer to fiscal years beginning 1 April. m 2014. n 2013. o Data are as at 1 January of reporting year. p Higher Education only. q Break in the time series. r Arrivals by air.

Bulgaria

Region	Eastern Europe	UN membership date	14 December 1955
Population (000, 2020)	6 948	Surface area (km2)	111 002 a
Pop. density (per km2, 2020)	64.0	Sex ratio (m per 100 f)	94.4
Capital city	Sofia	National currency	Bulgarian Lev (BGN)
Capital city pop. (000, 2020)	1 276.9 b	Exchange rate (per US$)	1.7 b

Economic indicators

	2010	2015	2020
GDP: Gross domestic product (million current US$)	50 364	50 631	66 199 c
GDP growth rate (annual %, const. 2015 prices)	0.6	4.0	3.1 c
GDP per capita (current US$)	6 783.0	7 032.3	9 387.8 c
Economy: Agriculture (% of Gross Value Added) d	4.6	4.7	3.9 c
Economy: Industry (% of Gross Value Added) d,e	26.8	27.4	25.8 c
Economy: Services and other activity (% of GVA) d,f,g	68.6	67.9	70.3 c
Employment in agriculture (% of employed)	6.8	6.9	6.3 h
Employment in industry (% of employed)	33.0	29.9	30.1 h
Employment in services & other sectors (% employed)	60.2	63.2	63.7 h
Unemployment rate (% of labour force) h	10.3	9.1	3.8
Labour force participation rate (female/male pop. %) h	47.7 / 59.5	48.6 / 60.1	49.1 / 61.9
CPI: Consumer Price Index (2010=100) i	100	107	114 b
Agricultural production index (2004-2006=100)	106	111	114 i
International trade: exports (million current US$)	20 608	25 779	33 638 h,b
International trade: imports (million current US$)	25 360	29 265	37 902 h,b
International trade: balance (million current US$)	- 4 752	- 3 486	- 4 264 h,b
Balance of payments, current account (million US$)	- 965	61	2 742 b

Major trading partners

						2019
Export partners (% of exports) h	Germany	14.6	Italy	8.5	Romania	8.4
Import partners (% of imports) h	Germany	12.4	Russian Federation	9.7	Italy	7.5

Social indicators

	2010	2015	2020
Population growth rate (average annual %) k	- 0.7	- 0.6	- 0.7
Urban population (% of total population)	72.3	74.0	75.3 b
Urban population growth rate (average annual %) k	- 0.3	- 0.2	...
Fertility rate, total (live births per woman) k	1.5	1.5	1.6
Life expectancy at birth (females/males, years) k	76.8 / 69.7	77.8 / 70.8	78.5 / 71.3
Population age distribution (0-14/60+ years old, %)	13.5 / 25.3	14.3 / 27.0	14.7 / 28.2
International migrant stock (000/% of total pop.)	76.3 / 1.0	123.8 / 1.7	168.5 / 2.4 b
Refugees and others of concern to the UNHCR (000)	6.9 l	19.0	21.2 b
Infant mortality rate (per 1 000 live births) k	9.5	8.3	6.3
Health: Current expenditure (% of GDP) m	7.1	8.2	8.1 a
Health: Physicians (per 1 000 pop.)	3.8	4.0	...
Education: Government expenditure (% of GDP)	3.9	4.1 n	...
Education: Primary gross enrol. ratio (f/m per 100 pop.)	108.2 / 108.5	93.7 / 94.7	89.1 / 89.6 a
Education: Secondary gross enrol. ratio (f/m per 100 pop.)	88.2 / 92.1	100.6 / 103.9	96.8 / 99.5 a
Education: Tertiary gross enrol. ratio (f/m per 100 pop.)	66.1 / 50.0	79.1 / 62.0	78.8 / 63.7 a
Intentional homicide rate (per 100 000 pop.)	2.0	1.8	1.3 c
Seats held by women in the National Parliament (%)	20.8	20.4	26.7 o

Environment and infrastructure indicators

	2010	2015	2020
Individuals using the Internet (per 100 inhabitants)	46.2 p	56.7 p	64.8 c
Research & Development expenditure (% of GDP)	0.6	1.0	0.8 c
Threatened species (number)	66	85	127
Forested area (% of land area) h	34.4	35.2	35.2 a
CO2 emission estimates (million tons/tons per capita)	44.4 / 6.0	43.7 / 6.1	42.8 / 6.1 a
Energy production, primary (Petajoules)	442	505	491 a
Energy supply per capita (Gigajoules)	100	108	110 a
Tourist/visitor arrivals at national borders (000)	6 047	7 099	9 273 c
Important sites for terrestrial biodiversity protected (%)	87.5	87.5	87.5 b
Pop. using safely managed sanitation (urban/rural %)	58.8 / ...	68.8 / ...	72.9 / ... a
Net Official Development Assist. disbursed (% of GNI)	0.09	0.09	0.11 a

a 2017. b 2019. c 2018. d Data classified according to ISIC Rev. 4. e Excludes publishing activities. Includes irrigation and canals. f Excludes repair of personal and household goods. g Excludes computer and related activities and radio/TV activities. h Estimate. i Calculated by the UN Statistics Division from national indices. j 2016. k Data refers to a 5-year period preceding the reference year. l Data as at the end of December. m Health expenditure data do not include funds from foreign origin flowing in the health financing system. n 2013. o Data are as at 1 January of reporting year. p Population aged 16 to 74 years.

Burkina Faso

Region	Western Africa	UN membership date	20 September 1960
Population (000, 2020)	20 903	Surface area (km2)	272 967 [a]
Pop. density (per km2, 2020)	76.4	Sex ratio (m per 100 f)	99.9
Capital city	Ouagadougou	National currency	CFA Franc, BCEAO (XOF) [b]
Capital city pop. (000, 2020)	2 652.7 [c]	Exchange rate (per US$)	583.9 [b]

Economic indicators

	2010	2015	2020
GDP: Gross domestic product (million current US$)	10 100	11 823	16 200 [d]
GDP growth rate (annual %, const. 2015 prices)	8.4	3.9	6.8 [d]
GDP per capita (current US$)	647.2	652.8	820.2 [d]
Economy: Agriculture (% of Gross Value Added)	26.2	24.9	24.3 [d]
Economy: Industry (% of Gross Value Added)	28.2	26.7	26.5 [d]
Economy: Services and other activity (% of GVA)	45.6	48.4	49.2 [d]
Employment in agriculture (% of employed) [e]	48.2	29.1	24.7
Employment in industry (% of employed) [e]	20.9	32.0	33.9
Employment in services & other sectors (% employed) [e]	31.0	38.9	41.4
Unemployment rate (% of labour force) [e]	4.7	6.4	6.4
Labour force participation rate (female/male pop. %) [e]	59.7 / 81.7	58.3 / 75.4	58.2 / 74.7
CPI: Consumer Price Index (2010=100) [f]	100	108	107 [c]
Agricultural production index (2004-2006=100)	118	121	125 [g]
International trade: exports (million current US$)	1 288	2 177	2 927 [e,c]
International trade: imports (million current US$)	2 048	2 980	5 193 [e,c]
International trade: balance (million current US$)	- 760	- 802	- 2 266 [e,c]
Balance of payments, current account (million current US$)	- 182	- 895	- 665 [d]

Major trading partners

						2019
Export partners (% of exports) [e]	Switzerland	52.7	India	15.4	Singapore	7.7
Import partners (% of imports) [e]	China	12.6	Ivory Coast	11.5	France	7.2

Social indicators

	2010	2015	2020
Population growth rate (average annual %) [h]	3.0	3.0	2.9
Urban population (% of total population)	24.6	27.5	30.0 [c]
Urban population growth rate (average annual %) [h]	5.7	5.2	...
Fertility rate, total (live births per woman) [h]	6.1	5.6	5.2
Life expectancy at birth (females/males, years) [h]	55.8 / 54.6	59.3 / 58.0	61.6 / 60.1
Population age distribution (0-14/60+ years old, %)	46.2 / 3.9	45.6 / 3.8	44.4 / 3.9
International migrant stock (000/% of total pop.) [i]	674.4 / 4.3	704.7 / 3.9	718.3 / 3.5 [c]
Refugees and others of concern to the UNHCR (000)	1.1 [i]	34.2	196.3 [c]
Infant mortality rate (per 1 000 live births) [h]	77.5	64.7	54.2
Health: Current expenditure (% of GDP)	5.9	5.8	6.9 [a]
Health: Physicians (per 1 000 pop.)	~0.0	0.1	0.1 [a]
Education: Government expenditure (% of GDP)	3.9	4.2	...
Education: Primary gross enrol. ratio (f/m per 100 pop.)	74.3 / 81.6	87.2 / 89.5	95.3 / 96.9 [d]
Education: Secondary gross enrol. ratio (f/m per 100 pop.)	18.9 / 24.8	32.3 / 35.1	40.7 / 40.7 [d]
Education: Tertiary gross enrol. ratio (f/m per 100 pop.)	2.3 / 4.8	3.5 / 6.6	4.8 / 8.2 [d]
Intentional homicide rate (per 100 000 pop.)	0.8	0.6	1.3 [a]
Seats held by women in the National Parliament (%)	15.3	13.3	13.4 [k]

Environment and infrastructure indicators

	2010	2015	2020
Individuals using the Internet (per 100 inhabitants)	2.4 [e]	14.0 [l,m]	16.0 [l,m,a]
Research & Development expenditure (% of GDP)	0.2 [n]	0.2 [o,p,q]	0.7 [o,a]
Threatened species (number)	24	29	36
Forested area (% of land area) [e]	20.6	19.6	19.6 [a]
Energy production, primary (Petajoules)	118	126	129 [a]
Energy supply per capita (Gigajoules)	9	10	10 [a]
Tourist/visitor arrivals at national borders (000)	274	163	144 [d]
Important sites for terrestrial biodiversity protected (%)	66.7	66.7	66.7 [c]
Net Official Development Assist. received (% of GNI)	11.95	9.90	7.94 [d]

a 2017. b African Financial Community (CFA) Franc, Central Bank of West African States (BCEAO). c 2019. d 2018. e estimate. f Ouagadougou g 2016. h Data refers to a 5-year period preceding the reference year. i Including refugees. Data as at the end of December. k Data are as at 1 January of reporting year. l At least once a month. m population aged 18 years and over. n 2009. o Excluding business enterprise. p Break in the time series. q 2014.

Burundi

Region	Eastern Africa	UN membership date	18 September 1962
Population (000, 2020)	11 891	Surface area (km2)	27 830 [a]
Pop. density (per km2, 2020)	463.0	Sex ratio (m per 100 f)	98.5
Capital city	Gitega	National currency	Burundi Franc (BIF)
Capital city pop. (000, 2020)	899.0 [b]	Exchange rate (per US$)	1 881.6 [c]

Economic indicators

	2010	2015	2020
GDP: Gross domestic product (million current US$)	2 032	2 811	3 285 [b]
GDP growth rate (annual %, const. 2015 prices)	5.1	- 0.4	0.1 [b]
GDP per capita (current US$)	234.2	276.6	294.0 [b]
Economy: Agriculture (% of Gross Value Added)	40.7	37.5	38.5 [b]
Economy: Industry (% of Gross Value Added)	16.3	16.4	17.4 [b]
Economy: Services and other activity (% of GVA)	43.0	46.2	44.1 [b]
Employment in agriculture (% of employed) [d]	92.1	92.0	92.0
Employment in industry (% of employed) [d]	1.8	1.6	1.4
Employment in services & other sectors (% employed) [d]	6.1	6.4	6.5
Unemployment rate (% of labour force) [d]	1.8	1.6	1.4
Labour force participation rate (female/male pop. %) [d]	80.2 / 77.3	80.0 / 77.1	80.4 / 77.8
CPI: Consumer Price Index (2010=100) [e]	100	154	183 [b]
Agricultural production index (2004-2006=100)	108	101	108 [f]
International trade: exports (million current US$)	118	114	155 [d,c]
International trade: imports (million current US$)	404	561	792 [d,c]
International trade: balance (million current US$)	- 286	- 447	- 637 [d,c]
Balance of payments, current account (million US$)	- 301	- 373	- 363 [b]

Major trading partners
						2019
Export partners (% of exports) [d]	United Arab Emirates	29.7	Dem. Rep. of Congo	11.2	Pakistan	7.8
Import partners (% of imports) [d]	Saudi Arabia	17.2	China		13.0	United Arab Emirates 8.8

Social indicators

	2010	2015	2020
Population growth rate (average annual %) [g]	3.3	3.2	3.1
Urban population (% of total population)	10.6	12.1	13.4 [c]
Urban population growth rate (average annual %) [g]	5.9	5.6	...
Fertility rate, total (live births per woman) [g]	6.4	6.0	5.4
Life expectancy at birth (females/males, years) [g]	57.0 / 53.6	60.7 / 57.1	62.8 / 59.2
Population age distribution (0-14/60+ years old, %)	45.1 / 3.3	45.5 / 3.7	45.3 / 4.1
International migrant stock (000/% of total pop.) [h]	235.3 / 2.7	289.8 / 2.9	321.0 / 2.8 [c]
Refugees and others of concern to the UNHCR (000)	200.8 [i]	137.7	121.2 [c]
Infant mortality rate (per 1 000 live births) [g]	70.0	52.3	42.4
Health: Current expenditure (% of GDP) [j]	11.3	6.6	7.5 [a]
Health: Physicians (per 1 000 pop.)	~0.0	~0.0	0.1 [a]
Education: Government expenditure (% of GDP)	6.8	6.4 [d]	4.8 [d,a]
Education: Primary gross enrol. ratio (f/m per 100 pop.)	136.4 / 138.0	132.8 / 129.0	122.2 / 120.7 [b]
Education: Secondary gross enrol. ratio (f/m per 100 pop.)	19.5 / 27.1	42.9 / 45.8	51.1 / 45.8 [b]
Education: Tertiary gross enrol. ratio (f/m per 100 pop.)	2.3 / 4.2	2.5 / 7.8 [k]	3.8 / 8.4 [a]
Intentional homicide rate (per 100 000 pop.)	4.0	4.5	6.1 [f]
Seats held by women in the National Parliament (%)	31.4	30.5	36.4 [l]

Environment and infrastructure indicators

	2010	2015	2020
Individuals using the Internet (per 100 inhabitants)	1.0 [d]	4.9 [d]	2.7 [a]
Research & Development expenditure (% of GDP)	0.1 [m]	0.1 [m,n]	0.2 [o,b]
Threatened species (number)	52	60	188
Forested area (% of land area) [d]	9.9	10.7	10.7 [a]
Energy production, primary (Petajoules)	54 [d]	56	56 [a]
Energy supply per capita (Gigajoules)	7 [d]	6	6 [a]
Tourist/visitor arrivals at national borders (000) [p]	142 [o]	131 [o]	299 [a]
Important sites for terrestrial biodiversity protected (%)	56.8	56.8	56.8 [c]
Net Official Development Assist. received (% of GNI)	31.05	11.81	14.66 [b]

a 2017. b 2018. c 2019. d Estimate. e Bujumbura f 2016. g Data refers to a 5-year period preceding the reference year. h Including refugees. i Data as at the end of December. j Data revision. k 2014. l Data are as at 1 January of reporting year. m Partial data. n 2012. o Break in the time series. p Including nationals residing abroad.

Cabo Verde

Region	Western Africa	UN membership date	16 September 1975
Population (000, 2020)	556	Surface area (km2)	4 033 [a]
Pop. density (per km2, 2020)	138.0	Sex ratio (m per 100 f)	100.8
Capital city	Praia	National currency	Cabo Verde Escudo (CVE)
Capital city pop. (000, 2020)	167.5 [b]	Exchange rate (per US$)	98.5 [c]

Economic indicators

	2010	2015	2020
GDP: Gross domestic product (million current US$)	1 664	1 596	1 977 [b]
GDP growth rate (annual %, const. 2015 prices)	1.5	1.0	5.1 [b]
GDP per capita (current US$)	3 378.3	3 041.8	3 635.4 [b]
Economy: Agriculture (% of Gross Value Added) [d]	9.2	10.0	6.2 [b]
Economy: Industry (% of Gross Value Added) [d,e]	20.8	20.7	22.6 [b]
Economy: Services and other activity (% of GVA) [d,f,g]	70.1	69.3	71.3 [b]
Employment in agriculture (% of employed) [h]	16.2	14.6	11.1
Employment in industry (% of employed) [h]	22.2	21.6	22.1
Employment in services & other sectors (% employed) [h]	61.5	63.8	66.8
Unemployment rate (% of labour force) [h]	10.7	11.9	12.3
Labour force participation rate (female/male pop. %) [h]	47.0 / 70.2	51.2 / 68.7	53.6 / 67.6
CPI: Consumer Price Index (2010=100) [i]	100	109	110 [c]
Agricultural production index (2004-2006=100)	106	96	97 [j]
International trade: exports (million current US$)	220	67	76 [h,c]
International trade: imports (million current US$)	731	603	941 [h,c]
International trade: balance (million current US$)	- 511	- 537	- 865 [h,c]
Balance of payments, current account (million current US$)	- 223	- 51	- 4 [c]

Major trading partners

						2019
Export partners (% of exports) [h]	Spain	65.0	Portugal	15.2	Italy	13.3
Import partners (% of imports) [h]	Portugal	43.2	Spain	14.5	Belgium	7.4

Social indicators

	2010	2015	2020
Population growth rate (average annual %) [k]	1.2	1.3	1.2
Urban population (% of total population)	61.8	64.3	66.2 [c]
Urban population growth rate (average annual %) [k]	2.5	2.0	...
Fertility rate, total (live births per woman) [k]	2.7	2.5	2.3
Life expectancy at birth (females/males, years) [k]	74.2 / 66.7	75.0 / 67.9	75.9 / 69.2
Population age distribution (0-14/60+ years old, %)	32.3 / 6.5	29.9 / 6.8	28.1 / 7.6
International migrant stock (000/% of total pop.)	14.4 / 2.9	14.9 / 2.8	15.7 / 2.8 [c]
Refugees and others of concern to the UNHCR (000)	~0.0 [l,m]	0.1	0.1 [c]
Infant mortality rate (per 1 000 live births) [k]	22.9	20.6	16.9
Health: Current expenditure (% of GDP)	4.5	4.8	5.2 [a]
Health: Physicians (per 1 000 pop.)	0.6	0.8	...
Education: Government expenditure (% of GDP)	5.6	5.3	5.2 [a]
Education: Primary gross enrol. ratio (f/m per 100 pop.)	107.0 / 115.2	101.7 / 109.2	100.5 / 107.5 [b]
Education: Secondary gross enrol. ratio (f/m per 100 pop.)	94.3 / 79.6	100.0 / 89.6	92.5 / 83.9 [b]
Education: Tertiary gross enrol. ratio (f/m per 100 pop.)	20.3 / 15.8	27.5 / 18.8	28.3 / 19.0 [b]
Intentional homicide rate (per 100 000 pop.)	7.9	8.8	6.8 [b]
Seats held by women in the National Parliament (%)	18.1	20.8	25.0 [n]

Environment and infrastructure indicators

	2010	2015	2020
Individuals using the Internet (per 100 inhabitants)	30.0 [h]	42.7	57.2 [o,a]
Research & Development expenditure (% of GDP)	...	0.1 [p,q,r]	...
Threatened species (number)	31	51	119
Forested area (% of land area)	21.1	22.3	22.3 [h,a]
Energy production, primary (Petajoules)	1	2 [h]	2 [h,a]
Energy supply per capita (Gigajoules)	18	16 [h]	18 [h,a]
Tourist/visitor arrivals at national borders (000) [s]	336	520	710 [b]
Important sites for terrestrial biodiversity protected (%)	9.4	12.0	12.0 [c]
Net Official Development Assist. received (% of GNI)	20.55	9.96	4.34 [b]

a 2017. b 2018. c 2019. d Data classified according to ISIC Rev. 4. e Excludes publishing activities. Includes irrigation and canals. f Excludes repair of personal and household goods. g Excludes computer and related activities and radio/TV activities. h Estimate. i Calculated by the UN Statistics Division from national indices. j 2016. k Data refers to a 5-year period preceding the reference year. l Data as at the end of December. m 2005. n Data are as at 1 January of reporting year. o Population aged 10 years and over. p Higher Education only. q Partial data. r 2011. s Non-resident tourists staying in hotels and similar establishments.

Cambodia

Region	South-eastern Asia	UN membership date	14 December 1955
Population (000, 2020)	16 719	Surface area (km2)	181 035[a]
Pop. density (per km2, 2020)	94.7	Sex ratio (m per 100 f)	95.4
Capital city	Phnom Penh	National currency	Riel (KHR)
Capital city pop. (000, 2020)	2 014.0[b,c]	Exchange rate (per US$)	4 084.0[c]

Economic indicators

	2010	2015	2020
GDP: Gross domestic product (million current US$)	11 242	18 050	24 572[d]
GDP growth rate (annual %, const. 2015 prices)	6.0	7.0	7.5[d]
GDP per capita (current US$)	785.5	1 162.9	1 512.1[d]
Economy: Agriculture (% of Gross Value Added)	36.0	28.2	23.5[d]
Economy: Industry (% of Gross Value Added)	23.3	29.4	34.4[d]
Economy: Services and other activity (% of GVA)	40.7	42.3	42.1[d]
Employment in agriculture (% of employed)	57.3[e]	42.5	31.2[e]
Employment in industry (% of employed)	16.0[e]	24.9	29.6[e]
Employment in services & other sectors (% employed)	26.7[e]	32.6	39.2[e]
Unemployment rate (% of labour force)[e]	0.8	0.4	0.7
Labour force participation rate (female/male pop. %)[e]	81.8 / 89.0	74.3 / 86.9	76.3 / 89.0
CPI: Consumer Price Index (2010=100)[f]	100	117	128[d]
Agricultural production index (2004-2006=100)	148	177	186[g]
International trade: exports (million current US$)	5 590	8 542	14 276[e,c]
International trade: imports (million current US$)	4 903	10 669	21 413[e,c]
International trade: balance (million current US$)	688	- 2 126	- 7 138[e,c]
Balance of payments, current account (million US$)	- 981	- 1 598	- 4 207[c]

Major trading partners

						2019
Export partners (% of exports)[e]	United States	24.0	Germany	8.6	Japan	8.5
Import partners (% of imports)[e]	China	35.1	Thailand	18.4	Viet Nam	12.7

Social indicators

	2010	2015	2020
Population growth rate (average annual %)[h]	1.5	1.6	1.5
Urban population (% of total population)	20.3	22.2	23.8[c]
Urban population growth rate (average annual %)[h]	2.6	3.4	...
Fertility rate, total (live births per woman)[h]	3.1	2.7	2.5
Life expectancy at birth (females/males, years)[h]	67.4 / 62.7	69.6 / 65.5	71.5 / 67.2
Population age distribution (0-14/60+ years old, %)	33.3 / 5.9	31.6 / 6.8	30.9 / 7.6
International migrant stock (000/% of total pop.)	82.0 / 0.6	74.0 / 0.5	78.6 / 0.5[c]
Refugees and others of concern to the UNHCR (000)	0.2[i]	0.2	57.4[c]
Infant mortality rate (per 1 000 live births)[h]	44.8	30.0	23.7
Health: Current expenditure (% of GDP)[j,k]	6.9	6.2	5.9[a]
Health: Physicians (per 1 000 pop.)	0.2	0.2[l]	...
Education: Government expenditure (% of GDP)	1.5	1.9[l]	...
Education: Primary gross enrol. ratio (f/m per 100 pop.)	120.2 / 127.4	116.7 / 117.5	106.1 / 108.7[d]
Education: Secondary gross enrol. ratio (f/m per 100 pop.)	41.6 / 48.7[e,m]	... / ...	... / ...
Education: Tertiary gross enrol. ratio (f/m per 100 pop.)	10.5 / 17.4	11.8 / 14.4	12.9 / 14.4[d]
Intentional homicide rate (per 100 000 pop.)	2.3	1.8[n]	...
Seats held by women in the National Parliament (%)	21.1	20.3	20.0[o]

Environment and infrastructure indicators

	2010	2015	2020
Individuals using the Internet (per 100 inhabitants)	1.3	6.4	40.0[d]
Research & Development expenditure (% of GDP)	...	0.1[p]	...
Threatened species (number)	204	243	280
Forested area (% of land area)[e]	57.2	53.6	53.6[a]
CO2 emission estimates (million tons/tons per capita)	4.6 / 0.3	8.0 / 0.5	10.8 / 0.7[a]
Energy production, primary (Petajoules)	152	184	198[a]
Energy supply per capita (Gigajoules)	16	19	21[a]
Tourist/visitor arrivals at national borders (000)[q]	2 508	4 775	6 201[d]
Important sites for terrestrial biodiversity protected (%)	39.5	39.5	39.5[c]
Pop. using safely managed drinking water (urban/rural, %)	51.2 / 14.3	55.0 / 16.0	56.6 / 16.7[a]
Net Official Development Assist. received (% of GNI)	6.35	4.01	3.37[d]

a 2017. b Refers to the municipality of Phnom Penh including suburban areas. c 2019. d 2018. e Estimate. f Phnom Penh g 2016. h Data refers to a 5-year period preceding the reference year. i Data as at the end of December. j Data refer to fiscal years beginning 1 July. k 2012 data are based on a health accounts study based on SHA2011. Numbers were converted to SHA 1.0 format for comparability. l 2014. m 2008. n 2011. o Data are as at 1 January of reporting year. p Break in the time series. q Arrivals by all means of transport.

Cameroon

Region	Middle Africa	
Population (000, 2020)	26 546	
Pop. density (per km2, 2020)	56.2	
Capital city	Yaoundé	
Capital city pop. (000, 2020)	3 822.4[c]	

UN membership date	20 September 1960	
Surface area (km2)	475 650[a]	
Sex ratio (m per 100 f)	100.1	
National currency	CFA Franc, BEAC (XAF)[b]	
Exchange rate (per US$)	583.9[c]	

Economic indicators	2010	2015	2020
GDP: Gross domestic product (million current US$)	26 144	30 905	38 694[d]
GDP growth rate (annual %, const. 2015 prices)	3.4	5.7	4.1[d]
GDP per capita (current US$)	1 285.3	1 326.5	1 534.5[d]
Economy: Agriculture (% of Gross Value Added)[e]	15.1	16.1	15.7[d]
Economy: Industry (% of Gross Value Added)[e,f]	29.1	27.4	28.1[d]
Economy: Services and other activity (% of GVA)[e,g,h]	55.8	56.6	56.2[d]
Employment in agriculture (% of employed)[i]	55.1	46.5	42.9
Employment in industry (% of employed)[i]	12.2	14.3	15.1
Employment in services & other sectors (% employed)[i]	32.8	39.1	42.1
Unemployment rate (% of labour force)[i]	4.1	3.5	3.4
Labour force participation rate (female/male pop. %)[i]	70.6 / 81.4	71.1 / 81.6	70.9 / 81.0
CPI: Consumer Price Index (2010=100)[i]	100	113	116[d]
Agricultural production index (2004-2006=100)	140	164	175[i]
International trade: exports (million current US$)	3 878	4 053	1 750[i,c]
International trade: imports (million current US$)	5 133	6 037	3 262[i,c]
International trade: balance (million current US$)	- 1 255	- 1 984	- 1 512[i,c]
Balance of payments, current account (million US$)	- 857	- 1 174	- 1 409[d]

Major trading partners					2019
Export partners (% of exports)[i]	Italy	13.9	China	12.1	France	10.5
Import partners (% of imports)[i]	China	17.2	France	9.8	Thailand	5.7

Social indicators	2010	2015	2020
Population growth rate (average annual %)[k]	2.7	2.7	2.6
Urban population (% of total population)	51.6	54.6	57.0[c]
Urban population growth rate (average annual %)[k]	3.9	3.8	...
Fertility rate, total (live births per woman)[k]	5.2	5.0	4.6
Life expectancy at birth (females/males, years)[k]	55.0 / 52.9	57.6 / 54.9	60.0 / 57.5
Population age distribution (0-14/60+ years old, %)	43.7 / 4.4	43.2 / 4.3	42.1 / 4.3
International migrant stock (000/% of total pop.)	291.5 / 1.4	508.3 / 2.2	505.7 / 2.0[c]
Refugees and others of concern to the UNHCR (000)	106.7[l]	391.8	1 463.2[c]
Infant mortality rate (per 1 000 live births)[k]	80.5	70.7	61.2
Health: Current expenditure (% of GDP)[i]	4.5	4.7	4.7[a]
Health: Physicians (per 1 000 pop.)	0.1	0.1[m]	2.3[i]
Education: Government expenditure (% of GDP)	3.0	2.8[i]	3.1[i,a]
Education: Primary gross enrol. ratio (f/m per 100 pop.)	100.2 / 116.0	109.9 / 122.4	98.0 / 108.7[d]
Education: Secondary gross enrol. ratio (f/m per 100 pop.)	36.8 / 44.1[n]	54.4 / 63.6	55.4 / 64.6[i]
Education: Tertiary gross enrol. ratio (f/m per 100 pop.)	10.0 / 12.3	15.1 / 18.8	11.4 / 14.1[a]
Intentional homicide rate (per 100 000 pop.)	4.9	1.2	1.4[a]
Seats held by women in the National Parliament (%)	13.9	31.1	31.1[o]

Environment and infrastructure indicators	2010	2015	2020
Individuals using the Internet (per 100 inhabitants)	4.3[i]	20.7[i]	23.2[a]
Threatened species (number)	624	697	890
Forested area (% of land area)[i]	42.1	39.8	39.8[a]
CO2 emission estimates (million tons/tons per capita)	5.1 / 0.3	5.9 / 0.3	6.2 / 0.3[a]
Energy production, primary (Petajoules)	351	493	472[a]
Energy supply per capita (Gigajoules)	15	17	16[a]
Tourist/visitor arrivals at national borders (000)	573	897	1 081[a]
Important sites for terrestrial biodiversity protected (%)	24.7	35.3	35.3[c]
Net Official Development Assist. received (% of GNI)	2.09	2.18	3.08[d]

a 2017. b African Financial Community (CFA) Franc, Bank of Central African States (BEAC). c 2019. d 2018. e Data classified according to ISIC Rev. 4. f Excludes publishing activities. Includes irrigation and canals. g Excludes computer and related activities and radio/TV activities. h Excludes repair of personal and household goods. i Estimate. j 2016. k Data refers to a 5-year period preceding the reference year. l Data as at the end of December. m 2011. n 2009. o Data are as at 1 January of reporting year.

Canada

Region	Northern America	UN membership date	09 November 1945
Population (000, 2020)	37 742	Surface area (km2)	9 984 670[a]
Pop. density (per km2, 2020)	4.2	Sex ratio (m per 100 f)	98.5
Capital city	Ottawa	National currency	Canadian Dollar (CAD)
Capital city pop. (000, 2020)	1 378.2[b,c]	Exchange rate (per US$)	1.3[c]

Economic indicators	2010	2015	2020
GDP: Gross domestic product (million current US$)	1 617 266	1 556 127	1 712 562[d]
GDP growth rate (annual %, const. 2015 prices)	3.1	0.7	1.9[d]
GDP per capita (current US$)	47 361.1	43 193.7	46 192.4[d]
Economy: Agriculture (% of Gross Value Added)[e]	1.6	2.0	2.0[d]
Economy: Industry (% of Gross Value Added)[e,f]	27.9	25.8	25.6[d]
Economy: Services and other activity (% of GVA)[e,g,h]	70.5	72.1	72.4[d]
Employment in agriculture (% of employed)	1.8	1.6	1.4[i]
Employment in industry (% of employed)	20.2	19.9	19.4[i]
Employment in services & other sectors (% employed)	78.0	78.4	79.2[i]
Unemployment rate (% of labour force)[i]	8.1	6.9	5.4
Labour force participation rate (female/male pop. %)[i]	61.9 / 71.5	60.8 / 70.5	60.7 / 69.2
CPI: Consumer Price Index (2010=100)[j]	100	109	117[c]
Agricultural production index (2004-2006=100)	103	110	113[k]
International trade: exports (million current US$)[l]	386 580	408 697	446 148[c]
International trade: imports (million current US$)[l]	392 109	419 375	453 234[c]
International trade: balance (million current US$)[l]	- 5 529	- 10 677	- 7 085[c]
Balance of payments, current account (million US$)	- 58 163	- 54 696	- 34 193[c]

Major trading partners						2019
Export partners (% of exports)	United States	75.4	China	3.9	United Kingdom	3.3
Import partners (% of imports)	United States	50.7	China	12.5	Mexico	6.1

Social indicators	2010	2015	2020
Population growth rate (average annual %)[m]	1.2	1.1	0.9
Urban population (% of total population)	80.9	81.3	81.5[c]
Urban population growth rate (average annual %)[m]	1.3	1.1	...
Fertility rate, total (live births per woman)[m]	1.6	1.6	1.5
Life expectancy at birth (females/males, years)[m]	83.0 / 78.4	83.8 / 79.6	84.2 / 80.2
Population age distribution (0-14/60+ years old, %)	16.5 / 19.9	16.0 / 22.3	15.8 / 24.9
International migrant stock (000/% of total pop.)	6 761.2 / 19.8	7 428.7 / 20.6	7 960.7 / 21.3[c]
Refugees and others of concern to the UNHCR (000)	216.6[n]	155.8[n]	189.8[c]
Infant mortality rate (per 1 000 live births)[m]	5.1	4.6	4.5
Health: Current expenditure (% of GDP)	10.7	10.5	10.6[a]
Education: Government expenditure (% of GDP)	5.4	5.3[o]	...
Education: Primary gross enrol. ratio (f/m per 100 pop.)	98.9 / 98.4	102.9 / 102.1	100.8 / 101.1[a]
Education: Secondary gross enrol. ratio (f/m per 100 pop.)	101.2 / 103.6	110.9 / 109.9	114.5 / 113.0[a]
Education: Tertiary gross enrol. ratio (f/m per 100 pop.)[i]	71.8 / 52.0	74.5 / 55.5	79.3 / 59.1[a]
Intentional homicide rate (per 100 000 pop.)	1.6	1.7	1.8[d]
Seats held by women in the National Parliament (%)	22.1	25.2	29.0[p]

Environment and infrastructure indicators	2010	2015	2020
Individuals using the Internet (per 100 inhabitants)	80.3[q]	90.0[r]	91.0[r,a]
Research & Development expenditure (% of GDP)	1.8	1.7	1.6[s,d]
Threatened species (number)	77	97	173
Forested area (% of land area)	38.7	38.7	38.7[i,a]
CO2 emission estimates (million tons/tons per capita)	528.6 / 15.5	557.7 / 15.6	547.8 / 15.0[a]
Energy production, primary (Petajoules)	16 662	19 754	21 327[a]
Energy supply per capita (Gigajoules)	318	327	330[a]
Tourist/visitor arrivals at national borders (000)	16 219	17 971	21 134[d]
Important sites for terrestrial biodiversity protected (%)	26.0	26.6	28.1[c]
Pop. using safely managed sanitation (urban/rural %)	82.0 / 81.5	82.3 / 81.6	82.2 / 81.4[a]
Net Official Development Assist. disbursed (% of GNI)[t]	0.34	0.28	0.26[a]

a 2017. b Refers to the Census Metropolitan Area. c 2019. d 2018. e Data classified according to ISIC Rev. 4. f Excludes publishing activities. Includes irrigation and canals. g Excludes repair of personal and household goods. h Excludes computer and related activities and radio/TV activities. i Estimate. j Calculated by the UN Statistics Division from national indices. k 2016. l Imports FOB. m Data refers to a 5-year period preceding the reference year. n Data as at the end of December. o 2011. p Data are as at 1 January of reporting year. q Population aged 16 years and over r Population aged 18 years and over. s Provisional data. t Development Assistance Committee member (OECD).

Cayman Islands

Region	Caribbean	Population (000, 2020)	64	
Surface area (km2)	264[a]	Pop. density (per km2, 2020)	266.2	
Sex ratio (m per 100 f)	100.4[b,c]	Capital city	George Town	
National currency	Cayman Islands Dollar (KYD)	Capital city pop. (000, 2020)	34.9[d]	
Exchange rate (per US$)	0.8[e]			

Economic indicators	2010	2015	2020
GDP: Gross domestic product (million current US$)	4 277	4 785	5 485[d]
GDP growth rate (annual %, const. 2015 prices)	- 2.7	2.8	3.3[d]
GDP per capita (current US$)	75 460.8	77 517.7	85 474.2[d]
Economy: Agriculture (% of Gross Value Added)[f]	0.3	0.4	0.4[d]
Economy: Industry (% of Gross Value Added)[f,g]	7.4	7.4	7.6[d]
Economy: Services and other activity (% of GVA)[f,h,i]	92.2	92.2	92.0[d]
Employment in agriculture (% of employed)[j]	0.6	0.8[k]	...
Employment in industry (% of employed)[j]	14.9	15.5[k]	...
Employment in services & other sectors (% employed)[j]	84.2	83.6[k]	...
Unemployment rate (% of labour force)	6.7	6.3[k]	...
Labour force participation rate (female/male pop. %)	80.6 / 88.0[j,l,m]	80.6 / 85.6[k]	... / ...
CPI: Consumer Price Index (2010=100)[n]	100	104	108[d]
Agricultural production index (2004-2006=100)	100	103	103[o]
International trade: exports (million current US$)[p]	24	65	39[e]
International trade: imports (million current US$)[p]	828[p]	915	1 393[p,e]
International trade: balance (million current US$)	- 804[p]	- 851	- 1 354[p,e]
Balance of payments, current account (million US$)	...	...	- 998[a]

Major trading partners						2019
Export partners (% of exports)[p]	Netherlands	79.5	Spain	11.0	United States	3.3
Import partners (% of imports)[p]	Netherlands	49.2	United States	24.8	Italy	7.3

Social indicators	2010	2015	2020
Population growth rate (average annual %)	2.6[q]	1.5[q]	1.3
Urban population (% of total population)	100.0	100.0	100.0[e]
Urban population growth rate (average annual %)[q]	2.6	1.5	...
Fertility rate, total (live births per woman)	1.6[r]	...	...
Life expectancy at birth (females/males, years)	83.8 / 76.3[s,t]	... / ...	... / ...
Population age distribution (0-14/60+ years old, %)	18.1 / 8.6[b,u]	18.3 / 6.7[b,v]	... / ...
International migrant stock (000/% of total pop.)[w]	24.1 / 42.4	26.2 / 42.4	29.0 / 44.6[e]
Refugees and others of concern to the UNHCR (000)	~0.0[x]	0.1	0.1[e]
Education: Government expenditure (% of GDP)	2.6[t]	...	...
Intentional homicide rate (per 100 000 pop.)	15.9	8.2[y]	...

Environment and infrastructure indicators	2010	2015	2020
Individuals using the Internet (per 100 inhabitants)[p]	66.0	77.0	81.1[a]
Threatened species (number)	34	71	83
Forested area (% of land area)[p]	52.9	52.9	52.9[a]
Energy supply per capita (Gigajoules)	144	133	135[a]
Tourist/visitor arrivals at national borders (000)[z]	288	385	463[d]
Important sites for terrestrial biodiversity protected (%)	31.7	32.5	32.5[e]

a 2017. b De jure population. c 2015. d 2018. e 2019. f Data classified according to ISIC Rev. 4. g Excludes publishing activities. Includes irrigation and canals. h Excludes computer and related activities and radio/TV activities. i Excludes repair of personal and household goods. j Break in the time series. k 2013. l Resident population (de jure). m 2009. n Calculated by the UN Statistics Division from national indices. o 2016. p Estimate. q Data refers to a 5-year period preceding the reference year. r 2007. s Data are based on a small number of deaths. t 2006. u Excluding the institutional population. v Population aged 65 years and over. w Refers to foreign citizens. x Data as at the end of December. y 2014. z Arrivals by air.

Central African Republic

Region	Middle Africa	UN membership date	20 September 1960
Population (000, 2020)	4 830	Surface area (km2)	622 984 [a]
Pop. density (per km2, 2020)	7.8	Sex ratio (m per 100 f)	98.3
Capital city	Bangui	National currency	CFA Franc, BEAC (XAF) [b]
Capital city pop. (000, 2020)	869.6 [c]	Exchange rate (per US$)	583.9 [c]

Economic indicators

	2010	2015	2020
GDP: Gross domestic product (million current US$)	2 034	1 632	2 243 [d]
GDP growth rate (annual %, const. 2015 prices)	3.6	4.8	4.3 [d]
GDP per capita (current US$)	463.6	363.2	480.7 [d]
Economy: Agriculture (% of Gross Value Added)	41.2	31.4	31.5 [d]
Economy: Industry (% of Gross Value Added)	24.0	26.0	25.8 [d]
Economy: Services and other activity (% of GVA)	34.8	42.6	42.8 [d]
Employment in agriculture (% of employed) [e]	78.8	78.5	77.1
Employment in industry (% of employed) [e]	6.2	5.3	5.4
Employment in services & other sectors (% employed) [e]	15.1	16.2	17.5
Unemployment rate (% of labour force) [e]	3.9	3.9	3.7
Labour force participation rate (female/male pop. %) [e]	65.0 / 80.4	64.7 / 81.2	64.4 / 79.8
CPI: Consumer Price Index (2010=100) [e,f]	100	187	...
Agricultural production index (2004-2006=100)	115	120	122 [g]
International trade: exports (million current US$)	90	97	324 [e,c]
International trade: imports (million current US$)	210	457	89 [e,c]
International trade: balance (million current US$)	- 120	- 360	236 [e,c]

Major trading partners

							2019
Export partners (% of exports) [e]	France	61.1	Benin	9.9	China	7.0	
Import partners (% of imports) [e]	France	26.1	Cameroon	12.1	Belgium	8.1	

Social indicators

	2010	2015	2020
Population growth rate (average annual %) [h]	1.7	0.5	1.4
Urban population (% of total population)	38.9	40.3	41.8 [c]
Urban population growth rate (average annual %) [h]	1.9	1.1	...
Fertility rate, total (live births per woman) [h]	5.3	5.1	4.8
Life expectancy at birth (females/males, years) [h]	47.4 / 44.6	50.5 / 47.3	54.9 / 50.5
Population age distribution (0-14/60+ years old, %)	44.1 / 4.6	45.2 / 4.4	43.5 / 4.5
International migrant stock (000/% of total pop.) [i]	93.5 / 2.1	81.6 / 1.8	90.6 / 1.9 [c]
Refugees and others of concern to the UNHCR (000)	215.3 [j]	517.2	712.6 [c]
Infant mortality rate (per 1 000 live births) [h]	99.7	90.3	81.9
Health: Current expenditure (% of GDP) [e]	3.7	6.3	5.8 [a]
Health: Physicians (per 1 000 pop.)	~0.0 [k]	0.1	...
Education: Government expenditure (% of GDP)	1.2	1.2 [l]	...
Education: Primary gross enrol. ratio (f/m per 100 pop.)	73.4 / 101.2	75.7 / 99.8 [m]	89.4 / 114.6 [g]
Education: Secondary gross enrol. ratio (f/m per 100 pop.)	9.8 / 17.4 [k]	11.9 / 22.9 [m]	13.8 / 20.5 [a]
Education: Tertiary gross enrol. ratio (f/m per 100 pop.)	1.3 / 4.0	1.6 / 4.4 [m]	... / ...
Intentional homicide rate (per 100 000 pop.)	...	...	20.1 [g]
Seats held by women in the National Parliament (%)	9.6	12.5 [n]	8.6 [o]

Environment and infrastructure indicators

	2010	2015	2020
Individuals using the Internet (per 100 inhabitants) [e]	2.0	3.8	4.3 [a]
Threatened species (number)	36	54	73
Forested area (% of land area)	35.7	35.6	35.6 [e,a]
Energy production, primary (Petajoules)	19	19	19 [a]
Energy supply per capita (Gigajoules)	5	5	5 [a]
Tourist/visitor arrivals at national borders (000) [p]	54	120	107 [a]
Important sites for terrestrial biodiversity protected (%)	74.2	74.2	74.2 [c]
Net Official Development Assist. received (% of GNI)	12.14	28.36	27.47 [d]

a 2017. b African Financial Community (CFA) Franc, Bank of Central African States (BEAC). c 2019. d 2018. e Estimate. f Bangui g 2016. h Data refers to a 5-year period preceding the reference year. i Refers to foreign citizens. j Data as at the end of December. k 2009. l 2011. m 2012. n 2013. o Data are as at 1 January of reporting year. p Arrivals by air at Bangui only.

Chad

Region	Middle Africa	UN membership date	20 September 1960
Population (000, 2020)	16 426	Surface area (km2)	1 284 000[a]
Pop. density (per km2, 2020)	13.0	Sex ratio (m per 100 f)	99.7
Capital city	N'Djamena	National currency	CFA Franc, BEAC (XAF)[b]
Capital city pop. (000, 2020)	1 371.5[c]	Exchange rate (per US$)	583.9[c]

Economic indicators

	2010	2015	2020
GDP: Gross domestic product (million current US$)	10 971	11 690	11 387[d]
GDP growth rate (annual %, const. 2015 prices)	15.0	4.6	2.4[d]
GDP per capita (current US$)	917.9	828.5	735.7[d]
Economy: Agriculture (% of Gross Value Added)	35.9	29.5	30.6[d]
Economy: Industry (% of Gross Value Added)	36.7	31.7	19.2[d]
Economy: Services and other activity (% of GVA)	27.4	38.8	50.2[d]
Employment in agriculture (% of employed)[e]	78.5	77.0	76.3
Employment in industry (% of employed)[e]	2.4	2.4	2.1
Employment in services & other sectors (% employed)[e]	19.1	20.7	21.6
Unemployment rate (% of labour force)[e]	1.6	1.8	1.9
Labour force participation rate (female/male pop. %)[e]	63.8 / 79.3	63.8 / 78.2	63.9 / 77.5
CPI: Consumer Price Index (2010=100)[e,f]	100	116	...
Agricultural production index (2004-2006=100)	147	141	150[g]
International trade: exports (million current US$)[e]	3 410	2 900	613[c]
International trade: imports (million current US$)[e]	2 507	2 200	319[c]
International trade: balance (million current US$)[e]	904	700	294[c]

Major trading partners

							2019
Export partners (% of exports)[e]	India	29.8	United Arab Emirates	16.1	United States		15.9
Import partners (% of imports)[e]	China	20.3	United Arab Emirates	13.1	France		10.6

Social indicators

	2010	2015	2020
Population growth rate (average annual %)[h]	3.4	3.3	3.0
Urban population (% of total population)	22.0	22.5	23.3[c]
Urban population growth rate (average annual %)[h]	3.5	3.8	...
Fertility rate, total (live births per woman)[h]	6.9	6.3	5.8
Life expectancy at birth (females/males, years)[h]	50.7 / 48.3	53.7 / 50.9	55.2 / 52.4
Population age distribution (0-14/60+ years old, %)	48.8 / 3.9	47.8 / 3.9	46.5 / 3.9
International migrant stock (000/% of total pop.)[i]	416.9 / 3.5	467.0 / 3.3	512.2 / 3.2[c]
Refugees and others of concern to the UNHCR (000)	533.0[j]	473.5	667.4[c]
Infant mortality rate (per 1 000 live births)[h]	97.5	84.1	74.5
Health: Current expenditure (% of GDP)[e]	4.1	4.5	4.5[a]
Health: Physicians (per 1 000 pop.)	~0.0[k]	~0.0	~0.0[a]
Education: Government expenditure (% of GDP)	2.0	2.9[l]	...
Education: Primary gross enrol. ratio (f/m per 100 pop.)	69.1 / 94.6	79.4 / 103.7	75.5 / 98.2[g]
Education: Secondary gross enrol. ratio (f/m per 100 pop.)	13.4 / 31.7	13.9 / 30.9	14.2 / 30.9[g]
Education: Tertiary gross enrol. ratio (f/m per 100 pop.)	0.6 / 3.6[e]	1.5 / 5.0	... / ...
Seats held by women in the National Parliament (%)	5.2	14.9	15.4[m]

Environment and infrastructure indicators

	2010	2015	2020
Individuals using the Internet (per 100 inhabitants)[e]	1.7	3.5	6.5[a]
Research & Development expenditure (% of GDP)	...	...	0.3[n,o,g]
Threatened species (number)	30	38	48
Forested area (% of land area)	4.4	3.9[e]	3.9[e,a]
Energy production, primary (Petajoules)	324	375	318[a]
Energy supply per capita (Gigajoules)	7	6	6[a]
Tourist/visitor arrivals at national borders (000)[p]	71	120	87[a]
Important sites for terrestrial biodiversity protected (%)	67.3	67.3	67.3[c]
Net Official Development Assist. received (% of GNI)	4.76	5.71	7.91[d]

a 2017. b African Financial Community (CFA) Franc, Bank of Central African States (BEAC). c 2019. d 2018. e estimate. f N'Djamena g 2016. h Data refers to a 5-year period preceding the reference year. i Including refugees. j Data as at the end of December. k 2006. l 2013. m Data are as at 1 January of reporting year. n Excluding private non-profit. o Excluding business enterprise. p Arrivals by air.

Channel Islands

Region	Northern Europe	Population (000, 2020)	174[a]	
Surface area (km2)	180[a,b]	Pop. density (per km2, 2020)	915.1[a]	
Sex ratio (m per 100 f)	98.0[a]	Capital city	Saint Helier[c]	
National currency	Pound Sterling (GBP)	Capital city pop. (000, 2020)	34.4[d]	
Exchange rate (per US$)	0.8[e]			

Economic indicators	2010	2015	2020
Employment in agriculture (% of employed)[f]	4.7	4.0	3.5
Employment in industry (% of employed)[f]	26.7	24.9	22.9
Employment in services & other sectors (% employed)[f]	68.6	71.1	73.6
Unemployment rate (% of labour force)[f]	8.4	8.1	7.5
Labour force participation rate (female/male pop. %)[f]	50.8 / 67.8	51.0 / 67.1	50.6 / 65.6

Social indicators	2010	2015	2020
Population growth rate (average annual %)[a,g]	1.0	0.7	1.0
Urban population (% of total population)[a]	31.1	31.0	30.9[e]
Urban population growth rate (average annual %)[a,g]	0.9	0.5	...
Fertility rate, total (live births per woman)[a,g]	1.6	1.6	1.5
Life expectancy at birth (females/males, years)[a,g]	83.4 / 78.4	84.1 / 79.8	84.7 / 80.9
Population age distribution (0-14/60+ years old, %)[a]	15.5 / 21.5	15.5 / 22.3	15.0 / 24.0
International migrant stock (000/% of total pop.)[a]	77.6 / 48.6	82.3 / 49.8	83.8 / 48.7[e]
Infant mortality rate (per 1 000 live births)[a,g]	7.6	6.7	6.1
Intentional homicide rate (per 100 000 pop.)	0.0	...	...

Environment and infrastructure indicators	2010	2015	2020
Forested area (% of land area)[f]	4.0	4.0	4.0[b]

a Refers to Guernsey and Jersey. b 2017. c The capital of the Bailiwick of Jersey. d 2018. e 2019. f Estimate. g Data refers to a 5-year period preceding the reference year.

Chile

Region	South America	UN membership date	24 October 1945
Population (000, 2020)	19 116	Surface area (km2)	756 102[a]
Pop. density (per km2, 2020)	25.7	Sex ratio (m per 100 f)	97.3
Capital city	Santiago	National currency	Chilean Peso (CLP)
Capital city pop. (000, 2020)	6 723.5[b,c]	Exchange rate (per US$)	744.6[c]

Economic indicators

	2010	2015	2020
GDP: Gross domestic product (million current US$)	218 538	243 919	298 231[d]
GDP growth rate (annual %, const. 2015 prices)	5.8	2.3	4.0[d]
GDP per capita (current US$)	12 808.0	13 574.2	15 923.4[d]
Economy: Agriculture (% of Gross Value Added)[e]	3.9	4.0	4.0[d]
Economy: Industry (% of Gross Value Added)[e,f]	38.8	32.6	32.8[d]
Economy: Services and other activity (% of GVA)[e,g,h]	57.3	63.4	63.3[d]
Employment in agriculture (% of employed)	10.6	9.4	8.8[i]
Employment in industry (% of employed)	23.0	23.3	22.0[i]
Employment in services & other sectors (% employed)	66.4	67.3	69.2[i]
Unemployment rate (% of labour force)[i]	8.4	6.5	7.1
Labour force participation rate (female/male pop. %)[i]	46.9 / 74.6	50.1 / 74.7	52.0 / 74.1
CPI: Consumer Price Index (2010=100)	101[j]	109[k]	102[l,c]
Agricultural production index (2004-2006=100)	108	111	114[m]
International trade: exports (million current US$)	71 106	62 033	69 681[c]
International trade: imports (million current US$)	59 007	62 387	69 591[c]
International trade: balance (million current US$)	12 099	- 354	90[c]
Balance of payments, current account (million US$)	3 069	- 5 647	- 9 157[d]

Major trading partners

						2019
Export partners (% of exports)	China	32.4	United States	13.6	Japan	9.1
Import partners (% of imports)	China	23.8	United States	19.3	Brazil	8.1

Social indicators

	2010	2015	2020
Population growth rate (average annual %)[n]	1.1	1.0	1.2
Urban population (% of total population)	87.1	87.4	87.6[c]
Urban population growth rate (average annual %)[n]	1.1	1.0	...
Fertility rate, total (live births per woman)[n]	1.9	1.8	1.6
Life expectancy at birth (females/males, years)[n]	81.1 / 75.1	82.1 / 76.3	82.3 / 77.4
Population age distribution (0-14/60+ years old, %)	22.1 / 13.3	20.6 / 15.3	19.2 / 17.4
International migrant stock (000/% of total pop.)	375.4 / 2.2	639.7 / 3.6	940.0 / 5.0[c]
Refugees and others of concern to the UNHCR (000)	1.9[o]	2.5	385.5[c]
Infant mortality rate (per 1 000 live births)[n]	7.7	7.2	6.7
Health: Current expenditure (% of GDP)	6.8	8.3	9.0[a]
Health: Physicians (per 1 000 pop.)	1.4	2.1	2.6[d]
Education: Government expenditure (% of GDP)	4.2	4.9	5.4[a]
Education: Primary gross enrol. ratio (f/m per 100 pop.)	102.2 / 105.2	99.1 / 102.2	99.9 / 102.9[a]
Education: Secondary gross enrol. ratio (f/m per 100 pop.)	91.4 / 88.7	102.1 / 101.5	102.0 / 101.6[a]
Education: Tertiary gross enrol. ratio (f/m per 100 pop.)	70.3 / 65.5	89.9 / 80.7	94.7 / 82.5[a]
Intentional homicide rate (per 100 000 pop.)	3.2	3.4	4.4[d]
Seats held by women in the National Parliament (%)	14.2	15.8	22.6[p]

Environment and infrastructure indicators

	2010	2015	2020
Individuals using the Internet (per 100 inhabitants)	45.0[i,q]	76.6	82.3[r,a]
Research & Development expenditure (% of GDP)	0.3	0.4	0.4[s,a]
Threatened species (number)	145	182	240
Forested area (% of land area)	21.8	23.9[i]	23.9[i,a]
CO2 emission estimates (million tons/tons per capita)	68.6 / 4.0	81.1 / 4.5	86.1 / 4.6[a]
Energy production, primary (Petajoules)	386	541	543[a]
Energy supply per capita (Gigajoules)	76	85	89[a]
Tourist/visitor arrivals at national borders (000)[t]	2 801	4 478	5 723[d]
Important sites for terrestrial biodiversity protected (%)	29.6	32.1	34.2[c]
Pop. using safely managed drinking water (urban/rural, %)	98.6 / ...	98.7 / ...	98.6 / ...[a]
Pop. using safely managed sanitation (urban/rural %)	66.7 / ...	81.1 / ...	81.4 / ...[a]
Net Official Development Assist. received (% of GNI)	0.09	0.02	0.03[a]

a 2017. b Refers to the urban population of Santiago Metropolitan Area Region. c 2019. d 2018. e Data classified according to ISIC Rev. 4. f Excludes publishing activities. Includes irrigation and canals. g Excludes computer and related activities and radio/TV activities. h Excludes repair of personal and household goods. i Estimate. j Base: 2009=100. k Index base: 2013=100. l Base: 2018=100. m 2016. n Data refers to a 5-year period preceding the reference year. o Data as at the end of December. p Data are as at 1 January of reporting year. q Population aged 5 years and over. r Population aged 15 years and over. s Provisional data. t Including nationals residing abroad.

China

Region	Eastern Asia	UN membership date	24 October 1945
Population (000, 2020)	1 439 324[a]	Surface area (km2)	9 600 000[b]
Pop. density (per km2, 2020)	153.3[a]	Sex ratio (m per 100 f)	105.3[a]
Capital city	Beijing	National currency	Yuan Renminbi (CNY)
Capital city pop. (000, 2020)	20 035.5[c,d]	Exchange rate (per US$)	7.0[a,d]

Economic indicators

	2010	2015	2020
GDP: Gross domestic product (million current US$)[a]	6 087 192	11 015 562	13 608 152[e]
GDP growth rate (annual %, const. 2015 prices)[a]	10.4	6.9	6.6[e]
GDP per capita (current US$)[a]	4 447.1	7 830.0	9 531.9[e]
Economy: Agriculture (% of Gross Value Added)[a,f]	9.6	8.7	7.5[e]
Economy: Industry (% of Gross Value Added)[a,f]	46.7	41.3	40.8[e]
Economy: Services and other activity (% of GVA)[a,f,g]	43.7	50.0	51.7[e]
Employment in agriculture (% of employed)[a,h]	36.7	28.6	24.7
Employment in industry (% of employed)[a,h]	28.7	29.2	28.2
Employment in services & other sectors (% employed)[a,h]	34.6	42.2	47.1
Unemployment rate (% of labour force)[a,h]	4.5	4.6	4.4
Labour force participation rate (female/male pop. %)[a,h]	64.0 / 78.3	62.5 / 76.9	59.8 / 74.8
CPI: Consumer Price Index (2010=100)	100	115	109[i,d]
Agricultural production index (2004-2006=100)[a]	120	136	139[i]
International trade: exports (million current US$)[a]	1 577 760	2 273 470	2 491 820[h,d]
International trade: imports (million current US$)[a]	1 396 000	1 679 560	2 070 150[h,d]
International trade: balance (million current US$)[a]	181 762	593 904	421 672[h,d]
Balance of payments, current account (million US$)[a]	237 810	304 164	141 335[d]

Major trading partners

						2019
Export partners (% of exports)[h]	United States	19.2	China, Hong Kong SAR	12.1	Japan	5.9
Import partners (% of imports)[h]	Rep. of Korea	9.6	Japan	8.4	Other Asia, nes	8.3

Social indicators

	2010	2015	2020
Population growth rate (average annual %)[a,k]	0.6	0.5	0.5
Urban population (% of total population)[a]	49.2	55.5	60.3[d]
Urban population growth rate (average annual %)[a,k]	3.5	2.9	...
Fertility rate, total (live births per woman)[a,k]	1.6	1.6	1.7
Life expectancy at birth (females/males, years)[a,k]	75.7 / 71.9	77.4 / 73.1	79.0 / 74.5
Population age distribution (0-14/60+ years old, %)[a]	18.7 / 12.2	18.1 / 15.0	17.7 / 17.4
International migrant stock (000/% of total pop.)[a,l]	849.9 / 0.1	978.0 / 0.1	1 030.9 / 0.1[d]
Refugees and others of concern to the UNHCR (000)[a]	301.1[m]	301.6	322.4[n,d]
Infant mortality rate (per 1 000 live births)[a,k]	18.1	12.3	9.9
Health: Current expenditure (% of GDP)[o]	4.2	4.9	5.2[b]
Health: Physicians (per 1 000 pop.)	1.5	1.8	2.0[b]
Education: Primary gross enrol. ratio (f/m per 100 pop.)	98.0 / 99.8	96.4 / 96.2	100.8 / 99.7[e]
Education: Secondary gross enrol. ratio (f/m per 100 pop.)	88.0 / 88.3	... / ...	... / ...
Education: Tertiary gross enrol. ratio (f/m per 100 pop.)	25.0 / 23.5	50.2 / 42.3	55.9 / 45.9[e]
Intentional homicide rate (per 100 000 pop.)	1.0	0.7	0.5[e]
Seats held by women in the National Parliament (%)	21.3	23.6	24.9[p]

Environment and infrastructure indicators

	2010	2015	2020
Individuals using the Internet (per 100 inhabitants)[a]	34.3	50.3[h,q,r,s]	54.3[b]
Research & Development expenditure (% of GDP)[a]	1.7	2.1	2.2[e]
Threatened species (number)[a]	859	1 040	1 172
Forested area (% of land area)	21.3	22.1	22.1[b]
CO2 emission estimates (million tons/tons per capita)[a]	7 832.7 / 5.9	9 101.4 / 6.6	9 257.9 / 6.7[b]
Energy production, primary (Petajoules)[a]	88 642	100 864	99 218[b]
Energy supply per capita (Gigajoules)[a]	75	86	88[b]
Tourist/visitor arrivals at national borders (000)[a]	55 664	56 886	62 900[e]
Important sites for terrestrial biodiversity protected (%)	8.6	9.4	9.9[d]
Pop. using safely managed drinking water (urban/rural, %)	92.7 / ...	92.4 / ...	92.3 / ...[b]
Pop. using safely managed sanitation (urban/rural %)[a]	58.3 / 37.1	76.3 / 49.9	83.7 / 56.1[b]
Net Official Development Assist. received (% of GNI)[a]	0.01	0.00	- 0.01[e]

a For statistical purposes, the data for China do not include those for the Hong Kong Special Administrative Region (Hong Kong SAR), Macao Special Administrative Region (Macao SAR) and Taiwan Province of China. **b** 2017. **c** Refer to all city districts (excluding Yanqing District) meeting the criteria such as contiguous built-up areas, being the location of the local government, being a Street or Having a Resident Committee. **d** 2019. **e** 2018. **f** Including taxes less subsidies on production and imports. **g** Excludes repair of motor vehicles and motorcycles, personal and household goods. **h** Estimate. **i** Index base: 2015=100. **j** 2016. **k** Data refers to a 5-year period preceding the reference year. **l** Refers to foreign citizens. **m** Data as at the end of December. **n** 321,500 Vietnamese refugees are well integrated and receive protection from the Government of China. **o** Data revision. **p** Data are as at 1 January of reporting year. **q** Population aged 6 years and over. **r** Data refer to permanent residents. **s** Users in the last 6 months

Region	Eastern Asia	
Surface area (km2)	1 106[a]	
Sex ratio (m per 100 f)	84.8	
National currency	Hong Kong Dollar (HKD)	
Exchange rate (per US$)	7.8[c]	

Population (000, 2020)	7 497
Pop. density (per km2, 2020)	7 140.0
Capital city	Hong Kong
Capital city pop. (000, 2020)	7 490.8[b,c]

Economic indicators

	2010	2015	2020
GDP: Gross domestic product (million current US$)	228 639	309 386	362 682[d]
GDP growth rate (annual %, const. 2015 prices)	6.8	2.4	3.0[d]
GDP per capita (current US$)	32 820.5	43 054.0	49 199.0[d]
Economy: Agriculture (% of Gross Value Added)[e,f,g]	0.1	0.1	0.1[d]
Economy: Industry (% of Gross Value Added)[f,g,h]	7.0	7.3	7.3[d]
Economy: Services and other activity (% of GVA)[g,i,j]	93.0	92.7	92.6[d]
Employment in agriculture (% of employed)[k]	0.2	0.2	0.2
Employment in industry (% of employed)[k]	12.8	12.0	11.5
Employment in services & other sectors (% employed)[k]	87.0	87.8	88.3
Unemployment rate (% of labour force)[k]	4.3	3.3	4.3
Labour force participation rate (female/male pop. %)[k]	51.4 / 68.1	54.3 / 68.5	53.7 / 67.0
CPI: Consumer Price Index (2010=100)	100	123	135[c]
Agricultural production index (2004-2006=100)	55	59	59[l]
International trade: exports (million current US$)	400 692	510 553	535 711[c]
International trade: imports (million current US$)	441 369	559 306	578 590[c]
International trade: balance (million current US$)	- 40 677	- 48 753	- 42 879[c]
Balance of payments, current account (million US$)	16 012	10 264	22 740[c]

Major trading partners

					2019
Export partners (% of exports)	China	55.3	United States	7.3	India	2.9
Import partners (% of imports)	China	45.7	Other Asia, nes	7.3	Singapore	6.5

Social indicators

	2010	2015	2020
Population growth rate (average annual %)[m]	0.6	0.6	0.8
Urban population (% of total population)	100.0	100.0	100.0[c]
Urban population growth rate (average annual %)[m]	0.6	0.6	...
Fertility rate, total (live births per woman)[m]	1.0	1.2	1.3
Life expectancy at birth (females/males, years)[m]	85.5 / 79.5	86.4 / 80.5	87.5 / 81.8
Population age distribution (0-14/60+ years old, %)	11.9 / 18.4	11.2 / 21.8	12.7 / 26.1
International migrant stock (000/% of total pop.)	2 780.0 / 39.9	2 838.7 / 39.5	2 942.3 / 39.6[c]
Refugees and others of concern to the UNHCR (000)	0.6[n]	10.1	0.1[c]
Infant mortality rate (per 1 000 live births)[m]	1.9	1.6	1.3
Education: Government expenditure (% of GDP)	3.5	3.3	3.3[d]
Education: Primary gross enrol. ratio (f/m per 100 pop.)	... / ...	111.2 / 109.3	111.2 / 106.4[d]
Education: Secondary gross enrol. ratio (f/m per 100 pop.)	88.2 / 87.9	101.4 / 103.1	105.8 / 109.1[d]
Education: Tertiary gross enrol. ratio (f/m per 100 pop.)	59.5 / 59.7[k]	74.0 / 65.2	81.1 / 72.9[d]
Intentional homicide rate (per 100 000 pop.)	0.5	0.3	0.7[d]

Environment and infrastructure indicators

	2010	2015	2020
Individuals using the Internet (per 100 inhabitants)	72.0[o]	84.9[o]	90.5[d]
Research & Development expenditure (% of GDP)	0.7	0.8	0.9[d]
Threatened species (number)	49	60	83
CO2 emission estimates (million tons/tons per capita)	42.0 / 6.0	43.9 / 6.0	44.0 / 6.0[a]
Energy supply per capita (Gigajoules)	77	79	80[a]
Tourist/visitor arrivals at national borders (000)	20 085	26 686	29 263[d]
Important sites for terrestrial biodiversity protected (%)	48.9	48.9	48.9[c]
Pop. using safely managed drinking water (urban/rural, %)	97.2 / ...	100.0 / ...	100.0 / ...[a]
Pop. using safely managed sanitation (urban/rural %)	91.9 / ...	91.8 / ...	91.8 / ...[a]

2017. **b** Consists of the population of Hong Kong Island, New Kowloon the new towns in New Territories and the marine areas. **c** 2019. **d** 2018. **e** Excluding hunting and forestry. **f** Excluding mining and quarrying. **g** Data classified according to ISIC Rev. 4. **h** Includes waste management. **i** Excludes repair of motor vehicles and motorcycles, personal and household goods. **j** Excluding waste management. **k** Estimate. **l** 2016. **m** Data refers to a 5-year period preceding the reference year. **n** Data as at the end of December. **o** Population aged 10 years and over.

China, Macao SAR

Region	Eastern Asia	Population (000, 2020)	649
Surface area (km2)	30 [a,b]	Pop. density (per km2, 2020)	21 716.9
Sex ratio (m per 100 f)	92.5	Capital city	Macao
National currency	Pataca (MOP)	Capital city pop. (000, 2020)	642.1 [c]
Exchange rate (per US$)	8.0 [c]		

Economic indicators

	2010	2015	2020
GDP: Gross domestic product (million current US$)	28 124	45 362	54 545 [d]
GDP growth rate (annual %, const. 2015 prices)	25.3	- 21.6	4.7 [d]
GDP per capita (current US$)	52 253.0	75 341.4	86 355.3 [d]
Economy: Industry (% of Gross Value Added) [e,f]	7.4	10.5	8.8 [d]
Economy: Services and other activity (% of GVA)	92.6	89.5	91.2 [d]
Employment in agriculture (% of employed)	0.4	0.4	0.4 [g]
Employment in industry (% of employed)	13.7	15.8	9.5 [g]
Employment in services & other sectors (% of employed)	85.9	83.8	90.1 [g]
Unemployment rate (% of labour force) [g]	2.8	1.8	2.5
Labour force participation rate (female/male pop. %) [g]	65.3 / 76.9	66.6 / 77.2	64.6 / 76.2
CPI: Consumer Price Index (2010=100)	100	131 [h]	144 [h,c]
Agricultural production index (2004-2006=100)	95	89	90 [i]
International trade: exports (million current US$)	870	1 339	1 024 [c]
International trade: imports (million current US$)	5 629	10 603	12 024 [c]
International trade: balance (million current US$)	- 4 760	- 9 264	- 11 000 [c]
Balance of payments, current account (million US$)	11 089	11 484	19 060 [d]

Major trading partners

						2019
Export partners (% of exports)	China, Hong Kong SAR	84.8	China	10.4	United States	1.6
Import partners (% of imports)	China	33.1	Italy	10.2	France	10.0

Social indicators

	2010	2015	2020
Population growth rate (average annual %) [j]	2.2	2.2	1.5
Urban population (% of total population)	100.0	100.0	100.0 [c]
Urban population growth rate (average annual %) [j]	2.1	2.3	...
Fertility rate, total (live births per woman) [j]	1.0	1.2	1.2
Life expectancy at birth (females/males, years) [j]	84.9 / 79.1	86.2 / 80.3	87.0 / 81.1
Population age distribution (0-14/60+ years old, %)	13.0 / 10.9	12.6 / 14.4	14.4 / 18.9
International migrant stock (000/% of total pop.)	318.5 / 59.2	376.1 / 62.5	399.6 / 62.4 [c]
Refugees and others of concern to the UNHCR (000)	~0.0 [k]	~0.0	~0.0 [c]
Infant mortality rate (per 1 000 live births) [j]	3.8	3.1	2.6
Education: Government expenditure (% of GDP)	2.6	3.0	2.7 [b]
Education: Primary gross enrol. ratio (f/m per 100 pop.)	94.0 / 95.8	98.5 / 100.1	100.1 / 100.7 [d]
Education: Secondary gross enrol. ratio (f/m per 100 pop.)	86.4 / 89.2	93.8 / 95.2	100.9 / 101.2 [d]
Education: Tertiary gross enrol. ratio (f/m per 100 pop.)	54.1 / 56.1	80.8 / 62.1	104.5 / 77.4 [d]
Intentional homicide rate (per 100 000 pop.)	0.4	0.2	0.3 [d]

Environment and infrastructure indicators

	2010	2015	2020
Individuals using the Internet (per 100 inhabitants)	55.2 [l]	77.6 [l]	83.8 [d]
Research & Development expenditure (% of GDP) [m]	0.1	0.1	0.2 [d]
Threatened species (number)	9	11	26
Energy production, primary (Petajoules) [g]	4	5	6 [b]
Energy supply per capita (Gigajoules)	60	74	78 [b]
Tourist/visitor arrivals at national borders (000) [n]	11 926	14 308	18 493 [d]
Important sites for terrestrial biodiversity protected (%)	0.0	0.0	0.0 [c]
Pop. using safely managed drinking water (urban/rural, %)	100.0 / ...	100.0 / ...	100.0 / ... [b]

a Inland waters include the reservoirs. b 2017. c 2019. d 2018. e Excluding mining and quarrying. f Includes waste management. g Estimate. h Calculated by the UN Statistics Division from national indices. i 2016. j Data refers to a 5-year period preceding the reference year. k Data as at the end of December. l Population aged 3 years and over. m Partial data. n Does not include other non-residents namely workers, students, etc.

Colombia

Region	South America	UN membership date	05 November 1945
Population (000, 2020)	50 883	Surface area (km2)	1 141 748[a]
Pop. density (per km2, 2020)	45.9	Sex ratio (m per 100 f)	96.5
Capital city	Bogota	National currency	Colombian Peso (COP)
Capital city pop. (000, 2020)	10 779.4[b,c]	Exchange rate (per US$)	3 294.0[c]

Economic indicators

	2010	2015	2020
GDP: Gross domestic product (million current US$)	286 104	293 482	330 228[d]
GDP growth rate (annual %, const. 2015 prices)	4.3	3.0	2.7[d]
GDP per capita (current US$)	6 326.5	6 175.9	6 649.6[d]
Economy: Agriculture (% of Gross Value Added)	7.0	6.6	6.9[d]
Economy: Industry (% of Gross Value Added)[e]	34.3	31.5	29.3[d]
Economy: Services and other activity (% of GVA)[f,g]	58.7	61.9	63.8[d]
Employment in agriculture (% of employed)	18.4	16.0	16.5[h]
Employment in industry (% of employed)	20.0	19.8	20.0[h]
Employment in services & other sectors (% employed)	61.6	64.2	63.5[h]
Unemployment rate (% of labour force)[h]	11.0	8.3	9.7
Labour force participation rate (female/male pop. %)[h]	55.7 / 81.6	58.5 / 82.0	57.5 / 81.0
CPI: Consumer Price Index (2010=100)[i]	100	118	141[c]
Agricultural production index (2004-2006=100)	100	119	115[j]
International trade: exports (million current US$)	39 820	35 691	39 489[c]
International trade: imports (million current US$)	40 683	54 036	52 696[c]
International trade: balance (million current US$)	- 863	- 18 345	- 13 207[c]
Balance of payments, current account (million US$)	- 8 732	- 18 564	- 13 800[c]

Major trading partners

						2019
Export partners (% of exports)	United States	31.1	China	11.6	Panama	6.0
Import partners (% of imports)	United States	25.4	China	20.8	Mexico	7.4

Social indicators

	2010	2015	2020
Population growth rate (average annual %)[k]	1.2	1.0	1.4
Urban population (% of total population)	78.0	79.8	81.1[c]
Urban population growth rate (average annual %)[k]	1.7	1.4	...
Fertility rate, total (live births per woman)[k]	2.1	1.9	1.8
Life expectancy at birth (females/males, years)[k]	77.9 / 71.7	78.9 / 73.1	79.8 / 74.2
Population age distribution (0-14/60+ years old, %)	27.3 / 9.7	24.5 / 11.5	22.2 / 13.2
International migrant stock (000/% of total pop.)	124.3 / 0.3	139.1 / 0.3	1 142.3 / 2.3[c]
Refugees and others of concern to the UNHCR (000)	3 672.4[l]	6 520.6	9 717.2[m,c]
Infant mortality rate (per 1 000 live births)[k]	16.9	14.4	12.6
Health: Current expenditure (% of GDP)[n]	7.1	7.3	7.2[a]
Health: Physicians (per 1 000 pop.)	1.6	2.0	2.2[d]
Education: Government expenditure (% of GDP)	4.8	4.5	4.5[a]
Education: Primary gross enrol. ratio (f/m per 100 pop.)	119.3 / 121.3	113.4 / 117.0	112.8 / 116.2[d]
Education: Secondary gross enrol. ratio (f/m per 100 pop.)	102.3 / 93.0	98.1 / 91.5	100.1 / 95.0[d]
Education: Tertiary gross enrol. ratio (f/m per 100 pop.)	41.3 / 37.5	57.4 / 49.3	59.7 / 51.1[d]
Intentional homicide rate (per 100 000 pop.)	34.2	26.9	25.3[d]
Seats held by women in the National Parliament (%)	8.4	19.9	18.3[o]

Environment and infrastructure indicators

	2010	2015	2020
Individuals using the Internet (per 100 inhabitants)	36.5[p]	55.9[p]	64.1[d]
Research & Development expenditure (% of GDP)	0.2	0.3	0.2[d]
Threatened species (number)	681	751	1 025
Forested area (% of land area)	52.8	52.7	52.7[h,a]
CO2 emission estimates (million tons/tons per capita)	60.2 / 1.3	77.6 / 1.6	75.3 / 1.5[a]
Energy production, primary (Petajoules)	4 486	5 367	5 171[a]
Energy supply per capita (Gigajoules)	31	32	34[a]
Tourist/visitor arrivals at national borders (000)	1 405	2 980	3 904[d]
Important sites for terrestrial biodiversity protected (%)	33.0	40.2	42.9[c]
Pop. using safely managed drinking water (urban/rural, %)	81.3 / 37.1	81.3 / 39.2	81.3 / 40.1[a]
Pop. using safely managed sanitation (urban/rural, %)	14.9 / ...	15.6 / ...	15.8 / ...[a]
Net Official Development Assist. received (% of GNI)	0.24	0.47	0.56[d]

2017. **b** Refers to the nuclei of Santa Fe de Bogotá, Soacha, Chia and Funza. **c** 2019. **d** 2018. **e** Excludes publishing activities. Includes irrigation and canals. **f** Excludes repair of personal and household goods. **g** Excludes computer and related activities and radio/TV activities. **h** Estimate. **i** Calculated by the UN Statistics Division from national indices. **j** 2016. **k** Data refers to a 5-year period preceding the reference year. **l** Data as at the end of December. **m** Figure of others of concern is provided by the Government of Colombia. **n** Data revision. **o** Data are as 1 January of reporting year. **p** Population aged 5 years and over.

Comoros

Region	Eastern Africa	UN membership date	12 November 1975
Population (000, 2020)	870	Surface area (km2)	2 235[a]
Pop. density (per km2, 2020)	467.3	Sex ratio (m per 100 f)	101.8
Capital city	Moroni	National currency	Comorian Franc (KMF)
Capital city pop. (000, 2020)	62.4[b]	Exchange rate (per US$)	437.9[c]

Economic indicators

	2010	2015	2020
GDP: Gross domestic product (million current US$)	907	988	1 166[b]
GDP growth rate (annual %, const. 2015 prices)	4.8	2.0	3.0[b]
GDP per capita (current US$)	1 315.2	1 271.1	1 400.5[b]
Economy: Agriculture (% of Gross Value Added)	31.6	31.1	31.5[b]
Economy: Industry (% of Gross Value Added)	12.2	11.8	12.4[b]
Economy: Services and other activity (% of GVA)	56.1	57.1	56.1[b]
Employment in agriculture (% of employed)[d]	53.7	51.8	49.9
Employment in industry (% of employed)[d]	13.7	13.4	13.0
Employment in services & other sectors (% employed)[d]	32.6	34.8	37.0
Unemployment rate (% of labour force)[d]	4.6	4.5	4.4
Labour force participation rate (female/male pop. %)[d]	34.5 / 49.7	35.7 / 49.8	36.8 / 50.0
CPI: Consumer Price Index (2010=100)	100	104[e]	...
Agricultural production index (2004-2006=100)	106	109	109[f]
International trade: exports (million current US$)	14	15	49[c]
International trade: imports (million current US$)	181	173	201[c]
International trade: balance (million current US$)	- 167	- 158	- 152[c]
Balance of payments, current account (million US$)	- 39	- 2	- 28[b]

Major trading partners

					2019
Export partners (% of exports)	France	45.8	India	18.9	Germany	10.0
Import partners (% of imports)	United Arab Emirates	21.7	France	15.2	Pakistan	15.1

Social indicators

	2010	2015	2020
Population growth rate (average annual %)[g]	2.4	2.4	2.2
Urban population (% of total population)	28.0	28.5	29.2[c]
Urban population growth rate (average annual %)[g]	2.5	2.7	...
Fertility rate, total (live births per woman)[g]	4.9	4.6	4.2
Life expectancy at birth (females/males, years)[g]	62.5 / 59.3	64.5 / 61.2	65.8 / 62.3
Population age distribution (0-14/60+ years old, %)	41.0 / 4.5	40.1 / 4.7	39.0 / 5.1
International migrant stock (000/% of total pop.)	12.6 / 1.8	12.6 / 1.6	12.5 / 1.5[c]
Refugees and others of concern to the UNHCR (000)	~0.0[h,i]	...	...
Infant mortality rate (per 1 000 live births)[g]	66.6	58.1	53.1
Health: Current expenditure (% of GDP)[j]	8.5	7.8	7.4[a]
Health: Physicians (per 1 000 pop.)	0.2[k]	0.2[l]	0.3[f]
Education: Government expenditure (% of GDP)	4.4[m]	2.5	...
Education: Primary gross enrol. ratio (f/m per 100 pop.)	104.1 / 113.0[m]	101.2 / 108.6[n]	99.4 / 99.6[b]
Education: Secondary gross enrol. ratio (f/m per 100 pop.)	... / ...	63.1 / 59.1[n]	61.4 / 57.6[b]
Education: Tertiary gross enrol. ratio (f/m per 100 pop.)	4.9 / 6.6	8.0 / 9.9[n]	... / ...
Seats held by women in the National Parliament (%)	3.0	3.0[n]	6.1[o]

Environment and infrastructure indicators

	2010	2015	2020
Individuals using the Internet (per 100 inhabitants)[d]	5.1	7.5	8.5[a]
Threatened species (number)	89	106	127
Forested area (% of land area)[d]	21.0	19.9	19.9[a]
Energy production, primary (Petajoules)	2	3	3[a]
Energy supply per capita (Gigajoules)	7[d]	7	8[d,a]
Tourist/visitor arrivals at national borders (000)[p]	15	24	36[b]
Important sites for terrestrial biodiversity protected (%)	8.3	8.3	8.3[c]
Net Official Development Assist. received (% of GNI)	7.72	6.63	7.82[b]

a 2017. b 2018. c 2019. d Estimate. e 2013. f 2016. g Data refers to a 5-year period preceding the reference year. h Data as at the end of December. i 2005. j Data revision. k 2009. l 2012. m 2008. n 2014. o Data are as at 1 January of reporting year. p Arrivals by air.

Congo

Region	Middle Africa	UN membership date	20 September 1960
Population (000, 2020)	5 518	Surface area (km2)	342 000[a]
Pop. density (per km2, 2020)	16.2	Sex ratio (m per 100 f)	99.8
Capital city	Brazzaville	National currency	CFA Franc, BEAC (XAF)[b]
Capital city pop. (000, 2020)	2 308.1[c]	Exchange rate (per US$)	583.9[c]

Economic indicators	2010	2015	2020
GDP: Gross domestic product (million current US$)	13 678	11 092	14 173[d]
GDP growth rate (annual %, const. 2015 prices)	15.0	- 13.2	1.0[d]
GDP per capita (current US$)	3 200.5	2 284.0	2 702.6[d]
Economy: Agriculture (% of Gross Value Added)	4.1	7.6	10.3[d]
Economy: Industry (% of Gross Value Added)	68.4	48.1	41.5[d]
Economy: Services and other activity (% of GVA)	27.6	44.4	48.1[d]
Employment in agriculture (% of employed)[e]	37.4	35.0	33.8
Employment in industry (% of employed)[e]	23.3	23.0	21.7
Employment in services & other sectors (% employed)[e]	39.2	42.0	44.5
Unemployment rate (% of labour force)[e]	14.0	9.9	9.3
Labour force participation rate (female/male pop. %)[e]	67.7 / 71.5	67.7 / 71.9	67.4 / 71.2
CPI: Consumer Price Index (2010=100)[e,f]	100	116	121[a]
Agricultural production index (2004-2006=100)	122	135	138[g]
International trade: exports (million current US$)	6 918	8 623	5 576[c]
International trade: imports (million current US$)	4 369	10 550	2 242[c]
International trade: balance (million current US$)	2 548	- 1 927	3 334[c]
Balance of payments, current account (million US$)	900	- 4 629	- 3 594[g]

Major trading partners						2019
Export partners (% of exports)	China	59.8	India	13.2	Netherlands	4.1
Import partners (% of imports)	France	15.0	China	11.4	Belgium	10.3

Social indicators	2010	2015	2020
Population growth rate (average annual %)[h]	3.3	2.6	2.6
Urban population (% of total population)	63.3	65.5	67.4[c]
Urban population growth rate (average annual %)[h]	4.0	3.3	...
Fertility rate, total (live births per woman)[h]	4.8	4.7	4.4
Life expectancy at birth (females/males, years)[h]	59.2 / 57.0	62.7 / 60.5	65.6 / 62.7
Population age distribution (0-14/60+ years old, %)	41.6 / 4.0	42.2 / 4.2	41.3 / 4.5
International migrant stock (000/% of total pop.)	425.2 / 9.9	390.1 / 8.0	402.1 / 7.5[c]
Refugees and others of concern to the UNHCR (000)	138.7[i]	65.8	189.8[c]
Infant mortality rate (per 1 000 live births)[h]	52.5	41.4	35.3
Health: Current expenditure (% of GDP)	2.0	3.4	2.9[a]
Health: Physicians (per 1 000 pop.)	0.1	0.2[j]	...
Education: Government expenditure (% of GDP)	6.2	4.6[e]	...
Education: Primary gross enrol. ratio (f/m per 100 pop.)	106.1 / 112.2	110.5 / 102.8[k]	... / ...
Education: Secondary gross enrol. ratio (f/m per 100 pop.)	... / ...	48.8 / 56.3[k]	... / ...
Education: Tertiary gross enrol. ratio (f/m per 100 pop.)	2.2 / 10.3[l]	8.0 / 10.6[m]	10.1 / 15.2[a]
Seats held by women in the National Parliament (%)	7.3	7.4	11.3[n]

Environment and infrastructure indicators	2010	2015	2020
Individuals using the Internet (per 100 inhabitants)[e]	5.0	7.6	8.6[a]
Threatened species (number)	103	119	155
Forested area (% of land area)[e]	65.6	65.4	65.4[a]
CO2 emission estimates (million tons/tons per capita)	1.8 / 0.4	3.2 / 0.6	2.8 / 0.5[a]
Energy production, primary (Petajoules)	724	609	686[a]
Energy supply per capita (Gigajoules)	16	24	24[a]
Tourist/visitor arrivals at national borders (000)[o]	194	220	156[c]
Important sites for terrestrial biodiversity protected (%)	49.0	53.8	56.5[c]
Pop. using safely managed drinking water (urban/rural, %)	55.4 / 12.4	58.5 / 17.0	58.6 / 19.1[a]
Net Official Development Assist. received (% of GNI)	14.57	1.05	1.45[d]

a 2017. b African Financial Community (CFA) Franc, Bank of Central African States (BEAC). c 2019. d 2018. e estimate. f Brazzaville g 2016. h Data refers to a 5-year period preceding the reference year. i Data as at the end of December. j 2011. k 2012. l 2009. m 2013. n Data are as at 1 January of reporting year. o Including nationals residing abroad.

Cook Islands

Region	Polynesia	Population (000, 2020)	18
Surface area (km2)	236 [a]	Pop. density (per km2, 2020)	73.0
Sex ratio (m per 100 f)	97.4 [b,c]	Capital city	Avarua
National currency	New Zealand Dollar (NZD)	Capital city pop. (000, 2020)	13.1 [d,e]
Exchange rate (per US$)	1.5 [f]		

Economic indicators	2010	2015	2020
GDP: Gross domestic product (million current US$)	241	302	363 [e]
GDP growth rate (annual %, const. 2015 prices)	- 4.9	5.7	5.7 [e]
GDP per capita (current US$)	13 092.7	17 182.6	20 705.2 [e]
Economy: Agriculture (% of Gross Value Added) [g]	3.4	3.2	3.1 [e]
Economy: Industry (% of Gross Value Added) [g,h]	7.9	11.3	7.8 [e]
Economy: Services and other activity (% of GVA) [g,i,j]	88.7	85.4	89.1 [e]
Employment in agriculture (% of employed)	...	4.3 [k,l]	...
Employment in industry (% of employed)	...	11.7 [k,l]	...
Employment in services & other sectors (% employed)	...	84.0 [k,l]	...
Unemployment rate (% of labour force) [k]	6.9 [b,m]	8.2 [l]	...
Labour force participation rate (female/male pop. %)	64.2 / 76.1 [b,k,m]	65.4 / 76.6 [k,l]	... / ...
CPI: Consumer Price Index (2010=100) [n,o]	100	112	111 [e]
Agricultural production index (2004-2006=100)	94	93	91 [c]
International trade: exports (million current US$)	5	14 [p]	6 [p,f]
International trade: imports (million current US$)	91	109 [p]	123 [p,f]
International trade: balance (million current US$)	- 85	- 95 [p]	- 117 [p,f]

Major trading partners						2019
Export partners (% of exports) [p]	Japan	36.2	Thailand	19.9	France	15.9
Import partners (% of imports) [p]	New Zealand	48.5	Italy	14.3	Fiji	9.6

Social indicators	2010	2015	2020
Population growth rate (average annual %)	- 1.2 [q]	- 1.2 [q]	0.1
Urban population (% of total population)	73.3	74.4	75.3 [f]
Urban population growth rate (average annual %) [q]	- 0.6	- 0.9	...
Fertility rate, total (live births per woman)	...	2.6 [l]	...
Life expectancy at birth (females/males, years)	76.2 / 69.5 [m]	79.6 / 71.7 [b,r,s]	... / ...
Population age distribution (0-14/60+ years old, %)	26.1 / 11.9 [t,m]	26.0 / 13.4 [l]	26.9 / 14.2 [b,c]
International migrant stock (000/% of total pop.)	3.8 / 20.5	3.5 / 19.8	3.5 / 19.9 [f]
Infant mortality rate (per 1 000 live births)	...	3.6 [r,s]	...
Health: Current expenditure (% of GDP) [u]	3.5	2.9	3.3 [a]
Health: Physicians (per 1 000 pop.)	1.3 [v]	1.4 [w]	...
Education: Government expenditure (% of GDP)	...	3.9	4.7 [c]
Education: Primary gross enrol. ratio (f/m per 100 pop.)	85.4 / 89.8	99.8 / 104.2	107.5 / 109.5 [c]
Education: Secondary gross enrol. ratio (f/m per 100 pop.)	86.4 / 78.3	90.6 / 85.4	88.6 / 84.8 [c]
Education: Tertiary gross enrol. ratio (f/m per 100 pop.)	... / ...	42.7 / 35.8 [x]	... / ...
Intentional homicide rate (per 100 000 pop.)	...	3.5 [x]	...

Environment and infrastructure indicators	2010	2015	2020
Threatened species (number)	53	73	77
Forested area (% of land area)	62.9	62.9	62.9 [p,a]
Energy production, primary (Petajoules) [p]	...	0	0 [a]
Energy supply per capita (Gigajoules) [p]	39	49	56 [a]
Tourist/visitor arrivals at national borders (000)	104	125	169 [e]
Important sites for terrestrial biodiversity protected (%)	0.0	0.0	5.7 [f]

a 2017. b Break in the time series. c 2016. d Refers to the island of Rarotonga. e 2018. f 2019. g At producers' prices. h Excludes publishing activities. Includes irrigation and canals. i Excludes computer and related activities and radio/TV activities. j Excludes repair of personal and household goods. k Resident population (de jure). l 2011. m 2006. n Calculated by the UN Statistics Division from national indices. o Rarotonga p Estimate. q Data refers to a 5-year period preceding the reference year. r Data refers to a 5-year period up to and including the reference year. s 2013. t Provisional data. u Data refer to fiscal years beginning 1 July. v 2009. w 2014. x 2012.

Costa Rica

Region	Central America	UN membership date	02 November 1945
Population (000, 2020)	5 094	Surface area (km2)	51 100[a]
Pop. density (per km2, 2020)	99.8	Sex ratio (m per 100 f)	99.8
Capital city	San José	National currency	Costa Rican Colon (CRC)
Capital city pop. (000, 2020)	1 378.5[b,c]	Exchange rate (per US$)	573.3[c]

Economic indicators

	2010	2015	2020
GDP: Gross domestic product (million current US$)	37 269	54 776	60 126[d]
GDP growth rate (annual %, const. 2015 prices)	5.0	3.6	2.7[d]
GDP per capita (current US$)	8 141.9	11 299.1	12 026.5[d]
Economy: Agriculture (% of Gross Value Added)[e]	7.2	5.4	5.0[d]
Economy: Industry (% of Gross Value Added)[e,f]	25.4	21.2	21.1[d]
Economy: Services and other activity (% of GVA)[e,g,h]	67.4	73.4	73.9[d]
Employment in agriculture (% of employed)	11.4[i]	12.3	11.9[i]
Employment in industry (% of employed)	20.0[i]	19.2	19.8[i]
Employment in services & other sectors (% employed)	68.6[i]	68.5	68.3[i]
Unemployment rate (% of labour force)[i]	7.2	9.0	12.7
Labour force participation rate (female/male pop. %)[i]	45.3 / 76.5	48.4 / 75.6	48.2 / 75.9
CPI: Consumer Price Index (2010=100)[j,k]	100	122	129[c]
Agricultural production index (2004-2006=100)	113	125	129[i]
International trade: exports (million current US$)	9 045	9 578	11 449[i,c]
International trade: imports (million current US$)	13 920	15 504	16 106[i,c]
International trade: balance (million current US$)	- 4 875	- 5 926	- 4 656[i,c]
Balance of payments, current account (million US$)	- 1 214	- 1 921	- 1 545[c]

Major trading partners

						2019
Export partners (% of exports)[i]	United States	41.1	Netherlands	6.0	Belgium	6.0
Import partners (% of imports)[i]	United States	39.1	China	13.7	Mexico	7.0

Social indicators

	2010	2015	2020
Population growth rate (average annual %)[m]	1.3	1.1	1.0
Urban population (% of total population)	71.7	76.9	80.1[c]
Urban population growth rate (average annual %)[m]	3.1	2.5	...
Fertility rate, total (live births per woman)[m]	1.9	1.9	1.8
Life expectancy at birth (females/males, years)[m]	80.8 / 76.1	81.7 / 76.7	82.7 / 77.4
Population age distribution (0-14/60+ years old, %)	24.3 / 10.8	22.1 / 12.6	20.8 / 15.0
International migrant stock (000/% of total pop.)[n]	405.4 / 8.9	411.7 / 8.5	417.8 / 8.3[c]
Refugees and others of concern to the UNHCR (000)	19.9[o]	7.9	79.2[c]
Infant mortality rate (per 1 000 live births)[m]	10.0	9.3	7.3
Health: Current expenditure (% of GDP)	8.1	7.8	7.3[a]
Health: Physicians (per 1 000 pop.)	2.3	1.4	2.9[d]
Education: Government expenditure (% of GDP)	6.6	7.1	7.4[a]
Education: Primary gross enrol. ratio (f/m per 100 pop.)	115.7 / 118.0	111.0 / 111.6	113.8 / 112.8[d]
Education: Secondary gross enrol. ratio (f/m per 100 pop.)	103.2 / 99.0	125.3 / 120.4	137.7 / 128.1[d]
Education: Tertiary gross enrol. ratio (f/m per 100 pop.)	... / ...	60.3 / 46.1	60.7 / 50.0[d]
Intentional homicide rate (per 100 000 pop.)	11.5	11.5	11.3[d]
Seats held by women in the National Parliament (%)	36.8	33.3	45.6[p]

Environment and infrastructure indicators

	2010	2015	2020
Individuals using the Internet (per 100 inhabitants)	36.5[q,r]	59.8[q,r]	74.1[d]
Research & Development expenditure (% of GDP)	0.5	0.4	0.4[a]
Threatened species (number)	285	323	363
Forested area (% of land area)[i]	51.0	54.0	54.0[a]
CO2 emission estimates (million tons/tons per capita)	6.6 / 1.5	6.9 / 1.4	7.6 / 1.5[a]
Energy production, primary (Petajoules)	104	110	102[a]
Energy supply per capita (Gigajoules)	45	43	43[a]
Tourist/visitor arrivals at national borders (000)	2 100	2 660	3 017[d]
Important sites for terrestrial biodiversity protected (%)	39.7	39.8	39.8[c]
Pop. using safely managed drinking water (urban/rural, %)	96.1 / 80.4	96.4 / 83.8	96.4 / 84.4[a]
Net Official Development Assist. received (% of GNI)	0.28	0.21	0.17[d]

2017. **b** Refers to the urban population of cantons. **c** 2019. **d** 2018. **e** Data classified according to ISIC Rev. 4. **f** Excludes publishing activities. Includes irrigation and canals. **g** Excludes computer and related activities and radio/TV activities. **h** Excludes repair of personal and household goods. **i** Estimate. **j** Calculated by the UN Statistics Division from national indices. **k** Central area. **l** 2016. **m** Data refers to a 5-year period preceding the reference year. **n** Including refugees. **o** Data as at the end of December. **p** Data are as at 1 January of reporting year. **q** Users in the last 3 months. **r** Population aged 5 years and over.

Côte d'Ivoire

Region	Western Africa	UN membership date	20 September 1960
Population (000, 2020)	26 378	Surface area (km2)	322 463[a]
Pop. density (per km2, 2020)	83.0	Sex ratio (m per 100 f)	101.7
Capital city	Yamoussoukro[b]	National currency	CFA Franc, BCEAO (XOF)[c]
Capital city pop. (000, 2020)	231.1[d]	Exchange rate (per US$)	583.9[e]

Economic indicators	2010	2015	2020
GDP: Gross domestic product (million current US$)	24 885	33 119	43 028[d]
GDP growth rate (annual %, const. 2015 prices)	2.0	8.8	7.4[d]
GDP per capita (current US$)	1 211.9	1 426.0	1 716.4[d]
Economy: Agriculture (% of Gross Value Added)	26.0	24.9	21.7[d]
Economy: Industry (% of Gross Value Added)	23.8	28.2	27.7[d]
Economy: Services and other activity (% of GVA)	50.2	46.9	50.5[d]
Employment in agriculture (% of employed)[f]	47.3	43.6	39.3
Employment in industry (% of employed)[f]	11.4	12.1	13.4
Employment in services & other sectors (% employed)[f]	41.4	44.4	47.3
Unemployment rate (% of labour force)[f]	6.7	3.1	3.4
Labour force participation rate (female/male pop. %)[f]	47.8 / 72.1	47.8 / 67.2	48.3 / 65.4
CPI: Consumer Price Index (2010=100)[f,g]	100	111	112[e]
Agricultural production index (2004-2006=100)	107	129	127[h]
International trade: exports (million current US$)	10 284	12 560	12 718[e]
International trade: imports (million current US$)	7 849	10 406	10 483[e]
International trade: balance (million current US$)	2 434	2 154	2 235[e]
Balance of payments, current account (million US$)	465	- 201	- 2 077[d]

Major trading partners						2019
Export partners (% of exports)	Netherlands	10.7	United States	6.0	France	5.9
Import partners (% of imports)	China	17.2	Nigeria	13.5	France	10.7

Social indicators	2010	2015	2020
Population growth rate (average annual %)[i]	2.2	2.5	2.5
Urban population (% of total population)	47.3	49.4	51.2[e]
Urban population growth rate (average annual %)[i]	3.0	3.4	...
Fertility rate, total (live births per woman)[i]	5.2	5.0	4.7
Life expectancy at birth (females/males, years)[i]	53.0 / 50.0	55.9 / 53.5	58.6 / 56.1
Population age distribution (0-14/60+ years old, %)	43.6 / 4.5	42.6 / 4.6	41.5 / 4.7
International migrant stock (000/% of total pop.)[j]	2 366.5 / 11.5	2 468.0 / 10.6	2 549.1 / 9.9[e]
Refugees and others of concern to the UNHCR (000)	564.5[k]	726.8	692.8[l,e]
Infant mortality rate (per 1 000 live births)[i]	77.2	67.5	60.4
Health: Current expenditure (% of GDP)	6.1	4.4	4.5[a]
Health: Physicians (per 1 000 pop.)	0.1[m]	0.2[n]	...
Education: Government expenditure (% of GDP)	4.6	4.8[f]	5.1[a]
Education: Primary gross enrol. ratio (f/m per 100 pop.)	64.1 / 79.5[o]	84.9 / 96.4	96.0 / 103.6[d]
Education: Secondary gross enrol. ratio (f/m per 100 pop.)	... / ...	35.1 / 49.9	44.3 / 57.7[d]
Education: Tertiary gross enrol. ratio (f/m per 100 pop.)	5.2 / 10.2	6.9 / 10.7	7.6 / 11.1[a]
Seats held by women in the National Parliament (%)	8.9	9.2	12.0[p]

Environment and infrastructure indicators	2010	2015	2020
Individuals using the Internet (per 100 inhabitants)	2.7[f]	38.4	46.8[d]
Research & Development expenditure (% of GDP)	...	...	0.1[q,r,h]
Threatened species (number)	210	226	280
Forested area (% of land area)[f]	32.7	32.7	32.7[a]
CO2 emission estimates (million tons/tons per capita)	6.2 / 0.3	9.5 / 0.4	10.2 / 0.4[a]
Energy production, primary (Petajoules)	467	526	438[a]
Energy supply per capita (Gigajoules)	21	24	19[a]
Tourist/visitor arrivals at national borders (000)[s]	252	1 441[t,u]	1 965[d]
Important sites for terrestrial biodiversity protected (%)	69.2	71.2	71.2[e]
Pop. using safely managed drinking water (urban/rural, %)	56.0 / 17.0	55.4 / 17.5	55.1 / 17.7[a]
Net Official Development Assist. received (% of GNI)	3.53	2.03	2.31[d]

a 2017. b Yamoussoukro is the capital and Abidjan is the administrative capital. c African Financial Community (CFA) Franc, Central Bank of West African States (BCEAO). d 2018. e 2019. f Estimate. g Abidjan h 2016. i Data refers to a 5-year period preceding the reference year. j Refers to foreign citizens. k Data as at the end of December. l Statelessness figure based on a Government estimate; adjusted to reflect the special acquisition of nationality by declaration' procedure until mid of 2019. Does not include individuals of unknown parentage who were abandoned as children and are not considered as nationals under Ivorian law. m 2008. n 2014. o 2009. p Data are as at 1 January of reporting year. q Excluding business enterprise. r Partial data. s Arrivals to Félix Houphouët Boigny Airport only. t Figures include arrivals by land (road and railway). u Break in the time series.

Croatia

Region	Southern Europe	UN membership date	22 May 1992
Population (000, 2020)	4 105	Surface area (km2)	56 594 [a]
Pop. density (per km2, 2020)	73.4	Sex ratio (m per 100 f)	93.1
Capital city	Zagreb	National currency	Kuna (HRK)
Capital city pop. (000, 2020)	685.2 [b,c]	Exchange rate (per US$)	6.6 [c]

Economic indicators

	2010	2015	2020
GDP: Gross domestic product (million current US$)	59 808	49 531	60 991 [d]
GDP growth rate (annual %, const. 2015 prices)	- 1.5	2.4	2.7 [d]
GDP per capita (current US$)	13 818.3	11 701.4	14 674.0 [d]
Economy: Agriculture (% of Gross Value Added) [e]	4.4	3.6	3.5 [d]
Economy: Industry (% of Gross Value Added) [e,f]	26.1	25.8	24.8 [d]
Economy: Services and other activity (% of GVA) [e,g,h]	69.5	70.6	71.7 [d]
Employment in agriculture (% of employed)	14.3	9.2	5.8 [i]
Employment in industry (% of employed)	27.5	26.7	27.5 [i]
Employment in services & other sectors (% employed)	58.3	64.1	66.8 [i]
Unemployment rate (% of labour force) [i]	11.6	16.2	7.1
Labour force participation rate (female/male pop. %) [i]	46.2 / 59.8	46.6 / 59.2	45.3 / 57.2
CPI: Consumer Price Index (2010=100)	100	107	110 [c]
Agricultural production index (2004-2006=100)	111	110	121 [j]
International trade: exports (million current US$)	11 811	12 844	17 063 [c]
International trade: imports (million current US$)	20 067	20 580	28 004 [c]
International trade: balance (million current US$)	- 8 256	- 7 737	- 10 941 [c]
Balance of payments, current account (million US$)	- 1 485	1 595	1 456 [c]

Major trading partners

						2019
Export partners (% of exports)	Italy	14.0	Germany	13.2	Slovenia	10.8
Import partners (% of imports)	Germany	15.5	Italy	13.9	Slovenia	11.5

Social indicators

	2010	2015	2020
Population growth rate (average annual %) [k]	- 0.2	- 0.4	- 0.6
Urban population (% of total population)	55.2	56.2	57.2 [c]
Urban population growth rate (average annual %) [k]	0.1	- 0.1	...
Fertility rate, total (live births per woman) [k]	1.5	1.5	1.4
Life expectancy at birth (females/males, years) [k]	79.5 / 72.6	80.6 / 74.2	81.4 / 75.0
Population age distribution (0-14/60+ years old, %)	15.4 / 23.8	14.5 / 26.3	14.5 / 28.3
International migrant stock (000/% of total pop.) [i]	573.2 / 13.2	561.1 / 13.3	518.1 / 12.5 [c]
Refugees and others of concern to the UNHCR (000)	25.5 [m]	17.5	8.3 [c]
Infant mortality rate (per 1 000 live births) [k]	5.8	4.3	4.0
Health: Current expenditure (% of GDP)	8.1	6.8 [n,o]	6.8 [o,a]
Health: Physicians (per 1 000 pop.)	2.8	3.2	3.0 [j]
Education: Government expenditure (% of GDP)	4.2	4.6 [p]	...
Education: Primary gross enrol. ratio (f/m per 100 pop.)	92.0 / 91.9	100.6 / 100.6	96.5 / 96.4 [a]
Education: Secondary gross enrol. ratio (f/m per 100 pop.)	103.4 / 96.6	101.0 / 96.5	101.8 / 97.1 [a]
Education: Tertiary gross enrol. ratio (f/m per 100 pop.)	62.1 / 46.3	76.7 / 56.7	78.8 / 57.4 [a]
Intentional homicide rate (per 100 000 pop.)	1.4	0.9	0.6 [d]
Seats held by women in the National Parliament (%)	23.5	25.8	19.2 [q]

Environment and infrastructure indicators

	2010	2015	2020
Individuals using the Internet (per 100 inhabitants)	56.6 [r]	69.8 [r]	75.3 [d]
Research & Development expenditure (% of GDP)	0.7	0.8	1.0 [s,d]
Threatened species (number)	101	159	212
Forested area (% of land area)	34.3	34.0	34.0 [i,a]
CO2 emission estimates (million tons/tons per capita)	18.2 / 4.1	15.5 / 3.7	16.2 / 3.9 [a]
Energy production, primary (Petajoules)	215	184	176 [a]
Energy supply per capita (Gigajoules)	90	83	87 [a]
Tourist/visitor arrivals at national borders (000) [t]	9 111	12 683	16 645 [d]
Important sites for terrestrial biodiversity protected (%)	24.4	76.5	76.5 [c]
Pop. using safely managed sanitation (urban/rural %)	64.2 / ...	64.2 / ...	64.3 / ... [a]
Net Official Development Assist. disbursed (% of GNI)	...	0.09	0.10 [a]
Net Official Development Assist. received (% of GNI)	0.23	...	...

2017. **b** Refers to the settlement of Zagreb. **c** 2019. **d** 2018. **e** Data classified according to ISIC Rev. 4. **f** Excludes publishing activities, includes irrigation and canals. **g** Excludes computer and related activities and radio/TV activities. Excludes repair of personal and household goods. **i** Estimate. **j** 2016. **k** Data refers to a 5-year period preceding the reference year. **l** Including refugees. **m** Data as at the end of December. **n** Break in the time series. **o** Data are based on SHA2011. **p** 2013. **q** Data are as at 1 January of reporting year. **r** Population aged 16 to 74 years. **s** Provisional data. **t** Excluding arrivals in ports of nautical tourism.

Cuba

Region	Caribbean	UN membership date	24 October 1945	
Population (000, 2020)	11 327	Surface area (km2)	109 884[a]	
Pop. density (per km2, 2020)	106.4	Sex ratio (m per 100 f)	98.6	
Capital city	Havana	National currency	Cuban Peso (CUP)[b]	
Capital city pop. (000, 2020)	2 138.4[c]	Exchange rate (per US$)	1.0[d,c]	

Economic indicators

	2010	2015	2020
GDP: Gross domestic product (million current US$)	64 328	87 206	100 023[e]
GDP growth rate (annual %, const. 2015 prices)	2.4	4.4	2.2[e]
GDP per capita (current US$)	5 730.4	7 700.4	8 821.8[e]
Economy: Agriculture (% of Gross Value Added)	3.7	3.9	3.8[e]
Economy: Industry (% of Gross Value Added)	23.1	22.6	25.2[e]
Economy: Services and other activity (% of GVA)	73.2	73.5	71.0[e]
Employment in agriculture (% of employed)	18.6	18.6[f]	17.3[f]
Employment in industry (% of employed)	17.1	17.1[f]	16.8[f]
Employment in services & other sectors (% employed)	64.3	64.3[f]	65.9[f]
Unemployment rate (% of labour force)[f]	2.5	2.4	1.6
Labour force participation rate (female/male pop. %)[f]	42.0 / 68.4	41.6 / 67.1	40.5 / 66.7
Agricultural production index (2004-2006=100)	88	100	103[g]
International trade: exports (million current US$)[f]	4 914	3 618	828[c]
International trade: imports (million current US$)[f]	11 488	12 638	7 498[c]
International trade: balance (million current US$)[f]	- 6 574	- 9 020	- 6 670[c]

Major trading partners

						2019
Export partners (% of exports)[f]	China	28.0	Canada	25.8	Spain	7.9
Import partners (% of imports)[f]	China	17.4	Spain	16.4	Mexico	5.7

Social indicators

	2010	2015	2020
Population growth rate (average annual %)[h]	- 0.1	0.2	~0.0
Urban population (% of total population)	76.6	76.9	77.1[c]
Urban population growth rate (average annual %)[h]	0.2	0.3	...
Fertility rate, total (live births per woman)[h]	1.6	1.7	1.6
Life expectancy at birth (females/males, years)[h]	80.1 / 76.1	80.4 / 76.5	80.7 / 76.7
Population age distribution (0-14/60+ years old, %)	17.7 / 17.3	16.7 / 19.4	15.9 / 21.3
International migrant stock (000/% of total pop.)	6.6 / 0.1	5.3 / ~0.0	4.9 / ~0.0[c]
Refugees and others of concern to the UNHCR (000)	0.4[i]	0.3	0.3[c]
Infant mortality rate (per 1 000 live births)[h]	5.3	4.8	4.5
Health: Current expenditure (% of GDP)	10.7	12.8	11.7[a]
Health: Physicians (per 1 000 pop.)	6.8	7.8	8.4[e]
Education: Government expenditure (% of GDP)	12.8	...	...
Education: Primary gross enrol. ratio (f/m per 100 pop.)	100.2 / 102.6	96.5 / 102.3	99.6 / 104.1[e]
Education: Secondary gross enrol. ratio (f/m per 100 pop.)	92.4 / 92.1	99.1 / 96.7	101.9 / 100.4[e]
Education: Tertiary gross enrol. ratio (f/m per 100 pop.)	118.6 / 72.2	42.5 / 30.2	51.0 / 32.3[e]
Intentional homicide rate (per 100 000 pop.)	4.5	5.5	5.0[g]
Seats held by women in the National Parliament (%)	43.2	48.9	53.2[i]

Environment and infrastructure indicators

	2010	2015	2020
Individuals using the Internet (per 100 inhabitants)	15.9[k]	37.3[l]	57.1[a]
Research & Development expenditure (% of GDP)	0.6	0.4	0.4[a]
Threatened species (number)	304	337	357
Forested area (% of land area)[f]	27.5	30.8	30.8[a]
CO2 emission estimates (million tons/tons per capita)	29.5 / 2.6	26.8 / 2.3	26.2 / 2.3[a]
Energy production, primary (Petajoules)	200	212	195[a]
Energy supply per capita (Gigajoules)	45	40	35[a]
Tourist/visitor arrivals at national borders (000)[m]	2 507	3 506	4 684[e]
Important sites for terrestrial biodiversity protected (%)	51.2	54.5	54.5[c]
Pop. using safely managed sanitation (urban/rural %)	36.2 / ...	40.2 / ...	41.9 / ...[a]
Net Official Development Assist. received (% of GNI)	0.21	0.65	...

a 2017. b The national currency of Cuba is the Cuban Peso (CUP). The convertible peso (CUC) is used by foreigners and tourists in Cuba. c 2019. d UN operational exchange rate. e 2018. f Estimate. g 2016. h Data refers to a 5-year period preceding the reference year. i Data as at the end of December. j Data are as at 1 January of reporting year. k Including users of the international network and also those having access only to the Cuban network. l Population aged 6 years and over. m Arrivals by air.

Curaçao

Region	Caribbean	Population (000, 2020)	164	
Surface area (km2)	444 [a]	Pop. density (per km2, 2020)	369.6	
Sex ratio (m per 100 f)	85.1	Capital city	Willemstad	
National currency	Neth. Ant. Guilder (ANG) [b]	Capital city pop. (000, 2020)	144.0 [c,d]	
Exchange rate (per US$)	1.8 [e]			

Economic indicators	2010	2015	2020
GDP: Gross domestic product (million current US$)	2 951	3 152	3 128 [d]
GDP growth rate (annual %, const. 2015 prices)	0.1	0.3	- 2.2 [d]
GDP per capita (current US$)	19 782.2	19 718.3	19 218.9 [d]
Economy: Agriculture (% of Gross Value Added) [f]	0.5	0.5	0.4 [d]
Economy: Industry (% of Gross Value Added)	16.2	20.2	18.5 [d]
Economy: Services and other activity (% of GVA)	83.3	79.3	81.1 [d]
Employment in agriculture (% of employed)	1.1 [g,h]	...	...
Employment in industry (% of employed)	17.6 [g,h]	...	...
Employment in services & other sectors (% employed)	81.3 [g,h]	...	...
Unemployment rate (% of labour force) [j]	9.6 [i,k]	13.0 [l]	...
Labour force participation rate (female/male pop. %)	53.2 / 66.5 [h]	... / ...	... / ...
CPI: Consumer Price Index (2010=100) [m]	100	108	116 [e]
Balance of payments, current account (million US$)	...	- 519	- 898 [d]

Social indicators	2010	2015	2020
Population growth rate (average annual %) [n]	2.7	1.4	0.5
Urban population (% of total population)	89.9	89.4	89.1 [e]
Urban population growth rate (average annual %) [n]	2.5	1.2	...
Fertility rate, total (live births per woman) [n]	2.2	2.1	1.8
Life expectancy at birth (females/males, years) [n]	79.4 / 72.6	80.7 / 74.5	81.4 / 75.5
Population age distribution (0-14/60+ years old, %)	20.7 / 18.6	19.8 / 21.6	18.2 / 24.5
International migrant stock (000/% of total pop.)	34.6 / 23.2	37.6 / 23.5	40.9 / 25.0 [e]
Refugees and others of concern to the UNHCR (000)	~0.0 [o]	0.1	26.1 [e]
Infant mortality rate (per 1 000 live births) [n]	13.0	10.3	9.0
Education: Government expenditure (% of GDP)	...	4.9 [l]	...
Education: Primary gross enrol. ratio (f/m per 100 pop.)	... / ...	157.7 / 164.2 [l]	... / ...
Education: Secondary gross enrol. ratio (f/m per 100 pop.)	... / ...	90.8 / 83.8 [l]	... / ...
Education: Tertiary gross enrol. ratio (f/m per 100 pop.)	... / ...	29.6 / 13.0 [l]	... / ...
Intentional homicide rate (per 100 000 pop.)	19.0 [p]	...	...

Environment and infrastructure indicators	2010	2015	2020
Individuals using the Internet (per 100 inhabitants)	...	...	68.1 [a]
Threatened species (number)	...	49	58
CO2 emission estimates (million tons/tons per capita)	... / ...	4.7 / 29.7	3.7 / 23.3 [a]
Energy production, primary (Petajoules)	...	1	1 [a]
Energy supply per capita (Gigajoules)	...	582	473 [a]
Tourist/visitor arrivals at national borders (000) [q]	342	468	432 [d]
Important sites for terrestrial biodiversity protected (%)	6.1	40.4	44.8 [e]

a 2017. **b** Netherlands Antillean Guilder. **c** Total population of Curaçao excluding some neighborhoods (see source). **d** 2018. **e** 2019. **f** Includes mining and handicrafts. **g** Data classified according to ISIC Rev. 3. **h** 2008. **i** Break in the time series. **j** Excluding the institutional population. **k** 2009. **l** 2013. **m** Calculated by the UN Statistics Division from national indices. **n** Data refers to a 5-year period preceding the reference year. **o** Data as at the end of December. **p** 2007. **q** Arrivals by air.

Cyprus

Region	Western Asia	UN membership date	20 September 1960
Population (000, 2020)	1 207[a]	Surface area (km2)	9 251[b]
Pop. density (per km2, 2020)	130.7[a]	Sex ratio (m per 100 f)	99.9[a]
Capital city	Nicosia	National currency	Euro (EUR)
Capital city pop. (000, 2020)	269.5[c]	Exchange rate (per US$)	0.9[d]

Economic indicators

	2010	2015	2020
GDP: Gross domestic product (million current US$)[e]	25 707	19 771	24 963[c]
GDP growth rate (annual %, const. 2015 prices)[e]	2.0	3.4	4.1[c]
GDP per capita (current US$)[e]	30 993.1	23 323.4	28 967.6[c]
Economy: Agriculture (% of Gross Value Added)[e,f]	2.3	2.1	2.3[c]
Economy: Industry (% of Gross Value Added)[e,f,g]	16.4	11.6	14.1[c]
Economy: Services and other activity (% of GVA)[e,f,h,i]	81.2	86.3	83.6[c]
Employment in agriculture (% of employed)	3.8	4.0	2.0[i]
Employment in industry (% of employed)	20.4	16.2	16.3[i]
Employment in services & other sectors (% employed)	75.8	79.8	81.7[i]
Unemployment rate (% of labour force)[j]	6.3	14.9	7.2
Labour force participation rate (female/male pop. %)[j]	57.6 / 70.6	57.9 / 67.4	57.8 / 68.0
CPI: Consumer Price Index (2010=100)[k,l]	100	102	103[d]
Agricultural production index (2004-2006=100)	84	81	79[m]
International trade: exports (million current US$)	1 506	3 367	3 528[d]
International trade: imports (million current US$)	8 645	7 133	9 219[d]
International trade: balance (million current US$)	- 7 138	- 3 766	- 5 691[d]
Balance of payments, current account (million US$)	- 2 799	- 84	- 1 655[d]

Major trading partners
						2019
Export partners (% of exports)	Netherlands	12.9	Libya	10.0	Greece	7.5
Import partners (% of imports)	Greece	20.3	Italy	10.3	United Kingdom	7.1

Social indicators

	2010	2015	2020
Population growth rate (average annual %)[a,n]	1.6	0.9	0.8
Urban population (% of total population)[a]	67.6	66.9	66.8[d]
Urban population growth rate (average annual %)[a,n]	1.4	0.7	...
Fertility rate, total (live births per woman)[a,n]	1.5	1.4	1.3
Life expectancy at birth (females/males, years)[a,n]	81.1 / 76.8	82.2 / 77.7	82.8 / 78.6
Population age distribution (0-14/60+ years old, %)[a]	17.8 / 16.1	16.9 / 17.7	16.6 / 19.8
International migrant stock (000/% of total pop.)[o]	191.9 / 17.2	192.0 / 16.5	191.9 / 16.0[d]
Refugees and others of concern to the UNHCR (000)	8.8[p]	14.1	33.3[q,d]
Infant mortality rate (per 1 000 live births)[a,n]	4.3	4.2	3.5
Health: Current expenditure (% of GDP)	6.3	6.8	6.7[b]
Health: Physicians (per 1 000 pop.)	2.2	2.6	2.0[m]
Education: Government expenditure (% of GDP)	6.6	6.4	...
Education: Primary gross enrol. ratio (f/m per 100 pop.)[j]	101.6 / 101.6	99.3 / 99.3	99.4 / 99.3[b]
Education: Secondary gross enrol. ratio (f/m per 100 pop.)[j]	92.0 / 90.9	99.4 / 100.1	99.5 / 101.1[b]
Education: Tertiary gross enrol. ratio (f/m per 100 pop.)[j]	45.6 / 50.9	69.4 / 51.1	82.4 / 69.6[b]
Intentional homicide rate (per 100 000 pop.)	0.7	1.3	1.3[c]
Seats held by women in the National Parliament (%)	12.5	12.5	19.6[r]

Environment and infrastructure indicators

	2010	2015	2020
Individuals using the Internet (per 100 inhabitants)	53.0[s]	71.7[s]	84.4[c]
Research & Development expenditure (% of GDP)	0.4	0.5	0.6[t,c]
Threatened species (number)	43	60	84
Forested area (% of land area)	18.7	18.7	18.7[i,b]
CO2 emission estimates (million tons/tons per capita)[e]	7.3 / 8.9	5.9 / 7.0	6.4 / 7.4[b]
Energy production, primary (Petajoules)	4	5	6[b]
Energy supply per capita (Gigajoules)	93	73	79[b]
Tourist/visitor arrivals at national borders (000)	2 173	2 659	3 939[c]
Important sites for terrestrial biodiversity protected (%)	61.9	70.8	74.1[d]
Pop. using safely managed sanitation (urban/rural %)	86.3 / ...	86.3 / ...	86.3 / ...[b]
Net Official Development Assist. disbursed (% of GNI)[k]	0.23	0.09	...

a Refers to the whole country. b 2017. c 2018. d 2019. e Excluding northern Cyprus. f Data classified according to ISIC Rev. 4. g Excludes publishing activities. Includes irrigation and canals. h Excludes computer and related activities and radio/TV activities. i Excludes repair of personal and household goods. j Estimate. k Data refer to government controlled areas. l Calculated by the UN Statistics Division from national indices. m 2016. n Data refers to a 5-year period preceding the reference year. o Including northern Cyprus. p Data as at the end of December. q UNHCR's assistance activities for IDPs ended in 1999. r Data are as at 1 January of reporting year. s Population aged 16 to 74 years. t Provisional data.

Czechia

Region	Eastern Europe	UN membership date	19 January 1993
Population (000, 2020)	10 709	Surface area (km2)	78 868[a]
Pop. density (per km2, 2020)	138.6	Sex ratio (m per 100 f)	97.0
Capital city	Prague	National currency	Czech Koruna (CZK)
Capital city pop. (000, 2020)	1 298.8[b]	Exchange rate (per US$)	22.6[b]

Economic indicators

	2010	2015	2020
GDP: Gross domestic product (million current US$)	207 478	186 830	245 226[c]
GDP growth rate (annual %, const. 2015 prices)	2.3	5.3	3.0[c]
GDP per capita (current US$)	19 691.3	17 623.1	22 992.1[c]
Economy: Agriculture (% of Gross Value Added)[d]	1.7	2.5	2.2[c]
Economy: Industry (% of Gross Value Added)[d,e]	36.8	37.8	35.8[c]
Economy: Services and other activity (% of GVA)[d,f,g]	61.5	59.7	62.0[c]
Employment in agriculture (% of employed)	3.1	2.9	2.6[h]
Employment in industry (% of employed)	38.0	38.0	37.1[h]
Employment in services & other sectors (% employed)	58.9	59.0	60.2[h]
Unemployment rate (% of labour force)[h]	7.3	5.0	1.9
Labour force participation rate (female/male pop. %)[h]	49.2 / 68.0	51.4 / 68.2	52.8 / 68.2
CPI: Consumer Price Index (2010=100)	100	108	117[b]
Agricultural production index (2004-2006=100)	91	96	100[i]
International trade: exports (million current US$)	132 141	157 194	198 852[b]
International trade: imports (million current US$)	125 691	140 716	178 552[b]
International trade: balance (million current US$)	6 450	16 478	20 300[b]
Balance of payments, current account (million US$)	- 7 351	461	- 866[b]

Major trading partners

						2019
Export partners (% of exports)	Germany	31.8	Slovakia	7.6	Poland	6.0
Import partners (% of imports)	Germany	24.7	China	15.8	Poland	7.5

Social indicators

	2010	2015	2020
Population growth rate (average annual %)[j]	0.5	0.1	0.2
Urban population (% of total population)	73.3	73.5	73.9[b]
Urban population growth rate (average annual %)[j]	0.4	0.2	...
Fertility rate, total (live births per woman)[j]	1.4	1.5	1.6
Life expectancy at birth (females/males, years)[j]	80.1 / 73.8	81.2 / 75.1	81.8 / 76.5
Population age distribution (0-14/60+ years old, %)	14.2 / 22.4	15.1 / 24.9	15.8 / 26.2
International migrant stock (000/% of total pop.)[k]	398.5 / 3.8	416.5 / 3.9	512.7 / 4.8[b]
Refugees and others of concern to the UNHCR (000)	3.5[l]	5.0	5.7[b]
Infant mortality rate (per 1 000 live births)[j]	3.1	2.5	2.3
Health: Current expenditure (% of GDP)[h]	6.9	7.2	7.2[a]
Health: Physicians (per 1 000 pop.)	3.5	4.0	4.1[c]
Education: Government expenditure (% of GDP)	4.1	5.8	5.6[i]
Education: Primary gross enrol. ratio (f/m per 100 pop.)	103.6 / 104.0	99.7 / 99.3	101.0 / 100.4[a]
Education: Secondary gross enrol. ratio (f/m per 100 pop.)	94.9 / 94.4	105.6 / 104.6	103.9 / 103.1[a]
Education: Tertiary gross enrol. ratio (f/m per 100 pop.)	74.9 / 53.6	75.7 / 53.8	75.3 / 53.4[a]
Intentional homicide rate (per 100 000 pop.)	1.0	0.8	0.6[a]
Seats held by women in the National Parliament (%)	15.5	19.0	22.5[m]

Environment and infrastructure indicators

	2010	2015	2020
Individuals using the Internet (per 100 inhabitants)	68.8[n]	75.7[o]	80.7[c]
Research & Development expenditure (% of GDP)	1.3	1.9	1.9[p,c]
Threatened species (number)	33	45	104
Forested area (% of land area)	34.4	34.5	34.5[h,a]
CO2 emission estimates (million tons/tons per capita)	112.5 / 10.7	99.4 / 9.4	101.7 / 9.6[a]
Energy production, primary (Petajoules)	1 340	1 207	1 157[a]
Energy supply per capita (Gigajoules)	180	166	171[a]
Tourist/visitor arrivals at national borders (000)	8 629	11 619	13 665[a]
Important sites for terrestrial biodiversity protected (%)	94.7	94.7	94.7[b]
Pop. using safely managed sanitation (urban/rural %)	92.4 / 80.8	96.8 / 84.3	97.8 / 85.1[a]
Net Official Development Assist. disbursed (% of GNI)[q]	0.13	0.12	0.15[a]

a 2017. b 2019. c 2018. d Data classified according to ISIC Rev. 4. e Excludes publishing activities. Includes irrigation and canals. f Excludes repair of personal and household goods. g Excludes computer and related activities and radio/TV activities. h Estimate. i 2016. j Data refers to a 5-year period preceding the reference year. k Refers to foreign citizens. l Data as at the end of December. m Data are as at 1 January of reporting year. n Population aged 16 to 74 years. o Population aged 16 years and over. p Provisional data. q Development Assistance Committee member (OECD).

Democratic People's Republic of Korea

Region	Eastern Asia	UN membership date	17 September 1991
Population (000, 2020)	25 779	Surface area (km2)	120 538 a
Pop. density (per km2, 2020)	214.1	Sex ratio (m per 100 f)	95.7
Capital city	Pyongyang	National currency	North Korean Won (KPW)
Capital city pop. (000, 2020)	3 060.9 b	Exchange rate (per US$)	107.7 c,b

Economic indicators	2010	2015	2020
GDP: Gross domestic product (million current US$)	13 945	16 283	17 487 d
GDP growth rate (annual %, const. 2015 prices)	- 0.5	- 1.1	- 4.1 d
GDP per capita (current US$)	571.0	649.9	687.9 d
Economy: Agriculture (% of Gross Value Added)	20.8	21.6	23.3 d
Economy: Industry (% of Gross Value Added)	48.2	46.2	43.7 d
Economy: Services and other activity (% of GVA)	53.3	54.5	53.7 d
Employment in agriculture (% of employed) e	53.5	52.0	51.1
Employment in industry (% of employed) e	15.4	14.5	13.2
Employment in services & other sectors (% employed) e	31.1	33.5	35.7
Unemployment rate (% of labour force) e	2.9	2.9	2.8
Labour force participation rate (female/male pop. %) e	74.2 / 88.0	73.7 / 87.7	73.3 / 87.7
Agricultural production index (2004-2006=100)	98	105	102 f
International trade: exports (million current US$) e	882	987	1 080 b
International trade: imports (million current US$) e	1 957	2 604	3 273 b
International trade: balance (million current US$) e	- 1 075	- 1 617	- 2 194 b

Major trading partners						2019
Export partners (% of exports) e	China	56.2	Suriname	5.5	Mali	5.2
Import partners (% of imports) e	China	94.9	Russian Federation	1.9	Brazil	0.9

Social indicators	2010	2015	2020
Population growth rate (average annual %) g	0.5	0.5	0.5
Urban population (% of total population)	60.4	61.3	62.1 b
Urban population growth rate (average annual %) g	0.8	0.8	...
Fertility rate, total (live births per woman) g	2.0	1.9	1.9
Life expectancy at birth (females/males, years) g	71.8 / 64.8	74.1 / 67.2	75.4 / 68.3
Population age distribution (0-14/60+ years old, %)	22.6 / 12.9	20.9 / 12.7	19.8 / 15.1
International migrant stock (000/% of total pop.) e	44.0 / 0.2	48.5 / 0.2	49.4 / 0.2 b
Infant mortality rate (per 1 000 live births) g	27.3	18.5	13.9
Health: Physicians (per 1 000 pop.)	3.3 h	3.5 i	3.7 a
Education: Primary gross enrol. ratio (f/m per 100 pop.)	99.4 / 99.4 j	94.7 / 94.5	112.8 / 112.8 d
Education: Secondary gross enrol. ratio (f/m per 100 pop.)	... / ...	93.3 / 92.3	... / ...
Education: Tertiary gross enrol. ratio (f/m per 100 pop.)	20.6 / 40.8 j	20.0 / 36.1	18.2 / 35.5 d
Seats held by women in the National Parliament (%)	15.6	16.3	17.6 k

Environment and infrastructure indicators	2010	2015	2020
Individuals using the Internet (per 100 inhabitants) e	0.0	0.0 l	...
Threatened species (number)	52	64	88
Forested area (% of land area) e	47.1	41.8	41.8 a
CO2 emission estimates (million tons/tons per capita)	49.3 / 2.0	22.5 / 0.9	19.6 / 0.8 a
Energy production, primary (Petajoules)	699	788	646 a
Energy supply per capita (Gigajoules)	25	13	12 a
Important sites for terrestrial biodiversity protected (%)	0.0	0.0	0.0 b
Pop. using safely managed drinking water (urban/rural, %)	78.0 / 52.4	77.4 / 50.4	77.2 / 49.6 a
Pop. using safely managed sanitation (urban/rural %)	... / 18.4	... / 9.0	... / 5.1 a

a 2017. b 2019. c UN operational exchange rate. d 2018. e Estimate. f 2016. g Data refers to a 5-year period preceding the reference year. h 2008. i 2014. j 2009. k Data are as at 1 January of reporting year. l 2012.

Democratic Republic of the Congo

Region	Middle Africa	UN membership date	20 September 1960
Population (000, 2020)	89 561	Surface area (km2)	2 344 858[a]
Pop. density (per km2, 2020)	39.5	Sex ratio (m per 100 f)	99.7
Capital city	Kinshasa	National currency	Congolese Franc (CDF)
Capital city pop. (000, 2020)	13 743.3[b]	Exchange rate (per US$)	1 672.9[b]

Economic indicators

	2010	2015	2020
GDP: Gross domestic product (million current US$)	21 566	37 918	47 146[c]
GDP growth rate (annual %, const. 2015 prices)	7.1	6.9	5.8[c]
GDP per capita (current US$)	334.0	497.3	560.8[c]
Economy: Agriculture (% of Gross Value Added)	22.4	19.7	20.0[c]
Economy: Industry (% of Gross Value Added)	40.5	44.8	46.0[c]
Economy: Services and other activity (% of GVA)[d]	38.9	38.4	37.5[c]
Employment in agriculture (% of employed)[e]	70.0	67.0	65.1
Employment in industry (% of employed)[e]	8.6	9.5	9.8
Employment in services & other sectors (% employed)[e]	21.4	23.5	25.1
Unemployment rate (% of labour force)[e]	4.0	4.4	4.2
Labour force participation rate (female/male pop. %)[e]	63.9 / 68.7	61.0 / 66.8	60.4 / 66.0
CPI: Consumer Price Index (2010=100)	100	130	134[f]
Agricultural production index (2004-2006=100)	104	110	109[f]
International trade: exports (million current US$)[e]	5 300	5 800	3 477[b]
International trade: imports (million current US$)[e]	4 500	6 200	5 159[b]
International trade: balance (million current US$)[e]	800	- 400	- 1 682[b]
Balance of payments, current account (million US$)	- 2 174	- 1 484	- 2 169[c]

Major trading partners

						2019
Export partners (% of exports)[e]	China	58.5	United Arab Emirates	9.0	Saudi Arabia	5.6
Import partners (% of imports)[e]	China	22.6	South Africa	13.5	Zambia	11.5

Social indicators

	2010	2015	2020
Population growth rate (average annual %)[g]	3.3	3.3	3.2
Urban population (% of total population)	40.0	42.7	45.0[b]
Urban population growth rate (average annual %)[g]	4.6	4.6	...
Fertility rate, total (live births per woman)[g]	6.6	6.4	6.0
Life expectancy at birth (females/males, years)[g]	56.9 / 54.0	59.5 / 56.7	61.7 / 58.7
Population age distribution (0-14/60+ years old, %)	46.1 / 4.7	46.3 / 4.7	45.8 / 4.7
International migrant stock (000/% of total pop.)[h]	589.0 / 0.9	824.5 / 1.1	963.8 / 1.1[b]
Refugees and others of concern to the UNHCR (000)	2 363.9[i]	2 001.0	5 057.8[b]
Infant mortality rate (per 1 000 live births)[g]	83.8	73.1	64.9
Health: Current expenditure (% of GDP)	4.0	3.9	4.0[a]
Health: Physicians (per 1 000 pop.)	0.1[i]	0.1[k]	0.1[f]
Education: Government expenditure (% of GDP)	1.5	2.2	1.5[e,a]
Education: Primary gross enrol. ratio (f/m per 100 pop.)	93.0 / 106.9	107.6 / 108.4	... / ...
Education: Secondary gross enrol. ratio (f/m per 100 pop.)	30.1 / 52.2	36.0 / 56.3	... / ...
Education: Tertiary gross enrol. ratio (f/m per 100 pop.)	3.2 / 10.3[i]	4.3 / 9.5[k]	4.7 / 8.5[f]
Seats held by women in the National Parliament (%)	8.4	8.9	12.8[l]

Environment and infrastructure indicators

	2010	2015	2020
Individuals using the Internet (per 100 inhabitants)[e]	0.7	3.8	8.6[a]
Research & Development expenditure (% of GDP)	0.1[m,n,j]	0.4[o,p,q]	...
Threatened species (number)	296	333	497
Forested area (% of land area)[e]	68.0	67.3	67.3[a]
CO2 emission estimates (million tons/tons per capita)	1.9 / ~0.0	2.7 / ~0.0	2.2 / ~0.0[a]
Energy production, primary (Petajoules)	856	1 218	1 264[a]
Energy supply per capita (Gigajoules)	13	16	15[a]
Tourist/visitor arrivals at national borders (000)	81[r]	354	351[f]
Important sites for terrestrial biodiversity protected (%)	52.7	52.7	52.7[b]
Net Official Development Assist. received (% of GNI)	16.87	7.40	5.52[c]

a 2017. b 2019. c 2018. d Excludes hotels and restaurants. e Estimate. f 2016. g Data refers to a 5-year period preceding the reference year. h Including refugees. i Data as at the end of December. j 2009. k 2013. l Data are as at 1 January of reporting year. m Government only. n S&T budget instead of R&D expenditure. o Excluding business enterprise. p Overestimated or based on overestimated data. q Break in the time series. r Arrivals by air.

Denmark

Region	Northern Europe	UN membership date	24 October 1945
Population (000, 2020)	5 792	Surface area (km2)	42 921 [a]
Pop. density (per km2, 2020)	136.5	Sex ratio (m per 100 f)	98.9
Capital city	Copenhagen	National currency	Danish Krone (DKK)
Capital city pop. (000, 2020)	1 333.9 [b,c]	Exchange rate (per US$)	6.7 [c]

Economic indicators

	2010	2015	2020
GDP: Gross domestic product (million current US$)	321 995	302 673	355 675 [d]
GDP growth rate (annual %, const. 2015 prices)	1.9	2.3	2.4 [d]
GDP per capita (current US$)	57 966.6	53 206.1	61 833.7 [d]
Economy: Agriculture (% of Gross Value Added) [e]	1.4	1.1	1.2 [d]
Economy: Industry (% of Gross Value Added) [e,f]	22.8	23.0	24.4 [d]
Economy: Services and other activity (% of GVA) [e,g,h]	102.1	107.9	107.5 [d]
Employment in agriculture (% of employed)	2.4	2.5	2.1 [i]
Employment in industry (% of employed)	19.6	19.3	18.3 [i]
Employment in services & other sectors (% employed)	78.0	78.2	79.6 [i]
Unemployment rate (% of labour force) [i]	7.5	6.2	4.8
Labour force participation rate (female/male pop. %) [i]	59.8 / 69.1	57.7 / 66.4	58.2 / 66.2
CPI: Consumer Price Index (2010=100) [j]	100	107	110 [c]
Agricultural production index (2004-2006=100)	101	105	101 [k]
International trade: exports (million current US$)	96 217	94 619	109 942 [c]
International trade: imports (million current US$)	82 724	85 327	97 196 [c]
International trade: balance (million current US$)	13 492	9 291	12 746 [c]
Balance of payments, current account (million US$)	21 051	24 953	27 581 [c]

Major trading partners

						2019
Export partners (% of exports)	Undisclosed [l]	17.6	Germany	13.4	Sweden	9.8
Import partners (% of imports)	Germany	21.6	Sweden	12.0	Netherlands	7.8

Social indicators

	2010	2015	2020
Population growth rate (average annual %) [m]	0.5	0.5	0.4
Urban population (% of total population)	86.8	87.5	88.0 [c]
Urban population growth rate (average annual %) [m]	0.7	0.6	...
Fertility rate, total (live births per woman) [m]	1.9	1.7	1.8
Life expectancy at birth (females/males, years) [m]	80.8 / 76.4	82.2 / 78.1	82.7 / 78.7
Population age distribution (0-14/60+ years old, %)	17.9 / 23.3	16.8 / 24.8	16.3 / 26.1
International migrant stock (000/% of total pop.)	500.8 / 9.0	595.9 / 10.5	722.9 / 12.5 [c]
Refugees and others of concern to the UNHCR (000)	24.5 [n]	27.3	47.4 [c]
Infant mortality rate (per 1 000 live births) [m]	3.5	3.5	3.1
Health: Current expenditure (% of GDP)	10.3	10.2	10.1 [a]
Health: Physicians (per 1 000 pop.)	3.7	3.9	4.0 [k]
Education: Government expenditure (% of GDP)	8.6	7.6 [o]	...
Education: Primary gross enrol. ratio (f/m per 100 pop.)	99.7 / 99.5	100.8 / 102.1	100.9 / 101.6 [a]
Education: Secondary gross enrol. ratio (f/m per 100 pop.)	120.0 / 119.0	133.4 / 127.3	129.8 / 128.4 [a]
Education: Tertiary gross enrol. ratio (f/m per 100 pop.)	87.4 / 60.4	96.3 / 68.7	93.6 / 68.4 [a]
Intentional homicide rate (per 100 000 pop.)	0.8	1.1	1.0 [d]
Seats held by women in the National Parliament (%)	38.0	38.0	39.7 [p]

Environment and infrastructure indicators

	2010	2015	2020
Individuals using the Internet (per 100 inhabitants)	88.7 [q]	96.3 [q]	97.3 [d]
Research & Development expenditure (% of GDP)	2.9	3.1	3.1 [r,d]
Threatened species (number)	33	36	77
Forested area (% of land area)	13.8	15.3	15.3 [i,a]
CO2 emission estimates (million tons/tons per capita) [s]	47.3 / 8.5	31.9 / 5.6	31.3 / 5.4 [a]
Energy production, primary (Petajoules) [s]	977	668	655 [a]
Energy supply per capita (Gigajoules) [s]	147	118	126 [a]
Tourist/visitor arrivals at national borders (000)	9 425	10 424 [t]	12 749 [d]
Important sites for terrestrial biodiversity protected (%)	86.2	86.2	86.2 [c]
Net Official Development Assist. disbursed (% of GNI) [u]	0.91	0.85	0.74 [a]

a 2017. **b** Refers to the Greater Copenhagen Region, consisting of (parts of) 16 municipalities. **c** 2019. **d** 2018. **e** Data classified according to ISIC Rev. 4. **f** Excludes publishing activities. Includes irrigation and canals. **g** Excludes repair of personal and household goods. **h** Excludes computer and related activities and radio/TV activities. **i** Estimate. **j** Calculated by the UN Statistics Division from national indices. **k** 2016. **l** Undisclosed (Special categories). **m** Data refers to a 5-year period preceding the reference year. **n** Data as at the end of December. **o** 2014. **p** Data are as at 1 January of reporting year. **q** Population aged 16 to 74 years. **r** Provisional data. **s** Excluding the Faroe Islands and Greenland. **t** Break in the time series. **u** Development Assistance Committee member (OECD).

Djibouti

Region	Eastern Africa	UN membership date	20 September 1977
Population (000, 2020)	988	Surface area (km2)	23 200 [a]
Pop. density (per km2, 2020)	42.6	Sex ratio (m per 100 f)	110.7
Capital city	Djibouti	National currency	Djibouti Franc (DJF)
Capital city pop. (000, 2020)	568.8 [b,c]	Exchange rate (per US$)	177.7 [c]

Economic indicators	2010	2015	2020
GDP: Gross domestic product (million current US$)	1 244	2 445	2 923 [d]
GDP growth rate (annual %, const. 2015 prices)	11.7	7.7	5.6 [d]
GDP per capita (current US$)	1 480.2	2 675.6	3 048.6 [d]
Economy: Agriculture (% of Gross Value Added)	2.8	1.3	1.4 [d]
Economy: Industry (% of Gross Value Added)	16.1	12.1	11.8 [d]
Economy: Services and other activity (% of GVA)	60.3	58.3	62.9 [d]
Employment in agriculture (% of employed) [e]	40.7	36.5	32.4
Employment in industry (% of employed) [e]	11.5	12.3	13.3
Employment in services & other sectors (% employed) [e]	47.8	51.2	54.3
Unemployment rate (% of labour force) [e]	10.7	10.6	10.3
Labour force participation rate (female/male pop. %) [e]	49.6 / 71.0	50.4 / 69.5	50.8 / 68.8
CPI: Consumer Price Index (2010=100)	100	112	120 [c]
Agricultural production index (2004-2006=100)	116	133	133 [f]
International trade: exports (million current US$) [e]	470	132	143 [c]
International trade: imports (million current US$) [e]	603	890	1 344 [c]
International trade: balance (million current US$) [e]	- 133	- 758	- 1 201 [c]
Balance of payments, current account (million US$)	50	714	541 [d]

Major trading partners						2019
Export partners (% of exports) [e]	Saudi Arabia	32.3	United States	20.4	India	14.0
Import partners (% of imports) [e]	China	35.2	United Arab Emirates	21.5	India	6.7

Social indicators	2010	2015	2020
Population growth rate (average annual %) [g]	1.4	1.7	1.6
Urban population (% of total population)	77.0	77.4	77.9 [c]
Urban population growth rate (average annual %) [g]	1.7	1.8	...
Fertility rate, total (live births per woman) [g]	3.6	3.1	2.8
Life expectancy at birth (females/males, years) [g]	60.5 / 57.6	63.2 / 60.0	68.7 / 64.6
Population age distribution (0-14/60+ years old, %)	32.6 / 6.1	30.6 / 6.5	28.9 / 7.4
International migrant stock (000/% of total pop.) [h]	101.6 / 12.1	112.4 / 12.3	115.3 / 11.8 [c]
Refugees and others of concern to the UNHCR (000)	15.8 [i]	17.4	30.1 [c]
Infant mortality rate (per 1 000 live births) [g]	63.4	55.7	33.4
Health: Current expenditure (% of GDP)	4.3	4.4	3.3 [a]
Health: Physicians (per 1 000 pop.)	0.2 [i]	0.2 [k]	...
Education: Government expenditure (% of GDP)	4.5	...	...
Education: Primary gross enrol. ratio (f/m per 100 pop.)	58.5 / 58.9 [i]	72.8 / 67.9	75.1 / 75.4 [c]
Education: Secondary gross enrol. ratio (f/m per 100 pop.)	31.1 / 38.5 [i]	45.3 / 48.0	52.9 / 51.2 [c]
Education: Tertiary gross enrol. ratio (f/m per 100 pop.)	3.1 / 4.1	4.6 / 6.0 [m]	... / ...
Seats held by women in the National Parliament (%)	13.8	12.7	26.2 [n]

Environment and infrastructure indicators	2010	2015	2020
Individuals using the Internet (per 100 inhabitants)	6.5 [e]	11.9 [e]	55.7 [a]
Threatened species (number)	81	94	110
Forested area (% of land area) [e]	0.2	0.2	0.2 [a]
Energy production, primary (Petajoules)	3	4	4 [a]
Energy supply per capita (Gigajoules)	13	9	9 [a]
Tourist/visitor arrivals at national borders (000)	51	63 [o]	...
Important sites for terrestrial biodiversity protected (%)	0.0	0.8	0.8 [c]
Pop. using safely managed sanitation (urban/rural %)	35.6 / 15.0	39.8 / 17.8	41.5 / 18.9 [a]
Net Official Development Assist. received (% of GNI)	...	9.81	8.65 [d]

2017. **b** Refers to the population of the "cercle". **c** 2019. **d** 2018. **e** Estimate. **f** 2016. **g** Data refers to a 5-year period preceding the reference year. **h** Including refugees. **i** Data as at the end of December. **j** 2006. **k** 2014. **l** 2009. **m** 2011. **n** Data are as at 1 January of reporting year. **o** 2013.

Dominica

Region	Caribbean	UN membership date	18 December 1978
Population (000, 2020)	75	Surface area (km2)	750 a
Pop. density (per km2, 2020)	100.1	Sex ratio (m per 100 f)	103.0 b
Capital city	Roseau	National currency	E. Caribbean Dollar (XCD) c
Capital city pop. (000, 2020)	14.9 d	Exchange rate (per US$)	2.7 e

Economic indicators	2010	2015	2020
GDP: Gross domestic product (million current US$)	494	541	551 d
GDP growth rate (annual %, const. 2015 prices)	- 2.8	- 2.6	2.3 d
GDP per capita (current US$)	6 967.3	7 597.7	7 691.3 d
Economy: Agriculture (% of Gross Value Added)	13.8	16.7	13.8 d
Economy: Industry (% of Gross Value Added)	14.4	14.0	19.7 d
Economy: Services and other activity (% of GVA)	71.8	68.5	60.7 d
CPI: Consumer Price Index (2010=100)	100	102	104 d
Agricultural production index (2004-2006=100)	108	112	113 f
International trade: exports (million current US$)	34	30 g	18 g.e
International trade: imports (million current US$)	225	214 g	304 g.e
International trade: balance (million current US$)	- 190	- 184 g	- 286 g.e
Balance of payments, current account (million US$)	- 80	- 41	- 225 d

Major trading partners						2019
Export partners (% of exports) g	Saudi Arabia	40.4	Belarus	8.3	Sri Lanka	3.8
Import partners (% of imports) g	United States	63.4	China	6.3	Italy	5.0

Social indicators	2010	2015	2020
Population growth rate (average annual %)	0.2 h	0.5 h	0.5
Urban population (% of total population)	68.1	69.6	70.8 e
Urban population growth rate (average annual %) h	0.7	0.9	...
Life expectancy at birth (females/males, years)	78.2 / 73.8 i	... / ...	... / ...
Population age distribution (0-14/60+ years old, %)	29.5 / 13.3 j	... / ...	... / ...
International migrant stock (000/% of total pop.)	8.1 / 11.4	8.1 / 11.4	8.3 / 11.5 e
Health: Current expenditure (% of GDP)	5.6	5.4	5.9 a
Health: Physicians (per 1 000 pop.)	...	...	1.1 a
Education: Government expenditure (% of GDP)	...	3.4	...
Education: Primary gross enrol. ratio (f/m per 100 pop.)	101.8 / 103.6	115.2 / 117.1	113.2 / 116.2 f
Education: Secondary gross enrol. ratio (f/m per 100 pop.)	93.0 / 85.1	93.8 / 94.7	... / ...
Intentional homicide rate (per 100 000 pop.)	21.2	12.6	26.6 a
Seats held by women in the National Parliament (%)	14.3	21.9	38.1 k.l

Environment and infrastructure indicators	2010	2015	2020
Individuals using the Internet (per 100 inhabitants)	47.4	65.0 g	69.6 g.a
Threatened species (number)	48	62	74
Forested area (% of land area) g	59.5	57.8	57.8 a
Energy production, primary (Petajoules)	0	0	0 a
Energy supply per capita (Gigajoules)	36	36 g	33 g.a
Tourist/visitor arrivals at national borders (000)	77	75	63 d
Important sites for terrestrial biodiversity protected (%)	40.0	40.0	40.0 e
Net Official Development Assist. received (% of GNI)	6.71	2.26	5.34 d

a 2017. b 2014. c East Caribbean Dollar. d 2018. e 2019. f 2016. g Estimate. h Data refers to a 5-year period preceding the reference year. i 2008. j 2006. k Data are as at 1 January of reporting year. l The figures correspond to the results of the December 2019 elections. They do not include 9 members to be appointed by the President and 2 ex officio members (the Speaker and the Attorney General).

Dominican Republic

Region	Caribbean	UN membership date	24 October 1945
Population (000, 2020)	10 848	Surface area (km2)	48 671 [a]
Pop. density (per km2, 2020)	224.5	Sex ratio (m per 100 f)	99.8
Capital city	Santo Domingo	National currency	Dominican Peso (DOP)
Capital city pop. (000, 2020)	3 245.0 [b,c]	Exchange rate (per US$)	53.0 [c]

Economic indicators

	2010	2015	2020
GDP: Gross domestic product (million current US$)	53 160	68 802	81 299 [d]
GDP growth rate (annual %, const. 2015 prices)	8.3	7.0	7.0 [d]
GDP per capita (current US$)	5 483.1	6 691.7	7 650.1 [d]
Economy: Agriculture (% of Gross Value Added) [e]	6.5	6.0	6.0 [d]
Economy: Industry (% of Gross Value Added) [e,f]	29.9	30.3	30.3 [d]
Economy: Services and other activity (% of GVA) [e,g,h]	54.7	56.3	56.2 [d]
Employment in agriculture (% of employed)	12.4	10.0	8.8 [i]
Employment in industry (% of employed)	18.5	18.5	19.9 [i]
Employment in services & other sectors (% employed)	69.1	71.5	71.3 [i]
Unemployment rate (% of labour force) [i]	5.2	7.6	5.9
Labour force participation rate (female/male pop. %) [i]	42.4 / 73.8	49.6 / 78.0	51.6 / 77.4
CPI: Consumer Price Index (2010=100) [j]	100	122	135 [c]
Agricultural production index (2004-2006=100)	123	142	145 [k]
International trade: exports (million current US$) [l]	4 767	8 384	11 117 [i,c]
International trade: imports (million current US$) [l]	15 138	17 348	20 599 [i,c]
International trade: balance (million current US$) [l]	- 10 371	- 8 964	- 9 482 [i,c]
Balance of payments, current account (million US$)	- 4 024	- 1 280	- 1 205 [c]

Major trading partners

						2019
Export partners (% of exports) [i]	United States	53.3	Haiti	9.6	Canada	8.9
Import partners (% of imports) [i]	United States	44.4	China	13.2	Mexico	4.6

Social indicators

	2010	2015	2020
Population growth rate (average annual %) [m]	1.3	1.2	1.1
Urban population (% of total population)	73.8	78.6	81.8 [c]
Urban population growth rate (average annual %) [m]	3.2	2.5	...
Fertility rate, total (live births per woman) [m]	2.6	2.4	2.4
Life expectancy at birth (females/males, years) [m]	74.6 / 68.5	75.9 / 69.6	77.1 / 70.7
Population age distribution (0-14/60+ years old, %)	30.6 / 8.5	28.8 / 9.6	27.4 / 11.1
International migrant stock (000/% of total pop.)	393.7 / 4.1	549.3 / 5.3	567.6 / 5.3 [c]
Refugees and others of concern to the UNHCR (000)	2.4 [n]	135.1 [o]	28.9 [p,c]
Infant mortality rate (per 1 000 live births) [m]	29.5	27.5	25.9
Health: Current expenditure (% of GDP)	5.6	6.0	6.1 [a]
Health: Physicians (per 1 000 pop.)	1.1 [q]	1.5 [r]	...
Education: Government expenditure (% of GDP)	2.0 [s]	...	...
Education: Primary gross enrol. ratio (f/m per 100 pop.) [i]	103.4 / 117.3	106.2 / 116.4	102.5 / 108.8 [d]
Education: Secondary gross enrol. ratio (f/m per 100 pop.) [i]	82.8 / 73.6	83.8 / 76.2	83.0 / 77.0 [d]
Education: Tertiary gross enrol. ratio (f/m per 100 pop.) [i]	... / ...	67.0 / 36.6	77.0 / 43.0 [a]
Intentional homicide rate (per 100 000 pop.)	25.5	17.8 [t]	10.0 [d]
Seats held by women in the National Parliament (%)	19.7	20.8	27.9 [u]

Environment and infrastructure indicators

	2010	2015	2020
Individuals using the Internet (per 100 inhabitants)	31.4 [i]	54.2 [v]	74.8 [d]
Threatened species (number)	126	153	203
Forested area (% of land area)	37.6	41.0 [i]	41.0 [i,a]
CO2 emission estimates (million tons/tons per capita)	19.0 / 1.9	21.5 / 2.0	21.4 / 2.0 [a]
Energy production, primary (Petajoules)	27	23	32 [a]
Energy supply per capita (Gigajoules)	30	31	32 [a]
Tourist/visitor arrivals at national borders (000) [w,x]	4 125	5 600	6 569 [d]
Important sites for terrestrial biodiversity protected (%)	76.7	81.1	81.1 [c]
Net Official Development Assist. received (% of GNI)	0.37	0.43	0.11 [d]

a 2017. b Refers to the urban population of the Municipalities of Santo Domingo de Guzmán, Santo Domingo Este, Santo Domingo Oeste, and Santo Domingo Norte. c 2019. d 2018. e Data classified according to ISIC Rev. 4. f Excludes publishing activities. Includes irrigation and canals. g Excludes computer and related activities and radio/TV activities. h Excludes repair of personal and household goods. i Estimate. j Calculated by the UN Statistics Division from national indices. k 2016. l Imports FOB. m Data refers to a 5-year period preceding the reference year. n Data is at the end of December. o Revised estimate includes only individuals born in the country where both parents were born abroad. p Official figure not available. UNHCR is currently working with authorities and other actors to determine the size of the population that found an effective nationality solution under Law 169-14. q 2008. r 2011. s 2007. t 2014. u Data are as at 1 January of reporting year. v Population aged 12 years and over. w Arrivals by air. x Including nationals residing abroad.

Ecuador

Region	South America	UN membership date	21 December 1945
Population (000, 2020)	17 643	Surface area (km2)	257 217 [a]
Pop. density (per km2, 2020)	71.0	Sex ratio (m per 100 f)	100.1
Capital city	Quito	National currency	US Dollar (USD)
Capital city pop. (000, 2020)	1 847.7 [b]	Exchange rate (per US$)	1.0 [b]

Economic indicators

	2010	2015	2020
GDP: Gross domestic product (million current US$)	69 555	99 290	108 398 [c]
GDP growth rate (annual %, const. 2015 prices)	3.5	0.1	1.4 [c]
GDP per capita (current US$)	4 633.6	6 124.5	6 344.9 [c]
Economy: Agriculture (% of Gross Value Added) [d]	10.2	10.2	9.9 [c]
Economy: Industry (% of Gross Value Added) [d,e]	36.3	34.4	34.9 [c]
Economy: Services and other activity (% of GVA) [d,f,g]	57.2	58.2	60.6 [c]
Employment in agriculture (% of employed)	27.9	26.2	29.4 [h]
Employment in industry (% of employed)	18.5	19.7	18.2 [h]
Employment in services & other sectors (% employed)	53.6	54.1	52.5 [h]
Unemployment rate (% of labour force) [h]	4.1	3.6	4.2
Labour force participation rate (female/male pop. %) [h]	49.9 / 80.5	52.1 / 81.0	55.3 / 81.0
CPI: Consumer Price Index (2010=100)	100	121	124 [b]
Agricultural production index (2004-2006=100)	123	122	115 [i]
International trade: exports (million current US$)	17 490	18 331	22 245 [h,b]
International trade: imports (million current US$)	20 591	21 387	22 425 [h,b]
International trade: balance (million current US$)	- 3 101	- 3 057	- 180 [h,b]
Balance of payments, current account (million US$)	- 1 582	- 2 221	- 79 [b]

Major trading partners

						2019
Export partners (% of exports) [h]	United States	30.9	Peru	7.5	China	6.9
Import partners (% of imports) [h]	United States	21.8	China	18.9	Colombia	7.9

Social indicators

	2010	2015	2020
Population growth rate (average annual %) [j]	1.6	1.5	1.7
Urban population (% of total population)	62.7	63.4	64.0 [b]
Urban population growth rate (average annual %) [j]	2.0	1.8	...
Fertility rate, total (live births per woman) [j]	2.7	2.6	2.4
Life expectancy at birth (females/males, years) [j]	77.6 / 71.7	78.5 / 72.8	79.6 / 74.0
Population age distribution (0-14/60+ years old, %)	31.0 / 8.6	29.1 / 9.8	27.4 / 11.0
International migrant stock (000/% of total pop.) [k]	325.4 / 2.2	387.5 / 2.4	381.5 / 2.2 [b]
Refugees and others of concern to the UNHCR (000)	171.1 [l]	133.1 [l]	420.5 [b]
Infant mortality rate (per 1 000 live births) [j]	19.1	15.1	13.6
Health: Current expenditure (% of GDP)	7.1	8.6	8.3 [a]
Health: Physicians (per 1 000 pop.)	2.1	2.1	2.0 [i]
Education: Government expenditure (% of GDP)	4.5	5.0	...
Education: Primary gross enrol. ratio (f/m per 100 pop.)	113.2 / 112.9	107.9 / 107.4	104.1 / 102.4 [c]
Education: Secondary gross enrol. ratio (f/m per 100 pop.)	94.5 / 90.3	106.2 / 102.0	102.8 / 100.1 [c]
Education: Tertiary gross enrol. ratio (f/m per 100 pop.)	41.6 / 36.0 [m]	48.4 / 41.5	... / ...
Intentional homicide rate (per 100 000 pop.)	17.5	6.5	5.8 [c]
Seats held by women in the National Parliament (%)	32.3	41.6	39.4 [n]

Environment and infrastructure indicators

	2010	2015	2020
Individuals using the Internet (per 100 inhabitants) [o]	29.0	48.9	57.3 [a]
Research & Development expenditure (% of GDP)	0.4	0.4 [p]	...
Threatened species (number)	2 255	2 308	2 501
Forested area (% of land area)	52.1	50.5 [h]	50.5 [h,a]
CO2 emission estimates (million tons/tons per capita)	32.7 / 2.2	37.4 / 2.3	34.3 / 2.1 [a]
Energy production, primary (Petajoules)	1 110	1 260	1 263 [a]
Energy supply per capita (Gigajoules)	35	37	37 [a]
Tourist/visitor arrivals at national borders (000)	1 047 [q]	1 676 [r]	2 535 [r,c]
Important sites for terrestrial biodiversity protected (%)	25.9	27.5	30.2 [b]
Pop. using safely managed drinking water (urban/rural, %)	82.0 / 54.4	84.4 / 56.9	84.9 / 57.9 [a]
Pop. using safely managed sanitation (urban/rural, %)	36.3 / 51.5	34.5 / 55.5	33.4 / 57.2 [a]
Net Official Development Assist. received (% of GNI)	0.25	0.33	0.38 [c]

a 2017. b 2019. c 2018. d Data classified according to ISIC Rev. 4. e Excludes publishing activities. Includes irrigation and canals. f Excludes repair of personal and household goods. g Excludes computer and related activities and radio/TV activities. h Estimate. i 2016. j Data refers to a 5-year period preceding the reference year. k Including refugees. l Data as at the end of December. m 2008. n Data are as at 1 January of reporting year. o Population aged 5 years and over. p 2014. q Excluding nationals residing abroad. r Including nationals residing abroad.

Egypt

Region	Northern Africa	UN membership date	24 October 1945
Population (000, 2020)	102 334	Surface area (km2)	1 002 000[a]
Pop. density (per km2, 2020)	102.8	Sex ratio (m per 100 f)	102.1
Capital city	Cairo	National currency	Egyptian Pound (EGP)
Capital city pop. (000, 2020)	20 485.0[b,c]	Exchange rate (per US$)	16.0[c]

Economic indicators

	2010	2015	2020
GDP: Gross domestic product (million current US$)	214 630	317 745	249 751[d]
GDP growth rate (annual %, const. 2015 prices)	5.1	4.4	5.3[d]
GDP per capita (current US$)	2 593.4	3 437.2	2 537.5[d]
Economy: Agriculture (% of Gross Value Added)[e]	14.0	11.3	11.5[d]
Economy: Industry (% of Gross Value Added)[e]	37.5	36.2	35.9[d]
Economy: Services and other activity (% of GVA)[e]	47.8	53.8	52.6[d]
Employment in agriculture (% of employed)	28.3	25.8	23.3[f]
Employment in industry (% of employed)	25.4	25.1	28.2[f]
Employment in services & other sectors (% employed)	46.3	49.1	48.6[f]
Unemployment rate (% of labour force)[f]	8.8	13.0	10.1
Labour force participation rate (female/male pop. %)[f]	22.6 / 75.6	22.4 / 73.3	22.1 / 70.9
CPI: Consumer Price Index (2010=100)[g]	100	157	289[h,c]
Agricultural production index (2004-2006=100)	109	121	124[i]
International trade: exports (million current US$)[j]	26 332	21 852	30 633[c]
International trade: imports (million current US$)[j]	53 003	73 975	78 658[c]
International trade: balance (million current US$)[j]	- 26 672	- 52 123	- 48 025[c]
Balance of payments, current account (million US$)	- 4 504	- 17 243	- 10 222[c]

Major trading partners

						2019
Export partners (% of exports)	United States	7.2	United Arab Emirates	6.8	Turkey	5.7
Import partners (% of imports)	China	15.3	United States	6.6	Saudi Arabia	6.6

Social indicators

	2010	2015	2020
Population growth rate (average annual %)[k]	1.8	2.2	2.0
Urban population (% of total population)	43.0	42.8	42.7[c]
Urban population growth rate (average annual %)[k]	1.8	2.1	...
Fertility rate, total (live births per woman)[k]	3.0	3.4	3.3
Life expectancy at birth (females/males, years)[k]	72.2 / 67.6	73.0 / 68.7	74.1 / 69.5
Population age distribution (0-14/60+ years old, %)	32.6 / 7.6	33.3 / 7.7	33.9 / 8.2
International migrant stock (000/% of total pop.)[l]	310.0 / 0.4	353.6 / 0.4	504.1 / 0.5[c]
Refugees and others of concern to the UNHCR (000)	109.9[m]	256.4	319.5[c]
Infant mortality rate (per 1 000 live births)[k]	23.5	18.9	15.6
Health: Current expenditure (% of GDP)	4.2	5.3	5.3[a]
Health: Physicians (per 1 000 pop.)	...	0.8	0.5[d]
Education: Government expenditure (% of GDP)	3.8[n]	...	...
Education: Primary gross enrol. ratio (f/m per 100 pop.)	100.7 / 103.7	103.7 / 104.0[o]	106.5 / 106.1[d]
Education: Secondary gross enrol. ratio (f/m per 100 pop.)	67.9 / 69.8	80.6 / 81.0[o]	87.3 / 88.5[d]
Education: Tertiary gross enrol. ratio (f/m per 100 pop.)	30.0 / 32.8	34.3 / 35.7	35.8 / 34.6[a]
Intentional homicide rate (per 100 000 pop.)	2.2	2.6[p]	...
Seats held by women in the National Parliament (%)	...	...	15.1[q]

Environment and infrastructure indicators

	2010	2015	2020
Individuals using the Internet (per 100 inhabitants)	21.6[r]	37.8[r]	46.9[d]
Research & Development expenditure (% of GDP)	0.4[s,t]	0.7	0.7[d]
Threatened species (number)	121	141	172
Forested area (% of land area)[f]	0.1	0.1	0.1[a]
CO2 emission estimates (million tons/tons per capita)[u]	176.4 / 2.1	199.5 / 2.1	209.2 / 2.1[a]
Energy production, primary (Petajoules)	3 692	3 051	3 418[a]
Energy supply per capita (Gigajoules)	39	37	41[a]
Tourist/visitor arrivals at national borders (000)	14 051	9 139	11 196[d]
Important sites for terrestrial biodiversity protected (%)	39.4	39.4	39.4[c]
Pop. using safely managed sanitation (urban/rural %)	67.0 / ...	69.4 / ...	70.7 / ...[a]
Net Official Development Assist. received (% of GNI)	0.28	0.77	0.85[d]

2017. **b** Refers to Greater Cairo as the sum of the Governorate of Al-Qahirah (Cairo) and the surrounding districts of the Governorates of Al-Jizah (Giza) and Al-Qalyūbyah (Qalyubia). **c** 2019. **d** 2018. **e** At factor cost. **f** Estimate. **g** Urban areas. **h** Calculated by the UN Statistics Division from national indices. **i** 2016. **j** Special trade system up to 2007. **k** Data refers to a 5-year period preceding the reference year. **l** Including refugees. **m** Data as at the end of December. **n** 2008. **o** 2014. **p** 2012. **q** Data are as at 1 January of reporting year. **r** Population aged 6 years and over. **s** Excluding business enterprise. **t** Excluding private non-profit. **u** Data refer to fiscal years beginning 1 July.

El Salvador

Region	Central America	UN membership date	24 October 1945
Population (000, 2020)	6 486	Surface area (km2)	21 041 [a,b]
Pop. density (per km2, 2020)	313.0	Sex ratio (m per 100 f)	88.0
Capital city	San Salvador	National currency	US Dollar (USD)
Capital city pop. (000, 2020)	1 105.7 [c,d]	Exchange rate (per US$)	1.0 [d]

Economic indicators	2010	2015	2020
GDP: Gross domestic product (million current US$)	18 448	23 438	26 057 [e]
GDP growth rate (annual %, const. 2015 prices)	1.4	2.4	2.5 [e]
GDP per capita (current US$)	2 983.2	3 705.6	4 058.2 [e]
Economy: Agriculture (% of Gross Value Added) [f]	7.6	6.1	5.4 [e]
Economy: Industry (% of Gross Value Added) [f,g]	27.5	27.8	28.0 [e]
Economy: Services and other activity (% of GVA) [f,h,i]	52.8	56.2	56.8 [e]
Employment in agriculture (% of employed)	20.8	18.1	16.0 [j]
Employment in industry (% of employed)	21.4	22.2	22.1 [j]
Employment in services & other sectors (% employed)	57.9	59.7	62.0 [j]
Unemployment rate (% of labour force) [j]	4.9	4.0	4.2
Labour force participation rate (female/male pop. %) [j]	46.0 / 76.6	45.2 / 75.3	45.5 / 75.8
CPI: Consumer Price Index (2010=100) [k]	100	108	111 [d]
Agricultural production index (2004-2006=100)	107	104	111 [d]
International trade: exports (million current US$)	4 499	5 509	5 943 [d]
International trade: imports (million current US$)	8 416	10 293	12 018 [d]
International trade: balance (million current US$)	- 3 917	- 4 784	- 6 074 [d]
Balance of payments, current account (million US$)	- 533	- 754	- 558 [d]

Major trading partners						2019
Export partners (% of exports)	United States	42.2	Guatemala	16.0	Honduras	15.9
Import partners (% of imports)	United States	30.4	China	14.3	Guatemala	10.6

Social indicators	2010	2015	2020
Population growth rate (average annual %) [m]	0.4	0.5	0.5
Urban population (% of total population)	65.5	69.7	72.7 [d]
Urban population growth rate (average annual %) [m]	1.6	1.7	...
Fertility rate, total (live births per woman) [m]	2.4	2.2	2.1
Life expectancy at birth (females/males, years) [m]	75.1 / 65.9	76.3 / 67.0	77.5 / 68.1
Population age distribution (0-14/60+ years old, %)	31.6 / 9.9	28.4 / 11.0	26.6 / 12.1
International migrant stock (000/% of total pop.) [n]	40.3 / 0.7	42.0 / 0.7	42.6 / 0.7 [d]
Refugees and others of concern to the UNHCR (000)	0.1 [o]	~0.0	75.3 [d]
Infant mortality rate (per 1 000 live births) [m]	21.6	17.7	14.6
Health: Current expenditure (% of GDP)	8.2	7.6	7.2 [b]
Health: Physicians (per 1 000 pop.)	1.9 [p]	...	1.6 [l]
Education: Government expenditure (% of GDP)	4.0	4.0	3.8 [b]
Education: Primary gross enrol. ratio (f/m per 100 pop.)	112.3 / 117.6	100.4 / 104.8	93.3 / 96.3 [e]
Education: Secondary gross enrol. ratio (f/m per 100 pop.)	69.0 / 69.3	75.6 / 75.0	71.4 / 71.9 [e]
Education: Tertiary gross enrol. ratio (f/m per 100 pop.)	27.4 / 24.8	29.4 / 26.5	31.1 / 27.5 [e]
Intentional homicide rate (per 100 000 pop.)	64.5	105.2	52.0 [e]
Seats held by women in the National Parliament (%)	19.0	27.4	33.3 [q]

Environment and infrastructure indicators	2010	2015	2020
Individuals using the Internet (per 100 inhabitants)	15.9 [r]	26.8	33.8 [b]
Research & Development expenditure (% of GDP)	0.1	0.1 [s]	0.2 [b]
Threatened species (number)	72	83	107
Forested area (% of land area) [j]	13.9	12.8	12.8 [b]
CO2 emission estimates (million tons/tons per capita)	5.8 / 0.9	6.4 / 1.0	5.7 / 0.9 [b]
Energy production, primary (Petajoules)	95	85	89 [b]
Energy supply per capita (Gigajoules)	29	28	27 [b]
Tourist/visitor arrivals at national borders (000)	1 150	1 402	1 677 [e]
Important sites for terrestrial biodiversity protected (%)	23.5	25.0	25.0 [d]
Pop. using safely managed drinking water (urban/rural, %)	76.1 / ...	77.0 / ...	77.3 / ... [b]
Net Official Development Assist. received (% of GNI)	1.69	0.40	1.03 [e]

a The total surface is 21 040.79 square kilometres, without taking into account the last ruling of The Hague. **b** 2017. **c** Refers to the urban parts of the municipalities San Salvador, Mejicanos, Soyapango, Delgado, Ilopango, Cuscatancingo, Ayutuxtepeque and San Marcos. **d** 2019. **e** 2018. **f** Data classified according to ISIC Rev. 4. **g** Excludes publishing activities. Includes irrigation and canals. **h** Excludes computer and related activities and radio/TV activities. **i** Excludes repair of personal and household goods. **j** Estimate. **k** Urban areas. **l** 2016. **m** Data refers to a 5-year period preceding the reference year. **n** Including refugees. **o** Data as at the end of December. **p** 2008. **q** Data are as at 1 January of reporting year. **r** Population aged 10 years and over. **s** Break in the time series.

Equatorial Guinea

Region	Middle Africa	UN membership date	12 November 1968
Population (000, 2020)	1 403	Surface area (km2)	28 052 [a]
Pop. density (per km2, 2020)	50.0	Sex ratio (m per 100 f)	125.3
Capital city	Malabo	National currency	CFA Franc, BEAC (XAF) [b]
Capital city pop. (000, 2020)	296.8 [c]	Exchange rate (per US$)	583.9 [d]

Economic indicators

	2010	2015	2020
GDP: Gross domestic product (million current US$)	16 299	13 176	13 324 [c]
GDP growth rate (annual %, const. 2015 prices)	- 8.9	- 9.1	- 4.7 [c]
GDP per capita (current US$)	17 272.0	11 274.9	10 179.2 [c]
Economy: Agriculture (% of Gross Value Added)	1.1	1.9	2.3 [c]
Economy: Industry (% of Gross Value Added)	74.3	59.0	57.1 [c]
Economy: Services and other activity (% of GVA)	43.4	55.7	56.7 [c]
Employment in agriculture (% of employed) [e]	41.7	42.0	42.5
Employment in industry (% of employed) [e]	22.9	20.9	18.5
Employment in services & other sectors (% employed) [e]	35.4	37.1	38.9
Unemployment rate (% of labour force) [e]	6.7	6.6	6.5
Labour force participation rate (female/male pop. %) [e]	54.0 / 67.7	54.9 / 67.8	55.0 / 67.5
CPI: Consumer Price Index (2010=100)	100 [f]	119	124 [d]
Agricultural production index (2004-2006=100)	109	115	115 [g]
International trade: exports (million current US$) [e]	9 964	9 570	3 939 [d]
International trade: imports (million current US$) [e]	5 679	6 010	3 902 [d]
International trade: balance (million current US$) [e]	4 285	3 560	37 [d]

Major trading partners

						2019
Export partners (% of exports) [e]	China	38.7	India	18.0	Spain	10.5
Import partners (% of imports) [e]	United States	21.1	Spain	18.6	China	14.2

Social indicators

	2010	2015	2020
Population growth rate (average annual %) [h]	4.6	4.3	3.7
Urban population (% of total population)	65.9	70.6	72.6 [d]
Urban population growth rate (average annual %) [h]	7.2	5.6	...
Fertility rate, total (live births per woman) [h]	5.4	5.0	4.6
Life expectancy at birth (females/males, years) [h]	56.0 / 53.8	57.8 / 55.4	59.4 / 57.3
Population age distribution (0-14/60+ years old, %)	38.5 / 4.4	37.5 / 4.1	36.8 / 3.8
International migrant stock (000/% of total pop.) [i]	8.7 / 0.9	209.6 / 17.9	227.6 / 16.8 [d]
Infant mortality rate (per 1 000 live births) [h]	84.6	73.8	66.1
Health: Current expenditure (% of GDP) [e]	1.8	2.9	3.1 [a]
Health: Physicians (per 1 000 pop.)	...	...	0.4 [a]
Education: Primary gross enrol. ratio (f/m per 100 pop.)	68.9 / 69.8	61.6 / 62.0	... / ...
Education: Secondary gross enrol. ratio (f/m per 100 pop.)	22.1 / 29.9 [j]	... / ...	... / ...
Seats held by women in the National Parliament (%)	10.0	24.0	21.0 [k]

Environment and infrastructure indicators

	2010	2015	2020
Individuals using the Internet (per 100 inhabitants)	6.0	21.3 [e]	26.2 [e,a]
Threatened species (number)	130	155	205
Forested area (% of land area)	58.0	55.9	55.9 [e,a]
Energy production, primary (Petajoules)	896	791	740 [a]
Energy supply per capita (Gigajoules)	86	54	39 [a]
Important sites for terrestrial biodiversity protected (%)	100.0	100.0	100.0 [d]
Net Official Development Assist. received (% of GNI)	0.89	0.08	0.06 [c]

a 2017. **b** African Financial Community (CFA) Franc, Bank of Central African States (BEAC). **c** 2018. **d** 2019. **e** estimate. **f** Break in the time series. **g** 2016. **h** Data refers to a 5-year period preceding the reference year. **i** Refers to foreign citizens. **j** 2005. **k** Data are as at 1 January of reporting year.

Eritrea

Region	Eastern Africa	UN membership date	28 May 1993
Population (000, 2020)	3 546	Surface area (km2)	117 600 [a]
Pop. density (per km2, 2020)	35.1	Sex ratio (m per 100 f)	100.5
Capital city	Asmara	National currency	Nakfa (ERN)
Capital city pop. (000, 2020)	928.8 [b]	Exchange rate (per US$)	15.1 [b]

Economic indicators

	2010	2015	2020
GDP: Gross domestic product (million current US$)	2 117	4 442	6 855 [c]
GDP growth rate (annual %, const. 2015 prices)	2.2	2.6	4.2 [c]
GDP per capita (current US$)	667.7	1 328.9	1 985.4 [c]
Economy: Agriculture (% of Gross Value Added)	19.1	17.2	17.3 [c]
Economy: Industry (% of Gross Value Added)	23.1	23.5	23.5 [c]
Economy: Services and other activity (% of GVA)	54.4	55.6	55.0 [c]
Employment in agriculture (% of employed) [d]	64.7	63.1	60.8
Employment in industry (% of employed) [d]	9.1	8.5	8.5
Employment in services & other sectors (% employed) [d]	26.3	28.4	30.7
Unemployment rate (% of labour force) [d]	5.4	5.3	5.2
Labour force participation rate (female/male pop. %) [d]	71.4 / 83.0	71.6 / 86.1	71.4 / 85.3
Agricultural production index (2004-2006=100) [d]	102	103	104 [e]
International trade: exports (million current US$) [d]	13	15	18 [b]
International trade: imports (million current US$) [d]	1 187	2 801	5 677 [b]
International trade: balance (million current US$) [d]	- 1 175	- 2 786	- 5 659 [b]

Major trading partners

					2019
Export partners (% of exports) [d]	China	53.6	United Arab Emirates 24.4	Rep. of Korea	20.5
Import partners (% of imports) [d]	Egypt	30.5	United Arab Emirates 22.1	China	11.2

Social indicators

	2010	2015	2020
Population growth rate (average annual %) [f]	2.3	1.1	1.2
Urban population (% of total population)	35.2	38.2	40.7 [b]
Urban population growth rate (average annual %) [f]	4.5	3.6	...
Fertility rate, total (live births per woman) [f]	4.8	4.4	4.1
Life expectancy at birth (females/males, years) [f]	62.7 / 58.7	65.6 / 61.4	68.0 / 63.6
Population age distribution (0-14/60+ years old, %)	39.5 / 6.2	42.3 / 6.5	41.1 / 6.4
International migrant stock (000/% of total pop.) [d]	15.7 / 0.5	15.9 / 0.5	16.1 / 0.5 [b]
Refugees and others of concern to the UNHCR (000)	5.0 [g]	3.0	0.9 [b]
Infant mortality rate (per 1 000 live births) [f]	51.6	45.0	34.7
Health: Current expenditure (% of GDP) [d]	3.5	2.9	2.9 [a]
Health: Physicians (per 1 000 pop.)	...	...	0.1 [e]
Education: Government expenditure (% of GDP)	2.1 [h]	...	...
Education: Primary gross enrol. ratio (f/m per 100 pop.)	76.9 / 90.2	70.4 / 81.7	63.1 / 73.6 [c]
Education: Secondary gross enrol. ratio (f/m per 100 pop.)	45.1 / 58.8	47.5 / 56.0	45.4 / 49.9 [c]
Education: Tertiary gross enrol. ratio (f/m per 100 pop.)	1.8 / 4.7	2.7 / 4.2	2.8 / 3.9 [e]
Seats held by women in the National Parliament (%)	22.0	22.0	22.0 [b]

Environment and infrastructure indicators

	2010	2015	2020
Individuals using the Internet (per 100 inhabitants) [d]	0.6	1.1	1.3 [a]
Threatened species (number)	97	113	143
Forested area (% of land area) [d]	15.2	15.0	15.0 [a]
CO2 emission estimates (million tons/tons per capita)	0.5 / 0.1	0.6 / 0.1	0.6 / 0.1 [a]
Energy production, primary (Petajoules)	24	27	28 [a]
Energy supply per capita (Gigajoules)	10	10	11 [a]
Tourist/visitor arrivals at national borders (000) [f]	84	114	142 [e]
Important sites for terrestrial biodiversity protected (%)	13.3	13.3	13.3 [b]
Net Official Development Assist. received (% of GNI)	7.74	5.16 [j]	...

a 2017. b 2019. c 2018. d Estimate. e 2016. f Data refers to a 5-year period preceding the reference year. g Data as at the end of December. h 2006. i Including nationals residing abroad. j 2011.

Estonia

Region	Northern Europe	UN membership date	17 September 1991
Population (000, 2020)	1 326	Surface area (km2)	45 227 [a]
Pop. density (per km2, 2020)	31.3	Sex ratio (m per 100 f)	90.0
Capital city	Tallinn	National currency	Euro (EUR)
Capital city pop. (000, 2020)	441.3 [b]	Exchange rate (per US$)	0.9 [b]

Economic indicators

	2010	2015	2020
GDP: Gross domestic product (million current US$)	19 697	23 049	30 747 [c]
GDP growth rate (annual %, const. 2015 prices)	2.7	1.8	4.8 [c]
GDP per capita (current US$)	14 786.2	17 523.3	23 241.9 [c]
Economy: Agriculture (% of Gross Value Added) [d]	3.6	3.3	3.1 [c]
Economy: Industry (% of Gross Value Added) [d,e]	27.6	27.3	27.7 [c]
Economy: Services and other activity (% of GVA) [d,f,g]	62.0	61.5	62.3 [c]
Employment in agriculture (% of employed)	4.2	3.9	3.1 [h]
Employment in industry (% of employed)	30.3	30.7	29.4 [h]
Employment in services & other sectors (% employed)	65.5	65.4	67.6 [h]
Unemployment rate (% of labour force) [h]	16.7	6.2	5.4
Labour force participation rate (female/male pop. %) [h]	55.0 / 67.1	56.0 / 69.5	56.8 / 70.7
CPI: Consumer Price Index (2010=100)	100	111	122 [b]
Agricultural production index (2004-2006=100)	110	150	128 [i]
International trade: exports (million current US$) [j]	12 811	13 908	16 811 [b]
International trade: imports (million current US$) [j]	13 197	15 732	18 659 [b]
International trade: balance (million current US$) [j]	- 385	- 1 824	- 1 848 [b]
Balance of payments, current account (million US$)	340	403	690 [b]

Major trading partners

							2019
Export partners (% of exports)	Finland	15.6	Sweden	10.0	Latvia	8.7
Import partners (% of imports)	Germany	9.8	Russian Federation	9.6	Finland	8.6

Social indicators

	2010	2015	2020
Population growth rate (average annual %) [k]	- 0.4	- 0.3	0.2
Urban population (% of total population)	68.1	68.4	69.1 [b]
Urban population growth rate (average annual %) [k]	- 0.5	- 0.2	...
Fertility rate, total (live births per woman) [k]	1.7	1.6	1.6
Life expectancy at birth (females/males, years) [k]	79.0 / 68.3	81.2 / 71.8	82.5 / 74.0
Population age distribution (0-14/60+ years old, %)	15.1 / 23.2	16.1 / 25.1	16.5 / 26.8
International migrant stock (000/% of total pop.)	217.9 / 16.4	194.7 / 14.8	190.2 / 14.4 [b]
Refugees and others of concern to the UNHCR (000)	101.0 [l]	86.8	77.0 [m,b]
Infant mortality rate (per 1 000 live births) [k]	4.7	3.2	2.0
Health: Current expenditure (% of GDP)	6.3	6.4	6.4 [a]
Health: Physicians (per 1 000 pop.)	3.2	3.4	4.5 [c]
Education: Government expenditure (% of GDP)	5.5	5.1	5.2 [i]
Education: Primary gross enrol. ratio (f/m per 100 pop.)	102.2 / 103.8	97.1 / 97.1	97.3 / 97.2 [a]
Education: Secondary gross enrol. ratio (f/m per 100 pop.)	105.3 / 105.2	110.8 / 111.3	118.9 / 116.2 [a]
Education: Tertiary gross enrol. ratio (f/m per 100 pop.)	85.9 / 51.6	87.5 / 57.7	84.8 / 55.4 [a]
Intentional homicide rate (per 100 000 pop.)	5.3	3.4	2.1 [c]
Seats held by women in the National Parliament (%)	22.8	19.8	28.7 [n]

Environment and infrastructure indicators

	2010	2015	2020
Individuals using the Internet (per 100 inhabitants)	74.1 [o,p]	88.4	89.4 [c]
Research & Development expenditure (% of GDP)	1.6	1.5	1.4 [q,c]
Threatened species (number)	11	17	48
Forested area (% of land area)	52.7	51.3	51.3 [h,a]
CO2 emission estimates (million tons/tons per capita)	18.6 / 13.9	15.1 / 11.5	16.0 / 12.1 [a]
Energy production, primary (Petajoules)	206	234	242 [a]
Energy supply per capita (Gigajoules)	179	176	185 [a]
Tourist/visitor arrivals at national borders (000) [r,s]	2 511	2 961	3 234 [c]
Important sites for terrestrial biodiversity protected (%)	94.8	94.8	94.9 [b]
Pop. using safely managed sanitation (urban/rural %)	97.4 / 93.9	98.4 / 94.2	98.7 / 94.4 [a]
Net Official Development Assist. disbursed (% of GNI)	0.10	0.15	0.16 [a]

[a] 2017. [b] 2019. [c] 2018. [d] Data classified according to ISIC Rev. 4. [e] Excludes publishing activities. Includes irrigation and canals. [f] Excludes repair of personal and household goods. [g] Excludes computer and related activities and radio/TV activities. [h] Estimate. [i] 2016. [j] General Extra-EU/Special Intra-EU [k] Data refers to a 5-year period preceding the reference year. [l] Data as at the end of December. [m] Most stateless people have permanent residence and enjoy more rights than foreseen in the 1954 Convention. [n] Data are as at 1 January of reporting year. [o] Users in the last 3 months. [p] Population aged 16 to 74 years. [q] Provisional data. [r] Border statistics are not collected any more, surveys used instead. [s] Based on mobile positioning data.

Eswatini

Region	Southern Africa	UN membership date	24 September 1968
Population (000, 2020)	1 160	Surface area (km2)	17 363[a]
Pop. density (per km2, 2020)	67.5	Sex ratio (m per 100 f)	96.7
Capital city	Mbabane[b]	National currency	Lilangeni (SZL)
Capital city pop. (000, 2020)	68.0[b,c]	Exchange rate (per US$)	14.1[d]

Economic indicators	2010	2015	2020
GDP: Gross domestic product (million current US$)	4 439	4 073	4 711[c]
GDP growth rate (annual %, const. 2015 prices)	3.8	2.3	2.4[c]
GDP per capita (current US$)	4 168.5	3 689.5	4 145.7[c]
Economy: Agriculture (% of Gross Value Added)[e]	10.4	9.8	9.0[c]
Economy: Industry (% of Gross Value Added)[e,f]	38.7	37.4	34.6[c]
Economy: Services and other activity (% of GVA)[e,g,h]	53.2	57.3	55.8[c]
Employment in agriculture (% of employed)[i]	15.2	13.5	12.3
Employment in industry (% of employed)[i]	25.3	24.6	23.5
Employment in services & other sectors (% employed)[i]	59.5	61.8	64.2
Unemployment rate (% of labour force)[i]	26.9	23.5	22.0
Labour force participation rate (female/male pop. %)[i]	45.5 / 57.4	47.0 / 56.4	48.6 / 56.9
CPI: Consumer Price Index (2010=100)	100	135	163[c]
Agricultural production index (2004-2006=100)	106	114	113[i]
International trade: exports (million current US$)	1 557[i]	1 820	2 002[d]
International trade: imports (million current US$)	1 710[i]	1 508	1 832[d]
International trade: balance (million current US$)	- 153[i]	312	169[d]
Balance of payments, current account (million US$)	- 388	533	196[d]

Major trading partners							2019
Export partners (% of exports)	South Africa	66.6	Kenya	6.3	Nigeria	5.0
Import partners (% of imports)	South Africa	73.0	China	7.2	Mozambique	2.4

Social indicators	2010	2015	2020
Population growth rate (average annual %)[k]	0.7	0.7	1.0
Urban population (% of total population)	22.5	23.3	24.0[d]
Urban population growth rate (average annual %)[k]	2.1	2.6	...
Fertility rate, total (live births per woman)[k]	3.6	3.1	3.0
Life expectancy at birth (females/males, years)[k]	46.0 / 42.0	54.0 / 47.8	63.9 / 55.2
Population age distribution (0-14/60+ years old, %)	40.2 / 5.6	39.1 / 5.7	37.4 / 5.7
International migrant stock (000/% of total pop.)[l]	32.6 / 3.1	32.4 / 2.9	32.3 / 2.8[d]
Refugees and others of concern to the UNHCR (000)	0.8[m]	0.9	1.8[d]
Infant mortality rate (per 1 000 live births)[k]	74.2	51.6	41.4
Health: Current expenditure (% of GDP)	8.6	7.1	6.9[a]
Health: Physicians (per 1 000 pop.)	0.2[n]	0.1[o]	0.3[j]
Education: Government expenditure (% of GDP)	6.1	7.1[p]	...
Education: Primary gross enrol. ratio (f/m per 100 pop.)	118.8 / 131.0	113.5 / 124.9	110.3 / 119.9[a]
Education: Secondary gross enrol. ratio (f/m per 100 pop.)	63.7 / 67.3	76.0 / 76.0	82.2 / 82.6[i]
Education: Tertiary gross enrol. ratio (f/m per 100 pop.)	4.6 / 5.3[q]	6.6 / 7.0[r]	... / ...
Intentional homicide rate (per 100 000 pop.)	19.5	10.1	11.6[a]
Seats held by women in the National Parliament (%)	13.6	6.2	9.6[s]

Environment and infrastructure indicators	2010	2015	2020
Individuals using the Internet (per 100 inhabitants)	11.0	25.6[i]	47.0[t,u,a]
Research & Development expenditure (% of GDP)	...	0.3	...
Threatened species (number)	29	34	41
Forested area (% of land area)[i]	32.7	34.1	34.1[a]
Energy production, primary (Petajoules)	33	36	37[i,a]
Energy supply per capita (Gigajoules)	41	43	39[i,a]
Tourist/visitor arrivals at national borders (000)	868	873	782[c]
Important sites for terrestrial biodiversity protected (%)	30.0	30.6	30.6[d]
Pop. using safely managed drinking water (urban/rural, %)	83.0 / ...	88.2 / ...	88.7 / ...[a]
Net Official Development Assist. received (% of GNI)	2.16	2.28	2.57[c]

a 2017. **b** Mbabane is the administrative capital and Lobamba is the legislative capital. **c** 2018. **d** 2019. **e** Data classified according to ISIC Rev. 4. **f** Excludes publishing activities. Includes irrigation and canals. **g** Excludes repair of personal and household goods. **h** Excludes computer and related activities and radio/TV activities. **i** Estimate. **j** 2016. **k** Data refers to a 5-year period preceding the reference year. **l** Including refugees. **m** Data as at the end of December. **n** 2009. **o** 2011. **p** 2014. **q** 2006. **r** 2013. **s** Data are as at 1 January of reporting year. **t** At least once a month. **u** Population aged 18 years and over.

Ethiopia

Region	Eastern Africa	
Population (000, 2020)	114 964	
Pop. density (per km2, 2020)	115.0	
Capital city	Addis Ababa	
Capital city pop. (000, 2020)	4 592.0 [b]	

UN membership date	13 November 1945	
Surface area (km2)	1 104 300 [a]	
Sex ratio (m per 100 f)	100.1	
National currency	Ethiopian Birr (ETB)	
Exchange rate (per US$)	31.8 [b]	

Economic indicators	2010	2015	2020
GDP: Gross domestic product (million current US$)	26 311	63 079	80 292 [c]
GDP growth rate (annual %, const. 2015 prices)	12.6	10.4	6.8 [c]
GDP per capita (current US$)	300.2	625.6	735.1 [c]
Economy: Agriculture (% of Gross Value Added)	45.3	38.8	32.8 [c]
Economy: Industry (% of Gross Value Added)	10.4	17.5	28.7 [c]
Economy: Services and other activity (% of GVA)	21.3	19.3	18.8 [c]
Employment in agriculture (% of employed) [d]	74.0	69.1	65.6
Employment in industry (% of employed) [d]	8.0	9.1	10.4
Employment in services & other sectors (% employed) [d]	18.0	21.8	24.0
Unemployment rate (% of labour force) [d]	2.3	2.2	2.1
Labour force participation rate (female/male pop. %) [d]	73.8 / 88.9	73.3 / 87.0	73.6 / 85.8
CPI: Consumer Price Index (2010=100) [d]	100	211	249 [a]
Agricultural production index (2004-2006=100)	138	170	164 [a]
International trade: exports (million current US$)	2 330	2 024	938 [d,b]
International trade: imports (million current US$)	8 602	17 686	9 675 [d,b]
International trade: balance (million current US$)	- 6 272	- 15 662	- 8 737 [d,b]
Balance of payments, current account (million US$)	- 635	- 7 567	- 4 611 [c]

Major trading partners						2019
Export partners (% of exports) [d]	China	8.9	Saudi Arabia	8.9	United States	7.8
Import partners (% of imports) [d]	China	28.3	United States	10.7	India	8.6

Social indicators	2010	2015	2020
Population growth rate (average annual %) [f]	2.8	2.8	2.6
Urban population (% of total population)	17.3	19.4	21.2 [b]
Urban population growth rate (average annual %) [f]	4.6	4.9	...
Fertility rate, total (live births per woman) [f]	5.4	4.8	4.3
Life expectancy at birth (females/males, years) [f]	60.6 / 57.6	65.5 / 61.9	67.9 / 64.1
Population age distribution (0-14/60+ years old, %)	44.9 / 5.1	42.2 / 5.2	39.9 / 5.3
International migrant stock (000/% of total pop.) [g]	568.7 / 0.6	1 161.6 / 1.2	1 253.1 / 1.1 [b]
Refugees and others of concern to the UNHCR (000)	155.4 [h]	705.7	5 444.5 [b]
Infant mortality rate (per 1 000 live births) [f]	59.8	45.8	37.0
Health: Current expenditure (% of GDP)	5.5	3.9	3.5 [a]
Health: Physicians (per 1 000 pop.)	~0.0 [i]	...	0.1 [c]
Education: Government expenditure (% of GDP)	4.5	4.7	...
Education: Primary gross enrol. ratio (f/m per 100 pop.)	88.0 / 95.2	96.1 / 105.8	... / ...
Education: Secondary gross enrol. ratio (f/m per 100 pop.)	31.6 / 38.0	34.2 / 35.6	... / ...
Education: Tertiary gross enrol. ratio (f/m per 100 pop.)	4.5 / 10.5	5.3 / 10.9 [j]	... / ...
Intentional homicide rate (per 100 000 pop.)	...	8.8 [k]	...
Seats held by women in the National Parliament (%)	21.9	27.8	38.8 [l]

Environment and infrastructure indicators	2010	2015	2020
Individuals using the Internet (per 100 inhabitants)	0.8 [d]	13.9	18.6 [d,a]
Research & Development expenditure (% of GDP)	0.2 [m]	0.6 [n]	0.3 [m,a]
Threatened species (number)	120	145	180
Forested area (% of land area) [d]	12.3	12.5	12.5 [a]
CO2 emission estimates (million tons/tons per capita) [o]	5.9 / 0.1	10.1 / 0.1	13.1 / 0.1 [a]
Energy production, primary (Petajoules)	1 212	1 330	1 371 [a]
Energy supply per capita (Gigajoules)	15	15	15 [a]
Tourist/visitor arrivals at national borders (000) [p,q]	468	864	849 [c]
Important sites for terrestrial biodiversity protected (%)	18.1	18.1	18.1 [b]
Pop. using safely managed drinking water (urban/rural, %)	37.0 / 1.7	38.0 / 3.6	38.4 / 4.6 [a]
Pop. using safely managed sanitation (urban/rural %)	... / 2.8	... / 3.5	... / 3.8 [a]
Net Official Development Assist. received (% of GNI)	11.58	5.04	5.90 [c]

a 2017. b 2019. c 2018. d Estimate. e 2016. f Data refers to a 5-year period preceding the reference year. g Including refugees. h Data as at the end of December. i 2009. j 2014. k 2012. l Data are as at 1 January of reporting year. m Break in the time series. n 2013. o Including Eritrea. p Including nationals residing abroad. q Arrivals through all ports of entry.

Falkland Islands (Malvinas)

Region	South America	Population (000, 2020)	3[a]
Surface area (km2)	12 173[a,b]	Pop. density (per km2, 2020)	0.2[a]
Sex ratio (m per 100 f)	110.5[a,c,d]	Capital city	Stanley
National currency	Falkland Islands Pound (FKP)	Capital city pop. (000, 2020)	2.3[a,e]
Exchange rate (per US$)	0.8[f]		

Economic indicators	2010	2015	2020
Unemployment rate (% of labour force)	...	1.2[g,h]	...
Labour force participation rate (female/male pop. %)	... / ...	77.2 / 86.0[g,i,h]	... / ...
Agricultural production index (2004-2006=100)	96	96	96[j]
International trade: exports (million current US$)[k]	9	4	2[f]
International trade: imports (million current US$)[k]	50	21	8[f]
International trade: balance (million current US$)[k]	- 41	- 17	- 6[f]

Major trading partners						2019
Export partners (% of exports)[k]	Spain	77.3	United States	6.1	Morocco	2.9
Import partners (% of imports)[k]	United Kingdom	78.9	Netherlands	15.5	Spain	1.3

Social indicators	2010	2015	2020
Population growth rate (average annual %)	- 0.6[l]	0.3[l]	0.2
Urban population (% of total population)[a]	73.7	76.3	78.1[f]
Urban population growth rate (average annual %)[a,l]	0.2	1.0	...
Population age distribution (0-14/60+ years old, %)	15.9 / 14.0[a,m]	16.4 / 15.7[c,a,d]	... / ...
International migrant stock (000/% of total pop.)[a]	1.4 / 49.5	1.6 / 55.4	1.9 / 56.3[f]

Environment and infrastructure indicators	2010	2015	2020
Individuals using the Internet (per 100 inhabitants)	95.8	98.3[k]	99.0[k,j]
Threatened species (number)	23	23	24
Forested area (% of land area)[k]	0.0	0.0	0.0[b]
Energy production, primary (Petajoules)	0[k]	0[k]	0[b]
Energy supply per capita (Gigajoules)	260[k]	197	183[b]
Important sites for terrestrial biodiversity protected (%)	10.9	10.9	10.9[f]

a A dispute exists between the Governments of Argentina and the United Kingdom of Great Britain and Northern Ireland concerning sovereignty over the Falkland Islands (Malvinas). b 2017. c Excluding military personnel and their families, visitors and transients. d 2012. e 2018. f 2019. g Population aged 16 to 65 years. h 2013. i Break in the time series. j 2016. k Estimate. l Data refers to a 5-year period preceding the reference year. m 2006.

Faroe Islands

Region	Northern Europe	Population (000, 2020)	50
Surface area (km2)	1 393[a]	Pop. density (per km2, 2020)	35.7
Sex ratio (m per 100 f)	107.2[b,c]	Capital city	Tórshavn
National currency	Danish Krone (DKK)	Capital city pop. (000, 2020)	20.8[d]
Exchange rate (per US$)	6.7[e]		

Economic indicators

	2010	2015	2020
Employment in agriculture (% of employed)	11.1[f,g,h]	...	...
Employment in industry (% of employed)	22.2[f,g,h]	...	...
Employment in services & other sectors (% employed)	66.7[f,g,h]	...	...
Unemployment rate (% of labour force)[i,k]	6.4[j]	4.0[l]	...
Labour force participation rate (female/male pop. %)	77.5 / 85.3[i,k]	79.4 / 86.0[i,k,l]	... / ...
Agricultural production index (2004-2006=100)	100	101	101[m]
International trade: exports (million current US$)[n]	839	1 024	1 950[e]
International trade: imports (million current US$)[n]	780	911	1 264[e]
International trade: balance (million current US$)[n]	59	113	686[e]
Balance of payments, current account (million US$)	144	194[o]	...

Major trading partners

							2019
Export partners (% of exports)[n]	United Kingdom	20.1	Russian Federation	20.0	Denmark	11.8	
Import partners (% of imports)[n]	Denmark	55.0	Germany	12.7	Norway	7.6	

Social indicators

	2010	2015	2020
Population growth rate (average annual %)	0.1[p]	0.2[p]	0.4
Urban population (% of total population)	40.9	41.6	42.2[e]
Urban population growth rate (average annual %)[p]	0.7	0.5	...
Fertility rate, total (live births per woman)	2.5	2.4	...
Life expectancy at birth (females/males, years)	82.3 / 76.8[q]	... / ...	84.5 / 78.3[r,m]
Population age distribution (0-14/60+ years old, %)	22.0 / 19.3[b,q]	21.0 / 22.5[b]	... / ...
International migrant stock (000/% of total pop.)	5.1 / 10.7	5.5 / 11.4	6.5 / 13.3[e]

Environment and infrastructure indicators

	2010	2015	2020
Individuals using the Internet (per 100 inhabitants)	75.2	94.2[n]	97.6[n,a]
Threatened species (number)	13	14	29
Forested area (% of land area)[n]	0.1	0.1	0.1[a]
Energy production, primary (Petajoules)	0	1	1[a]
Energy supply per capita (Gigajoules)[n]	184	185	210[a]
Important sites for terrestrial biodiversity protected (%)	0.0	15.8	15.8[e]

a 2017. b De jure population. c 2015. d 2018. e 2019. f Data classified according to ISIC Rev. 2. g Population aged 16 years and over. h 2005. i Population aged 15 to 74 years. j Break in the time series. k Excluding the institutional population. l 2013. m 2016. n Estimate. o 2011. p Data refers to a 5-year period preceding the reference year. q 2008. r Data refers to a 2-year period up to and including the reference year.

Fiji

Region	Melanesia	UN membership date	13 October 1970
Population (000, 2020)	896	Surface area (km2)	18 272[a]
Pop. density (per km2, 2020)	49.1	Sex ratio (m per 100 f)	102.6
Capital city	Suva	National currency	Fiji Dollar (FJD)
Capital city pop. (000, 2020)	178.3[b]	Exchange rate (per US$)	2.1[c]

Economic indicators

	2010	2015	2020
GDP: Gross domestic product (million current US$)	3 141	4 682	5 537[b]
GDP growth rate (annual %, const. 2015 prices)	3.0	4.7	3.5[b]
GDP per capita (current US$)	3 652.5	5 390.7	6 267.0[b]
Economy: Agriculture (% of Gross Value Added)[d]	10.2	10.2	13.4[b]
Economy: Industry (% of Gross Value Added)[d,e]	19.9	19.6	19.4[b]
Economy: Services and other activity (% of GVA)[d,f,g]	60.7	59.9	58.8[b]
Employment in agriculture (% of employed)[h]	43.9	39.4	35.7
Employment in industry (% of employed)[h]	14.4	13.2	13.3
Employment in services & other sectors (% employed)[h]	41.7	47.4	51.0
Unemployment rate (% of labour force)[h]	4.3	4.4	4.1
Labour force participation rate (female/male pop. %)[h]	43.1 / 79.2	40.1 / 77.0	38.6 / 76.2
CPI: Consumer Price Index (2010=100)[i]	100	116	132[c]
Agricultural production index (2004-2006=100)	81	85	84[i]
International trade: exports (million current US$)	841	895	1 137[h,c]
International trade: imports (million current US$)	1 808	2 081	2 650[h,c]
International trade: balance (million current US$)	- 967	- 1 186	- 1 513[h,c]
Balance of payments, current account (million current US$)	- 149	- 164	- 696[c]

Major trading partners

						2019
Export partners (% of exports)[h]	United States	17.9	Australia	12.9	Japan	7.4
Import partners (% of imports)[h]	Singapore	20.8	China	16.3	Australia	15.7

Social indicators

	2010	2015	2020
Population growth rate (average annual %)[k]	0.9	0.2	0.6
Urban population (% of total population)	52.2	54.7	56.8[c]
Urban population growth rate (average annual %)[k]	1.8	1.7	...
Fertility rate, total (live births per woman)[k]	2.8	2.8	2.8
Life expectancy at birth (females/males, years)[k]	68.0 / 64.9	68.6 / 65.4	69.1 / 65.6
Population age distribution (0-14/60+ years old, %)	29.0 / 7.9	29.8 / 8.1	29.0 / 9.6
International migrant stock (000/% of total pop.)	13.4 / 1.6	13.8 / 1.6	14.0 / 1.6[c]
Refugees and others of concern to the UNHCR (000)	~0.0[l]	~0.0	~0.0[c]
Infant mortality rate (per 1 000 live births)[k]	19.6	20.0	20.3
Health: Current expenditure (% of GDP)[m]	3.7	3.6	3.5[a]
Health: Physicians (per 1 000 pop.)	0.4[n]	0.9	...
Education: Government expenditure (% of GDP)	4.5[n]	3.9[o]	...
Education: Primary gross enrol. ratio (f/m per 100 pop.)	104.0 / 105.6[n]	105.5 / 107.9	105.2 / 107.6[j]
Education: Secondary gross enrol. ratio (f/m per 100 pop.)	90.7 / 82.9[n]	94.3 / 85.7[p]	... / ...
Education: Tertiary gross enrol. ratio (f/m per 100 pop.)	17.6 / 14.7[h,q]	... / ...	... / ...
Intentional homicide rate (per 100 000 pop.)	2.3	2.3[r]	...
Seats held by women in the National Parliament (%)	8.5[s]	14.0	19.6[t]

Environment and infrastructure indicators

	2010	2015	2020
Individuals using the Internet (per 100 inhabitants)[h]	20.0	42.5	50.0[a]
Threatened species (number)	192	278	321
Forested area (% of land area)[h]	54.3	55.7	55.7[a]
Energy production, primary (Petajoules)	5	7	7[a]
Energy supply per capita (Gigajoules)	25	41	38[h,a]
Tourist/visitor arrivals at national borders (000)[u]	632	755	870[b]
Important sites for terrestrial biodiversity protected (%)	11.2	11.2	11.2[c]
Net Official Development Assist. received (% of GNI)	2.49	2.29	2.28[b]

a 2017. b 2018. c 2019. d Data classified according to ISIC Rev. 4. e Excludes publishing activities. Includes irrigation and canals. f Excludes repair of personal and household goods. g Excludes computer and related activities and radio/TV activities. h Estimate. i Calculated by the UN Statistics Division from national indices. j 2016. k Data refers to a 5-year period preceding the reference year. l Data as at the end of December. m Data revision. n 2009. o 2013. p 2012. q 2005. r 2014. s 2006. t Data are as at 1 January of reporting year. u Excluding nationals residing abroad.

Finland

Region	Northern Europe	UN membership date	14 December 1955	
Population (000, 2020)	5 541 [a]	Surface area (km2)	338 440 [a,b]	
Pop. density (per km2, 2020)	18.2 [a]	Sex ratio (m per 100 f)	97.3 [a]	
Capital city	Helsinki	National currency	Euro (EUR)	
Capital city pop. (000, 2020)	1 292.2 [c]	Exchange rate (per US$)	0.9 [c]	

Economic indicators

	2010	2015	2020
GDP: Gross domestic product (million current US$)	249 181	234 585	276 878 [d]
GDP growth rate (annual %, const. 2015 prices)	3.2	0.6	1.7 [d]
GDP per capita (current US$)	46 438.9	42 798.8	50 135.7 [d]
Economy: Agriculture (% of Gross Value Added) [e]	2.8	2.6	2.8 [d]
Economy: Industry (% of Gross Value Added) [e,f]	29.9	27.0	28.4 [d]
Economy: Services and other activity (% of GVA) [e,g,h]	74.7	48.9	47.5 [d]
Employment in agriculture (% of employed)	4.4	4.2	3.5 [i]
Employment in industry (% of employed)	23.3	21.7	22.0 [i]
Employment in services & other sectors (% employed)	72.3	74.1	74.5 [i]
Unemployment rate (% of labour force) [i]	8.4	9.4	6.7
Labour force participation rate (female/male pop. %) [i]	56.0 / 63.9	55.5 / 62.3	55.3 / 62.5
CPI: Consumer Price Index (2010=100)	100 [j]	109 [j]	112 [c]
Agricultural production index (2004-2006=100)	94	98	97 [k]
International trade: exports (million current US$)	70 117	59 682	72 802 [i,c]
International trade: imports (million current US$)	68 767	60 174	73 335 [i,c]
International trade: balance (million current US$)	1 349	- 492	- 533 [i,c]
Balance of payments, current account (million US$)	2 792	- 1 683	- 2 060 [c]

Major trading partners

							2019
Export partners (% of exports) [i]	Germany	14.8	Sweden	10.2	Netherlands	6.5	
Import partners (% of imports) [i]	Germany	15.2	Russian Federation	13.9	Sweden	10.8	

Social indicators

	2010	2015	2020
Population growth rate (average annual %) [a,l]	0.4	0.4	0.2
Urban population (% of total population) [a]	83.8	85.2	85.4 [c]
Urban population growth rate (average annual %) [a,l]	0.6	0.8	...
Fertility rate, total (live births per woman) [a,l]	1.8	1.8	1.5
Life expectancy at birth (females/males, years) [a,l]	82.9 / 76.1	83.7 / 77.7	84.5 / 78.8
Population age distribution (0-14/60+ years old, %) [a]	16.5 / 24.8	16.4 / 27.0	15.9 / 29.0
International migrant stock (000/% of total pop.) [a]	228.5 / 4.3	314.9 / 5.7	383.1 / 6.9 [c]
Refugees and others of concern to the UNHCR (000)	14.0 [m]	16.3	35.0 [c]
Infant mortality rate (per 1 000 live births) [a,l]	2.7	2.1	1.7
Health: Current expenditure (% of GDP)	8.9	9.7	9.2 [b]
Health: Physicians (per 1 000 pop.)	3.3	3.3	3.8 [k]
Education: Government expenditure (% of GDP)	6.5	7.1	6.9 [k]
Education: Primary gross enrol. ratio (f/m per 100 pop.)	99.1 / 99.8	100.3 / 100.8	99.9 / 100.4 [b]
Education: Secondary gross enrol. ratio (f/m per 100 pop.)	110.1 / 105.2	157.5 / 142.9	161.5 / 146.8 [b]
Education: Tertiary gross enrol. ratio (f/m per 100 pop.)	103.1 / 84.3	95.8 / 79.8	95.7 / 81.0 [b]
Intentional homicide rate (per 100 000 pop.)	2.2	1.5	1.6 [d]
Seats held by women in the National Parliament (%)	40.0	42.5	46.0 [n]

Environment and infrastructure indicators

	2010	2015	2020
Individuals using the Internet (per 100 inhabitants)	86.9 [o]	86.4 [p]	88.9 [d]
Research & Development expenditure (% of GDP)	3.7	2.9	2.8 [d]
Threatened species (number)	18	25	61
Forested area (% of land area)	73.1	73.1	73.1 [i,b]
CO2 emission estimates (million tons/tons per capita)	62.0 / 11.6	42.4 / 7.7	42.6 / 7.7 [b]
Energy production, primary (Petajoules)	728	732	753 [b]
Energy supply per capita (Gigajoules)	285	246	251 [b]
Tourist/visitor arrivals at national borders (000)	2 319	2 622	3 224 [d]
Important sites for terrestrial biodiversity protected (%)	71.3	71.8	71.8 [c]
Pop. using safely managed sanitation (urban/rural %)	99.1 / ...	99.2 / ...	99.3 / ... [b]
Net Official Development Assist. disbursed (% of GNI) [q]	0.55	0.55	0.42 [b]

a Including Åland Islands. b 2017. c 2019. d 2018. e Data classified according to ISIC Rev. 4. f Excludes publishing activities. Includes irrigation and canals. g Excludes computer and related activities and radio/TV activities. h Excludes repair of personal and household goods. i Estimate. j Calculated by the UN Statistics Division from national indices. k 2016. l Data refers to a 5-year period preceding the reference year. m Data as at the end of December. n Data are as at 1 January of reporting year. o Population aged 16 to 74 years. p Population aged 16 to 89 years. q Development Assistance Committee member (OECD).

France

Region	Western Europe	UN membership date	24 October 1945
Population (000, 2020)	65 274	Surface area (km2)	551 500 [a]
Pop. density (per km2, 2020)	119.2	Sex ratio (m per 100 f)	93.8
Capital city	Paris	National currency	Euro (EUR)
Capital city pop. (000, 2020)	10 958.2 [b]	Exchange rate (per US$)	0.9 [b]

Economic indicators	2010	2015	2020
GDP: Gross domestic product (million current US$) [c]	2 642 610	2 438 208	2 778 892 [d]
GDP growth rate (annual %, const. 2015 prices) [c]	1.9	1.1	1.7 [d]
GDP per capita (current US$) [c]	40 685.3	36 611.8	41 358.1 [d]
Economy: Agriculture (% of Gross Value Added) [c,e]	1.8	1.8	1.8 [d]
Economy: Industry (% of Gross Value Added) [c,e,f]	19.8	19.8	19.0 [d]
Economy: Services and other activity (% of GVA) [c,e,g,h]	78.3	79.5	79.8 [d]
Employment in agriculture (% of employed)	2.9	2.7	2.4 [i]
Employment in industry (% of employed)	22.3	20.4	19.9 [i]
Employment in services & other sectors (% employed)	74.8	76.9	77.7 [i]
Unemployment rate (% of labour force) [i]	8.9	10.4	8.3
Labour force participation rate (female/male pop. %) [i]	50.8 / 61.9	50.8 / 60.6	50.6 / 59.6
CPI: Consumer Price Index (2010=100) [j,k]	100	106	110 [b]
Agricultural production index (2004-2006=100)	99	104	96 [l]
International trade: exports (million current US$)	511 651	493 941	569 757 [b]
International trade: imports (million current US$)	599 172	563 398	651 164 [b]
International trade: balance (million current US$)	- 87 520	- 69 457	- 81 407 [b]
Balance of payments, current account (million US$)	- 22 031	- 9 130	- 18 549 [b]

Major trading partners						2019
Export partners (% of exports)	Germany	13.8	United States	8.3	Italy	7.4
Import partners (% of imports)	Germany	17.7	Belgium	9.8	Italy	8.1

Social indicators	2010	2015	2020
Population growth rate (average annual %) [m]	0.6	0.5	0.3
Urban population (% of total population)	78.4	79.7	80.7 [b]
Urban population growth rate (average annual %) [m]	0.9	0.8	...
Fertility rate, total (live births per woman) [m]	2.0	2.0	1.9
Life expectancy at birth (females/males, years) [m]	84.3 / 77.5	85.0 / 78.7	85.4 / 79.4
Population age distribution (0-14/60+ years old, %)	18.5 / 23.1	18.4 / 25.0	17.7 / 26.8
International migrant stock (000/% of total pop.)	7 310.0 / 11.6	7 874.2 / 12.2	8 334.9 / 12.8 [b]
Refugees and others of concern to the UNHCR (000)	250.4 [n]	320.1	473.4 [b]
Infant mortality rate (per 1 000 live births) [m]	3.7	3.5	3.0
Health: Current expenditure (% of GDP)	11.2	11.5	11.3 [a]
Health: Physicians (per 1 000 pop.)	3.4	3.2	3.3 [d]
Education: Government expenditure (% of GDP)	5.7	5.5	5.4 [l]
Education: Primary gross enrol. ratio (f/m per 100 pop.) [i]	102.1 / 103.4	101.7 / 102.3	102.2 / 102.8 [a]
Education: Secondary gross enrol. ratio (f/m per 100 pop.) [i]	107.0 / 105.9	103.9 / 102.9	104.1 / 103.5 [a]
Education: Tertiary gross enrol. ratio (f/m per 100 pop.) [i]	61.2 / 48.7	69.7 / 56.1	72.8 / 58.7 [a]
Intentional homicide rate (per 100 000 pop.)	1.3	1.6	1.2 [d]
Seats held by women in the National Parliament (%)	18.9	26.2	39.5 [o]

Environment and infrastructure indicators	2010	2015	2020
Individuals using the Internet (per 100 inhabitants)	77.3 [p]	78.0 [q,r]	82.0 [d]
Research & Development expenditure (% of GDP)	2.2 [q]	2.3	2.2 [i,d]
Threatened species (number)	168	236	366
Forested area (% of land area) [i]	30.0	31.0	31.0 [a]
CO2 emission estimates (million tons/tons per capita) [s]	340.2 / 5.2	299.6 / 4.5 [t]	306.1 / 4.6 [a,t]
Energy production, primary (Petajoules) [s]	5 651	5 761 [t]	5 388 [t,a]
Energy supply per capita (Gigajoules) [s]	174	157 [t]	153 [t,a]
Tourist/visitor arrivals at national borders (000) [u]	76 647	84 452	89 322 [v,d]
Important sites for terrestrial biodiversity protected (%)	73.0	76.1	80.4 [b]
Net Official Development Assist. disbursed (% of GNI) [w]	0.50	0.37	0.43 [a]

a 2017. b 2019. c Including French Guiana, Guadeloupe, Martinique and Réunion. d 2018. e Data classified according to ISIC Rev. 4. f Excludes publishing activities. Includes irrigation and canals. g Excludes repair of personal and household goods. h Excludes computer and related activities and radio/TV activities. i Estimate. j Calculated by the UN Statistics Division from national indices. k Including French overseas departments and territories. l 2016. m Data refers to a 5-year period preceding the reference year. n Data as at the end of December. o Data are as at 1 January of reporting year. p Population aged 16 to 74 years. q Break in the time series. r Population aged 15 years and over. s Including Monaco. t From 2011 onwards, data include Monaco and the overseas departments (Guadeloupe, French Guiana, Martinique, Mayotte and Réunion), excluding the overseas collectivities: New Caledonia, French Polynesia, Saint Barthélemy, Saint Martin, St. Pierre and Miquelon, and Wallis and Futuna. u Arrivals of non-resident visitors. v Provisional data. w Development Assistance Committee member (OECD).

French Guiana

Region	South America	Population (000, 2020)	299	
Surface area (km2)	83 534[a]	Pop. density (per km2, 2020)	3.6	
Sex ratio (m per 100 f)	97.9	Capital city	Cayenne	
National currency	Euro (EUR)	Capital city pop. (000, 2020)	57.5[b]	
Exchange rate (per US$)	0.9[c]			

Economic indicators	2010	2015	2020
Employment in industry (% of employed)[d,e]	14.1	14.9[f]	...
Employment in services & other sectors (% employed)[d,e]	51.5	58.3[f]	...
Unemployment rate (% of labour force)[d]	21.0	21.3[g,h]	...
Labour force participation rate (female/male pop. %)	43.2 / 54.9[d]	48.4 / 58.8[d,g,h]	... / ...
CPI: Consumer Price Index (2010=100)[i]	100	105	108[c]
Agricultural production index (2004-2006=100)	103	133	127[j]

Social indicators	2010	2015	2020
Population growth rate (average annual %)[k]	2.8	2.3	2.7
Urban population (% of total population)	82.9	84.5	85.6[c]
Urban population growth rate (average annual %)[k]	3.2	3.1	...
Fertility rate, total (live births per woman)[k]	3.6	3.4	3.4
Life expectancy at birth (females/males, years)[k]	81.5 / 75.0	82.8 / 76.2	83.0 / 76.7
Population age distribution (0-14/60+ years old, %)	34.9 / 6.6	33.5 / 7.3	31.8 / 8.9
International migrant stock (000/% of total pop.)	96.3 / 41.3	106.1 / 40.7	117.4 / 40.4[c]
Infant mortality rate (per 1 000 live births)[k]	10.5	9.1	8.7
Intentional homicide rate (per 100 000 pop.)	13.2[l]	...	...

Environment and infrastructure indicators	2010	2015	2020
Threatened species (number)	56	67	79
Forested area (% of land area)	98.3[m]	98.2	98.2[m,a]
Energy production, primary (Petajoules)	3[n]	...	...
Tourist/visitor arrivals at national borders (000)[o]	83[l]	87	111[a]
Important sites for terrestrial biodiversity protected (%)	81.0	81.3	83.1[c]

a 2017. b 2018. c 2019. d Excluding the institutional population. e Population aged 15 to 64 years. f 2012. g Break in the time series. h 2013. i Calculated by the UN Statistics Division from national indices. j 2016. k Data refers to a 5-year period preceding the reference year. l 2009. m Estimate. n Data after 2010 are included in France. o Survey at Cayenne-Rochambeau airport on departure.

French Polynesia

Region	Polynesia	Population (000, 2020)	281
Surface area (km2)	4 000[a]	Pop. density (per km2, 2020)	76.8
Sex ratio (m per 100 f)	102.6	Capital city	Papeete
National currency	CFP Franc (XPF)[b]	Capital city pop. (000, 2020)	136.0[c,d]
Exchange rate (per US$)	106.2[e]		

Economic indicators	2010	2015	2020
GDP: Gross domestic product (million current US$)	6 081	5 324	6 100[d]
GDP growth rate (annual %, const. 2015 prices)	- 2.5	1.8	2.5[d]
GDP per capita (current US$)	22 820.8	19 491.9	21 967.5[d]
Economy: Agriculture (% of Gross Value Added)	2.5	3.1	3.1[d]
Economy: Industry (% of Gross Value Added)	12.3	11.8	11.8[d]
Economy: Services and other activity (% of GVA)	72.2	72.9	74.2[d]
Employment in agriculture (% of employed)[f]	8.7	7.7	6.8
Employment in industry (% of employed)[f]	16.4	15.1	14.6
Employment in services & other sectors (% employed)[f]	74.9	77.1	78.6
Unemployment rate (% of labour force)[f]	14.3	13.8	11.9
Labour force participation rate (female/male pop. %)[f]	48.6 / 64.2	48.6 / 62.4	47.4 / 60.1
CPI: Consumer Price Index (2010=100)	...	122[g,h]	...
Agricultural production index (2004-2006=100)	99	100	102[i]
International trade: exports (million current US$)	153	130	133[f,e]
International trade: imports (million current US$)	1 726	1 527	2 102[f,e]
International trade: balance (million current US$)	- 1 573	- 1 397	- 1 969[f,e]
Balance of payments, current account (million US$)	- 18	291	412[i]

Major trading partners						2019
Export partners (% of exports)[f]	Japan	38.6	United States	30.6	France	13.6
Import partners (% of imports)[f]	United States	33.0	France	31.8	New Zealand	6.0

Social indicators	2010	2015	2020
Population growth rate (average annual %)[j]	0.6	0.5	0.6
Urban population (% of total population)	60.3	61.7	61.9[e]
Urban population growth rate (average annual %)[j]	2.0	1.2	...
Fertility rate, total (live births per woman)[j]	2.2	2.0	2.0
Life expectancy at birth (females/males, years)[j]	77.4 / 72.8	78.6 / 74.0	79.6 / 75.3
Population age distribution (0-14/60+ years old, %)	25.5 / 9.3	23.6 / 11.4	22.2 / 13.6
International migrant stock (000/% of total pop.)	31.6 / 11.9	30.1 / 11.0	31.2 / 11.2[e]
Infant mortality rate (per 1 000 live births)[j]	8.8	6.9	6.7
Intentional homicide rate (per 100 000 pop.)	0.4[k]	...	...

Environment and infrastructure indicators	2010	2015	2020
Individuals using the Internet (per 100 inhabitants)	49.0	64.6[f]	72.7[f,a]
Threatened species (number)	160	175	181
Forested area (% of land area)[f]	42.3	42.3	42.3[a]
Energy production, primary (Petajoules)	1	1[f]	1[f,a]
Energy supply per capita (Gigajoules)	46	42	40[a]
Tourist/visitor arrivals at national borders (000)[l,m]	154	184	216[d]
Important sites for terrestrial biodiversity protected (%)	0.0	0.0	0.0[e]

a 2017. **b** Communauté financière du Pacifique (CFP) Franc. **c** Refers to the total population in the communes of Arue, Faaa, Mahina, Papara, Papeete, Pirae and Punaauia. **d** 2018. **e** 2019. **f** Estimate. **g** Base: 2000=100. **h** 2014. **i** 2016. **j** Data refers to a 5-year period preceding the reference year. **k** 2009. **l** Excluding nationals residing abroad. **m** Arrivals by air.

Gabon

Region	Middle Africa	UN membership date	20 September 1960
Population (000, 2020)	2 226	Surface area (km2)	267 668[a]
Pop. density (per km2, 2020)	8.6	Sex ratio (m per 100 f)	103.7
Capital city	Libreville	National currency	CFA Franc, BEAC (XAF)[b]
Capital city pop. (000, 2020)	823.9[c]	Exchange rate (per US$)	583.9[c]

Economic indicators

	2010	2015	2020
GDP: Gross domestic product (million current US$)	14 359	14 372	16 994[d]
GDP growth rate (annual %, const. 2015 prices)	7.1	3.9	1.2[d]
GDP per capita (current US$)	8 840.8	7 379.2	8 018.8[d]
Economy: Agriculture (% of Gross Value Added)	4.2	4.7	5.2[d]
Economy: Industry (% of Gross Value Added)	59.6	51.9	49.5[d]
Economy: Services and other activity (% of GVA)	64.5	73.7	79.2[d]
Employment in agriculture (% of employed)[e]	37.2	34.9	32.4
Employment in industry (% of employed)[e]	10.2	10.6	10.8
Employment in services & other sectors (% employed)[e]	52.6	54.5	56.9
Unemployment rate (% of labour force)[e]	20.4	20.3	20.2
Labour force participation rate (female/male pop. %)[e]	40.2 / 58.4	42.5 / 59.7	43.8 / 61.9
CPI: Consumer Price Index (2010=100)[e,f]	100	109	122[c]
Agricultural production index (2004-2006=100)	112	122	123[g]
International trade: exports (million current US$)[e]	8 539	5 074	486[c]
International trade: imports (million current US$)[e]	2 969	3 033	2 548[c]
International trade: balance (million current US$)[e]	5 570	2 040	- 2 062[c]
Balance of payments, current account (million US$)	2 453	141	...

Major trading partners

							2019
Export partners (% of exports)[e]	China	51.6	Singapore	6.8	Rep. of Korea	5.8
Import partners (% of imports)[e]	France	21.7	China	16.4	Belgium	6.1

Social indicators

	2010	2015	2020
Population growth rate (average annual %)[h]	3.1	3.6	2.7
Urban population (% of total population)	85.5	88.1	89.7[c]
Urban population growth rate (average annual %)[h]	3.9	3.9	...
Fertility rate, total (live births per woman)[h]	4.2	4.1	4.0
Life expectancy at birth (females/males, years)[h]	61.0 / 58.2	64.8 / 61.9	68.2 / 64.0
Population age distribution (0-14/60+ years old, %)	37.4 / 6.0	36.3 / 5.4	37.3 / 5.4
International migrant stock (000/% of total pop.)[i]	270.8 / 16.7	378.7 / 19.4	411.5 / 18.9[c]
Refugees and others of concern to the UNHCR (000)	13.2[i]	2.9	0.7[c]
Infant mortality rate (per 1 000 live births)[h]	49.9	41.9	35.3
Health: Current expenditure (% of GDP)	2.5	2.7	2.8[a]
Health: Physicians (per 1 000 pop.)	0.1[k]	...	0.7[a]
Education: Government expenditure (% of GDP)	3.1	2.7[l]	...
Education: Primary gross enrol. ratio (f/m per 100 pop.)	... / ...	137.7 / 142.1[m]	... / ...
Seats held by women in the National Parliament (%)	14.7	14.2	14.8[n]

Environment and infrastructure indicators

	2010	2015	2020
Individuals using the Internet (per 100 inhabitants)	13.0[e]	45.8[e]	62.0[o,p,a]
Research & Development expenditure (% of GDP)	0.6[q]	...	...
Threatened species (number)	204	231	329
Forested area (% of land area)	85.4	89.3	89.3[e,a]
CO2 emission estimates (million tons/tons per capita)	2.7 / 1.6	3.3 / 1.7	3.4 / 1.7[a]
Energy production, primary (Petajoules)	590	562	494[a]
Energy supply per capita (Gigajoules)	57	58	54[a]
Tourist/visitor arrivals at national borders (000)	269[r,s]	...	...
Important sites for terrestrial biodiversity protected (%)	61.2	61.2	61.7[c]
Net Official Development Assist. received (% of GNI)	0.85	0.75	0.74[d]

a 2017. b African Financial Community (CFA) Franc, Bank of Central African States (BEAC). c 2019. d 2018. e estimate. f Libreville and Owendo. g 2016. h Data refers to a 5-year period preceding the reference year. i Refers to foreign citizens. j Data as at the end of December. k 2008. l 2014. m 2011. n Data are as at 1 January of reporting year. o Population aged 18 years and over. p At least once a month. q 2009. r Arrivals of non-resident tourists at Libreville airport. s 2005.

Gambia

Region	Western Africa	UN membership date	21 September 1965
Population (000, 2020)	2 417	Surface area (km2)	11 295 [a]
Pop. density (per km2, 2020)	238.8	Sex ratio (m per 100 f)	98.4
Capital city	Banjul	National currency	Dalasi (GMD)
Capital city pop. (000, 2020)	443.4 [b,c]	Exchange rate (per US$)	49.5 [d]

Economic indicators	2010	2015	2020
GDP: Gross domestic product (million current US$)	1 543	1 378	1 633 [d]
GDP growth rate (annual %, const. 2015 prices)	5.9	4.1	6.5 [d]
GDP per capita (current US$)	860.6	660.7	716.1 [d]
Economy: Agriculture (% of Gross Value Added) [e]	37.4	24.3	21.6 [d]
Economy: Industry (% of Gross Value Added) [e,f]	10.4	18.8	16.9 [d]
Economy: Services and other activity (% of GVA) [e,g,h]	45.3	41.3	42.4 [d]
Employment in agriculture (% of employed) [i]	31.0	29.2	26.6
Employment in industry (% of employed) [i]	16.4	15.8	15.8
Employment in services & other sectors (% employed) [i]	52.6	54.9	57.7
Unemployment rate (% of labour force) [i]	9.4	9.3	9.1
Labour force participation rate (female/male pop. %) [i]	49.7 / 68.0	50.6 / 67.8	51.4 / 68.1
CPI: Consumer Price Index (2010=100) [j]	100	131	173 [c]
Agricultural production index (2004-2006=100)	133	101	106 [k]
International trade: exports (million current US$) [l]	68	90	25 [c]
International trade: imports (million current US$) [l]	284	402	494 [c]
International trade: balance (million current US$) [l]	- 215	- 312	- 469 [c]
Balance of payments, current account (million US$)	17	- 99	- 79 [d]

Major trading partners						2019
Export partners (% of exports)	Mali	48.5	Guinea-Bissau	18.9	China	13.5
Import partners (% of imports)	Ivory Coast	14.5	India	12.1	China	10.6

Social indicators	2010	2015	2020
Population growth rate (average annual %) [m]	3.0	3.0	2.9
Urban population (% of total population)	55.7	59.2	61.9 [c]
Urban population growth rate (average annual %) [m]	4.5	4.4	...
Fertility rate, total (live births per woman) [m]	5.6	5.5	5.2
Life expectancy at birth (females/males, years) [m]	60.2 / 57.6	61.6 / 59.1	63.0 / 60.2
Population age distribution (0-14/60+ years old, %)	45.1 / 4.3	44.5 / 4.1	44.0 / 3.9
International migrant stock (000/% of total pop.)	185.8 / 10.4	192.5 / 9.2	215.4 / 9.2 [c]
Refugees and others of concern to the UNHCR (000)	8.5 [n]	11.8	4.4 [c]
Infant mortality rate (per 1 000 live births) [m]	52.4	49.8	44.8
Health: Current expenditure (% of GDP)	3.4	3.1	3.3 [a]
Health: Physicians (per 1 000 pop.)	0.1 [o]	0.1	...
Education: Government expenditure (% of GDP)	4.2	2.2 [p]	2.1 [i,k]
Education: Primary gross enrol. ratio (f/m per 100 pop.)	80.8 / 78.8	93.0 / 87.1	102.5 / 93.6 [d]
Education: Secondary gross enrol. ratio (f/m per 100 pop.)	49.1 / 51.2 [i]	... / ...	... / ...
Education: Tertiary gross enrol. ratio (f/m per 100 pop.)	1.6 / 2.3	2.2 / 3.2 [q]	... / ...
Seats held by women in the National Parliament (%)	7.5	9.4	8.6 [r]

Environment and infrastructure indicators	2010	2015	2020
Individuals using the Internet (per 100 inhabitants)	9.2	16.5 [i]	19.8 [i,a]
Research & Development expenditure (% of GDP)	~0.0 [s,t]	0.1 [u,v]	0.1 [s,w,x,d]
Threatened species (number)	43	55	87
Forested area (% of land area)	47.4	48.2 [i]	48.2 [i,a]
Energy production, primary (Petajoules)	6	7	7 [a]
Energy supply per capita (Gigajoules)	7	7 [i]	7 [i,a]
Tourist/visitor arrivals at national borders (000) [y]	91 [z]	449	552 [d]
Important sites for terrestrial biodiversity protected (%)	34.6	34.6	34.6 [c]
Pop. using safely managed drinking water (urban/rural, %)	59.2 / ...	68.3 / ...	68.3 / ... [a]
Net Official Development Assist. received (% of GNI)	13.13	8.37	14.68 [d]

a 2017. b Refers to the local government areas of Banjul and Kanifing. c 2019. d 2018. e Data classified according to ISIC Rev. 4. f Excludes publishing activities. Includes irrigation and canals. g Excludes repair of personal and household goods. h Excludes computer and related activities and radio/TV activities. i Estimate. j Banjul, Kombo St. Mary k 2016. l As of 2009, merchandise trade includes re-exports. m Data refers to a 5-year period preceding the reference year. n Data as at the end of December. o 2008. p 2014. q 2012. r Data are as at 1 January of reporting year. s Partial data. t 2009. u Overestimated or based on overestimated data. v 2011. w Excluding private non-profit x Break in the time series. y Including nationals residing abroad. z Arrivals by air only.

Georgia

Region	Western Asia	UN membership date	31 July 1992
Population (000, 2020)	3 989[a]	Surface area (km2)	69 700[b]
Pop. density (per km2, 2020)	57.4[a]	Sex ratio (m per 100 f)	91.1[a]
Capital city	Tbilisi	National currency	Lari (GEL)
Capital city pop. (000, 2020)	1 077.3[c]	Exchange rate (per US$)	2.9[c]

Economic indicators

	2010	2015	2020
GDP: Gross domestic product (million current US$)	12 243	14 954	17 600[d]
GDP growth rate (annual %, const. 2015 prices)	6.2	3.0	4.8[d]
GDP per capita (current US$)	2 986.8	3 716.0	4 396.7[d]
Economy: Agriculture (% of Gross Value Added)	9.6	8.8	7.8[d]
Economy: Industry (% of Gross Value Added)[e]	19.1	21.5	22.9[d]
Economy: Services and other activity (% of GVA)[f,g]	60.4	63.9	62.2[d]
Employment in agriculture (% of employed)	48.1	44.0	41.3[h]
Employment in industry (% of employed)	10.6	11.0	14.2[h]
Employment in services & other sectors (% employed)	41.3	44.9	44.5[h]
Unemployment rate (% of labour force)[h]	20.2	16.5	14.7
Labour force participation rate (female/male pop. %)[h]	56.4 / 77.7	59.1 / 80.9	57.4 / 80.9
CPI: Consumer Price Index (2010=100)[i]	100	115	131[c]
Agricultural production index (2004-2006=100)	68	75	74[j]
International trade: exports (million current US$)	1 677	2 205	3 764[c]
International trade: imports (million current US$)	5 236	7 281	9 098[c]
International trade: balance (million current US$)	- 3 558	- 5 077	- 5 333[c]
Balance of payments, current account (million US$)	- 1 199	- 1 767	- 901[c]

Major trading partners

							2019
Export partners (% of exports)	Azerbaijan	13.2	Russian Federation	13.2	Armenia	11.0
Import partners (% of imports)	Turkey	17.7	Russian Federation	10.7	China	9.4

Social indicators

	2010	2015	2020
Population growth rate (average annual %)[a,k]	- 0.5	- 0.4	- 0.2
Urban population (% of total population)[a]	55.5	57.4	59.0[c]
Urban population growth rate (average annual %)[a,k]	- 0.5	- 0.7	...
Fertility rate, total (live births per woman)[a,k]	1.8	2.0	2.1
Life expectancy at birth (females/males, years)[a,k]	75.3 / 66.2	76.8 / 67.8	77.9 / 69.1
Population age distribution (0-14/60+ years old, %)[a]	18.0 / 18.9	19.0 / 20.1	20.2 / 21.5
International migrant stock (000/% of total pop.)[a]	73.0 / 1.8	76.7 / 1.9	79.0 / 2.0[c]
Refugees and others of concern to the UNHCR (000)	362.2[l]	268.3	287.4[c]
Infant mortality rate (per 1 000 live births)[a,k]	18.2	12.9	9.4
Health: Current expenditure (% of GDP)[m]	9.5	7.9	7.6[b]
Health: Physicians (per 1 000 pop.)	4.4	5.0	7.1[d]
Education: Government expenditure (% of GDP)	3.2[h,n]	2.0[o]	3.8[b]
Education: Primary gross enrol. ratio (f/m per 100 pop.)	104.1 / 102.7	102.8 / 102.7	99.2 / 98.1[d]
Education: Secondary gross enrol. ratio (f/m per 100 pop.)	100.9 / 97.8[p]	100.8 / 98.1	106.8 / 105.3[d]
Education: Tertiary gross enrol. ratio (f/m per 100 pop.)	37.0 / 28.4	51.6 / 41.6	68.1 / 60.2[c]
Intentional homicide rate (per 100 000 pop.)	4.6	2.7[q]	2.2[d]
Seats held by women in the National Parliament (%)	5.1	11.3	14.1[r]

Environment and infrastructure indicators

	2010	2015	2020
Individuals using the Internet (per 100 inhabitants)	26.9	47.6[s,t,u]	62.7[d]
Research & Development expenditure (% of GDP)	0.2[v]	0.3[w,x,y]	0.3[w,x,y,d]
Threatened species (number)	46	114	126
Forested area (% of land area)	40.6[h]	40.6	40.6[h,b]
CO2 emission estimates (million tons/tons per capita)	5.0 / 1.3	8.4 / 2.3	8.7 / 2.3[b]
Energy production, primary (Petajoules)	58	58	58[b]
Energy supply per capita (Gigajoules)	33	50	52[b]
Tourist/visitor arrivals at national borders (000)	1 067	3 012	4 757[d]
Important sites for terrestrial biodiversity protected (%)	34.4	40.3	40.3[c]
Pop. using safely managed sanitation (urban/rural %)	10.7 / ...	14.4 / ...	15.9 / ...[b]
Net Official Development Assist. received (% of GNI)	5.22	3.30	3.81[d]

Including Abkhazia and South Ossetia. **b** 2017. **c** 2019. **d** 2018. **e** Excludes publishing activities. Includes irrigation and canals. **f** Excludes repair of personal and household goods. **g** Excludes computer and related activities and radio/TV activities. **h** Estimate. **i** Data refer to 5 cities only. **j** 2016. **k** Data refers to a 5-year period preceding the reference year. **l** Data as at the end of December. **m** As a result of recent health-care reforms, public compulsory insurance has since 2008 been implemented by private insurance companies. The voucher cost of this insurance is treated as general government health expenditure. **n** 2009. **o** 2012. **p** 2008. **q** 2014. **r** Data are as at 1 January of reporting year. **s** Break in the time series. **t** Users in the last 3 months. **u** Population aged 6 years and over. **v** 2005. Partial data. **x** Excluding business enterprise. **y** Excluding private non-profit.

Germany

Region	Western Europe	UN membership date	18 September 1973
Population (000, 2020)	83 784	Surface area (km2)	357 376[a]
Pop. density (per km2, 2020)	240.4	Sex ratio (m per 100 f)	97.8
Capital city	Berlin	National currency	Euro (EUR)
Capital city pop. (000, 2020)	3 556.8[b]		

Economic indicators

	2010	2015	2020
GDP: Gross domestic product (million current US$)	3 396 354	3 360 550	3 949 549[c]
GDP growth rate (annual %, const. 2015 prices)	4.2	1.7	1.5[c]
GDP per capita (current US$)	42 020.0	41 088.8	47 513.7[c]
Economy: Agriculture (% of Gross Value Added)[d]	0.9	0.8	0.9[c]
Economy: Industry (% of Gross Value Added)[d,e]	29.9	30.1	30.5[c]
Economy: Services and other activity (% of GVA)[d,f,g]	72.4	72.8	76.9[c]
Employment in agriculture (% of employed)	1.6	1.4	1.2[h]
Employment in industry (% of employed)	28.3	27.7	26.8[h]
Employment in services & other sectors (% employed)	70.0	70.9	72.1[h]
Unemployment rate (% of labour force)[h]	7.0	4.6	3.0
Labour force participation rate (female/male pop. %)[h]	52.8 / 66.5	54.3 / 66.1	55.3 / 66.5
CPI: Consumer Price Index (2010=100)	100	107	105[i,b]
Agricultural production index (2004-2006=100)	103	108	107[j]
International trade: exports (million current US$)	1 267 740	1 328 500	1 493 090[b]
International trade: imports (million current US$)	1 060 670	1 057 540	1 240 700[b]
International trade: balance (million current US$)	207 071	270 964	252 398[b]
Balance of payments, current account (million US$)	196 172	288 621	274 847[b]

Major trading partners

							2019
Export partners (% of exports)	United States	8.9	France	8.0	China	7.3
Import partners (% of imports)	China	10.0	Netherlands	7.9	United States	6.6

Social indicators

	2010	2015	2020
Population growth rate (average annual %)[k]	- 0.2	0.2	0.5
Urban population (% of total population)	77.0	77.2	77.4[b]
Urban population growth rate (average annual %)[k]	0.1	0.3	...
Fertility rate, total (live births per woman)[k]	1.4	1.4	1.6
Life expectancy at birth (females/males, years)[k]	82.4 / 77.0	82.9 / 77.9	83.6 / 78.7
Population age distribution (0-14/60+ years old, %)	13.6 / 26.1	13.2 / 27.5	14.0 / 28.6
International migrant stock (000/% of total pop.)	9 812.3 / 12.1	10 220.4 / 12.5	13 132.1 / 15.7[b]
Refugees and others of concern to the UNHCR (000)	670.6[l]	573.8	1 461.0[b]
Infant mortality rate (per 1 000 live births)[k]	3.7	3.4	3.2
Health: Current expenditure (% of GDP)	11.0	11.1	11.2[a]
Health: Physicians (per 1 000 pop.)	3.8	4.1	4.2[a]
Education: Government expenditure (% of GDP)	4.9	4.8	4.8[i]
Education: Primary gross enrol. ratio (f/m per 100 pop.)	102.7 / 103.3	101.6 / 101.7	104.2 / 103.9[a]
Education: Secondary gross enrol. ratio (f/m per 100 pop.)	101.2 / 106.7	96.4 / 101.1	95.2 / 101.4[a]
Education: Tertiary gross enrol. ratio (f/m per 100 pop.)	... / ...	67.0 / 68.4	70.7 / 69.8[a]
Intentional homicide rate (per 100 000 pop.)	1.0	0.8	0.9[c]
Seats held by women in the National Parliament (%)	32.8	36.5	31.2[m]

Environment and infrastructure indicators

	2010	2015	2020
Individuals using the Internet (per 100 inhabitants)	82.0[n]	87.6[o]	89.7[c]
Research & Development expenditure (% of GDP)	2.7	2.9	3.1[h,c]
Threatened species (number)	79	107	200
Forested area (% of land area)	32.7	32.7	32.7[h,a]
CO2 emission estimates (million tons/tons per capita)	758.8 / 9.5	729.7 / 8.9	718.8 / 8.7[a]
Energy production, primary (Petajoules)	5 387	5 016	4 801[a]
Energy supply per capita (Gigajoules)	169	158	158[a]
Tourist/visitor arrivals at national borders (000)	26 875	34 970	38 881[c]
Important sites for terrestrial biodiversity protected (%)	77.9	78.4	78.8[b]
Pop. using safely managed sanitation (urban/rural %)	98.2 / 91.1	98.8 / 91.8	98.8 / 91.8[a]
Net Official Development Assist. disbursed (% of GNI)[p]	0.39	0.52	0.67[a]

a 2017. b 2019. c 2018. d Data classified according to ISIC Rev. 4. e Excludes publishing activities. Includes irrigation and canals. f Excludes computer and related activities and radio/TV activities. g Excludes repair of persona and household goods. h Estimate. i Index base: 2015=100. j 2016. k Data refers to a 5-year period preceding the reference year. l Data as at the end of December. m Data are as at 1 January of reporting year. n Population aged 16 to 74 years. o Users in the last 3 months. p Development Assistance Committee member (OECD).

Ghana

Region	Western Africa		UN membership date	08 March 1957	
Population (000, 2020)	31 073		Surface area (km2)	238 537[a]	
Pop. density (per km2, 2020)	136.6		Sex ratio (m per 100 f)	102.8	
Capital city	Accra		National currency	Ghana Cedi (GHS)	
Capital city pop. (000, 2020)	2 475.2[b]		Exchange rate (per US$)	5.5[b]	

Economic indicators

	2010	2015	2020
GDP: Gross domestic product (million current US$)	42 587	49 182	65 535[c]
GDP growth rate (annual %, const. 2015 prices)	7.9	2.2	6.3[c]
GDP per capita (current US$)	1 718.6	1 766.0	2 201.6[c]
Economy: Agriculture (% of Gross Value Added)[d]	28.9	22.1	19.7[c]
Economy: Industry (% of Gross Value Added)[d,e]	28.2	34.6	34.0[c]
Economy: Services and other activity (% of GVA)[d,f,g]	48.3	46.3	44.5[c]
Employment in agriculture (% of employed)	50.2[h]	35.2	28.5[h]
Employment in industry (% of employed)	13.7[h]	18.7	22.2[h]
Employment in services & other sectors (% employed)	36.1[h]	46.1	49.4[h]
Unemployment rate (% of labour force)[h]	5.3	6.8	4.5
Labour force participation rate (female/male pop. %)[h]	66.9 / 73.3	63.5 / 72.5	63.5 / 71.8
CPI: Consumer Price Index (2010=100)	100	176	255[c]
Agricultural production index (2004-2006=100)	127	151	153[i]
International trade: exports (million current US$)[j]	5 233	13 756	16 768[b]
International trade: imports (million current US$)[j]	8 057	14 687	10 440[b]
International trade: balance (million current US$)[j]	- 2 824	- 932	6 328[b]
Balance of payments, current account (million US$)	- 2 747	- 2 824	- 2 044[c]

Major trading partners

							2019
Export partners (% of exports)	China	16.7	Switzerland	14.7	India	14.2
Import partners (% of imports)	China	18.2	United States	9.4	United Kingdom	6.6

Social indicators

	2010	2015	2020
Population growth rate (average annual %)[k]	2.5	2.3	2.2
Urban population (% of total population)	50.7	54.1	56.7[b]
Urban population growth rate (average annual %)[k]	4.0	3.6	...
Fertility rate, total (live births per woman)[k]	4.4	4.2	3.9
Life expectancy at birth (females/males, years)[k]	61.1 / 59.2	62.7 / 60.9	64.7 / 62.6
Population age distribution (0-14/60+ years old, %)	39.3 / 4.6	38.2 / 4.8	37.1 / 5.3
International migrant stock (000/% of total pop.)	337.0 / 1.4	414.7 / 1.5	466.8 / 1.5[b]
Refugees and others of concern to the UNHCR (000)	14.8[l]	21.3	13.4[b]
Infant mortality rate (per 1 000 live births)[k]	53.7	44.8	35.6
Health: Current expenditure (% of GDP)	4.6	4.6	3.3[a]
Health: Physicians (per 1 000 pop.)	0.1	0.1[m]	0.1[a]
Education: Government expenditure (% of GDP)	5.5	4.5[h]	3.6[h,a]
Education: Primary gross enrol. ratio (f/m per 100 pop.)	99.5 / 101.1[n]	108.3 / 108.4	105.6 / 104.1[b]
Education: Secondary gross enrol. ratio (f/m per 100 pop.)	45.7 / 51.7[n]	66.1 / 69.6	64.5 / 64.6[b]
Education: Tertiary gross enrol. ratio (f/m per 100 pop.)	6.7 / 10.8[n]	12.9 / 18.4	13.6 / 17.7[c]
Intentional homicide rate (per 100 000 pop.)	1.7	1.9	2.1[a]
Seats held by women in the National Parliament (%)	8.3	10.9	13.1[o]

Environment and infrastructure indicators

	2010	2015	2020
Individuals using the Internet (per 100 inhabitants)	7.8[p,q]	25.0[r]	39.0[r,a]
Research & Development expenditure (% of GDP)	0.4[p]	...	...
Threatened species (number)	202	223	255
Forested area (% of land area)	40.4	41.0[h]	41.0[h,a]
CO2 emission estimates (million tons/tons per capita)	10.4 / 0.4	14.1 / 0.5	13.8 / 0.5[a]
Energy production, primary (Petajoules)	148	372	519[a]
Energy supply per capita (Gigajoules)	11	12	11[a]
Tourist/visitor arrivals at national borders (000)[s]	931	897	...
Important sites for terrestrial biodiversity protected (%)	80.6	80.6	80.6[b]
Pop. using safely managed drinking water (urban/rural, %)	44.3 / 5.9	52.9 / 9.8	56.5 / 11.5[a]
Net Official Development Assist. received (% of GNI)	5.36	3.65	1.66[c]

2017. **b** 2019. **c** 2018. **d** Data classified according to ISIC Rev. 4. **e** Excludes publishing activities. Includes irrigation and canals. **f** Excludes computer and related activities and radio/TV activities. **g** Excludes repair of personal and household goods. **h** Estimate. **i** 2016. **j** Since 2011, Ghana have been exporting crude petroleum & natural gas in relatively larger quantities. **k** Data refers to a 5-year period preceding the reference year. **l** Data as at the end of December. **m** 2012. **n** 2009. **o** Data are as at 1 January of reporting year. **p** Break in the time series. **q** Population aged 12 years and over. **r** Population aged 18 years and over. **s** Including nationals residing abroad.

Gibraltar

Region	Southern Europe	Population (000, 2020)	35
Surface area (km2)	6 [a]	Pop. density (per km2, 2020)	3 500.0
Sex ratio (m per 100 f)	101.8 [b,c]	Capital city	Gibraltar
National currency	Gibraltar Pound (GIP)	Capital city pop. (000, 2020)	34.7 [d]
Exchange rate (per US$)	0.8 [e]		

Economic indicators	2010	2015	2020
CPI: Consumer Price Index (2010=100)	...	142 [f,g]	...
International trade: exports (million current US$) [h]	259	295	436 [e]
International trade: imports (million current US$) [h]	627	737	1 052 [e]
International trade: balance (million current US$) [h]	- 368	- 442	- 615 [e]

Major trading partners						2019
Export partners (% of exports) [h]	Mauritania	39.7	Poland	18.3	Netherlands	15.3
Import partners (% of imports) [h]	Areas nes [i]	32.8	Netherlands	15.0	United States	12.9

Social indicators	2010	2015	2020
Population growth rate (average annual %)	0.7 [j]	0.6 [j]	0.4
Urban population (% of total population)	100.0	100.0	100.0 [e]
Urban population growth rate (average annual %) [j]	0.7	0.6	...
Population age distribution (0-14/60+ years old, %)	... / ...	18.1 / 22.4 [b,k,l]	... / ...
International migrant stock (000/% of total pop.)	10.4 / 30.9	11.1 / 32.8	11.2 / 33.2 [e]
Education: Primary gross enrol. ratio (f/m per 100 pop.)	112.8 / 110.9 [m]	... / ...	103.7 / 103.4 [a]
Education: Secondary gross enrol. ratio (f/m per 100 pop.)	83.2 / 85.2 [m]	... / ...	115.7 / 119.1 [a]
Intentional homicide rate (per 100 000 pop.)	3.0	...	...

Environment and infrastructure indicators	2010	2015	2020
Individuals using the Internet (per 100 inhabitants)	65.0	65.0 [h,j]	94.4 [h,n]
Threatened species (number)	22	26	36
Forested area (% of land area) [h]	0.0	0.0	0.0 [a]
CO2 emission estimates (million tons/tons per capita)	0.5 / 15.3	0.6 / 17.3	0.7 / 20.7 [a]
Energy supply per capita (Gigajoules)	220	262	309 [a]
Pop. using safely managed drinking water (urban/rural, %)	100.0 / ...	100.0 / ...	100.0 / ... [a]

a 2017. b Excluding military personnel, visitors and transients. c 2015. d 2018. e 2019. f Base: 2000=100. g 2014. h Estimate. i Areas not elsewhere specified. j Data refers to a 5-year period preceding the reference year. k De jure population. l 2012. m 2009. n 2016.

Greece

Region	Southern Europe	UN membership date	25 October 1945
Population (000, 2020)	10 423	Surface area (km2)	131 957 [a]
Pop. density (per km2, 2020)	80.9	Sex ratio (m per 100 f)	96.4
Capital city	Athens	National currency	Euro (EUR)
Capital city pop. (000, 2020)	3 154.2 [b,c]	Exchange rate (per US$)	0.9 [c]

Economic indicators

	2010	2015	2020
GDP: Gross domestic product (million current US$)	299 362	196 591	218 139 [d]
GDP growth rate (annual %, const. 2015 prices)	- 5.5	- 0.4	1.9 [d]
GDP per capita (current US$)	27 495.6	18 442.4	20 731.2 [d]
Economy: Agriculture (% of Gross Value Added) [e]	3.3	4.3	4.3 [d]
Economy: Industry (% of Gross Value Added) [e,f]	15.7	16.1	17.5 [d]
Economy: Services and other activity (% of GVA) [e,g,h]	75.2	76.2	74.7 [d]
Employment in agriculture (% of employed)	12.4	12.9	11.7 [i]
Employment in industry (% of employed)	19.6	14.9	15.2 [i]
Employment in services & other sectors (% employed)	68.0	72.2	73.1 [i]
Unemployment rate (% of labour force) [i]	12.7	24.9	15.5
Labour force participation rate (female/male pop. %) [i]	44.1 / 63.2	44.8 / 59.9	43.9 / 59.3
CPI: Consumer Price Index (2010=100) [i]	100	101	102 [c]
Agricultural production index (2004-2006=100)	94	88	93 [k]
International trade: exports (million current US$)	27 586	28 289	37 886 [c]
International trade: imports (million current US$)	66 453	47 264	62 198 [c]
International trade: balance (million current US$)	- 38 867	- 18 975	- 24 313 [c]
Balance of payments, current account (million US$)	- 30 263	- 1 611	- 2 928 [c]

Major trading partners

						2019
Export partners (% of exports)	Italy	10.8	Germany	6.6	Turkey	5.8
Import partners (% of imports)	Germany	10.6	Iraq	8.2	Italy	7.9

Social indicators

	2010	2015	2020
Population growth rate (average annual %) [i]	- 0.6	- 0.4	- 0.4
Urban population (% of total population)	76.3	78.0	79.4 [c]
Urban population growth rate (average annual %) [i]	0.7	0.1	...
Fertility rate, total (live births per woman) [i]	1.4	1.3	1.3
Life expectancy at birth (females/males, years) [i]	82.8 / 77.3	83.7 / 78.5	84.5 / 79.5
Population age distribution (0-14/60+ years old, %)	15.1 / 24.8	14.6 / 26.5	13.7 / 28.8
International migrant stock (000/% of total pop.)	1 321.1 / 12.1	1 242.9 / 11.7	1 211.4 / 11.6 [c]
Refugees and others of concern to the UNHCR (000)	57.4 [m]	37.6	147.1 [c]
Infant mortality rate (per 1 000 live births) [i]	3.5	3.3	2.8
Health: Current expenditure (% of GDP)	9.6	8.1	8.0 [a]
Health: Physicians (per 1 000 pop.)	3.9	5.3	5.5 [a]
Education: Government expenditure (% of GDP)	4.0 [n]	...	...
Education: Primary gross enrol. ratio (f/m per 100 pop.)	97.4 / 99.6	99.1 / 100.0	99.6 / 99.5 [a]
Education: Secondary gross enrol. ratio (f/m per 100 pop.)	104.4 / 108.1	98.4 / 105.8	101.4 / 107.5 [a]
Education: Tertiary gross enrol. ratio (f/m per 100 pop.)	107.3 / 100.5	125.0 / 120.1 [o]	137.0 / 136.2 [a]
Intentional homicide rate (per 100 000 pop.)	1.6	0.9	0.9 [d]
Seats held by women in the National Parliament (%)	17.3	23.0	20.7 [p]

Environment and infrastructure indicators

	2010	2015	2020
Individuals using the Internet (per 100 inhabitants)	44.4 [q]	66.8 [q]	73.0 [d]
Research & Development expenditure (% of GDP)	0.6 [i]	1.0	1.2 [r,d]
Threatened species (number)	156	291	520
Forested area (% of land area) [i]	30.3	31.5	31.5 [a]
CO2 emission estimates (million tons/tons per capita)	83.4 / 7.5	64.5 / 6.0	63.2 / 5.9 [a]
Energy production, primary (Petajoules)	395	354	301 [a]
Energy supply per capita (Gigajoules)	101	86	87 [a]
Tourist/visitor arrivals at national borders (000)	15 007	23 599	30 123 [d]
Important sites for terrestrial biodiversity protected (%)	86.0	86.0	86.0 [c]
Pop. using safely managed sanitation (urban/rural %)	90.8 / ...	95.0 / ...	96.6 / ... [a]
Net Official Development Assist. disbursed (% of GNI) [s]	0.17	0.12	0.16 [a]

[a] 2017. [b] Refers to the localities of Calithèa, Peristérion and Piraeus, among others. [c] 2019. [d] 2018. [e] Data classified according to ISIC Rev. 4. [f] Excludes publishing activities. Includes irrigation and canals. [g] Excludes computer and related activities and radio/TV activities. [h] Excludes repair of personal and household goods. [i] estimate. [j] Calculated by the UN Statistics Division from national indices. [k] 2016. [l] Data refers to a 5-year period preceding the reference year. [m] Data as at the end of December. [n] 2005. [o] 2014. [p] Data are as at 1 January of reporting year. [q] Population aged 16 to 74 years. [r] Provisional data. [s] Development Assistance Committee member (OECD).

Greenland

Region	Northern America	Population (000, 2020)	57
Surface area (km2)	2 166 086 [a]	Pop. density (per km2, 2020)	0.1
Sex ratio (m per 100 f)	112.1 [b,c,d]	Capital city	Nuuk
National currency	Danish Krone (DKK)	Capital city pop. (000, 2020)	18.4 [e]
Exchange rate (per US$)	6.7 [f]		

Economic indicators	2010	2015	2020
GDP: Gross domestic product (million current US$)	2 503	2 499	3 052 [e]
GDP growth rate (annual %, const. 2015 prices)	1.7	- 2.5	3.2 [e]
GDP per capita (current US$)	44 195.9	44 328.6	53 949.8 [e]
Economy: Agriculture (% of Gross Value Added)	13.8	17.6	18.6 [e]
Economy: Industry (% of Gross Value Added)	18.6	17.6	18.4 [e]
Economy: Services and other activity (% of GVA)	69.5	66.7	67.1 [e]
Employment in agriculture (% of employed)	...	4.6 [g,h,i]	...
Employment in industry (% of employed)	...	12.6 [g,h,i]	...
Employment in services & other sectors (% employed)	...	82.5 [g,h,i]	...
Unemployment rate (% of labour force)	8.4 [i]	9.7 [g,k,l,m]	...
Agricultural production index (2004-2006=100)	98	98	98 [d]
International trade: exports (million current US$)	389	406	771 [n,f]
International trade: imports (million current US$)	847	667	738 [n,f]
International trade: balance (million current US$)	- 458	- 261	32 [n,f]

Major trading partners						2019
Export partners (% of exports) [n]	Denmark	85.3	Areas nes [o]	7.7	Latvia	3.7
Import partners (% of imports) [n]	Denmark	54.2	Sweden	17.1	Spain	11.5

Social indicators	2010	2015	2020
Population growth rate (average annual %)	- 0.1 [p]	- 0.1 [p]	0.1
Urban population (% of total population)	84.4	86.1	87.1 [f]
Urban population growth rate (average annual %) [p]	0.3	0.3	...
Fertility rate, total (live births per woman)	2.3	2.0 [q]	
Life expectancy at birth (females/males, years) [r]	71.0 / 65.7	72.9 / 68.2	73.6 / 69.1 [e]
Population age distribution (0-14/60+ years old, %) [c,b]	22.6 / 10.9	21.1 / 12.7	21.0 / 13.2 [d]
International migrant stock (000/% of total pop.)	6.1 / 10.8	5.8 / 10.3	5.7 / 10.0 [f]
Intentional homicide rate (per 100 000 pop.)	19.4	7.1	5.3 [d]

Environment and infrastructure indicators	2010	2015	2020
Individuals using the Internet (per 100 inhabitants)	63.0	67.6 [n]	69.5 [n,a]
Threatened species (number)	14	17	27
Forested area (% of land area) [n]	~0.0	~0.0	~0.0 [a]
Energy production, primary (Petajoules)	1	2	1 [a]
Energy supply per capita (Gigajoules)	186	155	156 [a]
Important sites for terrestrial biodiversity protected (%)	26.3	26.3	26.3 [f]

a 2017. b De jure population. c Population statistics are compiled from registers. d 2016. e 2018. f 2019. g Nationals, residents. h Population aged 15 to 64 years. i 2011. j 2006. k Break in the time series. l Population aged 18 to 64 years. m 2013. n Estimate. o Areas not elsewhere specified. p Data refers to a 5-year period preceding the reference year. q 2014. r Data refers to a 5-year period up to and including the reference year.

Grenada

Region	Caribbean	UN membership date	17 September 1974
Population (000, 2020)	112	Surface area (km2)	345[a]
Pop. density (per km2, 2020)	331.0	Sex ratio (m per 100 f)	101.5
Capital city	Saint George's	National currency	E. Caribbean Dollar (XCD)[b]
Capital city pop. (000, 2020)	39.3[c,d]	Exchange rate (per US$)	2.7[e]

Economic indicators

	2010	2015	2020
GDP: Gross domestic product (million current US$)	771	997	1 169[d]
GDP growth rate (annual %, const. 2015 prices)	- 0.5	6.4	4.1[d]
GDP per capita (current US$)	7 257.8	9 096.9	10 485.9[d]
Economy: Agriculture (% of Gross Value Added)	5.2	8.6	6.3[d]
Economy: Industry (% of Gross Value Added)	16.8	14.2	16.2[d]
Economy: Services and other activity (% of GVA)	83.3	85.4	88.9[d]
CPI: Consumer Price Index (2010=100)	100	104	107[d]
Agricultural production index (2004-2006=100)	96	136	128[f]
International trade: exports (million current US$)[g]	25	33	32[e]
International trade: imports (million current US$)[g]	306	372	470[e]
International trade: balance (million current US$)[g]	- 281	- 339	- 438[e]
Balance of payments, current account (million US$)	- 204	- 122	- 116[d]

Major trading partners

							2019
Export partners (% of exports)[g]	United States	38.7	Saint Lucia	7.6	St.Vincent & Grenad.	5.8
Import partners (% of imports)[g]	United States	37.9	Canada	22.1	China	4.2

Social indicators

	2010	2015	2020
Population growth rate (average annual %)[h]	0.3	0.6	0.5
Urban population (% of total population)	35.9	36.0	36.4[e]
Urban population growth rate (average annual %)[h]	0.3	0.5	...
Fertility rate, total (live births per woman)[h]	2.3	2.2	2.1
Life expectancy at birth (females/males, years)[h]	75.7 / 70.6	75.2 / 70.3	75.0 / 70.1
Population age distribution (0-14/60+ years old, %)	24.0 / 13.3	23.2 / 13.5	23.8 / 14.9
International migrant stock (000/% of total pop.)	7.0 / 6.6	7.1 / 6.4	7.1 / 6.4[e]
Refugees and others of concern to the UNHCR (000)	~0.0[i]	...	~0.0[e]
Infant mortality rate (per 1 000 live births)[h]	12.3	13.7	15.0
Health: Current expenditure (% of GDP)	6.2	4.7	4.8[a]
Health: Physicians (per 1 000 pop.)	0.7[j]	...	1.4[a]
Education: Government expenditure (% of GDP)	...	...	3.2[a]
Education: Primary gross enrol. ratio (f/m per 100 pop.)	113.9 / 119.1	116.3 / 120.6	106.0 / 107.7[d]
Education: Secondary gross enrol. ratio (f/m per 100 pop.)	118.6 / 114.9	110.7 / 112.8	122.1 / 118.2[d]
Education: Tertiary gross enrol. ratio (f/m per 100 pop.)	75.3 / 54.2[k]	102.5 / 88.8	116.2 / 93.2[d]
Intentional homicide rate (per 100 000 pop.)	9.4	5.5	10.8[a]
Seats held by women in the National Parliament (%)	13.3	33.3	46.7[l]

Environment and infrastructure indicators

	2010	2015	2020
Individuals using the Internet (per 100 inhabitants)[g]	27.0	53.8	59.1[a]
Threatened species (number)	37	51	60
Forested area (% of land area)[g]	50.0	50.0	50.0[a]
Energy production, primary (Petajoules)	0	0	0[a]
Energy supply per capita (Gigajoules)	38	38	40[a]
Tourist/visitor arrivals at national borders (000)	110	155	185[d]
Important sites for terrestrial biodiversity protected (%)	34.5	34.5	34.5[e]
Net Official Development Assist. received (% of GNI)	4.63	2.73	2.89[d]

a 2017. **b** East Caribbean Dollar. **c** Refers to Saint George Parish. **d** 2018. **e** 2019. **f** 2016. **g** Estimate. **h** Data refers to a 5-year period preceding the reference year. **i** Data as at the end of December. **j** 2006. **k** 2009. **l** Data are as at 1 January of reporting year.

Guadeloupe

Region	Caribbean
Surface area (km2)	1 705[a]
Sex ratio (m per 100 f)	85.6
National currency	Euro (EUR)
Exchange rate (per US$)	0.9[c]

Population (000, 2020)	400
Pop. density (per km2, 2020)	245.8
Capital city	Basse-Terre
Capital city pop. (000, 2020)	58.4[b]

Economic indicators	2010	2015	2020
Employment in agriculture (% of employed)	...	3.3[d,e,f]	...
Employment in industry (% of employed)[d,e]	13.8	13.5[f]	...
Employment in services & other sectors (% employed)[d,e]	64.4	65.5[f]	...
Unemployment rate (% of labour force)[e]	23.8	26.1[g,h]	...
Labour force participation rate (female/male pop. %)	39.5 / 44.2[e]	49.6 / 56.5[e,g,h]	... / ...
CPI: Consumer Price Index (2010=100)[i]	100	106	109[c]
Agricultural production index (2004-2006=100)	89	96	92[j]

Social indicators	2010	2015	2020
Population growth rate (average annual %)[k]	0.2	- 0.3	-~0.0
Urban population (% of total population)[l]	98.4	98.4	98.5[c]
Urban population growth rate (average annual %)[k,l]	0.5	-~0.0	...
Fertility rate, total (live births per woman)[k]	2.2	2.2	2.2
Life expectancy at birth (females/males, years)[k]	82.9 / 75.7	84.0 / 76.8	85.2 / 78.1
Population age distribution (0-14/60+ years old, %)	22.5 / 19.1	20.4 / 22.7	18.4 / 26.1
International migrant stock (000/% of total pop.)[l]	94.9 / 21.0	98.5 / 22.1	100.0 / 22.3[c]
Infant mortality rate (per 1 000 live births)[k]	7.0	5.8	4.6
Intentional homicide rate (per 100 000 pop.)	8.9[m]	9.7	5.8[j]

Environment and infrastructure indicators	2010	2015	2020
Threatened species (number)[n]	54	70	83
Forested area (% of land area)[o]	43.1	43.0	43.0[a]
Energy production, primary (Petajoules)	2[o,p]	...	...
Tourist/visitor arrivals at national borders (000)[n,q]	392	512	735[b]
Important sites for terrestrial biodiversity protected (%)	82.3	82.4	82.4[c]

a 2017. b 2018. c 2019. d Population aged 15 to 64 years. e Excluding the institutional population. f 2012. g Break in the time series. h 2013. i Calculated by the UN Statistics Division from national indices. j 2016. k Data refers to a 5-year period preceding the reference year. l Including Saint Barthélemy and Saint Martin (French part). m 2009. n Excluding the north islands, Saint Barthélemy and Saint Martin (French part). o Estimate. p Data after 2010 are included in France. q Arrivals by air.

Guam

Region	Micronesia	Population (000, 2020)	169	
Surface area (km2)	549[a]	Pop. density (per km2, 2020)	312.5	
Sex ratio (m per 100 f)	101.8	Capital city	Hagåtña	
National currency	US Dollar (USD)	Capital city pop. (000, 2020)	146.9[b]	

Economic indicators	2010	2015	2020
Employment in agriculture (% of employed)	0.3	0.3[c]	0.2[c]
Employment in industry (% of employed)	15.1	14.8[c]	14.3[c]
Employment in services & other sectors (% employed)	84.6	84.9[c]	85.5[c]
Unemployment rate (% of labour force)[c]	8.2	6.9	5.7
Labour force participation rate (female/male pop. %)[c]	54.7 / 78.4	53.4 / 77.0	52.2 / 76.2
CPI: Consumer Price Index (2010=100)[d]	100	106	120[e,f]
Agricultural production index (2004-2006=100)	95	79	78[g]

Social indicators	2010	2015	2020
Population growth rate (average annual %)[h]	0.1	0.3	0.8
Urban population (% of total population)	94.1	94.5	94.9[f]
Urban population growth rate (average annual %)[h]	0.2	0.4	...
Fertility rate, total (live births per woman)[h]	2.5	2.4	2.3
Life expectancy at birth (females/males, years)[h]	80.3 / 74.7	81.8 / 75.5	83.3 / 76.5
Population age distribution (0-14/60+ years old, %)	27.5 / 11.1	25.5 / 13.1	23.9 / 15.2
International migrant stock (000/% of total pop.)	75.4 / 47.3	76.1 / 47.0	79.8 / 47.7[f]
Infant mortality rate (per 1 000 live births)[h]	11.4	10.1	8.7
Intentional homicide rate (per 100 000 pop.)	1.9	2.5[i]	...

Environment and infrastructure indicators	2010	2015	2020
Individuals using the Internet (per 100 inhabitants)[c]	54.0	73.1	80.5[a]
Research & Development expenditure (% of GDP)	0.3[j]	...	...
Threatened species (number)	34	95	107
Forested area (% of land area)[c]	46.3	46.3	46.3[a]
Energy production, primary (Petajoules)	...	0	0[a]
Energy supply per capita (Gigajoules)	...	0	1[a]
Tourist/visitor arrivals at national borders (000)	1 197	1 409	1 549[b]
Important sites for terrestrial biodiversity protected (%)	40.2	40.2	40.2[f]

a 2017. b 2018. c Estimate. d Calculated by the UN Statistics Division from national indices. e Monthly average for quarter or index for quarter. f 2019. g 2016. h Data refers to a 5-year period preceding the reference year. i 2011. j 2005.

Guatemala

Region	Central America	
Population (000, 2020)	17 916	
Pop. density (per km2, 2020)	167.2	
Capital city	Guatemala City	
Capital city pop. (000, 2020)	2 891.2 [b]	

UN membership date	21 November 1945	
Surface area (km2)	108 889 [a]	
Sex ratio (m per 100 f)	97.1	
National currency	Quetzal (GTQ)	
Exchange rate (per US$)	7.7 [b]	

Economic indicators	2010	2015	2020
GDP: Gross domestic product (million current US$)	41 338	63 767	78 461 [c]
GDP growth rate (annual %, const. 2015 prices)	2.9	4.1	3.1 [c]
GDP per capita (current US$)	2 825.5	3 923.6	4 549.0 [c]
Economy: Agriculture (% of Gross Value Added)	11.4	10.8	10.2 [c]
Economy: Industry (% of Gross Value Added)	28.0	27.2	25.2 [c]
Economy: Services and other activity (% of GVA)	57.0	56.8	53.4 [c]
Employment in agriculture (% of employed)	33.5	31.9	31.3 [d]
Employment in industry (% of employed)	22.0	18.9	18.4 [d]
Employment in services & other sectors (% employed)	44.5	49.2	50.3 [d]
Unemployment rate (% of labour force) [d]	3.5	2.5	2.5
Labour force participation rate (female/male pop. %) [d]	40.5 / 84.2	39.1 / 85.5	39.9 / 86.4
CPI: Consumer Price Index (2010=100)	100 [e]	122	143 [b]
Agricultural production index (2004-2006=100)	124	157	158 [f]
International trade: exports (million current US$)	8 460	10 677	11 289 [b]
International trade: imports (million current US$)	13 830	17 637	19 871 [b]
International trade: balance (million current US$)	- 5 370	- 6 960	- 8 581 [b]
Balance of payments, current account (million US$)	- 767	- 774	1 854 [b]

Major trading partners						2019
Export partners (% of exports)	United States	34.1	El Salvador	12.3	Honduras	8.9
Import partners (% of imports)	United States	37.1	China	11.2	Mexico	11.0

Social indicators	2010	2015	2020
Population growth rate (average annual %) [g]	2.2	2.1	1.9
Urban population (% of total population)	48.4	50.0	51.4 [b]
Urban population growth rate (average annual %) [g]	2.8	2.7	...
Fertility rate, total (live births per woman) [g]	3.6	3.2	2.9
Life expectancy at birth (females/males, years) [g]	73.7 / 67.2	75.6 / 69.2	76.8 / 71.0
Population age distribution (0-14/60+ years old, %)	39.4 / 6.1	36.2 / 6.7	33.3 / 7.2
International migrant stock (000/% of total pop.) [h]	66.4 / 0.5	78.4 / 0.5	80.4 / 0.5 [b]
Refugees and others of concern to the UNHCR (000)	0.1 [i]	0.3	146.8 [b]
Infant mortality rate (per 1 000 live births) [g]	31.3	26.9	20.7
Health: Current expenditure (% of GDP)	6.1	6.0	5.8 [a]
Health: Physicians (per 1 000 pop.)	0.9 [j]	...	0.4 [c]
Education: Government expenditure (% of GDP)	2.8	3.0	2.8 [a]
Education: Primary gross enrol. ratio (f/m per 100 pop.)	114.3 / 116.6	99.9 / 103.1	100.5 / 103.2 [c]
Education: Secondary gross enrol. ratio (f/m per 100 pop.)	50.7 / 53.9	52.6 / 55.8	51.4 / 54.0 [c]
Education: Tertiary gross enrol. ratio (f/m per 100 pop.)	17.5 / 17.1 [k]	23.6 / 20.0	... / ...
Intentional homicide rate (per 100 000 pop.)	40.7	29.4	22.5 [c]
Seats held by women in the National Parliament (%)	12.0	13.3	19.0 [l]

Environment and infrastructure indicators	2010	2015	2020
Individuals using the Internet (per 100 inhabitants)	10.5 [d]	28.8 [d]	65.0 [m,a]
Research & Development expenditure (% of GDP) [n]	~0.0	~0.0	~0.0 [a]
Threatened species (number)	230	282	352
Forested area (% of land area) [d]	34.7	33.0	33.0 [a]
CO2 emission estimates (million tons/tons per capita)	10.3 / 0.7	15.2 / 0.9	15.7 / 0.9 [a]
Energy production, primary (Petajoules)	279	289	343 [a]
Energy supply per capita (Gigajoules)	27	28	31 [a]
Tourist/visitor arrivals at national borders (000)	1 119	1 473	1 781 [c]
Important sites for terrestrial biodiversity protected (%)	25.3	28.9	30.0 [b]
Pop. using safely managed drinking water (urban/rural, %)	61.6 / 43.4	64.8 / 45.3	65.6 / 46.1 [a]
Net Official Development Assist. received (% of GNI)	1.00	0.66	0.52 [c]

a 2017. b 2019. c 2018. d Estimate. e Break in the time series. f 2016. g Data refers to a 5-year period preceding the reference year. h Including refugees. i Data as at the end of December. j 2009. k 2007. l Data are as at 1 January of reporting year. m Population aged 15 to 65 years. n Partial data.

Guinea

Region	Western Africa	UN membership date	12 December 1958
Population (000, 2020)	13 133	Surface area (km2)	245 857 [a]
Pop. density (per km2, 2020)	53.4	Sex ratio (m per 100 f)	93.7
Capital city	Conakry	National currency	Guinean Franc (GNF)
Capital city pop. (000, 2020)	1 889.2 [b]	Exchange rate (per US$)	9 400.8 [b]

Economic indicators

	2010	2015	2020
GDP: Gross domestic product (million current US$)	6 853	8 794	11 640 [c]
GDP growth rate (annual %, const. 2015 prices)	4.8	3.8	5.8 [c]
GDP per capita (current US$)	672.4	769.3	937.6 [c]
Economy: Agriculture (% of Gross Value Added)	18.6	20.1	19.5 [c]
Economy: Industry (% of Gross Value Added)	34.3	28.6	32.7 [c]
Economy: Services and other activity (% of GVA)	44.1	46.1	44.4 [c]
Employment in agriculture (% of employed) [d]	67.5	64.9	61.3
Employment in industry (% of employed) [d]	5.3	5.4	6.2
Employment in services & other sectors (% employed) [d]	27.2	29.7	32.5
Unemployment rate (% of labour force) [d]	4.5	4.4	4.3
Labour force participation rate (female/male pop. %) [d]	62.5 / 63.6	62.6 / 62.0	62.8 / 60.3
CPI: Consumer Price Index (2010=100) [e]	100	186	263 [b]
Agricultural production index (2004-2006=100)	120	132	135 [f]
International trade: exports (million current US$)	1 471 [d]	1 574	2 384 [d,b]
International trade: imports (million current US$)	1 402 [d]	2 139	2 032 [d,b]
International trade: balance (million current US$)	69 [d]	- 565	351 [d,b]
Balance of payments, current account (million US$)	- 327	- 1 020	- 190 [c]

Major trading partners

						2019
Export partners (% of exports) [d]	United Arab Emirates	35.8	China	33.8	India	6.1
Import partners (% of imports) [d]	China	32.3	India	8.4	Netherlands	6.2

Social indicators

	2010	2015	2020
Population growth rate (average annual %) [g]	2.2	2.3	2.8
Urban population (% of total population)	33.7	35.1	36.5 [b]
Urban population growth rate (average annual %) [g]	3.0	3.1	...
Fertility rate, total (live births per woman) [g]	5.5	5.1	4.7
Life expectancy at birth (females/males, years) [g]	56.4 / 54.5	58.4 / 57.4	61.5 / 60.3
Population age distribution (0-14/60+ years old, %)	46.2 / 4.6	45.0 / 4.7	43.0 / 4.7
International migrant stock (000/% of total pop.) [h,i]	178.0 / 1.7	126.4 / 1.1	120.6 / 0.9 [b]
Refugees and others of concern to the UNHCR (000)	15.0 [j]	9.0	6.4 [b]
Infant mortality rate (per 1 000 live births) [g]	77.7	65.7	51.6
Health: Current expenditure (% of GDP)	3.0	5.8	4.1 [a]
Health: Physicians (per 1 000 pop.)	...	0.1	0.1 [f]
Education: Government expenditure (% of GDP)	2.6	2.5	2.2 [a]
Education: Primary gross enrol. ratio (f/m per 100 pop.)	76.0 / 92.3	85.0 / 100.4 [k]	82.4 / 100.5 [f]
Education: Secondary gross enrol. ratio (f/m per 100 pop.)	24.6 / 43.1 [l]	31.0 / 47.5 [k]	... / ...
Education: Tertiary gross enrol. ratio (f/m per 100 pop.)	5.2 / 16.8	7.0 / 16.2 [k]	... / ...
Seats held by women in the National Parliament (%)	19.3 [l]	21.9	22.8 [m]

Environment and infrastructure indicators

	2010	2015	2020
Individuals using the Internet (per 100 inhabitants)	1.0 [d]	8.2 [d]	18.0 [n,o,a]
Threatened species (number)	134	163	365
Forested area (% of land area) [d]	26.6	25.9	25.9 [a]
Energy production, primary (Petajoules)	112	114	115 [a]
Energy supply per capita (Gigajoules)	14	12	12 [a]
Tourist/visitor arrivals at national borders (000) [p]	12	35	99 [a]
Important sites for terrestrial biodiversity protected (%)	71.2	71.2	71.2 [b]
Net Official Development Assist. received (% of GNI)	3.45	6.31	5.73 [c]

a 2017. b 2019. c 2018. d Estimate. e Conakry f 2016. g Data refers to a 5-year period preceding the reference year. h Including refugees. i Refers to foreign citizens. j Data as at the end of December. k 2014. l 2008. m Data are as at 1 January of reporting year. n At least once a month. o Population aged 18 years and over. p Arrivals by air at Conakry airport.

Guinea-Bissau

Region	Western Africa	UN membership date	17 September 1974	
Population (000, 2020)	1 968	Surface area (km2)	36 125[a]	
Pop. density (per km2, 2020)	70.0	Sex ratio (m per 100 f)	95.8	
Capital city	Bissau	National currency	CFA Franc, BCEAO (XOF)[b]	
Capital city pop. (000, 2020)	578.8[c]	Exchange rate (per US$)	583.9[c]	

Economic indicators

	2010	2015	2020
GDP: Gross domestic product (million current US$)	849	1 047	1 459[d]
GDP growth rate (annual %, const. 2015 prices)	4.6	6.1	3.8[d]
GDP per capita (current US$)	557.6	602.9	778.4[d]
Economy: Agriculture (% of Gross Value Added)	46.2	49.0	49.9[d]
Economy: Industry (% of Gross Value Added)	13.5	12.8	13.3[d]
Economy: Services and other activity (% of GVA)	42.5	38.5	38.1[d]
Employment in agriculture (% of employed)[e]	71.0	69.7	67.8
Employment in industry (% of employed)[e]	7.1	6.9	7.0
Employment in services & other sectors (% employed)[e]	21.8	23.4	25.2
Unemployment migrant rate (% of labour force)[e]	2.7	2.6	2.5
Labour force participation rate (female/male pop. %)[e]	65.1 / 78.7	65.6 / 78.8	65.9 / 78.6
CPI: Consumer Price Index (2010=100)[f]	100	108	112[a]
Agricultural production index (2004-2006=100)	128	140	143[g]
International trade: exports (million current US$)[e]	120	548	3 731[c]
International trade: imports (million current US$)[e]	197	221	188[c]
International trade: balance (million current US$)[e]	- 77	327	3 544[c]
Balance of payments, current account (million US$)	- 71	21	- 54[d]

Major trading partners

							2019
Export partners (% of exports)[e]	India	49.9	Belgium	28.3	Ivory Coast	8.5
Import partners (% of imports)[e]	Portugal	31.1	Senegal	19.9	China	9.1

Social indicators

	2010	2015	2020
Population growth rate (average annual %)[h]	2.5	2.6	2.5
Urban population (% of total population)	40.1	42.1	43.8[c]
Urban population growth rate (average annual %)[h]	3.4	3.6	...
Fertility rate, total (live births per woman)[h]	5.2	4.9	4.5
Life expectancy at birth (females/males, years)[h]	55.6 / 50.9	58.2 / 53.6	59.7 / 55.8
Population age distribution (0-14/60+ years old, %)	43.1 / 4.3	42.7 / 4.5	41.9 / 4.6
International migrant stock (000/% of total pop.)[i]	21.1 / 1.4	22.3 / 1.3	26.9 / 1.4[c]
Refugees and others of concern to the UNHCR (000)	8.0[j]	8.8	1.9[c]
Infant mortality rate (per 1 000 live births)[h]	85.2	68.1	57.1
Health: Current expenditure (% of GDP)[e]	6.6	8.6	7.2[a]
Health: Physicians (per 1 000 pop.)	0.1[k]	0.2	0.1[g]
Education: Government expenditure (% of GDP)	1.9	2.1[l]	...
Education: Primary gross enrol. ratio (f/m per 100 pop.)	114.5 / 122.9	... / ...	... / ...
Intentional homicide rate (per 100 000 pop.)	...	2.8	1.1[a]
Seats held by women in the National Parliament (%)	10.0	13.7	13.7[m]

Environment and infrastructure indicators

	2010	2015	2020
Individuals using the Internet (per 100 inhabitants)[e]	2.4	3.5	3.9[a]
Threatened species (number)	52	66	92
Forested area (% of land area)[e]	71.9	70.1	70.1[a]
Energy production, primary (Petajoules)	24	25	26[a]
Energy supply per capita (Gigajoules)	18	17	17[a]
Tourist/visitor arrivals at national borders (000)[n]	22	44	45[g]
Important sites for terrestrial biodiversity protected (%)	52.2	52.6	52.6[c]
Net Official Development Assist. received (% of GNI)	15.27	8.86	10.55[d]

a 2017. b African Financial Community (CFA) Franc, Central Bank of West African States (BCEAO). c 2019. d 2018. e Estimate. f Bissau g 2016. h Data refers to a 5-year period preceding the reference year. i Including refugees. j Data as at the end of December. k 2009. l 2013. m Data are as at 1 January of reporting year. n Arrivals by air.

Guyana

Region	South America	UN membership date	20 September 1966
Population (000, 2020)	787	Surface area (km2)	214 969 [a]
Pop. density (per km2, 2020)	4.0	Sex ratio (m per 100 f)	101.2
Capital city	Georgetown	National currency	Guyana Dollar (GYD)
Capital city pop. (000, 2020)	109.9 [b]	Exchange rate (per US$)	208.5 [c]

Economic indicators

	2010	2015	2020
GDP: Gross domestic product (million current US$)	2 259	3 179	3 818 [b]
GDP growth rate (annual %, const. 2015 prices)	4.1	3.1	3.4 [b]
GDP per capita (current US$)	3 014.7	4 142.5	4 900.8 [b]
Economy: Agriculture (% of Gross Value Added)	17.6	18.9	14.7 [b]
Economy: Industry (% of Gross Value Added)	34.5	32.9	38.4 [b]
Economy: Services and other activity (% of GVA)	60.4	64.1	64.4 [b]
Employment in agriculture (% of employed) [d]	20.6	18.0	16.8
Employment in industry (% of employed) [d]	23.5	23.2	22.9
Employment in services & other sectors (% employed) [d]	55.9	58.7	60.3
Unemployment rate (% of labour force) [d]	11.4	12.0	11.8
Labour force participation rate (female/male pop. %) [d]	39.3 / 73.8	42.4 / 70.1	44.1 / 68.4
CPI: Consumer Price Index (2010=100) [d,e]	100	109	116 [c]
Agricultural production index (2004-2006=100)	108	145	130 [f]
International trade: exports (million current US$)	901	1 169	1 405 [d,c]
International trade: imports (million current US$)	1 452	1 484	3 467 [d,c]
International trade: balance (million current US$)	- 551	- 315	- 2 062 [d,c]
Balance of payments, current account (million current US$)	- 246	- 39	- 1 072 [b]

Major trading partners

						2019
Export partners (% of exports) [d]	Canada	26.9	United States	15.4	Panama	10.9
Import partners (% of imports) [d]	United States	57.0	Trinidad and Tobago	18.2	China	5.5

Social indicators

	2010	2015	2020
Population growth rate (average annual %) [g]	0.1	0.5	0.5
Urban population (% of total population)	26.6	26.4	26.7 [c]
Urban population growth rate (average annual %) [g]	- 1.0	0.4	...
Fertility rate, total (live births per woman) [g]	2.7	2.6	2.5
Life expectancy at birth (females/males, years) [g]	70.8 / 64.2	72.2 / 65.4	72.9 / 66.7
Population age distribution (0-14/60+ years old, %)	32.2 / 7.3	29.3 / 8.8	27.7 / 10.8
International migrant stock (000/% of total pop.)	13.1 / 1.8	15.4 / 2.0	15.7 / 2.0 [c]
Refugees and others of concern to the UNHCR (000)	~0.0 [h]	~0.0	36.5 [c]
Infant mortality rate (per 1 000 live births) [g]	32.0	31.7	26.8
Health: Current expenditure (% of GDP) [i]	5.5	4.5	4.9 [a]
Health: Physicians (per 1 000 pop.)	0.7	...	0.8 [b]
Education: Government expenditure (% of GDP)	3.6	5.2	6.3 [a]
Education: Primary gross enrol. ratio (f/m per 100 pop.)	95.0 / 97.9	96.0 / 99.6 [j]	... / ...
Education: Secondary gross enrol. ratio (f/m per 100 pop.)	91.9 / 88.4	99.2 / 96.3 [j]	... / ...
Education: Tertiary gross enrol. ratio (f/m per 100 pop.)	16.3 / 6.9	15.4 / 7.8 [j]	... / ...
Intentional homicide rate (per 100 000 pop.)	18.7	19.4	14.2 [b]
Seats held by women in the National Parliament (%)	30.0	31.3	34.8 [k]

Environment and infrastructure indicators

	2010	2015	2020
Individuals using the Internet (per 100 inhabitants)	29.9	34.0 [d]	37.3 [d,a]
Threatened species (number)	69	87	122
Forested area (% of land area) [d]	84.2	84.0	84.0 [a]
Energy production, primary (Petajoules)	8	7	7 [a]
Energy supply per capita (Gigajoules)	46	45	47 [a]
Tourist/visitor arrivals at national borders (000)	152	207	287 [b]
Net Official Development Assist. received (% of GNI)	4.71	1.01	2.87 [b]

2017. **b** 2018. **c** 2019. **d** Estimate. **e** Georgetown **f** 2016. **g** Data refers to a 5-year period preceding the reference year. **h** Data as at the end of December. **i** Data revision. **j** 2012. **k** Data are as at 1 January of reporting year.

Haiti

Region	Caribbean	UN membership date	24 October 1945
Population (000, 2020)	11 402	Surface area (km2)	27 750[a]
Pop. density (per km2, 2020)	413.7	Sex ratio (m per 100 f)	97.4
Capital city	Port-au-Prince	National currency	Gourde (HTG)
Capital city pop. (000, 2020)	2 704.2[b]	Exchange rate (per US$)	92.0[b]

Economic indicators

	2010	2015	2020
GDP: Gross domestic product (million current US$)	6 708	8 355	9 287[c]
GDP growth rate (annual %, const. 2015 prices)	- 5.5	1.2	1.5[c]
GDP per capita (current US$)	674.2	781.2	834.9[c]
Economy: Agriculture (% of Gross Value Added)	25.7	17.3	18.6[c]
Economy: Industry (% of Gross Value Added)	27.4	34.7	31.7[c]
Economy: Services and other activity (% of GVA)	32.6	33.2	32.6[c]
Employment in agriculture (% of employed)[d]	33.6	30.3	28.3
Employment in industry (% of employed)[d]	6.5	7.1	6.6
Employment in services & other sectors (% employed)[d]	59.9	62.6	65.0
Unemployment rate (% of labour force)[d]	15.4	14.0	13.9
Labour force participation rate (female/male pop. %)[d]	59.3 / 71.6	61.2 / 72.0	62.1 / 72.9
CPI: Consumer Price Index (2010=100)	100	139	181[a]
Agricultural production index (2004-2006=100)	132	159	155[e]
International trade: exports (million current US$)[d]	579	1 018	746[b]
International trade: imports (million current US$)[d]	3 147	3 523	3 118[b]
International trade: balance (million current US$)[d]	- 2 568	- 2 505	- 2 372[b]
Balance of payments, current account (million US$)	- 102	- 271	- 343[c]

Major trading partners

						2019
Export partners (% of exports)[d]	United States	78.0	Canada	6.5	Dominican Rep.	3.2
Import partners (% of imports)[d]	United States	31.0	Dominican Rep.	26.9	China	15.5

Social indicators

	2010	2015	2020
Population growth rate (average annual %)[f]	1.6	1.4	1.3
Urban population (% of total population)	47.5	52.4	56.2[b]
Urban population growth rate (average annual %)[f]	3.7	3.3	...
Fertility rate, total (live births per woman)[f]	3.6	3.3	3.0
Life expectancy at birth (females/males, years)[f]	61.6 / 57.7	63.5 / 59.3	65.7 / 61.4
Population age distribution (0-14/60+ years old, %)	36.3 / 6.5	34.4 / 7.1	32.5 / 7.7
International migrant stock (000/% of total pop.)	17.2 / 0.2	18.0 / 0.2	18.8 / 0.2[b]
Refugees and others of concern to the UNHCR (000)	~0.0[g]	~0.0	3.0[h,b]
Infant mortality rate (per 1 000 live births)[f]	63.8	61.0	54.3
Health: Current expenditure (% of GDP)	8.1	8.6[i]	8.0[a]
Health: Physicians (per 1 000 pop.)	...	0.1	0.2[c]
Education: Government expenditure (% of GDP)	...	3.2	2.4[e]
Intentional homicide rate (per 100 000 pop.)	6.8	10.0	6.7[c]
Seats held by women in the National Parliament (%)	4.1	4.2	2.5[j,k]

Environment and infrastructure indicators

	2010	2015	2020
Individuals using the Internet (per 100 inhabitants)	8.4[d]	12.2[d]	32.5[c]
Threatened species (number)	137	169	269
Forested area (% of land area)[d]	3.7	3.5	3.5[a]
CO2 emission estimates (million tons/tons per capita)	2.1 / 0.2	3.2 / 0.3	3.3 / 0.3[a]
Energy production, primary (Petajoules)	131	139	142[a]
Energy supply per capita (Gigajoules)	16	17	17[a]
Tourist/visitor arrivals at national borders (000)[l,m]	255	516	447[c]
Important sites for terrestrial biodiversity protected (%)	24.3	36.8	41.0[b]
Net Official Development Assist. received (% of GNI)	43.49	11.93	10.26[c]

a 2017. **b** 2019. **c** 2018. **d** Estimate. **e** 2016. **f** Data refers to a 5-year period preceding the reference year. **g** Data as at the end of December. **h** Figure refers to individuals without a nationality who were born in the Dominican Republic prior to January 2010 and who were identified by UNHCR in Haiti since June 2015. **i** Break in the time series. **j** The term of all members in the 119-member Chamber of Deputies and 20 of 30 senators expired on 13 January 2020. There are currently only 10 sitting senators. **k** Data are as at 1 January of reporting year. **l** Arrivals by air. **m** Including nationals residing abroad.

Holy See

Region	Southern Europe	Population (000, 2020)	1
Surface area (km2)	~0 [a,b]	Pop. density (per km2, 2020)	1 820.5
Sex ratio (m per 100 f)	219.2 [c]	Capital city	Vatican City
National currency	Euro (EUR)	Capital city pop. (000, 2020)	0.8 [d]
Exchange rate (per US$)	0.9 [e]		

Social indicators	2010	2015	2020
Population growth rate (average annual %)	–0.0 [f]	–0.0 [f]	0.1
Urban population (% of total population)	100.0	100.0	100.0 [e]
Urban population growth rate (average annual %) [f]	- 0.1	0.2	...
International migrant stock (000/% of total pop.) [g,h]	0.8 / 100.0	0.8 / 100.0	0.8 / 100.0 [e]
Intentional homicide rate (per 100 000 pop.)	0.0	0.0	...

Environment and infrastructure indicators	2010	2015	2020
Threatened species (number)	1	1	1

a Surface area is 0.44 Km2. **b** 2017. **c** 2009. **d** 2018. **e** 2019. **f** Data refers to a 5-year period preceding the reference year. **g** Data refer to the Vatican City State. **h** Estimate.

Honduras

Region	Central America	UN membership date	17 December 1945
Population (000, 2020)	9 905	Surface area (km2)	112 492 [a]
Pop. density (per km2, 2020)	88.5	Sex ratio (m per 100 f)	99.9
Capital city	Tegucigalpa	National currency	Lempira (HNL)
Capital city pop. (000, 2020)	1 403.2 [b]	Exchange rate (per US$)	24.6 [b]

Economic indicators

	2010	2015	2020
GDP: Gross domestic product (million current US$)	15 839	20 980	23 970 [c]
GDP growth rate (annual %, const. 2015 prices)	3.7	3.8	3.7 [c]
GDP per capita (current US$)	1 904.3	2 302.2	2 500.1 [c]
Economy: Agriculture (% of Gross Value Added)	11.9	12.6	12.3 [c]
Economy: Industry (% of Gross Value Added)	26.2	26.5	28.0 [c]
Economy: Services and other activity (% of GVA)	61.3	59.4	58.9 [c]
Employment in agriculture (% of employed)	36.5	28.7	30.1 [d]
Employment in industry (% of employed)	19.1	21.8	19.7 [d]
Employment in services & other sectors (% employed)	44.5	49.5	50.2 [d]
Unemployment rate (% of labour force) [d]	4.1	6.2	5.2
Labour force participation rate (female/male pop. %) [d]	44.5 / 84.8	48.3 / 85.3	52.1 / 85.8
CPI: Consumer Price Index (2010=100) [d]	100	129	150 [b]
Agricultural production index (2004-2006=100)	111	122	124 [e]
International trade: exports (million current US$)	3 104	4 201	4 161 [d,b]
International trade: imports (million current US$)	6 895	8 381	10 059 [d,b]
International trade: balance (million current US$)	- 3 791	- 4 179	- 5 898 [d,b]
Balance of payments, current account (million US$)	- 804	- 980	- 163 [b]

Major trading partners

							2019
Export partners (% of exports) [d]	United States	40.2	Germany	7.9	Belgium	7.0
Import partners (% of imports) [d]	United States	34.7	China	15.0	Guatemala	8.6

Social indicators

	2010	2015	2020
Population growth rate (average annual %) [f]	2.2	1.8	1.7
Urban population (% of total population)	51.9	55.2	57.7 [b]
Urban population growth rate (average annual %) [f]	3.4	3.0	...
Fertility rate, total (live births per woman) [f]	3.2	2.7	2.5
Life expectancy at birth (females/males, years) [f]	75.0 / 70.3	76.3 / 71.6	77.3 / 72.7
Population age distribution (0-14/60+ years old, %)	37.6 / 5.8	33.7 / 6.5	30.6 / 7.4
International migrant stock (000/% of total pop.) [g]	27.3 / 0.3	38.3 / 0.4	38.9 / 0.4 [b]
Refugees and others of concern to the UNHCR (000)	~0.0 [h]	~0.0	251.6 [b]
Infant mortality rate (per 1 000 live births) [f]	23.3	18.4	15.0
Health: Current expenditure (% of GDP)	8.7	7.7	7.9 [a]
Health: Physicians (per 1 000 pop.)	0.3	1.0 [i]	0.3 [a]
Education: Government expenditure (% of GDP)	...	6.4	6.0 [a]
Education: Primary gross enrol. ratio (f/m per 100 pop.)	100.7 / 100.6	92.5 / 93.0	91.5 / 91.6 [a]
Education: Secondary gross enrol. ratio (f/m per 100 pop.)	72.8 / 59.1	55.4 / 46.2	55.9 / 48.6 [a]
Education: Tertiary gross enrol. ratio (f/m per 100 pop.)	20.9 / 18.1	23.6 / 17.3	30.3 / 22.2 [c]
Intentional homicide rate (per 100 000 pop.)	75.0	56.5	38.9 [c]
Seats held by women in the National Parliament (%)	18.0	25.8	21.1 [j]

Environment and infrastructure indicators

	2010	2015	2020
Individuals using the Internet (per 100 inhabitants)	11.1	27.1 [k]	31.7 [k,a]
Research & Development expenditure (% of GDP)	...	~0.0 [l,m]	~0.0 [a]
Threatened species (number)	240	294	342
Forested area (% of land area) [d]	46.4	41.0	41.0 [a]
CO2 emission estimates (million tons/tons per capita)	7.5 / 0.9	9.6 / 1.1	9.4 / 1.0 [a]
Energy production, primary (Petajoules)	93	118	126 [a]
Energy supply per capita (Gigajoules)	24	28	27 [a]
Tourist/visitor arrivals at national borders (000)	863	880	851 [a]
Important sites for terrestrial biodiversity protected (%)	57.1	59.0	59.0 [b]
Pop. using safely managed drinking water (urban/rural, %)	... / 17.4	... / 18.2	... / 18.5 [a]
Pop. using safely managed sanitation (urban/rural %)	34.0 / ...	34.4 / ...	34.5 / ... [a]
Net Official Development Assist. received (% of GNI)	3.14	2.79	2.99 [c]

a 2017. b 2019. c 2018. d Estimate. e 2016. f Data refers to a 5-year period preceding the reference year. g Including refugees. h Data as at the end of December. i 2013. j Data are as at 1 January of reporting year. k Users in the last 3 months. l Break in the time series. m Partial data.

Hungary

Region	Eastern Europe	UN membership date	14 December 1955
Population (000, 2020)	9 660	Surface area (km2)	93 024[a]
Pop. density (per km2, 2020)	106.7	Sex ratio (m per 100 f)	90.8
Capital city	Budapest	National currency	Forint (HUF)
Capital city pop. (000, 2020)	1 763.9[b]	Exchange rate (per US$)	294.7[b]

Economic indicators

	2010	2015	2020
GDP: Gross domestic product (million current US$)	131 136	124 530	157 883[c]
GDP growth rate (annual %, const. 2015 prices)	0.7	3.8	5.1[c]
GDP per capita (current US$)	13 209.5	12 735.8	16 264.0[c]
Economy: Agriculture (% of Gross Value Added)[d]	3.6	4.5	4.2[c]
Economy: Industry (% of Gross Value Added)[d,e]	29.9	31.4	30.1[c]
Economy: Services and other activity (% of GVA)[d,f,g]	63.3	64.3	66.5[c]
Employment in agriculture (% of employed)	4.5	4.9	4.6[h]
Employment in industry (% of employed)	30.7	30.3	32.8[h]
Employment in services & other sectors (% employed)	64.8	64.8	62.6[h]
Unemployment rate (% of labour force)[h]	11.2	6.8	3.5
Labour force participation rate (female/male pop. %)[h]	43.8 / 58.2	47.3 / 63.4	48.5 / 65.3
CPI: Consumer Price Index (2010=100)	100	111	122[b]
Agricultural production index (2004-2006=100)	80	92	88[i]
International trade: exports (million current US$)	94 749	100 297	121 995[b]
International trade: imports (million current US$)	87 432	90 761	116 556[b]
International trade: balance (million current US$)	7 317	9 536	5 439[b]
Balance of payments, current account (million US$)	342	2 926	- 1 247[b]

Major trading partners

						2019
Export partners (% of exports)	Germany	27.7	Italy	5.2	Slovakia	5.2
Import partners (% of imports)	Germany	25.3	China	6.1	Austria	6.1

Social indicators

	2010	2015	2020
Population growth rate (average annual %)[j]	- 0.3	- 0.3	- 0.2
Urban population (% of total population)	68.9	70.5	71.6[b]
Urban population growth rate (average annual %)[j]	0.4	0.2	...
Fertility rate, total (live births per woman)[j]	1.3	1.3	1.5
Life expectancy at birth (females/males, years)[j]	77.8 / 69.6	78.7 / 71.6	80.1 / 73.0
Population age distribution (0-14/60+ years old, %)	14.9 / 22.1	14.4 / 25.0	14.4 / 26.8
International migrant stock (000/% of total pop.)[k]	436.6 / 4.4	475.5 / 4.9	512.0 / 5.3[b]
Refugees and others of concern to the UNHCR (000)	5.8[l]	28.8	6.4[b]
Infant mortality rate (per 1 000 live births)[j]	5.7	5.0	4.1
Health: Current expenditure (% of GDP)[h]	7.5	7.0	6.9[a]
Health: Physicians (per 1 000 pop.)	2.9	3.1	3.4[c]
Education: Government expenditure (% of GDP)	4.8	4.6	4.7[i]
Education: Primary gross enrol. ratio (f/m per 100 pop.)	100.5 / 101.2	102.2 / 102.5	100.5 / 101.1[a]
Education: Secondary gross enrol. ratio (f/m per 100 pop.)	96.4 / 97.7	103.3 / 102.7	103.6 / 103.4[a]
Education: Tertiary gross enrol. ratio (f/m per 100 pop.)	73.8 / 54.1	54.7 / 43.5	53.9 / 43.3[a]
Intentional homicide rate (per 100 000 pop.)	1.4	2.3	2.5[a]
Seats held by women in the National Parliament (%)	11.1	10.1	12.1[m]

Environment and infrastructure indicators

	2010	2015	2020
Individuals using the Internet (per 100 inhabitants)	65.0[n]	72.8[n]	76.1[c]
Research & Development expenditure (% of GDP)	1.1	1.4	1.6[c]
Threatened species (number)	47	67	123
Forested area (% of land area)	22.6	22.7	22.7[h,a]
CO2 emission estimates (million tons/tons per capita)	47.1 / 4.7	42.7 / 4.3	45.8 / 4.7[a]
Energy production, primary (Petajoules)	495	471	472[a]
Energy supply per capita (Gigajoules)	112	108	115[a]
Tourist/visitor arrivals at national borders (000)	9 510	14 316	17 552[c]
Important sites for terrestrial biodiversity protected (%)	82.5	82.5	82.5[b]
Pop. using safely managed sanitation (urban/rural %)	95.0 / 98.2	94.8 / 98.2	94.7 / 98.2[a]
Net Official Development Assist. disbursed (% of GNI)[o]	0.09	0.13	0.11[a]

a 2017. b 2019. c 2018. d Data classified according to ISIC Rev. 4. e Excludes publishing activities. Includes irrigation and canals. f Excludes repair of personal and household goods. g Excludes computer and related activities and radio/TV activities. h Estimate. i 2016. j Data refers to a 5-year period preceding the reference year. k Including refugees. l Data as at the end of December. m Data are as at 1 January of reporting year. n Population aged 16 to 74 years. o Development Assistance Committee member (OECD).

Iceland

Region	Northern Europe	
Population (000, 2020)	341	
Pop. density (per km2, 2020)	3.4	
Capital city	Reykjavik	
Capital city pop. (000, 2020)	216.4[b]	

UN membership date	19 November 1946
Surface area (km2)	103 000[a]
Sex ratio (m per 100 f)	100.9
National currency	Iceland Krona (ISK)
Exchange rate (per US$)	121.1[c]

Economic indicators	2010	2015	2020
GDP: Gross domestic product (million current US$)	13 684	17 389	25 882[b]
GDP growth rate (annual %, const. 2015 prices)	- 3.4	4.7	4.6[b]
GDP per capita (current US$)	42 717.7	52 655.5	76 867.3[b]
Economy: Agriculture (% of Gross Value Added)[d]	7.1	6.0	5.2[b]
Economy: Industry (% of Gross Value Added)[d,e]	24.1	22.3	22.4[b]
Economy: Services and other activity (% of GVA)[d,f,g]	65.9	70.1	66.0[b]
Employment in agriculture (% of employed)	5.6	4.2	3.8[h]
Employment in industry (% of employed)	18.4	17.8	16.1[h]
Employment in services & other sectors (% employed)	76.0	77.9	80.1[h]
Unemployment rate (% of labour force)[h]	7.6	4.0	3.2
Labour force participation rate (female/male pop. %)[h]	70.6 / 79.1	73.1 / 81.0	70.6 / 78.9
CPI: Consumer Price Index (2010=100)	100	118	129[c]
Agricultural production index (2004-2006=100)	110	122	126[i]
International trade: exports (million current US$)	4 603	4 722	5 228[c]
International trade: imports (million current US$)	3 914	5 285	6 579[c]
International trade: balance (million current US$)	689	- 563	- 1 351[c]
Balance of payments, current account (million current US$)	- 881	894	1 404[c]

Major trading partners						2019
Export partners (% of exports)	Netherlands	26.3	United Kingdom	10.4	Spain	9.5
Import partners (% of imports)	Norway	11.3	United States	8.5	Germany	8.3

Social indicators	2010	2015	2020
Population growth rate (average annual %)[j]	1.6	0.6	0.7
Urban population (% of total population)	93.6	93.7	93.9[c]
Urban population growth rate (average annual %)[j]	1.8	0.6	...
Fertility rate, total (live births per woman)[j]	2.1	2.0	1.8
Life expectancy at birth (females/males, years)[j]	83.2 / 79.6	83.8 / 80.6	84.3 / 81.2
Population age distribution (0-14/60+ years old, %)	20.8 / 16.9	20.3 / 19.1	19.4 / 21.6
International migrant stock (000/% of total pop.)	35.1 / 11.0	39.1 / 11.8	52.4 / 15.5[c]
Refugees and others of concern to the UNHCR (000)	0.2[k]	0.4	1.2[c]
Infant mortality rate (per 1 000 live births)[j]	2.0	1.6	1.3
Health: Current expenditure (% of GDP)[h]	8.5	8.2	8.3[a]
Health: Physicians (per 1 000 pop.)	3.6	3.8	4.1[h]
Education: Government expenditure (% of GDP)	7.0	7.5	7.5[i]
Education: Primary gross enrol. ratio (f/m per 100 pop.)	99.6 / 99.0	98.6 / 98.7	100.3 / 100.4[a]
Education: Secondary gross enrol. ratio (f/m per 100 pop.)	108.2 / 106.5	119.6 / 118.6	116.9 / 118.1[a]
Education: Tertiary gross enrol. ratio (f/m per 100 pop.)	101.5 / 56.8	98.0 / 54.7	94.4 / 50.6[a]
Intentional homicide rate (per 100 000 pop.)	0.6	0.9	0.9[b]
Seats held by women in the National Parliament (%)	42.9	41.3	38.1[l]

Environment and infrastructure indicators	2010	2015	2020
Individuals using the Internet (per 100 inhabitants)	93.4[m,n]	98.2[h]	99.0[b]
Research & Development expenditure (% of GDP)	2.6[o]	2.2	2.0[b]
Threatened species (number)	17	21	36
Forested area (% of land area)	0.4	0.5[h]	0.5[h,a]
CO2 emission estimates (million tons/tons per capita)	1.9 / 6.1	2.1 / 6.2	2.2 / 6.3[a]
Energy production, primary (Petajoules)	252	285	299[a]
Energy supply per capita (Gigajoules)	869	949	977[a]
Tourist/visitor arrivals at national borders (000)	489	1 289	2 344[b]
Important sites for terrestrial biodiversity protected (%)	16.7	19.1	19.1[c]
Net Official Development Assist. disbursed (% of GNI)[p]	0.26	0.24	0.28[a]

a 2017. b 2018. c 2019. d Data classified according to ISIC Rev. 4. e Excludes publishing activities. Includes irrigation and canals. f Excludes repair of personal and household goods. g Excludes computer and related activities and radio/TV activities. h Estimate. i 2016. j Data refers to a 5-year period preceding the reference year. k Data as at the end of December. l Data are as at 1 January of reporting year. m Users in the last 3 months. n Population age 16 to 74 years. o 2009. p Development Assistance Committee member (OECD).

India

Region	Southern Asia	UN membership date	30 October 1945
Population (000, 2020)	1 380 004	Surface area (km2)	3 287 263 [a]
Pop. density (per km2, 2020)	464.1	Sex ratio (m per 100 f)	108.2
Capital city	New Delhi	National currency	Indian Rupee (INR)
Capital city pop. (000, 2020)	29 399.1 [b,c]	Exchange rate (per US$)	71.3 [c]

Economic indicators

	2010	2015	2020
GDP: Gross domestic product (million current US$)	1 669 620	2 146 759	2 779 352 [d]
GDP growth rate (annual %, const. 2015 prices)	8.5	8.0	6.8 [d]
GDP per capita (current US$)	1 352.7	1 638.6	2 054.8 [d]
Economy: Agriculture (% of Gross Value Added) [e]	18.4	17.7	16.1 [d]
Economy: Industry (% of Gross Value Added) [e,f]	33.1	30.0	29.6 [d]
Economy: Services and other activity (% of GVA) [e,g,h]	56.0	55.7	62.0 [d]
Employment in agriculture (% of employed)	51.5	45.7 [i]	41.5 [i]
Employment in industry (% of employed)	21.8	24.1 [i]	26.2 [i]
Employment in services & other sectors (% employed)	26.7	30.3 [i]	32.3 [i]
Unemployment rate (% of labour force) [i]	5.6	5.6	5.4
Labour force participation rate (female/male pop. %) [i]	25.7 / 80.5	21.7 / 77.9	20.3 / 76.0
CPI: Consumer Price Index (2010=100) [j]	100	149	180 [c]
Agricultural production index (2004-2006=100)	124	142	145 [k]
International trade: exports (million current US$)	220 408	264 381	323 251 [c]
International trade: imports (million current US$)	350 029	390 745	478 884 [c]
International trade: balance (million current US$)	- 129 621	- 126 364	- 155 633 [c]
Balance of payments, current account (million US$)	- 54 516	- 22 457	- 26 894 [c]

Major trading partners

						2019
Export partners (% of exports)	United States	16.8	United Arab Emirates	9.1	China	5.3
Import partners (% of imports)	China	14.3	United States	7.3	United Arab Emirates	6.3

Social indicators

	2010	2015	2020
Population growth rate (average annual %) [l]	1.5	1.2	1.0
Urban population (% of total population)	30.9	32.8	34.5 [c]
Urban population growth rate (average annual %) [l]	2.6	2.4	...
Fertility rate, total (live births per woman) [l]	2.8	2.4	2.2
Life expectancy at birth (females/males, years) [l]	66.4 / 64.7	69.0 / 66.7	70.5 / 68.1
Population age distribution (0-14/60+ years old, %)	30.8 / 7.8	28.4 / 8.9	26.2 / 10.1
International migrant stock (000/% of total pop.) [m]	5 439.8 / 0.4	5 241.0 / 0.4	5 154.7 / 0.4 [c]
Refugees and others of concern to the UNHCR (000)	193.7 [n]	205.8	206.6 [c]
Infant mortality rate (per 1 000 live births) [l]	49.5	39.1	32.0
Health: Current expenditure (% of GDP) [i,o]	3.3	3.6 [p]	3.5 [a]
Health: Physicians (per 1 000 pop.)	0.7	0.7 [q]	0.9 [d]
Education: Government expenditure (% of GDP)	3.4	3.8 [r]	...
Education: Primary gross enrol. ratio (f/m per 100 pop.)	110.7 / 107.7 [i]	114.8 / 102.8	121.1 / 105.6 [a]
Education: Secondary gross enrol. ratio (f/m per 100 pop.)	61.1 / 64.9	74.7 / 73.1	76.6 / 73.9 [i,d]
Education: Tertiary gross enrol. ratio (f/m per 100 pop.)	15.1 / 20.3	26.8 / 26.7	29.1 / 27.2 [d]
Intentional homicide rate (per 100 000 pop.)	3.8	3.4	3.1 [d]
Seats held by women in the National Parliament (%)	10.8	12.0	14.4 [s]

Environment and infrastructure indicators

	2010	2015	2020
Individuals using the Internet (per 100 inhabitants)	7.5 [i]	17.0 [t]	34.4 [a]
Research & Development expenditure (% of GDP)	0.8	0.7	0.6 [d]
Threatened species (number)	758	1 039	1 118
Forested area (% of land area) [i]	23.5	23.8	23.8 [a]
CO2 emission estimates (million tons/tons per capita)	1 583.4 / 1.3	2 026.7 / 1.5	2 161.6 / 1.6 [a]
Energy production, primary (Petajoules)	22 888	22 818	23 410 [a]
Energy supply per capita (Gigajoules)	24	28	28 [a]
Tourist/visitor arrivals at national borders (000)	5 776 [u]	13 284 [v]	17 423 [v,d]
Important sites for terrestrial biodiversity protected (%)	17.7	21.0	21.0 [a]
Pop. using safely managed drinking water (urban/rural, %)	... / 40.0	... / 51.3	... / 56.0 [a]
Pop. using safely managed sanitation (urban/rural %)	... / 22.6	... / 34.3	... / 39.0 [a]
Net Official Development Assist. received (% of GNI)	0.17	0.15	0.09 [d]

[a] 2017. **b** Refers to the Delhi metropolitan area that is not restricted to state boundaries (National Capital Territory), includes contiguous suburban cities and towns, such as Faridabad, Gurgaon, and Ghaziabad. **c** 2019. **d** 2018. **e** Data classified according to ISIC Rev. 4. **f** Excludes publishing activities. Includes irrigation and canals. **g** Excludes computer and related activities and radio/TV activities. **h** Excludes repair of personal and household goods. **i** Estimate. **j** Industrial workers. **k** 2016. **l** Data refers to a 5-year period preceding the reference year. **m** Including refugees. **n** Data as at the end of December. **o** Data refer to fiscal years beginning 1 April. **p** Break in the time series. **q** 2014. **r** 2013. **s** Data are as at 1 January of reporting year. **t** Population aged 18 years and over. **u** Excluding nationals residing abroad. **v** Including nationals residing abroad.

Indonesia

Region	South-eastern Asia	UN membership date	28 September 1950
Population (000, 2020)	273 524	Surface area (km2)	1 910 931 [a]
Pop. density (per km2, 2020)	151.0	Sex ratio (m per 100 f)	101.4
Capital city	Jakarta	National currency	Rupiah (IDR)
Capital city pop. (000, 2020)	10 638.7 [b,c]	Exchange rate (per US$)	13 901.0 [c]

Economic indicators

	2010	2015	2020
GDP: Gross domestic product (million current US$)	755 094	860 854	1 042 173 [d]
GDP growth rate (annual %, const. 2015 prices)	6.2	4.9	5.2 [d]
GDP per capita (current US$)	3 122.4	3 331.7	3 893.5 [d]
Economy: Agriculture (% of Gross Value Added) [e]	14.3	13.9	13.3 [d]
Economy: Industry (% of Gross Value Added) [e,f]	43.9	41.4	41.4 [d]
Economy: Services and other activity (% of GVA) [e,g,h]	38.9	43.1	42.7 [d]
Employment in agriculture (% of employed)	39.1	33.0	27.7 [i]
Employment in industry (% of employed)	18.7	22.0	22.7 [i]
Employment in services & other sectors (% employed)	42.2	44.9	49.6 [i]
Unemployment rate (% of labour force) [i]	5.6	4.5	4.8
Labour force participation rate (female/male pop. %) [i]	51.2 / 83.2	50.6 / 82.4	53.2 / 81.8
CPI: Consumer Price Index (2010=100)	100	132	151 [c]
Agricultural production index (2004-2006=100)	123	142	143 [i]
International trade: exports (million current US$) [k]	157 779	150 366	167 003 [c]
International trade: imports (million current US$) [k]	135 663	142 695	170 727 [c]
International trade: balance (million current US$) [k]	22 116	7 671	- 3 724 [c]
Balance of payments, current account (million US$)	5 144	- 17 519	- 30 387 [c]

Major trading partners

						2019
Export partners (% of exports)	China	16.7	United States	10.6	Japan	9.5
Import partners (% of imports)	China	26.3	Singapore	10.1	Japan	9.2

Social indicators

	2010	2015	2020
Population growth rate (average annual %) [i]	1.3	1.3	1.1
Urban population (% of total population)	49.9	53.3	56.0 [c]
Urban population growth rate (average annual %) [i]	3.0	2.6	...
Fertility rate, total (live births per woman) [i]	2.5	2.4	2.3
Life expectancy at birth (females/males, years) [i]	70.3 / 66.4	72.2 / 67.9	73.6 / 69.3
Population age distribution (0-14/60+ years old, %)	28.8 / 7.5	27.5 / 8.5	25.9 / 10.1
International migrant stock (000/% of total pop.) [m]	305.4 / 0.1	338.1 / 0.1	353.1 / 0.1 [c]
Refugees and others of concern to the UNHCR (000)	2.9 [n]	13.2	14.0 [c]
Infant mortality rate (per 1 000 live births) [i]	30.4	25.0	18.9
Health: Current expenditure (% of GDP)	3.0	3.0 [o]	3.0 [a]
Health: Physicians (per 1 000 pop.)	0.1	0.3	0.4 [d]
Education: Government expenditure (% of GDP)	2.8	3.6	...
Education: Primary gross enrol. ratio (f/m per 100 pop.)	111.0 / 107.4	104.4 / 107.4	104.6 / 108.1 [d]
Education: Secondary gross enrol. ratio (f/m per 100 pop.)	76.7 / 76.2	86.3 / 86.0	90.0 / 87.8 [d]
Education: Tertiary gross enrol. ratio (f/m per 100 pop.)	22.5 / 25.7	35.0 / 31.5	39.0 / 33.8 [d]
Intentional homicide rate (per 100 000 pop.)	0.4	0.6	0.4 [a]
Seats held by women in the National Parliament (%)	18.0	17.1	20.4 [p]

Environment and infrastructure indicators

	2010	2015	2020
Individuals using the Internet (per 100 inhabitants)	10.9	22.0 [q]	39.9 [d]
Research & Development expenditure (% of GDP)	0.1 [r,s,t]	0.1 [u]	0.2 [d]
Threatened species (number)	1 142	1 246	1 654
Forested area (% of land area) [i]	52.1	50.2	48.5 [a]
CO2 emission estimates (million tons/tons per capita)	357.6 / 1.5	459.1 / 1.8	496.4 / 1.9 [a]
Energy production, primary (Petajoules)	16 863	18 140	19 187 [a]
Energy supply per capita (Gigajoules)	34	37	38 [a]
Tourist/visitor arrivals at national borders (000)	7 003	10 407	15 810 [d]
Important sites for terrestrial biodiversity protected (%)	17.4	23.1	26.1 [c]
Net Official Development Assist. received (% of GNI)	0.18	0.00	0.10 [d]

a 2017. b Refers to the functional urban area. c 2019. d 2018. e Data classified according to ISIC Rev. 4. f Excludes publishing activities. Includes irrigation and canals. g Excludes computer and related activities and radio/TV activities. h Excludes repair of personal and household goods. i Estimate. j 2016. k Merchandise imports data follows special trade system up to 2007. l Data refers to a 5-year period preceding the reference year. m Including refugees. n Data as at the end of December. o Provisional data. p Data are as at 1 January of reporting year. q Population aged 5 years and over. r Break in the time series. s Partial data. t 2009. u 2013.

Iran (Islamic Republic of)

Region	Southern Asia	UN membership date	24 October 1945
Population (000, 2020)	83 993	Surface area (km2)	1 628 750 [a,b]
Pop. density (per km2, 2020)	51.6	Sex ratio (m per 100 f)	102.0
Capital city	Tehran	National currency	Iranian Rial (IRR)
Capital city pop. (000, 2020)	9 013.7 [c]	Exchange rate (per US$)	42 000.0 [c]

Economic indicators

	2010	2015	2020
GDP: Gross domestic product (million current US$)	491 099	393 436	473 091 [d]
GDP growth rate (annual %, const. 2015 prices)	5.8	- 1.3	- 4.8 [d]
GDP per capita (current US$)	6 657.8	5 012.4	5 783.5 [d]
Economy: Agriculture (% of Gross Value Added)	6.4	10.6	10.0 [d]
Economy: Industry (% of Gross Value Added)	43.4	33.2	34.3 [d]
Economy: Services and other activity (% of GVA)	42.2	53.7	50.5 [d]
Employment in agriculture (% of employed)	19.2	18.0	17.8 [e]
Employment in industry (% of employed)	32.2	32.5	30.3 [e]
Employment in services & other sectors (% employed)	48.6	49.4	51.9 [e]
Unemployment rate (% of labour force) [e]	13.5	11.1	11.2
Labour force participation rate (female/male pop. %) [e]	15.7 / 69.9	14.8 / 69.7	17.3 / 71.1
CPI: Consumer Price Index (2010=100) [f]	...	92	175 [c]
Agricultural production index (2004-2006=100)	102	110	110 [g]
International trade: exports (million current US$) [h,i]	83 785	64 084 [e]	17 394 [e,c]
International trade: imports (million current US$) [h,i]	54 697	41 453 [e]	20 502 [e,c]
International trade: balance (million current US$) [h,i]	29 088	22 631 [e]	- 3 108 [e,c]

Major trading partners

					2019
Export partners (% of exports) [e]	Other Asia, nes	42.4	Other Europe, nes	14.0	China 8.6
Import partners (% of imports) [e]	China	25.4	United Arab Emirates	15.8	Rep. of Korea 7.1

Social indicators

	2010	2015	2020
Population growth rate (average annual %) [j]	1.1	1.2	1.4
Urban population (% of total population)	70.6	73.4	75.4 [c]
Urban population growth rate (average annual %) [j]	2.0	2.0	...
Fertility rate, total (live births per woman) [j]	1.8	1.9	2.2
Life expectancy at birth (females/males, years) [j]	74.6 / 71.0	76.2 / 74.0	77.6 / 75.3
Population age distribution (0-14/60+ years old, %)	24.0 / 7.5	23.9 / 8.9	24.7 / 10.3
International migrant stock (000/% of total pop.) [k]	2 761.6 / 3.7	2 726.4 / 3.5	2 682.2 / 3.2 [c]
Refugees and others of concern to the UNHCR (000)	1 085.3 [l]	979.5	979.5 [c]
Infant mortality rate (per 1 000 live births) [j]	19.1	15.2	12.8
Health: Current expenditure (% of GDP) [m]	6.8	7.8	8.7 [b]
Health: Physicians (per 1 000 pop.)	0.5 [n]	1.2	1.6 [d]
Education: Government expenditure (% of GDP)	3.7	2.8	4.0 [d]
Education: Primary gross enrol. ratio (f/m per 100 pop.)	99.6 / 101.7	112.3 / 105.7	113.9 / 107.7 [b]
Education: Secondary gross enrol. ratio (f/m per 100 pop.)	78.0 / 83.2	83.0 / 88.7	84.7 / 87.9 [b]
Education: Tertiary gross enrol. ratio (f/m per 100 pop.)	44.1 / 44.2	63.8 / 70.9 [o]	62.9 / 73.3 [b]
Intentional homicide rate (per 100 000 pop.)	3.0 [p]	2.5 [o]	...
Seats held by women in the National Parliament (%)	2.8	3.1	5.9 [q]

Environment and infrastructure indicators

	2010	2015	2020
Individuals using the Internet (per 100 inhabitants)	15.9 [r]	45.3 [e]	70.0 [d]
Research & Development expenditure (% of GDP)	0.3 [s,t]	0.4	0.8 [u,b]
Threatened species (number)	102	121	161
Forested area (% of land area)	6.6	6.6	6.6 [e,b]
CO2 emission estimates (million tons/tons per capita) [v]	498.6 / 6.7	553.3 / 7.0	567.1 / 7.0 [b]
Energy production, primary (Petajoules)	14 283	13 637	17 740 [b]
Energy supply per capita (Gigajoules)	115	126	135 [b]
Tourist/visitor arrivals at national borders (000)	2 938	5 237	7 295 [d]
Important sites for terrestrial biodiversity protected (%)	43.6	43.6	43.6 [c]
Pop. using safely managed drinking water (urban/rural, %)	95.1 / 82.9	94.9 / 82.7	94.9 / 82.7 [b]
Net Official Development Assist. received (% of GNI)	0.02	0.03	0.03 [b]

Land area only. **b** 2017. **c** 2019. **d** 2018. **e** Estimate. **f** Index base: fiscal (solar) year 2016 (21 March 2016 - 20 March 2017)=100. **g** 2016. **h** Data include oil and gas. The value of oil exports and total exports are rough estimates based on information published in various petroleum industry journals. **i** Year ending 20 March of the year stated. **j** Data refers to a 5-year period preceding the reference year. **k** Including refugees. **l** Data as at the end of December. **m** Provisional data. **n** 2006. **o** 2014. **p** 2009. **q** Data are as at 1 January of reporting year. **r** Population aged 6 years and over. **s** Excluding private non-profit. **t** Excluding government. **u** Break in the time series. **v** Data refer to the Iranian Year which begins on 21 March and ends on 20 March of the following year.

Iraq

Region	Western Asia	UN membership date	21 December 1945
Population (000, 2020)	40 222	Surface area (km2)	435 052 [a]
Pop. density (per km2, 2020)	92.6	Sex ratio (m per 100 f)	102.5
Capital city	Baghdad	National currency	Iraqi Dinar (IQD)
Capital city pop. (000, 2020)	6 974.4 [b]	Exchange rate (per US$)	1 182.0 [b]

Economic indicators

	2010	2015	2020
GDP: Gross domestic product (million current US$)	138 517	166 774	212 272 [c]
GDP growth rate (annual %, const. 2015 prices)	6.4	4.7	- 1.0 [c]
GDP per capita (current US$)	4 657.3	4 688.3	5 523.1 [c]
Economy: Agriculture (% of Gross Value Added)	5.1	4.2	1.9 [c]
Economy: Industry (% of Gross Value Added)	55.4	45.0	55.3 [c]
Economy: Services and other activity (% of GVA)	51.5	51.2	48.4 [c]
Employment in agriculture (% of employed) [d]	21.9	19.4	17.8
Employment in industry (% of employed) [d]	21.7	22.8	22.4
Employment in services & other sectors (% employed) [d]	56.4	57.9	59.9
Unemployment rate (% of labour force) [d]	8.4	10.7	12.8
Labour force participation rate (female/male pop. %) [d]	12.0 / 72.3	14.1 / 73.8	11.8 / 74.3
CPI: Consumer Price Index (2010=100)	100	119	120 [c]
Agricultural production index (2004-2006=100)	103	73	75 [e]
International trade: exports (million current US$)	52 483	49 403	4 658 [d,b]
International trade: imports (million current US$)	43 915	32 665	31 372 [d,b]
International trade: balance (million current US$)	8 568	16 738	- 26 714 [d,b]
Balance of payments, current account (million US$)	6 488	- 2 762	15 675 [b]

Major trading partners

						2019
Export partners (% of exports) [d]	India	24.9	China	24.6	Rep. of Korea	9.0
Import partners (% of imports) [d]	Areas nes [f]	68.2	United Arab Emirates	7.8	Turkey	6.7

Social indicators

	2010	2015	2020
Population growth rate (average annual %) [g]	2.0	3.6	2.5
Urban population (% of total population)	69.1	69.9	70.7 [b]
Urban population growth rate (average annual %) [g]	2.7	3.4	...
Fertility rate, total (live births per woman) [g]	4.4	4.2	3.7
Life expectancy at birth (females/males, years) [g]	71.3 / 64.9	71.6 / 67.2	72.4 / 68.3
Population age distribution (0-14/60+ years old, %)	41.8 / 4.8	39.3 / 5.1	37.7 / 5.1
International migrant stock (000/% of total pop.) [h,i]	117.4 / 0.4	359.4 / 1.0	368.1 / 0.9 [b]
Refugees and others of concern to the UNHCR (000)	1 796.3 [j]	4 311.7	2 132.4 [k,b]
Infant mortality rate (per 1 000 live births) [g]	31.7	28.5	24.1
Health: Current expenditure (% of GDP)	3.2	3.1	4.2 [a]
Health: Physicians (per 1 000 pop.)	0.7	1.0 [l]	0.7 [c]
Education: Primary gross enrol. ratio (f/m per 100 pop.)	99.1 / 117.8 [m]	... / ...	... / ...
Education: Secondary gross enrol. ratio (f/m per 100 pop.)	46.0 / 61.4 [m]	... / ...	... / ...
Education: Tertiary gross enrol. ratio (f/m per 100 pop.)	12.0 / 20.1 [d,n]	... / ...	... / ...
Intentional homicide rate (per 100 000 pop.)	9.0	10.1 [o]	...
Seats held by women in the National Parliament (%)	25.5	26.5	26.4 [p]

Environment and infrastructure indicators

	2010	2015	2020
Individuals using the Internet (per 100 inhabitants)	2.5	58.0 [q,r]	75.0 [c]
Research & Development expenditure (% of GDP)	~0.0 [s,t,u]	~0.0	~0.0 [c]
Threatened species (number)	60	69	80
Forested area (% of land area) [d]	1.9	1.9	1.9 [a]
CO2 emission estimates (million tons/tons per capita)	103.6 / 3.4	130.8 / 3.6	139.9 / 3.7 [a]
Energy production, primary (Petajoules)	5 274	7 565	9 881 [a]
Energy supply per capita (Gigajoules)	47	55	66 [a]
Tourist/visitor arrivals at national borders (000)	1 518	892 [o]	...
Important sites for terrestrial biodiversity protected (%)	3.0	5.7	5.8 [b]
Pop. using safely managed drinking water (urban/rural, %)	62.6 / 38.5	63.7 / 44.2	64.1 / 46.5 [a]
Pop. using safely managed sanitation (urban/rural %)	35.1 / 39.2	38.2 / 43.3	39.4 / 45.0 [a]
Net Official Development Assist. received (% of GNI)	1.55	0.84	1.03 [c]

a 2017. b 2019. c 2018. d Estimate. e 2016. f Areas not elsewhere specified. g Data refers to a 5-year period preceding the reference year. h Including refugees. i Refers to foreign citizens. j Data as at the end of December. k Estimate of stateless persons adjusted to reflect reduction of statelessness in line with Law 26 of 2006, which allows stateless persons to apply for nationality in certain circumstances. l 2014. m 2007. n 2005. o 2013. p Data are as at 1 January of reporting year. q Population aged 15 years and over. r Last week. s Excluding business enterprise. t Based on R&D budget instead of R&D expenditure. u Excluding private non-profit.

Ireland

Region	Northern Europe	UN membership date	14 December 1955
Population (000, 2020)	4 938	Surface area (km2)	69 797 [a]
Pop. density (per km2, 2020)	71.7	Sex ratio (m per 100 f)	98.6
Capital city	Dublin	National currency	Euro (EUR)
Capital city pop. (000, 2020)	1 214.7 [b]	Exchange rate (per US$)	0.9 [b]

Economic indicators

	2010	2015	2020
GDP: Gross domestic product (million current US$)	222 149	291 500	382 674 [c]
GDP growth rate (annual %, const. 2015 prices)	1.8	25.2	8.2 [c]
GDP per capita (current US$)	48 777.6	62 655.5	79 414.6 [c]
Economy: Agriculture (% of Gross Value Added) [d]	1.0	1.0	1.0 [c]
Economy: Industry (% of Gross Value Added) [d,e]	25.6	41.0	39.3 [c]
Economy: Services and other activity (% of GVA) [d,f,g]	69.9	60.1	60.0 [c]
Employment in agriculture (% of employed)	5.8	5.3	4.5 [h]
Employment in industry (% of employed)	18.1	18.1	18.5 [h]
Employment in services & other sectors (% employed)	76.2	76.6	77.0 [h]
Unemployment rate (% of labour force) [h]	14.5	9.9	5.2
Labour force participation rate (female/male pop. %) [h]	55.6 / 70.5	55.1 / 69.5	55.8 / 67.9
CPI: Consumer Price Index (2010=100) [i]	100	105	107 [b]
Agricultural production index (2004-2006=100)	101	109	110 [i]
International trade: exports (million current US$)	120 645	124 731	170 743 [b]
International trade: imports (million current US$)	64 601	77 795	101 473 [b]
International trade: balance (million current US$)	56 045	46 935	69 270 [b]
Balance of payments, current account (million US$)	2 320	31 682	- 36 374 [b]

Major trading partners

						2019
Export partners (% of exports)	United States	30.8	United Kingdom	10.3	Belgium	10.2
Import partners (% of imports)	United Kingdom	22.5	United States	15.5	France	13.6

Social indicators

	2010	2015	2020
Population growth rate (average annual %) [k]	1.9	0.4	1.2
Urban population (% of total population)	61.5	62.5	63.4 [b]
Urban population growth rate (average annual %) [k]	2.2	0.6	...
Fertility rate, total (live births per woman) [k]	2.0	2.0	1.8
Life expectancy at birth (females/males, years) [k]	82.0 / 77.4	82.5 / 78.7	83.7 / 80.4
Population age distribution (0-14/60+ years old, %)	20.8 / 15.9	21.9 / 17.9	20.8 / 19.6
International migrant stock (000/% of total pop.)	730.5 / 16.0	759.3 / 16.3	833.6 / 17.1 [b]
Refugees and others of concern to the UNHCR (000)	14.2 [l]	10.5 [l]	14.4 [b]
Infant mortality rate (per 1 000 live births) [k]	3.7	3.4	2.7
Health: Current expenditure (% of GDP)	10.5	7.3	7.2 [a]
Health: Physicians (per 1 000 pop.)	4.1	3.1	3.3 [c]
Education: Government expenditure (% of GDP)	6.0	3.8	3.7 [i]
Education: Primary gross enrol. ratio (f/m per 100 pop.) [h]	103.3 / 102.3	101.0 / 101.4	100.7 / 101.0 [a]
Education: Secondary gross enrol. ratio (f/m per 100 pop.) [h]	121.7 / 114.8	118.7 / 115.4	124.3 / 126.3 [a]
Education: Tertiary gross enrol. ratio (f/m per 100 pop.) [h]	65.4 / 60.8	80.6 / 74.0	82.0 / 73.7 [e]
Intentional homicide rate (per 100 000 pop.)	1.2	0.7	0.9 [c]
Seats held by women in the National Parliament (%)	13.9	16.3	20.9 [m]

Environment and infrastructure indicators

	2010	2015	2020
Individuals using the Internet (per 100 inhabitants)	69.8 [n]	83.5 [n,o]	84.5 [c]
Research & Development expenditure (% of GDP)	1.6 [h]	1.2 [h]	1.1 [p,c]
Threatened species (number)	27	39	79
Forested area (% of land area)	10.5	10.9	10.9 [h,a]
CO2 emission estimates (million tons/tons per capita)	39.5 / 8.7	35.3 / 7.5	35.7 / 7.4 [a]
Energy production, primary (Petajoules)	78	81	204 [a]
Energy supply per capita (Gigajoules)	132	119	121 [a]
Tourist/visitor arrivals at national borders (000) [r]	7 134 [q]	9 528	10 926 [c]
Important sites for terrestrial biodiversity protected (%)	85.4	86.0	86.0 [b]
Pop. using safely managed sanitation (urban/rural %)	74.2 / 68.8	88.2 / 72.1	88.5 / 72.1 [a]
Net Official Development Assist. disbursed (% of GNI) [s]	0.52	0.32	0.32 [a]

2017. **b** 2019. **c** 2018. **d** Data classified according to ISIC Rev. 4. **e** Excludes publishing activities. Includes irrigation and canals. **f** Excludes repair of personal and household goods. **g** Excludes computer and related activities and radio/TV activities. **h** Estimate. **i** Calculated by the UN Statistics Division from national indices. **j** 2016. **k** Data refers to a 5-year period preceding the reference year. **l** Data as at the end of December. **m** Data are as at 1 January reporting year. **n** Population aged 16 to 74 years. **o** Users in the last 3 months. **p** Provisional data. **q** Break in the time series. **r** Including tourists from Northern Ireland. **s** Development Assistance Committee member (OECD).

Isle of Man

Region	Northern Europe	Population (000, 2020)	86
Surface area (km2)	572[a]	Pop. density (per km2, 2020)	150.7
Sex ratio (m per 100 f)	98.2[b,c]	Capital city	Douglas
National currency	Pound Sterling (GBP)	Capital city pop. (000, 2020)	27.2[d]
Exchange rate (per US$)	0.8[e]		

Economic indicators	2010	2015	2020
Employment in agriculture (% of employed)	1.9[f,g]	...	...
Employment in industry (% of employed)	14.8[f,g]	...	...
Employment in services & other sectors (% employed)	83.3[f,g]	...	...
Unemployment rate (% of labour force)	2.4[g]	2.6[h,i,j]	...
Labour force participation rate (female/male pop. %)	56.3 / 69.9[g]	57.5 / 69.3[h,k,l]	... / ...
CPI: Consumer Price Index (2010=100)	...	161[m,n]	...

Social indicators	2010	2015	2020
Population growth rate (average annual %)	1.0[o]	0.8[o]	0.6
Urban population (% of total population)	52.0	52.2	52.7[e]
Urban population growth rate (average annual %)[o]	1.0	0.9	...
Population age distribution (0-14/60+ years old, %)[b]	16.4 / 24.1[p]	16.3 / 25.7	16.0 / 26.9[c]
International migrant stock (000/% of total pop.)	43.4 / 51.2	42.2 / 50.7	42.9 / 50.7[e]
Intentional homicide rate (per 100 000 pop.)	...	1.2	0.0[c]

Environment and infrastructure indicators	2010	2015	2020
Threatened species (number)	2	3	6
Forested area (% of land area)[q]	6.1	6.1	6.1[a]
Energy production, primary (Petajoules)[q]	0	0	0[a]
Energy supply per capita (Gigajoules)	50	49	53[a]

a 2017. b De jure population. c 2016. d 2018. e 2019. f Data classified according to ISIC Rev. 3. g 2006. h Break in the time series. i Population aged 15 to 64 years. j 2013. k Population aged 16 years and over. l 2011. m Base: 2000=100. n 2014. o Data refers to a 5-year period preceding the reference year. p 2009. q Estimate.

Israel

Region	Western Asia	UN membership date	11 May 1949
Population (000, 2020)	8 656	Surface area (km2)	22 072 [a]
Pop. density (per km2, 2020)	400.0	Sex ratio (m per 100 f)	99.1
Capital city	Jerusalem [b]	National currency	New Israeli Sheqel (ILS)
Capital city pop. (000, 2020)	919.4 [c,d]	Exchange rate (per US$)	3.5 [d]

Economic indicators

	2010	2015	2020
GDP: Gross domestic product (million current US$)	233 996	299 813	370 588 [e]
GDP growth rate (annual %, const. 2015 prices)	5.6	2.3	3.4 [e]
GDP per capita (current US$)	31 851.5	37 577.7	44 214.9 [e]
Economy: Agriculture (% of Gross Value Added) [f]	1.7	1.3	1.3 [e]
Economy: Industry (% of Gross Value Added) [f,g]	23.6	22.5	21.5 [e]
Economy: Services and other activity (% of GVA) [f,h,i]	77.1	76.5	78.2 [e]
Employment in agriculture (% of employed)	1.3 [j]	1.0	0.9 [j]
Employment in industry (% of employed)	19.1 [j]	17.6	16.8 [j]
Employment in services & other sectors (% employed)	79.6 [j]	81.4	82.3 [j]
Unemployment rate (% of labour force) [j]	8.5	5.2	3.8
Labour force participation rate (female/male pop. %) [j]	57.0 / 69.4	59.0 / 69.5	59.7 / 68.5
CPI: Consumer Price Index (2010=100)	100	107	108 [d]
Agricultural production index (2004-2006=100)	104	106	109 [k]
International trade: exports (million current US$)	58 413	64 062	58 488 [d]
International trade: imports (million current US$)	59 194	62 068	76 579 [d]
International trade: balance (million current US$)	- 781	1 994	- 18 090 [d]
Balance of payments, current account (million US$)	8 091	15 429	14 051 [d]

Major trading partners

						2019
Export partners (% of exports)	United States	27.3	United Kingdom	8.5	China	7.6
Import partners (% of imports)	United States	16.7	China	13.4	Germany	6.3

Social indicators

	2010	2015	2020
Population growth rate (average annual %) [l]	2.4	1.7	1.6
Urban population (% of total population)	91.8	92.2	92.5 [d]
Urban population growth rate (average annual %) [l]	2.4	1.7	...
Fertility rate, total (live births per woman) [l]	2.9	3.0	3.0
Life expectancy at birth (females/males, years) [l]	82.8 / 79.0	83.7 / 80.0	84.3 / 81.0
Population age distribution (0-14/60+ years old, %)	27.3 / 14.9	27.9 / 15.8	27.8 / 16.5
International migrant stock (000/% of total pop.) [m]	1 950.6 / 26.6	2 011.7 / 25.2	1 956.3 / 23.0 [d]
Refugees and others of concern to the UNHCR (000)	31.1 [n]	45.2	55.1 [d]
Infant mortality rate (per 1 000 live births) [l]	4.0	3.4	2.7
Health: Current expenditure (% of GDP)	7.0	7.1	7.4 [a]
Health: Physicians (per 1 000 pop.)	3.5	3.5	4.6 [e]
Education: Government expenditure (% of GDP)	5.5	5.9	5.8 [k]
Education: Primary gross enrol. ratio (f/m per 100 pop.)	105.7 / 105.2	106.0 / 105.3	105.4 / 104.4 [a]
Education: Secondary gross enrol. ratio (f/m per 100 pop.)	104.5 / 102.0	104.2 / 103.2	106.0 / 104.2 [a]
Education: Tertiary gross enrol. ratio (f/m per 100 pop.)	74.6 / 57.6	76.3 / 55.2	74.5 / 52.8 [a]
Intentional homicide rate (per 100 000 pop.)	2.0	1.4	1.5 [a]
Seats held by women in the National Parliament (%)	19.2	22.5	23.3 [o]

Environment and infrastructure indicators

	2010	2015	2020
Individuals using the Internet (per 100 inhabitants)	67.5 [p]	77.4 [p]	83.7 [e]
Research & Development expenditure (% of GDP) [q]	3.9	4.3	5.0 [j,e]
Threatened species (number)	131	152	207
Forested area (% of land area)	7.1	7.6	7.6 [j,a]
CO2 emission estimates (million tons/tons per capita)	68.4 / 9.0	63.9 / 7.6	63.8 / 7.3 [a]
Energy production, primary (Petajoules)	162	308	375 [a]
Energy supply per capita (Gigajoules)	131	118	116 [a]
Tourist/visitor arrivals at national borders (000) [r]	2 803	2 799	4 121 [e]
Important sites for terrestrial biodiversity protected (%)	20.3	20.3	20.3 [d]
Pop. using safely managed drinking water (urban/rural, %)	99.8 / 99.7	99.5 / 99.4	99.4 / 99.2 [a]
Pop. using safely managed sanitation (urban/rural, %)	87.9 / 86.1	92.1 / 90.2	93.8 / 91.8 [a]
Net Official Development Assist. disbursed (% of GNI)	0.07	0.08	0.12 [a]

2017. **b** Designation and data provided by Israel. The position of the UN on Jerusalem is stated in A/RES/181 (II) and subsequent General Assembly and Security Council resolutions. **c** Including East Jerusalem. **d** 2019. **e** 2018. **f** Data classified according to ISIC Rev. 4. **g** Excludes publishing activities. Includes irrigation and canals. **h** Excludes repair of personal and household goods. **i** Excludes computer and related activities and radio/TV activities. **j** Estimate. **k** 2016. **l** Data refers to a 5-year period preceding the reference year. **m** Including refugees. **n** Data as at the end of December. **o** Data are as at 1 January of reporting year. **p** Population aged 20 years and over. **q** Do not correspond exactly to Frascati Manual recommendations. **r** Excluding nationals residing abroad.

Italy

Region	Southern Europe	UN membership date	14 December 1955
Population (000, 2020)	60 462	Surface area (km2)	302 073[a]
Pop. density (per km2, 2020)	205.6	Sex ratio (m per 100 f)	94.9
Capital city	Rome	National currency	Euro (EUR)
Capital city pop. (000, 2020)	4 234.0[b,c]	Exchange rate (per US$)	0.9[c]

Economic indicators

	2010	2015	2020
GDP: Gross domestic product (million current US$)	2 134 018	1 835 899	2 084 882[d]
GDP growth rate (annual %, const. 2015 prices)	1.7	0.8	0.8[d]
GDP per capita (current US$)	35 971.5	30 306.1	34 388.5[d]
Economy: Agriculture (% of Gross Value Added)[e]	2.0	2.3	2.2[d]
Economy: Industry (% of Gross Value Added)[e,f]	24.3	23.2	23.9[d]
Economy: Services and other activity (% of GVA)[e,g,h]	81.3	81.4	78.8[d]
Employment in agriculture (% of employed)	3.8	3.8	3.6[i]
Employment in industry (% of employed)	28.6	26.6	25.6[i]
Employment in services & other sectors (% employed)	67.6	69.6	70.8[i]
Unemployment rate (% of labour force)[i]	8.4	11.9	9.8
Labour force participation rate (female/male pop. %)[i]	37.9 / 59.0	39.5 / 58.7	40.7 / 58.7
CPI: Consumer Price Index (2010=100)	100	107	111[i,c]
Agricultural production index (2004-2006=100)	97	92	92[k]
International trade: exports (million current US$)	446 840	456 989	532 684[c]
International trade: imports (million current US$)	486 984	410 933	473 562[c]
International trade: balance (million current US$)	- 40 145	46 055	59 121[c]
Balance of payments, current account (million US$)	- 70 819	25 379	58 933[c]

Major trading partners

						2019
Export partners (% of exports)	Germany	12.2	France	10.5	United States	9.6
Import partners (% of imports)	Germany	16.5	France	8.7	China	7.5

Social indicators

	2010	2015	2020
Population growth rate (average annual %)[l]	0.4	0.4	~0.0
Urban population (% of total population)	68.3	69.6	70.7[c]
Urban population growth rate (average annual %)[l]	0.5	0.3	...
Fertility rate, total (live births per woman)[l]	1.4	1.4	1.3
Life expectancy at birth (females/males, years)[l]	84.1 / 78.8	84.7 / 79.9	85.4 / 81.0
Population age distribution (0-14/60+ years old, %)	14.1 / 26.7	13.7 / 28.0	13.0 / 29.8
International migrant stock (000/% of total pop.)	5 787.9 / 9.8	5 805.3 / 9.6	6 273.7 / 10.4[c]
Refugees and others of concern to the UNHCR (000)	61.3[m]	142.6	261.4[c]
Infant mortality rate (per 1 000 live births)[l]	3.4	3.0	2.6
Health: Current expenditure (% of GDP)	9.0	9.0	8.8[a]
Health: Physicians (per 1 000 pop.)	3.8	3.8	4.0[d]
Education: Government expenditure (% of GDP)	4.4	4.1	3.8[k]
Education: Primary gross enrol. ratio (f/m per 100 pop.)	102.5 / 103.5	100.2 / 100.6	100.3 / 103.4[a]
Education: Secondary gross enrol. ratio (f/m per 100 pop.)	102.4 / 103.4	102.1 / 102.4	100.9 / 101.6[a]
Education: Tertiary gross enrol. ratio (f/m per 100 pop.)	77.7 / 54.4	70.8 / 51.6	71.5 / 53.0[a]
Intentional homicide rate (per 100 000 pop.)	0.9	0.8	0.6[d]
Seats held by women in the National Parliament (%)	21.3	31.0	35.7[n]

Environment and infrastructure indicators

	2010	2015	2020
Individuals using the Internet (per 100 inhabitants)	53.7[o]	58.1[p]	74.4[d]
Research & Development expenditure (% of GDP)	1.2	1.3	1.4[q,d]
Threatened species (number)	174	279	482
Forested area (% of land area)[l]	30.7	31.6	31.6[a]
CO2 emission estimates (million tons/tons per capita)[r]	392.0 / 6.6	329.7 / 5.4	321.5 / 5.3[a]
Energy production, primary (Petajoules)[s]	1 384	1 509	1 421[a]
Energy supply per capita (Gigajoules)[s]	123	108	108[a]
Tourist/visitor arrivals at national borders (000)[t]	43 626	50 732	61 567[d]
Important sites for terrestrial biodiversity protected (%)	77.3	77.3	77.3[c]
Pop. using safely managed sanitation (urban/rural %)	96.2 / 96.1	96.3 / 96.1	96.3 / 96.1[a]
Net Official Development Assist. disbursed (% of GNI)[u]	0.15	0.22	0.30[a]

a 2017. b Refers to the official Metropolitan City. c 2019. d 2018. e Data classified according to ISIC Rev. 4. f Excludes publishing activities. Includes irrigation and canals. g Excludes repair of personal and household goods. h Excludes computer and related activities and radio/TV activities. i Estimate. j Calculated by the UN Statistics Divisio from national indices. k 2016. l Data refers to a 5-year period preceding the reference year. m Data as at the end of December. n Data are as at 1 January of reporting year. o Population aged 16 to 74 years. p Population aged 6 years and over. q Provisional data. r Including San Marino. s Data include San Marino and the Holy See. t Excluding seasonal and border workers. u Development Assistance Committee member (OECD).

Jamaica

Region	Caribbean	
Population (000, 2020)	2 961	
Pop. density (per km2, 2020)	273.4	
Capital city	Kingston	
Capital city pop. (000, 2020)	589.8 [b]	

UN membership date	18 September 1962
Surface area (km2)	10 990 [a]
Sex ratio (m per 100 f)	98.5
National currency	Jamaican Dollar (JMD)
Exchange rate (per US$)	131.2 [b]

Economic indicators

	2010	2015	2020
GDP: Gross domestic product (million current US$)	13 221	14 196	15 714 [c]
GDP growth rate (annual %, const. 2015 prices)	- 1.5	0.9	1.9 [c]
GDP per capita (current US$)	4 704.1	4 910.5	5 354.3 [c]
Economy: Agriculture (% of Gross Value Added)	5.9	7.2	7.7 [c]
Economy: Industry (% of Gross Value Added)	20.0	22.0	23.5 [c]
Economy: Services and other activity (% of GVA)	68.6	66.1	65.7 [c]
Employment in agriculture (% of employed)	17.8 [d]	17.7	15.7 [d]
Employment in industry (% of employed)	16.2 [d]	14.9	16.2 [d]
Employment in services & other sectors (% employed)	66.0 [d]	67.3	68.1 [d]
Unemployment rate (% of labour force) [d]	12.4	13.5	8.0
Labour force participation rate (female/male pop. %) [d]	55.6 / 71.1	57.4 / 71.5	60.0 / 72.6
CPI: Consumer Price Index (2010=100) [e]	100	141	163 [b]
Agricultural production index (2004-2006=100)	98	101	105 [f]
International trade: exports (million current US$)	1 328	1 263	1 586 [b]
International trade: imports (million current US$)	5 225	4 993	6 339 [b]
International trade: balance (million current US$)	- 3 898	- 3 730	- 4 753 [b]
Balance of payments, current account (million US$)	- 934	- 430	- 288 [c]

Major trading partners

							2019
Export partners (% of exports)	United States	38.8	Netherlands	13.8	Canada	8.8
Import partners (% of imports)	United States	45.2	China	7.8	Colombia	5.2

Social indicators

	2010	2015	2020
Population growth rate (average annual %) [g]	0.5	0.6	0.5
Urban population (% of total population)	53.7	54.8	56.0 [b]
Urban population growth rate (average annual %) [g]	0.9	0.8	...
Fertility rate, total (live births per woman) [g]	2.3	2.1	2.0
Life expectancy at birth (females/males, years) [g]	75.6 / 72.8	75.5 / 72.5	75.9 / 72.8
Population age distribution (0-14/60+ years old, %)	27.0 / 11.4	24.6 / 11.9	23.4 / 13.3
International migrant stock (000/% of total pop.)	23.7 / 0.8	23.2 / 0.8	23.5 / 0.8 [b]
Refugees and others of concern to the UNHCR (000)	~0.0 [h]	~0.0	~0.0 [b]
Infant mortality rate (per 1 000 live births) [g]	16.7	14.9	11.8
Health: Current expenditure (% of GDP)	5.0	5.7	6.0 [a]
Health: Physicians (per 1 000 pop.)	0.4 [i]	0.4	1.3 [a]
Education: Government expenditure (% of GDP)	6.4	5.4	...
Education: Primary gross enrol. ratio (f/m per 100 pop.)	... / ...	94.5 / 89.3	88.9 / 93.0 [c]
Education: Secondary gross enrol. ratio (f/m per 100 pop.)	95.5 / 88.2	83.8 / 78.2	83.6 / 81.0 [c]
Education: Tertiary gross enrol. ratio (f/m per 100 pop.)	37.8 / 16.4	34.7 / 19.9	... / ...
Intentional homicide rate (per 100 000 pop.)	51.5	41.8	43.9 [c]
Seats held by women in the National Parliament (%)	13.3	12.7	17.5 [i]

Environment and infrastructure indicators

	2010	2015	2020
Individuals using the Internet (per 100 inhabitants)	27.7 [k]	42.2 [d]	55.1 [d,a]
Threatened species (number)	282	298	323
Forested area (% of land area) [d]	31.1	31.0	31.0 [a]
CO2 emission estimates (million tons/tons per capita)	6.9 / 2.5	7.0 / 2.4	7.0 / 2.4 [a]
Energy production, primary (Petajoules)	5	7	6 [d,a]
Energy supply per capita (Gigajoules)	39	39	38 [a]
Tourist/visitor arrivals at national borders (000) [i,m]	1 922	2 123	2 473 [c]
Important sites for terrestrial biodiversity protected (%)	29.4	29.5	29.5 [b]
Net Official Development Assist. received (% of GNI)	1.11	0.43	0.66 [c]

2017. **b** 2019. **c** 2018. **d** Estimate. **e** Calculated by the UN Statistics Division from national indices. **f** 2016. **g** Data refers to a 5-year period preceding the reference year. **h** Data as at the end of December. **i** 2008. **j** Data are as at 1 January of reporting year. **k** Population aged 14 years and over. **l** Arrivals of non-resident tourists by air. **m** Including nationals residing abroad; E/D cards.

Japan

Region	Eastern Asia	UN membership date	18 December 1956	
Population (000, 2020)	126 476	Surface area (km2)	377 930 [a,b]	
Pop. density (per km2, 2020)	346.9	Sex ratio (m per 100 f)	95.4	
Capital city	Tokyo	National currency	Yen (JPY)	
Capital city pop. (000, 2020)	37 435.2 [c,d]	Exchange rate (per US$)	109.1 [d]	

Economic indicators

	2010	2015	2020
GDP: Gross domestic product (million current US$)	5 700 098	4 389 476	4 971 323 [e]
GDP growth rate (annual %, const. 2015 prices)	4.2	1.2	0.8 [e]
GDP per capita (current US$)	44 344.1	34 296.8	39 082.1 [e]
Economy: Agriculture (% of Gross Value Added) [f,g]	1.1	1.1	1.1 [e]
Economy: Industry (% of Gross Value Added) [f,g,h]	28.5	29.2	28.5 [e]
Economy: Services and other activity (% of GVA) [f,g,i,j]	63.7	62.4	62.8 [e]
Employment in agriculture (% of employed)	4.1	3.6	3.4 [k]
Employment in industry (% of employed)	25.6	25.0	24.1 [k]
Employment in services & other sectors (% employed)	70.4	71.4	72.6 [k]
Unemployment rate (% of labour force) [k]	5.1	3.4	2.3
Labour force participation rate (female/male pop. %) [k]	48.7 / 72.1	49.8 / 70.8	52.7 / 71.0
CPI: Consumer Price Index (2010=100) [l]	100	104	105 [d]
Agricultural production index (2004-2006=100)	97	96	92 [m]
International trade: exports (million current US$)	769 774	624 874	705 640 [d]
International trade: imports (million current US$)	694 059	625 568	720 895 [d]
International trade: balance (million current US$)	75 715	- 695	- 15 255 [d]
Balance of payments, current account (million US$)	220 888	136 472	184 540 [d]

Major trading partners

						2019
Export partners (% of exports)	United States	19.9	China	19.1	Rep. of Korea	6.6
Import partners (% of imports)	China	23.5	United States	11.3	Australia	6.3

Social indicators

	2010	2015	2020
Population growth rate (average annual %) [n]	~0.0	- 0.1	- 0.2
Urban population (% of total population)	90.8	91.4	91.7 [d]
Urban population growth rate (average annual %) [n]	1.1	~0.0	...
Fertility rate, total (live births per woman) [n]	1.3	1.4	1.4
Life expectancy at birth (females/males, years) [n]	86.0 / 79.2	86.5 / 80.0	87.5 / 81.3
Population age distribution (0-14/60+ years old, %)	13.4 / 30.3	13.0 / 32.8	12.4 / 34.3
International migrant stock (000/% of total pop.) [o]	2 134.2 / 1.7	2 232.2 / 1.7	2 498.9 / 2.0 [d]
Refugees and others of concern to the UNHCR (000)	7.0 [p]	13.8 [k]	31.5 [k,d]
Infant mortality rate (per 1 000 live births) [n]	2.6	2.5	1.8
Health: Current expenditure (% of GDP) [k]	9.2	10.9	10.9 [q]
Health: Physicians (per 1 000 pop.)	2.2	2.3 [r]	2.4 [m]
Education: Government expenditure (% of GDP)	3.6	3.6 [f]	...
Intentional homicide rate (per 100 000 pop.)	0.4	0.3	0.3 [e]
Seats held by women in the National Parliament (%)	11.2	9.5	9.9 [s]

Environment and infrastructure indicators

	2010	2015	2020
Individuals using the Internet (per 100 inhabitants)	78.2 [t]	91.1	91.3 [e]
Research & Development expenditure (% of GDP)	3.1	3.3	3.3 [u,e]
Threatened species (number)	330	364	470
Forested area (% of land area) [k]	68.5	68.5	68.5 [d]
CO2 emission estimates (million tons/tons per capita) [v]	1 127.2 / 8.8	1 155.7 / 9.1	1 132.4 / 8.9 [q]
Energy production, primary (Petajoules) [v]	4 228	1 345	1 727 [q]
Energy supply per capita (Gigajoules) [v]	163	141	142 [q]
Tourist/visitor arrivals at national borders (000) [w]	8 611	19 737	31 192 [e]
Important sites for terrestrial biodiversity protected (%)	60.9	64.8	64.8 [d]
Net Official Development Assist. disbursed (% of GNI) [x]	0.20	0.20	0.23 [d]

a Data refer to 1 October. b 2007. c Major metropolitan areas. d 2019. e 2018. f At producers' prices. g Data classified according to ISIC Rev. 4. h Excludes publishing activities. Includes irrigation and canals. i Excludes repair of personal and household goods. j Excludes computer and related activities and radio/TV activities. k Estimate. l Calculated by the UN Statistics Division from national indices. m 2016. n Data refers to a 5-year period preceding the reference year. o Refers to foreign citizens. p Data as at the end of December, q 2017. r 2014. s Data are as at 1 January of reporting year. t Population aged 6 years and over. u Break in the time series. v Data include Okinawa. w Excluding nationals residing abroad. x Development Assistance Committee member (OECD).

Jordan

Region	Western Asia	UN membership date	14 December 1955
Population (000, 2020)	10 203	Surface area (km2)	89 318 [a]
Pop. density (per km2, 2020)	114.9	Sex ratio (m per 100 f)	102.6
Capital city	Amman	National currency	Jordanian Dinar (JOD)
Capital city pop. (000, 2020)	2 108.5 [b]	Exchange rate (per US$)	0.7 [b]

Economic indicators

	2010	2015	2020
GDP: Gross domestic product (million current US$)	26 520	37 923	42 231 [c]
GDP growth rate (annual %, const. 2015 prices)	2.7	2.6	1.9 [c]
GDP per capita (current US$)	3 652.1	4 092.4	4 237.8 [c]
Economy: Agriculture (% of Gross Value Added)	4.5	5.4	5.9 [c]
Economy: Industry (% of Gross Value Added) [d]	31.0	29.9	29.0 [c]
Economy: Services and other activity (% of GVA) [e,f]	70.4	76.3	75.8 [c]
Employment in agriculture (% of employed) [g]	3.5	3.3	3.0
Employment in industry (% of employed) [g]	26.4	25.4	24.4
Employment in services & other sectors (% employed) [g]	70.1	71.3	72.6
Unemployment rate (% of labour force) [g]	12.5	13.1	14.6
Labour force participation rate (female/male pop. %) [g]	15.3 / 67.2	14.0 / 63.9	14.4 / 63.5
CPI: Consumer Price Index (2010=100)	100	116	125 [b]
Agricultural production index (2004-2006=100)	127	150	145 [h]
International trade: exports (million current US$)	7 023	7 833	8 146 [g,b]
International trade: imports (million current US$)	15 262	20 475	19 669 [g,b]
International trade: balance (million current US$)	- 8 239	- 12 642	- 11 523 [g,b]
Balance of payments, current account (million US$)	- 1 882	- 3 406	- 2 850 [c]

Major trading partners

					2019
Export partners (% of exports) [g]	United States	22.8	Saudi Arabia	9.9	Iraq	9.1
Import partners (% of imports) [g]	Saudi Arabia	16.6	China	13.6	United States	8.7

Social indicators

	2010	2015	2020
Population growth rate (average annual %) [i]	4.6	4.9	1.9
Urban population (% of total population)	86.1	90.3	91.2 [b]
Urban population growth rate (average annual %) [i]	6.2	5.8	...
Fertility rate, total (live births per woman) [i]	3.8	3.4	2.8
Life expectancy at birth (females/males, years) [i]	74.6 / 71.5	75.5 / 72.2	76.1 / 72.7
Population age distribution (0-14/60+ years old, %)	37.5 / 5.4	36.0 / 5.5	32.9 / 6.1
International migrant stock (000/% of total pop.) [j,k]	2 723.0 / 37.5	3 112.0 / 33.6	3 346.7 / 33.1 [b]
Refugees and others of concern to the UNHCR (000)	453.2 [l]	684.8	756.1 [m,b]
Infant mortality rate (per 1 000 live births) [i]	19.7	17.1	14.6
Health: Current expenditure (% of GDP)	8.4	7.6	8.1 [a]
Health: Physicians (per 1 000 pop.)	2.2	2.8	2.3 [a]
Education: Government expenditure (% of GDP)	...	...	3.6 [a]
Education: Primary gross enrol. ratio (f/m per 100 pop.)	81.1 / 82.7	79.1 / 79.9 [n]	80.7 / 82.2 [c]
Education: Secondary gross enrol. ratio (f/m per 100 pop.)	81.6 / 78.6	70.3 / 68.0 [n]	64.2 / 62.1 [c]
Education: Tertiary gross enrol. ratio (f/m per 100 pop.)	39.6 / 34.8	38.2 / 35.1	37.4 / 31.5 [c]
Intentional homicide rate (per 100 000 pop.)	1.6	1.6	1.4 [a]
Seats held by women in the National Parliament (%)	6.4	12.0	15.4 [o]

Environment and infrastructure indicators

	2010	2015	2020
Individuals using the Internet (per 100 inhabitants)	27.2 [p]	60.1 [g]	66.8 [g,a]
Research & Development expenditure (% of GDP)	0.4 [q]	...	0.7 [r,s,h]
Threatened species (number)	90	102	121
Forested area (% of land area) [g]	1.1	1.1	1.1 [a]
CO2 emission estimates (million tons/tons per capita)	18.8 / 2.6	23.8 / 2.6	25.6 / 2.6 [a]
Energy production, primary (Petajoules)	9	8	11 [a]
Energy supply per capita (Gigajoules)	42	39	40 [a]
Tourist/visitor arrivals at national borders (000) [t]	4 207	3 761 [r]	4 150 [c]
Important sites for terrestrial biodiversity protected (%)	7.3	10.2	13.5 [b]
Pop. using safely managed sanitation (urban/rural %)	83.3 / ...	83.3 / ...	83.2 / ... [a]
Net Official Development Assist. received (% of GNI)	3.62	5.70	6.00 [c]

a 2017. b 2019. c 2018. d Excludes publishing activities. Includes irrigation and canals. e Excludes repair of personal and household goods. f Excludes computer and related activities and radio/TV activities. g Estimate. h 2016. i Data refers to a 5-year period preceding the reference year. j Refers to foreign citizens. k Including refugees. l Data as at the end of December. m Includes 34,500 Iraqi refugees registered with UNHCR in Jordan. n 2014. o Data are as at 1 January of reporting year. p Population aged 5 years and over. q 2008. r Break in the time series. s Underestimated or based on overestimated data. t Including nationals residing abroad.

Kazakhstan

Region	Central Asia	UN membership date	02 March 1992
Population (000, 2020)	18 777	Surface area (km2)	2 724 902 a
Pop. density (per km2, 2020)	7.0	Sex ratio (m per 100 f)	94.3
Capital city	Nur-Sultan	National currency	Tenge (KZT)
Capital city pop. (000, 2020)	1 117.6 b	Exchange rate (per US$)	382.6 b

Economic indicators

	2010	2015	2020
GDP: Gross domestic product (million current US$)	148 047	184 388	179 340 c
GDP growth rate (annual %, const. 2015 prices)	7.3	1.2	4.1 c
GDP per capita (current US$)	9 109.3	10 493.3	9 789.5 c
Economy: Agriculture (% of Gross Value Added) d	4.7	5.0	4.7 c
Economy: Industry (% of Gross Value Added) d,e	41.9	32.5	35.9 c
Economy: Services and other activity (% of GVA) d,f,g	47.5	50.6	48.2 c
Employment in agriculture (% of employed)	28.3	18.0	15.4 h
Employment in industry (% of employed)	18.7	20.6	20.5 h
Employment in services & other sectors (% employed)	53.0	61.4	64.1 h
Unemployment rate (% of labour force) h	5.8	4.9	4.6
Labour force participation rate (female/male pop. %) h	65.4 / 75.9	65.4 / 77.0	62.2 / 75.1
CPI: Consumer Price Index (2010=100)	100	138	169 a
Agricultural production index (2004-2006=100)	106	131	139 i
International trade: exports (million current US$)	57 244	45 954	57 723 b
International trade: imports (million current US$)	24 024	30 567	38 357 b
International trade: balance (million current US$)	33 220	15 387	19 366 b
Balance of payments, current account (million US$)	1 386	- 6 012	- 6 498 b

Major trading partners

							2019
Export partners (% of exports)	Italy	14.5	China	13.6	Russian Federation	9.7
Import partners (% of imports)	Russian Federation	36.7	China	17.1	Rep. of Korea	8.9

Social indicators

	2010	2015	2020
Population growth rate (average annual %) j	1.1	1.6	1.3
Urban population (% of total population)	56.8	57.2	57.5 b
Urban population growth rate (average annual %) j	1.2	1.7	...
Fertility rate, total (live births per woman) j	2.5	2.7	2.8
Life expectancy at birth (females/males, years) j	71.9 / 60.6	73.9 / 64.3	77.4 / 68.8
Population age distribution (0-14/60+ years old, %)	24.1 / 9.9	26.7 / 10.7	29.1 / 12.2
International migrant stock (000/% of total pop.)	3 334.9 / 20.5	3 546.1 / 20.2	3 705.6 / 20.0 b
Refugees and others of concern to the UNHCR (000)	12.7 k	7.8	8.9 b
Infant mortality rate (per 1 000 live births) j	23.9	14.1	7.7
Health: Current expenditure (% of GDP) l	2.7	3.0	3.1 a
Health: Physicians (per 1 000 pop.)	3.9	4.0 m	...
Education: Government expenditure (% of GDP)	3.1 n	2.8	2.8 a
Education: Primary gross enrol. ratio (f/m per 100 pop.)	109.1 / 108.5	111.7 / 111.5	105.3 / 103.5 b
Education: Secondary gross enrol. ratio (f/m per 100 pop.)	98.8 / 98.2	112.2 / 108.5	113.8 / 112.7 b
Education: Tertiary gross enrol. ratio (f/m per 100 pop.)	51.7 / 40.7	52.1 / 40.8	68.4 / 55.4 b
Intentional homicide rate (per 100 000 pop.)	8.5	4.9	5.1 a
Seats held by women in the National Parliament (%)	17.8	26.2	27.1 o

Environment and infrastructure indicators

	2010	2015	2020
Individuals using the Internet (per 100 inhabitants)	31.6 p	70.8 q	78.9 c
Research & Development expenditure (% of GDP)	0.2	0.2	0.1 c
Threatened species (number)	73	78	81
Forested area (% of land area) h	1.2	1.2	1.2 a
CO2 emission estimates (million tons/tons per capita)	221.1 / 13.5	245.8 / 14.0	255.8 / 14.2 a
Energy production, primary (Petajoules)	6 770	6 629	7 359 a
Energy supply per capita (Gigajoules)	205	169	183 a
Tourist/visitor arrivals at national borders (000)	2 991	4 560 m	...
Important sites for terrestrial biodiversity protected (%)	10.4	10.4	11.1 b
Pop. using safely managed sanitation (urban/rural %)	91.6 / ...	90.9 / ...	90.5 / ... a
Net Official Development Assist. disbursed (% of GNI)	...	0.02	0.02 a
Net Official Development Assist. received (% of GNI)	0.17	0.05	0.05 c

a 2017. b 2019. c 2018. d Data classified according to ISIC Rev. 4. e Excludes publishing activities. Includes irrigation and canals. f Excludes repair of personal and household goods. g Excludes computer and related activities and radio/TV activities. h Estimate. i 2016. j Data refers to a 5-year period preceding the reference year. k Data as at the end of December. l Data revision. m 2014. n 2009. o Data are as at 1 January of reporting year. p Population aged 16 to 74 years. q Population aged 6 to 74 years.

Kenya

Region	Eastern Africa	
Population (000, 2020)	53 771	
Pop. density (per km2, 2020)	94.5	
Capital city	Nairobi	
Capital city pop. (000, 2020)	4 556.4 [b]	
UN membership date	16 December 1963	
Surface area (km2)	591 958 [a]	
Sex ratio (m per 100 f)	98.8	
National currency	Kenyan Shilling (KES)	
Exchange rate (per US$)	101.3 [b]	

Economic indicators	2010	2015	2020
GDP: Gross domestic product (million current US$)	40 000	64 008	87 906 [c]
GDP growth rate (annual %, const. 2015 prices)	8.4	5.7	6.3 [c]
GDP per capita (current US$)	951.7	1 336.9	1 710.5 [c]
Economy: Agriculture (% of Gross Value Added) [d]	27.1	32.2	36.7 [c]
Economy: Industry (% of Gross Value Added) [d,e]	20.3	18.5	17.6 [c]
Economy: Services and other activity (% of GVA) [d,f,g]	50.7	45.1	41.8 [c]
Employment in agriculture (% of employed) [h]	60.3	57.3	53.8
Employment in industry (% of employed) [h]	6.3	6.7	7.4
Employment in services & other sectors (% employed) [h]	33.4	36.0	38.7
Unemployment rate (% of labour force) [h]	2.8	2.8	2.6
Labour force participation rate (female/male pop. %) [h]	66.4 / 75.0	71.0 / 77.9	72.3 / 77.5
CPI: Consumer Price Index (2010=100)	100	150	181 [c]
Agricultural production index (2004-2006=100)	123	127	126 [i]
International trade: exports (million current US$)	5 169	5 908 [h]	6 526 [h,b]
International trade: imports (million current US$)	12 093	16 097 [h]	19 845 [h,b]
International trade: balance (million current US$)	- 6 924	- 10 189 [h]	- 13 319 [h,b]
Balance of payments, current account (million US$)	- 2 369	- 4 289	- 5 018 [a]

Major trading partners						2019
Export partners (% of exports) [h]	Uganda	10.1	Pakistan	9.7	United States	7.7
Import partners (% of imports) [h]	China	21.1	India	10.5	Saudi Arabia	9.8

Social indicators	2010	2015	2020
Population growth rate (average annual %) [j]	2.8	2.6	2.3
Urban population (% of total population)	23.6	25.7	27.5 [b]
Urban population growth rate (average annual %) [j]	4.4	4.4	...
Fertility rate, total (live births per woman) [j]	4.6	4.1	3.5
Life expectancy at birth (females/males, years) [j]	60.3 / 56.7	65.2 / 60.6	68.5 / 63.8
Population age distribution (0-14/60+ years old, %)	43.4 / 3.2	41.4 / 3.6	38.6 / 4.2
International migrant stock (000/% of total pop.) [k]	954.9 / 2.3	1 126.9 / 2.4	1 044.9 / 2.0 [b]
Refugees and others of concern to the UNHCR (000)	751.0 [l]	613.8	492.5 [b]
Infant mortality rate (per 1 000 live births) [j]	51.1	41.6	36.3
Health: Current expenditure (% of GDP)	6.1	5.2 [m]	4.8 [a]
Health: Physicians (per 1 000 pop.)	0.2	0.2 [n]	0.2 [c]
Education: Government expenditure (% of GDP)	5.5	5.3	5.2 [h,a]
Education: Primary gross enrol. ratio (f/m per 100 pop.)	102.7 / 105.1 [o]	103.6 / 103.7	103.4 / 103.0 [i]
Education: Secondary gross enrol. ratio (f/m per 100 pop.)	53.7 / 59.9 [o]	... / ...	... / ...
Education: Tertiary gross enrol. ratio (f/m per 100 pop.)	3.3 / 4.7 [o]	7.7 / 10.8	9.7 / 13.2 [a]
Intentional homicide rate (per 100 000 pop.)	4.6	4.7	4.9 [c]
Seats held by women in the National Parliament (%)	9.8	19.7	21.8 [p]

Environment and infrastructure indicators	2010	2015	2020
Individuals using the Internet (per 100 inhabitants)	7.2	16.6	17.8 [h,a]
Research & Development expenditure (% of GDP)	0.8 [m]	...	...
Threatened species (number)	338	463	549
Forested area (% of land area) [h]	7.4	7.8	7.8 [a]
CO2 emission estimates (million tons/tons per capita)	11.2 / 0.3	14.7 / 0.3	16.3 / 0.3 [a]
Energy production, primary (Petajoules)	650 [h]	761	738 [a]
Energy supply per capita (Gigajoules)	19 [h]	20	19 [a]
Tourist/visitor arrivals at national borders (000) [q]	1 470	1 114	1 364 [a]
Important sites for terrestrial biodiversity protected (%)	34.4	34.5	34.5 [b]
Pop. using safely managed drinking water (urban/rural, %)	55.9 / ...	51.7 / ...	50.0 / ... [a]
Net Official Development Assist. received (% of GNI)	4.09	3.89	2.86 [c]

2017. **b** 2019. **c** 2018. **d** Data classified according to ISIC Rev. 4. **e** Excludes publishing activities. Includes irrigation and canals. **f** Excludes repair of personal and household goods. **g** Excludes computer and related activities and radio/TV activities. **h** Estimate. **i** 2016. **j** Data refers to a 5-year period preceding the reference year. **k** Including refugees. **l** Data as at the end of December. **m** Break in the time series. **n** 2014. **o** 2009. **p** Data are as at 1 January reporting year. **q** Excluding nationals residing abroad.

Kiribati

Region	Micronesia	UN membership date	14 September 1999
Population (000, 2020)	119	Surface area (km2)	726 [a,b]
Pop. density (per km2, 2020)	147.5	Sex ratio (m per 100 f)	96.8
Capital city	Bairiki	National currency	Australian Dollar (AUD)
Capital city pop. (000, 2020)	3.2 [c]	Exchange rate (per US$)	1.4 [d]

Economic indicators

	2010	2015	2020
GDP: Gross domestic product (million current US$)	156	169	189 [e]
GDP growth rate (annual %, const. 2015 prices)	- 0.9	10.3	2.3 [e]
GDP per capita (current US$)	1 516.9	1 524.8	1 627.4 [e]
Economy: Agriculture (% of Gross Value Added) [f]	24.2	22.6	24.0 [e]
Economy: Industry (% of Gross Value Added) [f]	11.9	15.7	15.6 [e]
Economy: Services and other activity (% of GVA) [f]	66.8	69.9	70.5 [e]
Employment in agriculture (% of employed)	22.1	...	...
Employment in industry (% of employed)	16.1	...	...
Employment in services & other sectors (% employed)	61.8	...	...
Unemployment rate (% of labour force)	30.6 [g]	...	...
Labour force participation rate (female/male pop. %)	52.3 / 66.8 [h]	... / ...	... / ...
CPI: Consumer Price Index (2010=100) [i]	100	100	...
Agricultural production index (2004-2006=100)	60	61	61 [j]
International trade: exports (million current US$)	4	10	10 [i,d]
International trade: imports (million current US$)	73	111	554 [i,d]
International trade: balance (million current US$)	- 69	- 101	- 544 [i,d]
Balance of payments, current account (million US$)	~0	56	77 [e]

Major trading partners

						2019
Export partners (% of exports) [i]	Thailand	54.7	Philippines	17.1	Rep. of Korea	9.6
Import partners (% of imports) [i]	Fiji	21.3	China	18.2	Australia	13.6

Social indicators

	2010	2015	2020
Population growth rate (average annual %) [k]	2.2	1.5	1.5
Urban population (% of total population)	47.4	51.6	54.8 [d]
Urban population growth rate (average annual %) [k]	3.8	3.5	...
Fertility rate, total (live births per woman) [k]	3.9	3.8	3.6
Life expectancy at birth (females/males, years) [k]	68.6 / 61.5	70.6 / 62.5	72.0 / 63.9
Population age distribution (0-14/60+ years old, %)	36.1 / 5.5	35.0 / 5.7	35.9 / 6.8
International migrant stock (000/% of total pop.)	2.9 / 2.8	2.9 / 2.6	3.0 / 2.6 [d]
Infant mortality rate (per 1 000 live births) [k]	51.4	47.9	43.0
Health: Current expenditure (% of GDP) [l,m]	9.2	8.0	10.8 [b]
Health: Physicians (per 1 000 pop.)	0.4	0.2 [n]	...
Education: Primary gross enrol. ratio (f/m per 100 pop.)	113.2 / 107.2 [o]	106.6 / 104.5	104.9 / 97.9 [b]
Education: Secondary gross enrol. ratio (f/m per 100 pop.)	91.4 / 82.7 [p]	... / ...	... / ...
Intentional homicide rate (per 100 000 pop.)	3.9	7.5 [q]	...
Seats held by women in the National Parliament (%)	4.3	8.7	6.5 [r]

Environment and infrastructure indicators

	2010	2015	2020
Individuals using the Internet (per 100 inhabitants)	9.1	13.0 [i]	14.6 [i,b]
Threatened species (number)	90	100	108
Forested area (% of land area) [i]	15.0	15.0	15.0 [b]
Energy production, primary (Petajoules) [i]	1	1	1 [b]
Energy supply per capita (Gigajoules)	13	12 [i]	12 [i,b]
Tourist/visitor arrivals at national borders (000) [s]	5	4	7 [e]
Important sites for terrestrial biodiversity protected (%)	40.0	40.0	40.0 [d]
Net Official Development Assist. received (% of GNI)	10.38	18.51	20.67 [e]

a Land area only. Excluding 84 square km of uninhabited islands. b 2017. c 2015. d 2019. e 2018. f At factor cost. g De facto population. h Persons present (de facto). i Estimate. j 2016. k Data refers to a 5-year period preceding the reference year. l General government expenditure (GGE) can be larger than the Gross domestic product (GDP) because government accounts for a very large part of domestic consumption and because a large part of domestic consumption in the country is accounted for by imports. m Data refer to fiscal years beginning 1 July. n 2013. o 2009. p 2008. q 2012. r Data are as at 1 January of reporting year. s Air arrivals. Tarawa and Christmas Island.

Kuwait

Region	Western Asia	UN membership date	14 May 1963
Population (000, 2020)	4 271	Surface area (km2)	17 818[a]
Pop. density (per km2, 2020)	239.7	Sex ratio (m per 100 f)	157.9
Capital city	Kuwait City	National currency	Kuwaiti Dinar (KWD)
Capital city pop. (000, 2020)	3 052.5[b,c]	Exchange rate (per US$)	0.3[c]

Economic indicators	2010	2015	2020
GDP: Gross domestic product (million current US$)	115 416	114 585	141 698[d]
GDP growth rate (annual %, const. 2015 prices)	- 2.4	0.6	1.2[d]
GDP per capita (current US$)	38 576.4	29 874.0	34 248.8[d]
Economy: Agriculture (% of Gross Value Added)	0.4	0.5	0.4[d]
Economy: Industry (% of Gross Value Added)	58.2	48.7	54.7[d]
Economy: Services and other activity (% of GVA)	59.0	71.1	65.0[d]
Employment in agriculture (% of employed)[e]	2.5	2.2	2.0
Employment in industry (% of employed)[e]	24.5	24.8	24.4
Employment in services & other sectors (% of employed)[e]	73.0	73.0	73.7
Unemployment rate (% of labour force)[e]	1.8	2.2	2.3
Labour force participation rate (female/male pop. %)[e]	46.6 / 84.7	50.0 / 87.2	49.3 / 87.3
CPI: Consumer Price Index (2010=100)[e]	100	118	125[d]
Agricultural production index (2004-2006=100)	131	189	191[f]
International trade: exports (million current US$)	62 698	54 121	81 282[e,c]
International trade: imports (million current US$)	22 691	30 957	40 063[e,c]
International trade: balance (million current US$)	40 007	23 164	41 219[e,c]
Balance of payments, current account (million US$)	36 989	8 584	24 049[d]

Major trading partners						2019
Export partners (% of exports)[e]	Areas nes[g]	90.9	India	1.6	China	1.3
Import partners (% of imports)[e]	China	16.7	United States	8.7	United Arab Emirates	8.6

Social indicators	2010	2015	2020
Population growth rate (average annual %)[h]	5.5	5.0	2.1
Urban population (% of total population)	100.0	100.0	100.0[c]
Urban population growth rate (average annual %)[h]	5.5	5.4	...
Fertility rate, total (live births per woman)[h]	2.4	2.1	2.1
Life expectancy at birth (females/males, years)[h]	74.9 / 73.1	75.9 / 74.1	76.4 / 74.6
Population age distribution (0-14/60+ years old, %)	23.2 / 3.4	21.2 / 4.2	21.5 / 6.5
International migrant stock (000/% of total pop.)[i,j]	1 871.5 / 62.6	2 866.1 / 74.7	3 034.8 / 72.1[c]
Refugees and others of concern to the UNHCR (000)	96.5[k]	94.6	93.7[c]
Infant mortality rate (per 1 000 live births)[h]	9.7	8.2	7.1
Health: Current expenditure (% of GDP)	2.8	4.0	5.3[a]
Health: Physicians (per 1 000 pop.)	2.4	2.6	...
Education: Government expenditure (% of GDP)	3.8[e,l]	...	...
Education: Primary gross enrol. ratio (f/m per 100 pop.)	101.2 / 103.2	104.3 / 101.0	97.2 / 88.1[d]
Education: Secondary gross enrol. ratio (f/m per 100 pop.)	98.8 / 97.0	101.0 / 94.9	... / ...
Education: Tertiary gross enrol. ratio (f/m per 100 pop.)	... / ...	76.5 / 36.9	76.1 / 35.8[d]
Intentional homicide rate (per 100 000 pop.)	2.0	1.8[m]	...
Seats held by women in the National Parliament (%)	7.7	1.5	6.4[n]

Environment and infrastructure indicators	2010	2015	2020
Individuals using the Internet (per 100 inhabitants)	61.4[e]	72.0[e]	99.6[d]
Research & Development expenditure (% of GDP)[o]	0.1[p]	0.1[q,r,s]	0.1[q,r,d]
Threatened species (number)	41	42	57
Forested area (% of land area)[e]	0.4	0.4	0.4[a]
CO2 emission estimates (million tons/tons per capita)	77.0 / 25.7	91.6 / 23.3	89.4 / 21.6[a]
Energy production, primary (Petajoules)[t]	5 557	7 004	6 919[a]
Energy supply per capita (Gigajoules)[t]	450	369	383[a]
Tourist/visitor arrivals at national borders (000)	5 208	6 941	8 508[d]
Important sites for terrestrial biodiversity protected (%)	31.0	42.1	51.6[c]
Net Official Development Assist. disbursed (% of GNI)	...	...	0.41[a]

2017. **b** Data refers to the Governorates of Capital, Hawalli, Al-Farwaniya and Mubarak Al-Kabeer. **c** 2019. **d** 2018. Estimate. **f** 2016. **g** Areas not elsewhere specified. **h** Data refers to a 5-year period preceding the reference year. **i** Including refugees. **j** Refers to foreign citizens. **k** Data as at the end of December. **l** 2006. **m** 2012. **n** Data are as at 1 January of reporting year. **o** Partial data. **p** Government only. **q** Excluding business enterprise. **r** Excluding private non-profit. **s** Break in the time series. **t** The data for crude oil production include 50 per cent of the output of the neutral Zone.

Kyrgyzstan

Region	Central Asia	UN membership date	02 March 1992
Population (000, 2020)	6 524	Surface area (km2)	199 949 a
Pop. density (per km2, 2020)	34.0	Sex ratio (m per 100 f)	97.9
Capital city	Bishkek	National currency	Som (KGS)
Capital city pop. (000, 2020)	1 017.2 b	Exchange rate (per US$)	69.6 b

Economic indicators

	2010	2015	2020
GDP: Gross domestic product (million current US$)	4 794	6 678	8 093 c
GDP growth rate (annual %, const. 2015 prices)	- 0.5	3.9	3.5 c
GDP per capita (current US$)	884.2	1 120.7	1 283.8 c
Economy: Agriculture (% of Gross Value Added) d	18.8	15.4	13.1 c
Economy: Industry (% of Gross Value Added) d,e	28.2	27.5	30.9 c
Economy: Services and other activity (% of GVA) d,f,g	45.6	46.0	45.8 c
Employment in agriculture (% of employed)	32.3 h	29.3	20.4 h
Employment in industry (% of employed)	21.0 h	20.9	24.7 h
Employment in services & other sectors (% employed)	46.7 h	49.8	54.9 h
Unemployment rate (% of labour force) h	8.6	7.6	6.6
Labour force participation rate (female/male pop. %) h	52.2 / 76.6	49.9 / 75.5	44.5 / 75.6
CPI: Consumer Price Index (2010=100)	100	146	156 b
Agricultural production index (2004-2006=100)	105	114	117 i
International trade: exports (million current US$)	1 488	1 441	2 517 h,b
International trade: imports (million current US$)	3 223	4 068	5 906 h,b
International trade: balance (million current US$)	- 1 734	- 2 627	- 3 390 h,b
Balance of payments, current account (million US$)	- 475	- 1 052	- 962 c

Major trading partners

						2019
Export partners (% of exports) h	United Kingdom	36.5	Russian Federation	19.4	Kazakhstan	14.7
Import partners (% of imports) h	China	36.7	Russian Federation	28.5	Kazakhstan	11.4

Social indicators

	2010	2015	2020
Population growth rate (average annual %) j	1.3	1.9	1.8
Urban population (% of total population)	35.3	35.8	36.6 b
Urban population growth rate (average annual %) j	1.3	1.8	...
Fertility rate, total (live births per woman) j	2.8	3.3	3.0
Life expectancy at birth (females/males, years) j	71.7 / 63.5	74.3 / 66.4	75.4 / 67.2
Population age distribution (0-14/60+ years old, %)	29.9 / 6.4	31.5 / 7.0	32.6 / 8.1
International migrant stock (000/% of total pop.)	232.1 / 4.3	204.4 / 3.4	200.3 / 3.1 b
Refugees and others of concern to the UNHCR (000)	304.2 k	14.3	0.6 b
Infant mortality rate (per 1 000 live births) j	30.2	19.5	15.5
Health: Current expenditure (% of GDP)	7.0	7.1	6.2 a
Health: Physicians (per 1 000 pop.)	2.3	2.2 i	...
Education: Government expenditure (% of GDP)	5.8	6.0	6.1 a
Education: Primary gross enrol. ratio (f/m per 100 pop.)	99.1 / 99.8	105.0 / 105.8	107.2 / 107.9 c
Education: Secondary gross enrol. ratio (f/m per 100 pop.)	87.4 / 87.7	91.7 / 90.5	95.0 / 95.1 c
Education: Tertiary gross enrol. ratio (f/m per 100 pop.)	47.8 / 36.6	53.0 / 40.6	46.7 / 36.0 c
Intentional homicide rate (per 100 000 pop.)	16.8	5.1	2.2 c
Seats held by women in the National Parliament (%)	25.6	23.3	19.2 m

Environment and infrastructure indicators

	2010	2015	2020
Individuals using the Internet (per 100 inhabitants)	16.3 h	30.2 h	38.0 n,a
Research & Development expenditure (% of GDP)	0.2	0.1 o	0.1 o,a
Threatened species (number)	40	41	43
Forested area (% of land area) h	3.5	3.3	3.3 a
CO2 emission estimates (million tons/tons per capita)	6.0 / 1.1	9.9 / 1.7	8.9 / 1.4 a
Energy production, primary (Petajoules)	53	75	88 a
Energy supply per capita (Gigajoules)	21	29	27 a
Tourist/visitor arrivals at national borders (000)	1 224	4 000	6 947 c
Important sites for terrestrial biodiversity protected (%)	25.7	25.7	25.7 b
Pop. using safely managed drinking water (urban/rural, %)	87.5 / 40.7	92.7 / 51.6	93.5 / 53.9 a
Net Official Development Assist. received (% of GNI)	8.29	12.07	5.27 c

a 2017. b 2019. c 2018. d Data classified according to ISIC Rev. 4. e Excludes publishing activities. Includes irrigation and canals. f Excludes computer and related activities and radio/TV activities. g Excludes repair of personal and household goods. h Estimate. i 2016. j Data refers to a 5-year period preceding the reference year. k Data as at the end of December. l 2014. m Data are as at 1 January of reporting year. n Population aged 18 years and over. o Excluding private non-profit.

Lao People's Democratic Republic

Region	South-eastern Asia	UN membership date	14 December 1955
Population (000, 2020)	7 276	Surface area (km2)	236 800 [a]
Pop. density (per km2, 2020)	31.5	Sex ratio (m per 100 f)	100.8
Capital city	Vientiane	National currency	Lao Kip (LAK)
Capital city pop. (000, 2020)	673.1 [b]	Exchange rate (per US$)	8 861.0 [b]

Economic indicators

	2010	2015	2020
GDP: Gross domestic product (million current US$)	7 313	14 390	17 954 [c]
GDP growth rate (annual %, const. 2015 prices)	8.1	7.3	6.2 [c]
GDP per capita (current US$)	1 170.3	2 134.7	2 542.5 [c]
Economy: Agriculture (% of Gross Value Added) [d]	23.6	19.7	17.7 [c]
Economy: Industry (% of Gross Value Added) [d,e]	30.9	31.0	35.5 [c]
Economy: Services and other activity (% of GVA) [d,f,g]	57.4	59.2	57.3 [c]
Employment in agriculture (% of employed)	71.5	65.9 [h]	61.7 [h]
Employment in industry (% of employed)	8.3	10.6 [h]	12.2 [h]
Employment in services & other sectors (% employed)	20.2	23.5 [h]	26.2 [h]
Unemployment rate (% of labour force) [h]	0.7	0.7	0.6
Labour force participation rate (female/male pop. %) [h]	76.8 / 79.4	76.8 / 80.2	76.8 / 80.2
CPI: Consumer Price Index (2010=100) [h]	100 [i]	126	131 [c]
Agricultural production index (2004-2006=100)	132	212	219 [j]
International trade: exports (million current US$)	1 909	2 985	5 809 [b]
International trade: imports (million current US$)	1 837	3 778	5 797 [b]
International trade: balance (million current US$)	72	- 793	12 [b]
Balance of payments, current account (million US$)	29	- 2 268	- 1 430 [c]

Major trading partners

						2019
Export partners (% of exports)	Thailand	41.4	China	28.8	Viet Nam	18.2
Import partners (% of imports)	Thailand	50.3	China	29.0	Viet Nam	7.8

Social indicators

	2010	2015	2020
Population growth rate (average annual %) [k]	1.7	1.5	1.5
Urban population (% of total population)	30.1	33.1	35.6 [b]
Urban population growth rate (average annual %) [k]	3.7	3.2	...
Fertility rate, total (live births per woman) [k]	3.4	2.9	2.7
Life expectancy at birth (females/males, years) [k]	64.8 / 61.2	67.3 / 63.7	69.2 / 65.7
Population age distribution (0-14/60+ years old, %)	36.4 / 5.6	33.6 / 6.1	31.9 / 6.8
International migrant stock (000/% of total pop.) [l,m]	33.0 / 0.5	45.5 / 0.7	48.3 / 0.7 [b]
Refugees and others of concern to the UNHCR (000)	...	...	~0.0 [b]
Infant mortality rate (per 1 000 live births) [k]	57.5	47.0	38.8
Health: Current expenditure (% of GDP) [n]	2.9	2.5 [i,o]	2.5 [o,a]
Health: Physicians (per 1 000 pop.)	0.8	0.5 [p]	0.4 [a]
Education: Government expenditure (% of GDP)	1.7	2.9 [p]	...
Education: Primary gross enrol. ratio (f/m per 100 pop.)	117.9 / 128.9	111.3 / 116.6	100.4 / 104.3 [c]
Education: Secondary gross enrol. ratio (f/m per 100 pop.)	42.3 / 51.5	60.7 / 66.1	65.0 / 69.6 [h,c]
Education: Tertiary gross enrol. ratio (f/m per 100 pop.)	14.4 / 18.9	17.7 / 18.7	15.5 / 14.4 [c]
Seats held by women in the National Parliament (%)	25.2	25.0	27.5 [q]

Environment and infrastructure indicators

	2010	2015	2020
Individuals using the Internet (per 100 inhabitants)	7.0	18.2 [h]	25.5 [h,a]
Threatened species (number)	132	210	250
Forested area (% of land area) [h]	77.2	81.3	81.3 [a]
Energy production, primary (Petajoules)	98	162	276 [a]
Energy supply per capita (Gigajoules)	16	25	35 [a]
Tourist/visitor arrivals at national borders (000)	1 670	3 543	3 770 [c]
Important sites for terrestrial biodiversity protected (%)	44.0	44.0	44.0 [b]
Pop. using safely managed drinking water (urban/rural, %)	24.3 / 8.6	25.7 / 10.1	26.3 / 10.8 [a]
Pop. using safely managed sanitation (urban/rural %)	55.5 / 39.5	60.4 / 51.2	62.4 / 55.8 [a]
Net Official Development Assist. received (% of GNI)	5.83	3.43	3.29 [c]

[a] 2017. [b] 2019. [c] 2018. [d] Data classified according to ISIC Rev. 4. [e] Excludes publishing activities. Includes irrigation and canals. [f] Excludes computer and related activities and radio/TV activities. [g] Excludes repair of personal and household goods. [h] Estimate. [i] Break in the time series. [j] 2016. [k] Data refers to a 5-year period preceding the reference year. [l] Refers to foreign citizens. [m] Including refugees. [n] Data refer to fiscal years ending 30 September. [o] Data are based on SHA2011. [p] 2014. [q] Data are as at 1 January of reporting year.

Latvia

Region	Northern Europe	UN membership date	17 September 1991
Population (000, 2020)	1 886	Surface area (km2)	64 573[a]
Pop. density (per km2, 2020)	30.3	Sex ratio (m per 100 f)	85.5
Capital city	Riga	National currency	Euro (EUR)
Capital city pop. (000, 2020)	633.8[b]	Exchange rate (per US$)	0.9[b]

Economic indicators

	2010	2015	2020
GDP: Gross domestic product (million current US$)	23 804	27 090	34 426[c]
GDP growth rate (annual %, const. 2015 prices)	- 4.5	3.3	4.6[c]
GDP per capita (current US$)	11 234.3	13 560.8	17 851.6[c]
Economy: Agriculture (% of Gross Value Added)[d]	4.5	4.0	4.1[c]
Economy: Industry (% of Gross Value Added)[d,e]	23.1	22.1	22.5[c]
Economy: Services and other activity (% of GVA)[d,f,g]	66.8	68.4	66.9[c]
Employment in agriculture (% of employed)	8.6	7.9	6.5[h]
Employment in industry (% of employed)	23.1	23.6	23.7[h]
Employment in services & other sectors (% employed)	68.3	68.4	69.8[h]
Unemployment rate (% of labour force)[h]	19.5	9.9	6.5
Labour force participation rate (female/male pop. %)[h]	53.8 / 65.3	54.0 / 67.5	55.3 / 67.9
CPI: Consumer Price Index (2010=100)	100	108	117[b]
Agricultural production index (2004-2006=100)	108	152	139[i]
International trade: exports (million current US$)	8 851	11 650	14 447[b]
International trade: imports (million current US$)	11 143	14 096	17 768[b]
International trade: balance (million current US$)	- 2 292	- 2 446	- 3 320[b]
Balance of payments, current account (million US$)	435	- 241	- 176[b]

Major trading partners   2019

Export partners (% of exports)	Lithuania	17.1	Estonia	11.7	Russian Federation	9.2
Import partners (% of imports)	Lithuania	17.6	Germany	10.9	Poland	9.4

Social indicators

	2010	2015	2020
Population growth rate (average annual %)[j]	- 1.2	- 1.2	- 1.1
Urban population (% of total population)	67.8	68.0	68.2[b]
Urban population growth rate (average annual %)[j]	- 1.3	- 1.2	...
Fertility rate, total (live births per woman)[j]	1.5	1.5	1.7
Life expectancy at birth (females/males, years)[j]	77.0 / 66.0	78.8 / 69.0	79.8 / 69.9
Population age distribution (0-14/60+ years old, %)	14.1 / 23.6	15.1 / 25.6	16.4 / 27.6
International migrant stock (000/% of total pop.)	313.8 / 14.8	265.4 / 13.3	237.3 / 12.4[b]
Refugees and others of concern to the UNHCR (000)	327.0[k]	263.2	225.5[l,b]
Infant mortality rate (per 1 000 live births)[j]	7.8	5.2	3.3
Health: Current expenditure (% of GDP)[h]	6.1	5.7	6.0[a]
Health: Physicians (per 1 000 pop.)	3.1	3.2	3.2[a]
Education: Government expenditure (% of GDP)	5.1	5.3	4.7[i]
Education: Primary gross enrol. ratio (f/m per 100 pop.)[h]	101.9 / 103.9	99.4 / 99.4	99.5 / 99.3[a]
Education: Secondary gross enrol. ratio (f/m per 100 pop.)[h]	102.1 / 103.5	111.2 / 113.5	110.2 / 111.3[a]
Education: Tertiary gross enrol. ratio (f/m per 100 pop.)[h]	88.4 / 50.4	91.1 / 58.4	105.1 / 72.0[a]
Intentional homicide rate (per 100 000 pop.)	3.3	3.4	4.4[c]
Seats held by women in the National Parliament (%)	22.0	18.0	30.0[m]

Environment and infrastructure indicators

	2010	2015	2020
Individuals using the Internet (per 100 inhabitants)	68.4[n]	79.2[n]	83.6[c]
Research & Development expenditure (% of GDP)	0.6	0.6	0.6[c]
Threatened species (number)	18	25	40
Forested area (% of land area)	53.9	54.0	54.0[h,a]
CO2 emission estimates (million tons/tons per capita)	8.1 / 3.9	6.8 / 3.5	6.7 / 3.4[a]
Energy production, primary (Petajoules)	83	98	108[a]
Energy supply per capita (Gigajoules)	89	90	95[a]
Tourist/visitor arrivals at national borders (000)[o]	1 373	2 024	1 946[c]
Important sites for terrestrial biodiversity protected (%)	97.2	97.2	97.2[b]
Pop. using safely managed sanitation (urban/rural %)	86.9 / 70.9	89.4 / 75.2	90.2 / 76.5[a]
Net Official Development Assist. disbursed (% of GNI)	0.06	0.09	0.11[a]

a 2017. **b** 2019. **c** 2018. **d** Data classified according to ISIC Rev. 4. **e** Excludes publishing activities. Includes irrigation and canals. **f** Excludes repair of personal and household goods. **g** Excludes computer and related activities and radio/TV activities. **h** Estimate. **i** 2016. **j** Data refers to a 5-year period preceding the reference year. **k** Data as at the end of December. **l** Figure includes persons under UNHCR's statelessness mandate and covered by two separate Latvian laws. **m** Data are as at 1 January of reporting year. **n** Population aged 16 to 74 years. **o** Non-resident departures. Survey of persons crossing the state border.

Lebanon

Region	Western Asia	
Population (000, 2020)	6 825	
Pop. density (per km2, 2020)	667.2	
Capital city	Beirut	
Capital city pop. (000, 2020)	2 406.9 [b,c,d]	

UN membership date	24 October 1945	
Surface area (km2)	10 452 [a]	
Sex ratio (m per 100 f)	101.4	
National currency	Lebanese Pound (LBP)	
Exchange rate (per US$)	1 507.5 [d]	

Economic indicators

	2010	2015	2020
GDP: Gross domestic product (million current US$)	38 420	49 974	56 409 [e]
GDP growth rate (annual %, const. 2015 prices)	8.0	0.4	0.2 [e]
GDP per capita (current US$)	7 756.7	7 649.8	8 223.7 [e]
Economy: Agriculture (% of Gross Value Added) [f]	4.3	3.7	3.3 [e]
Economy: Industry (% of Gross Value Added) [f,g]	15.7	16.6	16.3 [e]
Economy: Services and other activity (% of GVA) [f,h,i]	72.7	73.5	73.8 [e]
Employment in agriculture (% of employed) [j]	14.7	14.4	13.4
Employment in industry (% of employed) [j]	25.2	23.5	22.3
Employment in services & other sectors (% employed) [j]	60.1	62.1	64.3
Unemployment rate (% of labour force) [j]	6.4	6.4	6.3
Labour force participation rate (female/male pop. %) [j]	22.8 / 69.8	22.6 / 71.4	22.9 / 71.3
CPI: Consumer Price Index (2010=100) [j]	100	115	126 [e]
Agricultural production index (2004-2006=100)	93	91	89 [k]
International trade: exports (million current US$)	4 254	2 953	3 154 [j,d]
International trade: imports (million current US$)	17 970	18 600	18 472 [j,d]
International trade: balance (million current US$)	- 13 716	- 15 646	- 15 317 [j,d]
Balance of payments, current account (million US$)	- 7 552	- 8 542	- 12 445 [e]

Major trading partners

						2019
Export partners (% of exports) [j]	United Arab Emirates	15.5	Saudi Arabia	7.2	Syria	7.0
Import partners (% of imports) [j]	China	10.3	Greece	8.5	Italy	8.0

Social indicators

	2010	2015	2020
Population growth rate (average annual %) [l]	1.1	5.5	0.9
Urban population (% of total population)	87.3	88.1	88.8 [d]
Urban population growth rate (average annual %) [l]	1.8	6.2	...
Fertility rate, total (live births per woman) [l]	1.9	2.1	2.1
Life expectancy at birth (females/males, years) [l]	79.7 / 76.0	80.6 / 76.9	80.8 / 77.0
Population age distribution (0-14/60+ years old, %)	25.8 / 9.2	27.3 / 9.6	25.1 / 11.2
International migrant stock (000/% of total pop.) [m]	820.7 / 16.6	1 973.2 / 30.2	1 863.9 / 27.2 [d]
Refugees and others of concern to the UNHCR (000)	9.5 [n]	1 189.1	949.6 [d]
Infant mortality rate (per 1 000 live births) [l]	10.6	9.6	9.4
Health: Current expenditure (% of GDP)	7.4	7.7	8.2 [a]
Health: Physicians (per 1 000 pop.)	2.3	2.1	2.1 [e]
Education: Government expenditure (% of GDP)	1.6	2.5 [o]	...
Intentional homicide rate (per 100 000 pop.)	3.3	3.5	2.5 [e]
Seats held by women in the National Parliament (%)	3.1	3.1	4.7 [p]

Environment and infrastructure indicators

	2010	2015	2020
Individuals using the Internet (per 100 inhabitants) [j]	43.7 [q]	74.0	78.2 [a]
Threatened species (number)	50	69	109
Forested area (% of land area) [j]	13.4	13.4	13.4 [a]
CO2 emission estimates (million tons/tons per capita)	18.3 / 4.2	24.6 / 4.2	26.9 / 4.4 [a]
Energy production, primary (Petajoules)	9	8	8 [i,a]
Energy supply per capita (Gigajoules)	53	52	54 [a]
Tourist/visitor arrivals at national borders (000) [r]	2 168	1 518	1 964 [e]
Important sites for terrestrial biodiversity protected (%)	11.4	12.3	12.3 [d]
Net Official Development Assist. received (% of GNI)	1.17	1.95	2.60 [e]

a 2017. b Estimates should be viewed with caution as these are derived from scarce data. c Excluding Syrian refugees. d 2019. e 2018. f Data classified according to ISIC Rev. 4. g Excludes publishing activities. Includes irrigation and canals. h Excludes computer and related activities and radio/TV activities. i Excludes repair of personal and household goods. j Estimate. k 2016. l Data refers to a 5-year period preceding the reference year. m Including refugees. n Data as at the end of December. o 2013. p Data are as at 1 January of reporting year. q Population aged 5 years and over. r Excluding the Lebanon, Syria and Palestine nationalities.

Lesotho

Region	Southern Africa	UN membership date	17 October 1966
Population (000, 2020)	2 142	Surface area (km2)	30 355 [a]
Pop. density (per km2, 2020)	70.6	Sex ratio (m per 100 f)	97.4
Capital city	Maseru	National currency	Loti (LSL)
Capital city pop. (000, 2020)	201.9 [b]	Exchange rate (per US$)	14.1 [c]

Economic indicators

	2010	2015	2020
GDP: Gross domestic product (million current US$)	2 386	2 465	2 631 [b]
GDP growth rate (annual %, const. 2015 prices)	6.1	1.6	1.2 [b]
GDP per capita (current US$)	1 195.6	1 197.0	1 248.0 [b]
Economy: Agriculture (% of Gross Value Added) [d]	5.6	5.6	6.0 [b]
Economy: Industry (% of Gross Value Added) [d]	32.9	34.8	34.0 [b]
Economy: Services and other activity (% of GVA) [d,e,f]	52.2	52.9	53.2 [b]
Employment in agriculture (% of employed) [g]	11.3	9.4	8.4
Employment in industry (% of employed) [g]	42.4	42.9	41.9
Employment in services & other sectors (% employed) [g]	46.3	47.7	49.6
Unemployment rate (% of labour force) [g]	26.8	24.4	22.8
Labour force participation rate (female/male pop. %) [g]	60.6 / 76.5	59.8 / 76.0	60.1 / 76.1
CPI: Consumer Price Index (2010=100)	100	127	156 [c]
Agricultural production index (2004-2006=100)	107	98	96 [h]
International trade: exports (million current US$)	503	604	345 [g,c]
International trade: imports (million current US$)	1 277	1 410	1 171 [g,c]
International trade: balance (million current US$)	- 773	- 806	- 826 [g,c]
Balance of payments, current account (million US$)	- 158	- 78	- 80 [c]

Major trading partners

						2019
Export partners (% of exports) [g]	South Africa	49.2	United States	45.5	Eswatini	1.7
Import partners (% of imports) [g]	South Africa	70.7	China	14.8	Other Asia, nes	5.3

Social indicators

	2010	2015	2020
Population growth rate (average annual %) [i]	~0.0	0.6	0.8
Urban population (% of total population)	24.8	26.9	28.6 [c]
Urban population growth rate (average annual %) [i]	3.1	2.9	...
Fertility rate, total (live births per woman) [i]	3.4	3.3	3.2
Life expectancy at birth (females/males, years) [i]	45.8 / 40.6	51.3 / 45.2	56.8 / 50.4
Population age distribution (0-14/60+ years old, %)	34.9 / 7.0	33.4 / 7.2	32.2 / 7.5
International migrant stock (000/% of total pop.) [j,k]	6.4 / 0.3	6.6 / 0.3	6.9 / 0.3 [c]
Refugees and others of concern to the UNHCR (000)	...	~0.0	0.1 [c]
Infant mortality rate (per 1 000 live births) [i]	74.9	65.4	62.3
Health: Current expenditure (% of GDP) [g]	7.6	8.4	8.8 [a]
Health: Physicians (per 1 000 pop.)	0.1	...	...
Education: Government expenditure (% of GDP)	12.1 [l]	...	6.5 [b]
Education: Primary gross enrol. ratio (f/m per 100 pop.)	122.1 / 127.4	113.7 / 119.6	117.8 / 124.1 [a]
Education: Secondary gross enrol. ratio (f/m per 100 pop.)	65.4 / 47.1	69.7 / 51.8	71.3 / 52.8 [a]
Education: Tertiary gross enrol. ratio (f/m per 100 pop.)	3.9 / 3.3 [m]	12.2 / 8.2	12.4 / 8.0 [b]
Intentional homicide rate (per 100 000 pop.)	38.3	43.6	...
Seats held by women in the National Parliament (%)	24.2	26.7	23.3 [n]

Environment and infrastructure indicators

	2010	2015	2020
Individuals using the Internet (per 100 inhabitants)	3.9 [g]	25.0 [g]	29.0 [o,p,a]
Research & Development expenditure (% of GDP)	~0.0 [q,r]	~0.0 [s,t]	...
Threatened species (number)	16	17	19
Forested area (% of land area) [g]	1.4	1.6	1.6 [a]
Energy production, primary (Petajoules)	27	20 [g]	18 [a]
Energy supply per capita (Gigajoules)	25	22 [g]	21 [g,a]
Tourist/visitor arrivals at national borders (000)	426	1 082 [u]	1 173 [u,b]
Important sites for terrestrial biodiversity protected (%)	16.4	16.4	16.4 [c]
Net Official Development Assist. received (% of GNI)	8.54	3.10	4.91 [b]

a 2017. b 2018. c 2019. d Data classified according to ISIC Rev. 4. e Excludes computer and related activities and radio/TV activities. f Excludes repair of personal and household goods. g Estimate. h 2016. i Data refers to a 5-year period preceding the reference year. j Including refugees. k Refers to foreign citizens. l 2008. m 2006. n Data are as at 1 January of reporting year. o At least once a month. p Population aged 18 years and over. q Partial data. r 2009. s Excluding business enterprise. t Excluding private non-profit. u Break in the time series.

Liberia

Region	Western Africa	UN membership date	02 November 1945
Population (000, 2020)	5 058	Surface area (km2)	111 369[a]
Pop. density (per km2, 2020)	52.5	Sex ratio (m per 100 f)	101.1
Capital city	Monrovia	National currency	Liberian Dollar (LRD)
Capital city pop. (000, 2020)	1 467.0[b]	Exchange rate (per US$)	187.9[b]

Economic indicators

	2010	2015	2020
GDP: Gross domestic product (million current US$)	1 292	2 075	2 122[c]
GDP growth rate (annual %, const. 2015 prices)	7.3	5.2[d]	1.2[c]
GDP per capita (current US$)	332.0	463.9	440.3[c]
Economy: Agriculture (% of Gross Value Added)	70.2	70.0	72.5[c]
Economy: Industry (% of Gross Value Added)	11.9	9.9	9.4[c]
Economy: Services and other activity (% of GVA)	15.9	16.5	15.6[c]
Employment in agriculture (% of employed)	47.3	44.2[e]	43.0[e]
Employment in industry (% of employed)	10.8	11.0[e]	10.1[e]
Employment in services & other sectors (% employed)	41.9	44.9[e]	46.9[e]
Unemployment rate (% of labour force)[e]	2.3	2.1	2.7
Labour force participation rate (female/male pop. %)[e]	70.1 / 81.1	70.2 / 80.1	72.1 / 80.6
CPI: Consumer Price Index (2010=100)	100	148	223[c]
Agricultural production index (2004-2006=100)	104	112	113[f]
International trade: exports (million current US$)[e]	222	626	841[b]
International trade: imports (million current US$)[e]	710	901	345[b]
International trade: balance (million current US$)[e]	- 488	- 275	496[b]
Balance of payments, current account (million US$)	- 853	171	- 674[c]

Major trading partners

						2019
Export partners (% of exports)[e]	Areas nes[g]	20.0	Switzerland	13.5	France	8.6
Import partners (% of imports)[e]	Areas nes[g]	59.9	China	16.5	India	4.5

Social indicators

	2010	2015	2020
Population growth rate (average annual %)[h]	3.8	2.8	2.5
Urban population (% of total population)	47.8	49.8	51.6[b]
Urban population growth rate (average annual %)[h]	4.6	3.4	...
Fertility rate, total (live births per woman)[h]	5.2	4.8	4.4
Life expectancy at birth (females/males, years)[h]	59.8 / 56.4	62.2 / 59.2	65.0 / 62.2
Population age distribution (0-14/60+ years old, %)	43.0 / 5.0	42.1 / 5.0	40.4 / 5.2
International migrant stock (000/% of total pop.)	99.1 / 2.5	113.8 / 2.5	94.4 / 1.9[b]
Refugees and others of concern to the UNHCR (000)	26.6[i]	40.4	8.8[b]
Infant mortality rate (per 1 000 live births)[h]	72.9	60.1	54.1
Health: Current expenditure (% of GDP)[j]	8.8	10.3	8.2[a]
Health: Physicians (per 1 000 pop.)	~0.0	~0.0	...
Education: Government expenditure (% of GDP)	1.7[k]	2.3[e,d]	...
Education: Primary gross enrol. ratio (f/m per 100 pop.)	96.5 / 108.0[l]	90.2 / 100.3	84.7 / 85.5[a]
Education: Secondary gross enrol. ratio (f/m per 100 pop.)	... / ...	32.9 / 42.8	... / ...
Education: Tertiary gross enrol. ratio (f/m per 100 pop.)	6.6 / 12.4	9.2 / 14.7[m]	... / ...
Intentional homicide rate (per 100 000 pop.)	3.3	3.3[m]	...
Seats held by women in the National Parliament (%)	12.5	11.0	12.3[n]

Environment and infrastructure indicators

	2010	2015	2020
Individuals using the Internet (per 100 inhabitants)	2.3	33.0[o,p]	8.0[e,a]
Threatened species (number)	147	158	218
Forested area (% of land area)	44.9	43.4	43.4[e,a]
Energy production, primary (Petajoules)	64	76	81[a]
Energy supply per capita (Gigajoules)	19	20	21[a]
Important sites for terrestrial biodiversity protected (%)	15.8	15.8	15.8[b]
Net Official Development Assist. received (% of GNI)	77.85	37.78	20.38[c]

2017. **b** 2019. **c** 2018. **d** 2014. **e** Estimate. **f** 2016. **g** Areas not elsewhere specified. **h** Data refers to a 5-year period preceding the reference year. **i** Data as at the end of December. **j** Data revision. **k** 2008. **l** 2009. **m** 2012. **n** Data are as at 1 January of reporting year. **o** Population aged 18 years and over. **p** Users in the last month.

Libya

Region	Northern Africa	UN membership date	14 December 1955
Population (000, 2020)	6 871	Surface area (km2)	1 676 198 a
Pop. density (per km2, 2020)	3.9	Sex ratio (m per 100 f)	101.9
Capital city	Tripoli	National currency	Libyan Dinar (LYD)
Capital city pop. (000, 2020)	1 160.9 b	Exchange rate (per US$)	1.4 b

Economic indicators	2010	2015	2020
GDP: Gross domestic product (million current US$)	80 942	17 666	34 377 c
GDP growth rate (annual %, const. 2015 prices)	4.3	- 45.5	17.9 c
GDP per capita (current US$)	13 060.2	2 752.4	5 147.3 c
Economy: Agriculture (% of Gross Value Added)	2.5	0.9	0.9 c
Economy: Industry (% of Gross Value Added)	74.0	67.1	67.1 c
Economy: Services and other activity (% of GVA)	24.6	33.0	33.4 c
Employment in agriculture (% of employed) d	19.1	20.3	18.8
Employment in industry (% of employed) d	27.5	22.3	21.7
Employment in services & other sectors (% employed) d	53.4	57.4	59.5
Unemployment rate (% of labour force) d	19.0	18.9	18.6
Labour force participation rate (female/male pop. %) d	33.6 / 62.9	34.0 / 64.8	33.8 / 65.2
CPI: Consumer Price Index (2010=100)	100	126 e	...
Agricultural production index (2004-2006=100)	112	117	117 f
International trade: exports (million current US$)	36 440	10 200 d	489 d,b
International trade: imports (million current US$)	17 674	12 999 d	2 450 d,b
International trade: balance (million current US$)	18 766	- 2 799 d	- 1 961 d,b
Balance of payments, current account (million US$)	16 801	- 9 346	11 276 c

Major trading partners						2019
Export partners (% of exports) d	Italy	18.6	China	16.2	Germany	15.5
Import partners (% of imports) d	Turkey	14.1	United Arab Emirates	10.5	China	9.8

Social indicators	2010	2015	2020
Population growth rate (average annual %) g	1.3	0.7	1.4
Urban population (% of total population)	78.1	79.3	80.4 b
Urban population growth rate (average annual %) g	1.5	0.5	...
Fertility rate, total (live births per woman) g	2.5	2.4	2.2
Life expectancy at birth (females/males, years) g	74.9 / 70.1	74.9 / 68.9	75.7 / 69.9
Population age distribution (0-14/60+ years old, %)	28.8 / 5.9	28.9 / 6.3	27.8 / 6.9
International migrant stock (000/% of total pop.) h	684.0 / 11.0	771.1 / 12.0	818.2 / 12.1 b
Refugees and others of concern to the UNHCR (000)	11.2 i	471.7	321.4 b
Infant mortality rate (per 1 000 live births) g	17.6	13.0	10.5
Health: Current expenditure (% of GDP) d	3.6	6.1 i	...
Health: Physicians (per 1 000 pop.)	2.0 k	1.9	2.1 a
Education: Primary gross enrol. ratio (f/m per 100 pop.)	106.6 / 111.3 l	... / ...	... / ...
Education: Secondary gross enrol. ratio (f/m per 100 pop.)	106.0 / 90.2 l	... / ...	... / ...
Seats held by women in the National Parliament (%)	7.7	16.0	16.0 m

Environment and infrastructure indicators	2010	2015	2020
Individuals using the Internet (per 100 inhabitants) d	14.0	19.0	21.8 a
Threatened species (number)	44	54	75
Forested area (% of land area) d	0.1	0.1	0.1 a
CO2 emission estimates (million tons/tons per capita)	48.2 / 7.8	42.7 / 6.9	41.5 / 6.5 a
Energy production, primary (Petajoules)	4 294	1 314	2 233 a
Energy supply per capita (Gigajoules)	139	101	87 a
Tourist/visitor arrivals at national borders (000)	34 n	...	...
Important sites for terrestrial biodiversity protected (%)	0.0	0.0	0.0 b
Net Official Development Assist. received (% of GNI)	0.01	0.54	0.62 c

a 2017. b 2019. c 2018. d Estimate. e 2013. f 2016. g Data refers to a 5-year period preceding the reference year. h Refers to foreign citizens. i Data as at the end of December. j 2011. k 2009. l 2006. m Data are as at 1 January of reporting year. n 2008.

Liechtenstein

Region	Western Europe	UN membership date	18 September 1990
Population (000, 2020)	39	Surface area (km2)	160[a]
Pop. density (per km2, 2020)	241.5	Sex ratio (m per 100 f)	98.4[b,c]
Capital city	Vaduz	National currency	Swiss Franc (CHF)
Capital city pop. (000, 2020)	5.5[d]	Exchange rate (per US$)	1.0[e]

Economic indicators	2010	2015	2020
GDP: Gross domestic product (million current US$)	5 621	6 269	6 796[d]
GDP growth rate (annual %, const. 2015 prices)	7.4	~0.0	2.0[d]
GDP per capita (current US$)	156 166.5	167 294.2	179 258.2[d]
Economy: Agriculture (% of Gross Value Added)	0.1	0.1	0.1[d]
Economy: Industry (% of Gross Value Added)[f]	45.2	43.6	44.5[d]
Economy: Services and other activity (% of GVA)[g,h]	79.6	81.9	81.5[d]
Unemployment rate (% of labour force)[i]	2.6	2.6[j]	...
Labour force participation rate (female/male pop. %)	52.6 / 70.9	53.5 / 70.6[j]	... / ...
Agricultural production index (2004-2006=100)	101	100	97[c]

Social indicators	2010	2015	2020
Population growth rate (average annual %)	0.7[k]	0.8[k]	0.7
Urban population (% of total population)	14.5	14.3	14.4[e]
Urban population growth rate (average annual %)[k]	0.3	0.5	...
Fertility rate, total (live births per woman)	1.4	1.5[l]	...
Population age distribution (0-14/60+ years old, %)	16.0 / 20.1	15.0 / 22.5[b]	14.9 / 22.7[b,c]
International migrant stock (000/% of total pop.)	22.3 / 62.1	23.8 / 63.5	25.5 / 67.0[e]
Refugees and others of concern to the UNHCR (000)	0.1[m]	0.2	0.2[e]
Education: Government expenditure (% of GDP)	2.0[n]	2.6[o]	...
Education: Primary gross enrol. ratio (f/m per 100 pop.)[p]	102.3 / 108.6	104.8 / 106.5	102.9 / 106.3[a]
Education: Secondary gross enrol. ratio (f/m per 100 pop.)[p]	100.0 / 117.6	101.7 / 130.7	105.1 / 129.1[a]
Education: Tertiary gross enrol. ratio (f/m per 100 pop.)[p]	27.4 / 44.3	21.9 / 44.8	27.4 / 43.6[a]
Intentional homicide rate (per 100 000 pop.)	2.8	0.0	2.6[d]
Seats held by women in the National Parliament (%)	24.0	20.0	12.0[q]

Environment and infrastructure indicators	2010	2015	2020
Individuals using the Internet (per 100 inhabitants)[p]	80.0	96.6	98.1[a]
Threatened species (number)	2	4	13
Forested area (% of land area)[p]	43.1	43.1	43.1[a]
Energy production, primary (Petajoules)[p]	1	1	1[a]
Energy supply per capita (Gigajoules)	92	88	89[a]
Tourist/visitor arrivals at national borders (000)	64	57[r]	85[r,d]
Important sites for terrestrial biodiversity protected (%)	80.8	80.8	80.8[e]
Net Official Development Assist. disbursed (% of GNI)	0.62	0.50[s]	...

a 2017. b De jure population. c 2016. d 2018. e 2019. f Excludes publishing activities. Includes irrigation and canals. g Excludes computer and related activities and radio/TV activities. h Excludes repair of personal and household goods. i Population aged 15 to 64 years. j 2013. k Data refers to a 5-year period preceding the reference year. l 2012. m Data as at the end of December. n 2008. o 2011. p Estimate. q Data are as at 1 January of reporting year. r Excluding long term tourists on campgrounds and in holiday flats. s 2014.

Lithuania

Region	Northern Europe	UN membership date	17 September 1991
Population (000, 2020)	2 722	Surface area (km2)	65 286 [a]
Pop. density (per km2, 2020)	43.4	Sex ratio (m per 100 f)	86.2
Capital city	Vilnius	National currency	Euro (EUR)
Capital city pop. (000, 2020)	537.6 [b]	Exchange rate (per US$)	0.9 [b]

Economic indicators

	2010	2015	2020
GDP: Gross domestic product (million current US$)	37 034	41 392	53 455 [c]
GDP growth rate (annual %, const. 2015 prices)	1.5	2.0	3.6 [c]
GDP per capita (current US$)	11 855.5	14 118.0	19 082.5 [c]
Economy: Agriculture (% of Gross Value Added) [d,e]	3.4	3.8	3.2 [c]
Economy: Industry (% of Gross Value Added) [d,e,f]	29.1	29.6	28.4 [c]
Economy: Services and other activity (% of GVA) [e,g,h]	56.4	54.8	55.8 [c]
Employment in agriculture (% of employed)	8.8	9.1	6.6 [i]
Employment in industry (% of employed)	24.6	25.1	25.9 [i]
Employment in services & other sectors (% employed)	66.6	65.9	67.4 [i]
Unemployment rate (% of labour force) [i]	17.8	9.1	6.3
Labour force participation rate (female/male pop. %) [i]	52.6 / 62.3	54.6 / 65.0	56.2 / 67.6
CPI: Consumer Price Index (2010=100) [j]	100	108	118 [b]
Agricultural production index (2004-2006=100)	100	138	131 [k]
International trade: exports (million current US$)	20 814	25 411	33 123 [b]
International trade: imports (million current US$)	23 378	28 176	35 612 [b]
International trade: balance (million current US$)	- 2 564	- 2 765	- 2 489 [b]
Balance of payments, current account (million US$)	72	- 1 015	2 298 [b]

Major trading partners

						2019
Export partners (% of exports)	Russian Federation	14.0	Latvia	9.5	Poland	7.9
Import partners (% of imports)	Russian Federation	14.7	Poland	11.9	Germany	11.6

Social indicators

	2010	2015	2020
Population growth rate (average annual %) [l]	- 1.4	- 1.3	- 1.5
Urban population (% of total population)	66.8	67.2	67.9 [b]
Urban population growth rate (average annual %) [l]	- 1.3	- 1.1	...
Fertility rate, total (live births per woman) [l]	1.4	1.6	1.7
Life expectancy at birth (females/males, years) [l]	77.8 / 66.0	79.3 / 68.5	81.1 / 70.0
Population age distribution (0-14/60+ years old, %)	14.8 / 22.4	14.6 / 24.5	15.5 / 27.5
International migrant stock (000/% of total pop.)	160.8 / 5.1	136.0 / 4.6	117.2 / 4.2 [b]
Refugees and others of concern to the UNHCR (000)	4.6 [m]	4.7	5.1 [b]
Infant mortality rate (per 1 000 live births) [l]	6.0	4.4	4.0
Health: Current expenditure (% of GDP) [i]	6.8	6.5	6.5 [a]
Health: Physicians (per 1 000 pop.)	3.4	4.3	6.4 [c]
Education: Government expenditure (% of GDP)	5.3	4.2	4.0 [k]
Education: Primary gross enrol. ratio (f/m per 100 pop.) [i]	99.8 / 101.1	101.9 / 102.2	103.9 / 103.9 [a]
Education: Secondary gross enrol. ratio (f/m per 100 pop.) [i]	104.1 / 106.0	105.4 / 109.8	106.0 / 110.6 [a]
Education: Tertiary gross enrol. ratio (f/m per 100 pop.) [i]	104.6 / 69.2	82.7 / 57.5	84.0 / 61.4 [a]
Intentional homicide rate (per 100 000 pop.)	7.0	5.9	4.6 [c]
Seats held by women in the National Parliament (%)	19.1	23.4	24.1 [n]

Environment and infrastructure indicators

	2010	2015	2020
Individuals using the Internet (per 100 inhabitants)	62.1 [o,p]	71.4 [o]	79.7 [c]
Research & Development expenditure (% of GDP)	0.8	1.0	0.9 [q,c]
Threatened species (number)	17	22	41
Forested area (% of land area)	34.6	34.8	34.8 [i,a]
CO2 emission estimates (million tons/tons per capita)	12.3 / 4.0	10.6 / 3.6	10.8 / 3.8 [a]
Energy production, primary (Petajoules)	64	77	86 [a]
Energy supply per capita (Gigajoules)	94	100	108 [a]
Tourist/visitor arrivals at national borders (000)	1 507	2 071	2 825 [c]
Important sites for terrestrial biodiversity protected (%)	91.1	91.1	91.1 [b]
Pop. using safely managed sanitation (urban/rural %)	93.5 / 75.8	94.7 / 81.1	95.2 / 83.3 [a]
Net Official Development Assist. disbursed (% of GNI)	0.10	0.12	0.13 [a]

a 2017. **b** 2019. **c** 2018. **d** Includes publishing activities and landscaping care. **e** Data classified according to ISIC Rev. 4. **f** Excludes publishing activities. Includes irrigation and canals. **g** Excludes repair of personal and household goods. **h** Excludes computer and related activities and radio/TV activities. **i** Estimate. **j** Calculated by the UN Statistics Division from national indices. **k** 2016. **l** Data refers to a 5-year period preceding the reference year. **m** Data as at the end of December. **n** Data are as at 1 January of reporting year. **o** Population aged 16 to 74 years. **p** Users in the last 12 months. **q** Provisional data.

Luxembourg

Region	Western Europe	
Population (000, 2020)	626	
Pop. density (per km2, 2020)	241.7	
Capital city	Luxembourg	
Capital city pop. (000, 2020)	119.8[b]	

UN membership date	24 October 1945	
Surface area (km2)	2 586[a]	
Sex ratio (m per 100 f)	102.3	
National currency	Euro (EUR)	
Exchange rate (per US$)	0.9[c]	

Economic indicators

	2010	2015	2020
GDP: Gross domestic product (million current US$)	53 212	57 744	70 920[b]
GDP growth rate (annual %, const. 2015 prices)	4.9	4.3	3.1[b]
GDP per capita (current US$)	104 771.9	101 888.6	117 369.5[b]
Economy: Agriculture (% of Gross Value Added)[d]	0.3	0.2	0.3[b]
Economy: Industry (% of Gross Value Added)[d,e]	12.7	12.2	13.0[b]
Economy: Services and other activity (% of GVA)[d,f,g]	89.5	89.7	87.6[b]
Employment in agriculture (% of employed)	1.1	1.0	1.0[h]
Employment in industry (% of employed)	13.3	12.5	11.5[h]
Employment in services & other sectors (% employed)	85.6	86.4	87.5[h]
Unemployment rate (% of labour force)[h]	4.4	6.7	5.2
Labour force participation rate (female/male pop. %)[h]	48.8 / 65.4	53.6 / 65.2	55.1 / 63.7
CPI: Consumer Price Index (2010=100)[i]	100	109	115[c]
Agricultural production index (2004-2006=100)	94	102	103[i]
International trade: exports (million current US$)	13 911	12 626	15 433[h,c]
International trade: imports (million current US$)	20 400	19 296	23 057[h,c]
International trade: balance (million current US$)	- 6 489	- 6 671	- 7 623[h,c]
Balance of payments, current account (million US$)	3 584	2 949	3 095[c]

Major trading partners

						2019
Export partners (% of exports)[h]	Germany	26.3	France	14.7	Belgium	11.8
Import partners (% of imports)[h]	Belgium	25.5	Germany	23.3	France	12.5

Social indicators

	2010	2015	2020
Population growth rate (average annual %)[k]	2.1	2.2	2.0
Urban population (% of total population)	88.5	90.2	91.2[c]
Urban population growth rate (average annual %)[k]	2.5	2.6	...
Fertility rate, total (live births per woman)[k]	1.6	1.5	1.4
Life expectancy at birth (females/males, years)[k]	82.2 / 76.7	83.4 / 78.8	84.2 / 79.8
Population age distribution (0-14/60+ years old, %)	17.6 / 19.0	16.4 / 19.1	15.6 / 19.9
International migrant stock (000/% of total pop.)	163.1 / 32.1	248.9 / 43.9	291.7 / 47.4[c]
Refugees and others of concern to the UNHCR (000)	4.1[l]	2.1	5.7[c]
Infant mortality rate (per 1 000 live births)[k]	2.3	3.4	2.9
Health: Current expenditure (% of GDP)	7.0	5.5	5.5[a]
Health: Physicians (per 1 000 pop.)	2.8	2.9	3.0[a]
Education: Government expenditure (% of GDP)	...	4.0	...
Education: Primary gross enrol. ratio (f/m per 100 pop.)	98.1 / 97.1	98.9 / 99.0	102.0 / 102.6[a]
Education: Secondary gross enrol. ratio (f/m per 100 pop.)	102.8 / 99.8	104.2 / 100.5	104.8 / 102.6[a]
Education: Tertiary gross enrol. ratio (f/m per 100 pop.)	19.2 / 17.3	20.8 / 18.8	20.1 / 18.2[a]
Intentional homicide rate (per 100 000 pop.)	2.0	0.9	0.3[a]
Seats held by women in the National Parliament (%)	20.0	28.3	30.0[m]

Environment and infrastructure indicators

	2010	2015	2020
Individuals using the Internet (per 100 inhabitants)	90.6[n]	96.4	97.1[b]
Research & Development expenditure (% of GDP)	1.5	1.3	1.2[o,b]
Threatened species (number)	5	9	16
Forested area (% of land area)[h]	35.7	35.7	35.7[a]
CO2 emission estimates (million tons/tons per capita)	10.7 / 21.0	8.8 / 15.5	8.6 / 14.5[a]
Energy production, primary (Petajoules)	5	6	8[a]
Energy supply per capita (Gigajoules)	352	279	274[a]
Tourist/visitor arrivals at national borders (000)	805	1 090	1 018[b]
Important sites for terrestrial biodiversity protected (%)	78.1	81.7	81.9[c]
Pop. using safely managed drinking water (urban/rural, %)	100.0 / 100.0	100.0 / 98.0	100.0 / 97.0[a]
Pop. using safely managed sanitation (urban/rural, %)	93.4 / 85.8	96.2 / 88.3	97.4 / 89.3[a]
Net Official Development Assist. disbursed (% of GNI)[p]	1.05	0.95	1.00[a]

2017. **b** 2018. **c** 2019. **d** Data classified according to ISIC Rev. 4. **e** Excludes publishing activities. Includes irrigation and canals. **f** Excludes repair of personal and household goods. **g** Excludes computer and related activities and radio/TV activities. **h** Estimate. **i** Calculated by the UN Statistics Division from national indices. **j** 2016. **k** Data refers to a 5-year period preceding the reference year. **l** Data as at the end of December. **m** Data are as at 1 January of reporting year. **n** Population aged 16 to 74 years. **o** Provisional data. **p** Development Assistance Committee member (OECD).

Madagascar

Region	Eastern Africa	UN membership date	20 September 1960
Population (000, 2020)	27 691	Surface area (km2)	587 295 a
Pop. density (per km2, 2020)	47.6	Sex ratio (m per 100 f)	99.6
Capital city	Antananarivo	National currency	Malagasy Ariary (MGA)
Capital city pop. (000, 2020)	3 210.4 b	Exchange rate (per US$)	3 627.3 b

Economic indicators

	2010	2015	2020
GDP: Gross domestic product (million current US$)	9 983	11 323	13 851 c
GDP growth rate (annual %, const. 2015 prices)	0.6	3.1	4.6 c
GDP per capita (current US$)	472.0	467.2	527.4 c
Economy: Agriculture (% of Gross Value Added)	30.3	27.0	25.2 c
Economy: Industry (% of Gross Value Added)	18.8	19.9	24.4 c
Economy: Services and other activity (% of GVA)	50.4	56.3	55.3 c
Employment in agriculture (% of employed) d	73.4	66.4	63.8
Employment in industry (% of employed) d	6.0	8.4	9.1
Employment in services & other sectors (% employed) d	20.6	25.1	27.1
Unemployment rate (% of labour force) d	4.3	1.8	1.8
Labour force participation rate (female/male pop. %) d	87.1 / 91.0	83.5 / 89.6	83.4 / 89.0
CPI: Consumer Price Index (2010=100)	100	140	125 e,f,b
Agricultural production index (2004-2006=100)	123	117	118 g
International trade: exports (million current US$)	1 082	2 164	2 689 b
International trade: imports (million current US$)	2 546	2 961	3 603 b
International trade: balance (million current US$)	- 1 464	- 796	- 914 b
Balance of payments, current account (million US$)	- 917	- 281	80 c

Major trading partners

						2019
Export partners (% of exports)	France	20.2	United States	19.8	China	6.3
Import partners (% of imports)	China	19.1	France	14.1	United Arab Emirates	10.0

Social indicators

	2010	2015	2020
Population growth rate (average annual %) h	2.9	2.7	2.7
Urban population (% of total population)	31.9	35.2	37.9 b
Urban population growth rate (average annual %) h	4.9	4.7	...
Fertility rate, total (live births per woman) h	4.8	4.4	4.1
Life expectancy at birth (females/males, years) h	63.7 / 60.8	66.0 / 63.0	68.1 / 64.9
Population age distribution (0-14/60+ years old, %)	43.5 / 4.3	41.6 / 4.6	40.1 / 5.0
International migrant stock (000/% of total pop.) i	28.9 / 0.1	32.1 / 0.1	34.9 / 0.1 b
Refugees and others of concern to the UNHCR (000)	~0.0 i	~0.0	0.2 b
Infant mortality rate (per 1 000 live births) h	45.5	36.8	29.0
Health: Current expenditure (% of GDP) k	5.3	5.7	5.5 a
Health: Physicians (per 1 000 pop.)	0.2	0.2 l	...
Education: Government expenditure (% of GDP)	3.2 m	2.8 d,l	...
Education: Primary gross enrol. ratio (f/m per 100 pop.)	142.4 / 145.0	147.3 / 147.3	143.1 / 142.0 c
Education: Secondary gross enrol. ratio (f/m per 100 pop.)	29.7 / 31.6 m,d	38.3 / 38.7 d	37.1 / 36.0 c
Education: Tertiary gross enrol. ratio (f/m per 100 pop.)	3.5 / 3.8	4.6 / 5.0	5.2 / 5.5 c
Seats held by women in the National Parliament (%)	7.9 m	20.5	15.9 n

Environment and infrastructure indicators

	2010	2015	2020
Individuals using the Internet (per 100 inhabitants)	1.7 d	4.2 d	9.8 a
Research & Development expenditure (% of GDP) o	0.1	~0.0 p,q,l	~0.0 p,a
Threatened species (number)	663	965	2 910
Forested area (% of land area) d	21.6	21.4	21.4 a
Energy production, primary (Petajoules)	174 d	209	272 a
Energy supply per capita (Gigajoules)	9 d	10	13 a
Tourist/visitor arrivals at national borders (000) r	196	244	291 c
Important sites for terrestrial biodiversity protected (%)	22.4	23.0	25.0 b
Net Official Development Assist. received (% of GNI)	5.53	7.23	5.92 c

a 2017. b 2019. c 2018. d Estimate. e Base: 2016 = 100 f Data refer to 7 cities only. g 2016. h Data refers to a 5-year period preceding the reference year. i Refers to foreign citizens. j Data as at the end of December. k Data revision. l 2014. m 2009. n Data are as at 1 January of reporting year. o Partial data. p Government only. q Break in the time series. r Arrivals of non-resident tourists by air.

Malawi

Region	Eastern Africa	UN membership date	01 December 1964
Population (000, 2020)	19 130	Surface area (km2)	118 484[a]
Pop. density (per km2, 2020)	202.9	Sex ratio (m per 100 f)	97.3
Capital city	Lilongwe	National currency	Malawi Kwacha (MWK)
Capital city pop. (000, 2020)	1 074.7[b]	Exchange rate (per US$)	733.7[c]

Economic indicators

	2010	2015	2020
GDP: Gross domestic product (million current US$)	6 960	6 431	7 196[c]
GDP growth rate (annual %, const. 2015 prices)	6.9	3.3	4.0[c]
GDP per capita (current US$)	478.7	384.1	396.6[c]
Economy: Agriculture (% of Gross Value Added)[d]	31.9	32.4	31.0[c]
Economy: Industry (% of Gross Value Added)[d,e]	16.4	16.4	15.9[c]
Economy: Services and other activity (% of GVA)[d,f,g]	51.2	50.9	53.6[c]
Employment in agriculture (% of employed)[h]	48.1	45.6	43.2
Employment in industry (% of employed)[h]	14.2	14.0	13.8
Employment in services & other sectors (% employed)[h]	37.7	40.4	43.0
Unemployment rate (% of labour force)[h]	5.9	5.8	5.7
Labour force participation rate (female/male pop. %)[h]	73.3 / 82.1	72.6 / 82.2	72.6 / 81.3
CPI: Consumer Price Index (2010=100)[h]	100	251	383[c]
Agricultural production index (2004-2006=100)	156	152	146[i]
International trade: exports (million current US$)	1 066	1 080	819[h,b]
International trade: imports (million current US$)	2 173	2 312	360[h,b]
International trade: balance (million current US$)	- 1 107	- 1 232	459[h,b]
Balance of payments, current account (million US$)	- 969	- 930	- 1 427[c]

Major trading partners   2019

Export partners (% of exports)[h]	Belgium	22.0	South Africa	7.8	United Rep. of Tanzania	7.7
Import partners (% of imports)[h]	South Africa	17.8	China	14.7	India	10.9

Social indicators

	2010	2015	2020
Population growth rate (average annual %)[j]	2.8	2.8	2.7
Urban population (% of total population)	15.5	16.3	17.2[b]
Urban population growth rate (average annual %)[j]	3.7	3.9	...
Fertility rate, total (live births per woman)[j]	5.7	4.9	4.2
Life expectancy at birth (females/males, years)[j]	54.0 / 48.7	62.5 / 56.6	66.6 / 60.3
Population age distribution (0-14/60+ years old, %)	46.4 / 4.2	45.1 / 4.0	43.0 / 4.1
International migrant stock (000/% of total pop.)[k]	217.7 / 1.5	232.8 / 1.4	247.7 / 1.3[b]
Refugees and others of concern to the UNHCR (000)	15.2[l]	22.6	39.3[b]
Infant mortality rate (per 1 000 live births)[j]	68.4	52.6	41.3
Health: Current expenditure (% of GDP)	7.2	9.3	9.6[a]
Health: Physicians (per 1 000 pop.)	~0.0[m]	...	~0.0[c]
Education: Government expenditure (% of GDP)	3.5	5.6	4.0[h,a]
Education: Primary gross enrol. ratio (f/m per 100 pop.)	140.2 / 137.3	147.9 / 144.9	143.1 / 141.8[c]
Education: Secondary gross enrol. ratio (f/m per 100 pop.)	31.9 / 36.1	38.9 / 42.6[h]	39.9 / 40.6[c]
Education: Tertiary gross enrol. ratio (f/m per 100 pop.)	0.5 / 0.9	0.6 / 1.0[n]	... / ...
Intentional homicide rate (per 100 000 pop.)	3.6	1.8[o]	...
Seats held by women in the National Parliament (%)	20.8	16.7	22.9[p]

Environment and infrastructure indicators

	2010	2015	2020
Individuals using the Internet (per 100 inhabitants)	2.3	5.3[h]	13.8[h,a]
Threatened species (number)	158	171	130
Forested area (% of land area)	34.3	33.4[h]	33.4[h,a]
Energy production, primary (Petajoules)	64	68	68[a]
Energy supply per capita (Gigajoules)	5	5	5[a]
Tourist/visitor arrivals at national borders (000)[q]	746	805	871[c]
Important sites for terrestrial biodiversity protected (%)	73.7	73.7	73.7[b]
Net Official Development Assist. received (% of GNI)	14.84	16.93	18.10[c]

2017. **b** 2019. **c** 2018. **d** Data classified according to ISIC Rev. 4. **e** Excludes publishing activities. Includes irrigation and canals. **f** Excludes computer and related activities and radio/TV activities. **g** Excludes repair of personal and household goods. **h** Estimate. **i** 2016. **j** Data refers to a 5-year period preceding the reference year. **k** Including refugees. **l** Data as at the end of December. **m** 2009. **n** 2011. **o** 2012. **p** Data are as at 1 January of reporting year. **q** Departures.

Malaysia

Region	South-eastern Asia	UN membership date	17 September 1957
Population (000, 2020)	32 366 [a]	Surface area (km2)	330 323 [b]
Pop. density (per km2, 2020)	98.5 [a]	Sex ratio (m per 100 f)	105.7 [a]
Capital city	Kuala Lumpur [c]	National currency	Malaysian Ringgit (MYR)
Capital city pop. (000, 2020)	7 780.3 [d,e]	Exchange rate (per US$)	4.1 [e]

Economic indicators

	2010	2015	2020
GDP: Gross domestic product (million current US$)	255 018	301 355	358 579 [f]
GDP growth rate (annual %, const. 2015 prices)	7.4	5.1	4.7 [f]
GDP per capita (current US$)	9 040.6	9 955.2	11 373.3 [f]
Economy: Agriculture (% of Gross Value Added)	10.2	8.4	7.6 [f]
Economy: Industry (% of Gross Value Added) [g,h]	40.9	38.9	38.8 [f]
Economy: Services and other activity (% of GVA) [g,i,j]	71.6	71.3	68.1 [f]
Employment in agriculture (% of employed)	14.2	12.5	10.1 [k]
Employment in industry (% of employed)	27.7	27.5	26.8 [k]
Employment in services & other sectors (% employed)	58.0	60.0	63.1 [k]
Unemployment rate (% of labour force) [k]	3.2	3.1	3.4
Labour force participation rate (female/male pop. %) [k]	43.5 / 76.2	50.5 / 77.6	50.9 / 77.2
CPI: Consumer Price Index (2010=100)	100	113	121 [e]
Agricultural production index (2004-2006=100)	111	122	123 [l]
International trade: exports (million current US$)	198 791	200 211	238 089 [e]
International trade: imports (million current US$)	164 586	176 175	204 906 [e]
International trade: balance (million current US$)	34 204	24 036	33 183 [e]
Balance of payments, current account (million US$)	25 644	9 068	7 590 [f]

Major trading partners

						2019
Export partners (% of exports)	China	14.2	Singapore	13.9	United States	9.7
Import partners (% of imports)	China	20.7	Singapore	10.5	United States	8.1

Social indicators

	2010	2015	2020
Population growth rate (average annual %) [a,m]	1.9	1.4	1.3
Urban population (% of total population) [a]	70.9	74.2	76.6 [e]
Urban population growth rate (average annual %) [a,m]	3.1	2.7	...
Fertility rate, total (live births per woman) [a,m]	2.2	2.1	2.0
Life expectancy at birth (females/males, years) [a,m]	76.3 / 72.0	77.2 / 73.0	78.1 / 74.0
Population age distribution (0-14/60+ years old, %) [a]	28.0 / 7.9	25.1 / 9.3	23.4 / 11.0
International migrant stock (000/% of total pop.) [a,n,o]	2 417.4 / 8.6	3 280.7 / 10.8	3 430.4 / 10.7 [e]
Refugees and others of concern to the UNHCR (000)	212.9 [p]	272.0	266.5 [q,e]
Infant mortality rate (per 1 000 live births) [a,m]	7.0	6.4	5.9
Health: Current expenditure (% of GDP) [r]	3.2	3.9	3.9 [b]
Health: Physicians (per 1 000 pop.)	1.2	1.5	...
Education: Government expenditure (% of GDP)	5.0	5.0	4.7 [b]
Education: Primary gross enrol. ratio (f/m per 100 pop.)	100.2 / 99.3	104.1 / 103.5	106.0 / 104.6 [b]
Education: Secondary gross enrol. ratio (f/m per 100 pop.)	80.2 / 74.5	88.7 / 81.4	85.4 / 78.8 [f]
Education: Tertiary gross enrol. ratio (f/m per 100 pop.)	43.0 / 31.4	51.7 / 39.8	49.9 / 40.7 [f]
Intentional homicide rate (per 100 000 pop.)	1.9	2.1 [s]	...
Seats held by women in the National Parliament (%)	9.9	10.4	14.4 [t]

Environment and infrastructure indicators

	2010	2015	2020
Individuals using the Internet (per 100 inhabitants)	56.3	71.1 [u]	81.2 [f]
Research & Development expenditure (% of GDP)	1.0	1.3	1.4 [l]
Threatened species (number)	1 180	1 252	1 662
Forested area (% of land area) [k]	67.3	67.6	67.6 [b]
CO2 emission estimates (million tons/tons per capita)	189.9 / 6.8	220.4 / 7.2	211.0 / 6.7 [b]
Energy production, primary (Petajoules)	3 450	3 748	3 830 [b]
Energy supply per capita (Gigajoules)	105	111	110 [b]
Tourist/visitor arrivals at national borders (000) [v]	24 577	25 721	25 832 [f]
Important sites for terrestrial biodiversity protected (%)	28.5	28.5	28.5 [e]
Net Official Development Assist. received (% of GNI)	0.00	0.00	- 0.01 [f]

a Including Sabah and Sarawak. b 2017. c Kuala Lumpur is the capital and Putrajaya is the administrative capital. d Refers to the Greater Kuala Lumpur. e 2019. f 2018. g At producers' prices. h Excludes publishing activities. Include irrigation and canals. i Excludes computer and related activities and radio/TV activities. j Excludes repair of personal and household goods. k Estimate. l 2016. m Data refers to a 5-year period preceding the reference year. n Including refugees. o Refers to foreign citizens. p Data as at the end of December. q Updated figure based on registration and community legal assistance programme in West Malaysia by a local NGO with UNHCR technical support since 2014. During 2017, 906 persons of those registered acquired Malaysian nationality. r Provisional data. s 2013. t Data are as at 1 January of reporting year. u Population aged 15 years and over. v Including Singapore residents crossing the frontier by road through Johore Causeway.

Maldives

Region	Southern Asia	UN membership date	21 September 1965
Population (000, 2020)	540	Surface area (km2)	300 [a]
Pop. density (per km2, 2020)	1 801.8	Sex ratio (m per 100 f)	173.5
Capital city	Male	National currency	Rufiyaa (MVR)
Capital city pop. (000, 2020)	176.9 [b]	Exchange rate (per US$)	15.4 [c]

Economic indicators

	2010	2015	2020
GDP: Gross domestic product (million current US$)	2 588	4 109	5 327 [b]
GDP growth rate (annual %, const. 2015 prices)	7.3	2.9	6.9 [b]
GDP per capita (current US$)	7 076.7	9 033.4	10 330.6 [b]
Economy: Agriculture (% of Gross Value Added) [d]	6.1	6.3	6.5 [b]
Economy: Industry (% of Gross Value Added) [d,e]	10.2	12.1	15.0 [b]
Economy: Services and other activity (% of GVA) [d,f,g]	54.6	53.1	52.8 [b]
Employment in agriculture (% of employed) [h]	12.8	9.8	8.2
Employment in industry (% of employed) [h]	20.9	19.1	18.3
Employment in services & other sectors (% employed) [h]	66.4	71.2	73.4
Unemployment rate (% of labour force) [h]	4.1	5.7	6.4
Labour force participation rate (female/male pop. %) [h]	44.1 / 77.1	45.0 / 82.4	41.6 / 85.2
CPI: Consumer Price Index (2010=100) [h]	100	132	136 [b]
Agricultural production index (2004-2006=100)	76	67	67 [i]
International trade: exports (million current US$)	74	144	163 [h,c]
International trade: imports (million current US$)	1 095	1 897	2 883 [h,c]
International trade: balance (million current US$)	- 1 021	- 1 753	- 2 720 [h,c]
Balance of payments, current account (million US$)	- 196	- 302	- 1 388 [b]

Major trading partners

						2019
Export partners (% of exports) [h]	Thailand	36.3	Germany	12.7	United Kingdom	9.2
Import partners (% of imports) [h]	United Arab Emirates	18.1	China	16.5	Singapore	12.5

Social indicators

	2010	2015	2020
Population growth rate (average annual %) [j]	2.7	4.4	3.4
Urban population (% of total population)	36.4	38.5	40.2 [c]
Urban population growth rate (average annual %) [j]	4.2	3.9	...
Fertility rate, total (live births per woman) [j]	2.3	2.1	1.9
Life expectancy at birth (females/males, years) [j]	76.2 / 73.7	78.4 / 75.5	80.4 / 77.1
Population age distribution (0-14/60+ years old, %)	25.3 / 6.2	21.2 / 5.8	19.6 / 5.7
International migrant stock (000/% of total pop.) [k]	54.7 / 14.9	64.3 / 14.1	69.2 / 13.0 [c]
Infant mortality rate (per 1 000 live births) [j]	14.8	9.0	6.8
Health: Current expenditure (% of GDP)	8.5 [l,m]	8.7	9.0 [a]
Health: Physicians (per 1 000 pop.)	1.4	2.9	4.6 [b]
Education: Government expenditure (% of GDP)	4.1	4.4	4.1 [i]
Education: Primary gross enrol. ratio (f/m per 100 pop.)	108.6 / 112.7 [n]	100.0 / 103.0	98.1 / 96.2 [a]
Education: Tertiary gross enrol. ratio (f/m per 100 pop.)	13.0 / 9.7 [o]	20.1 / 8.5 [p]	59.8 / 16.6 [a]
Intentional homicide rate (per 100 000 pop.)	1.6	0.7 [q]	...
Seats held by women in the National Parliament (%)	6.5	5.9	4.6 [r]

Environment and infrastructure indicators

	2010	2015	2020
Individuals using the Internet (per 100 inhabitants)	26.5 [s]	54.5 [h]	63.2 [h,a]
Threatened species (number)	59	69	80
Forested area (% of land area) [h]	3.3	3.3	3.3 [a]
Energy production, primary (Petajoules)	0	0	0 [a]
Energy supply per capita (Gigajoules)	37	41	43 [a]
Tourist/visitor arrivals at national borders (000) [t]	792	1 234	1 484 [b]
Important sites for terrestrial biodiversity protected (%)	0.0	0.0	0.0 [c]
Net Official Development Assist. received (% of GNI)	3.88	0.64	2.45 [b]

2017. **b** 2018. **c** 2019. **d** Data classified according to ISIC Rev. 4. **e** Excludes publishing activities. Includes irrigation and canals. **f** Excludes repair of personal and household goods. **g** Excludes computer and related activities and radio/TV activities. **h** Estimate. **i** 2016. **j** Data refers to a 5-year period preceding the reference year. **k** Refers to foreign citizens. **l** Break in the time series. **m** Data revision. **n** 2009. **o** 2008. **p** 2014. **q** 2013. **r** Data are as at 1 January of reporting year. **s** Population aged 15 years and over. **t** Arrivals by air.

Mali

Region	Western Africa	UN membership date	28 September 1960
Population (000, 2020)	20 251	Surface area (km2)	1 240 192 [a]
Pop. density (per km2, 2020)	16.6	Sex ratio (m per 100 f)	100.4
Capital city	Bamako	National currency	CFA Franc, BCEAO (XOF) [b]
Capital city pop. (000, 2020)	2 529.3 [c]	Exchange rate (per US$)	583.9 [c]

Economic indicators

	2010	2015	2020
GDP: Gross domestic product (million current US$)	10 679	13 095	17 172 [d]
GDP growth rate (annual %, const. 2015 prices)	10.9	7.6	6.7 [d]
GDP per capita (current US$)	709.6	750.9	900.1 [d]
Economy: Agriculture (% of Gross Value Added)	34.9	40.2	39.9 [d]
Economy: Industry (% of Gross Value Added)	25.3	19.5	20.5 [d]
Economy: Services and other activity (% of GVA)	48.5	51.8	49.2 [d]
Employment in agriculture (% of employed)	68.6 [e]	62.3	62.3 [e]
Employment in industry (% of employed)	8.8 [e]	8.3	7.6 [e]
Employment in services & other sectors (% employed)	22.5 [e]	29.5	30.2 [e]
Unemployment rate (% of labour force) [e]	8.1	7.7	7.3
Labour force participation rate (female/male pop. %) [e]	60.3 / 81.9	61.2 / 81.2	61.2 / 80.6
CPI: Consumer Price Index (2010=100) [f]	100	110	110 [g]
Agricultural production index (2004-2006=100)	126	157	171 [g]
International trade: exports (million current US$)	1 996	2 530 [e]	879 [e,c]
International trade: imports (million current US$)	4 704	3 169 [e]	8 277 [e,c]
International trade: balance (million current US$)	- 2 707	- 639 [e]	- 7 397 [e,c]
Balance of payments, current account (million US$)	- 1 190	- 697	- 836 [d]

Major trading partners

						2019
Export partners (% of exports) [e]	South Africa	41.0	Switzerland	21.4	Burkina Faso	6.1
Import partners (% of imports) [e]	Senegal	20.5	China	15.2	Ivory Coast	9.7

Social indicators

	2010	2015	2020
Population growth rate (average annual %) [h]	3.3	2.9	3.0
Urban population (% of total population)	36.0	40.0	43.1 [c]
Urban population growth rate (average annual %) [h]	5.6	5.0	...
Fertility rate, total (live births per woman) [h]	6.7	6.4	5.9
Life expectancy at birth (females/males, years) [h]	54.6 / 53.4	56.9 / 55.6	59.5 / 58.0
Population age distribution (0-14/60+ years old, %)	47.5 / 4.2	47.9 / 4.0	47.0 / 3.9
International migrant stock (000/% of total pop.) [i]	339.4 / 2.3	420.5 / 2.4	468.2 / 2.4 [c]
Refugees and others of concern to the UNHCR (000)	15.3 [j]	148.3	182.9 [c]
Infant mortality rate (per 1 000 live births) [h]	89.1	78.5	65.8
Health: Current expenditure (% of GDP)	4.6	4.1	3.8 [a]
Health: Physicians (per 1 000 pop.)	0.1	0.1 [k]	0.1 [d]
Education: Government expenditure (% of GDP)	3.3	3.8	3.19
Education: Primary gross enrol. ratio (f/m per 100 pop.)	77.0 / 89.7	71.5 / 79.7	71.6 / 79.5 [d]
Education: Secondary gross enrol. ratio (f/m per 100 pop.)	31.9 / 46.5	36.8 / 46.5	37.0 / 45.0 [d]
Education: Tertiary gross enrol. ratio (f/m per 100 pop.)	3.6 / 8.6	3.2 / 7.7	2.7 / 6.3 [a]
Seats held by women in the National Parliament (%)	10.2	9.5	9.5 [l]

Environment and infrastructure indicators

	2010	2015	2020
Individuals using the Internet (per 100 inhabitants)	2.0 [e]	10.3 [e]	13.0 [m,n,a]
Research & Development expenditure (% of GDP)	0.6	0.3 [o]	0.3 [o,p,a]
Threatened species (number)	29	39	62
Forested area (% of land area) [e]	4.2	3.9	3.9 [a]
Energy production, primary (Petajoules)	52	56	57 [a]
Energy supply per capita (Gigajoules)	5	5	5 [a]
Tourist/visitor arrivals at national borders (000)	169	159	193 [a]
Important sites for terrestrial biodiversity protected (%)	8.1	8.1	8.1 [c]
Pop. using safely managed sanitation (urban/rural %)	8.3 / 16.9	8.9 / 23.0	9.1 / 25.5 [a]
Net Official Development Assist. received (% of GNI)	10.64	9.38	9.03 [d]

a 2017. b African Financial Community (CFA) Franc, Central Bank of West African States (BCEAO). c 2019. d 2018. e Estimate. f Bamako g 2016. h Data refers to a 5-year period preceding the reference year. i Including refugees. j Data as at the end of December. k 2012. l Data are as at 1 January of reporting year. m Population aged 18 years and over. n At least once a month. o Excluding business enterprise. p Partial data.

Malta

Region	Southern Europe	UN membership date	01 December 1964
Population (000, 2020)	442	Surface area (km2)	315[a]
Pop. density (per km2, 2020)	1 379.8	Sex ratio (m per 100 f)	100.6
Capital city	Valletta	National currency	Euro (EUR)
Capital city pop. (000, 2020)	212.8[b,c]	Exchange rate (per US$)	0.9[d]

Economic indicators

	2010	2015	2020
GDP: Gross domestic product (million current US$)	8 741	10 702	14 549[c]
GDP growth rate (annual %, const. 2015 prices)	3.5	10.7	6.6[c]
GDP per capita (current US$)	21 099.5	24 685.0	33 122.8[c]
Economy: Agriculture (% of Gross Value Added)[e]	1.7	1.2	1.0[c]
Economy: Industry (% of Gross Value Added)[e,f]	19.0	13.3	12.7[c]
Economy: Services and other activity (% of GVA)[e,g,h]	76.9	83.5	84.6[c]
Employment in agriculture (% of employed)	1.3	1.5	0.9[i]
Employment in industry (% of employed)	25.5	20.0	18.0[i]
Employment in services & other sectors (% employed)	73.1	78.5	81.0[i]
Unemployment rate (% of labour force)[i]	6.8	5.4	3.4
Labour force participation rate (female/male pop. %)[i]	34.0 / 66.4	42.2 / 67.0	45.9 / 66.8
CPI: Consumer Price Index (2010=100)	100	108	113[d]
Agricultural production index (2004-2006=100)	98	93	90[i]
International trade: exports (million current US$)	3 717	3 915	4 143[d]
International trade: imports (million current US$)	5 732	6 788	8 211[d]
International trade: balance (million current US$)	- 2 015	- 2 873	- 4 068[d]
Balance of payments, current account (million US$)	- 420	301	1 436[d]

Major trading partners

						2019
Export partners (% of exports)	Germany	13.4	Italy	7.7	France	7.3
Import partners (% of imports)	United Kingdom	18.5	Italy	16.9	Germany	6.6

Social indicators

	2010	2015	2020
Population growth rate (average annual %)[k]	0.5	0.9	0.4
Urban population (% of total population)	94.1	94.4	94.7[d]
Urban population growth rate (average annual %)[k]	0.5	0.6	...
Fertility rate, total (live births per woman)[k]	1.4	1.4	1.4
Life expectancy at birth (females/males, years)[k]	82.4 / 78.1	83.4 / 79.4	84.1 / 80.4
Population age distribution (0-14/60+ old, %)	15.0 / 23.0	14.2 / 25.4	14.4 / 28.1
International migrant stock (000/% of total pop.)	33.0 / 8.0	52.6 / 12.1	84.9 / 19.3[d]
Refugees and others of concern to the UNHCR (000)	7.4[l]	6.5	10.7
Infant mortality rate (per 1 000 live births)[k]	5.6	5.5	5.0
Health: Current expenditure (% of GDP)	8.2	9.2	9.3[a]
Health: Physicians (per 1 000 pop.)	2.2	2.9	...
Education: Government expenditure (% of GDP)	6.5	5.3	...
Education: Primary gross enrol. ratio (f/m per 100 pop.)	101.9 / 101.6	104.3 / 102.8	105.1 / 104.9[a]
Education: Secondary gross enrol. ratio (f/m per 100 pop.)	98.2 / 110.0	97.8 / 92.1	104.7 / 104.8[a]
Education: Tertiary gross enrol. ratio (f/m per 100 pop.)	42.9 / 32.0	55.0 / 39.9	63.2 / 46.0[e]
Intentional homicide rate (per 100 000 pop.)	1.0	0.9	1.6[c]
Seats held by women in the National Parliament (%)	8.7	12.9	13.4[m]

Environment and infrastructure indicators

	2010	2015	2020
Individuals using the Internet (per 100 inhabitants)	63.0[n]	76.0[o]	81.7[c]
Research & Development expenditure (% of GDP)	0.6	0.7	0.6[p,c]
Threatened species (number)	26	31	49
Forested area (% of land area)[i]	1.1	1.1	1.1[a]
CO2 emission estimates (million tons/tons per capita)	2.6 / 6.2	1.6 / 3.7	1.5 / 3.3[a]
Energy production, primary (Petajoules)	0	1	1[a]
Energy supply per capita (Gigajoules)	85	63	66[a]
Tourist/visitor arrivals at national borders (000)[q]	1 339	1 783	2 599[c]
Important sites for terrestrial biodiversity protected (%)	77.5	78.8	84.5[d]
Pop. using safely managed sanitation (urban/rural %)	93.0 / 93.0	93.0 / 93.0	93.0 / 93.0[a]
Net Official Development Assist. disbursed (% of GNI)	0.18	0.17	0.21[a]

2017. **b** Refers to the localities of the Northern Harbour and Southern Harbour. **c** 2018. **d** 2019. **e** Data classified according to ISIC Rev. 4. **f** Excludes publishing activities. Includes irrigation and canals. **g** Excludes computer and related activities and radio/TV activities. **h** Excludes repair of personal and household goods. **i** Estimate. **j** 2016. **k** Data refers to a 5-year period preceding the reference year. **l** Data as at the end of December. **m** Data are as at 1 January of reporting year. **n** Population aged 16 to 74 years. **o** Users in the last 3 months. **p** Provisional data. **q** Departures by air and by sea.

Marshall Islands

Region	Micronesia	UN membership date	17 September 1991
Population (000, 2020)	53	Surface area (km2)	181 [a]
Pop. density (per km2, 2020)	295.8	Sex ratio (m per 100 f)	104.5 [b,c]
Capital city	Majuro	National currency	US Dollar (USD)
Capital city pop. (000, 2020)	30.7 [d]		

Economic indicators

	2010	2015	2020
GDP: Gross domestic product (million current US$)	168	181	214 [d]
GDP growth rate (annual %, const. 2015 prices)	7.1	- 0.6	2.6 [d]
GDP per capita (current US$)	2 986.1	3 159.2	3 666.9 [d]
Economy: Agriculture (% of Gross Value Added)	15.4	14.4	15.7 [d]
Economy: Industry (% of Gross Value Added)	12.4	10.3	12.1 [d]
Economy: Services and other activity (% of GVA)	65.3	71.5	68.7 [d]
Employment in agriculture (% of employed)	11.0 [b,e]	...	...
Employment in industry (% of employed)	9.4 [b,e]	...	...
Employment in services & other sectors (% employed)	79.6 [b,e]	...	...
Unemployment rate (% of labour force)	...	4.7 [b,f]	...
Agricultural production index (2004-2006=100)	112	110	104 [c]
International trade: exports (million current US$) [g]	17	25	34 [h]
International trade: imports (million current US$) [g]	76	84	71 [h]
International trade: balance (million current US$) [g]	- 60	- 59	- 37 [h]
Balance of payments, current account (million US$)	- 14	- 7	53 [d]

Major trading partners

							2019
Export partners (% of exports) [g]	Thailand	18.8	Malaysia	18.2	China	17.3
Import partners (% of imports) [g]	Areas nes [i]	77.4	China	10.2	Brazil	3.8

Social indicators

	2010	2015	2020
Population growth rate (average annual %)	0.1 [i]	0.2 [i]	0.1
Urban population (% of total population)	73.6	75.8	77.4 [h]
Urban population growth rate (average annual %) [j]	0.8	0.8	...
Fertility rate, total (live births per woman)	...	4.1 [f]	...
Life expectancy at birth (females/males, years)	... / ...	72.5 / 71.3 [b,f]	... / ...
Population age distribution (0-14/60+ years old, %)	40.9 / 4.5 [k,l]	... / ...	39.0 / 5.5 [b,c]
International migrant stock (000/% of total pop.)	3.1 / 5.5	3.3 / 5.7	3.3 / 5.6 [h]
Infant mortality rate (per 1 000 live births)	...	25.4 [m,f]	...
Health: Current expenditure (% of GDP) [n,o]	15.2	17.6	16.4 [a]
Health: Physicians (per 1 000 pop.)	0.6	0.4 [p]	...
Education: Primary gross enrol. ratio (f/m per 100 pop.)	97.4 / 98.8 [q]	86.5 / 88.5	84.6 / 84.9 [c]
Education: Secondary gross enrol. ratio (f/m per 100 pop.)	79.3 / 75.6 [q]	68.8 / 64.1	66.6 / 62.4 [c]
Education: Tertiary gross enrol. ratio (f/m per 100 pop.)	... / ...	23.8 / 23.5 [p]	... / ...
Seats held by women in the National Parliament (%)	3.0	3.0	6.1 [r]

Environment and infrastructure indicators

	2010	2015	2020
Individuals using the Internet (per 100 inhabitants) [g]	7.0	19.3	38.7 [a]
Threatened species (number)	84	95	104
Forested area (% of land area) [g]	70.2	70.2	70.2 [a]
Energy production, primary (Petajoules) [g]	0	0	0 [a]
Energy supply per capita (Gigajoules) [g]	41	42	43 [a]
Tourist/visitor arrivals at national borders (000) [s]	5	6	7 [d]
Important sites for terrestrial biodiversity protected (%)	8.4	10.1	10.1 [h]
Net Official Development Assist. received (% of GNI)	12.53	23.01	19.49 [d]

a 2017. b Break in the time series. c 2016. d 2018. e Data classified according to ISIC Rev. 3. f 2011. g Estimate. h 2019. i Areas not elsewhere specified. j Data refers to a 5-year period preceding the reference year. k Projections are prepared by the Secretariat of the Pacific Community based on 1999 census of population and housing. l Estimates should be viewed with caution as these are derived from scarce data. m Data refers to a 3-year period up to and including the reference year. n Data refer to fiscal years ending 30 September. o Health expenditure indicators are high as they spend a lot on health using direct funding from the United States and also from their domestic funds. Current health expenditure is mostly government. p 2012. q 2009. r Data are as at 1 January of reporting year. s Arrivals by air.

Martinique

Region	Caribbean	Population (000, 2020)	375
Surface area (km2)	1 128ª	Pop. density (per km2, 2020)	354.0
Sex ratio (m per 100 f)	85.2	Capital city	Fort-de-France
National currency	Euro (EUR)	Capital city pop. (000, 2020)	79.4ᵇ
Exchange rate (per US$)	0.9ᶜ		

Economic indicators	2010	2015	2020
Employment in agriculture (% of employed)ᵈ,ᵉ	4.1	3.9ᶠ	...
Employment in industry (% of employed)ᵈ,ᵉ	11.9	11.8ᶠ	...
Employment in services & other sectors (% of employed)ᵈ,ᵉ	65.3	69.0ᶠ	...
Unemployment rate (% of labour force)ᵈ	21.0	22.8ᵍ,ʰ	...
Labour force participation rate (female/male pop. %)	43.3 / 49.1ᵈ	52.6 / 53.8ᵈ,ᵍ,ʰ	... / ...
CPI: Consumer Price Index (2010=100)ⁱ	100	106	109ᶜ
Agricultural production index (2004-2006=100)	82	80	79ʲ

Social indicators	2010	2015	2020
Population growth rate (average annual %)ᵏ	- 0.1	- 0.8	- 0.2
Urban population (% of total population)	89.0	89.0	89.1ᶜ
Urban population growth rate (average annual %)ᵏ	- 0.2	- 0.5	...
Fertility rate, total (live births per woman)ᵏ	2.0	2.0	1.9
Life expectancy at birth (females/males, years)ᵏ	83.2 / 76.7	84.4 / 77.8	85.4 / 78.9
Population age distribution (0-14/60+ years old, %)	19.5 / 20.6	17.3 / 25.4	15.7 / 29.2
International migrant stock (000/% of total pop.)	59.6 / 15.1	61.7 / 16.3	61.6 / 16.4ᶜ
Infant mortality rate (per 1 000 live births)ᵏ	7.6	6.4	5.6
Intentional homicide rate (per 100 000 pop.)	2.8ˡ	...	...

Environment and infrastructure indicators	2010	2015	2020
Threatened species (number)	31	45	62
Forested area (% of land area)ᵐ	45.8	45.8	45.8ª
Energy production, primary (Petajoules)	1ᵐ,ⁿ	...	...
Tourist/visitor arrivals at national borders (000)	478	487	537ᵇ
Important sites for terrestrial biodiversity protected (%)	97.2	97.2	99.7ᶜ

a 2017. b 2018. c 2019. d Excluding the institutional population. e Population aged 15 to 64 years. f 2012. g Break in the time series. h 2013. i Calculated by the UN Statistics Division from national indices. j 2016. k Data refers to a 5-year period preceding the reference year. l 2009. m Estimate. n Data after 2010 are included in France.

Mauritania

Region	Western Africa	UN membership date	27 October 1961
Population (000, 2020)	4 650	Surface area (km2)	1 030 700 [a]
Pop. density (per km2, 2020)	4.5	Sex ratio (m per 100 f)	100.9
Capital city	Nouakchott	National currency	Ouguiya (MRU)
Capital city pop. (000, 2020)	1 259.0 [b]	Exchange rate (per US$)	37.3 [b]

Economic indicators

	2010	2015	2020
GDP: Gross domestic product (million current US$)	5 450	6 321	7 620 [c]
GDP growth rate (annual %, const. 2015 prices)	6.9	4.1	3.6 [c]
GDP per capita (current US$)	1 559.6	1 562.1	1 730.4 [c]
Economy: Agriculture (% of Gross Value Added)	17.8	22.4	24.1 [c]
Economy: Industry (% of Gross Value Added)	42.2	25.3	26.8 [c]
Economy: Services and other activity (% of GVA)	50.9	57.6	56.8 [c]
Employment in agriculture (% of employed) [d]	56.9	53.8	50.6
Employment in industry (% of employed) [d]	11.9	12.5	13.1
Employment in services & other sectors (% employed) [d]	31.2	33.7	36.3
Unemployment rate (% of labour force) [d]	9.8	9.8	9.6
Labour force participation rate (female/male pop. %) [d]	28.0 / 64.5	28.4 / 63.1	28.9 / 63.0
CPI: Consumer Price Index (2010=100)	...	...	110 [e,b]
Agricultural production index (2004-2006=100)	109	125	120 [f]
International trade: exports (million current US$)	1 819	1 522 [d]	2 301 [d,b]
International trade: imports (million current US$)	1 708	3 677 [d]	3 525 [d,b]
International trade: balance (million current US$)	111	- 2 156 [d]	- 1 224 [d,b]
Balance of payments, current account (million current US$)	...	- 956	- 973 [c]

Major trading partners

							2019
Export partners (% of exports) [d]	China	35.1	Switzerland	15.4	Spain		11.6
Import partners (% of imports) [d]	Rep. of Korea	18.1	United Arab Emirates	8.9	Norway		7.8

Social indicators

	2010	2015	2020
Population growth rate (average annual %) [g]	2.9	2.9	2.8
Urban population (% of total population)	46.6	51.1	54.5 [b]
Urban population growth rate (average annual %) [g]	4.9	4.8	...
Fertility rate, total (live births per woman) [g]	5.1	4.9	4.6
Life expectancy at birth (females/males, years) [g]	63.7 / 60.1	65.0 / 61.4	66.2 / 63.0
Population age distribution (0-14/60+ years old, %)	41.2 / 4.8	40.5 / 4.9	39.7 / 5.1
International migrant stock (000/% of total pop.) [h,i]	84.7 / 2.4	166.6 / 4.1	173.0 / 3.8 [b]
Refugees and others of concern to the UNHCR (000)	27.0 [i]	77.3	87.3 [b]
Infant mortality rate (per 1 000 live births) [g]	65.6	58.9	53.4
Health: Current expenditure (% of GDP)	3.4	4.7	4.4 [a]
Health: Physicians (per 1 000 pop.)	0.2	0.2	0.2 [c]
Education: Government expenditure (% of GDP)	3.6	2.9 [k]	2.6 [d,f]
Education: Primary gross enrol. ratio (f/m per 100 pop.)	102.0 / 97.5	107.0 / 102.0	102.8 / 97.1 [c]
Education: Secondary gross enrol. ratio (f/m per 100 pop.)	19.1 / 22.4 [d]	30.3 / 32.5	37.1 / 36.5 [c]
Education: Tertiary gross enrol. ratio (f/m per 100 pop.)	2.5 / 6.2	3.7 / 7.4	3.3 / 6.6 [a]
Seats held by women in the National Parliament (%)	22.1	25.2	20.3 [l]

Environment and infrastructure indicators

	2010	2015	2020
Individuals using the Internet (per 100 inhabitants) [d]	4.0	15.2	20.8 [a]
Research & Development expenditure (% of GDP)	...	...	~0.0 [m,n,c]
Threatened species (number)	58	69	94
Forested area (% of land area)	0.2	0.2	0.2 [d,a]
Energy production, primary (Petajoules)	34	30	30 [a]
Energy supply per capita (Gigajoules)	12	14 [d]	17 [a]
Important sites for terrestrial biodiversity protected (%)	11.2	11.2	11.2 [b]
Net Official Development Assist. received (% of GNI)	8.75	7.08	8.39 [c]

a 2017. b 2019. c 2018. d Estimate. e Index base: 2014=100. f 2016. g Data refers to a 5-year period preceding the reference year. h Including refugees. i Refers to foreign citizens. j Data as at the end of December. k 2013. l Data are as at 1 January of reporting year. m Partial data. n Higher Education only.

Mauritius

Region	Eastern Africa	UN membership date	24 April 1968
Population (000, 2020)	1 272 [a]	Surface area (km2)	1 969 [b,c]
Pop. density (per km2, 2020)	626.5 [a]	Sex ratio (m per 100 f)	97.4 [a]
Capital city	Port Louis	National currency	Mauritius Rupee (MUR)
Capital city pop. (000, 2020)	149.4 [d]	Exchange rate (per US$)	36.6 [e]

Economic indicators

	2010	2015	2020
GDP: Gross domestic product (million current US$)	10 004	11 692	14 220 [d]
GDP growth rate (annual %, const. 2015 prices)	4.4	3.6	3.8 [d]
GDP per capita (current US$)	8 016.1	9 283.6	11 222.0 [d]
Economy: Agriculture (% of Gross Value Added) [f]	4.1	3.6	3.2 [d]
Economy: Industry (% of Gross Value Added) [g]	25.3	21.7	20.1 [d]
Economy: Services and other activity (% of GVA) [h,i]	69.6	76.0	77.3 [d]
Employment in agriculture (% of employed)	8.6	6.9 [j]	5.9 [j]
Employment in industry (% of employed)	28.7	26.6 [j]	25.1 [j]
Employment in services & other sectors (% employed)	62.7	66.5 [j]	69.0 [j]
Unemployment rate (% of labour force) [j]	7.6	7.4	6.7
Labour force participation rate (female/male pop. %) [j]	43.0 / 74.1	45.7 / 73.4	45.1 / 71.7
CPI: Consumer Price Index (2010=100) [k]	100	120	130 [e]
Agricultural production index (2004-2006=100)	99	94	92 [l]
International trade: exports (million current US$)	1 850	2 481	1 876 [e]
International trade: imports (million current US$)	4 402	4 458	5 601 [e]
International trade: balance (million current US$)	- 2 553	- 1 977	- 3 725 [e]
Balance of payments, current account (million US$)	- 1 006	- 417	- 816 [d]

Major trading partners

							2019
Export partners (% of exports)	France	12.6	United Kingdom	11.1	United States	10.8
Import partners (% of imports)	China	16.7	India	13.9	South Africa	8.1

Social indicators

	2010	2015	2020
Population growth rate (average annual %) [a,m]	0.4	0.2	0.2
Urban population (% of total population) [a]	41.6	41.0	40.8 [e]
Urban population growth rate (average annual %) [a,m]	0.2	- 0.1	...
Fertility rate, total (live births per woman) [a,m]	1.7	1.5	1.4
Life expectancy at birth (females/males, years) [a,m]	76.2 / 69.4	77.7 / 70.7	78.2 / 71.4
Population age distribution (0-14/60+ years old, %) [a]	21.9 / 12.1	19.4 / 15.4	16.8 / 18.4
International migrant stock (000/% of total pop.) [e,n]	24.8 / 2.0	28.6 / 2.3	28.8 / 2.3 [e]
Refugees and others of concern to the UNHCR (000)	...	...	~0.0 [e]
Infant mortality rate (per 1 000 live births) [a,m]	13.2	12.0	11.2
Health: Current expenditure (% of GDP)	4.6	5.7	5.7 [c]
Health: Physicians (per 1 000 pop.)	1.2	2.0	2.5 [d]
Education: Government expenditure (% of GDP)	3.6	4.9	4.8 [d]
Education: Primary gross enrol. ratio (f/m per 100 pop.)	103.1 / 102.5	103.8 / 102.0	102.5 / 99.8 [d]
Education: Secondary gross enrol. ratio (f/m per 100 pop.)	91.3 / 87.2 [i]	99.5 / 95.3	97.8 / 92.5 [d]
Education: Tertiary gross enrol. ratio (f/m per 100 pop.)	36.9 / 30.5	42.5 / 32.4	47.5 / 33.9 [c]
Intentional homicide rate (per 100 000 pop.)	2.6	1.7	2.9 [d]
Seats held by women in the National Parliament (%)	17.1	11.6	20.0 [o]

Environment and infrastructure indicators

	2010	2015	2020
Individuals using the Internet (per 100 inhabitants)	28.3 [p]	50.1 [p]	58.6 [d]
Research & Development expenditure (% of GDP)	0.4 [q,r,s]	0.2 [q,t,u]	0.3 [d]
Threatened species (number)	222	249	272
Forested area (% of land area)	18.9	19.0	19.0 [j,c]
CO2 emission estimates (million tons/tons per capita)	3.7 / 2.9	4.0 / 3.1	4.2 / 3.3 [c]
Energy production, primary (Petajoules)	11	12	10 [c]
Energy supply per capita (Gigajoules)	50	53	55 [c]
Tourist/visitor arrivals at national borders (000)	935	1 151	1 399 [d]
Important sites for terrestrial biodiversity protected (%)	9.0	9.6	9.6 [e]
Net Official Development Assist. received (% of GNI)	1.26	0.62	0.44 [d]

Including Agalega, Rodrigues and Saint Brandon. **b** Excluding the islands of Saint Brandon and Agalega. **c** 2017. **d** 18, **e** 2019. **f** Data classified according to ISIC Rev. 4. **g** Excludes publishing activities. Includes irrigation and canals. **h** Excludes computer and related activities and radio/TV activities. **i** Excludes repair of personal and household goods. **j** Estimate. **k** Calculated by the UN Statistics Division from national indices. **l** 2016. **m** Data refers to a 5-year period preceding the reference year. **n** Refers to foreign citizens. **o** Data are as at 1 January of reporting year. **p** Population aged 5 years and over. **q** Overestimated or based on overestimated data. **r** Based on R&D budget instead of R&D expenditure. **s** 2005. **t** Break in the time series. **u** 2012.

Mayotte

Region	Eastern Africa	Population (000, 2020)	273	
Pop. density (per km2, 2020)	727.5	Sex ratio (m per 100 f)	96.8	
Capital city	Mamoudzou	National currency	Euro (EUR)	
Capital city pop. (000, 2020)	6.2 [a]	Exchange rate (per US$)	0.9 [b]	

Economic indicators	2010	2015	2020
International trade: exports (million current US$)	6 [c]	...	...
International trade: imports (million current US$)	309 [c]	...	...
International trade: balance (million current US$)	- 303 [c]	...	...

Social indicators	2010	2015	2020
Population growth rate (average annual %) [d]	3.2	2.8	2.6
Urban population (% of total population)	49.0	47.0	45.9 [b]
Urban population growth rate (average annual %) [d]	2.7	2.0	...
Fertility rate, total (live births per woman) [d]	4.6	4.1	3.7
Life expectancy at birth (females/males, years) [d]	81.9 / 74.5	82.9 / 76.0	82.9 / 76.0
Population age distribution (0-14/60+ years old, %)	42.9 / 5.1	41.7 / 5.6	39.0 / 6.1
International migrant stock (000/% of total pop.)	72.8 / 34.9	74.0 / 30.8	74.6 / 28.0 [b]
Infant mortality rate (per 1 000 live births) [d]	5.6	4.2	4.2
Intentional homicide rate (per 100 000 pop.)	5.9 [e]	...	...

Environment and infrastructure indicators	2010	2015	2020
Threatened species (number)	69	84	102
Forested area (% of land area) [f]	18.2	15.6	15.6 [g]
Energy production, primary (Petajoules)	0 [h]	...	...
Important sites for terrestrial biodiversity protected (%)	64.1	64.1	64.3 [b]

a 2018. b 2019. c 2005. d Data refers to a 5-year period preceding the reference year. e 2009. f Estimate. g 2017. h Data after 2010 are included in France.

Mexico

Region	Central America	UN membership date	07 November 1945
Population (000, 2020)	128 933	Surface area (km2)	1 964 375 a
Pop. density (per km2, 2020)	66.3	Sex ratio (m per 100 f)	95.8
Capital city	Mexico City	National currency	Mexican Peso (MXN)
Capital city pop. (000, 2020)	21 671.9 b,c	Exchange rate (per US$)	18.8 c

Economic indicators	2010	2015	2020
GDP: Gross domestic product (million current US$)	1 057 801	1 170 567	1 223 401 d
GDP growth rate (annual %, const. 2015 prices)	5.1	3.3	2.0 d
GDP per capita (current US$)	9 271.4	9 606.0	9 694.9 d
Economy: Agriculture (% of Gross Value Added) e	3.4	3.4	3.5 d
Economy: Industry (% of Gross Value Added) e,f	33.7	31.8	31.9 d
Economy: Services and other activity (% of GVA) e,g,h	56.4	55.1	54.6 d
Employment in agriculture (% of employed)	13.9	13.4	12.4 i
Employment in industry (% of employed)	24.4	25.2	26.2 i
Employment in services & other sectors (% employed)	61.7	61.4	61.4 i
Unemployment rate (% of labour force) i	5.3	4.3	3.6
Labour force participation rate (female/male pop. %) i	43.1 / 79.7	43.9 / 79.0	44.2 / 78.3
CPI: Consumer Price Index (2010=100)	100	119	142 c
Agricultural production index (2004-2006=100)	108	120	126 k
International trade: exports (million current US$) i	298 305	380 550	472 273 c
International trade: imports (million current US$) i	301 482	395 234	467 293 c
International trade: balance (million current US$) i	- 3 177	- 14 684	4 980 c
Balance of payments, current account (million US$)	- 4 872	- 31 011	- 2 444 c

Major trading partners						2019
Export partners (% of exports)	United States	76.0	Areas nes m	6.2	Canada	3.0
Import partners (% of imports)	United States	44.1	China	17.8	Japan	3.8

Social indicators	2010	2015	2020
Population growth rate (average annual %) n	1.5	1.3	1.1
Urban population (% of total population)	77.8	79.3	80.4 c
Urban population growth rate (average annual %) n	2.0	1.8	...
Fertility rate, total (live births per woman) n	2.4	2.3	2.1
Life expectancy at birth (females/males, years) n	78.0 / 72.4	77.9 / 72.0	77.8 / 72.1
Population age distribution (0-14/60+ years old, %)	29.5 / 8.8	27.6 / 10.0	25.8 / 11.2
International migrant stock (000/% of total pop.) o	969.5 / 0.8	1 028.8 / 0.8	1 060.7 / 0.8 c
Refugees and others of concern to the UNHCR (000)	1.6 p	2.2	302.1 c
Infant mortality rate (per 1 000 live births) n	17.1	15.2	13.5
Health: Current expenditure (% of GDP)	6.0	5.8	5.5 a
Health: Physicians (per 1 000 pop.)	2.2	2.3	2.4 a
Education: Government expenditure (% of GDP)	5.2	5.2	4.9 k
Education: Primary gross enrol. ratio (f/m per 100 pop.)	109.8 / 111.4	106.5 / 106.7	106.0 / 105.5 a
Education: Secondary gross enrol. ratio (f/m per 100 pop.)	90.4 / 83.8	104.1 / 97.6	108.2 / 100.7 a
Education: Tertiary gross enrol. ratio (f/m per 100 pop.)	27.3 / 27.9	31.6 / 32.1	40.6 / 39.8 a
Intentional homicide rate (per 100 000 pop.)	22.6	17.0	29.1 d
Seats held by women in the National Parliament (%)	27.6	38.0	48.2 q

Environment and infrastructure indicators	2010	2015	2020
Individuals using the Internet (per 100 inhabitants)	31.0 i	57.4 r,s	65.8 d
Research & Development expenditure (% of GDP)	0.5	0.4	0.3 i,d
Threatened species (number)	943	1 109	1 656
Forested area (% of land area)	34.2	34.0	34.0 i,a
CO2 emission estimates (million tons/tons per capita)	440.5 / 3.9	442.4 / 3.7	446.0 / 3.6 a
Energy production, primary (Petajoules)	9 403	8 031	6 989 a
Energy supply per capita (Gigajoules)	64	62	59 a
Tourist/visitor arrivals at national borders (000) t	23 290	32 093	41 313 d
Important sites for terrestrial biodiversity protected (%)	34.0	35.1	37.1 c
Pop. using safely managed sanitation (urban/rural %)	35.3 / ...	47.2 / ...	52.3 / ... a
Net Official Development Assist. received (% of GNI)	0.04	0.03	0.05 d

a 2017. b Refers to the total population in 76 municipalities of the Metropolitan Area of Mexico City. c 2019. d 2018. e Data classified according to ISIC Rev. 4. f Excludes publishing activities. Includes irrigation and canals. g Includes repair of personal and household goods. h Excludes computer and related activities and radio/TV activities. i Estimate. j Calculated by the UN Statistics Division from national indices. k 2016. l Imports FOB. m Areas not elsewhere specified. n Data refers to a 5-year period preceding the reference year. o Including refugees. p Data as at the end of December. q Data are as at 1 January of reporting year. r Break in the time series. s Population aged 6 years and over. t Including nationals residing abroad.

Micronesia (Federated States of)

Region	Micronesia	UN membership date	17 September 1991
Population (000, 2020)	115	Surface area (km2)	702 [a]
Pop. density (per km2, 2020)	164.3	Sex ratio (m per 100 f)	103.4
Capital city	Palikir	National currency	US Dollar (USD)
Capital city pop. (000, 2020)	7.0 [b]	Exchange rate (per US$)	1.0 [c]

Economic indicators	2010	2015	2020
GDP: Gross domestic product (million current US$)	297	315	371 [b]
GDP growth rate (annual %, const. 2015 prices)	2.1	4.9	1.4 [b]
GDP per capita (current US$)	2 884.0	2 893.6	3 296.4 [b]
Economy: Agriculture (% of Gross Value Added)	26.7	27.7	28.0 [b]
Economy: Industry (% of Gross Value Added)	7.8	6.5	6.5 [b]
Economy: Services and other activity (% of GVA)	79.6	75.2	76.5 [b]
CPI: Consumer Price Index (2010=100)	100	113	112 [a]
Agricultural production index (2004-2006=100)	96	127	101 [d]
International trade: exports (million current US$)	23	11 [e]	1 [e,c]
International trade: imports (million current US$)	168	67 [e]	8 [e,c]
International trade: balance (million current US$)	- 145	- 56 [e]	- 7 [e,c]
Balance of payments, current account (million US$)	- 25	22 [f]	...

Major trading partners						2019
Export partners (% of exports) [e]	Thailand	68.3	China	14.4	Japan	9.4
Import partners (% of imports) [e]	United States	36.2	China	14.8	Japan	14.4

Social indicators	2010	2015	2020
Population growth rate (average annual %) [g]	- 0.6	1.1	1.1
Urban population (% of total population)	22.3	22.5	22.8 [c]
Urban population growth rate (average annual %) [g]	- 0.5	0.3	...
Fertility rate, total (live births per woman) [g]	3.6	3.3	3.1
Life expectancy at birth (females/males, years) [g]	67.7 / 64.4	68.6 / 65.2	69.4 / 66.1
Population age distribution (0-14/60+ years old, %)	35.7 / 5.4	32.8 / 6.5	31.2 / 7.8
International migrant stock (000/% of total pop.)	2.8 / 2.7	2.8 / 2.5	2.8 / 2.5 [c]
Refugees and others of concern to the UNHCR (000)	...	~0.0	~0.0 [a]
Infant mortality rate (per 1 000 live births) [g]	35.0	30.3	23.5
Health: Current expenditure (% of GDP) [h]	13.1	12.5	12.4 [a]
Health: Physicians (per 1 000 pop.)	0.2 [i]	...	...
Education: Government expenditure (% of GDP)	...	12.5	...
Education: Primary gross enrol. ratio (f/m per 100 pop.)	113.8 / 112.4 [j]	96.0 / 98.3	... / ...
Education: Secondary gross enrol. ratio (f/m per 100 pop.)	86.6 / 79.9 [k]	... / ...	... / ...
Seats held by women in the National Parliament (%)	0.0	0.0	0.0 [l]

Environment and infrastructure indicators	2010	2015	2020
Individuals using the Internet (per 100 inhabitants) [e]	20.0	31.5	35.3 [a]
Threatened species (number)	148	163	170
Forested area (% of land area) [e]	91.6	91.8	91.8 [a]
Energy production, primary (Petajoules)	0	0	0 [a]
Energy supply per capita (Gigajoules)	15	20	20 [e,a]
Tourist/visitor arrivals at national borders (000) [m]	45	31	19 [b]
Important sites for terrestrial biodiversity protected (%)	~0.0	~0.0	~0.0 [c]

a 2017. **b** 2018. **c** 2019. **d** 2016. **e** Estimate. **f** 2014. **g** Data refers to a 5-year period preceding the reference year. **h** Data refer to fiscal years ending 30 September. **i** 2009. **j** 2007. **k** 2005. **l** Data are as at 1 January of reporting year. **m** Arrivals in the States of Kosrae, Chuuk, Pohnpei and Yap; excluding FSM citizens.

Monaco

Region	Western Europe	UN membership date	28 May 1993
Population (000, 2020)	39	Surface area (km2)	2 [a]
Pop. density (per km2, 2020)	26 373.8	Sex ratio (m per 100 f)	94.7 [b,c]
Capital city	Monaco	National currency	Euro (EUR)
Capital city pop. (000, 2020)	38.9 [d]	Exchange rate (per US$)	0.9 [e]

Economic indicators	2010	2015	2020
GDP: Gross domestic product (million current US$)	5 362	6 259	7 188 [d]
GDP growth rate (annual %, const. 2015 prices)	- 1.4	4.9	6.1 [d]
GDP per capita (current US$)	150 577.0	165 945.5	185 835.0 [d]
Economy: Industry (% of Gross Value Added) [f,g]	12.9	17.6	13.1 [d]
Economy: Services and other activity (% of GVA) [f,g]	76.5	73.9	74.6 [d]

Social indicators	2010	2015	2020
Population growth rate (average annual %)	1.9 [h]	0.6 [h]	0.5
Urban population (% of total population)	100.0	100.0	100.0 [e]
Urban population growth rate (average annual %) [h]	1.9	0.6	...
Population age distribution (0-14/60+ years old, %)	12.7 / 31.2 [b,c]	... / ...	... / ...
International migrant stock (000/% of total pop.)	21.1 / 59.3	26.0 / 68.9	26.5 / 68.0 [e]
Refugees and others of concern to the UNHCR (000)	~0.0 [i]	~0.0	~0.0 [e]
Health: Current expenditure (% of GDP) [j]	2.3	2.0	1.8 [a]
Health: Physicians (per 1 000 pop.)	...	7.5 [k]	...
Education: Government expenditure (% of GDP)	1.3	1.0 [k]	1.5 [a]
Intentional homicide rate (per 100 000 pop.)	0.0	0.0	...
Seats held by women in the National Parliament (%)	26.1	20.8	33.3 [l]

Environment and infrastructure indicators	2010	2015	2020
Individuals using the Internet (per 100 inhabitants)	75.0	93.4 [j]	97.1 [j,a]
Research & Development expenditure (% of GDP)	~0.0 [m,n]	...	...
Threatened species (number)	11	16	34
Tourist/visitor arrivals at national borders (000)	279	331	347 [d]
Pop. using safely managed drinking water (urban/rural, %)	100.0 / ...	100.0 / ...	100.0 / ... [a]
Pop. using safely managed sanitation (urban/rural %)	100.0 / ...	100.0 / ...	100.0 / ... [a]

a 2017. **b** De jure population. **c** 2008. **d** 2018. **e** 2019. **f** Data classified according to ISIC Rev. 4. **g** At producers' prices. **h** Data refers to a 5-year period preceding the reference year. **i** Data as at the end of December. **j** Estimate. **k** 2014. **l** Data are as at 1 January of reporting year. **m** Partial data. **n** 2005.

Mongolia

Region	Eastern Asia	UN membership date	27 October 1961
Population (000, 2020)	3 278	Surface area (km2)	1 564 116 [a]
Pop. density (per km2, 2020)	2.1	Sex ratio (m per 100 f)	97.1
Capital city	Ulaanbaatar	National currency	Tugrik (MNT)
Capital city pop. (000, 2020)	1 552.7 [b]	Exchange rate (per US$)	2 734.3 [b]

Economic indicators

	2010	2015	2020
GDP: Gross domestic product (million current US$)	7 189	11 750	13 010 [c]
GDP growth rate (annual %, const. 2015 prices)	6.4	2.4	6.7 [c]
GDP per capita (current US$)	2 643.3	3 918.6	4 103.7 [c]
Economy: Agriculture (% of Gross Value Added) [d]	13.1	14.5	12.2 [c]
Economy: Industry (% of Gross Value Added) [d,e]	37.0	33.8	42.8 [c]
Economy: Services and other activity (% of GVA) [d,f,g]	57.0	63.5	59.5 [c]
Employment in agriculture (% of employed)	33.5	28.5	26.9 [h]
Employment in industry (% of employed)	16.2	20.3	19.5 [h]
Employment in services & other sectors (% employed)	50.2	51.3	53.6 [h]
Unemployment rate (% of labour force) [h]	6.6	4.9	6.0
Labour force participation rate (female/male pop. %) [h]	53.1 / 65.1	53.8 / 67.2	53.1 / 66.1
CPI: Consumer Price Index (2010=100)	100 [i]	164 [i]	120 [j,b]
Agricultural production index (2004-2006=100)	114	153	161 [k]
International trade: exports (million current US$)	2 908 [h]	4 669	7 433 [h,b]
International trade: imports (million current US$)	3 200 [h]	3 797	6 039 [h,b]
International trade: balance (million current US$)	- 291 [h]	873	1 394 [h,b]
Balance of payments, current account (million US$)	- 885	- 948	- 2 162 [b]

Major trading partners

						2019
Export partners (% of exports) [h]	China	92.8	United Kingdom	2.5	Russian Federation	1.2
Import partners (% of imports) [h]	China	33.5	Russian Federation	29.1	Japan	9.6

Social indicators

	2010	2015	2020
Population growth rate (average annual %) [l]	1.5	2.0	1.8
Urban population (% of total population)	67.6	68.2	68.5 [b]
Urban population growth rate (average annual %) [l]	3.0	2.1	...
Fertility rate, total (live births per woman) [l]	2.4	2.8	2.9
Life expectancy at birth (females/males, years) [l]	70.3 / 62.4	72.7 / 64.5	73.8 / 65.5
Population age distribution (0-14/60+ years old, %)	27.0 / 5.6	28.9 / 6.2	31.1 / 7.3
International migrant stock (000/% of total pop.) [m]	16.1 / 0.6	19.9 / 0.7	21.1 / 0.7 [b]
Refugees and others of concern to the UNHCR (000)	0.3 [n]	~0.0	0.1 [b]
Infant mortality rate (per 1 000 live births) [l]	30.5	22.8	18.1
Health: Current expenditure (% of GDP)	3.7	4.2	4.0 [a]
Health: Physicians (per 1 000 pop.)	2.8	3.2	2.9 [k]
Education: Government expenditure (% of GDP)	4.6	4.2	4.1 [a]
Education: Primary gross enrol. ratio (f/m per 100 pop.)	124.3 / 127.2	99.4 / 101.3	102.8 / 105.3 [c]
Education: Secondary gross enrol. ratio (f/m per 100 pop.)	94.8 / 88.3	... / ...	... / ...
Education: Tertiary gross enrol. ratio (f/m per 100 pop.)	65.1 / 42.5	78.9 / 57.4	76.7 / 54.7 [c]
Intentional homicide rate (per 100 000 pop.)	8.8	7.1	6.2 [c]
Seats held by women in the National Parliament (%)	3.9	14.9	17.3 [o]

Environment and infrastructure indicators

	2010	2015	2020
Individuals using the Internet (per 100 inhabitants)	10.2	22.5	47.2 [c]
Research & Development expenditure (% of GDP) [p]	0.2	0.2	0.1 [c]
Threatened species (number)	36	36	43
Forested area (% of land area) [h]	8.4	8.1	8.1 [a]
CO2 emission estimates (million tons/tons per capita)	14.1 / 5.2	17.1 / 5.8	19.3 / 6.3 [a]
Energy production, primary (Petajoules)	655	654	1 311 [a]
Energy supply per capita (Gigajoules)	61	91	128 [a]
Tourist/visitor arrivals at national borders (000)	456	386	529 [c]
Important sites for terrestrial biodiversity protected (%)	37.2	40.0	41.7 [b]
Net Official Development Assist. received (% of GNI)	4.34	2.19	2.88 [c]

a 2017. b 2019. c 2018. d Data classified according to ISIC Rev. 4. e Excludes publishing activities. Includes irrigation and canals. f Excludes computer and related activities and radio/TV activities. g Excludes repair of personal and household goods. h Estimate. i Calculated by the UN Statistics Division from national indices. j Index base: 2015=100. k 2016. l Data refers to a 5-year period preceding the reference year. m Refers to foreign citizens. n Data as at the end of December. o Data are as at 1 January of reporting year. p Partial data.

Montenegro

Region	Southern Europe	UN membership date	28 June 2006
Population (000, 2020)	628	Surface area (km2)	13 812 [a]
Pop. density (per km2, 2020)	46.7	Sex ratio (m per 100 f)	97.8
Capital city	Podgorica	National currency	Euro (EUR)
Capital city pop. (000, 2020)	177.2 [b,c]	Exchange rate (per US$)	0.9 [d]

Economic indicators	2010	2015	2020
GDP: Gross domestic product (million current US$)	4 139	4 053	5 507 [c]
GDP growth rate (annual %, const. 2015 prices)	2.7	3.4	5.1 [c]
GDP per capita (current US$)	6 630.0	6 464.7	8 771.7 [c]
Economy: Agriculture (% of Gross Value Added) [e]	9.2	9.8	8.2 [c]
Economy: Industry (% of Gross Value Added) [e,f]	20.5	17.4	19.5 [c]
Economy: Services and other activity (% of GVA) [e,g,h]	52.5	57.1	55.6 [c]
Employment in agriculture (% of employed)	6.2 [i]	7.7	7.8 [i]
Employment in industry (% of employed)	18.7 [i]	17.5	19.2 [i]
Employment in services & other sectors (% employed)	75.1 [i]	74.8	73.0 [i]
Unemployment rate (% of labour force) [i]	19.6	17.5	14.8
Labour force participation rate (female/male pop. %) [i]	41.4 / 55.8	46.6 / 59.4	46.6 / 62.7
CPI: Consumer Price Index (2010=100)	100	111	117 [j,d]
Agricultural production index (2004-2006=100)	63	71	66 [k]
International trade: exports (million current US$)	437	353	459 [i,d]
International trade: imports (million current US$)	2 182	2 050	2 903 [i,d]
International trade: balance (million current US$)	- 1 745	- 1 697	- 2 444 [i,d]
Balance of payments, current account (million US$)	- 852	- 443	- 837 [d]

Major trading partners						2019
Export partners (% of exports) [i]	Serbia	23.6	Hungary	11.7	Areas nes [l]	8.6
Import partners (% of imports) [i]	Serbia	19.3	China	10.1	Germany	9.2

Social indicators	2010	2015	2020
Population growth rate (average annual %) [m]	0.3	0.1	-0.0
Urban population (% of total population)	64.1	65.8	67.2 [d]
Urban population growth rate (average annual %) [m]	0.8	0.6	...
Fertility rate, total (live births per woman) [m]	1.8	1.7	1.8
Life expectancy at birth (females/males, years) [m]	76.5 / 71.9	78.5 / 73.6	79.1 / 74.2
Population age distribution (0-14/60+ years old, %)	19.2 / 17.9	18.5 / 20.3	18.0 / 22.1
International migrant stock (000/% of total pop.)	78.5 / 12.6	71.7 / 11.4	71.0 / 11.3 [d]
Refugees and others of concern to the UNHCR (000)	18.3 [n]	19.8	13.6 [d]
Infant mortality rate (per 1 000 live births) [m]	10.9	4.3	2.8
Health: Physicians (per 1 000 pop.)	2.0	2.4	2.8 [c]
Education: Primary gross enrol. ratio (f/m per 100 pop.)	110.6 / 110.3	95.5 / 95.3	97.6 / 102.2 [c]
Education: Secondary gross enrol. ratio (f/m per 100 pop.)	101.9 / 99.0	93.5 / 92.0	90.5 / 89.3 [c]
Education: Tertiary gross enrol. ratio (f/m per 100 pop.)	58.3 / 46.5	... / ...	64.9 / 47.9 [c]
Intentional homicide rate (per 100 000 pop.)	2.4	2.7	2.2 [c]
Seats held by women in the National Parliament (%)	11.1	17.3	29.6 [o]

Environment and infrastructure indicators	2010	2015	2020
Individuals using the Internet (per 100 inhabitants)	37.5 [i]	68.1 [p]	71.5 [c]
Research & Development expenditure (% of GDP)	1.1 [q]	0.4	0.4 [c]
Threatened species (number)	72	85	113
Forested area (% of land area) [i]	61.5	61.5	61.5 [a]
CO2 emission estimates (million tons/tons per capita)	2.6 / 4.2	2.4 / 3.8	2.2 / 3.5 [a]
Energy production, primary (Petajoules)	35	30	27 [a]
Energy supply per capita (Gigajoules)	77	67	68 [a]
Tourist/visitor arrivals at national borders (000)	1 088	1 560	2 077 [c]
Important sites for terrestrial biodiversity protected (%)	11.1	11.1	11.1 [d]
Pop. using safely managed drinking water (urban/rural, %)	94.6 / ...	93.8 / ...	93.8 / ... [a]
Pop. using safely managed sanitation (urban/rural %)	30.6 / ...	30.1 / ...	29.8 / ... [a]
Net Official Development Assist. received (% of GNI)	1.95	2.41	2.83 [c]

2017. **b** Refers to the urban population of Podgorica municipality. **c** 2018. **d** 2019. **e** Data classified according to ISIC Rev. 4. **f** Excludes publishing activities. Includes irrigation and canals. **g** Excludes repair of personal and household goods. **h** Excludes computer and related activities and radio/TV activities. **i** Estimate. **j** Calculated by the UN Statistics Division from national indices. **k** 2016. **l** Areas not elsewhere specified. **m** Data refers to a 5-year period preceding the reference year. **n** Data as at the end of December. **o** Data are as at 1 January of reporting year. **p** Population aged 16 to 74 years. **q** 2007.

Montserrat

Region	Caribbean	Population (000, 2020)	5
Surface area (km2)	103[a]	Pop. density (per km2, 2020)	52.4
Sex ratio (m per 100 f)	106.0[b]	Capital city	Brades Estate
National currency	E. Caribbean Dollar (XCD)[c]	Capital city pop. (000, 2020)	0.5[d]
Exchange rate (per US$)	2.7[e]		

Economic indicators	2010	2015	2020
GDP: Gross domestic product (million current US$)	56	61	64[d]
GDP growth rate (annual %, const. 2015 prices)	- 2.8	- 1.9	3.7[d]
GDP per capita (current US$)	11 331.1	12 357.9	12 753.6[d]
Economy: Agriculture (% of Gross Value Added)	1.1	1.4	1.4[d]
Economy: Industry (% of Gross Value Added)	13.3	12.4	13.4[d]
Economy: Services and other activity (% of GVA)	91.2	86.5	86.5[d]
Unemployment rate (% of labour force)	...	5.6[f]	...
CPI: Consumer Price Index (2010=100)[g]	100	108	110[d]
Agricultural production index (2004-2006=100)	98	104	104[b]
International trade: exports (million current US$)	1	3[g]	6[g,e]
International trade: imports (million current US$)[g]	29	39	35[e]
International trade: balance (million current US$)[g]	- 28	- 36	- 28[e]
Balance of payments, current account (million US$)	- 19	- 1	- 1[d]

Major trading partners						2019
Export partners (% of exports)[g]	United States	19.5	Antigua and Barbuda	17.2	France	13.9
Import partners (% of imports)[g]	United States	74.3	United Kingdom	5.1	Egypt	2.9

Social indicators	2010	2015	2020
Population growth rate (average annual %)	0.7[h]	0.7[h]	0.5
Urban population (% of total population)	9.2	9.0	9.1[e]
Urban population growth rate (average annual %)[h]	0.3	0.5	...
Population age distribution (0-14/60+ years old, %)	19.6 / 19.0[i,j]	19.7 / 19.6[k,f]	... / ...
International migrant stock (000/% of total pop.)	1.3 / 26.4	1.4 / 27.2	1.4 / 27.6[e]
Refugees and others of concern to the UNHCR (000)	~0.0[l]	...	...
Education: Government expenditure (% of GDP)	5.1[m]	...	...
Education: Primary gross enrol. ratio (f/m per 100 pop.)	163.4 / 154.0[m]	96.0 / 92.9[n]	114.8 / 104.6[d]
Education: Secondary gross enrol. ratio (f/m per 100 pop.)	123.7 / 124.0[m]	180.4 / 173.5[n]	105.9 / 94.5[d]
Education: Tertiary gross enrol. ratio (f/m per 100 pop.)	30.2 / 4.9	... / ...	... / ...
Intentional homicide rate (per 100 000 pop.)	20.4[o]	20.3[p]	...

Environment and infrastructure indicators	2010	2015	2020
Individuals using the Internet (per 100 inhabitants)	35.0	54.6[f]	...
Threatened species (number)	35	54	62
Forested area (% of land area)[g]	25.0	25.0	25.0[a]
Energy supply per capita (Gigajoules)	175	149	72[a]
Tourist/visitor arrivals at national borders (000)	6	9	9[d]
Important sites for terrestrial biodiversity protected (%)	0.0	30.6	30.6[e]

a 2017. **b** 2016. **c** East Caribbean Dollar. **d** 2018. **e** 2019. **f** 2011. **g** Estimate. **h** Data refers to a 5-year period preceding the reference year. **i** Intercensus data. **j** 2006. **k** De jure population. **l** Data as at the end of December. **m** 2009. **n** 2014. **o** 2008. **p** 2012.

Morocco

Region	Northern Africa	UN membership date	12 November 1956
Population (000, 2020)	36 911	Surface area (km2)	446 550 [a]
Pop. density (per km2, 2020)	82.7	Sex ratio (m per 100 f)	98.5
Capital city	Rabat	National currency	Moroccan Dirham (MAD)
Capital city pop. (000, 2020)	1 864.9 [b,c]	Exchange rate (per US$)	9.6 [c]

Economic indicators

	2010	2015	2020
GDP: Gross domestic product (million current US$) [d]	93 217	101 179	117 921 [e]
GDP growth rate (annual %, const. 2015 prices) [d]	4.0	4.9	3.7 [e]
GDP per capita (current US$) [d]	2 882.1	2 918.9	3 272.9 [e]
Economy: Agriculture (% of Gross Value Added) [d]	14.4	14.3	13.9 [e]
Economy: Industry (% of Gross Value Added) [d]	28.6	29.5	29.4 [e]
Economy: Services and other activity (% of GVA) [d]	64.0	64.3	60.8 [e]
Employment in agriculture (% of employed) [f]	40.5	37.2	34.1
Employment in industry (% of employed) [f]	21.5	21.7	21.8
Employment in services & other sectors (% employed) [f]	38.0	41.1	44.0
Unemployment rate (% of labour force) [f]	9.1	9.5	9.0
Labour force participation rate (female/male pop. %) [f]	25.5 / 75.5	23.0 / 72.5	21.4 / 69.9
CPI: Consumer Price Index (2010=100) [g]	100	106	111 [c]
Agricultural production index (2004-2006=100)	126	142	122 [h]
International trade: exports (million current US$)	17 765	22 337	29 328 [c]
International trade: imports (million current US$)	35 379	38 146	51 075 [c]
International trade: balance (million current US$)	- 17 614	- 15 809	- 21 747 [c]
Balance of payments, current account (million US$)	- 3 925	- 2 161	- 4 915 [c]

Major trading partners

						2019
Export partners (% of exports)	Spain	24.1	France	21.6	Italy	4.7
Import partners (% of imports)	Spain	15.6	France	12.2	China	10.1

Social indicators

	2010	2015	2020
Population growth rate (average annual %) [i]	1.2	1.4	1.3
Urban population (% of total population)	58.0	60.8	63.0 [c]
Urban population growth rate (average annual %) [i]	2.2	2.4	...
Fertility rate, total (live births per woman) [i]	2.5	2.6	2.4
Life expectancy at birth (females/males, years) [i]	74.7 / 72.1	76.3 / 73.7	77.5 / 75.1
Population age distribution (0-14/60+ years old, %)	28.5 / 8.6	27.7 / 9.9	26.8 / 11.9
International migrant stock (000/% of total pop.) [j]	70.9 / 0.2	92.4 / 0.3	98.6 / 0.3 [c]
Refugees and others of concern to the UNHCR (000)	1.1 [k]	4.4	9.1 [c]
Infant mortality rate (per 1 000 live births) [i]	26.6	24.2	19.9
Health: Current expenditure (% of GDP)	5.9	5.1	5.2 [a]
Health: Physicians (per 1 000 pop.)	0.6 [l]	0.9 [m]	0.7 [a]
Education: Government expenditure (% of GDP)	5.3 [l]	...	...
Education: Primary gross enrol. ratio (f/m per 100 pop.)	106.3 / 113.0	106.6 / 112.3	111.5 / 116.1 [e]
Education: Secondary gross enrol. ratio (f/m per 100 pop.)	58.8 / 67.6	64.1 / 75.1 [n]	76.6 / 83.7 [e]
Education: Tertiary gross enrol. ratio (f/m per 100 pop.)	13.8 / 15.3	27.8 / 29.0	35.7 / 36.2 [e]
Intentional homicide rate (per 100 000 pop.)	1.4	1.2	1.4 [e]
Seats held by women in the National Parliament (%)	10.5	17.0	20.5 [o]

Environment and infrastructure indicators

	2010	2015	2020
Individuals using the internet (per 100 inhabitants)	52.0 [p,q]	57.1 [r,s]	64.8 [e]
Research & Development expenditure (% of GDP)	0.7	...	...
Threatened species (number)	157	176	238
Forested area (% of land area) [f]	12.7	12.6	12.6 [a]
CO2 emission estimates (million tons/tons per capita)	46.4 / 1.4	55.4 / 1.6	58.1 / 1.6 [a]
Energy production, primary (Petajoules)	84	62	89 [a]
Energy supply per capita (Gigajoules)	23	23	24 [a]
Tourist/visitor arrivals at national borders (000) [t]	9 288	10 177	12 289 [e]
Important sites for terrestrial biodiversity protected (%)	20.7	53.8	53.8 [c]
Pop. using safely managed drinking water (urban/rural, %)	87.9 / 32.1	88.8 / 38.6	88.9 / 39.9 [a]
Pop. using safely managed sanitation (urban/rural %)	39.4 / ...	40.3 / ...	40.2 / ... [a]
Net Official Development Assist. received (% of GNI)	1.07	1.53	0.70 [c]

2017. **b** Including Salé and Temara. **c** 2019. **d** Including Western Sahara. **e** 2018. **f** Estimate. **g** Calculated by the UN Statistics Division from national indices. **h** 2016. **i** Data refers to a 5-year period preceding the reference year. **j** Refers to foreign citizens. **k** Data as at the end of December. **l** 2009. **m** 2014. **n** 2012. **o** Data are as at 1 January of reporting year. **p** Population aged 6 to 74 years. **q** Living in electrified areas. **r** Users in the last 3 months. **s** Population aged 5 years and over. **t** Including nationals residing abroad.

Mozambique

Region	Eastern Africa	UN membership date	16 September 1975
Population (000, 2020)	31 255	Surface area (km2)	799 380 [a]
Pop. density (per km2, 2020)	39.7	Sex ratio (m per 100 f)	94.5
Capital city	Maputo	National currency	Mozambique Metical (MZN)
Capital city pop. (000, 2020)	1 104.3 [b]	Exchange rate (per US$)	61.5 [b]

Economic indicators	2010	2015	2020
GDP: Gross domestic product (million current US$)	11 121	15 951	14 717 [c]
GDP growth rate (annual %, const. 2015 prices)	6.7	6.7	3.4 [c]
GDP per capita (current US$)	472.6	589.9	498.9 [c]
Economy: Agriculture (% of Gross Value Added) [d]	29.8	25.9	27.4 [c]
Economy: Industry (% of Gross Value Added) [d,e]	18.3	20.5	27.2 [c]
Economy: Services and other activity (% of GVA) [d,f,g]	57.5	60.0	55.6 [c]
Employment in agriculture (% of employed)	76.4 [h]	72.1	69.9 [h]
Employment in industry (% of employed)	5.3 [h]	7.7	8.6 [h]
Employment in services & other sectors (% employed)	18.3 [h]	20.1	21.5 [h]
Unemployment rate (% of labour force) [h]	3.3	3.4	3.2
Labour force participation rate (female/male pop. %) [h]	82.8 / 82.0	77.8 / 80.0	77.0 / 79.0
CPI: Consumer Price Index (2010=100) [i]	100	126	182 [b]
Agricultural production index (2004-2006=100)	146	141	149 [i]
International trade: exports (million current US$)	2 243	3 649 [h]	5 878 [h,b]
International trade: imports (million current US$)	3 564	7 852 [h]	8 270 [h,b]
International trade: balance (million current US$)	- 1 321	- 4 203 [h]	- 2 392 [h,b]
Balance of payments, current account (million US$)	- 1 679	- 5 968	- 4 501 [c]

Major trading partners						2019
Export partners (% of exports) [h]	India	27.6	Netherlands	21.2	South Africa	17.2
Import partners (% of imports) [h]	South Africa	26.1	China	11.8	United Arab Emirates	7.6

Social indicators	2010	2015	2020
Population growth rate (average annual %) [k]	2.8	2.8	2.9
Urban population (% of total population)	31.8	34.4	36.5 [b]
Urban population growth rate (average annual %) [k]	4.1	4.5	...
Fertility rate, total (live births per woman) [k]	5.5	5.2	4.9
Life expectancy at birth (females/males, years) [k]	53.3 / 48.8	56.8 / 51.5	62.8 / 57.0
Population age distribution (0-14/60+ years old, %)	45.7 / 4.7	45.4 / 4.5	44.1 / 4.4
International migrant stock (000/% of total pop.) [i]	306.5 / 1.3	321.8 / 1.2	334.7 / 1.1 [b]
Refugees and others of concern to the UNHCR (000)	10.0 [m]	18.8	25.1 [b]
Infant mortality rate (per 1 000 live births) [k]	78.7	62.8	53.9
Health: Current expenditure (% of GDP) [n]	5.1	5.3	4.9 [a]
Health: Physicians (per 1 000 pop.)	~0.0	~0.0	0.1 [c]
Education: Government expenditure (% of GDP)	4.3 [o]	6.5 [p]	...
Education: Primary gross enrol. ratio (f/m per 100 pop.)	105.9 / 119.2	103.4 / 113.8 [h]	108.4 / 116.8 [c]
Education: Secondary gross enrol. ratio (f/m per 100 pop.)	22.5 / 28.0	31.9 / 35.2 [h]	33.4 / 37.4 [a]
Education: Tertiary gross enrol. ratio (f/m per 100 pop.)	3.7 / 5.7	5.6 / 7.8	6.5 / 8.1 [c]
Intentional homicide rate (per 100 000 pop.)	3.7	3.5 [q]	...
Seats held by women in the National Parliament (%)	39.2	39.6	41.2 [r]

Environment and infrastructure indicators	2010	2015	2020
Individuals using the Internet (per 100 inhabitants)	4.2	16.9 [h]	10.0 [s,a]
Research & Development expenditure (% of GDP)	0.4 [t,u]	0.3	...
Threatened species (number)	209	268	426
Forested area (% of land area)	49.6	48.2	48.2 [h,a]
CO2 emission estimates (million tons/tons per capita)	2.4 / 0.1	6.2 / 0.2	7.6 / 0.3 [a]
Energy production, primary (Petajoules)	398	718	831 [a]
Energy supply per capita (Gigajoules)	13	16	15 [a]
Tourist/visitor arrivals at national borders (000) [v]	1 718 [u]	1 552	2 743 [c]
Important sites for terrestrial biodiversity protected (%)	17.4	21.7	21.7 [b]
Pop. using safely managed sanitation (urban/rural %)	... / 9.8	... / 14.4	... / 16.3 [a]
Net Official Development Assist. received (% of GNI)	19.80	12.54	12.89 [c]

a 2017. **b** 2019. **c** 2018. **d** Data classified according to ISIC Rev. 4. **e** Excludes publishing activities. Includes irrigation and canals. **f** Excludes repair of personal and household goods. **g** Excludes computer and related activities and radio/TV activities. **h** Estimate. **i** Calculated by the UN Statistics Division from national indices. **j** 2016. **k** Data refers to a 5-year period preceding the reference year. **l** Including refugees. **m** Data as at the end of December. **n** Data revision. **o** 2006. **p** 2013. **q** 2011. **r** Data are as at 1 January of reporting year. **s** Population aged 15 to 65 years. **t** Excluding business enterprise. **u** Break in the time series. **v** The data of all the border posts of the country are used.

Myanmar

Region	South-eastern Asia
Population (000, 2020)	54 410
Pop. density (per km2, 2020)	83.3
Capital city	Nay Pyi Taw
Capital city pop. (000, 2020)	546.5 [b]

UN membership date	19 April 1948
Surface area (km2)	676 577 [a]
Sex ratio (m per 100 f)	93.0
National currency	Kyat (MMK)
Exchange rate (per US$)	1 465.5 [b]

Economic indicators

	2010	2015	2020
GDP: Gross domestic product (million current US$)	41 445	62 543	72 745 [c]
GDP growth rate (annual %, const. 2015 prices)	10.2	7.0	6.2 [c]
GDP per capita (current US$)	819.1	1 187.2	1 354.4 [c]
Economy: Agriculture (% of Gross Value Added) [d]	36.9	26.8	26.3 [c]
Economy: Industry (% of Gross Value Added) [d]	26.5	34.5	34.7 [c]
Economy: Services and other activity (% of GVA) [d,e]	23.6	25.9	23.6 [c]
Employment in agriculture (% of employed)	53.5 [f]	51.7	48.1 [f]
Employment in industry (% of employed)	17.7 [f]	16.8	16.3 [f]
Employment in services & other sectors (% employed)	28.8 [f]	31.5	35.6 [f]
Unemployment rate (% of labour force) [f]	0.8	0.8	1.7
Labour force participation rate (female/male pop. %) [f]	53.6 / 82.3	51.9 / 80.7	47.3 / 77.2
CPI: Consumer Price Index (2010=100)	100	129	155 [c]
Agricultural production index (2004-2006=100)	135	136	137 [g]
International trade: exports (million current US$)	8 873	11 432	17 997 [b]
International trade: imports (million current US$)	4 866	16 913	18 578 [b]
International trade: balance (million current US$)	4 008	- 5 481	- 581 [b]
Balance of payments, current account (million US$)	1 574	- 2 838	- 2 137 [c]

Major trading partners

						2019
Export partners (% of exports)	China	31.7	Thailand	17.9	Japan	7.9
Import partners (% of imports)	China	34.7	Singapore	18.2	Thailand	11.7

Social indicators

	2010	2015	2020
Population growth rate (average annual %) [h]	0.7	0.8	0.6
Urban population (% of total population)	28.9	29.9	30.9 [b]
Urban population growth rate (average annual %) [h]	1.3	1.5	...
Fertility rate, total (live births per woman) [h]	2.5	2.2	2.2
Life expectancy at birth (females/males, years) [h]	65.8 / 59.1	68.0 / 61.3	69.8 / 63.7
Population age distribution (0-14/60+ years old, %)	30.0 / 7.3	27.8 / 8.5	25.5 / 10.0
International migrant stock (000/% of total pop.) [i]	76.4 / 0.2	73.3 / 0.1	76.0 / 0.1 [b]
Refugees and others of concern to the UNHCR (000)	859.4 [j]	1 466.5	883.5 [k,b]
Infant mortality rate (per 1 000 live births) [h]	52.0	43.7	38.4
Health: Current expenditure (% of GDP) [l,m,n]	1.8	5.2	4.7 [a]
Health: Physicians (per 1 000 pop.)	0.5	0.6 [o]	0.7 [c]
Education: Government expenditure (% of GDP)	...	0.8 [p]	2.2 [a]
Education: Primary gross enrol. ratio (f/m per 100 pop.)	97.6 / 98.6	100.3 / 103.3 [q]	109.7 / 114.8 [c]
Education: Secondary gross enrol. ratio (f/m per 100 pop.)	49.2 / 47.1	52.3 / 51.3 [q]	71.3 / 65.6 [c]
Education: Tertiary gross enrol. ratio (f/m per 100 pop.)	12.2 / 9.0 [r]	14.9 / 12.2 [o]	22.0 / 15.6 [c]
Intentional homicide rate (per 100 000 pop.)	1.6	2.2	2.3 [g]
Seats held by women in the National Parliament (%)	...	6.2	11.1 [s]

Environment and infrastructure indicators

	2010	2015	2020
Individuals using the Internet (per 100 inhabitants)	0.2	21.7 [f]	30.7 [f,a]
Research & Development expenditure (% of GDP)	...	...	~0.0 [t,u,v,w,a]
Threatened species (number)	249	301	357
Forested area (% of land area)	48.6	44.5 [f]	44.5 [f,a]
CO2 emission estimates (million tons/tons per capita)	7.9 / 0.2	18.7 / 0.4	30.4 / 0.6 [a]
Energy production, primary (Petajoules)	969	1 176	1 186 [a]
Energy supply per capita (Gigajoules)	13	16	16 [a]
Tourist/visitor arrivals at national borders (000)	792	4 681	3 551 [c]
Important sites for terrestrial biodiversity protected (%)	21.9	24.2	24.9 [b]
Net Official Development Assist. received (% of GNI)	0.72	2.02	2.44 [c]

2017. **b** 2019. **c** 2018. **d** At producers' prices. **e** Excludes hotels and restaurants. **f** Estimate. **g** 2016. **h** Data refers to a 5-year period preceding the reference year. **i** Refers to foreign citizens. **j** Data as at the end of December. The figure of persons of concern under the statelessness mandate relates to stateless persons in Rakhine state and persons of undetermined nationality residing in other states in Myanmar. The figure of stateless persons in Rakhine state has been estimated on the basis of the 2014 census report and 2017 General Administration Department (GAD) Ministry of Home Affairs (MoHA) data. **l** Data revision. **m** Country is still reporting data based on SHA 1.0. **n** Data refer to fiscal years beginning 1 April. **o** 2012. **p** 2011. **q** 2014. **r** 2007. **s** Data are as at 1 January of reporting year. **t** Break in the time series. **u** Excluding business enterprise. **v** Excluding private non-profit. **w** Partial data.

Namibia

Region	Southern Africa	UN membership date	23 April 1990
Population (000, 2020)	2 541	Surface area (km2)	824 116[a]
Pop. density (per km2, 2020)	3.1	Sex ratio (m per 100 f)	94.1
Capital city	Windhoek	National currency	Namibia Dollar (NAD)
Capital city pop. (000, 2020)	417.4[b]	Exchange rate (per US$)	14.1[b]

Economic indicators

	2010	2015	2020
GDP: Gross domestic product (million current US$)	11 282	11 651	14 519[c]
GDP growth rate (annual %, const. 2015 prices)	6.0	6.1	- 0.1[c]
GDP per capita (current US$)	5 324.6	5 032.9	5 930.1[c]
Economy: Agriculture (% of Gross Value Added)	9.2	6.3	7.6[c]
Economy: Industry (% of Gross Value Added)	29.8	30.5	31.1[c]
Economy: Services and other activity (% of GVA)	65.7	81.9	84.8[c]
Employment in agriculture (% of employed)[d]	28.1	24.5	21.8
Employment in industry (% of employed)[d]	13.9	17.0	16.4
Employment in services & other sectors (% employed)[d]	57.9	58.5	61.8
Unemployment rate (% of labour force)[d]	22.1	20.9	20.6
Labour force participation rate (female/male pop. %)[d]	52.6 / 63.0	56.4 / 65.4	56.6 / 63.6
CPI: Consumer Price Index (2010=100)[e]	100	129	158[b]
Agricultural production index (2004-2006=100)	90	92	93[f]
International trade: exports (million current US$)	5 848	4 628	6 258[b]
International trade: imports (million current US$)	5 980	7 697	8 086[b]
International trade: balance (million current US$)	- 131	- 3 069	- 1 828[b]
Balance of payments, current account (million US$)	- 389	- 1 559	- 284[b]

Major trading partners

						2019
Export partners (% of exports)	China	24.0	South Africa	16.2	Botswana	9.8
Import partners (% of imports)	South Africa	43.2	Zambia	14.9	China	3.9

Social indicators

	2010	2015	2020
Population growth rate (average annual %)[g]	1.8	1.8	1.9
Urban population (% of total population)	41.6	46.9	51.0[b]
Urban population growth rate (average annual %)[g]	3.9	4.6	...
Fertility rate, total (live births per woman)[g]	3.6	3.6	3.4
Life expectancy at birth (females/males, years)[g]	54.4 / 51.5	63.0 / 57.7	65.8 / 60.0
Population age distribution (0-14/60+ years old, %)	37.4 / 5.8	36.9 / 5.6	36.8 / 5.6
International migrant stock (000/% of total pop.)	103.8 / 4.9	101.6 / 4.4	107.6 / 4.3[b]
Refugees and others of concern to the UNHCR (000)	8.8[h]	4.4	4.3[b]
Infant mortality rate (per 1 000 live births)[g]	43.5	38.6	33.4
Health: Current expenditure (% of GDP)	9.7	9.9	8.6[a]
Health: Physicians (per 1 000 pop.)	0.4[i]	...	0.4[c]
Education: Government expenditure (% of GDP)	8.3	3.1[j]	...
Education: Primary gross enrol. ratio (f/m per 100 pop.)	112.9 / 117.5	118.4 / 123.7[k]	122.1 / 126.4[c]
Education: Secondary gross enrol. ratio (f/m per 100 pop.)	70.0 / 61.5[i]	... / ...	... / ...
Education: Tertiary gross enrol. ratio (f/m per 100 pop.)	10.3 / 8.1[l]	26.0 / 15.1	30.3 / 15.3[a]
Intentional homicide rate (per 100 000 pop.)	14.8	17.7[m]	...
Seats held by women in the National Parliament (%)	26.9	41.3	42.7[n,o]

Environment and infrastructure indicators

	2010	2015	2020
Individuals using the Internet (per 100 inhabitants)	11.6	25.7[d]	51.0[p,q,a]
Research & Development expenditure (% of GDP)[s]	0.1[r]	0.3[i]	...
Threatened species (number)	92	105	117
Forested area (% of land area)[d]	8.9	8.4	8.4[a]
CO2 emission estimates (million tons/tons per capita)	3.1 / 1.4	3.9 / 1.6	4.0 / 1.6[a]
Energy production, primary (Petajoules)	17	20	21[a]
Energy supply per capita (Gigajoules)	30	32	32[a]
Tourist/visitor arrivals at national borders (000)	984	1 388	1 499[a]
Important sites for terrestrial biodiversity protected (%)	83.3	86.1	86.1[b]
Net Official Development Assist. received (% of GNI)	2.41	1.23	1.07[c]

a 2017. b 2019. c 2018. d Estimate. e Calculated by the UN Statistics Division from national indices. f 2016. g Data refers to a 5-year period preceding the reference year. h Data as at the end of December. i 2007. j 2014. k 2013. l 2008. m 2012. n Data are as at 1 January of reporting year. o The figures on the National Assembly correspond to the provisional results of the November 2019 elections, excluding members yet to be appointed. Newl elected members are due to be sworn in March 2020. p At least once a month. q Population aged 18 years and over r Excluding government. s Partial data.

Nauru

Region	Micronesia	UN membership date	14 September 1999
Population (000, 2020)	11	Surface area (km2)	21 [a]
Pop. density (per km2, 2020)	561.4	Sex ratio (m per 100 f)	101.9 [b,c]
Capital city	Yaren	National currency	Australian Dollar (AUD)
Capital city pop. (000, 2020)	11.3 [d,e]	Exchange rate (per US$)	1.4 [f]

Economic indicators	2010	2015	2020
GDP: Gross domestic product (million current US$)	59	104	127 [e]
GDP growth rate (annual %, const. 2015 prices)	13.6	2.8	- 4.0 [e]
GDP per capita (current US$)	5 924.8	10 050.4	11 875.9 [e]
Economy: Agriculture (% of Gross Value Added) [g]	4.2	2.4	2.4 [e]
Economy: Industry (% of Gross Value Added) [g]	43.6	40.7	37.5 [e]
Economy: Services and other activity (% of GVA) [g]	52.8	43.8	42.3 [e]
Unemployment rate (% of labour force)	...	23.0 [b,h]	...
Labour force participation rate (female/male pop. %)	... / ...	49.3 / 78.9 [h]	... / ...
Agricultural production index (2004-2006=100)	106	113	114 [c]
Balance of payments, current account (million US$)	24	- 17	8 [e]

Social indicators	2010	2015	2020
Population growth rate (average annual %)	- 0.2 [i]	2.3 [i]	- 0.1
Urban population (% of total population)	100.0	100.0	100.0 [f]
Urban population growth rate (average annual %) [i]	- 0.2	2.3	...
Fertility rate, total (live births per woman)	...	3.9 [j,k]	...
Life expectancy at birth (females/males, years)	58.2 / 52.5 [l,m]	64.8 / 57.8 [b,j,k]	... / ...
Population age distribution (0-14/60+ years old, %)	... / ...	... / ...	39.5 / 4.0 [b,c]
International migrant stock (000/% of total pop.) [n]	1.2 / 11.8	1.9 / 18.2	2.1 / 19.7 [f]
Refugees and others of concern to the UNHCR (000)	...	0.8	1.2 [f]
Infant mortality rate (per 1 000 live births)	...	18.0 [j,k]	...
Health: Current expenditure (% of GDP) [o,p,q]	10.4	13.3	11.0 [a]
Health: Physicians (per 1 000 pop.)	1.1	1.3	...
Education: Government expenditure (% of GDP)	4.9 [r,m]	...	...
Education: Primary gross enrol. ratio (f/m per 100 pop.)	93.4 / 93.8 [s]	111.6 / 121.3 [t]	123.2 / 129.7 [c]
Education: Secondary gross enrol. ratio (f/m per 100 pop.)	67.9 / 63.9 [s]	83.2 / 86.0 [t]	83.6 / 81.9 [c]
Seats held by women in the National Parliament (%)	0.0	5.3	10.5 [u]

Environment and infrastructure indicators	2010	2015	2020
Individuals using the Internet (per 100 inhabitants)	...	54.0 [v,h]	57.0 [r,a]
Threatened species (number)	74	80	86
Forested area (% of land area) [r]	0.0	0.0	0.0 [a]
Energy production, primary (Petajoules)	0 [r]	0 [r]	0 [a]
Energy supply per capita (Gigajoules)	58	63 [r]	55 [r,a]
Important sites for terrestrial biodiversity protected (%)	0.0	0.0	0.0 [f]
Net Official Development Assist. received (% of GNI)	48.74	25.20	21.49 [e]

a 2017. b Break in the time series. c 2016. d Refers to Nauru. e 2018. f 2019. g At producers' prices. h 2011. i Data refers to a 5-year period preceding the reference year. j Data refers to a 3-year period up to and including the reference year. k 2013. l Data refers to a 6-year period up to and including the reference year. m 2007. n Refers to foreign citizens. o Data refer to fiscal years beginning 1 July. p Indicators are sensitive to external funds flowing in to the country. q General government expenditure (GGE) can be larger than the Gross domestic product (GDP) because government accounts for a very large part of domestic consumption and because a large part of domestic consumption in the country is accounted for by imports. r Estimate. s 2008. t 2014. u Data are as at 1 January of reporting year. v Population aged 15 years and over.

Nepal

Region	Southern Asia	UN membership date	14 December 1955	
Population (000, 2020)	29 137	Surface area (km2)	147 181 [a]	
Pop. density (per km2, 2020)	203.3	Sex ratio (m per 100 f)	84.5	
Capital city	Kathmandu	National currency	Nepalese Rupee (NPR)	
Capital city pop. (000, 2020)	1 376.1 [b,c]	Exchange rate (per US$)	113.3 [c]	

Economic indicators

	2010	2015	2020
GDP: Gross domestic product (million current US$)	16 281	20 801	27 830 [d]
GDP growth rate (annual %, const. 2015 prices)	4.8	3.3	6.7 [d]
GDP per capita (current US$)	602.7	770.0	990.6 [d]
Economy: Agriculture (% of Gross Value Added)	35.4	31.7	28.1 [d]
Economy: Industry (% of Gross Value Added)	15.1	14.8	14.9 [d]
Economy: Services and other activity (% of GVA)	48.5	53.4	59.4 [d]
Employment in agriculture (% of employed) [e]	70.2	67.3	64.5
Employment in industry (% of employed) [e]	13.3	14.3	15.3
Employment in services & other sectors (% employed) [e]	16.5	18.5	20.2
Unemployment rate (% of labour force) [e]	1.5	1.5	1.5
Labour force participation rate (female/male pop. %) [e]	79.5 / 87.4	81.5 / 85.3	82.9 / 85.2
CPI: Consumer Price Index (2010=100) [f]	...	104	128 [c]
Agricultural production index (2004-2006=100)	114	138	140 [g]
International trade: exports (million current US$) [h]	874	660	588 [e,c]
International trade: imports (million current US$) [h]	5 116	6 612	4 737 [e,c]
International trade: balance (million current US$) [h]	- 4 242	- 5 952	- 4 149 [e,c]
Balance of payments, current account (million US$)	- 128	2 447	- 2 775 [d]

Major trading partners

					2019
Export partners (% of exports) [e]	India	56.7	United States	11.2	Turkey 6.4
Import partners (% of imports) [e]	India	65.0	China	12.6	Areas nes [i] 2.0

Social indicators

	2010	2015	2020
Population growth rate (average annual %) [j]	1.0	-0.0	1.5
Urban population (% of total population)	16.8	18.6	20.2 [c]
Urban population growth rate (average annual %) [j]	3.1	3.2	...
Fertility rate, total (live births per woman) [j]	2.8	2.3	1.9
Life expectancy at birth (females/males, years) [j]	67.8 / 65.2	70.0 / 67.3	71.7 / 68.8
Population age distribution (0-14/60+ years old, %)	36.3 / 7.5	33.4 / 8.3	28.8 / 8.7
International migrant stock (000/% of total pop.) [k]	578.7 / 2.1	509.5 / 1.9	490.8 / 1.7 [c]
Refugees and others of concern to the UNHCR (000)	891.3 [l]	36.8	19.3 [m,c]
Infant mortality rate (per 1 000 live births) [j]	42.6	33.8	27.9
Health: Current expenditure (% of GDP) [n]	5.0	6.2	5.6 [a]
Health: Physicians (per 1 000 pop.)	...	0.6 [o]	0.7 [d]
Education: Government expenditure (% of GDP)	3.6	3.7	5.2 [d]
Education: Primary gross enrol. ratio (f/m per 100 pop.)	149.9 / 139.3	148.6 / 139.9	143.5 / 140.8 [c]
Education: Secondary gross enrol. ratio (f/m per 100 pop.)	56.9 / 58.3 [e]	69.4 / 66.3 [e]	83.0 / 77.4 [c]
Education: Tertiary gross enrol. ratio (f/m per 100 pop.)	11.3 / 17.6	14.5 / 15.5	12.8 / 12.0 [d]
Intentional homicide rate (per 100 000 pop.)	3.0	2.1 [p]	2.3 [q]
Seats held by women in the National Parliament (%)	33.2	29.5	32.7 [q]

Environment and infrastructure indicators

	2010	2015	2020
Individuals using the Internet (per 100 inhabitants)	7.9 [l]	17.6 [e]	34.0 [a]
Research & Development expenditure (% of GDP)	0.3 [r,s]	...	...
Threatened species (number)	93	105	109
Forested area (% of land area)	25.4	25.4	25.4 [e,a]
CO2 emission estimates (million tons/tons per capita)	4.1 / 0.2	5.7 / 0.2	10.1 / 0.3 [a]
Energy production, primary (Petajoules)	384	424	438 [a]
Energy supply per capita (Gigajoules)	16	17	19 [a]
Tourist/visitor arrivals at national borders (000) [t]	603	539	1 173 [d]
Important sites for terrestrial biodiversity protected (%)	50.7	50.7	50.7 [c]
Pop. using safely managed drinking water (urban/rural, %)	34.5 / 24.2	34.2 / 25.2	34.1 / 25.6 [a]
Net Official Development Assist. received (% of GNI)	4.76	5.63	5.00 [d]

a. 2017. b. Refers to the municipality. c. 2019. d. 2018. e. Estimate. f. Index base: 2014/2015=100. g. 2016. h. Merchandise trade data up to 2009 reported by fiscal year and beginning 2010 reported by calendar year. i. Areas not elsewhere specified. j. Data refers to a 5-year period preceding the reference year. k. Including refugees. l. Data as at the end of December. m. Various studies estimate a large number of individuals without citizenship certificates in Nepal, who are not all necessarily stateless. UNHCR has been working closely with the Government of Nepal and partners to address this situation. n. Data refer to fiscal years ending 15 July. o. 2013. p. 2014. q. Data are as at 1 January of reporting year. r. Based on R&D budget instead of R&D expenditure. s. Break in the time series. t. Including arrivals from India.

Netherlands

Region	Western Europe	UN membership date	10 December 1945	
Population (000, 2020)	17 135	Surface area (km2)	41 542[a]	
Pop. density (per km2, 2020)	508.2	Sex ratio (m per 100 f)	99.3	
Capital city	Amsterdam[b]	National currency	Euro (EUR)	
Capital city pop. (000, 2020)	1 140.3[c]	Exchange rate (per US$)	0.9[c]	

Economic indicators

	2010	2015	2020
GDP: Gross domestic product (million current US$)	846 555	765 265	914 105[d]
GDP growth rate (annual %, const. 2015 prices)	1.3	2.0	2.6[d]
GDP per capita (current US$)	50 743.8	45 179.0	53 583.1[d]
Economy: Agriculture (% of Gross Value Added)[e]	2.0	1.9	1.8[d]
Economy: Industry (% of Gross Value Added)[e,f]	21.9	20.2	20.0[d]
Economy: Services and other activity (% of GVA)[e,g,h]	72.1	72.3	71.9[d]
Employment in agriculture (% of employed)	3.1	2.3	2.0[i]
Employment in industry (% of employed)	17.7	16.4	15.8[i]
Employment in services & other sectors (% employed)	79.2	81.2	82.2[i]
Unemployment rate (% of labour force)[i]	5.0	6.9	3.0
Labour force participation rate (female/male pop. %)[i]	58.0 / 71.0	58.2 / 70.1	58.1 / 68.7
CPI: Consumer Price Index (2010=100)	100	109	116[c]
Agricultural production index (2004-2006=100)	112	116	118[i]
International trade: exports (million current US$)	492 646	437 329	577 617[c]
International trade: imports (million current US$)	439 987	393 728	514 513[c]
International trade: balance (million current US$)	52 659	43 601	63 103[c]
Balance of payments, current account (million US$)	61 803	48 501	92 805[c]

Major trading partners

						2019
Export partners (% of exports)	Germany	22.2	Belgium	10.1	France	7.8
Import partners (% of imports)	Germany	17.1	Belgium	9.9	China	9.4

Social indicators

	2010	2015	2020
Population growth rate (average annual %)[k]	0.4	0.3	0.2
Urban population (% of total population)	87.1	90.2	91.9[c]
Urban population growth rate (average annual %)[k]	1.4	1.0	...
Fertility rate, total (live births per woman)[k]	1.7	1.7	1.7
Life expectancy at birth (females/males, years)[k]	82.2 / 78.0	83.1 / 79.4	83.8 / 80.3
Population age distribution (0-14/60+ years old, %)	17.5 / 22.0	16.8 / 24.1	15.7 / 26.6
International migrant stock (000/% of total pop.)	1 832.5 / 11.0	1 996.3 / 11.8	2 282.8 / 13.4[c]
Refugees and others of concern to the UNHCR (000)	90.1[l]	92.5	109.1[c]
Infant mortality rate (per 1 000 live births)[k]	4.1	3.5	2.5
Health: Current expenditure (% of GDP)[i]	10.2	10.3	10.1[a]
Health: Physicians (per 1 000 pop.)	3.0	3.5	3.6[a]
Education: Government expenditure (% of GDP)	5.5	5.3	5.5[i]
Education: Primary gross enrol. ratio (f/m per 100 pop.)	108.1 / 108.5	102.7 / 102.7	104.2 / 104.2[a]
Education: Secondary gross enrol. ratio (f/m per 100 pop.)	121.2 / 122.9	134.6 / 132.6	136.5 / 134.7[a]
Education: Tertiary gross enrol. ratio (f/m per 100 pop.)	67.3 / 60.3	86.1 / 75.2	90.9 / 79.3[a]
Intentional homicide rate (per 100 000 pop.)	0.9	0.6	0.6[d]
Seats held by women in the National Parliament (%)	42.0	37.3	33.3[m]

Environment and infrastructure indicators

	2010	2015	2020
Individuals using the Internet (per 100 inhabitants)	90.7[n,o]	91.7[p]	94.7[d]
Research & Development expenditure (% of GDP)	1.7	2.0	2.2[q,r,d]
Threatened species (number)	24	29	71
Forested area (% of land area)	11.1	11.2	11.2[i,a]
CO2 emission estimates (million tons/tons per capita)	170.8 / 10.3	157.9 / 9.3	155.6 / 9.1[a]
Energy production, primary (Petajoules)[s]	2 979	2 006	1 748[a]
Energy supply per capita (Gigajoules)[s]	206	176	181[a]
Tourist/visitor arrivals at national borders (000)	10 883	15 007	18 780[d]
Important sites for terrestrial biodiversity protected (%)	97.2	97.3	97.9[c]
Pop. using safely managed sanitation (urban/rural %)	97.5 / 97.4	97.5 / 97.4	97.5 / 97.4[a]
Net Official Development Assist. disbursed (% of GNI)[t]	0.81	0.75	0.60[a]

a 2017. b Amsterdam is the capital and The Hague is the seat of government. c 2019. d 2018. e Data classified according to ISIC Rev. 4. f Excludes publishing activities. Includes irrigation and canals. g Excludes repair of personal and household goods. h Excludes computer and related activities and radio/TV activities. i Estimate. j 2016. k Data refers to a 5-year period preceding the reference year. l Data as at the end of December. m Data are as at 1 January reporting year. n Users in the last 12 months. o Population aged 16 to 74 years. p Population aged 12 years and over. q Provisional data. r Break in the time series. s Data exclude Suriname and the Netherlands Antilles (former) t Development Assistance Committee member (OECD).

New Caledonia

Region	Melanesia	Population (000, 2020)	286
Surface area (km2)	18 575[a]	Pop. density (per km2, 2020)	15.6
Sex ratio (m per 100 f)	101.1	Capital city	Nouméa
National currency	CFP Franc (XPF)[b]	Capital city pop. (000, 2020)	197.8[c]
Exchange rate (per US$)	106.2[d]		

Economic indicators	2010	2015	2020
GDP: Gross domestic product (million current US$)	9 355	8 772	10 174[c]
GDP growth rate (annual %, const. 2015 prices)	6.9	0.6	1.6[c]
GDP per capita (current US$)	36 900.3	32 362.6	36 334.8[c]
Economy: Agriculture (% of Gross Value Added)	1.5	2.1	2.0[c]
Economy: Industry (% of Gross Value Added)	28.3	23.9	24.6[c]
Economy: Services and other activity (% of GVA)[e]	70.5	75.3	74.6[c]
Employment in agriculture (% of employed)[f]	2.6	2.2	1.9
Employment in industry (% of employed)[f]	22.0	21.6	20.7
Employment in services & other sectors (% employed)[f]	75.5	76.2	77.5
Unemployment rate (% of labour force)[f]	14.4	14.1	12.8
Labour force participation rate (female/male pop. %)[f]	61.0 / 71.0	58.7 / 68.8	57.5 / 68.2
CPI: Consumer Price Index (2010=100)[g]	100	106	110[d]
Agricultural production index (2004-2006=100)	98	104	105[h]
International trade: exports (million current US$)	1 268	1 239	1 674[f,d]
International trade: imports (million current US$)	3 303	2 529	2 951[f,d]
International trade: balance (million current US$)	- 2 036	- 1 291	- 1 277[f,d]
Balance of payments, current account (million US$)	- 1 360	- 1 119	- 654[h]

Major trading partners						2019
Export partners (% of exports)[f]	China	57.2	Rep. of Korea	13.4	Japan	11.6
Import partners (% of imports)[f]	France	42.4	Australia	12.9	Singapore	11.6

Social indicators	2010	2015	2020
Population growth rate (average annual %)[i]	1.4	1.3	1.0
Urban population (% of total population)	67.1	69.4	71.1[d]
Urban population growth rate (average annual %)[i]	2.5	2.1	...
Fertility rate, total (live births per woman)[i]	2.3	2.2	2.0
Life expectancy at birth (females/males, years)[i]	78.3 / 72.4	79.3 / 73.7	80.2 / 74.7
Population age distribution (0-14/60+ years old, %)	25.8 / 11.0	23.8 / 12.4	22.1 / 14.2
International migrant stock (000/% of total pop.)	61.2 / 24.1	68.9 / 25.4	72.5 / 25.7[d]
Infant mortality rate (per 1 000 live births)[i]	15.1	13.0	11.5
Intentional homicide rate (per 100 000 pop.)	3.2[j]	...	...

Environment and infrastructure indicators	2010	2015	2020
Individuals using the Internet (per 100 inhabitants)[f]	42.0	74.0	82.0[a]
Threatened species (number)	415	493	759
Forested area (% of land area)[f]	45.9	45.9	45.9[a]
Energy production, primary (Petajoules)	1	2	2[a]
Energy supply per capita (Gigajoules)	184	228	246[a]
Tourist/visitor arrivals at national borders (000)[k]	99	114	120[c]
Important sites for terrestrial biodiversity protected (%)	26.6	36.4	36.4[d]

a 2017. b Communauté financière du Pacifique (CFP) Franc. c 2018. d 2019. e Excludes hotels and restaurants. f Estimate. g Calculated by the UN Statistics Division from national indices. h 2016. i Data refers to a 5-year period preceding the reference year. j 2009. k Including nationals residing abroad.

New Zealand

Region	Oceania	UN membership date	24 October 1945
Population (000, 2020)	4 822	Surface area (km2)	268 107 [a]
Pop. density (per km2, 2020)	18.3	Sex ratio (m per 100 f)	96.7
Capital city	Wellington	National currency	New Zealand Dollar (NZD)
Capital city pop. (000, 2020)	413.0 [b]	Exchange rate (per US$)	1.5 [b]

Economic indicators	2010	2015	2020
GDP: Gross domestic product (million current US$)	146 584	177 468	207 921 [c]
GDP growth rate (annual %, const. 2015 prices)	1.0	4.2	2.8 [c]
GDP per capita (current US$)	33 542.7	38 458.4	43 836.2 [c]
Economy: Agriculture (% of Gross Value Added) [d]	7.1	4.9	5.8 [c]
Economy: Industry (% of Gross Value Added) [d,e]	23.0	23.2	22.5 [c]
Economy: Services and other activity (% of GVA) [d,f,g]	73.0	73.1	72.2 [c]
Employment in agriculture (% of employed)	6.7	6.1	5.6 [h]
Employment in industry (% of employed)	20.6	21.6	19.4 [h]
Employment in services & other sectors (% employed)	72.6	72.3	75.1 [h]
Unemployment rate (% of labour force) [h]	6.6	5.4	4.0
Labour force participation rate (female/male pop. %) [h]	61.0 / 73.8	62.8 / 74.1	64.7 / 75.2
CPI: Consumer Price Index (2010=100) [i]	100	108	114 [b]
Agricultural production index (2004-2006=100)	104	118	117 [j]
International trade: exports (million current US$)	31 393	34 357	39 540 [b]
International trade: imports (million current US$)	30 616	36 528	42 271 [b]
International trade: balance (million current US$)	777	- 2 171	- 2 731 [b]
Balance of payments, current account (million US$)	- 3 429	- 4 655	- 5 966 [b]

Major trading partners						2019
Export partners (% of exports)	China	27.9	Australia	14.5	United States	9.4
Import partners (% of imports)	China	20.2	Australia	11.5	United States	10.0

Social indicators	2010	2015	2020
Population growth rate (average annual %) [k]	1.1	1.1	0.9
Urban population (% of total population)	86.2	86.3	86.6 [b]
Urban population growth rate (average annual %) [k]	1.1	1.1	...
Fertility rate, total (live births per woman) [k]	2.1	2.0	1.9
Life expectancy at birth (females/males, years) [k]	82.3 / 78.3	83.1 / 79.5	83.8 / 80.3
Population age distribution (0-14/60+ years old, %)	20.5 / 18.4	20.0 / 20.0	19.4 / 22.2
International migrant stock (000/% of total pop.)	947.4 / 21.7	1 039.7 / 22.5	1 068.7 / 22.3 [b]
Refugees and others of concern to the UNHCR (000)	2.5 [l]	1.6	2.6 [b]
Infant mortality rate (per 1 000 live births) [k]	5.0	4.4	3.8
Health: Current expenditure (% of GDP) [h]	9.6	9.3	9.2 [a]
Health: Physicians (per 1 000 pop.)	3.1	3.3	3.6 [c]
Education: Government expenditure (% of GDP)	7.0	6.3	6.4 [i]
Education: Primary gross enrol. ratio (f/m per 100 pop.)	101.3 / 101.0	98.2 / 97.7	100.2 / 99.8 [a]
Education: Secondary gross enrol. ratio (f/m per 100 pop.)	121.8 / 116.4	118.1 / 111.5	118.2 / 111.1 [a]
Education: Tertiary gross enrol. ratio (f/m per 100 pop.)	... / ...	94.9 / 67.3	97.2 / 67.9 [a]
Intentional homicide rate (per 100 000 pop.)	1.0	1.0	0.7 [a]
Seats held by women in the National Parliament (%)	33.6	31.4	40.8 [m]

Environment and infrastructure indicators	2010	2015	2020
Individuals using the Internet (per 100 inhabitants)	80.5	88.2	90.8 [a]
Research & Development expenditure (% of GDP)	1.3 [n]	1.2	1.4 [a]
Threatened species (number)	153	197	261
Forested area (% of land area)	38.6	38.6	38.6 [h,a]
CO2 emission estimates (million tons/tons per capita)	30.3 / 7.0	31.3 / 6.7	32.2 / 6.7 [a]
Energy production, primary (Petajoules)	775	780	758 [a]
Energy supply per capita (Gigajoules)	192	206	203 [a]
Tourist/visitor arrivals at national borders (000)	2 435	3 039	3 686 [c]
Important sites for terrestrial biodiversity protected (%)	45.7	46.4	46.4 [b]
Net Official Development Assist. disbursed (% of GNI) [o]	0.26	0.27	0.23 [a]

2017. **b** 2019. **c** 2018. **d** Data classified according to ISIC Rev. 4. **e** Excludes publishing activities. Includes irrigation and canals. **f** Excludes repair of personal and household goods. **g** Excludes computer and related activities of radio/TV activities. **h** Estimate. **i** Calculated by the UN Statistics Division from national indices. **j** 2016. **k** Data refers to a 5-year period preceding the reference year. **l** Data as at the end of December. **m** Data are as at 1 January of reporting year. **n** 2009. **o** Development Assistance Committee member (OECD).

Nicaragua

Region	Central America	UN membership date	24 October 1945	
Population (000, 2020)	6 625	Surface area (km2)	130 373[a]	
Pop. density (per km2, 2020)	55.0	Sex ratio (m per 100 f)	97.2	
Capital city	Managua	National currency	Cordoba Oro (NIO)	
Capital city pop. (000, 2020)	1 055.5[b]	Exchange rate (per US$)	33.8[b]	

Economic indicators

	2010	2015	2020
GDP: Gross domestic product (million current US$)	8 759	12 757	13 118[c]
GDP growth rate (annual %, const. 2015 prices)	4.4	4.8	- 3.8[c]
GDP per capita (current US$)	1 503.9	2 049.8	2 028.9[c]
Economy: Agriculture (% of Gross Value Added)	18.7	17.8	16.9[c]
Economy: Industry (% of Gross Value Added)	24.2	28.5	28.2[c]
Economy: Services and other activity (% of GVA)	56.5	53.2	54.6[c]
Employment in agriculture (% of employed)[d]	29.4	31.0	30.6
Employment in industry (% of employed)[d]	18.4	17.6	15.6
Employment in services & other sectors (% employed)[d]	52.2	51.4	53.8
Unemployment rate (% of labour force)[d]	7.8	4.7	7.4
Labour force participation rate (female/male pop. %)[d]	47.1 / 83.0	49.4 / 84.2	49.9 / 84.2
CPI: Consumer Price Index (2010=100)	100	137	163[b]
Agricultural production index (2004-2006=100)	118	127	132[e]
International trade: exports (million current US$)	1 848	4 667	3 998[d,b]
International trade: imports (million current US$)	4 191	5 866	8 426[d,b]
International trade: balance (million current US$)	- 2 343	- 1 199	- 4 429[d,b]
Balance of payments, current account (million US$)	- 780	- 1 145	83[c]

Major trading partners

						2019
Export partners (% of exports)[d]	United States	61.1	El Salvador	5.7	Mexico	5.6
Import partners (% of imports)[d]	United States	27.8	China	13.2	Mexico	10.1

Social indicators

	2010	2015	2020
Population growth rate (average annual %)[f]	1.4	1.3	1.2
Urban population (% of total population)	56.9	57.9	58.8[b]
Urban population growth rate (average annual %)[f]	1.6	1.5	1.5
Fertility rate, total (live births per woman)[f]	2.7	2.5	2.4
Life expectancy at birth (females/males, years)[f]	74.9 / 68.6	76.4 / 69.8	77.7 / 70.6
Population age distribution (0-14/60+ years old, %)	33.3 / 6.3	31.3 / 7.4	29.5 / 8.7
International migrant stock (000/% of total pop.)[g]	37.3 / 0.6	40.3 / 0.6	42.2 / 0.6[b]
Refugees and others of concern to the UNHCR (000)	0.1[h]	0.4	0.8[b]
Infant mortality rate (per 1 000 live births)[f]	23.1	17.8	16.8
Health: Current expenditure (% of GDP)	7.0	8.0	8.6[a]
Health: Physicians (per 1 000 pop.)	0.7	0.9	1.0[c]
Education: Government expenditure (% of GDP)	4.5	4.1	4.3[a]
Education: Primary gross enrol. ratio (f/m per 100 pop.)	120.1 / 121.1	... / ...	... / ...
Education: Secondary gross enrol. ratio (f/m per 100 pop.)	78.0 / 69.1	... / ...	... / ...
Intentional homicide rate (per 100 000 pop.)	13.5	8.4	7.2[e]
Seats held by women in the National Parliament (%)	20.7	39.1	47.2[i]

Environment and infrastructure indicators

	2010	2015	2020
Individuals using the Internet (per 100 inhabitants)[d]	10.0	19.7	27.9[a]
Research & Development expenditure (% of GDP)	...	0.1[i]	...
Threatened species (number)	121	141	161
Forested area (% of land area)	25.9	25.9	25.9[d,a]
CO2 emission estimates (million tons/tons per capita)	4.3 / 0.7	5.1 / 0.8	5.1 / 0.8[a]
Energy production, primary (Petajoules)	66	92	93[a]
Energy supply per capita (Gigajoules)	22	27	27[a]
Tourist/visitor arrivals at national borders (000)[k]	1 011	1 386	1 256[c]
Important sites for terrestrial biodiversity protected (%)	70.4	70.4	70.4[b]
Pop. using safely managed drinking water (urban/rural, %)	67.0 / 29.8	67.3 / 29.6	67.4 / 29.5[a]
Net Official Development Assist. received (% of GNI)	6.01	3.69	2.76[c]

a 2017. **b** 2019. **c** 2018. **d** Estimate. **e** 2016. **f** Data refers to a 5-year period preceding the reference year. **g** Including refugees. **h** Data as at the end of December. **i** Data are as at 1 January of reporting year. **j** Higher Education only. **k** Including nationals residing abroad.

Niger

Region	Western Africa	UN membership date	20 September 1960
Population (000, 2020)	24 207	Surface area (km2)	1 267 000[a]
Pop. density (per km2, 2020)	19.1	Sex ratio (m per 100 f)	101.1
Capital city	Niamey	National currency	CFA Franc, BCEAO (XOF)[b]
Capital city pop. (000, 2020)	1 251.5[c]	Exchange rate (per US$)	583.9[c]

Economic indicators

	2010	2015	2020
GDP: Gross domestic product (million current US$)	7 620	9 659	12 821[d]
GDP growth rate (annual %, const. 2015 prices)	8.4	4.3	7.0[d]
GDP per capita (current US$)	462.8	482.9	571.3[d]
Economy: Agriculture (% of Gross Value Added)[e]	39.2	34.9	40.7[d]
Economy: Industry (% of Gross Value Added)[e,f]	19.8	23.1	19.2[d]
Economy: Services and other activity (% of GVA)[e,g,h]	47.7	53.6	49.4[d]
Employment in agriculture (% of employed)[i]	77.1	75.9	74.8
Employment in industry (% of employed)[i]	7.5	7.4	7.2
Employment in services & other sectors (% employed)[i]	15.4	16.7	18.0
Unemployment rate (% of labour force)[i]	0.6	0.5	0.5
Labour force participation rate (female/male pop. %)[i]	68.6 / 91.0	61.0 / 84.3	60.3 / 83.5
CPI: Consumer Price Index (2010=100)[l]	...	107[j,k]	102[m,c]
Agricultural production index (2004-2006=100)	146	161	173[n]
International trade: exports (million current US$)	479	790	232[i,c]
International trade: imports (million current US$)	2 273	2 458	1 127[i,c]
International trade: balance (million current US$)	- 1 794	- 1 669	- 895[i,c]
Balance of payments, current account (million US$)	- 1 137	- 1 486	- 1 625[d]

Major trading partners

						2019
Export partners (% of exports)[i]	United Arab Emirates	32.9	Mali	21.6	China	18.5
Import partners (% of imports)[i]	Nigeria	10.0	France	10.0	China	8.1

Social indicators

	2010	2015	2020
Population growth rate (average annual %)[o]	3.8	3.9	3.8
Urban population (% of total population)	16.2	16.2	16.5[c]
Urban population growth rate (average annual %)[o]	3.7	3.9	...
Fertility rate, total (live births per woman)[o]	7.6	7.4	7.0
Life expectancy at birth (females/males, years)[o]	56.2 / 54.5	60.3 / 58.1	63.0 / 60.7
Population age distribution (0-14/60+ years old, %)	50.0 / 4.2	50.2 / 4.2	49.7 / 4.1
International migrant stock (000/% of total pop.)[p]	126.5 / 0.8	253.0 / 1.3	294.2 / 1.3[c]
Refugees and others of concern to the UNHCR (000)	0.3[q]	202.2	411.2[c]
Infant mortality rate (per 1 000 live births)[o]	67.6	55.9	46.3
Health: Current expenditure (% of GDP)	6.9	7.1	7.7[a]
Health: Physicians (per 1 000 pop.)	~0.0[r]	~0.0	~0.0[n]
Education: Government expenditure (% of GDP)	3.7	6.0	3.5[a]
Education: Primary gross enrol. ratio (f/m per 100 pop.)	55.9 / 69.2	65.6 / 77.4	69.2 / 80.1[a]
Education: Secondary gross enrol. ratio (f/m per 100 pop.)	10.7 / 15.3	17.0 / 23.1	20.7 / 27.7[a]
Education: Tertiary gross enrol. ratio (f/m per 100 pop.)	0.8 / 2.0	2.1 / 4.4	2.6 / 6.2[d]
Intentional homicide rate (per 100 000 pop.)	...	4.4[s]	...
Seats held by women in the National Parliament (%)	9.7	13.3	17.0[t]

Environment and infrastructure indicators

	2010	2015	2020
Individuals using the Internet (per 100 inhabitants)	0.8[i]	2.5[i]	5.3[d]
Threatened species (number)	26	31	37
Forested area (% of land area)[i]	1.0	0.9	0.9[a]
CO2 emission estimates (million tons/tons per capita)	1.4 / 0.1	2.0 / 0.1	2.0 / 0.1[a]
Energy production, primary (Petajoules)	56	100	98[i,a]
Energy supply per capita (Gigajoules)	4	5	4[i,a]
Tourist/visitor arrivals at national borders (000)	74	135	157[d]
Important sites for terrestrial biodiversity protected (%)	24.9	33.1	33.1[c]
Pop. using safely managed sanitation (urban/rural %)	20.3 / 5.0	22.6 / 6.4	23.4 / 6.9[a]
Net Official Development Assist. received (% of GNI)	13.06	12.30	13.24[d]

2017. **b** African Financial Community (CFA) Franc, Central Bank of West African States (BCEAO). **c** 2019. **d** 2018. **e** Data classified according to ISIC Rev. 4. **f** Excludes publishing activities. Includes irrigation and canals. **g** Excludes repair of personal and household goods. **h** Excludes computer and related activities and radio/TV activities. **i** Estimate. **j** Index base: 2008=100. **k** Niamey **l** WAEMU harmonized consumer price index. **m** Index base: 2014=100. 2016. **o** Data refers to a 5-year period preceding the reference year. **p** Including refugees. **q** Data as at the end of December. **r** 2009. **s** 2012. **t** Data are as at 1 January of reporting year.

Nigeria

Region	Western Africa	UN membership date	07 October 1960
Population (000, 2020)	206 140	Surface area (km2)	923 768 a
Pop. density (per km2, 2020)	226.3	Sex ratio (m per 100 f)	102.8
Capital city	Abuja	National currency	Naira (NGN)
Capital city pop. (000, 2020)	3 095.1 b,c	Exchange rate (per US$)	307.0 c

Economic indicators

	2010	2015	2020
GDP: Gross domestic product (million current US$)	363 360	494 583	421 821 d
GDP growth rate (annual %, const. 2015 prices)	8.0	2.7	1.9 d
GDP per capita (current US$)	2 292.4	2 730.4	2 153.5 d
Economy: Agriculture (% of Gross Value Added) e	23.9	20.9	21.4 d
Economy: Industry (% of Gross Value Added) e,f	25.3	20.4	26.0 d
Economy: Services and other activity (% of GVA) e,g,h	44.1	50.2	50.7 d
Employment in agriculture (% of employed) i	41.4	36.9	34.7
Employment in industry (% of employed) i	10.3	12.2	12.2
Employment in services & other sectors (% employed) i	48.4	50.9	53.1
Unemployment rate (% of labour force) i	3.8	4.3	8.0
Labour force participation rate (female/male pop. %) i	55.3 / 64.5	48.8 / 58.9	47.6 / 57.8
CPI: Consumer Price Index (2010=100) j	100	159	268 c
Agricultural production index (2004-2006=100)	105	120	119 k
International trade: exports (million current US$)	86 568	50 108 i	79 964 i,c
International trade: imports (million current US$)	44 235	34 912 i	72 765 i,c
International trade: balance (million current US$)	42 333	15 196 i	7 199 i,c
Balance of payments, current account (million US$)	13 111	- 15 439	5 334 d

Major trading partners

						2019
Export partners (% of exports) i	India	15.9	Netherlands	10.7	Spain	10.1
Import partners (% of imports) i	China	19.4	Netherlands	11.4	Rep. of Korea	10.8

Social indicators

	2010	2015	2020
Population growth rate (average annual %) l	2.6	2.7	2.6
Urban population (% of total population)	43.5	47.8	51.2 c
Urban population growth rate (average annual %) l	4.8	4.6	...
Fertility rate, total (live births per woman) l	5.9	5.7	5.4
Life expectancy at birth (females/males, years) l	50.5 / 49.0	52.8 / 51.2	55.1 / 53.3
Population age distribution (0-14/60+ years old, %)	44.0 / 4.5	44.1 / 4.5	43.5 / 4.5
International migrant stock (000/% of total pop.) m,n	988.7 / 0.6	1 199.1 / 0.7	1 256.4 / 0.6 c
Refugees and others of concern to the UNHCR (000)	10.6 o	1 510.2	2 211.1 c
Infant mortality rate (per 1 000 live births) l	89.3	75.0	62.1
Health: Current expenditure (% of GDP)	3.3	3.6	3.8 a
Health: Physicians (per 1 000 pop.)	0.4 p	0.4 q	0.4 d
Education: Primary gross enrol. ratio (f/m per 100 pop.)	81.0 / 89.1 i	89.4 / 90.8 r	82.2 / 87.2 k
Education: Secondary gross enrol. ratio (f/m per 100 pop.)	41.2 / 47.2	44.7 / 48.8	39.8 / 44.1 k
Education: Tertiary gross enrol. ratio (f/m per 100 pop.)	8.1 / 11.0	8.3 / 12.0 s	... / ...
Intentional homicide rate (per 100 000 pop.)	...	...	34.5 k
Seats held by women in the National Parliament (%)	7.0	6.7	3.4 t

Environment and infrastructure indicators

	2010	2015	2020
Individuals using the Internet (per 100 inhabitants)	11.5 i	36.0 u	42.0 u,a
Research & Development expenditure (% of GDP)	0.1 v	...	...
Threatened species (number)	297	333	380
Forested area (% of land area) i	9.9	7.7	7.7 a
CO2 emission estimates (million tons/tons per capita)	55.4 / 0.3	82.6 / 0.5	86.0 / 0.4 a
Energy production, primary (Petajoules)	10 591	10 677	10 402 a
Energy supply per capita (Gigajoules)	34	33	34 a
Tourist/visitor arrivals at national borders (000)	1 555	1 255	1 889 k
Important sites for terrestrial biodiversity protected (%)	80.4	80.4	80.4 c
Pop. using safely managed drinking water (urban/rural, %)	24.1 / 14.0	24.5 / 15.2	24.6 / 15.7 a
Pop. using safely managed sanitation (urban/rural %)	27.4 / 24.6	29.0 / 24.1	29.5 / 23.9 a
Net Official Development Assist. received (% of GNI)	0.60	0.51	0.87 d

a 2017. b Data refers to the urban agglomeration. c 2019. d 2018. e Data classified according to ISIC Rev. 4. f Excludes publishing activities. Includes irrigation and canals. g Excludes repair of personal and household goods. h Excludes computer and related activities and radio/TV activities. i Estimate. j Rural and urban areas. k 2016. l Data refers to a 5-year period preceding the reference year. m Including refugees. n Refers to foreign citizens. o Data as the end of December. p 2009. q 2013. r 2014. s 2011. t Data are as at 1 January of reporting year. u Population aged 18 years and over. v 2007.

Niue

Region	Polynesia	Population (000, 2020)	2
Surface area (km2)	260 [a]	Pop. density (per km2, 2020)	6.3
Sex ratio (m per 100 f)	100.0 [b,c]	Capital city	Alofi
National currency	New Zealand Dollar (NZD)	Capital city pop. (000, 2020)	0.7 [d]
Exchange rate (per US$)	1.5 [e]		

Economic indicators	2010	2015	2020
Agricultural production index (2004-2006=100)	97	101	101 [c]

Social indicators	2010	2015	2020
Population growth rate (average annual %)	- 0.7 [f]	- 0.1 [f]	0.1
Urban population (% of total population)	38.7	42.6	45.5 [e]
Urban population growth rate (average annual %) [f]	1.2	1.9	...
Fertility rate, total (live births per woman)	...	2.6 [g,h]	
Life expectancy at birth (females/males, years)	76.0 / 67.0 [i]	76.3 / 70.1 [b,j,h]	... / ...
Population age distribution (0-14/60+ years old, %)	25.7 / 16.8 [k]	26.4 / 16.4 [h]	22.8 / 20.1 [b,c]
International migrant stock (000/% of total pop.)	0.6 / 36.4	0.6 / 36.3	0.6 / 36.4 [e]
Infant mortality rate (per 1 000 live births)	...	8.1 [j,h]	...
Health: Current expenditure (% of GDP) [l,m,n]	10.3	8.2	8.6 [a]
Health: Physicians (per 1 000 pop.)	1.9 [o]	...	...
Education: Primary gross enrol. ratio (f/m per 100 pop.)	100.0 / 103.5 [p]	127.8 / 127.7	126.9 / 127.5 [c]
Education: Secondary gross enrol. ratio (f/m per 100 pop.)	90.8 / 82.9 [p]	109.4 / 89.5	... / ...

Environment and infrastructure indicators	2010	2015	2020
Individuals using the Internet (per 100 inhabitants) [q]	77.0	79.6 [h]	...
Threatened species (number)	43	50	56
Forested area (% of land area) [q]	71.5	69.6	69.6 [a]
Energy production, primary (Petajoules)	0	0	0 [q,a]
Energy supply per capita (Gigajoules)	52	63	60 [q,a]
Tourist/visitor arrivals at national borders (000) [r]	6	8	10 [a]
Important sites for terrestrial biodiversity protected (%)	0.0	0.0	0.0 [e]

a 2017. b Break in the time series. c 2016. d 2018. e 2019. f Data refers to a 5-year period preceding the reference year. g Data refers to a 3-year period up to and including the reference year. h 2011. i 2006. j Data refers to a 5-year period up to and including the reference year. k De jure population. l Indicators are sensitive to external funds flowing in to the country. m General government expenditure (GGE) can be larger than the Gross domestic product (GDP) because government accounts for a very large part of domestic consumption and because a large part of domestic consumption in the country is accounted for by imports. n Data refer to fiscal years beginning 1 July. o 2008. p 2005. q Estimate. r Including Niueans residing usually in New Zealand.

North Macedonia

Region	Southern Europe	UN membership date	08 April 1993
Population (000, 2020)	2 083	Surface area (km2)	25 713ᵃ
Pop. density (per km2, 2020)	82.6	Sex ratio (m per 100 f)	100.1
Capital city	Skopje	National currency	Denar (MKD)
Capital city pop. (000, 2020)	589.8ᵇ	Exchange rate (per US$)	55.0ᵇ

Economic indicators

	2010	2015	2020
GDP: Gross domestic product (million current US$)	9 407	10 065	12 629ᶜ
GDP growth rate (annual %, const. 2015 prices)	3.4	3.9	3.3ᶜ
GDP per capita (current US$)	4 542.9	4 840.3	6 062.9ᶜ
Economy: Agriculture (% of Gross Value Added)	11.7	11.1	8.4ᶜ
Economy: Industry (% of Gross Value Added)ᵈ	24.4	27.4	27.4ᶜ
Economy: Services and other activity (% of GVA)ᵉ,ᶠ	60.3	55.9	54.8ᶜ
Employment in agriculture (% of employed)	18.6ᵍ	17.9	15.1ᵍ
Employment in industry (% of employed)	30.3ᵍ	30.5	31.4ᵍ
Employment in services & other sectors (% employed)	51.1ᵍ	51.6	53.5ᵍ
Unemployment rate (% of labour force)ᵍ	32.0	26.1	16.4
Labour force participation rate (female/male pop. %)ᵍ	42.8 / 68.6	43.5 / 67.6	43.0 / 67.2
CPI: Consumer Price Index (2010=100)	100	110	113ᵇ
Agricultural production index (2004-2006=100)	115	122	123ʰ
International trade: exports (million current US$)	3 351	4 530	7 186ᵇ
International trade: imports (million current US$)	5 474	6 427	9 470ᵇ
International trade: balance (million current US$)	- 2 123	- 1 897	- 2 284ᵇ
Balance of payments, current account (million US$)	- 198	- 193	- 353ᵇ

Major trading partners

						2019
Export partners (% of exports)	Germany	48.7	Serbia	8.5	Bulgaria	4.9
Import partners (% of imports)	United Kingdom	11.5	Germany	11.4	Greece	8.1

Social indicators

	2010	2015	2020
Population growth rate (average annual %)ⁱ	0.1	0.1	-0.0
Urban population (% of total population)	57.1	57.4	58.2ᵇ
Urban population growth rate (average annual %)ⁱ	- 0.1	0.2	...
Fertility rate, total (live births per woman)ⁱ	1.5	1.5	1.5
Life expectancy at birth (females/males, years)ⁱ	76.3 / 72.1	77.2 / 73.1	77.6 / 73.6
Population age distribution (0-14/60+ years old, %)	17.9 / 16.4	16.8 / 18.6	16.3 / 20.7
International migrant stock (000/% of total pop.)	129.7 / 6.3	130.7 / 6.3	131.2 / 6.3ᵇ
Refugees and others of concern to the UNHCR (000)	3.3ʲ	1.6	17.6ᵇ
Infant mortality rate (per 1 000 live births)ⁱ	10.8	8.9	10.7
Health: Current expenditure (% of GDP)	6.7	6.3	6.1ᵃ
Health: Physicians (per 1 000 pop.)	2.7	2.9	...
Education: Primary gross enrol. ratio (f/m per 100 pop.)	86.7 / 88.0	94.0 / 93.7	97.1 / 97.2ᵃ
Education: Secondary gross enrol. ratio (f/m per 100 pop.)	81.0 / 83.3	81.2 / 82.6	80.3 / 82.5ᵃ
Education: Tertiary gross enrol. ratio (f/m per 100 pop.)	40.4 / 34.7	45.9 / 36.7	48.6 / 36.7ᵃ
Intentional homicide rate (per 100 000 pop.)	2.1	1.2	1.2ᶜ
Seats held by women in the National Parliament (%)	32.5	33.3	40.0ᵏ

Environment and infrastructure indicators

	2010	2015	2020
Individuals using the Internet (per 100 inhabitants)	51.9ˡ	70.4ᵐ	79.2ᶜ
Research & Development expenditure (% of GDP)	0.2	0.4	0.4ᶜ
Threatened species (number)	90	100	133
Forested area (% of land area)ᵍ	39.6	39.6	39.6ᵃ
CO2 emission estimates (million tons/tons per capita)	8.3 / 4.0	7.1 / 3.4	7.4 / 3.6ᵃ
Energy production, primary (Petajoules)	68	58	53ᵃ
Energy supply per capita (Gigajoules)	58	56	57ᵃ
Tourist/visitor arrivals at national borders (000)	262	486	707ᶜ
Important sites for terrestrial biodiversity protected (%)	26.0	26.0	26.0ᵇ
Pop. using safely managed drinking water (urban/rural, %)	92.9 / 89.1	89.9 / 74.6	89.9 / 68.8ᵃ
Pop. using safely managed sanitation (urban/rural %)	8.6 / ...	8.2 / ...	8.2 / ...ᵃ
Net Official Development Assist. received (% of GNI)	2.10	2.20	1.40ᶜ

a 2017. b 2019. c 2018. d Excludes publishing activities. Includes irrigation and canals. e Excludes repair of personal and household goods. f Excludes computer and related activities and radio/TV activities. g Estimate. h 2016. i Data refers to a 5-year period preceding the reference year. j Data as at the end of December. k Data are as at 1 January of reporting year. l Population aged 15 to 74 years. m Population aged 16 to 74 years.

Northern Mariana Islands

Region	Micronesia	Population (000, 2020)	55
Surface area (km2)	457[a]	Pop. density (per km2, 2020)	120.3
Sex ratio (m per 100 f)	107.1[b,c]	Capital city	Garapan
National currency	US Dollar (USD)	Capital city pop. (000, 2020)	4.0[d]

Economic indicators

	2010	2015	2020
Unemployment rate (% of labour force)	11.2[b,e]	...	...
Labour force participation rate (female/male pop. %)	66.6 / 77.6[b,e]	... / ...	... / ...
International trade: exports (million current US$)[f]	1 453	1 685	1 895[g]
International trade: imports (million current US$)[f]	2 867	4 215	5 734[g]
International trade: balance (million current US$)[f]	- 1 414	- 2 530	- 3 838[g]

Major trading partners

					2019
Export partners (% of exports)[f]	Areas nes[h]	91.1	Rep. of Korea	6.6	Peru	0.4
Import partners (% of imports)[f]	Areas nes[h]	66.1	China, Hong Kong SAR	14.8	Singapore	4.7

Social indicators

	2010	2015	2020
Population growth rate (average annual %)	- 3.2[i]	0.1[i]	0.2
Urban population (% of total population)	90.9	91.4	91.7[g]
Urban population growth rate (average annual %)[i]	- 3.1	0.2[i]	...
Fertility rate, total (live births per woman)	2.2	1.6[j]	...
Life expectancy at birth (females/males, years)	79.9 / 74.4[k]	77.9 / 74.9[b,l]	... / ...
Population age distribution (0-14/60+ years old, %)	26.7 / 5.8	26.0 / 6.7[m]	23.5 / 10.0[b,c]
International migrant stock (000/% of total pop.)	24.2 / 44.8	21.6 / 38.8	21.8 / 38.1[g]
Infant mortality rate (per 1 000 live births)	...	6.4[l]	...

Environment and infrastructure indicators

	2010	2015	2020
Threatened species (number)	85	99	105
Forested area (% of land area)[f]	65.9	64.1	64.1[a]
Tourist/visitor arrivals at national borders (000)[n]	375	475	517[o]
Important sites for terrestrial biodiversity protected (%)	40.6	40.6	40.6[g]

a 2017. **b** Break in the time series. **c** 2016. **d** 2010. **e** Population aged 16 years and over. **f** Estimate. **g** 2019. **h** Areas not elsewhere specified. **i** Data refers to a 5-year period preceding the reference year. **j** 2013. **k** 2009. **l** 2012. **m** 2011. **n** Arrivals by air. **o** 2018.

Norway

Region	Northern Europe	UN membership date	27 November 1945
Population (000, 2020)	5 421[a]	Surface area (km2)	386 194[a,b]
Pop. density (per km2, 2020)	14.8[a]	Sex ratio (m per 100 f)	102.2[a]
Capital city	Oslo	National currency	Norwegian Krone (NOK)
Capital city pop. (000, 2020)	1 026.8[c]	Exchange rate (per US$)	8.8[c]

Economic indicators	2010	2015	2020
GDP: Gross domestic product (million current US$)	428 757	385 802	434 167[d]
GDP growth rate (annual %, const. 2015 prices)	0.7	2.0	1.3[d]
GDP per capita (current US$)	87 754.3	74 194.9	81 335.7[d]
Economy: Agriculture (% of Gross Value Added)[e]	1.8	1.7	2.3[d]
Economy: Industry (% of Gross Value Added)[e,f]	39.0	34.8	39.0[d]
Economy: Services and other activity (% of GVA)[e,g,h]	53.7	59.8	54.4[d]
Employment in agriculture (% of employed)	2.5	2.0	2.0[i]
Employment in industry (% of employed)	19.7	20.1	19.1[i]
Employment in services & other sectors (% employed)	77.8	77.9	78.9[i]
Unemployment rate (% of labour force)[i]	3.5	4.3	3.3
Labour force participation rate (female/male pop. %)[i]	61.8 / 69.6	61.3 / 68.4	60.3 / 67.0
CPI: Consumer Price Index (2010=100)	100	109	120[c]
Agricultural production index (2004-2006=100)	102	107	107[i]
International trade: exports (million current US$)	130 657	103 785	104 030[c]
International trade: imports (million current US$)	77 330	76 399	86 145[c]
International trade: balance (million current US$)	53 327	27 386	17 885[c]
Balance of payments, current account (million US$)	50 258	31 106	16 065[c]

Major trading partners						2019
Export partners (% of exports)	United Kingdom	20.1	Germany	14.5	Netherlands	11.1
Import partners (% of imports)	Sweden	11.7	Germany	10.8	China	10.2

Social indicators	2010	2015	2020
Population growth rate (average annual %)[a,k]	1.1	1.2	0.8
Urban population (% of total population)[a]	79.1	81.1	82.6[c]
Urban population growth rate (average annual %)[a,k]	1.4	1.7	...
Fertility rate, total (live births per woman)[a,k]	1.9	1.8	1.7
Life expectancy at birth (females/males, years)[a,k]	82.8 / 78.3	83.6 / 79.5	84.2 / 80.2
Population age distribution (0-14/60+ years old, %)[a]	18.8 / 21.0	18.0 / 21.8	17.3 / 23.3
International migrant stock (000/% of total pop.)[a]	526.8 / 10.8	746.4 / 14.4	867.8 / 16.1[c]
Refugees and others of concern to the UNHCR (000)	55.9[l]	54.9	59.9[c]
Infant mortality rate (per 1 000 live births)[a,k]	3.0	2.4	2.1
Health: Current expenditure (% of GDP)[i]	8.9	10.1	10.4[b]
Health: Physicians (per 1 000 pop.)	2.5	2.6	2.9[d]
Education: Government expenditure (% of GDP)	6.7	7.6	8.0[i]
Education: Primary gross enrol. ratio (f/m per 100 pop.)	99.2 / 98.9	99.8 / 100.0	100.2 / 100.3[b]
Education: Secondary gross enrol. ratio (f/m per 100 pop.)	111.7 / 113.5	113.2 / 116.0	114.2 / 119.4[b]
Education: Tertiary gross enrol. ratio (f/m per 100 pop.)	91.2 / 56.5	92.9 / 63.8	98.7 / 66.3[b]
Intentional homicide rate (per 100 000 pop.)	0.6	0.5	0.5[d]
Seats held by women in the National Parliament (%)	39.6	39.6	41.4[m]

Environment and infrastructure indicators	2010	2015	2020
Individuals using the Internet (per 100 inhabitants)	93.4[n]	96.8[n]	96.5[d]
Research & Development expenditure (% of GDP)	1.6	1.9	2.1[o,d]
Threatened species (number)	36	44	115
Forested area (% of land area)	33.1	33.2	33.2[i,b]
CO2 emission estimates (million tons/tons per capita)	37.3 / 7.6	35.9 / 6.9	34.8 / 6.6[b]
Energy production, primary (Petajoules)[a]	8 734	8 629	8 923[b]
Energy supply per capita (Gigajoules)[a]	257	231	233[b]
Tourist/visitor arrivals at national borders (000)	4 767[p]	5 361[q]	5 688[q,d]
Important sites for terrestrial biodiversity protected (%)	54.4	56.1	57.7[c]
Net Official Development Assist. disbursed (% of GNI)[r]	1.05	1.05	0.99[b]

a Including Svalbard and Jan Mayen Islands. b 2017. c 2019. d 2018. e Data classified according to ISIC Rev. 4. f Excludes publishing activities. Includes irrigation and canals. g Excludes computer and related activities and radio/TV activities. h Excludes repair of personal and household goods. i Estimate. j 2016. k Data refers to a 5-year period preceding the reference year. l Data as at the end of December. m Data are as at 1 January of reporting year. n Population aged 16 to 74 years. o Provisional data. p Arrivals of non-resident tourists at national borders. q Non-resident tourists staying in all types of accommodation establishments. r Development Assistance Committee member (OECD).

Oman

Region	Western Asia	UN membership date	07 October 1971
Population (000, 2020)	5 107	Surface area (km2)	309 500 a
Pop. density (per km2, 2020)	16.5	Sex ratio (m per 100 f)	194.1
Capital city	Muscat	National currency	Rial Omani (OMR)
Capital city pop. (000, 2020)	1 501.6 b,c	Exchange rate (per US$)	0.4 c

Economic indicators

	2010	2015	2020
GDP: Gross domestic product (million current US$)	56 913	65 481	92 111 d
GDP growth rate (annual %, const. 2015 prices)	1.7	5.1	2.1 d
GDP per capita (current US$)	18 712.6	15 344.5	19 072.8 d
Economy: Agriculture (% of Gross Value Added)	1.4	2.2	2.2 d
Economy: Industry (% of Gross Value Added)	62.6	45.7	48.6 d
Economy: Services and other activity (% of GVA)	56.0	68.6	66.1 d
Employment in agriculture (% of employed)	5.2	4.9 e	4.4 e
Employment in industry (% of employed)	36.9	33.6 e	32.8 e
Employment in services & other sectors (% employed)	58.0	61.4 e	62.7 e
Unemployment rate (% of labour force) e	5.0	3.6	2.6
Labour force participation rate (female/male pop. %) e	27.0 / 82.2	30.3 / 88.3	31.0 / 90.4
CPI: Consumer Price Index (2010=100)	100	109	114 c
Agricultural production index (2004-2006=100)	119	143	144 f
International trade: exports (million current US$)	36 600	35 686	38 723 e,c
International trade: imports (million current US$)	19 775	29 007	23 383 e,c
International trade: balance (million current US$)	16 825	6 679	15 340 e,c
Balance of payments, current account (million US$)	4 634	- 10 954	- 4 347 d

Major trading partners

						2019
Export partners (% of exports) e	Areas nes g	65.3	United Arab Emirates	6.9	Qatar	4.3
Import partners (% of imports) e	United Arab Emirates	45.9	China	5.9	India	4.4

Social indicators

	2010	2015	2020
Population growth rate (average annual %) h	3.8	6.8	3.6
Urban population (% of total population)	75.2	81.4	85.4 c
Urban population growth rate (average annual %) h	4.6	8.0	...
Fertility rate, total (live births per woman) h	2.9	2.9	2.9
Life expectancy at birth (females/males, years) h	77.5 / 73.2	78.7 / 74.5	80.0 / 75.8
Population age distribution (0-14/60+ years old, %)	25.7 / 3.9	21.8 / 3.8	22.5 / 4.3
International migrant stock (000/% of total pop.) i	816.2 / 26.8	1 856.2 / 43.5	2 286.2 / 46.0 c
Refugees and others of concern to the UNHCR (000)	0.1 j	0.4	0.6 c
Infant mortality rate (per 1 000 live births) h	9.8	9.6	7.3
Health: Current expenditure (% of GDP)	2.8	4.3	3.8 a
Health: Physicians (per 1 000 pop.)	1.9	2.1	2.0 d
Education: Government expenditure (% of GDP)	4.2 k	5.0 l	6.8 a
Education: Primary gross enrol. ratio (f/m per 100 pop.)	100.8 / 105.4 k	110.7 / 106.0	108.6 / 98.6 d
Education: Secondary gross enrol. ratio (f/m per 100 pop.)	97.2 / 102.3 k	102.4 / 104.2	102.5 / 111.0 d
Education: Tertiary gross enrol. ratio (f/m per 100 pop.)	28.5 / 19.8	54.2 / 28.3	55.6 / 26.4 d
Intentional homicide rate (per 100 000 pop.)	1.6	0.4	0.3 d
Seats held by women in the National Parliament (%)	0.0	1.2	2.3 m

Environment and infrastructure indicators

	2010	2015	2020
Individuals using the Internet (per 100 inhabitants)	35.8 n	73.5 e	80.2 e,a
Research & Development expenditure (% of GDP)	...	0.2	0.2 o,d
Threatened species (number)	79	90	112
Forested area (% of land area)	~0.0	~0.0	~0.0 e,a
CO2 emission estimates (million tons/tons per capita)	42.4 / 13.9	63.6 / 15.2	65.5 / 14.1 a
Energy production, primary (Petajoules)	2 793	3 228	3 242 a
Energy supply per capita (Gigajoules)	256	249	238 a
Tourist/visitor arrivals at national borders (000)	1 441	1 909	2 301 d
Important sites for terrestrial biodiversity protected (%)	8.5	11.8	11.8 c
Net Official Development Assist. received (% of GNI)	- 0.04		

2017. **b** Refers to Muscat governorate. **c** 2019. **d** 2018. **e** Estimate. **f** 2016. **g** Areas not elsewhere specified. **h** Data refers to a 5-year period preceding the reference year. **i** Refers to foreign citizens. **j** Data as at the end of December. **k** 2009. **l** 2013. **m** Data are as at 1 January of reporting year. **n** Population aged 5 years and over. **o** Partial data.

Pakistan

Region	Southern Asia	UN membership date	30 September 1947
Population (000, 2020)	220 892	Surface area (km2)	796 095[a]
Pop. density (per km2, 2020)	286.5	Sex ratio (m per 100 f)	106.0
Capital city	Islamabad	National currency	Pakistan Rupee (PKR)
Capital city pop. (000, 2020)	1 095.1[b]	Exchange rate (per US$)	154.9[b]

Economic indicators	2010	2015	2020
GDP: Gross domestic product (million current US$)	174 508	267 035	282 346[c]
GDP growth rate (annual %, const. 2015 prices)	1.6	4.7	5.4[c]
GDP per capita (current US$)	972.6	1 339.0	1 330.4[c]
Economy: Agriculture (% of Gross Value Added)[d]	24.3	25.1	24.0[c]
Economy: Industry (% of Gross Value Added)[d,e]	20.6	20.1	19.3[c]
Economy: Services and other activity (% of GVA)[d,f,g]	57.0	67.6	66.7[c]
Employment in agriculture (% of employed)	43.4	41.0	35.9[h]
Employment in industry (% of employed)	21.4	24.0	25.8[h]
Employment in services & other sectors (% employed)	35.2	35.0	38.3[h]
Unemployment rate (% of labour force)[h]	0.6	3.6	4.4
Labour force participation rate (female/male pop. %)[h]	21.7 / 79.9	23.9 / 80.8	22.2 / 81.7
CPI: Consumer Price Index (2010=100)	100[i]	145	182[b]
Agricultural production index (2004-2006=100)	111	128	128[i]
International trade: exports (million current US$)	21 413	22 089	23 759[b]
International trade: imports (million current US$)	37 537	43 990	50 047[b]
International trade: balance (million current US$)	- 16 124	- 21 901	- 26 288[b]
Balance of payments, current account (million US$)	- 1 354	- 2 803	- 7 143[b]

Major trading partners						2019
Export partners (% of exports)	United States	17.0	China	8.6	United Kingdom	7.1
Import partners (% of imports)	China	24.8	United Arab Emirates	12.6	United States	5.2

Social indicators	2010	2015	2020
Population growth rate (average annual %)[k]	2.3	2.1	2.0
Urban population (% of total population)	35.0	36.0	36.9[b]
Urban population growth rate (average annual %)[k]	2.6	2.7	...
Fertility rate, total (live births per woman)[k]	4.2	3.8	3.6
Life expectancy at birth (females/males, years)[k]	65.4 / 63.6	67.0 / 65.1	68.0 / 66.1
Population age distribution (0-14/60+ years old, %)	37.7 / 6.3	35.9 / 6.4	34.8 / 6.7
International migrant stock (000/% of total pop.)[l]	3 941.6 / 2.2	3 506.5 / 1.8	3 258.0 / 1.5[b]
Refugees and others of concern to the UNHCR (000)	4 151.0[m]	3 440.0	1 518.4[b]
Infant mortality rate (per 1 000 live births)[k]	75.6	68.1	61.3
Health: Current expenditure (% of GDP)	2.6	2.7	2.9[a]
Health: Physicians (per 1 000 pop.)	0.8	0.9	1.0[c]
Education: Government expenditure (% of GDP)	2.3	2.6	2.9[a]
Education: Primary gross enrol. ratio (f/m per 100 pop.)	77.6 / 91.0	78.3 / 91.4	86.1 / 102.0[c]
Education: Secondary gross enrol. ratio (f/m per 100 pop.)	28.8 / 37.3	34.9 / 44.0	39.1 / 45.9[c]
Education: Tertiary gross enrol. ratio (f/m per 100 pop.)	6.2 / 7.3[h,n]	8.6 / 9.8	8.3 / 9.6[c]
Intentional homicide rate (per 100 000 pop.)	7.4	4.8	3.9[c]
Seats held by women in the National Parliament (%)	22.2	20.7	20.2[o]

Environment and infrastructure indicators	2010	2015	2020
Individuals using the Internet (per 100 inhabitants)	8.0[h]	14.0[h]	15.5[a]
Research & Development expenditure (% of GDP)[p,q]	0.4[n]	0.2	0.2[a]
Threatened species (number)	109	129	155
Forested area (% of land area)[h]	2.2	1.9	1.9[a]
CO2 emission estimates (million tons/tons per capita)	129.2 / 0.8	150.7 / 0.8	183.4 / 0.9[a]
Energy production, primary (Petajoules)	2 040	2 174	2 175[h,a]
Energy supply per capita (Gigajoules)	17	18	22[a]
Tourist/visitor arrivals at national borders (000)	907	966[r]	...
Important sites for terrestrial biodiversity protected (%)	34.8	34.8	34.8[b]
Pop. using safely managed drinking water (urban/rural, %)	45.4 / 32.2	41.5 / 32.5	40.0 / 32.6[a]
Net Official Development Assist. received (% of GNI)	1.59	1.31	0.42[c]

a 2017. b 2019. c 2018. d Data classified according to ISIC Rev. 4. e Excludes publishing activities. Includes irrigation and canals. f Excludes repair of personal and household goods. g Excludes computer and related activities and radio/TV activities. h Estimate. i Break in the time series. j 2016. k Data refers to a 5-year period preceding the reference year. l Including refugees. m Data as at the end of December. n 2009. o Data are as at 1 January of reporting year. p Excluding business enterprise. q Excluding private non-profit. r 2012.

Palau

Region	Micronesia	
Population (000, 2020)	22	
Pop. density (per km2, 2020)	48.8	
Capital city	Melekeok	
Capital city pop. (000, 2020)	11.4[d,e]	

UN membership date	15 December 1994
Surface area (km2)	459[a]
Sex ratio (m per 100 f)	113.3[b,c]
National currency	US Dollar (USD)
Exchange rate (per US$)	1.0[f]

Economic indicators	2010	2015	2020
GDP: Gross domestic product (million current US$)	183	280	284[e]
GDP growth rate (annual %, const. 2015 prices)	0.3	10.1	1.7[e]
GDP per capita (current US$)	10 219.9	15 871.8	15 859.4[e]
Economy: Agriculture (% of Gross Value Added)[g]	4.2	3.3	3.5[e]
Economy: Industry (% of Gross Value Added)[g,h]	11.0	8.3	8.8[e]
Economy: Services and other activity (% of GVA)[g,i,j]	88.7	80.6	81.6[e]
Employment in agriculture (% of employed)	2.4[k,l,m]	...	...
Employment in industry (% of employed)	11.8[k,l,m]	...	...
Employment in services & other sectors (% employed)	85.9[k,l,m]	...	...
Unemployment rate (% of labour force)	4.2[l,n]	...	...
Labour force participation rate (female/male pop. %)	58.1 / 75.4[l,n]	... / ...	... / ...
CPI: Consumer Price Index (2010=100)	100	118	118[a]
International trade: exports (million current US$)[o]	12[p]	6	8[p,f]
International trade: imports (million current US$)[o]	107	150	169[p,f]
International trade: balance (million current US$)[o]	- 96	- 144	- 161[p,f]
Balance of payments, current account (million US$)	- 19	- 24	- 52[a]

Major trading partners						2019
Export partners (% of exports)[p]	Japan	77.2	Areas nes[q]	8.9	Panama	4.7
Import partners (% of imports)[p]	United States	34.8	Singapore	17.0	Rep. of Korea	10.3

Social indicators	2010	2015	2020
Population growth rate (average annual %)	0.6[r]	0.8[r]	1.1
Urban population (% of total population)	74.8	78.2	80.5[f]
Urban population growth rate (average annual %)[r]	1.6	1.7	...
Fertility rate, total (live births per woman)	...	2.2[b,s]	...
Life expectancy at birth (females/males, years)	72.1 / 66.3[n]	77.8 / 68.1[b]	... / ...
Population age distribution (0-14/60+ years old, %)	24.1 / 8.2[t,n]	20.5 / 12.1[t]	20.3 / 13.1[b,c]
International migrant stock (000/% of total pop.)	5.5 / 30.6	4.9 / 27.9	5.1 / 28.1[f]
Refugees and others of concern to the UNHCR (000)	...	~0.0	~0.0[a]
Infant mortality rate (per 1 000 live births)	...	13.3	...
Health: Current expenditure (% of GDP)[u,v]	11.6	10.9	12.0[a]
Health: Physicians (per 1 000 pop.)	1.6	1.4[w]	...
Education: Primary gross enrol. ratio (f/m per 100 pop.)	... / ...	105.2 / 119.6[w]	... / ...
Education: Secondary gross enrol. ratio (f/m per 100 pop.)	... / ...	122.9 / 110.8[w]	... / ...
Education: Tertiary gross enrol. ratio (f/m per 100 pop.)	... / ...	66.4 / 43.9[x]	... / ...
Intentional homicide rate (per 100 000 pop.)	...	17.0	11.2[e]
Seats held by women in the National Parliament (%)	0.0	0.0	12.5[y]

Environment and infrastructure indicators	2010	2015	2020
Threatened species (number)	128	177	189
Forested area (% of land area)[p]	87.6	87.6	87.6[a]
Energy production, primary (Petajoules)	...	...	0[a]
Energy supply per capita (Gigajoules)	161	174[p]	182[p,a]
Tourist/visitor arrivals at national borders (000)[z]	85	162	106[e]
Important sites for terrestrial biodiversity protected (%)	44.0	44.0	44.0[f]
Net Official Development Assist. received (% of GNI)	15.80	5.07	27.99[e]

2017. **b** Break in the time series. **c** 2016. **d** Refers to Koror. **e** 2018. **f** 2019. **g** Data classified according to ISIC Rev. 4. **h** Excludes publishing activities. Includes irrigation and canals. **i** Excludes repair of personal and household goods. **j** Excludes computer and related activities and radio/TV activities. **k** Data classified according to ISIC Rev. 3. 1. **l** population aged 16 years and over. **m** 2008. **n** 2005. **o** Imports FOB. **p** Estimate. **q** Areas not elsewhere specified. **r** Data refers to a 5-year period preceding the reference year. **s** Preliminary census results. **t** De jure population. **u** Data revision. **v** Data refer to fiscal years ending 30 September. **w** 2014. **x** 2013. **y** Data are as at 1 January of reporting year. **z** Air arrivals (Palau International Airport).

Panama

Region	Central America	UN membership date	13 November 1945
Population (000, 2020)	4 315	Surface area (km2)	75 320[a]
Pop. density (per km2, 2020)	58.0	Sex ratio (m per 100 f)	100.2
Capital city	Panama City	National currency	Balboa (PAB)
Capital city pop. (000, 2020)	1 821.7[b,c]	Exchange rate (per US$)	1.0[c]

Economic indicators	2010	2015	2020
GDP: Gross domestic product (million current US$)	29 440	54 092	65 055[d]
GDP growth rate (annual %, const. 2015 prices)	5.8	5.7	3.7[d]
GDP per capita (current US$)	8 082.0	13 630.3	15 575.1[d]
Economy: Agriculture (% of Gross Value Added)	3.8	2.9	2.3[d]
Economy: Industry (% of Gross Value Added)	20.1	28.7	30.2[d]
Economy: Services and other activity (% of GVA)	55.2	50.1	50.4[d]
Employment in agriculture (% of employed)	17.4	14.7	13.7[e]
Employment in industry (% of employed)	18.7	18.7	18.8[e]
Employment in services & other sectors (% employed)	63.9	66.6	67.5[e]
Unemployment rate (% of labour force)[e]	3.7	3.0	3.8
Labour force participation rate (female/male pop. %)[e]	47.1 / 80.0	50.7 / 79.2	53.4 / 79.8
CPI: Consumer Price Index (2010=100)[f]	100	120	122[c]
Agricultural production index (2004-2006=100)	106	114	112[g]
International trade: exports (million current US$)[h]	10 987	11 348	713[e,c]
International trade: imports (million current US$)[h]	16 737	10 375	12 836[e,c]
International trade: balance (million current US$)[h]	- 5 751	973	- 12 123[e,c]
Balance of payments, current account (million US$)	- 3 113	- 4 848	- 3 500[c]

Major trading partners						2019
Export partners (% of exports)[e]	Ecuador	21.5	Guatemala	13.2	United States	9.2
Import partners (% of imports)[e]	United States	18.8	China	16.9	Japan	14.8

Social indicators	2010	2015	2020
Population growth rate (average annual %)[i]	1.8	1.7	1.7
Urban population (% of total population)	65.1	66.7	68.1[c]
Urban population growth rate (average annual %)[i]	2.2	2.2	...
Fertility rate, total (live births per woman)[i]	2.6	2.6	2.5
Life expectancy at birth (females/males, years)[i]	79.3 / 73.5	80.4 / 74.4	81.5 / 75.1
Population age distribution (0-14/60+ years old, %)	29.1 / 9.7	27.8 / 10.8	26.5 / 12.2
International migrant stock (000/% of total pop.)	157.3 / 4.3	184.7 / 4.7	185.1 / 4.4[c]
Refugees and others of concern to the UNHCR (000)	17.6[j]	19.3	113.5[c]
Infant mortality rate (per 1 000 live births)[i]	17.8	16.0	14.1
Health: Current expenditure (% of GDP)	7.2	6.8	7.3[a]
Health: Physicians (per 1 000 pop.)	1.4	1.6[k]	1.6[g]
Education: Government expenditure (% of GDP)	3.5[l]	3.2[m]	...
Education: Primary gross enrol. ratio (f/m per 100 pop.)	103.1 / 107.0	94.9 / 97.2	93.4 / 95.4[a]
Education: Secondary gross enrol. ratio (f/m per 100 pop.)	73.5 / 69.2	77.9 / 73.9	78.3 / 74.1[a]
Education: Tertiary gross enrol. ratio (f/m per 100 pop.)	53.7 / 35.1	58.0 / 36.8	58.6 / 37.3[g]
Intentional homicide rate (per 100 000 pop.)	12.6	11.9	9.4[d]
Seats held by women in the National Parliament (%)	8.5	19.3	22.5[n]

Environment and infrastructure indicators	2010	2015	2020
Individuals using the Internet (per 100 inhabitants)	40.1[o]	51.2[p]	57.9[e,a]
Research & Development expenditure (% of GDP)	0.1	0.1	0.1[a]
Threatened species (number)	347	373	400
Forested area (% of land area)	63.2[e]	62.3	62.3[e,a]
CO2 emission estimates (million tons/tons per capita)	8.9 / 2.4	10.1 / 2.5	9.6 / 2.3[a]
Energy production, primary (Petajoules)	26	36	42[a]
Energy supply per capita (Gigajoules)	39	43	48[a]
Tourist/visitor arrivals at national borders (000)	1 324	2 110	1 785[d]
Important sites for terrestrial biodiversity protected (%)	34.4	34.4	34.4[c]
Net Official Development Assist. received (% of GNI)	0.49	0.02	0.06[d]

a 2017. b Refers to the metropolitan area of Panama City. c 2019. d 2018. e Estimate. f Urban areas. g 2016. h From 2004 to 2011 merchandise data including Zona Libre de Colon. i Data refers to a 5-year period preceding the reference year. j Data as at the end of December. k 2013. l 2008. m 2011. n Data are as at 1 January of reporting year. o Multipliers were applied to residential and commercial subscriptions, taking into account the average size of households and employees per business. p Population aged 10 years and over.

Papua New Guinea

Region	Melanesia	UN membership date	10 October 1975
Population (000, 2020)	8 947	Surface area (km2)	462 840 a
Pop. density (per km2, 2020)	19.8	Sex ratio (m per 100 f)	104.3
Capital city	Port Moresby	National currency	Kina (PGK)
Capital city pop. (000, 2020)	374.5 b	Exchange rate (per US$)	3.4 b

Economic indicators	2010	2015	2020
GDP: Gross domestic product (million current US$)	14 251	22 962	23 077 c
GDP growth rate (annual %, const. 2015 prices)	10.1	6.9	–0.0 c
GDP per capita (current US$)	1 949.4	2 832.0	2 681.4 c
Economy: Agriculture (% of Gross Value Added)	20.2	19.6	19.5 c
Economy: Industry (% of Gross Value Added)	34.2	29.9	30.5 c
Economy: Services and other activity (% of GVA)	50.8	53.9	53.5 c
Employment in agriculture (% of employed) d	66.4	61.3	57.8
Employment in industry (% of employed) d	4.8	6.4	6.7
Employment in services & other sectors (% employed) d	28.8	32.3	35.5
Unemployment rate (% of labour force) d	2.0	2.6	2.5
Labour force participation rate (female/male pop. %) d	47.2 / 49.3	46.6 / 48.2	46.0 / 47.9
CPI: Consumer Price Index (2010=100)	100 e	128	151 c
Agricultural production index (2004-2006=100)	112	121	122 f
International trade: exports (million current US$) d	5 742	8 425	11 798 b
International trade: imports (million current US$) d	3 950	2 537	3 130 b
International trade: balance (million current US$) d	1 792	5 888	8 669 b
Balance of payments, current account (million US$)	- 642	4 407	5 451 c

Major trading partners						2019
Export partners (% of exports) d	Australia	25.4	China	24.2	Japan	23.3
Import partners (% of imports) d	Australia	37.8	China	16.9	Singapore	12.8

Social indicators	2010	2015	2020
Population growth rate (average annual %) g	2.4	2.1	2.0
Urban population (% of total population)	13.0	13.0	13.2 b
Urban population growth rate (average annual %) g	2.2	2.2	
Fertility rate, total (live births per woman) g	4.1	3.8	3.6
Life expectancy at birth (females/males, years) g	62.7 / 60.0	64.1 / 61.4	65.4 / 62.9
Population age distribution (0-14/60+ years old, %)	38.3 / 5.3	36.8 / 5.5	35.1 / 6.0
International migrant stock (000/% of total pop.) h,i	30.4 / 0.4	30.9 / 0.4	31.2 / 0.4 b
Refugees and others of concern to the UNHCR (000)	9.7 i	9.9	9.9 b
Infant mortality rate (per 1 000 live births) g	54.5	48.3	41.9
Health: Current expenditure (% of GDP)	2.1	1.9	2.5 a
Health: Physicians (per 1 000 pop.)	0.1	...	0.1 c
Education: Primary gross enrol. ratio (f/m per 100 pop.)	54.3 / 61.4 k	95.7 / 107.7 l	103.6 / 113.2 f
Education: Secondary gross enrol. ratio (f/m per 100 pop.)	... / ...	33.0 / 44.0 l	39.9 / 54.7 f
Intentional homicide rate (per 100 000 pop.)	9.8	...	...
Seats held by women in the National Parliament (%)	0.9	2.7	0.0 m

Environment and infrastructure indicators	2010	2015	2020
Individuals using the Internet (per 100 inhabitants)	1.3 n	7.9 d	11.2 d,a
Research & Development expenditure (% of GDP)	...	...	–0.0 o,p,f
Threatened species (number)	453	478	585
Forested area (% of land area) d	74.1	74.1	74.1 a
Energy production, primary (Petajoules)	95	228	232 a
Energy supply per capita (Gigajoules)	20	21	20 a
Tourist/visitor arrivals at national borders (000)	140	183	140 c
Important sites for terrestrial biodiversity protected (%)	6.9	6.9	6.9 b
Net Official Development Assist. received (% of GNI)	3.92	2.78	3.50 c

2017. **b** 2019. **c** 2018. **d** Estimate. **e** Break in the time series. **f** 2016. **g** Data refers to a 5-year period preceding the reference year. **h** Refers to foreign citizens. **i** Including refugees. **j** Data as at the end of December. **k** 2008. **l** 2012. **m** Data are as at 1 January of reporting year. **n** Population aged 10 years and over. **o** Excluding business enterprise. **p** Partial data.

Paraguay

Region	South America	UN membership date	24 October 1945
Population (000, 2020)	7 132	Surface area (km2)	406 752 [a]
Pop. density (per km2, 2020)	18.0	Sex ratio (m per 100 f)	103.3
Capital city	Asunción	National currency	Guarani (PYG)
Capital city pop. (000, 2020)	3 279.2 [b,c]	Exchange rate (per US$)	6 453.1 [c]

Economic indicators

	2010	2015	2020
GDP: Gross domestic product (million current US$)	27 239	36 164	40 307 [d]
GDP growth rate (annual %, const. 2015 prices)	11.1	3.1	4.0 [d]
GDP per capita (current US$)	4 359.6	5 406.7	5 794.6 [d]
Economy: Agriculture (% of Gross Value Added)	14.0	10.2	11.0 [d]
Economy: Industry (% of Gross Value Added)	37.3	37.4	37.2 [d]
Economy: Services and other activity (% of GVA)	49.3	56.8	55.6 [d]
Employment in agriculture (% of employed)	25.6	19.7	19.9 [e]
Employment in industry (% of employed)	19.2	19.7	17.9 [e]
Employment in services & other sectors (% employed)	55.2	60.6	62.1 [e]
Unemployment rate (% of labour force) [e]	4.6	4.6	4.8
Labour force participation rate (female/male pop. %) [e]	53.8 / 83.8	55.9 / 82.9	59.4 / 84.5
CPI: Consumer Price Index (2010=100) [f,g]	100	125	144 [c]
Agricultural production index (2004-2006=100)	138	162	164 [h]
International trade: exports (million current US$)	6 517	8 328	12 425 [e,c]
International trade: imports (million current US$)	10 033	10 291	12 360 [e,c]
International trade: balance (million current US$)	- 3 517	- 1 964	64 [e,c]
Balance of payments, current account (million US$)	49	- 145	- 447 [c]

Major trading partners

							2019
Export partners (% of exports) [e]	Brazil	31.1	Argentina	24.1	Russian Federation	8.7
Import partners (% of imports) [e]	China	28.2	Brazil	22.3	Argentina	10.0

Social indicators

	2010	2015	2020
Population growth rate (average annual %) [i]	1.4	1.4	1.3
Urban population (% of total population)	59.3	60.8	61.9 [c]
Urban population growth rate (average annual %) [i]	1.9	1.8	
Fertility rate, total (live births per woman) [i]	2.9	2.6	2.4
Life expectancy at birth (females/males, years) [i]	74.2 / 70.2	75.2 / 71.3	76.2 / 72.1
Population age distribution (0-14/60+ years old, %)	32.9 / 7.8	30.4 / 8.8	28.9 / 9.9
International migrant stock (000/% of total pop.)	160.3 / 2.6	156.5 / 2.3	160.5 / 2.3 [c]
Refugees and others of concern to the UNHCR (000)	0.1 [i]	0.2	4.3 [c]
Infant mortality rate (per 1 000 live births) [i]	24.1	20.8	19.0
Health: Current expenditure (% of GDP)	4.6	6.7 [k]	6.7 [k,a]
Health: Physicians (per 1 000 pop.)	...	1.3 [l]	1.4 [d]
Education: Government expenditure (% of GDP)	2.8	3.7 [l]	3.4 [h]
Education: Primary gross enrol. ratio (f/m per 100 pop.)	100.9 / 104.3	103.0 / 105.7 [l]	... / ...
Education: Secondary gross enrol. ratio (f/m per 100 pop.)	69.8 / 65.7	78.6 / 73.3 [l]	... / ...
Education: Tertiary gross enrol. ratio (f/m per 100 pop.)	40.9 / 28.6	... / ...	... / ...
Intentional homicide rate (per 100 000 pop.)	11.9	9.2	7.1 [d]
Seats held by women in the National Parliament (%)	12.5	15.0	16.2 [m]

Environment and infrastructure indicators

	2010	2015	2020
Individuals using the Internet (per 100 inhabitants)	19.8 [n,o]	49.7 [o]	65.0 [d]
Research & Development expenditure (% of GDP)	~0.0 [p]	0.1 [q]	0.1 [q,a]
Threatened species (number)	48	58	67
Forested area (% of land area) [e]	42.7	38.6	38.6 [a]
CO2 emission estimates (million tons/tons per capita)	4.8 / 0.8	5.8 / 0.9	7.7 / 1.1 [a]
Energy production, primary (Petajoules)	324	324	338 [a]
Energy supply per capita (Gigajoules)	37	38	42 [a]
Tourist/visitor arrivals at national borders (000) [r]	465	1 215	1 181 [d]
Important sites for terrestrial biodiversity protected (%)	36.2	36.3	36.3 [c]
Pop. using safely managed drinking water (urban/rural, %)	70.3 / 41.0	71.7 / 48.2	72.2 / 50.7 [a]
Pop. using safely managed sanitation (urban/rural, %)	51.9 / 54.1	53.1 / 62.8	53.6 / 66.2 [a]
Net Official Development Assist. received (% of GNI)	0.43	0.17	0.41 [d]

a 2017. b Refers to the district of Asuncion and the 19 districts of Central Department. c 2019. d 2018. e Estimate
f For Greater Asuncion only. g Calculated by the UN Statistics Division from national indices. h 2016. i Data refers
a 5-year period preceding the reference year. j Data as at the end of December. k Data revision. l 2012. m Data are
as at 1 January of reporting year. n Users in the last 3 months. o Population aged 10 years and over. p 2008. q
Excluding business enterprise. r Excluding nationals residing abroad and crew members.

Peru

Region	South America	UN membership date	31 October 1945
Population (000, 2020)	32 972	Surface area (km2)	1 285 216[a]
Pop. density (per km2, 2020)	25.8	Sex ratio (m per 100 f)	98.7
Capital city	Lima	National currency	Sol (PEN)
Capital city pop. (000, 2020)	10 554.7[b,c]	Exchange rate (per US$)	3.3[c]

Economic indicators

	2010	2015	2020
GDP: Gross domestic product (million current US$)	147 528	189 757	222 237[d]
GDP growth rate (annual %, const. 2015 prices)	8.3	3.3	4.0[d]
GDP per capita (current US$)	5 082.3	6 227.5	6 947.3[d]
Economy: Agriculture (% of Gross Value Added)[e]	7.5	7.7	7.5[d]
Economy: Industry (% of Gross Value Added)[e,f]	39.1	33.2	33.9[d]
Economy: Services and other activity (% of GVA)[e,g,h]	55.0	59.2	59.5[d]
Employment in agriculture (% of employed)	27.7	28.3	27.2[i]
Employment in industry (% of employed)	16.9	16.6	15.3[i]
Employment in services & other sectors (% employed)	55.4	55.2	57.5[i]
Unemployment rate (% of labour force)[i]	3.5	3.0	3.2
Labour force participation rate (female/male pop. %)[i]	72.1 / 85.9	67.9 / 83.8	70.6 / 85.5
CPI: Consumer Price Index (2010=100)[i]	100	118	130[c]
Agricultural production index (2004-2006=100)	129	148	150[k]
International trade: exports (million current US$)	35 807	33 667	46 132[c]
International trade: imports (million current US$)	29 966	38 026	42 376[c]
International trade: balance (million current US$)	5 842	- 4 359	3 755[c]
Balance of payments, current account (million US$)	- 3 564	- 9 526	- 3 594[d]

Major trading partners

							2019
Export partners (% of exports)	China	29.4	United States	12.5	Canada	5.2
Import partners (% of imports)	China	24.2	United States	20.8	Brazil	5.7

Social indicators

	2010	2015	2020
Population growth rate (average annual %)[i]	0.8	1.0	1.6
Urban population (% of total population)	76.4	77.4	78.1[c]
Urban population growth rate (average annual %)[i]	1.6	1.6	...
Fertility rate, total (live births per woman)[i]	2.7	2.4	2.3
Life expectancy at birth (females/males, years)[i]	76.1 / 71.3	77.7 / 72.6	79.2 / 73.7
Population age distribution (0-14/60+ years old, %)	30.1 / 8.9	28.1 / 10.7	24.7 / 12.5
International migrant stock (000/% of total pop.)	104.7 / 0.4	154.8 / 0.5	782.2 / 2.4[c]
Refugees and others of concern to the UNHCR (000)	1.4[m]	1.8	860.1[c]
Infant mortality rate (per 1 000 live births)[i]	18.1	14.1	12.8
Health: Current expenditure (% of GDP)	4.7	5.0[i]	5.0[i,a]
Health: Physicians (per 1 000 pop.)	0.9[n]	1.1[o]	1.3[k]
Education: Government expenditure (% of GDP)	2.9	4.0	3.9[a]
Education: Primary gross enrol. ratio (f/m per 100 pop.)	110.0 / 109.8	100.3 / 100.2	105.1 / 108.8[d]
Education: Secondary gross enrol. ratio (f/m per 100 pop.)	93.5 / 91.1	97.4 / 97.8	103.6 / 109.3[d]
Education: Tertiary gross enrol. ratio (f/m per 100 pop.)	35.6 / 32.9[p]	... / ...	72.7 / 68.7[a]
Intentional homicide rate (per 100 000 pop.)	...	7.4	7.9[a]
Seats held by women in the National Parliament (%)	27.5	22.3	30.0[q,r]

Environment and infrastructure indicators

	2010	2015	2020
Individuals using the Internet (per 100 inhabitants)	34.8[s]	40.9	52.5[d]
Research & Development expenditure (% of GDP)	...	0.1	0.1[d]
Threatened species (number)	551	643	819
Forested area (% of land area)[i]	58.4	57.8	57.8[a]
CO2 emission estimates (million tons/tons per capita)	41.5 / 1.4	49.7 / 1.6	49.7 / 1.5[a]
Energy production, primary (Petajoules)	810	938	912[a]
Energy supply per capita (Gigajoules)	27	28	30[a]
Tourist/visitor arrivals at national borders (000)[t,u]	2 299	3 456	4 419[d]
Important sites for terrestrial biodiversity protected (%)	26.5	27.7	29.1[c]
Pop. using safely managed drinking water (urban/rural, %)	57.9 / 18.0	58.6 / 20.0	58.8 / 20.8[a]
Pop. using safely managed sanitation (urban/rural, %)	34.9 / ...	46.5 / ...	51.2 / ...[a]
Net Official Development Assist. received (% of GNI)	- 0.22	0.18	0.21[d]

2017. **b** Refers to the Province of Lima and the Constitutional Province of Callao. **c** 2019. **d** 2018. **e** Data classified according to ISIC Rev. 4. **f** Excludes publishing activities. Includes irrigation and canals. **g** Excludes repair of personal and household goods. **h** Excludes computer and related activities and radio/TV activities. **i** Estimate. **j** Metropolitan area. **k** 2016. **l** Data refers to a 5-year period preceding the reference year. **m** Data as at the end of December. **n** 2009. **o** 2012. **p** 2006. **q** Data are as at 1 January of reporting year. **r** The figures correspond to the situation prior to dissolution of Parliament in September 2019. New elections were held in January 2020 (final results are still pending). **s** Population aged 6 years and over. **t** Including tourists with identity document other than a passport. **u** Excluding nationals residing abroad.

Philippines

Region	South-eastern Asia	UN membership date	24 October 1945	
Population (000, 2020)	109 581	Surface area (km2)	300 000 a	
Pop. density (per km2, 2020)	367.5	Sex ratio (m per 100 f)	100.9	
Capital city	Manila	National currency	Philippine Piso (PHP)	
Capital city pop. (000, 2020)	13 698.9 b,c	Exchange rate (per US$)	50.7 c	

Economic indicators

	2010	2015	2020
GDP: Gross domestic product (million current US$)	199 591	292 774	330 910 d
GDP growth rate (annual %, const. 2015 prices)	7.6	6.1	6.2 d
GDP per capita (current US$)	2 124.1	2 867.1	3 102.7 d
Economy: Agriculture (% of Gross Value Added) e	12.3	10.3	9.3 d
Economy: Industry (% of Gross Value Added) e,f,g	32.6	30.9	30.8 d
Economy: Services and other activity (% of GVA) e,g,h,i	58.9	61.9	63.9 d
Employment in agriculture (% of employed)	32.8 i	29.2	22.5 i
Employment in industry (% of employed)	15.5 i	16.2	19.8 i
Employment in services & other sectors (% employed)	51.6 i	54.6	57.6 i
Unemployment rate (% of labour force) i	3.6	3.1	2.2
Labour force participation rate (female/male pop. %) i	48.5 / 76.0	49.3 / 75.2	46.2 / 73.2
CPI: Consumer Price Index (2010=100) k	...	107	120 c
Agricultural production index (2004-2006=100)	112	116	113 l
International trade: exports (million current US$)	51 498	58 648	70 927 c
International trade: imports (million current US$)	58 468	70 153	117 247 c
International trade: balance (million current US$)	- 6 970	- 11 505	- 46 321 c
Balance of payments, current account (million US$)	7 179	7 266	- 464 c

Major trading partners

						2019
Export partners (% of exports)	United States	16.3	Japan	15.1	China	13.8
Import partners (% of imports)	China	22.8	Japan	9.6	Rep. of Korea	7.5

Social indicators

	2010	2015	2020
Population growth rate (average annual %) m	1.7	1.7	1.4
Urban population (% of total population)	45.3	46.3	47.1 c
Urban population growth rate (average annual %) m	1.5	2.1	...
Fertility rate, total (live births per woman) m	3.3	3.0	2.6
Life expectancy at birth (females/males, years) m	73.4 / 65.8	74.6 / 66.2	75.3 / 67.1
Population age distribution (0-14/60+ years old, %)	34.0 / 6.5	32.3 / 7.3	30.0 / 8.6
International migrant stock (000/% of total pop.) n,o	208.6 / 0.2	211.9 / 0.2	218.5 / 0.2 c
Refugees and others of concern to the UNHCR (000)	139.9 p	386.2	226.8 c
Infant mortality rate (per 1 000 live births) m	25.5	23.7	19.7
Health: Current expenditure (% of GDP) q	4.3	4.3	4.4 a
Health: Physicians (per 1 000 pop.)	1.3	...	0.6 a
Education: Government expenditure (% of GDP)	2.7 r	...	...
Education: Primary gross enrol. ratio (f/m per 100 pop.)	107.1 / 108.3 r	110.5 / 113.9	105.5 / 109.4 a
Education: Secondary gross enrol. ratio (f/m per 100 pop.)	87.5 / 80.9 r	91.5 / 84.4	90.6 / 82.0 a
Education: Tertiary gross enrol. ratio (f/m per 100 pop.)	32.9 / 26.3	40.1 / 31.3 s	40.4 / 30.8 a
Intentional homicide rate (per 100 000 pop.)	9.2	9.4	6.5 d
Seats held by women in the National Parliament (%)	21.0	27.2	28.0 t

Environment and infrastructure indicators

	2010	2015	2020
Individuals using the Internet (per 100 inhabitants)	25.0	36.0 u	60.1 i,a
Research & Development expenditure (% of GDP)	0.1 r	0.2	...
Threatened species (number)	697	767	884
Forested area (% of land area)	22.9	27.0	27.0 i,a
CO2 emission estimates (million tons/tons per capita)	77.1 / 0.8	103.9 / 1.0	126.5 / 1.2 a
Energy production, primary (Petajoules)	924	999	1 098 a
Energy supply per capita (Gigajoules)	17	20	22 a
Tourist/visitor arrivals at national borders (000) v	3 520	5 361	7 168 d
Important sites for terrestrial biodiversity protected (%)	39.9	40.1	40.1 c
Pop. using safely managed drinking water (urban/rural, %)	60.8 / 32.3	61.3 / 33.3	61.5 / 33.7 a
Pop. using safely managed sanitation (urban/rural %)	50.7 / 42.9	53.0 / 47.6	54.0 / 49.6 a
Net Official Development Assist. received (% of GNI)	0.24	0.14	0.14 d

a 2017. b Refers to the National Capital Region. c 2019. d 2018. e Data classified according to ISIC Rev. 4. f Excludes publishing activities. Includes irrigation and canals. g Including taxes less subsidies on production and imports. h Excludes computer and related activities and radio/TV activities. i Excludes repair of personal and household goods. j Estimate. k Base: 2012=100. l 2016. m Data refers to a 5-year period preceding the reference year. n Refers to foreign citizens. o Including refugees. p Data as at the end of December. q Data revision. r 2009. 2014. t Data are as at 1 January of reporting year. u Population aged 18 years and over. v Including nationals resid abroad.

Poland

Region	Eastern Europe	
Population (000, 2020)	37 847	
Pop. density (per km2, 2020)	123.6	
Capital city	Warsaw	
Capital city pop. (000, 2020)	1 775.9[b]	

UN membership date	24 October 1945
Surface area (km2)	312 679[a]
Sex ratio (m per 100 f)	94.0
National currency	Zloty (PLN)
Exchange rate (per US$)	3.8[b]

Economic indicators

	2010	2015	2020
GDP: Gross domestic product (million current US$)	479 321	477 581	585 661[c]
GDP growth rate (annual %, const. 2015 prices)	3.6	3.8	5.1[c]
GDP per capita (current US$)	12 505.2	12 556.7	15 444.0[c]
Economy: Agriculture (% of Gross Value Added)[d]	2.9	2.5	2.4[c]
Economy: Industry (% of Gross Value Added)[d,e]	33.9	33.9	32.7[c]
Economy: Services and other activity (% of GVA)[d,f,g]	60.3	62.4	62.9[c]
Employment in agriculture (% of employed)	13.1	11.5	8.9[h]
Employment in industry (% of employed)	30.3	30.5	32.0[h]
Employment in services & other sectors (% employed)	56.6	57.9	59.1[h]
Unemployment rate (% of labour force)[h]	9.6	7.5	3.0
Labour force participation rate (female/male pop. %)[h]	48.3 / 64.3	48.8 / 65.2	48.3 / 65.1
CPI: Consumer Price Index (2010=100)[i]	100	108	114[b]
Agricultural production index (2004-2006=100)	101	107	113[j]
International trade: exports (million current US$)	157 065	194 461	251 865[b]
International trade: imports (million current US$)	174 128	189 696	246 654[b]
International trade: balance (million current US$)	- 17 063	4 765	5 211[b]
Balance of payments, current account (million US$)	- 25 843	- 2 626	2 776[b]

Major trading partners

						2019
Export partners (% of exports)	Germany	27.5	Czechia	6.2	United Kingdom	6.0
Import partners (% of imports)	Germany	21.4	China	12.3	Russian Federation	6.5

Social indicators

	2010	2015	2020
Population growth rate (average annual %)[k]	---0.0	- 0.2	- 0.1
Urban population (% of total population)	60.9	60.3	60.0[b]
Urban population growth rate (average annual %)[k]	- 0.2	- 0.2	...
Fertility rate, total (live births per woman)[k]	1.4	1.3	1.4
Life expectancy at birth (females/males, years)[k]	79.8 / 71.3	81.2 / 73.1	82.4 / 74.5
Population age distribution (0-14/60+ years old, %)	15.2 / 19.4	14.8 / 22.7	15.2 / 25.9
International migrant stock (000/% of total pop.)	642.4 / 1.7	619.4 / 1.6	656.0 / 1.7[b]
Refugees and others of concern to the UNHCR (000)	18.4[l]	29.0	26.5[b]
Infant mortality rate (per 1 000 live births)[k]	5.5	4.4	3.3
Health: Current expenditure (% of GDP)[h]	6.4	6.4	6.5[a]
Health: Physicians (per 1 000 pop.)	2.2	2.3	2.4[a]
Education: Government expenditure (% of GDP)	5.1	4.8	4.6[j]
Education: Primary gross enrol. ratio (f/m per 100 pop.)	96.1 / 96.9	100.3 / 100.0[m]	100.0 / 100.0[a]
Education: Secondary gross enrol. ratio (f/m per 100 pop.)	95.7 / 96.2	105.7 / 109.7	108.1 / 111.7[a]
Education: Tertiary gross enrol. ratio (f/m per 100 pop.)	90.7 / 59.6	81.1 / 53.5	81.9 / 54.4[a]
Intentional homicide rate (per 100 000 pop.)	1.0	0.8	0.7[c]
Seats held by women in the National Parliament (%)	20.0	24.1	28.7[n]

Environment and infrastructure indicators

	2010	2015	2020
Individuals using the Internet (per 100 inhabitants)	62.3[o]	68.0[o,p]	77.5[c]
Research & Development expenditure (% of GDP)	0.7	1.0	1.2[q,c]
Threatened species (number)	37	51	95
Forested area (% of land area)	30.5	30.8	30.8[h,a]
CO2 emission estimates (million tons/tons per capita)	307.5 / 8.0	282.7 / 7.4	305.8 / 8.0[a]
Energy production, primary (Petajoules)	2 809	2 843	2 690[a]
Energy supply per capita (Gigajoules)	111	105	115[a]
Tourist/visitor arrivals at national borders (000)	12 470[r]	16 728	19 622[c]
Important sites for terrestrial biodiversity protected (%)	86.5	87.3	87.3[b]
Net Official Development Assist. disbursed (% of GNI)[s]	0.08	0.10	0.13[a]

a 2017. b 2019. c 2018. d Data classified according to ISIC Rev. 4. e Excludes publishing activities. Includes irrigation and canals. f Excludes computer and related activities and radio/TV activities. g Excludes repair of personal and household goods. h Estimate. i Calculated by the UN Statistics Division from national indices. j 2016. k Data refers to a 5-year period preceding the reference year. l Data as at the end of December. m 2014. n Data are as at 1 January of reporting year. o Population aged 16 to 74 years. p Users in the last 3 months. q Provisional data. r Border statistics are not collected any more, surveys used instead. s Development Assistance Committee member (OECD).

Portugal

Region	Southern Europe	UN membership date	14 December 1955
Population (000, 2020)	10 197	Surface area (km2)	92 226 [a]
Pop. density (per km2, 2020)	111.3	Sex ratio (m per 100 f)	89.8
Capital city	Lisbon	National currency	Euro (EUR)
Capital city pop. (000, 2020)	2 942.1 [b,c]	Exchange rate (per US$)	0.9 [c]

Economic indicators

	2010	2015	2020
GDP: Gross domestic product (million current US$)	237 881	199 314	240 792 [d]
GDP growth rate (annual %, const. 2015 prices)	1.7	1.8	2.4 [d]
GDP per capita (current US$)	22 449.9	19 223.3	23 477.7 [d]
Economy: Agriculture (% of Gross Value Added) [e]	2.2	2.4	2.4 [d]
Economy: Industry (% of Gross Value Added) [e,f]	22.7	22.3	22.2 [d]
Economy: Services and other activity (% of GVA) [e,g,h]	61.7	60.2	60.9 [d]
Employment in agriculture (% of employed)	11.2	7.5	5.7 [i]
Employment in industry (% of employed)	27.3	24.3	24.6 [i]
Employment in services & other sectors (% employed)	61.5	68.1	69.8 [i]
Unemployment rate (% of labour force) [i]	10.8	12.4	5.9
Labour force participation rate (female/male pop. %) [i]	55.8 / 66.9	53.8 / 64.2	53.8 / 63.6
CPI: Consumer Price Index (2010=100) [j,k]	100	107	111 [c]
Agricultural production index (2004-2006=100)	105	116	108 [l]
International trade: exports (million current US$)	49 414	55 045	67 012 [c]
International trade: imports (million current US$)	77 682	66 909	89 929 [c]
International trade: balance (million current US$)	- 28 268	- 11 864	- 22 917 [c]
Balance of payments, current account (million US$)	- 24 407	471	- 236 [c]

Major trading partners

						2019
Export partners (% of exports)	Spain	24.9	France	13.0	Germany	12.0
Import partners (% of imports)	Spain	30.4	Germany	13.3	France	9.8

Social indicators

	2010	2015	2020
Population growth rate (average annual %) [m]	0.2	- 0.4	- 0.3
Urban population (% of total population)	60.6	63.5	65.8 [c]
Urban population growth rate (average annual %) [m]	1.2	0.5	...
Fertility rate, total (live births per woman) [m]	1.4	1.3	1.3
Life expectancy at birth (females/males, years) [m]	82.5 / 76.0	83.6 / 77.4	84.6 / 78.7
Population age distribution (0-14/60+ years old, %)	15.0 / 24.7	14.1 / 27.0	13.1 / 29.4
International migrant stock (000/% of total pop.)	762.8 / 7.2	864.8 / 8.3	888.2 / 8.7 [c]
Refugees and others of concern to the UNHCR (000)	0.5 [n]	1.4	3.0 [c]
Infant mortality rate (per 1 000 live births) [m]	3.3	2.9	3.0
Health: Current expenditure (% of GDP)	9.8	9.0	9.0 [a]
Health: Physicians (per 1 000 pop.)	4.0	4.7	5.1 [a]
Education: Government expenditure (% of GDP)	5.4	4.9	...
Education: Primary gross enrol. ratio (f/m per 100 pop.)	109.9 / 113.2	104.9 / 109.0	104.4 / 107.9 [a]
Education: Secondary gross enrol. ratio (f/m per 100 pop.)	108.3 / 105.3	116.9 / 120.6	118.7 / 121.1 [a]
Education: Tertiary gross enrol. ratio (f/m per 100 pop.)	71.2 / 60.2	65.6 / 57.9	67.7 / 60.1 [a]
Intentional homicide rate (per 100 000 pop.)	1.2	1.0	0.8 [d]
Seats held by women in the National Parliament (%)	27.4	31.3	40.0 [o]

Environment and infrastructure indicators

	2010	2015	2020
Individuals using the Internet (per 100 inhabitants)	53.3 [p]	68.6 [p]	74.7 [d]
Research & Development expenditure (% of GDP)	1.5	1.2	1.4 [q,d]
Threatened species (number)	171	256	465
Forested area (% of land area) [i]	35.4	34.7	34.7 [a]
CO2 emission estimates (million tons/tons per capita) [r]	47.6 / 4.5	46.9 / 4.5	50.8 / 4.9 [a]
Energy production, primary (Petajoules) [r]	242	224	220 [a]
Energy supply per capita (Gigajoules) [r]	92	88	92 [a]
Tourist/visitor arrivals at national borders (000)	6 756	11 723 [s]	16 186 [s,d]
Important sites for terrestrial biodiversity protected (%)	70.6	73.1	73.3 [c]
Pop. using safely managed sanitation (urban/rural %)	74.1 / ...	89.7 / ...	92.7 / ... [a]
Net Official Development Assist. disbursed (% of GNI) [t]	0.29	0.16	0.18 [a]

a 2017. b Refers to Grande Lisboa, the Peninsula of Setúbal, and the municipality Azambuja. c 2019. d 2018. e Data classified according to ISIC Rev. 4. f Excludes publishing activities. Includes irrigation and canals. g Excludes computer and related activities and radio/TV activities. h Excludes repair of personal and household goods. i Estimate. j Excluding rent. k Calculated by the UN Statistics Division from national indices. l 2016. m Data refers to a 5-year period preceding the reference year. n Data as at the end of December. o Data are as at 1 January of reporting year. p Population aged 16 to 74 years. q Provisional data. r Data includes the Azores and Madeira. s Include hotels, apartment hotels, "pousadas", tourist apartments, tourist villages, camping sites, recreation centres, tourism in rural areas and local accommodation. t Development Assistance Committee member (OECD).

Puerto Rico

Region	Caribbean	Population (000, 2020)	2 861	
Surface area (km2)	8 868[a]	Pop. density (per km2, 2020)	322.5	
Sex ratio (m per 100 f)	90.0	Capital city	San Juan	
National currency	US Dollar (USD)	Capital city pop. (000, 2020)	2 451.4[b,c]	

Economic indicators	2010	2015	2020
GDP: Gross domestic product (million current US$)	98 381	103 376	101 131[d]
GDP growth rate (annual %, const. 2015 prices)	- 0.4	- 1.0	- 4.9[d]
GDP per capita (current US$)	27 482.0	30 570.7	33 271.2[d]
Economy: Agriculture (% of Gross Value Added)[e]	0.8	0.8	0.8[d]
Economy: Industry (% of Gross Value Added)[e]	50.7	51.1	49.9[d]
Economy: Services and other activity (% of GVA)[e]	46.4	49.6	48.4[d]
Employment in agriculture (% of employed)[f]	1.4	1.2	1.0
Employment in industry (% of employed)[f]	17.4	16.3	15.5
Employment in services & other sectors (% employed)[f]	81.3	82.5	83.5
Unemployment rate (% of labour force)[f]	16.1	12.0	8.4
Labour force participation rate (female/male pop. %)[f]	35.5 / 54.9	32.5 / 50.1	30.9 / 46.9
CPI: Consumer Price Index (2010=100)[g]	100	105	107[a]
Agricultural production index (2004-2006=100)	104	102	102[h]

Social indicators	2010	2015	2020
Population growth rate (average annual %)[i]	- 0.3	- 1.1	- 3.3
Urban population (% of total population)	93.8	93.6	93.6[c]
Urban population growth rate (average annual %)[i]	- 0.3	- 0.3	...
Fertility rate, total (live births per woman)[i]	1.7	1.5	1.2
Life expectancy at birth (females/males, years)[i]	81.8 / 74.0	82.7 / 75.4	83.3 / 76.2
Population age distribution (0-14/60+ years old, %)	20.6 / 18.3	18.6 / 21.3	15.8 / 27.7
International migrant stock (000/% of total pop.)	305.0 / 8.5	280.5 / 8.3	266.8 / 9.1[c]
Infant mortality rate (per 1 000 live births)[i]	7.2	6.4	5.5
Education: Government expenditure (% of GDP)	...	6.1[j]	...
Education: Primary gross enrol. ratio (f/m per 100 pop.)	99.3 / 95.7	89.1 / 89.0	82.8 / 83.2[h]
Education: Secondary gross enrol. ratio (f/m per 100 pop.)	88.3 / 83.6	98.4 / 91.0	85.4 / 78.7[h]
Education: Tertiary gross enrol. ratio (f/m per 100 pop.)	106.9 / 72.4	114.5 / 79.5	116.2 / 79.8[h]
Intentional homicide rate (per 100 000 pop.)	28.8	18.2	21.1[d]

Environment and infrastructure indicators	2010	2015	2020
Individuals using the Internet (per 100 inhabitants)	45.3[k]	63.5	70.6[f,a]
Research & Development expenditure (% of GDP)	0.5[l]	0.4	...
Threatened species (number)	103	127	146
Forested area (% of land area)[f]	54.0	55.9	55.9[a]
Energy production, primary (Petajoules)	0	1	1[f,a]
Energy supply per capita (Gigajoules)	8	16	16[a]
Tourist/visitor arrivals at national borders (000)[m]	3 186	3 542	3 068[d]
Important sites for terrestrial biodiversity protected (%)	32.8	32.8	32.8[c]

2017. **b** Refers to the Metropolitan Statistical Area. **c** 2019. **d** 2018. **e** At producers' prices. **f** Estimate. **g** Calculated by the UN Statistics Division from national indices. **h** 2016. **i** Data refers to a 5-year period preceding the reference year. **j** 2014. **k** Population aged 12 years and over. **l** 2009. **m** Arrivals of non-resident tourists by air.

Qatar

Region	Western Asia	UN membership date	21 September 1971
Population (000, 2020)	2 881	Surface area (km2)	11 607 a
Pop. density (per km2, 2020)	248.2	Sex ratio (m per 100 f)	302.4
Capital city	Doha	National currency	Qatari Rial (QAR)
Capital city pop. (000, 2020)	637.3 b,c	Exchange rate (per US$)	3.6 c

Economic indicators

	2010	2015	2020
GDP: Gross domestic product (million current US$)	125 122	161 740	191 362 d
GDP growth rate (annual %, const. 2015 prices)	16.7	3.7	1.5 d
GDP per capita (current US$)	67 403.2	63 039.1	68 793.7 d
Economy: Agriculture (% of Gross Value Added) e	0.1	0.2	0.2 d
Economy: Industry (% of Gross Value Added) e,f,g	67.5	55.4	58.8 d
Economy: Services and other activity (% of GVA) e,f,h,i	40.8	48.8	46.6 d
Employment in agriculture (% of employed)	1.5 i	1.2	1.2 i
Employment in industry (% of employed)	56.4 i	54.1	54.4 i
Employment in services & other sectors (% employed)	42.1 i	44.6	44.5 i
Unemployment rate (% of labour force) j	0.4	0.2	0.1
Labour force participation rate (female/male pop. %) j	51.4 / 96.3	58.9 / 95.2	56.8 / 95.1
CPI: Consumer Price Index (2010=100) k	...	105	108 c
Agricultural production index (2004-2006=100)	132	167	166 l
International trade: exports (million current US$)	74 964	77 971	72 935 c
International trade: imports (million current US$)	23 240	32 610	29 178 c
International trade: balance (million current US$)	51 725	45 361	43 757 c
Balance of payments, current account (million US$)	...	13 751	4 229 c

Major trading partners

						2019
Export partners (% of exports)	Japan	18.6	Rep. of Korea	15.6	China	12.4
Import partners (% of imports)	United States	18.7	China	11.9	Germany	7.1

Social indicators

	2010	2015	2020
Population growth rate (average annual %) m	15.3	6.5	2.3
Urban population (% of total population)	98.5	98.9	99.2 c
Urban population growth rate (average annual %) m	14.7	6.7	...
Fertility rate, total (live births per woman) m	2.2	2.0	1.9
Life expectancy at birth (females/males, years) m	80.3 / 77.6	81.1 / 78.3	81.8 / 78.9
Population age distribution (0-14/60+ years old, %)	12.9 / 1.6	13.4 / 2.2	13.6 / 3.6
International migrant stock (000/% of total pop.) n	1 456.4 / 78.5	1 687.6 / 65.8	2 229.7 / 78.7 c
Refugees and others of concern to the UNHCR (000)	1.3 o	1.4	1.5 c
Infant mortality rate (per 1 000 live births) m	8.3	7.3	6.3
Health: Current expenditure (% of GDP)	1.8	3.1	2.6 a
Health: Physicians (per 1 000 pop.)	3.7	1.7 p	2.5 d
Education: Government expenditure (% of GDP)	4.5	3.6 p	2.9 a
Education: Primary gross enrol. ratio (f/m per 100 pop.)	104.4 / 100.9	103.0 / 102.2	104.4 / 103.3 d
Education: Secondary gross enrol. ratio (f/m per 100 pop.)	102.7 / 108.3	... / ...	... / ...
Education: Tertiary gross enrol. ratio (f/m per 100 pop.)	26.3 / 4.5	45.0 / 6.4	54.9 / 7.0 d
Intentional homicide rate (per 100 000 pop.)	0.2	0.4 p	...
Seats held by women in the National Parliament (%)	0.0	0.0	9.8 q

Environment and infrastructure indicators

	2010	2015	2020
Individuals using the Internet (per 100 inhabitants)	69.0	92.9 r	99.7 d
Research & Development expenditure (% of GDP)	...	0.5	0.5 d
Threatened species (number)	32	35	50
Forested area (% of land area) j	0.0	0.0	0.0 a
CO2 emission estimates (million tons/tons per capita)	55.5 / 31.2	77.6 / 31.3	80.1 / 30.4 a
Energy production, primary (Petajoules)	7 428	9 316	9 387 a
Energy supply per capita (Gigajoules)	655	737	681 a
Tourist/visitor arrivals at national borders (000)	1 700	2 941	1 819 d
Important sites for terrestrial biodiversity protected (%)	40.0	40.0	40.0 c

a 2017. b Does not include the populations from the industrial area and zone 58. c 2019. d 2018. e Data classified according to ISIC Rev. 4. f At producers' prices. g Excludes publishing activities. Includes irrigation and canals. h Excludes computer and related activities and radio/TV activities. i Excludes repair of personal and household goods. Estimate. k Index base: 2013=100. l 2016. m Data refers to a 5-year period preceding the reference year. n Refers foreign citizens. o Data as at the end of December. p 2014. q Data are as at 1 January of reporting year. r Populati aged 15 years and over.

Republic of Korea

Region	Eastern Asia	UN membership date	17 September 1991
Population (000, 2020)	51 269	Surface area (km2)	100 284 [a]
Pop. density (per km2, 2020)	527.3	Sex ratio (m per 100 f)	100.2
Capital city	Seoul	National currency	South Korean Won (KRW)
Capital city pop. (000, 2020)	9 962.4 [b,c]	Exchange rate (per US$)	1 157.8 [c]

Economic indicators

	2010	2015	2020
GDP: Gross domestic product (million current US$)	1 144 067	1 465 773	1 720 489 [d]
GDP growth rate (annual %, const. 2015 prices)	6.8	2.8	2.7 [d]
GDP per capita (current US$)	23 091.2	28 840.7	33 621.9 [d]
Economy: Agriculture (% of Gross Value Added) [e]	2.4	2.2	2.0 [d]
Economy: Industry (% of Gross Value Added) [e,f]	37.5	37.2	37.3 [d]
Economy: Services and other activity (% of GVA) [e,g,h]	67.6	69.5	72.1 [d]
Employment in agriculture (% of employed)	6.6	5.1	4.8 [i]
Employment in industry (% of employed)	25.0	25.2	25.0 [i]
Employment in services & other sectors (% employed)	68.4	69.7	70.2 [i]
Unemployment rate (% of labour force) [i]	3.7	3.6	4.6
Labour force participation rate (female/male pop. %) [i]	49.5 / 72.2	51.9 / 73.3	52.8 / 73.1
CPI: Consumer Price Index (2010=100) [j]	100	110	115 [c]
Agricultural production index (2004-2006=100)	101	104	103 [k]
International trade: exports (million current US$)	466 381	526 753	542 172 [c]
International trade: imports (million current US$)	425 208	436 487	503 263 [c]
International trade: balance (million current US$)	41 173	90 266	38 909 [c]
Balance of payments, current account (million US$)	27 950	105 119	59 971 [c]

Major trading partners

						2019
Export partners (% of exports)	China	25.1	United States	13.6	Viet Nam	8.9
Import partners (% of imports)	China	21.3	United States	12.3	Japan	9.5

Social indicators

	2010	2015	2020
Population growth rate (average annual %) [l]	0.3	0.5	0.2
Urban population (% of total population)	81.9	81.6	81.4 [c]
Urban population growth rate (average annual %) [l]	0.5	0.3	...
Fertility rate, total (live births per woman) [l]	1.2	1.2	1.1
Life expectancy at birth (females/males, years) [l]	82.7 / 76.0	84.4 / 77.9	85.7 / 79.6
Population age distribution (0-14/60+ years old, %)	16.1 / 15.3	13.8 / 18.3	12.5 / 23.2
International migrant stock (000/% of total pop.) [m]	920.0 / 1.9	1 143.1 / 2.2	1 163.7 / 2.3 [c]
Refugees and others of concern to the UNHCR (000)	1.2 [n]	6.6	27.7 [c]
Infant mortality rate (per 1 000 live births) [l]	3.5	3.0	2.1
Health: Current expenditure (% of GDP) [i]	6.2	7.0	7.6 [a]
Health: Physicians (per 1 000 pop.)	2.0	2.2	2.4 [a]
Education: Primary gross enrol. ratio (f/m per 100 pop.)	101.8 / 101.7	98.7 / 98.9	98.0 / 98.2 [a]
Education: Secondary gross enrol. ratio (f/m per 100 pop.)	96.1 / 96.6	99.7 / 100.3	100.0 / 100.6 [a]
Education: Tertiary gross enrol. ratio (f/m per 100 pop.)	86.8 / 116.7	82.0 / 105.3	82.8 / 104.8 [a]
Intentional homicide rate (per 100 000 pop.)	1.0	0.7	0.6 [d]
Seats held by women in the National Parliament (%)	14.7	16.3	17.3 [o]

Environment and infrastructure indicators

	2010	2015	2020
Individuals using the Internet (per 100 inhabitants)	83.7 [p]	89.9 [q]	96.0 [d]
Research & Development expenditure (% of GDP)	3.5	4.2	4.8 [d]
Threatened species (number)	64	76	136
Forested area (% of land area) [i]	64.0	63.5	63.4 [a]
CO2 emission estimates (million tons/tons per capita)	550.9 / 11.1	582.0 / 11.4	600.0 / 11.7 [a]
Energy production, primary (Petajoules)	1 863	2 125	2 028 [a]
Energy supply per capita (Gigajoules)	212	226	232 [a]
Tourist/visitor arrivals at national borders (000) [r]	8 798	13 232	15 347 [d]
Important sites for terrestrial biodiversity protected (%)	33.8	36.4	37.5 [c]
Net Official Development Assist. disbursed (% of GNI) [s]	0.12	0.14	0.14 [a]

a 2017. b Refers to Seoul Special City. c 2019. d 2018. e Data classified according to ISIC Rev. 4. f Excludes publishing activities. Includes irrigation and canals. g Excludes computer and related activities and radio/TV activities. h Excludes repair of personal and household goods. i Estimate. j Calculated by the UN Statistics Division from national indices. k 2016. l Data refers to a 5-year period preceding the reference year. m Refers to foreign citizens. n Data as at the end of December. o Data are as at 1 January of reporting year. p Population aged 3 years and over. q Population aged 16 to 74 years. r Including nationals residing abroad and crew members. s Development Assistance Committee member (OECD).

Republic of Moldova

Region	Eastern Europe	UN membership date	02 March 1992
Population (000, 2020)	4 034 [a]	Surface area (km2)	33 846 [b]
Pop. density (per km2, 2020)	122.8 [a]	Sex ratio (m per 100 f)	91.9 [a]
Capital city	Chisinau	National currency	Moldovan Leu (MDL)
Capital city pop. (000, 2020)	504.3 [c]	Exchange rate (per US$)	17.2 [c]

Economic indicators	2010	2015	2020
GDP: Gross domestic product (million current US$)	6 975	7 745	11 309 [d]
GDP growth rate (annual %, const. 2015 prices)	7.1	- 0.3	2.8 [d]
GDP per capita (current US$)	1 707.0	1 902.7	2 791.0 [d]
Economy: Agriculture (% of Gross Value Added) [e]	13.0	13.2	11.8 [d]
Economy: Industry (% of Gross Value Added) [e,f]	23.7	26.0	26.6 [d]
Economy: Services and other activity (% of GVA) [e,g,h]	54.1	58.0	57.8 [d]
Employment in agriculture (% of employed)	27.5	34.2	35.4 [i]
Employment in industry (% of employed)	18.7	17.8	17.1 [i]
Employment in services & other sectors (% employed)	53.8	48.0	47.5 [i]
Unemployment rate (% of labour force) [i]	7.4	3.7	5.4
Labour force participation rate (female/male pop. %) [i]	38.6 / 45.2	41.3 / 47.3	40.0 / 45.8
CPI: Consumer Price Index (2010=100) [i,k]	100	136	166 [c]
Agricultural production index (2004-2006=100)	93	95	111 [l]
International trade: exports (million current US$)	1 541	1 967	2 779 [c]
International trade: imports (million current US$)	3 855	3 987	5 842 [c]
International trade: balance (million current US$)	- 2 314	- 2 020	- 3 063 [c]
Balance of payments, current account (million US$)	- 481	- 463	- 1 159 [c]

Major trading partners						2019
Export partners (% of exports)	Romania	27.5	Italy	9.6	Russian Federation	9.0
Import partners (% of imports)	Romania	14.4	Russian Federation	11.9	China	10.3

Social indicators	2010	2015	2020
Population growth rate (average annual %) [a,m]	- 0.4	- 0.1	- 0.2
Urban population (% of total population) [a]	42.6	42.5	42.7 [c]
Urban population growth rate (average annual %) [a,m]	- 0.4	- 0.2	...
Fertility rate, total (live births per woman) [a,m]	1.3	1.3	1.3
Life expectancy at birth (females/males, years) [a,m]	72.1 / 64.4	75.2 / 66.7	75.9 / 67.4
Population age distribution (0-14/60+ years old, %) [a]	16.5 / 14.1	15.8 / 16.5	15.9 / 18.9
International migrant stock (000/% of total pop.) [a]	129.5 / 3.2	106.4 / 2.6	104.7 / 2.6 [c]
Refugees and others of concern to the UNHCR (000)	2.3 [n]	6.8	4.2 [c]
Infant mortality rate (per 1 000 live births) [a,m]	15.6	14.2	12.4
Health: Current expenditure (% of GDP) [o]	10.1	8.6	7.0 [b]
Health: Physicians (per 1 000 pop.)	2.4	2.5	3.2 [b]
Education: Government expenditure (% of GDP)	9.1	7.5 [p]	6.7 [b]
Education: Primary gross enrol. ratio (f/m per 100 pop.) [i]	93.3 / 93.7	91.9 / 92.9	90.6 / 90.6 [d]
Education: Secondary gross enrol. ratio (f/m per 100 pop.) [i]	89.0 / 87.0	86.5 / 85.8	86.5 / 87.3 [d]
Education: Tertiary gross enrol. ratio (f/m per 100 pop.) [i]	43.7 / 32.7	47.4 / 35.3	45.7 / 34.2 [d]
Intentional homicide rate (per 100 000 pop.)	6.5	4.6	4.1 [d]
Seats held by women in the National Parliament (%)	23.8	20.8	24.8 [q]

Environment and infrastructure indicators	2010	2015	2020
Individuals using the Internet (per 100 inhabitants)	32.3 [i]	69.0	76.1 [i,b]
Research & Development expenditure (% of GDP)	0.4	0.3	0.3 [d]
Threatened species (number)	27	29	33
Forested area (% of land area) [i]	11.8	12.4	12.4 [b]
CO2 emission estimates (million tons/tons per capita)	7.9 / 2.2	7.6 / 2.1	7.5 / 2.1 [b]
Energy production, primary (Petajoules) [o]	8	31	37 [b]
Energy supply per capita (Gigajoules) [o]	20	25	28 [b]
Tourist/visitor arrivals at national borders (000) [k]	64	94	160 [d]
Important sites for terrestrial biodiversity protected (%)	0.0	0.0	0.0 [c]
Pop. using safely managed sanitation (urban/rural %)	75.2 / ...	76.6 / ...	77.9 / ... [b]
Net Official Development Assist. received (% of GNI)	6.32	3.81	1.94 [d]

a Including the Transnistria region. b 2017. c 2019. d 2018. e Data classified according to ISIC Rev. 4. f Excludes publishing activities. Includes irrigation and canals. g Excludes repair of personal and household goods. h Excludes computer and related activities and radio/TV activities. i Estimate. j Data refer to 8 cities only. k Excluding the left side of the river Nistru and the municipality of Bender. l 2016. m Data refers to a 5-year period preceding the reference year. n Data as at the end of December. o Excluding the Transnistria region. p 2014. q Data are as at 1 January of reporting year.

Réunion

Region	Eastern Africa	Population (000, 2020)	895	
Surface area (km2)	2 513[a]	Pop. density (per km2, 2020)	358.1	
Sex ratio (m per 100 f)	93.8	Capital city	Saint-Denis	
National currency	Euro (EUR)	Capital city pop. (000, 2020)	147.2[b]	
Exchange rate (per US$)	0.9[c]			

Economic indicators	2010	2015	2020
Employment in agriculture (% of employed)[e]	4.2[d]	4.3[f,g]	...
Employment in industry (% of employed)[e]	14.1[d]	12.7[f,g]	...
Employment in services & other sectors (% of employed)[e]	67.1[d]	81.7[f,g]	...
Unemployment rate (% of labour force)[e]	28.9	28.9[f,h]	...
Labour force participation rate (female/male pop. %)	45.3 / 59.9[e]	49.1 / 61.3[e,f,h]	... / ...
CPI: Consumer Price Index (2010=100)[i]	100	105	108[c]
Agricultural production index (2004-2006=100)	105	101	102[j]

Social indicators	2010	2015	2020
Population growth rate (average annual %)[k]	1.0	0.8	0.7
Urban population (% of total population)	98.5	99.3	99.6[c]
Urban population growth rate (average annual %)[k]	1.4	0.9	...
Fertility rate, total (live births per woman)[k]	2.4	2.4	2.3
Life expectancy at birth (females/males, years)[k]	81.9 / 74.5	82.9 / 76.0	83.8 / 77.3
Population age distribution (0-14/60+ years old, %)	25.4 / 12.2	24.3 / 15.3	22.4 / 18.3
International migrant stock (000/% of total pop.)	123.0 / 14.8	127.2 / 14.7	129.2 / 14.5[c]
Infant mortality rate (per 1 000 live births)[k]	5.6	4.2	2.7
Intentional homicide rate (per 100 000 pop.)	1.8[l]	...	...

Environment and infrastructure indicators	2010	2015	2020
Threatened species (number)	104	126	145
Forested area (% of land area)[m]	35.2	35.1	35.1[a]
Energy production, primary (Petajoules)	8[n]	...	...
Tourist/visitor arrivals at national borders (000)[o]	420	426	535[b]
Important sites for terrestrial biodiversity protected (%)	47.1	47.1	47.1[c]

a 2017. **b** 2018. **c** 2019. **d** Population aged 15 to 64 years. **e** Excluding the institutional population. **f** Break in the time series. **g** 2012. **h** 2013. **i** Calculated by the UN Statistics Division from national indices. **j** 2016. **k** Data refers to a 5-year period preceding the reference year. **l** 2009. **m** Estimate. **n** Data after 2010 are included in France. **o** Arrivals by air.

Romania

Region	Eastern Europe	UN membership date	14 December 1955	
Population (000, 2020)	19 238	Surface area (km2)	238 391 [a]	
Pop. density (per km2, 2020)	83.6	Sex ratio (m per 100 f)	94.6	
Capital city	Bucharest	National currency	Romanian Leu (RON)	
Capital city pop. (000, 2020)	1 812.3 [b]	Exchange rate (per US$)	4.3 [b]	

Economic indicators

	2010	2015	2020
GDP: Gross domestic product (million current US$)	166 225	177 895	239 552 [c]
GDP growth rate (annual %, const. 2015 prices)	- 3.9	3.9	4.0 [c]
GDP per capita (current US$)	8 119.7	8 928.1	12 280.8 [c]
Economy: Agriculture (% of Gross Value Added) [d]	5.6	4.8	4.8 [c]
Economy: Industry (% of Gross Value Added) [d,e]	42.4	34.1	32.0 [c]
Economy: Services and other activity (% of GVA) [d,f,g]	64.0	61.1	61.4 [c]
Employment in agriculture (% of employed)	31.0	25.6	21.3 [h]
Employment in industry (% of employed)	28.3	28.5	30.1 [h]
Employment in services & other sectors (% employed)	40.7	46.0	48.6 [h]
Unemployment rate (% of labour force) [h]	7.0	6.8	3.9
Labour force participation rate (female/male pop. %) [h]	46.3 / 64.3	45.2 / 64.4	44.9 / 64.4
CPI: Consumer Price Index (2010=100)	100 [i]	114 [i]	124 [i,b]
Agricultural production index (2004-2006=100)	90	91	95 [k]
International trade: exports (million current US$)	49 413	60 605	77 299 [b]
International trade: imports (million current US$)	62 007	69 858	96 644 [b]
International trade: balance (million current US$)	- 12 593	- 9 253	- 19 346 [b]
Balance of payments, current account (million US$)	- 8 478	- 1 015	- 11 384 [b]

Major trading partners

						2019
Export partners (% of exports)	Germany	22.4	Italy	11.3	France	6.9
Import partners (% of imports)	Germany	20.2	Italy	9.1	Hungary	7.0

Social indicators

	2010	2015	2020
Population growth rate (average annual %) [l]	- 0.9	- 0.5	- 0.7
Urban population (% of total population)	53.8	53.9	54.1 [b]
Urban population growth rate (average annual %) [l]	- 0.7	- 0.5	...
Fertility rate, total (live births per woman) [l]	1.5	1.5	1.6
Life expectancy at birth (females/males, years) [l]	76.7 / 69.5	78.4 / 71.5	79.3 / 72.4
Population age distribution (0-14/60+ years old, %)	15.8 / 21.3	15.5 / 23.8	15.5 / 25.9
International migrant stock (000/% of total pop.)	177.2 / 0.9	281.0 / 1.4	462.6 / 2.4 [b]
Refugees and others of concern to the UNHCR (000)	1.7 [m]	2.9	4.8 [b]
Infant mortality rate (per 1 000 live births) [l]	12.0	8.4	6.7
Health: Current expenditure (% of GDP) [h]	5.8	4.9	5.2 [a]
Health: Physicians (per 1 000 pop.)	2.5	2.6 [n]	3.0 [a]
Education: Government expenditure (% of GDP)	3.5	3.1	...
Education: Primary gross enrol. ratio (f/m per 100 pop.)	99.1 / 100.8	88.5 / 89.8	84.6 / 85.7 [a]
Education: Secondary gross enrol. ratio (f/m per 100 pop.)	97.2 / 98.1	92.9 / 92.9	91.4 / 91.1 [a]
Education: Tertiary gross enrol. ratio (f/m per 100 pop.)	74.4 / 54.2	52.2 / 41.7	55.4 / 43.8 [a]
Intentional homicide rate (per 100 000 pop.)	1.3	1.7	1.3 [c]
Seats held by women in the National Parliament (%)	11.4	13.7	21.9 [o]

Environment and infrastructure indicators

	2010	2015	2020
Individuals using the Internet (per 100 inhabitants)	39.9 [p]	55.8 [p]	70.7 [c]
Research & Development expenditure (% of GDP)	0.5	0.5	0.5 [c]
Threatened species (number)	64	85	140
Forested area (% of land area)	28.3	29.8	29.8 [h,a]
CO2 emission estimates (million tons/tons per capita)	74.7 / 3.7	69.6 / 3.5	70.8 / 3.6 [a]
Energy production, primary (Petajoules)	1 155	1 116	1 071 [a]
Energy supply per capita (Gigajoules)	72	67	71 [a]
Tourist/visitor arrivals at national borders (000)	7 498	9 331	11 720 [c]
Important sites for terrestrial biodiversity protected (%)	65.0	76.0	76.0 [b]
Net Official Development Assist. disbursed (% of GNI)	0.07	0.09	0.11 [a]

a 2017. b 2019. c 2018. d Data classified according to ISIC Rev. 4. e Excludes publishing activities. Includes irrigation and canals. f Excludes computer and related activities and radio/TV activities. g Excludes repair of personal and household goods. h Estimate. i Break in the time series. j Calculated by the UN Statistics Division from national indices. k 2016. l Data refers to a 5-year period preceding the reference year. m Data as at the end of December. n 2013. o Data are as at 1 January of reporting year. p Population aged 16 to 74 years.

Russian Federation

Region	Eastern Europe	
Population (000, 2020)	145 934	
Pop. density (per km2, 2020)	8.9	
Capital city	Moscow	
Capital city pop. (000, 2020)	12 476.2 [b]	

UN membership date	24 October 1945	
Surface area (km2)	17 098 246 [a]	
Sex ratio (m per 100 f)	86.4	
National currency	Russian Ruble (RUB)	
Exchange rate (per US$)	61.9 [b]	

Economic indicators

	2010	2015	2020
GDP: Gross domestic product (million current US$)	1 539 845	1 366 031	1 660 514 [c]
GDP growth rate (annual %, const. 2015 prices)	4.5	- 2.3	2.3 [c]
GDP per capita (current US$)	10 732.2	9 421.9	11 394.1 [c]
Economy: Agriculture (% of Gross Value Added)	3.8	4.3	3.5 [c]
Economy: Industry (% of Gross Value Added)	34.8	33.3	35.9 [c]
Economy: Services and other activity (% of GVA)	48.3	53.6	52.4 [c]
Employment in agriculture (% of employed)	7.7	6.7	5.6 [d]
Employment in industry (% of employed)	27.8	27.3	26.6 [d]
Employment in services & other sectors (% employed)	64.5	66.0	67.8 [d]
Unemployment rate (% of labour force) [d]	7.4	5.6	4.4
Labour force participation rate (female/male pop. %) [d]	55.9 / 70.3	55.5 / 71.2	54.4 / 69.8
CPI: Consumer Price Index (2010=100)	100	152	181 [b]
Agricultural production index (2004-2006=100)	99	131	139 [d]
International trade: exports (million current US$) [f]	397 068	343 908	426 720 [b]
International trade: imports (million current US$) [f]	228 912	182 782	247 161 [b]
International trade: balance (million current US$) [f]	168 156	161 126	179 559 [b]
Balance of payments, current account (million US$)	67 452	67 777	64 607 [b]

Major trading partners

						2019
Export partners (% of exports) [f]	China	13.4	Netherlands	10.5	Germany	6.6
Import partners (% of imports) [f]	China	21.9	Germany	10.2	Belarus	5.5

Social indicators

	2010	2015	2020
Population growth rate (average annual %) [g]	-0.0	0.2	0.1
Urban population (% of total population)	73.7	74.0	74.6 [b]
Urban population growth rate (average annual %) [g]	-0.0	0.2	...
Fertility rate, total (live births per woman) [g]	1.5	1.7	1.8
Life expectancy at birth (females/males, years) [g]	73.7 / 61.0	76.0 / 64.6	77.5 / 66.8
Population age distribution (0-14/60+ years old, %)	14.9 / 18.0	16.9 / 20.0	18.4 / 22.4
International migrant stock (000/% of total pop.)	11 194.7 / 7.8	11 643.3 / 8.0	11 640.6 / 8.0 [b]
Refugees and others of concern to the UNHCR (000)	132.6 [h]	431.2	135.5 [i,b]
Infant mortality rate (per 1 000 live births) [g]	10.7	8.3	5.8
Health: Current expenditure (% of GDP)	5.0	5.3 [j]	5.3 [j,a]
Health: Physicians (per 1 000 pop.)	2.4	3.7	...
Education: Government expenditure (% of GDP)	4.1 [k]	3.8	3.7 [e]
Education: Primary gross enrol. ratio (f/m per 100 pop.)	99.6 / 99.1 [l]	99.5 / 98.7	102.3 / 102.8 [a]
Education: Secondary gross enrol. ratio (f/m per 100 pop.)	84.1 / 85.4 [l]	101.0 / 103.4	102.1 / 104.7 [a]
Education: Tertiary gross enrol. ratio (f/m per 100 pop.)	86.8 / 64.2 [l]	87.6 / 72.7	89.1 / 75.0 [a]
Intentional homicide rate (per 100 000 pop.)	11.6	11.5	8.2 [c]
Seats held by women in the National Parliament (%)	14.0	13.6	15.8 [m]

Environment and infrastructure indicators

	2010	2015	2020
Individuals using the Internet (per 100 inhabitants)	43.0 [n]	70.1 [o,p]	80.9 [c]
Research & Development expenditure (% of GDP)	1.1	1.1	1.0 [c]
Threatened species (number)	126	217	279
Forested area (% of land area) [d]	49.8	49.8	49.8 [a]
CO2 emission estimates (million tons/tons per capita)	1 529.2 / 10.7	1 534.5 / 10.6	1 536.9 / 10.6 [a]
Energy production, primary (Petajoules)	53 679	56 024	59 485 [a]
Energy supply per capita (Gigajoules)	202	207	217 [a]
Tourist/visitor arrivals at national borders (000)	22 281	33 729	24 551 [c]
Important sites for terrestrial biodiversity protected (%)	25.1	25.1	25.1 [b]
Pop. using safely managed sanitation (urban/rural %)	62.2 / 48.4	63.1 / 53.2	63.4 / 55.2 [a]
Net Official Development Assist. disbursed (% of GNI)	0.03	0.09 [q]	0.08 [q,a]

a 2017. b 2019. c 2018. d Estimate. e 2016. f Russian data provided by the Russian Federation. Includes statistical data for the Autonomous Republic of Crimea and the city of Sevastopol, Ukraine, temporarily occupied by the Russian Federation. g Data refers to a 5-year period preceding the reference year. h Data as at the end of December. i Statelessness figure based on census figure from 2010 adjusted to reflect number of stateless persons who acquired nationality between 2011 and mid-2019. j From 2015 the data is adjusted by WHO in accordance with UN General Assembly Resolution A/RES/68/262. k 2008. l 2009. m Data are as at 1 January of reporting year. n Population aged 16 to 74 years. o Population aged 15 to 72 years. p Users in the last 3 months. q Some of the debt relief reported correspond to the credits. Statistics currently published on ODA by Russia and the estimates from the previous Chairman's reports should not be used at the same time.

Rwanda

Region	Eastern Africa	UN membership date	18 September 1962	
Population (000, 2020)	12 952	Surface area (km2)	26 338[a]	
Pop. density (per km2, 2020)	525.0	Sex ratio (m per 100 f)	96.7	
Capital city	Kigali	National currency	Rwanda Franc (RWF)	
Capital city pop. (000, 2020)	1 094.8[b]	Exchange rate (per US$)	922.5[b]	

Economic indicators

	2010	2015	2020
GDP: Gross domestic product (million current US$)	5 772	8 278	9 510[c]
GDP growth rate (annual %, const. 2015 prices)	7.3	8.9	8.6[c]
GDP per capita (current US$)	575.0	728.1	773.0[c]
Economy: Agriculture (% of Gross Value Added)[d]	30.2	30.1	31.2[c]
Economy: Industry (% of Gross Value Added)[d,e]	15.8	18.3	17.4[c]
Economy: Services and other activity (% of GVA)[d,f,g]	65.5	63.4	62.8[c]
Employment in agriculture (% of employed)[h]	79.5	66.7	61.7
Employment in industry (% of employed)[h]	5.7	8.3	9.1
Employment in services & other sectors (% employed)[h]	14.8	25.0	29.2
Unemployment rate (% of labour force)[h]	1.1	1.1	1.0
Labour force participation rate (female/male pop. %)[h]	84.1 / 84.9	83.9 / 84.0	84.0 / 83.3
CPI: Consumer Price Index (2010=100)[i,j]	100	122	141[b]
Agricultural production index (2004-2006=100)	139	149	140[k]
International trade: exports (million current US$)	242	579	992[b]
International trade: imports (million current US$)	1 405	1 858	3 214[b]
International trade: balance (million current US$)	- 1 163	- 1 279	- 2 221[b]
Balance of payments, current account (million US$)	- 427	- 1 267	- 746[c]

Major trading partners

						2019
Export partners (% of exports)	Dem. Rep. of Congo	38.0	United Arab Emirates	13.5	Burundi	9.6
Import partners (% of imports)	China	22.5	India	10.1	United Arab Emirates	8.7

Social indicators

	2010	2015	2020
Population growth rate (average annual %)[l]	2.5	2.5	2.6
Urban population (% of total population)	16.9	17.0	17.3[b]
Urban population growth rate (average annual %)[l]	2.6	2.6	...
Fertility rate, total (live births per woman)[l]	4.8	4.2	4.1
Life expectancy at birth (females/males, years)[l]	61.5 / 58.5	67.6 / 63.8	70.5 / 66.3
Population age distribution (0-14/60+ years old, %)	41.5 / 4.1	40.6 / 4.5	39.5 / 5.1
International migrant stock (000/% of total pop.)[m]	426.9 / 4.3	514.6 / 4.5	539.9 / 4.3[b]
Refugees and others of concern to the UNHCR (000)	55.7[n]	135.6	150.1[b]
Infant mortality rate (per 1 000 live births)[l]	62.7	39.4	29.2
Health: Current expenditure (% of GDP)[o]	8.6	6.5[p]	6.6[a]
Health: Physicians (per 1 000 pop.)	...	0.1	0.1[c]
Education: Government expenditure (% of GDP)	4.9	3.8[h]	3.1[c]
Education: Primary gross enrol. ratio (f/m per 100 pop.)	150.1 / 146.4	140.6 / 138.7	132.1 / 134.0[c]
Education: Secondary gross enrol. ratio (f/m per 100 pop.)	31.6 / 31.6	39.4 / 36.3	43.3 / 38.5[c]
Education: Tertiary gross enrol. ratio (f/m per 100 pop.)	5.2 / 6.7	6.7 / 8.5	6.0 / 7.5[c]
Intentional homicide rate (per 100 000 pop.)	2.9	2.6	...
Seats held by women in the National Parliament (%)	56.2	63.8	61.2[q]

Environment and infrastructure indicators

	2010	2015	2020
Individuals using the Internet (per 100 inhabitants)	8.0	18.0[h]	21.8[h,a]
Research & Development expenditure (% of GDP)	...	...	0.7[k]
Threatened species (number)	55	61	168
Forested area (% of land area)[h]	18.1	19.5	19.5[a]
Energy production, primary (Petajoules)	76	85[h]	86[h,a]
Energy supply per capita (Gigajoules)	8	8[h]	8[h,a]
Tourist/visitor arrivals at national borders (000)	504	987	932[k]
Important sites for terrestrial biodiversity protected (%)	51.7	51.7	51.7[b]
Pop. using safely managed drinking water (urban/rural, %)	35.2 / ...	41.1 / ...	43.4 / ...[a]
Net Official Development Assist. received (% of GNI)	18.00	13.47	12.02[c]

a 2017. b 2019. c 2018. d Data classified according to ISIC Rev. 4. e Excludes publishing activities. Includes irrigation and canals. f Excludes repair of personal and household goods. g Excludes computer and related activities and radio/TV activities. h Estimate. i Urban areas. j Calculated by the UN Statistics Division from national indices. 2016. l Data refers to a 5-year period preceding the reference year. m Including refugees. n Data as at the end of December. o Data revision. p Break in the time series. q Data are as at 1 January of reporting year.

Saint Helena

Region	Western Africa	Population (000, 2020)	4[a]	
Surface area (km2)	308[a,b]	Pop. density (per km2, 2020)	10.6[a]	
Capital city	Jamestown	National currency	Saint Helena Pound (SHP)	
Capital city pop. (000, 2020)	0.6[c]	Exchange rate (per US$)	0.8[d]	

Economic indicators	2010	2015	2020
Employment in agriculture (% of employed)	7.3[e,f,g]	...	...
Employment in industry (% of employed)	20.0[e,f,g]	...	...
Employment in services & other sectors (% employed)	72.7[e,f,g]	...	...
Unemployment rate (% of labour force)	2.0	...	...
International trade: exports (million current US$)[h]	–0	–0	–0[d]
International trade: imports (million current US$)[h]	20	41	71[d]
International trade: balance (million current US$)[h]	- 20	- 40	- 71[d]

Major trading partners						2019
Export partners (% of exports)[h]	United States	50.5	Japan	12.2	Rep. of Korea	10.2
Import partners (% of imports)[h]	United Kingdom	65.0	South Africa	21.2	Brazil	3.0

Social indicators	2010	2015	2020
Population growth rate (average annual %)[a]	- 0.5[i]	- 0.7[i]	0.5
Urban population (% of total population)[a]	39.5	39.5	39.9[d]
Urban population growth rate (average annual %)[a,i]	- 0.7	- 0.7	...
International migrant stock (000/% of total pop.)[a,j]	0.2 / 4.8	0.4 / 6.4	0.4 / 7.1[d]
Intentional homicide rate (per 100 000 pop.)	0.0[k]	...	...

Environment and infrastructure indicators	2010	2015	2020
Individuals using the Internet (per 100 inhabitants)	24.9	37.6[h,l]	...
Threatened species (number)[a]	60	80	173
Forested area (% of land area)[h]	5.1	5.1	5.1[b]
Energy production, primary (Petajoules)	0	0	0[b]
Energy supply per capita (Gigajoules)	30	25[h]	26[h,b]

a Including Ascension and Tristan da Cunha. b 2017. c 2018. d 2019. e Data classified according to ISIC Rev. 3. f Population aged 15 to 69 years. g 2008. h Estimate. i Data refers to a 5-year period preceding the reference year. j Refers to foreign citizens. k 2009. l 2012.

Saint Kitts and Nevis

Region	Caribbean	UN membership date	23 September 1983
Population (000, 2020)	57	Surface area (km2)	261 [a]
Pop. density (per km2, 2020)	218.5	Sex ratio (m per 100 f)	97.0 [b,c]
Capital city	Basseterre	National currency	E. Caribbean Dollar (XCD) [d]
Capital city pop. (000, 2020)	14.4 [e]	Exchange rate (per US$)	2.7 [f]

Economic indicators

	2010	2015	2020
GDP: Gross domestic product (million current US$)	760	923	1 011 [e]
GDP growth rate (annual %, const. 2015 prices)	- 0.6	1.0	2.9 [e]
GDP per capita (current US$)	15 508.6	18 029.3	19 275.4 [e]
Economy: Agriculture (% of Gross Value Added)	1.4	1.1	1.2 [e]
Economy: Industry (% of Gross Value Added)	25.2	26.1	27.7 [e]
Economy: Services and other activity (% of GVA)	86.8	87.8	87.3 [e]
CPI: Consumer Price Index (2010=100) [g]	100	106	105 [e]
Agricultural production index (2004-2006=100)	35	38	39 [h]
International trade: exports (million current US$)	32	32	63 [i,f]
International trade: imports (million current US$)	270	297	338 [i,f]
International trade: balance (million current US$)	- 238	- 265	- 275 [i,f]
Balance of payments, current account (million US$)	- 139	- 80	- 72 [e]

Major trading partners

						2019
Export partners (% of exports) [i]	United States	68.7	Saint Lucia	6.8	Trinidad and Tobago	6.5
Import partners (% of imports) [i]	United States	67.0	Trinidad and Tobago	4.4	Canada	2.7

Social indicators

	2010	2015	2020
Population growth rate (average annual %)	1.1 [j]	1.1 [j]	0.9
Urban population (% of total population)	31.3	30.8	30.8 [f]
Urban population growth rate (average annual %) [j]	0.7	0.8	...
International migrant stock (000/% of total pop.)	7.2 / 14.8	7.4 / 14.5	7.6 / 14.4 [f]
Refugees and others of concern to the UNHCR (000)	...	~0.0	~0.0 [f]
Health: Current expenditure (% of GDP)	5.3	4.9	5.0 [a]
Health: Physicians (per 1 000 pop.)	...	2.7	...
Education: Government expenditure (% of GDP)	4.0 [k]	2.6	...
Education: Primary gross enrol. ratio (f/m per 100 pop.)	110.6 / 116.5	107.9 / 108.7	107.1 / 110.4 [h]
Education: Secondary gross enrol. ratio (f/m per 100 pop.)	105.2 / 107.4 [i]	107.5 / 108.3	108.7 / 105.1 [h]
Education: Tertiary gross enrol. ratio (f/m per 100 pop.)	27.6 / 12.8 [l]	115.9 / 57.7	... / ...
Intentional homicide rate (per 100 000 pop.)	42.8	36.1 [m]	...
Seats held by women in the National Parliament (%)	6.7	6.7	20.0 [n]

Environment and infrastructure indicators

	2010	2015	2020
Individuals using the Internet (per 100 inhabitants)	63.0	75.7 [i]	80.7 [i,a]
Threatened species (number)	36	51	57
Forested area (% of land area)	42.3	42.3	42.3 [i,a]
Energy production, primary (Petajoules)	0	0 [i]	0 [a]
Energy supply per capita (Gigajoules)	62	62 [i]	63 [i,a]
Tourist/visitor arrivals at national borders (000) [o]	98	118	125 [e]
Important sites for terrestrial biodiversity protected (%)	22.3	23.3	56.8 [f]
Net Official Development Assist. received (% of GNI)	1.56	3.60 [p]	...

a 2017. b Provisional data. c 2011. d East Caribbean Dollar. e 2018. f 2019. g Calculated by the UN Statistics Division from national indices. h 2016. i Estimate. j Data refers to a 5-year period preceding the reference year. k 2007. l 2008. m 2012. n Data are as at 1 January of reporting year. o Arrivals of non-resident tourists by air. p 2013.

Saint Lucia

Region	Caribbean	UN membership date	18 September 1979
Population (000, 2020)	184	Surface area (km2)	539 a,b
Pop. density (per km2, 2020)	301.0	Sex ratio (m per 100 f)	97.0
Capital city	Castries	National currency	E. Caribbean Dollar (XCD) c
Capital city pop. (000, 2020)	22.3 d	Exchange rate (per US$)	2.7 e

Economic indicators	2010	2015	2020
GDP: Gross domestic product (million current US$)	1 400	1 659	1 922 d
GDP growth rate (annual %, const. 2015 prices)	0.4	0.2	0.9 d
GDP per capita (current US$)	8 044.1	9 262.3	10 566.0 d
Economy: Agriculture (% of Gross Value Added)	2.5	2.1	1.8 d
Economy: Industry (% of Gross Value Added)	13.7	13.0	11.6 d
Economy: Services and other activity (% of GVA)	86.0	85.3	88.7 d
Employment in agriculture (% of employed) f	19.8	18.5	17.0
Employment in industry (% of employed) f	18.6	17.9	18.3
Employment in services & other sectors (% employed) f	61.7	63.7	64.7
Unemployment rate (% of labour force) f	17.1	24.1	20.2
Labour force participation rate (female/male pop. %) f	57.0 / 74.9	58.5 / 75.2	59.7 / 74.9
CPI: Consumer Price Index (2010=100) g	100	111	110 d
Agricultural production index (2004-2006=100)	87	66	65 h
International trade: exports (million current US$)	215	181	55 f,e
International trade: imports (million current US$)	647	583	598 f,e
International trade: balance (million current US$)	- 432	- 403	- 543 f,e
Balance of payments, current account (million current US$)	- 203	38	103 d

Major trading partners						2019
Export partners (% of exports) f	United States	32.2	Trinidad and Tobago	7.9	Areas nes i	7.9
Import partners (% of imports) f	United States	43.8	Trinidad and Tobago	15.0	Areas nes i	6.0

Social indicators	2010	2015	2020
Population growth rate (average annual %) j	1.3	0.6	0.5
Urban population (% of total population)	18.4	18.5	18.8 e
Urban population growth rate (average annual %) j	- 3.4	0.6	...
Fertility rate, total (live births per woman) j	1.6	1.5	1.4
Life expectancy at birth (females/males, years) j	76.0 / 73.0	76.6 / 73.9	77.4 / 74.7
Population age distribution (0-14/60+ years old, %)	23.2 / 11.9	19.8 / 12.9	18.0 / 14.9
International migrant stock (000/% of total pop.)	9.1 / 5.2	8.7 / 4.8	8.4 / 4.6 e
Refugees and others of concern to the UNHCR (000)	~0.0 k	0.1	~0.0 e
Infant mortality rate (per 1 000 live births) j	16.3	16.0	12.5
Health: Current expenditure (% of GDP)	5.4	4.8	4.5 b
Health: Physicians (per 1 000 pop.)	1.6	2.7 l	0.6 b
Education: Government expenditure (% of GDP)	3.9 f	4.5	3.8 d
Education: Primary gross enrol. ratio (f/m per 100 pop.)	98.0 / 103.2 m	99.5 / 102.8	103.2 / 102.1 d
Education: Secondary gross enrol. ratio (f/m per 100 pop.)	93.3 / 94.4	88.1 / 88.9	89.4 / 89.3 d
Education: Tertiary gross enrol. ratio (f/m per 100 pop.)	17.8 / 6.9	21.4 / 11.3	18.7 / 9.4 d
Intentional homicide rate (per 100 000 pop.)	25.3	15.6	21.4 d
Seats held by women in the National Parliament (%)	11.1	16.7	16.7 n

Environment and infrastructure indicators	2010	2015	2020
Individuals using the Internet (per 100 inhabitants) f	32.5	42.5	50.8 b
Threatened species (number)	46	58	69
Forested area (% of land area) f	33.8	33.3	33.3 b
Energy production, primary (Petajoules)	0	0	0 b
Energy supply per capita (Gigajoules)	31	30	29 b
Tourist/visitor arrivals at national borders (000) o	306	345	395 d
Important sites for terrestrial biodiversity protected (%)	45.6	45.6	45.6 e
Net Official Development Assist. received (% of GNI)	3.03	0.93	0.49 d

Refers to habitable area. Excludes Saint Lucia's Forest Reserve. **b** 2017. **c** East Caribbean Dollar. **d** 2018. **e** 2019. Estimate. **g** Calculated by the UN Statistics Division from national indices. **h** 2016. **i** Areas not elsewhere specified. Data refers to a 5-year period preceding the reference year. **k** Data as at the end of December. **l** 2014. **m** 2007. **n** ta are as at 1 January of reporting year. **o** Excluding nationals residing abroad.

Saint Pierre and Miquelon

Region	Northern America	Population (000, 2020)	6	
Surface area (km2)	242 a	Pop. density (per km2, 2020)	27.9	
Sex ratio (m per 100 f)	98.2 b	Capital city	Saint-Pierre	
National currency	Euro (EUR)	Capital city pop. (000, 2020)	5.7 c	
Exchange rate (per US$)	0.9 d			

Economic indicators	2010	2015	2020
Agricultural production index (2004-2006=100)	110	114	115 e
International trade: exports (million current US$) f	137	533	1 112 d
International trade: imports (million current US$) f	747	2 259	3 870 d
International trade: balance (million current US$) f	- 610	- 1 726	- 2 758 d

Major trading partners						2019
Export partners (% of exports) f	Canada	75.4	France	9.1	Belgium	5.3
Import partners (% of imports) f	France	68.4	Canada	23.2	Netherlands	2.7

Social indicators	2010	2015	2020
Population growth rate (average annual %)	~0.0 g	~0.0 g	0.4
Urban population (% of total population)	89.9	89.9	89.9 d
Urban population growth rate (average annual %) g	~0.0	0.1	...
Population age distribution (0-14/60+ years old, %)	19.1 / 17.8 b	... / ...	... / ...
International migrant stock (000/% of total pop.)	1.0 / 16.0	1.0 / 16.5	1.0 / 17.0 d
Intentional homicide rate (per 100 000 pop.)	15.8 h	...	...

Environment and infrastructure indicators	2010	2015	2020
Threatened species (number)	4	7	19
Forested area (% of land area) f	12.6	12.2	12.2 a
Energy production, primary (Petajoules)	0	0	0 a
Energy supply per capita (Gigajoules)	160 f	171 f	171 a

a 2017. b 2006. c 2018. d 2019. e 2016. f Estimate. g Data refers to a 5-year period preceding the reference year.
h 2009.

Saint Vincent and the Grenadines

Region	Caribbean	UN membership date	16 September 1980
Population (000, 2020)	111	Surface area (km2)	389 [a]
Pop. density (per km2, 2020)	284.5	Sex ratio (m per 100 f)	102.7
Capital city	Kingstown	National currency	E. Caribbean Dollar (XCD) [b]
Capital city pop. (000, 2020)	26.6 [c]	Exchange rate (per US$)	2.7 [d]

Economic indicators

	2010	2015	2020
GDP: Gross domestic product (million current US$)	681	755	811 [c]
GDP growth rate (annual %, const. 2015 prices)	- 3.3	1.3	2.2 [c]
GDP per capita (current US$)	6 292.8	6 920.9	7 361.3 [c]
Economy: Agriculture (% of Gross Value Added)	7.1	7.3	8.6 [c]
Economy: Industry (% of Gross Value Added)	19.2	18.0	17.8 [c]
Economy: Services and other activity (% of GVA)	73.3	77.3	78.0 [c]
Employment in agriculture (% of employed) [e]	12.9	11.7	10.5
Employment in industry (% of employed) [e]	20.5	20.0	19.9
Employment in services & other sectors (% employed) [e]	66.6	68.4	69.5
Unemployment rate (% of labour force) [e]	19.4	19.3	18.9
Labour force participation rate (female/male pop. %) [e]	52.9 / 78.4	53.4 / 77.6	54.4 / 76.9
CPI: Consumer Price Index (2010=100) [e]	100 [f]	105	110 [c]
Agricultural production index (2004-2006=100)	119	111	110 [g]
International trade: exports (million current US$)	42	47	37 [e,d]
International trade: imports (million current US$)	379	334	335 [e,d]
International trade: balance (million current US$)	- 338	- 287	- 298 [e,d]
Balance of payments, current account (million US$)	- 208	- 116	- 99 [c]

Major trading partners

							2019
Export partners (% of exports) [e]	Dominica	17.9	Barbados	15.0	Antigua and Barbuda	12.5
Import partners (% of imports) [e]	United States	38.6	Trinidad and Tobago	17.9	United Kingdom	7.3

Social indicators

	2010	2015	2020
Population growth rate (average annual %) [h]	- 0.1	0.2	0.3
Urban population (% of total population)	49.0	51.0	52.6 [d]
Urban population growth rate (average annual %) [h]	0.9	0.8	...
Fertility rate, total (live births per woman) [h]	2.1	2.0	1.9
Life expectancy at birth (females/males, years) [h]	74.1 / 69.4	74.5 / 69.6	74.9 / 70.1
Population age distribution (0-14/60+ years old, %)	25.8 / 11.3	23.7 / 13.2	21.9 / 14.7
International migrant stock (000/% of total pop.)	4.6 / 4.2	4.6 / 4.2	4.7 / 4.2 [d]
Infant mortality rate (per 1 000 live births) [h]	19.5	17.4	14.6
Health: Current expenditure (% of GDP)	4.6	4.3	4.5 [a]
Health: Physicians (per 1 000 pop.)	0.7	...	...
Education: Government expenditure (% of GDP)	5.1	...	5.8 [a]
Education: Primary gross enrol. ratio (f/m per 100 pop.)	106.2 / 111.9	109.7 / 110.7	112.7 / 114.1 [c]
Education: Secondary gross enrol. ratio (f/m per 100 pop.)	110.7 / 105.5	107.7 / 107.1	108.7 / 105.9 [c]
Education: Tertiary gross enrol. ratio (f/m per 100 pop.)	... / ...	29.8 / 17.8	... / ...
Intentional homicide rate (per 100 000 pop.)	23.1	25.8 [i]	36.5 [g]
Seats held by women in the National Parliament (%)	21.7	13.0	13.0 [j]

Environment and infrastructure indicators

	2010	2015	2020
Individuals using the Internet (per 100 inhabitants)	33.7 [e]	17.1	22.4 [c]
Threatened species (number)	38	54	65
Forested area (% of land area) [e]	69.2	69.2	69.2 [a]
Energy production, primary (Petajoules)	0	0	0 [a]
Energy supply per capita (Gigajoules)	31	29	35 [e,a]
Tourist/visitor arrivals at national borders (000) [k]	72	75	80 [c]
Important sites for terrestrial biodiversity protected (%)	43.0	43.0	43.0 [d]
Net Official Development Assist. received (% of GNI)	2.52	1.63	2.08 [a]

2017. **b** East Caribbean Dollar. **c** 2018. **d** 2019. **e** Estimate. **f** Break in the time series. **g** 2016. **h** Data refers to a year period preceding the reference year. **i** 2012. **j** Data are as at 1 January of reporting year. **k** Arrivals of non-resident tourists by air.

Samoa

Region	Polynesia	UN membership date	15 December 1976
Population (000, 2020)	198	Surface area (km2)	2 842 a
Pop. density (per km2, 2020)	70.1	Sex ratio (m per 100 f)	107.3
Capital city	Apia	National currency	Tala (WST)
Capital city pop. (000, 2020)	36.1 b	Exchange rate (per US$)	2.6 c

Economic indicators

	2010	2015	2020
GDP: Gross domestic product (million current US$)	692	787	833 b
GDP growth rate (annual %, const. 2015 prices)	2.4	6.7	0.7 b
GDP per capita (current US$)	3 722.1	4 066.3	4 249.6 b
Economy: Agriculture (% of Gross Value Added) d	9.1	8.9	9.4 b
Economy: Industry (% of Gross Value Added) e,f	18.1	18.1	14.6 b
Economy: Services and other activity (% of GVA) g,h,i	48.6	48.9	51.2 b
Employment in agriculture (% of employed) j	34.5	32.3	29.9
Employment in industry (% of employed) j	23.1	22.6	23.3
Employment in services & other sectors (% employed) j	42.4	45.1	46.9
Unemployment rate (% of labour force) j	5.6	8.7	8.4
Labour force participation rate (female/male pop. %) j	31.6 / 56.0	31.7 / 56.5	31.0 / 55.2
CPI: Consumer Price Index (2010=100) j,k	100	108	118 c
Agricultural production index (2004-2006=100)	107	119	118 l
International trade: exports (million current US$)	70	59	32 j,c
International trade: imports (million current US$)	310	371	390 j,c
International trade: balance (million current US$)	- 240	- 312	- 358 j,c
Balance of payments, current account (million US$)	- 44	- 13	20 b

Major trading partners

							2019
Export partners (% of exports) j	American Samoa	26.7	New Zealand	17.7	Tokelau	13.8
Import partners (% of imports) j	New Zealand	24.9	Singapore	18.4	China	11.9

Social indicators

	2010	2015	2020
Population growth rate (average annual %) m	0.7	0.8	0.5
Urban population (% of total population)	20.1	18.9	18.1 c
Urban population growth rate (average annual %) m	- 0.4	- 0.4	...
Fertility rate, total (live births per woman) m	4.5	4.2	3.9
Life expectancy at birth (females/males, years) m	73.5 / 68.8	74.5 / 70.2	75.2 / 71.1
Population age distribution (0-14/60+ years old, %)	38.3 / 7.1	38.8 / 7.0	37.2 / 8.0
International migrant stock (000/% of total pop.)	5.1 / 2.8	4.3 / 2.2	4.0 / 2.0 c
Refugees and others of concern to the UNHCR (000)	...	...	~0.0 c
Infant mortality rate (per 1 000 live births) m	16.6	15.1	13.4
Health: Current expenditure (% of GDP) n	5.5	5.7	5.5 a
Health: Physicians (per 1 000 pop.)	0.3	0.5 o	0.3 l
Education: Government expenditure (% of GDP)	5.1 p	...	4.1 l
Education: Primary gross enrol. ratio (f/m per 100 pop.)	109.9 / 111.5	106.4 / 106.4	110.4 / 110.6 b
Education: Secondary gross enrol. ratio (f/m per 100 pop.)	93.6 / 82.3	99.1 / 89.3	98.0 / 88.8 l
Intentional homicide rate (per 100 000 pop.)	8.6	3.1 o	...
Seats held by women in the National Parliament (%)	8.2	6.1	10.0 q

Environment and infrastructure indicators

	2010	2015	2020
Individuals using the Internet (per 100 inhabitants) j	7.0	25.4	33.6 a
Threatened species (number)	78	90	100
Forested area (% of land area) j	60.4	60.4	60.4 a
Energy production, primary (Petajoules)	1	1	1 a
Energy supply per capita (Gigajoules)	21 j	24	25 j,a
Tourist/visitor arrivals at national borders (000)	122	128	164 b
Important sites for terrestrial biodiversity protected (%)	8.3	8.3	13.7 c
Pop. using safely managed sanitation (urban/rural %)	39.6 / 51.8	38.3 / 51.1	37.7 / 50.9 a
Net Official Development Assist. received (% of GNI)	19.98	11.89	14.49 b

a 2017. b 2018. c 2019. d At producers' prices. e Including taxes less subsidies on production and imports. f Excludes publishing activities. Includes irrigation and canals. g Excludes computer and related activities and radio/TV activities. h Excludes repair of personal and household goods. i Data classified according to ISIC Rev. 4. j Estimate. k Excluding rent. l 2016. m Data refers to a 5-year period preceding the reference year. n Data refer to fiscal years beginning 1 July. o 2013. p 2008. q Data are as at 1 January of reporting year.

San Marino

Region	Southern Europe	UN membership date	02 March 1992
Population (000, 2020)	34	Surface area (km2)	61 [a]
Pop. density (per km2, 2020)	563.5	Sex ratio (m per 100 f)	94.9 [b,c]
Capital city	San Marino	National currency	Euro (EUR)
Capital city pop. (000, 2020)	4.5 [d]	Exchange rate (per US$)	0.9 [e]

Economic indicators	2010	2015	2020
GDP: Gross domestic product (million current US$)	2 139	1 419	1 638 [d]
GDP growth rate (annual %, const. 2015 prices)	- 4.6	- 6.2	1.1 [d]
GDP per capita (current US$)	68 505.0	42 643.4	48 472.7 [d]
Economy: Agriculture (% of Gross Value Added) [f]	0.1	0.0	0.0 [d]
Economy: Industry (% of Gross Value Added) [f,g]	35.6	34.4	34.7 [d]
Economy: Services and other activity (% of GVA) [f,h,i]	91.4	89.4	86.8 [d]
Employment in agriculture (% of employed)	0.3 [i]	...	...
Employment in industry (% of employed)	34.3 [i]	...	...
Employment in services & other sectors (% employed)	65.4 [i]	...	...
Unemployment rate (% of labour force)	4.4	6.6 [j,k,l]	...
CPI: Consumer Price Index (2010=100) [m]	...	108	112 [e]

Social indicators	2010	2015	2020
Population growth rate (average annual %)	1.2 [n]	1.2 [n]	0.5
Urban population (% of total population)	95.7	96.7	97.4 [e]
Urban population growth rate (average annual %) [n]	1.5	1.4	...
Life expectancy at birth (females/males, years)	... / ...	86.4 / 81.7 [o]	... / ...
Population age distribution (0-14/60+ years old, %)	20.9 / 21.6 [p,q,r]	15.0 / 24.1 [b]	... / ...
International migrant stock (000/% of total pop.) [s]	4.9 / 15.6	5.2 / 15.6	5.5 / 16.3 [e]
Health: Current expenditure (% of GDP)	6.6	7.4	7.4 [a]
Health: Physicians (per 1 000 pop.)	...	6.1 [l]	...
Education: Government expenditure (% of GDP)	2.3	2.4 [t]	3.0 [a]
Education: Primary gross enrol. ratio (f/m per 100 pop.)	120.3 / 106.4	103.8 / 109.5 [u]	116.9 / 100.4 [d]
Education: Secondary gross enrol. ratio (f/m per 100 pop.)	93.9 / 91.2	98.3 / 97.1 [u]	63.8 / 71.5 [d]
Education: Tertiary gross enrol. ratio (f/m per 100 pop.)	69.7 / 46.6	58.7 / 41.9 [u]	36.0 / 48.6 [d]
Intentional homicide rate (per 100 000 pop.)	0.0	0.0 [t]	...
Seats held by women in the National Parliament (%)	16.7	16.7	31.7 [v]

Environment and infrastructure indicators	2010	2015	2020
Individuals using the Internet (per 100 inhabitants)	54.2 [w]	49.6 [t]	60.2 [x,a]
Threatened species (number)	0	1	2
Forested area (% of land area) [x]	0.0	0.0	0.0 [a]
Tourist/visitor arrivals at national borders (000) [y]	120	54	84 [d]

a 2017. b Population statistics are compiled from registers. c 2015. d 2018. e 2019. f Data classified according to
SIC Rev. 4. g Excludes publishing activities. Includes irrigation and canals. h Excludes computer and related activities
and radio/TV activities. i Excludes repair of personal and household goods. j Break in the time series. k Population
aged 14 years and over. l 2014. m Index base: December 2010=100. n Data refers to a 5-year period preceding the
reference year. o 2013. p Population aged 0 to 20 years. q Provisional data. r Population aged 61 years and over. s
refers to foreign citizens. t 2011. u 2012. v Data are as at 1 January of reporting year. w 2009. x Estimate. y
including Italian tourists.

Sao Tome and Principe

Region	Middle Africa	UN membership date	16 September 1975
Population (000, 2020)	219	Surface area (km2)	964 a
Pop. density (per km2, 2020)	228.3	Sex ratio (m per 100 f)	100.2
Capital city	Sao Tome	National currency	Dobra (STN)
Capital city pop. (000, 2020)	80.1 b	Exchange rate (per US$)	21.9 c

Economic indicators

	2010	2015	2020
GDP: Gross domestic product (million current US$)	197	308	411 b
GDP growth rate (annual %, const. 2015 prices)	4.6	3.6	2.2 b
GDP per capita (current US$)	1 094.7	1 544.9	1 948.1 b
Economy: Agriculture (% of Gross Value Added)	11.8	12.2	11.3 b
Economy: Industry (% of Gross Value Added)	18.2	15.7	15.4 b
Economy: Services and other activity (% of GVA)	37.4	46.7	46.1 b
Employment in agriculture (% of employed) d	24.3	21.1	18.7
Employment in industry (% of employed) d	17.8	18.3	18.4
Employment in services & other sectors (% employed) d	57.9	60.5	62.9
Unemployment rate (% of labour force) d	14.7	13.5	13.7
Labour force participation rate (female/male pop. %) d	41.5 / 76.2	41.6 / 76.1	41.2 / 74.0
CPI: Consumer Price Index (2010=100)	100	154	185 b
Agricultural production index (2004-2006=100)	104	111	109 e
International trade: exports (million current US$)	6	9	14 d,c
International trade: imports (million current US$)	112	142	165 d,c
International trade: balance (million current US$)	- 106	- 133	- 151 d,c
Balance of payments, current account (million US$)	- 88	- 69	- 75 b

Major trading partners

						2019
Export partners (% of exports) d	Netherlands	37.8	Portugal	24.1	Belgium	17.7
Import partners (% of imports) d	Portugal	53.7	Angola	23.2	China	5.8

Social indicators

	2010	2015	2020
Population growth rate (average annual %) f	2.7	2.0	1.9
Urban population (% of total population)	65.0	70.2	73.6 c
Urban population growth rate (average annual %) f	4.2	3.8	...
Fertility rate, total (live births per woman) f	4.8	4.6	4.4
Life expectancy at birth (females/males, years) f	68.3 / 63.9	70.8 / 66.2	72.4 / 67.7
Population age distribution (0-14/60+ years old, %)	43.4 / 4.4	43.3 / 4.5	41.8 / 5.0
International migrant stock (000/% of total pop.) g	2.7 / 1.5	2.4 / 1.2	2.2 / 1.0 c
Infant mortality rate (per 1 000 live births) f	42.1	32.1	26.4
Health: Current expenditure (% of GDP) h	6.8	5.4	6.2 a
Health: Physicians (per 1 000 pop.)	...	0.3	0.1 a
Education: Government expenditure (% of GDP)	9.7	3.9	4.9 a
Education: Primary gross enrol. ratio (f/m per 100 pop.)	116.2 / 117.0	103.2 / 107.3	105.0 / 108.5 a
Education: Secondary gross enrol. ratio (f/m per 100 pop.)	52.3 / 51.2	86.9 / 78.2	95.9 / 82.9 a
Education: Tertiary gross enrol. ratio (f/m per 100 pop.)	4.3 / 4.4	13.7 / 13.1	... / ...
Intentional homicide rate (per 100 000 pop.)	3.3	3.3 i	...
Seats held by women in the National Parliament (%)	7.3	18.2	14.6 i

Environment and infrastructure indicators

	2010	2015	2020
Individuals using the Internet (per 100 inhabitants)	18.8	25.8 d	29.9 d,a
Threatened species (number)	70	81	108
Forested area (% of land area) d	55.8	55.8	55.8 a
Energy production, primary (Petajoules)	1	1	1 a
Energy supply per capita (Gigajoules)	14	14 d	14 d,a
Tourist/visitor arrivals at national borders (000)	8	26	33 b
Important sites for terrestrial biodiversity protected (%)	79.5	79.5	79.5 c
Net Official Development Assist. received (% of GNI)	25.35	15.44	10.88 b

a 2017. b 2018. c 2019. d Estimate. e 2016. f Data refers to a 5-year period preceding the reference year. g Refers to foreign citizens. h Data revision. i 2011. j Data are as at 1 January of reporting year.

Saudi Arabia

Region	Western Asia	UN membership date	24 October 1945
Population (000, 2020)	34 814	Surface area (km2)	2 206 714 a
Pop. density (per km2, 2020)	16.2	Sex ratio (m per 100 f)	137.1
Capital city	Riyadh	National currency	Saudi Riyal (SAR)
Capital city pop. (000, 2020)	7 070.7 b	Exchange rate (per US$)	3.8 b

Economic indicators

	2010	2015	2020
GDP: Gross domestic product (million current US$)	528 207	654 270	782 483 c
GDP growth rate (annual %, const. 2015 prices)	5.0	4.1	2.2 c
GDP per capita (current US$)	19 262.6	20 627.9	23 217.2 c
Economy: Agriculture (% of Gross Value Added) d	2.6	2.6	2.2 c
Economy: Industry (% of Gross Value Added) d,e	58.2	45.3	49.6 c
Economy: Services and other activity (% of GVA) d,f,g	50.4	60.0	57.4 c
Employment in agriculture (% of employed)	4.2 h	6.1	2.3 h
Employment in industry (% of employed)	21.1 h	22.7	24.8 h
Employment in services & other sectors (% employed)	74.7 h	71.2	72.9 h
Unemployment rate (% of labour force) h	5.6	5.6	5.9
Labour force participation rate (female/male pop. %) h	18.3 / 74.6	22.2 / 79.5	22.3 / 78.7
CPI: Consumer Price Index (2010=100) i	100	114	117 b
Agricultural production index (2004-2006=100)	103	102	106 j
International trade: exports (million current US$)	250 577	203 689	259 208 h,b
International trade: imports (million current US$)	103 622	174 786	136 472 h,b
International trade: balance (million current US$)	146 955	28 903	122 736 h,b
Balance of payments, current account (million US$)	66 751	- 56 724	49 842 b

Major trading partners

							2019
Export partners (% of exports) h	Areas nes k	78.6	China	3.3	United Arab Emirates	2.8
Import partners (% of imports) h	China	16.5	United States	13.3	United Arab Emirates	8.9

Social indicators

	2010	2015	2020
Population growth rate (average annual %) l	2.8	2.9	1.9
Urban population (% of total population)	82.1	83.2	84.1 b
Urban population growth rate (average annual %) l	3.0	3.1	...
Fertility rate, total (live births per woman) l	3.2	2.7	2.3
Life expectancy at birth (females/males, years) l	75.1 / 72.1	76.0 / 73.1	76.5 / 73.7
Population age distribution (0-14/60+ years old, %)	29.7 / 4.5	25.8 / 5.2	24.7 / 5.9
International migrant stock (000/% of total pop.) m,n	8 430.0 / 30.7	10 771.4 / 34.0	13 122.3 / 38.3 b
Refugees and others of concern to the UNHCR (000)	70.7 o	70.3	72.5 b
Infant mortality rate (per 1 000 live births) l	12.2	8.7	6.3
Health: Current expenditure (% of GDP)	3.6	6.0	5.8 j
Health: Physicians (per 1 000 pop.)	2.4	2.6 p	2.6 c
Education: Government expenditure (% of GDP)	5.1 q	...	...
Education: Primary gross enrol. ratio (f/m per 100 pop.)	106.2 / 107.1	112.1 / 108.7	100.3 / 99.2 c
Education: Secondary gross enrol. ratio (f/m per 100 pop.)	89.0 / 100.4 h,r	115.0 / 117.9	106.8 / 113.2 c
Education: Tertiary gross enrol. ratio (f/m per 100 pop.)	39.3 / 34.1	61.4 / 60.7	69.9 / 66.3 c
Intentional homicide rate (per 100 000 pop.)	1.1 s	1.5	1.3 a
Seats held by women in the National Parliament (%)	0.0	19.9	19.9 t

Environment and infrastructure indicators

	2010	2015	2020
Individuals using the Internet (per 100 inhabitants)	41.0	69.6 u	93.3 c
Research & Development expenditure (% of GDP) v,x	0.9 w	0.8 y	...
Threatened species (number)	103	119	144
Forested area (% of land area) h	0.5	0.5	0.5 a
CO2 emission estimates (million tons/tons per capita)	419.2 / 15.3	531.6 / 16.8	532.2 / 16.2 a
Energy production, primary (Petajoules) z	22 115	27 184	27 155 a
Energy supply per capita (Gigajoules) z	281	308	272 a
Tourist/visitor arrivals at national borders (000)	10 850	17 994	15 334 c
Important sites for terrestrial biodiversity protected (%)	22.0	22.0	22.0 b
Net Official Development Assist. received (% of GNI)	- 0.03 s		

2017. **b** 2019. **c** 2018. **d** Data classified according to ISIC Rev. 4. **e** Excludes publishing activities. Includes [irri]gation and canals. **f** Excludes computer and related activities and radio/TV activities. **g** Excludes repair of personal [and] household goods. **h** Estimate. **i** Calculated by the UN Statistics Division from national indices. **j** 2016. **k** Areas [not] elsewhere specified. **l** Data refers to a 5-year period preceding the reference year. **m** Refers to foreign citizens. **n** [Inc]luding refugees. **o** Data as at the end of December. **p** 2014. **r** 2009. **s** 2007. **t** Data are as at 1 January of [rep]orting year. **u** Population aged 12 to 65 years. **y** Based on R&D budget instead of R&D expenditure. **w** Break in the [tim]e series. **x** Overestimated or based on overestimated data. **y** 2013. **z** The data for crude oil production include 50 [per] cent of the output of the Neutral Zone.

Senegal

Region	Western Africa	UN membership date	28 September 1960
Population (000, 2020)	16 744	Surface area (km2)	196 712 [a,b]
Pop. density (per km2, 2020)	87.0	Sex ratio (m per 100 f)	95.3
Capital city	Dakar	National currency	CFA Franc, BCEAO (XOF) [c]
Capital city pop. (000, 2020)	3 057.1 [d,e]	Exchange rate (per US$)	583.9 [e]

Economic indicators

	2010	2015	2020
GDP: Gross domestic product (million current US$)	16 725	17 761	23 809 [f]
GDP growth rate (annual %, const. 2015 prices)	4.2	6.4	6.8 [f]
GDP per capita (current US$)	1 319.2	1 218.3	1 501.7 [f]
Economy: Agriculture (% of Gross Value Added) [g]	16.6	16.0	17.3 [f]
Economy: Industry (% of Gross Value Added) [g,h]	25.6	26.4	25.7 [f]
Economy: Services and other activity (% of GVA) [g,i,j]	55.7	56.4	55.4 [f]
Employment in agriculture (% of employed)	38.2 [k]	33.3	29.4 [k]
Employment in industry (% of employed)	12.8 [k]	13.0	13.6 [k]
Employment in services & other sectors (% employed)	49.0 [k]	53.7	56.9 [k]
Unemployment rate (% of labour force) [k]	10.4	6.8	6.7
Labour force participation rate (female/male pop. %) [k]	34.3 / 64.4	34.7 / 58.0	35.1 / 57.4
CPI: Consumer Price Index (2010=100) [l]	100 [m]	105 [m]	104 [n,f]
Agricultural production index (2004-2006=100)	151	159	145 [o]
International trade: exports (million current US$)	2 086	2 612	4 175 [e]
International trade: imports (million current US$)	4 777	5 595	8 143 [e]
International trade: balance (million current US$)	- 2 691	- 2 984	- 3 969 [e]
Balance of payments, current account (million US$)	- 589	- 945	- 2 215 [f]

Major trading partners

							2019
Export partners (% of exports)	Mali	23.0	Switzerland	14.7	India	8.7
Import partners (% of imports)	France	16.8	China	10.7	Belgium	6.9

Social indicators

	2010	2015	2020
Population growth rate (average annual %) [p]	2.7	2.8	2.8
Urban population (% of total population)	43.8	45.9	47.7 [e]
Urban population growth rate (average annual %) [p]	3.7	3.9	...
Fertility rate, total (live births per woman) [p]	5.1	5.0	4.6
Life expectancy at birth (females/males, years) [p]	63.9 / 61.1	67.5 / 63.8	69.4 / 65.3
Population age distribution (0-14/60+ years old, %)	43.5 / 4.8	43.5 / 4.8	42.6 / 4.8
International migrant stock (000/% of total pop.) [q]	256.1 / 2.0	266.5 / 1.8	275.2 / 1.7 [e]
Refugees and others of concern to the UNHCR (000)	24.2 [r]	17.3	16.2 [e]
Infant mortality rate (per 1 000 live births) [p]	47.5	38.3	32.7
Health: Current expenditure (% of GDP)	4.0	4.4	4.1 [b]
Health: Physicians (per 1 000 pop.)	0.1 [s]	0.2	0.1 [b]
Education: Government expenditure (% of GDP)	5.2	5.5	4.8 [k,b]
Education: Primary gross enrol. ratio (f/m per 100 pop.)	86.4 / 81.7	89.8 / 80.2	86.1 / 75.9 [f]
Education: Secondary gross enrol. ratio (f/m per 100 pop.)	33.8 / 38.7	50.1 / 50.4 [t]	45.7 / 41.7 [f]
Education: Tertiary gross enrol. ratio (f/m per 100 pop.)	5.6 / 9.6 [k]	8.0 / 13.5	10.3 / 15.2 [f]
Intentional homicide rate (per 100 000 pop.)	...	0.3	...
Seats held by women in the National Parliament (%)	22.7	42.7	43.0 [u]

Environment and infrastructure indicators

	2010	2015	2020
Individuals using the Internet (per 100 inhabitants)	8.0 [k,v]	27.0 [w]	46.0 [w,b]
Research & Development expenditure (% of GDP)	0.4	0.6 [x]	...
Threatened species (number)	82	106	145
Forested area (% of land area) [k]	44.0	43.0	43.0 [b]
CO2 emission estimates (million tons/tons per capita)	5.5 / 0.4	7.5 / 0.5	8.3 / 0.5 [b]
Energy production, primary (Petajoules)	86	78	67 [b]
Energy supply per capita (Gigajoules)	13	12	11 [b]
Tourist/visitor arrivals at national borders (000) [k]	900	1 007	1 365 [b]
Important sites for terrestrial biodiversity protected (%)	31.5	31.5	37.8 [e]
Pop. using safely managed sanitation (urban/rural %)	16.9 / 17.8	20.4 / 20.2	21.9 / 21.1 [b]
Net Official Development Assist. received (% of GNI)	5.83	5.00	4.25 [f]

a Surface area is based on the 2002 population and housing census. b 2017. c African Financial Community (CFA) Franc, Central Bank of West African States (BCEAO). d Refers to the sum of the Departments of Dakar, Pikinie and Guédiawaye, in Dakar Region. e 2019. f 2018. g Data classified according to ISIC Rev. 4. h Excludes publishing activities. Includes irrigation and canals. i Excludes repair of personal and household goods. j Excludes computer ar related activities and radio/TV activities. k Estimate. l Data refer to the national index. m Calculated by the UN Statistics Division from national indices. n Index base: 2014=100. o 2016. p Data refers to a 5-year period precedir the reference year. q Including refugees. r Data as at the end of December. s 2008. t 2014. u Data are as at 1 January of reporting year. v Population aged 12 years and over. w Population aged 18 years and over. x Excluding business enterprise.

Serbia

Region	Southern Europe	UN membership date	01 November 2000
Population (000, 2020)	8 737 [a]	Surface area (km2)	88 499 [b,c]
Pop. density (per km2, 2020)	99.9 [a]	Sex ratio (m per 100 f)	96.0 [a]
Capital city	Belgrade	National currency	Serbian Dinar (RSD)
Capital city pop. (000, 2020)	1 393.7 [d,e]	Exchange rate (per US$)	104.9 [e]

Economic indicators

	2010	2015	2020
GDP: Gross domestic product (million current US$)	39 460	37 160	50 597 [f]
GDP growth rate (annual %, const. 2015 prices)	0.6	0.8	4.4 [f]
GDP per capita (current US$)	5 411.9	5 237.3	7 208.8 [f]
Economy: Agriculture (% of Gross Value Added) [g]	10.2	8.2	7.7 [f]
Economy: Industry (% of Gross Value Added) [g,h]	28.4	31.4	30.8 [f]
Economy: Services and other activity (% of GVA) [g,i,j]	79.1	78.2	79.2 [f]
Employment in agriculture (% of employed)	22.3	19.4	15.1 [k]
Employment in industry (% of employed)	25.6	24.5	27.4 [k]
Employment in services & other sectors (% employed)	52.1	56.1	57.6 [k]
Unemployment rate (% of labour force) [k]	19.2	17.7	12.7
Labour force participation rate (female/male pop. %) [k]	42.9 / 59.2	44.2 / 60.4	47.3 / 62.6
CPI: Consumer Price Index (2010=100)	100	133	144 [e]
Agricultural production index (2004-2006=100)	103	95	105 [f]
International trade: exports (million current US$) [m]	9 795	13 379	19 630 [e]
International trade: imports (million current US$) [m]	16 735	18 210	26 730 [e]
International trade: balance (million current US$) [m]	- 6 940	- 4 831	- 7 100 [e]
Balance of payments, current account (million US$)	- 2 692	- 1 370	- 3 536 [e]

Major trading partners

							2019
Export partners (% of exports)	Germany	12.6	Italy	10.1	Bosnia Herzegovina	7.7
Import partners (% of imports)	Germany	12.9	Russian Federation	9.7	China	9.4

Social indicators

	2010	2015	2020
Population growth rate (average annual %) [a,n]	- 0.4	- 0.3	- 0.3
Urban population (% of total population) [a]	55.0	55.7	56.3 [e]
Urban population growth rate (average annual %) [a,n]	~0.0	- 0.1	...
Fertility rate, total (live births per woman) [a,n]	1.6	1.5	1.5
Life expectancy at birth (females/males, years) [a,n]	76.2 / 70.8	77.4 / 72.1	78.4 / 73.2
Population age distribution (0-14/60+ years old, %) [a]	17.3 / 21.1	16.2 / 24.3	15.4 / 25.3
International migrant stock (000/% of total pop.) [a]	826.3 / 9.2	807.4 / 9.1	820.3 / 9.4 [e]
Refugees and others of concern to the UNHCR (000) [a]	312.6 [o]	259.7	250.7 [f]
Infant mortality rate (per 1 000 live births) [a,n]	7.1	6.1	4.9
Health: Current expenditure (% of GDP) [p]	9.5	8.8	8.4 [c]
Health: Physicians (per 1 000 pop.)	2.5	2.5	3.1 [l]
Education: Government expenditure (% of GDP)	4.6	4.0	4.0 [c]
Education: Primary gross enrol. ratio (f/m per 100 pop.) [k]	95.6 / 96.1	101.2 / 101.5	100.3 / 100.3 [f]
Education: Secondary gross enrol. ratio (f/m per 100 pop.) [k]	92.4 / 90.5	97.4 / 96.0	95.6 / 94.6 [f]
Education: Tertiary gross enrol. ratio (f/m per 100 pop.) [k]	55.6 / 42.8	66.9 / 50.2	78.3 / 56.7 [f]
Intentional homicide rate (per 100 000 pop.)	1.4	1.2	1.2 [f]
Seats held by women in the National Parliament (%)	21.6	34.0	37.6 [q]

Environment and infrastructure indicators

	2010	2015	2020
Individuals using the Internet (per 100 inhabitants)	40.9	65.3 [r]	73.4 [f]
Research & Development expenditure (% of GDP) [s]	0.7	0.8	0.9 [f]
Threatened species (number)	46	56	86
Forested area (% of land area) [k]	31.0	31.1	31.1 [c]
CO2 emission estimates (million tons/tons per capita)	45.6 / 6.3	44.5 / 6.3	46.1 / 6.6 [c]
Energy production, primary (Petajoules) [t]	440	449	438 [c]
Energy supply per capita (Gigajoules) [t]	89	87	93 [c]
Tourist/visitor arrivals at national borders (000)	683	1 132	1 711 [f]
Important sites for terrestrial biodiversity protected (%)	22.3	26.1	26.1 [e]
Pop. using safely managed drinking water (urban/rural, %)	81.4 / 66.4	81.3 / 66.4	81.3 / 66.4 [c]
Pop. using safely managed sanitation (urban/rural, %)	20.2 / ...	22.5 / ...	23.2 / ... [c]
Net Official Development Assist. received (% of GNI)	1.62	0.83	2.23 [f]

a Including Kosovo. b Changes in total area per year are the result of new measuring and correcting of the administrative borders between former Yugoslavian countries. c 2017. d Refers to the urban population of Belgrade area. e 2019. f 2018. g Data classified according to ISIC Rev. 4. h Excludes publishing activities. Includes irrigation canals. i Excludes repair of personal and household goods. j Excludes computer and related activities and radio/TV activities. k Estimate. l 2016. m Special trade system up to 2008. n Data refers to a 5-year period preceding the reference year. o Data as at the end of December. p Excluding Kosovo and Metohija. q Data are as at 1 January of reporting year. r Population aged 16 to 74 years. s Excluding data from some regions, provinces or states. t Excluding Kosovo.

Seychelles

Region	Eastern Africa	UN membership date	21 September 1976
Population (000, 2020)	98	Surface area (km2)	457 [a]
Pop. density (per km2, 2020)	213.8	Sex ratio (m per 100 f)	105.3
Capital city	Victoria	National currency	Seychelles Rupee (SCR)
Capital city pop. (000, 2020)	28.1 [b]	Exchange rate (per US$)	14.1 [c]

Economic indicators

	2010	2015	2020
GDP: Gross domestic product (million current US$)	970	1 377	1 590 [b]
GDP growth rate (annual %, const. 2015 prices)	5.9	4.9	7.9 [b]
GDP per capita (current US$)	10 628.1	14 503.3	16 377.9 [b]
Economy: Agriculture (% of Gross Value Added) [d]	2.7	2.4	2.4 [b]
Economy: Industry (% of Gross Value Added) [d,e]	16.5	14.0	13.4 [b]
Economy: Services and other activity (% of GVA) [d,f,g]	55.4	55.4	53.2 [b]
Employment in agriculture (% of employed)	...	3.6 [h,i,j]	...
Employment in industry (% of employed)	...	17.9 [h,i,j]	...
Employment in services & other sectors (% employed)	...	78.2 [h,i,j]	...
Unemployment rate (% of labour force)	5.5 [k]	4.1 [h,i,l,j]	...
Labour force participation rate (female/male pop. %)	... / ...	61.9 / 68.3 [h,i,l,j]	... / ...
CPI: Consumer Price Index (2010=100) [m]	100	121	130 [c]
Agricultural production index (2004-2006=100)	92	100	99 [n]
International trade: exports (million current US$)	418	474	824 [c]
International trade: imports (million current US$)	1 180	975	1 438 [c]
International trade: balance (million current US$)	- 763	- 501	- 614 [c]
Balance of payments, current account (million US$)	- 214	- 256	- 278 [c]

Major trading partners

						2019
Export partners (% of exports)	United Arab Emirates	36.7	United Kingdom	14.8	British Virgin Islands	12.6
Import partners (% of imports)	United Arab Emirates	22.2	Qatar	13.9	France	7.9

Social indicators

	2010	2015	2020
Population growth rate (average annual %) [o]	0.6	0.8	0.7
Urban population (% of total population)	53.3	55.4	57.1 [c]
Urban population growth rate (average annual %) [o]	1.2	1.3	...
Fertility rate, total (live births per woman) [o]	2.3	2.4	2.5
Life expectancy at birth (females/males, years) [o]	76.6 / 68.9	77.0 / 69.6	77.3 / 69.8
Population age distribution (0-14/60+ years old, %)	22.8 / 9.9	23.2 / 10.8	23.8 / 13.0
International migrant stock (000/% of total pop.)	11.4 / 12.5	12.8 / 13.5	12.9 / 13.2 [c]
Refugees and others of concern to the UNHCR (000)	...	...	~0.0 [b]
Infant mortality rate (per 1 000 live births) [o]	12.2	12.4	10.9
Health: Current expenditure (% of GDP)	4.8	4.6	5.0 [a]
Health: Physicians (per 1 000 pop.)	1.1	1.0 [p]	2.1 [n]
Education: Government expenditure (% of GDP)	4.8 [q]	4.1 [r]	4.4 [n]
Education: Primary gross enrol. ratio (f/m per 100 pop.)	112.1 / 108.8	106.0 / 102.8	103.3 / 97.6 [b]
Education: Secondary gross enrol. ratio (f/m per 100 pop.)	77.1 / 72.5 [s]	84.4 / 78.6	84.2 / 78.8 [b]
Education: Tertiary gross enrol. ratio (f/m per 100 pop.)	... / ...	20.0 / 9.2	23.3 / 11.2 [b]
Intentional homicide rate (per 100 000 pop.)	9.9	7.4	12.5 [n]
Seats held by women in the National Parliament (%)	23.5	43.8	21.2 [t]

Environment and infrastructure indicators

	2010	2015	2020
Individuals using the Internet (per 100 inhabitants) [s]	41.0	54.3	58.8 [a]
Research & Development expenditure (% of GDP)	0.3 [k]	...	0.2 [l,n]
Threatened species (number)	190	435	451
Forested area (% of land area) [s]	88.4	88.4	88.4 [a]
Energy production, primary (Petajoules)	0	0	0 [a]
Energy supply per capita (Gigajoules)	67	72	86 [a]
Tourist/visitor arrivals at national borders (000)	175	276	362 [b]
Important sites for terrestrial biodiversity protected (%)	28.6	28.6	28.6 [c]
Net Official Development Assist. received (% of GNI)	5.89	0.52	1.17 [a]

a 2017. b 2018. c 2019. d Data classified according to ISIC Rev. 4. e Excludes publishing activities. Includes irrigation and canals. f Excludes repair of personal and household goods. g Excludes computer and related activities and radio/TV activities. h Excluding some areas. i Excluding the institutional population. j 2011. k 2005. l Break in the time series. m Calculated by the UN Statistics Division from national indices. n 2016. o Data refers to a 5-year period preceding the reference year. p 2012. q 2006. r 2014. s Estimate. t Data are as at 1 January of reporting ye

Sierra Leone

Region	Western Africa	UN membership date	27 September 1961
Population (000, 2020)	7 977	Surface area (km2)	72 300[a]
Pop. density (per km2, 2020)	110.5	Sex ratio (m per 100 f)	99.6
Capital city	Freetown	National currency	Leone (SLL)
Capital city pop. (000, 2020)	1 168.4[b]	Exchange rate (per US$)	9 716.7[b]

Economic indicators	2010	2015	2020
GDP: Gross domestic product (million current US$)	2 578	4 248	4 101[c]
GDP growth rate (annual %, const. 2015 prices)	5.3	- 20.5	4.6[c]
GDP per capita (current US$)	401.8	592.3	536.1[c]
Economy: Agriculture (% of Gross Value Added)	55.2	60.5	61.0[c]
Economy: Industry (% of Gross Value Added)	8.1	4.6	5.5[c]
Economy: Services and other activity (% of GVA)	54.3	51.3	51.9[c]
Employment in agriculture (% of employed)[d]	63.9	57.9	54.4
Employment in industry (% of employed)[d]	5.3	5.8	6.5
Employment in services & other sectors (% employed)[d]	30.8	36.3	39.1
Unemployment rate (% of labour force)[d]	4.2	4.6	4.4
Labour force participation rate (female/male pop. %)[d]	59.8 / 61.6	57.1 / 59.3	57.2 / 58.4
CPI: Consumer Price Index (2010=100)[e]	100	134	234[b]
Agricultural production index (2004-2006=100)	147	169	195[f]
International trade: exports (million current US$)	319[d]	93	44[d,b]
International trade: imports (million current US$)	776[d]	1 759	741[d,b]
International trade: balance (million current US$)	- 457[d]	- 1 666	- 697[d,b]
Balance of payments, current account (million US$)	- 585	- 1 003	- 646[c]

Major trading partners						2019
Export partners (% of exports)[d]	Netherlands	23.0	China	13.0	Ivory Coast	12.2
Import partners (% of imports)[d]	China	16.8	India	7.8	Turkey	7.2

Social indicators	2010	2015	2020
Population growth rate (average annual %)[g]	2.6	2.2	2.1
Urban population (% of total population)	38.9	40.8	42.5[b]
Urban population growth rate (average annual %)[g]	3.7	3.3	
Fertility rate, total (live births per woman)[g]	5.6	4.8	4.3
Life expectancy at birth (females/males, years)[g]	47.8 / 46.2	52.3 / 50.5	54.8 / 53.2
Population age distribution (0-14/60+ years old, %)	43.0 / 4.8	41.9 / 4.7	40.3 / 4.6
International migrant stock (000/% of total pop.)[h]	79.1 / 1.2	58.8 / 0.8	54.3 / 0.7[b]
Refugees and others of concern to the UNHCR (000)	8.6[i]	1.4	0.4[b]
Infant mortality rate (per 1 000 live births)[g]	122.1	97.1	80.8
Health: Current expenditure (% of GDP)	10.9	20.4	13.4[a]
Health: Physicians (per 1 000 pop.)	~0.0	~0.0[j]	...
Education: Government expenditure (% of GDP)	2.6	2.7[k]	4.6[a]
Education: Primary gross enrol. ratio (f/m per 100 pop.)	... / ...	116.9 / 115.3	114.7 / 110.8[c]
Education: Secondary gross enrol. ratio (f/m per 100 pop.)	... / ...	36.5 / 41.6	41.1 / 42.5[a]
Intentional homicide rate (per 100 000 pop.)	2.5	1.7	...
Seats held by women in the National Parliament (%)	13.2	12.4	12.3[l]

Environment and infrastructure indicators	2010	2015	2020
Individuals using the Internet (per 100 inhabitants)	0.6[d]	6.3[d]	9.0[m,a]
Threatened species (number)	131	158	236
Forested area (% of land area)[d]	37.8	42.2	42.2[a]
Energy production, primary (Petajoules)	52	54	55[a]
Energy supply per capita (Gigajoules)	9	9	9[a]
Tourist/visitor arrivals at national borders (000)	39[n]	24[n]	57[c]
Important sites for terrestrial biodiversity protected (%)	55.1	57.3	57.3[b]
Pop. using safely managed drinking water (urban/rural, %)	11.5 / 4.8	11.9 / 7.2	12.1 / 8.3[a]
Pop. using safely managed sanitation (urban/rural %)	18.6 / 6.7	19.8 / 7.9	20.3 / 8.4[a]
Net Official Development Assist. received (% of GNI)	17.59	22.75	13.37[c]

2017. **b** 2019. **c** 2018. **d** Estimate. **e** Calculated by the UN Statistics Division from national indices. **f** 2016. **g** Data refers to a 5-year period preceding the reference year. **h** Including refugees. **i** Data as at the end of December. **j** 2011. **k** 2014. **l** Data are as at 1 January of reporting year. **m** Users in the last 3 months. **n** Arrivals by air.

Singapore

Region	South-eastern Asia	UN membership date	21 September 1965
Population (000, 2020)	5 850	Surface area (km2)	719[a,b]
Pop. density (per km2, 2020)	8 357.6	Sex ratio (m per 100 f)	109.8
Capital city	Singapore	National currency	Singapore Dollar (SGD)
Capital city pop. (000, 2020)	5 868.1[c]	Exchange rate (per US$)	1.3[c]

Economic indicators	2010	2015	2020
GDP: Gross domestic product (million current US$)	236 420	306 254	361 115[d]
GDP growth rate (annual %, const. 2015 prices)	15.2	2.5	3.2[d]
GDP per capita (current US$)	46 075.3	54 765.0	62 720.9[d]
Economy: Agriculture (% of Gross Value Added)[e]	0.0	0.0	0.0[d]
Economy: Industry (% of Gross Value Added)[e,f,g]	27.6	25.6	26.1[d]
Economy: Services and other activity (% of GVA)[e,h,i]	76.3	82.1	80.1[d]
Employment in agriculture (% of employed)[j]	0.9	0.8	0.7
Employment in industry (% of employed)[j]	21.6	17.3	15.2
Employment in services & other sectors (% employed)[j]	77.5	81.9	84.1
Unemployment rate (% of labour force)[j]	4.1	3.8	4.4
Labour force participation rate (female/male pop. %)[j]	58.1 / 78.6	62.6 / 79.4	61.8 / 78.2
CPI: Consumer Price Index (2010=100)	100	113	114[c]
Agricultural production index (2004-2006=100)	92	109	115[k]
International trade: exports (million current US$)	353 240	357 941	390 332[c]
International trade: imports (million current US$)	313 071	308 122	358 975[c]
International trade: balance (million current US$)	40 169	49 820	31 357[c]
Balance of payments, current account (million US$)	54 996	57 574	63 139[c]

Major trading partners						2019
Export partners (% of exports)	China	13.2	China, Hong Kong SAR	11.4	Malaysia	10.5
Import partners (% of imports)	China	13.7	United States	12.2	Malaysia	11.6

Social indicators	2010	2015	2020
Population growth rate (average annual %)[l]	3.7	1.7	0.9
Urban population (% of total population)	100.0	100.0	100.0[c]
Urban population growth rate (average annual %)[l]	2.4	1.7	...
Fertility rate, total (live births per woman)[l]	1.3	1.2	1.2
Life expectancy at birth (females/males, years)[l]	83.7 / 78.7	84.5 / 80.1	85.5 / 81.2
Population age distribution (0-14/60+ years old, %)	14.0 / 12.7	12.6 / 15.7	12.3 / 20.9
International migrant stock (000/% of total pop.)	2 164.8 / 42.2	2 543.6 / 45.5	2 155.7 / 37.1[c]
Refugees and others of concern to the UNHCR (000)	~0.0[m]	~0.0	1.3[c]
Infant mortality rate (per 1 000 live births)[l]	2.2	2.1	1.6
Health: Current expenditure (% of GDP)[n,o,p]	3.2	4.2	4.4[b]
Health: Physicians (per 1 000 pop.)	1.7	2.0[q]	2.3[k]
Education: Government expenditure (% of GDP)	3.1	2.9[r]	...
Education: Primary gross enrol. ratio (f/m per 100 pop.)	... / ...	... / ...	100.6 / 100.7[j,b]
Education: Secondary gross enrol. ratio (f/m per 100 pop.)	... / ...	... / ...	107.0 / 108.1[j,b]
Education: Tertiary gross enrol. ratio (f/m per 100 pop.)	... / ...	... / ...	91.2 / 78.9[j,b]
Intentional homicide rate (per 100 000 pop.)	0.4	0.3	0.2[d]
Seats held by women in the National Parliament (%)	23.4	25.3	24.0[s]

Environment and infrastructure indicators	2010	2015	2020
Individuals using the Internet (per 100 inhabitants)	71.0[j,t]	79.0	88.2[d]
Research & Development expenditure (% of GDP)	1.9	2.2	1.9[b]
Threatened species (number)	277	287	326
Forested area (% of land area)[j]	23.3	23.1	23.1[b]
CO2 emission estimates (million tons/tons per capita)	42.4 / 8.4	45.5 / 8.2	47.4 / 8.4[b]
Energy production, primary (Petajoules)	25	28	28[b]
Energy supply per capita (Gigajoules)	213	223	204[b]
Tourist/visitor arrivals at national borders (000)[u]	9 161	12 051	14 673[d]
Important sites for terrestrial biodiversity protected (%)	21.1	21.1	21.1[c]
Pop. using safely managed drinking water (urban/rural, %)	100.0 / ...	100.0 / ...	100.0 / ...[b]
Pop. using safely managed sanitation (urban/rural, %)	100.0 / ...	100.0 / ...	100.0 / ...[b]

a The land area of Singapore comprises the mainland and other islands. b 2017. c 2019. d 2018. e Data classified according to ISIC Rev. 4. f Excludes publishing activities. Includes irrigation and canals. g Excluding mining and quarrying. h Excludes repair of personal and household goods. i Excludes computer and related activities and radio/TV activities. j Estimate. k 2016. l Data refers to a 5-year period preceding the reference year. m Data as at the end of December. n Medisave is classified as Social insurance scheme, considering that it is a compulsory payment. o Data refer to fiscal years beginning 1 April. p Provisional data. q 2014. r 2013. s Data are as at 1 January of reporting year. t Population aged 7 years and over. u Excluding Malaysian citizens arriving by land.

Sint Maarten (Dutch part)

Region	Caribbean	Population (000, 2020)		41
Surface area (km2)	34 [a]	Pop. density (per km2, 2020)		1 216.6
Sex ratio (m per 100 f)	95.7 [b,c]	Capital city		Philipsburg
National currency	Neth. Ant. Guilder (ANG) [d]	Capital city pop. (000, 2020)		40.6 [e,f]
Exchange rate (per US$)	1.8 [f]			

Economic indicators	2010	2015	2020
GDP: Gross domestic product (million current US$)	896	1 066	980 [f]
GDP growth rate (annual %, const. 2015 prices)	1.1	0.5	- 8.5 [f]
GDP per capita (current US$)	26 237.8	26 682.0	23 366.7 [f]
Economy: Agriculture (% of Gross Value Added)	0.1	0.1	0.1 [f]
Economy: Industry (% of Gross Value Added)	13.4	9.8	9.9 [f]
Economy: Services and other activity (% of GVA)	74.3	76.3	76.8 [f]
Balance of payments, current account (million US$)	...	18	64 [f]

Social indicators	2010	2015	2020
Population growth rate (average annual %)	0.4 [g]	3.1 [g]	1.3
Urban population (% of total population)	100.0	100.0	100.0 [h]
Urban population growth rate (average annual %) [g]	0.4	3.1	...
Life expectancy at birth (females/males, years)	77.2 / 72.0 [i]	77.1 / 69.2 [j,k]	... / ...
Population age distribution (0-14/60+ years old, %)	... / ...	21.0 / 10.4 [b,k]	... / ...
International migrant stock (000/% of total pop.)	26.2 / 76.7	27.3 / 68.3	28.3 / 66.7 [h]
Refugees and others of concern to the UNHCR (000)	~0.0 [l]	~0.0	0.1 [h]
Education: Primary gross enrol. ratio (f/m per 100 pop.)	... / ...	128.9 / 127.5 [c]	... / ...
Education: Secondary gross enrol. ratio (f/m per 100 pop.)	... / ...	88.5 / 92.7 [c]	... / ...
Education: Tertiary gross enrol. ratio (f/m per 100 pop.)	... / ...	9.0 / 2.6	... / ...

Environment and infrastructure indicators	2010	2015	2020
Threatened species (number)	...	49	58
Energy supply per capita (Gigajoules) [m]	...	305	292 [a]
Tourist/visitor arrivals at national borders (000) [n]	443	505	178 [f]
Important sites for terrestrial biodiversity protected (%)	5.1	5.1	5.1 [h]

a 2017. **b** De jure population. **c** 2014. **d** Netherlands Antillean Guilder. **e** Refers to the total population of Sint Maarten. **f** 2018. **g** Data refers to a 5-year period preceding the reference year. **h** 2019. **i** Data refers to a 3-year period up to and including the reference year. **j** Data refers to a 2-year period up to and including the reference year. **k** 2013. **l** Data as at the end of December. **m** Estimate. **n** Arrivals by air. Including arrivals to Saint Martin (French part).

Slovakia

Region	Eastern Europe	UN membership date	19 January 1993
Population (000, 2020)	5 460	Surface area (km2)	49 035 [a,b]
Pop. density (per km2, 2020)	113.5	Sex ratio (m per 100 f)	94.9
Capital city	Bratislava	National currency	Euro (EUR)
Capital city pop. (000, 2020)	432.5 [c]	Exchange rate (per US$)	0.9 [c]

Economic indicators

	2010	2015	2020
GDP: Gross domestic product (million current US$)	90 184	88 457	105 956 [d]
GDP growth rate (annual %, const. 2015 prices)	5.7	4.8	4.0 [d]
GDP per capita (current US$)	16 687.5	16 273.6	19 430.8 [d]
Economy: Agriculture (% of Gross Value Added) [e]	1.8	2.9	2.6 [d]
Economy: Industry (% of Gross Value Added) [e,f]	33.9	33.9	33.6 [d]
Economy: Services and other activity (% of GVA) [e,g,h]	63.3	63.3	64.5 [d]
Employment in agriculture (% of employed)	3.2	3.2	2.1 [i]
Employment in industry (% of employed)	37.1	36.1	36.1 [i]
Employment in services & other sectors (% employed)	59.6	60.7	61.8 [i]
Unemployment rate (% of labour force) [i]	14.4	11.5	5.1
Labour force participation rate (female/male pop. %) [i]	50.6 / 67.6	52.0 / 67.8	52.0 / 67.1
CPI: Consumer Price Index (2010=100)	100	109	115 [c]
Agricultural production index (2004-2006=100)	82	86	98 [i]
International trade: exports (million current US$)	65 306	74 970	90 050 [c]
International trade: imports (million current US$)	65 644	73 053	90 979 [c]
International trade: balance (million current US$)	- 338	1 916	- 930 [c]
Balance of payments, current account (million US$)	- 4 210	- 1 849	- 3 019 [c]

Major trading partners

						2019
Export partners (% of exports)	Germany	22.3	Czechia	11.0	Poland	7.5
Import partners (% of imports)	Germany	16.4	Czechia	10.1	Other Europe, nes	8.6

Social indicators

	2010	2015	2020
Population growth rate (average annual %) [k]	~0.0	0.1	0.1
Urban population (% of total population)	54.7	53.9	53.7 [c]
Urban population growth rate (average annual %) [k]	- 0.3	- 0.2	...
Fertility rate, total (live births per woman) [k]	1.3	1.4	1.5
Life expectancy at birth (females/males, years) [k]	78.6 / 70.8	79.8 / 72.5	80.8 / 73.7
Population age distribution (0-14/60+ years old, %)	15.3 / 17.8	15.3 / 20.7	15.6 / 23.3
International migrant stock (000/% of total pop.)	146.3 / 2.7	177.6 / 3.3	188.0 / 3.4 [c]
Refugees and others of concern to the UNHCR (000)	1.6 [l]	2.5	2.5 [c]
Infant mortality rate (per 1 000 live births) [k]	6.2	5.4	4.8
Health: Current expenditure (% of GDP) [i]	7.8	6.8	6.7 [b]
Health: Physicians (per 1 000 pop.)	3.4	3.4	3.4 [b]
Education: Government expenditure (% of GDP)	4.1	4.6	3.9 [i]
Education: Primary gross enrol. ratio (f/m per 100 pop.)	101.0 / 101.9	98.1 / 98.9	98.4 / 99.0 [b]
Education: Secondary gross enrol. ratio (f/m per 100 pop.)	92.8 / 91.8	91.5 / 90.5	91.6 / 90.5 [b]
Education: Tertiary gross enrol. ratio (f/m per 100 pop.)	69.6 / 45.0	61.8 / 40.1	56.6 / 37.1 [b]
Intentional homicide rate (per 100 000 pop.)	1.5	0.8	1.1 [d]
Seats held by women in the National Parliament (%)	18.0	18.7	20.7 [m]

Environment and infrastructure indicators

	2010	2015	2020
Individuals using the Internet (per 100 inhabitants)	75.7 [n,o]	77.6 [n,o]	80.7 [d]
Research & Development expenditure (% of GDP)	0.6	1.2	0.8 [d]
Threatened species (number)	34	45	116
Forested area (% of land area)	40.3	40.3	40.3 [i,b]
CO2 emission estimates (million tons/tons per capita)	34.6 / 6.4	29.4 / 5.4	32.2 / 5.9 [b]
Energy production, primary (Petajoules)	250	265	265 [b]
Energy supply per capita (Gigajoules)	136	124	132 [b]
Tourist/visitor arrivals at national borders (000) [p]	1 327	1 721	2 256 [d]
Important sites for terrestrial biodiversity protected (%)	77.6	85.7	85.8 [c]
Pop. using safely managed sanitation (urban/rural %)	89.0 / 76.2	88.6 / 75.9	88.4 / 75.7 [b]
Net Official Development Assist. disbursed (% of GNI) [q]	0.09	0.10	0.13 [b]

a Excluding inland water. **b** 2017. **c** 2019. **d** 2018. **e** Data classified according to ISIC Rev. 4. **f** Excludes publishing activities. Includes irrigation and canals. **g** Excludes repair of personal and household goods. **h** Excludes computer and related activities and radio/TV activities. **i** Estimate. **j** 2016. **k** Data refers to a 5-year period preceding the reference year. **l** Data as at the end of December. **m** Data are as at 1 January of reporting year. **n** Population aged 1 to 74 years. **o** Users in the last 3 months. **p** Non-resident tourists staying in commercial accommodation only (representing approximately 25% of all tourists). **q** Development Assistance Committee member (OECD).

Slovenia

Region	Southern Europe	UN membership date	22 May 1992
Population (000, 2020)	2 079	Surface area (km2)	20 273 [a]
Pop. density (per km2, 2020)	103.2	Sex ratio (m per 100 f)	99.2
Capital city	Ljubljana	National currency	Euro (EUR)
Capital city pop. (000, 2020)	286.5 [b]	Exchange rate (per US$)	0.9 [c]

Economic indicators	2010	2015	2020
GDP: Gross domestic product (million current US$)	48 161	43 090	54 034 [b]
GDP growth rate (annual %, const. 2015 prices)	1.3	2.2	4.1 [b]
GDP per capita (current US$)	23 569.9	20 804.5	26 005.1 [b]
Economy: Agriculture (% of Gross Value Added) [d]	2.2	2.4	2.4 [b]
Economy: Industry (% of Gross Value Added) [d,e]	30.4	32.4	32.7 [b]
Economy: Services and other activity (% of GVA) [d,f,g]	69.0	68.6	67.8 [b]
Employment in agriculture (% of employed)	8.8	7.1	5.1 [h]
Employment in industry (% of employed)	32.6	32.0	33.5 [h]
Employment in services & other sectors (% employed)	58.6	60.9	61.5 [h]
Unemployment rate (% of labour force) [h]	7.2	9.0	3.8
Labour force participation rate (female/male pop. %) [h]	53.1 / 65.5	52.0 / 62.9	53.0 / 62.8
CPI: Consumer Price Index (2010=100)	100	106	111 [c]
Agricultural production index (2004-2006=100)	91	91	88 [i]
International trade: exports (million current US$)	24 435	26 587	37 557 [c]
International trade: imports (million current US$)	26 592	25 870	38 179 [c]
International trade: balance (million current US$)	- 2 157	717	- 622 [c]
Balance of payments, current account (million US$)	- 357	1 645	3 525 [c]

Major trading partners						2019
Export partners (% of exports)	Germany	18.9	Italy	11.5	Croatia	8.6
Import partners (% of imports)	Germany	14.5	Italy	12.6	Switzerland	9.3

Social indicators	2010	2015	2020
Population growth rate (average annual %) [j]	0.5	0.3	0.1
Urban population (% of total population)	52.7	53.8	54.8 [c]
Urban population growth rate (average annual %) [j]	0.9	0.7	...
Fertility rate, total (live births per woman) [j]	1.4	1.6	1.6
Life expectancy at birth (females/males, years) [j]	82.0 / 75.0	83.1 / 77.1	83.8 / 78.2
Population age distribution (0-14/60+ years old, %)	14.0 / 22.2	14.7 / 25.1	15.1 / 27.7
International migrant stock (000/% of total pop.)	253.8 / 12.4	237.6 / 11.5	253.1 / 12.2 [c]
Refugees and others of concern to the UNHCR (000)	4.6 [k]	0.3	1.2 [c]
Infant mortality rate (per 1 000 live births) [j]	3.2	2.2	1.9
Health: Current expenditure (% of GDP) [h]	8.6	8.5	8.2 [a]
Health: Physicians (per 1 000 pop.)	2.4	2.8	3.1 [a]
Education: Government expenditure (% of GDP)	5.6	4.9	4.8 [i]
Education: Primary gross enrol. ratio (f/m per 100 pop.)	99.5 / 99.5	100.3 / 99.6	100.6 / 100.2 [a]
Education: Secondary gross enrol. ratio (f/m per 100 pop.)	98.6 / 99.3	111.0 / 109.7	117.1 / 114.2 [a]
Education: Tertiary gross enrol. ratio (f/m per 100 pop.)	107.4 / 72.3	96.0 / 65.4	93.0 / 64.9 [a]
Intentional homicide rate (per 100 000 pop.)	0.7	1.0	0.5 [b]
Seats held by women in the National Parliament (%)	14.4	36.7	27.8 [l]

Environment and infrastructure indicators	2010	2015	2020
Individuals using the Internet (per 100 inhabitants)	70.0 [m]	73.1 [m]	79.8 [b]
Research & Development expenditure (% of GDP)	2.1	2.2	1.9 [n,b]
Threatened species (number)	95	125	175
Forested area (% of land area)	61.9	62.0	62.0 [h,a]
CO2 emission estimates (million tons/tons per capita)	15.4 / 7.5	12.8 / 6.2	13.4 / 6.5 [a]
Energy production, primary (Petajoules)	157	142	153 [a]
Energy supply per capita (Gigajoules)	150	133	139 [a]
Tourist/visitor arrivals at national borders (000)	2 049	3 022	4 425 [b]
Important sites for terrestrial biodiversity protected (%)	86.1	88.7	88.7 [c]
Net Official Development Assist. disbursed (% of GNI) [o]	0.13	0.15	0.16 [a]

2017. **b** 2018. **c** 2019. **d** Data classified according to ISIC Rev. 4. **e** Excludes publishing activities. Includes [navi]gation and canals. **f** Excludes repair of personal and household goods. **g** Excludes computer and related activities [an]d radio/TV activities. **h** Estimate. **i** 2016. **j** Data refers to a 5-year period preceding the reference year. **k** Data as [t]he end of December. **l** Data are as at 1 January of reporting year. **m** Population aged 16 to 74 years. **n** Provisional [dat]a. **o** Development Assistance Committee member (OECD).

Solomon Islands

Region	Melanesia	UN membership date	19 September 1978		
Population (000, 2020)	687	Surface area (km2)	28 896 [a]		
Pop. density (per km2, 2020)	24.5	Sex ratio (m per 100 f)	103.4		
Capital city	Honiara	National currency	Solomon Is. Dollar (SBD) [b]		
Capital city pop. (000, 2020)	91.8 [c]	Exchange rate (per US$)	8.2 [d]		

Economic indicators

	2010	2015	2020
GDP: Gross domestic product (million current US$)	720	1 059	1 271 [c]
GDP growth rate (annual %, const. 2015 prices)	10.6	2.5	3.9 [c]
GDP per capita (current US$)	1 363.3	1 756.1	1 946.9 [c]
Economy: Agriculture (% of Gross Value Added)	28.7	25.0	25.4 [c]
Economy: Industry (% of Gross Value Added)	13.3	15.5	15.2 [c]
Economy: Services and other activity (% of GVA)	52.3	51.6	51.5 [c]
Employment in agriculture (% of employed) [e]	44.8	39.9	37.1
Employment in industry (% of employed) [e]	8.2	9.4	9.6
Employment in services & other sectors (% employed) [e]	47.0	50.7	53.4
Unemployment rate (% of labour force) [e]	1.7	0.7	0.5
Labour force participation rate (female/male pop. %) [e]	82.7 / 86.0	82.2 / 85.6	82.0 / 85.5
CPI: Consumer Price Index (2010=100)	100	125	131 [c]
Agricultural production index (2004-2006=100)	111	116	113 [f]
International trade: exports (million current US$)	215	400	611 [e,d]
International trade: imports (million current US$)	328	466	348 [e,d]
International trade: balance (million current US$)	- 112	- 65	263 [e,d]
Balance of payments, current account (million US$)	- 144	- 36	- 142 [d]

Major trading partners

						2019
Export partners (% of exports) [e]	China	66.8	Italy	7.2	India	5.1
Import partners (% of imports) [e]	Australia	18.2	Singapore	16.3	China	14.9

Social indicators

	2010	2015	2020
Population growth rate (average annual %) [g]	2.3	2.7	2.6
Urban population (% of total population)	20.0	22.4	24.2 [d]
Urban population growth rate (average annual %) [g]	4.7	4.3	...
Fertility rate, total (live births per woman) [g]	4.4	4.4	4.4
Life expectancy at birth (females/males, years) [g]	71.7 / 68.3	73.3 / 69.8	74.6 / 71.1
Population age distribution (0-14/60+ years old, %)	40.8 / 5.1	40.4 / 5.3	40.0 / 5.6
International migrant stock (000/% of total pop.)	2.8 / 0.5	2.6 / 0.4	2.5 / 0.4 [d]
Refugees and others of concern to the UNHCR (000)	...	~0.0	~0.0 [d]
Infant mortality rate (per 1 000 live births) [g]	23.0	20.2	15.5
Health: Current expenditure (% of GDP) [h]	7.3	5.2	4.7 [a]
Health: Physicians (per 1 000 pop.)	0.2 [i]	0.2 [j]	0.2 [f]
Education: Government expenditure (% of GDP)	9.9	...	...
Education: Primary gross enrol. ratio (f/m per 100 pop.)	113.2 / 116.0	113.0 / 114.2	106.0 / 106.4 [c]
Education: Secondary gross enrol. ratio (f/m per 100 pop.)	44.9 / 51.9	47.0 / 49.5 [k]	... / ...
Intentional homicide rate (per 100 000 pop.)	3.8 [i]	...	...
Seats held by women in the National Parliament (%)	0.0	2.0	6.1 [l]

Environment and infrastructure indicators

	2010	2015	2020
Individuals using the Internet (per 100 inhabitants) [e]	5.0	10.0	11.9 [a]
Threatened species (number)	220	238	256
Forested area (% of land area) [e]	79.1	78.1	78.1 [a]
Energy production, primary (Petajoules) [e]	3	3	3 [a]
Energy supply per capita (Gigajoules)	15 [e]	13	12 [e,a]
Tourist/visitor arrivals at national borders (000)	20	22	28 [c]
Important sites for terrestrial biodiversity protected (%)	4.4	4.4	4.4 [d]
Net Official Development Assist. received (% of GNI)	66.97	16.95	14.64 [c]

a 2017. b Solomon Islands Dollar. c 2018. d 2019. e Estimate. f 2016. g Data refers to a 5-year period preceding the reference year. h Data revision. i 2008. j 2013. k 2012. l Data are as at 1 January of reporting year.

Somalia

Region	Eastern Africa	UN membership date	20 September 1960
Population (000, 2020)	15 893	Surface area (km2)	637 657 a
Pop. density (per km2, 2020)	25.3	Sex ratio (m per 100 f)	99.4
Capital city	Mogadishu	National currency	Somali Shilling (SOS)
Capital city pop. (000, 2020)	2 179.9 b,c	Exchange rate (per US$)	23 605.0 a

Economic indicators

	2010	2015	2020
GDP: Gross domestic product (million current US$)	1 093	1 455	1 494 d
GDP growth rate (annual %, const. 2015 prices)	2.6	2.7	3.1 d
GDP per capita (current US$)	90.7	105.4	99.6 d
Economy: Agriculture (% of Gross Value Added)	60.2	60.2	60.2 d
Economy: Industry (% of Gross Value Added)	7.4	7.4	7.4 d
Economy: Services and other activity (% of GVA)	36.5	37.7	37.3 d
Employment in agriculture (% of employed) e	83.8	83.4	83.0
Employment in industry (% of employed) e	4.1	3.8	3.5
Employment in services & other sectors (% employed) e	12.1	12.8	13.4
Unemployment rate (% of labour force) e	11.7	11.6	11.4
Labour force participation rate (female/male pop. %) e	20.5 / 74.8	21.2 / 73.6	21.8 / 73.7
Agricultural production index (2004-2006=100)	105	109	108 f
International trade: exports (million current US$) e	568	853	1 179 c
International trade: imports (million current US$) e	496	525	549 c
International trade: balance (million current US$) e	72	328	630 c

Major trading partners

						2019
Export partners (% of exports) e	United Arab Emirates	29.4	Oman	25.6	Saudi Arabia	14.6
Import partners (% of imports) e	United Arab Emirates	29.1	China	17.0	India	16.4

Social indicators

	2010	2015	2020
Population growth rate (average annual %) g	2.8	2.7	2.8
Urban population (% of total population)	39.3	43.2	45.6 c
Urban population growth rate (average annual %) g	4.5	4.8	...
Fertility rate, total (live births per woman) g	7.1	6.6	6.1
Life expectancy at birth (females/males, years) g	54.8 / 51.6	56.5 / 53.3	58.7 / 55.3
Population age distribution (0-14/60+ years old, %)	48.2 / 4.4	47.2 / 4.5	46.1 / 4.6
International migrant stock (000/% of total pop.) e,h	48.1 / 0.4	41.0 / 0.3	52.1 / 0.3 c
Refugees and others of concern to the UNHCR (000)	1 489.8 i	1 165.0	2 694.7 c
Infant mortality rate (per 1 000 live births) g	89.8	79.4	69.3
Health: Physicians (per 1 000 pop.)	~0.0 i	~0.0 k	...
Education: Primary gross enrol. ratio (f/m per 100 pop.)	16.6 / 30.1 l	... / ...	... / ...
Education: Secondary gross enrol. ratio (f/m per 100 pop.)	3.7 / 8.1 l	... / ...	... / ...
Seats held by women in the National Parliament (%)	6.9	13.8	24.4 m

Environment and infrastructure indicators

	2010	2015	2020
Individuals using the Internet (per 100 inhabitants) e	1.2 n	1.8	2.0 a
Threatened species (number)	128	165	199
Forested area (% of land area) e	10.8	10.1	10.1 a
Energy production, primary (Petajoules)	124	129	139 a
Energy supply per capita (Gigajoules)	10	10	10 a
Important sites for terrestrial biodiversity protected (%)	0.0	0.0	0.0 c
Net Official Development Assist. received (% of GNI)	...	31.36	33.61 d

2017. **b** Data refers to the urban agglomeration. **c** 2019. **d** 2018. **e** Estimate. **f** 2016. **g** Data refers to a 5-year period preceding the reference year. **h** Including refugees. **i** Data as at the end of December. **j** 2006. **k** 2014. **l** 2007. Data are as at 1 January of reporting year. **n** 2009.

South Africa

Region	Southern Africa	UN membership date	07 November 1945
Population (000, 2020)	59 309	Surface area (km2)	1 221 037 [a]
Pop. density (per km2, 2020)	48.9	Sex ratio (m per 100 f)	97.1
Capital city	Pretoria [b]	National currency	Rand (ZAR)
Capital city pop. (000, 2020)	2 472.6 [c]	Exchange rate (per US$)	14.0 [c]

Economic indicators

	2010	2015	2020
GDP: Gross domestic product (million current US$)	375 348	317 416	368 094 [d]
GDP growth rate (annual %, const. 2015 prices)	3.0	1.2	0.8 [d]
GDP per capita (current US$)	7 328.6	5 730.9	6 369.2 [d]
Economy: Agriculture (% of Gross Value Added)	2.6	2.3	2.4 [d]
Economy: Industry (% of Gross Value Added)	30.2	29.1	29.0 [d]
Economy: Services and other activity (% of GVA)	56.6	64.8	61.8 [d]
Employment in agriculture (% of employed)	4.9	5.6	5.0 [e]
Employment in industry (% of employed)	24.4	23.8	22.7 [e]
Employment in services & other sectors (% employed)	70.7	70.6	72.3 [e]
Unemployment rate (% of labour force) [e]	24.7	25.2	28.5
Labour force participation rate (female/male pop. %) [e]	44.9 / 60.4	48.6 / 62.5	49.7 / 62.6
CPI: Consumer Price Index (2010=100) [f,g]	100	130	159 [c]
Agricultural production index (2004-2006=100)	117	122	117 [h]
International trade: exports (million current US$) [i]	82 631	80 265	89 396 [c]
International trade: imports (million current US$) [i]	83 100	85 510	88 037 [c]
International trade: balance (million current US$) [i]	- 469	- 5 244	1 358 [c]
Balance of payments, current account (million US$)	- 5 492	- 14 568	- 10 667 [c]

Major trading partners

					2019
Export partners (% of exports)	China	10.7	Germany	8.0	United States	7.0
Import partners (% of imports)	China	18.5	Germany	9.9	United States	6.6

Social indicators

	2010	2015	2020
Population growth rate (average annual %) [j]	1.3	1.6	1.4
Urban population (% of total population)	62.2	64.8	66.9 [c]
Urban population growth rate (average annual %) [j]	2.0	2.2	...
Fertility rate, total (live births per woman) [j]	2.6	2.6	2.4
Life expectancy at birth (females/males, years) [j]	57.3 / 52.3	64.2 / 57.8	67.1 / 60.2
Population age distribution (0-14/60+ years old, %)	29.7 / 7.2	29.3 / 7.9	28.8 / 8.5
International migrant stock (000/% of total pop.) [k]	2 114.8 / 4.1	3 816.5 / 6.9	4 224.3 / 7.2 [c]
Refugees and others of concern to the UNHCR (000)	229.7 [l]	912.6	273.5 [m,c]
Infant mortality rate (per 1 000 live births) [j]	48.1	32.9	27.2
Health: Current expenditure (% of GDP) [n]	7.4	8.2	8.1 [a]
Health: Physicians (per 1 000 pop.)	0.7	0.8	0.9 [a]
Education: Government expenditure (% of GDP)	5.7	6.0	6.2 [d]
Education: Primary gross enrol. ratio (f/m per 100 pop.)	102.7 / 106.8	101.9 / 109.2	99.1 / 102.6 [a]
Education: Secondary gross enrol. ratio (f/m per 100 pop.)	96.6 / 91.0	108.8 / 110.1	109.0 / 100.4 [a]
Education: Tertiary gross enrol. ratio (f/m per 100 pop.)	... / ...	23.2 / 16.5 [o]	26.4 / 18.4 [a]
Intentional homicide rate (per 100 000 pop.)	31.0	33.7	36.4 [d]
Seats held by women in the National Parliament (%)	44.5	41.5	46.4 [p]

Environment and infrastructure indicators

	2010	2015	2020
Individuals using the Internet (per 100 inhabitants) [e]	24.0	51.9	56.2 [a]
Research & Development expenditure (% of GDP)	0.7	0.8	0.8 [a]
Threatened species (number)	441	527	597
Forested area (% of land area)	7.6	7.6 [e]	7.6 [e,a]
CO2 emission estimates (million tons/tons per capita)	418.8 / 8.1	418.3 / 7.6	421.7 / 7.4 [a]
Energy production, primary (Petajoules)	6 569	6 595	6 653 [a]
Energy supply per capita (Gigajoules)	114	103	104 [a]
Tourist/visitor arrivals at national borders (000)	8 074 [q]	8 904 [q,r]	10 472 [r,d]
Important sites for terrestrial biodiversity protected (%)	29.0	30.8	32.5 [c]
Pop. using safely managed drinking water (urban/rural, %)	87.3 / ...	83.4 / ...	81.9 / ... [a]
Net Official Development Assist. received (% of GNI)	0.28	0.46	0.26 [d]

a 2017. b Pretoria is the administrative capital, Cape Town is the legislative capital and Bloemfontein is the judicial capital. c 2019. d 2018. e Estimate. f Calculated by the UN Statistics Division from national indices. g Urban area. h 2016. i Imports FOB. j Data refers to a 5-year period preceding the reference year. k Including refugees. l Data at the end of December. m All data relate to end of 2018. n Data refer to fiscal years beginning 1 April. o 2014. p Data are as at 1 January of reporting year. q Break in the time series. r Excluding transit.

South Sudan

Region	Eastern Africa
Population (000, 2020)	11 194
Pop. density (per km2, 2020)	18.3
Capital city	Juba
Capital city pop. (000, 2020)	385.8 c

UN membership date	14 July 2011
Surface area (km2)	658 841 a
Sex ratio (m per 100 f)	100.2
National currency	S. Sudanese Pound (SSP) b
Exchange rate (per US$)	161.1 c

Economic indicators	2010	2015	2020
GDP: Gross domestic product (million current US$)	14 986	13 216	8 207 d
GDP growth rate (annual %, const. 2015 prices)	- 0.9	3.4	3.4 d
GDP per capita (current US$)	1 576.1	1 233.3	747.7 d
Economy: Agriculture (% of Gross Value Added) e	5.1	4.2	1.9 d
Economy: Industry (% of Gross Value Added) e	55.4	45.0	55.3 d
Economy: Services and other activity (% of GVA) e	52.4	56.5	52.1 d
Employment in agriculture (% of employed) f	56.4	56.8	56.1
Employment in industry (% of employed) f	16.8	15.2	14.1
Employment in services & other sectors (% employed) f	26.8	28.0	29.7
Unemployment rate (% of labour force) f	12.7	12.6	12.3
Labour force participation rate (female/male pop. %) f	70.6 / 76.0	70.7 / 74.6	71.0 / 73.8
CPI: Consumer Price Index (2010=100)	100	332	4 584 a
International trade: exports (million current US$) f	...	3 103	1 091 c
International trade: imports (million current US$) f	...	635	1 238 c
International trade: balance (million current US$) f	...	2 468	- 147 c
Balance of payments, current account (million US$)	...	- 500	- 316 d

Major trading partners						2019
Export partners (% of exports) f	China	89.9	United States	4.1	United Arab Emirates	2.8
Import partners (% of imports) f	Uganda	41.4	United Arab Emirates	17.5	Kenya	13.8

Social indicators	2010	2015	2020
Population growth rate (average annual %) g	4.6	2.4	0.9
Urban population (% of total population)	17.9	18.9	19.9 c
Urban population growth rate (average annual %) g	5.1	4.4	...
Fertility rate, total (live births per woman) g	5.6	5.2	4.7
Life expectancy at birth (females/males, years) g	54.4 / 52.2	57.5 / 54.6	58.9 / 56.0
Population age distribution (0-14/60+ years old, %)	43.5 / 5.2	42.5 / 5.1	41.3 / 5.2
International migrant stock (000/% of total pop.) h	257.9 / 2.7	844.1 / 7.9	865.6 / 7.8 c
Refugees and others of concern to the UNHCR (000)	...	2 058.5	2 189.6 c
Infant mortality rate (per 1 000 live births) g	78.6	65.8	64.4
Health: Current expenditure (% of GDP)	...	...	9.8 f,a
Education: Government expenditure (% of GDP)	...	1.4	1.0 a
Education: Primary gross enrol. ratio (f/m per 100 pop.)	... / ...	60.4 / 85.3	... / ...
Education: Secondary gross enrol. ratio (f/m per 100 pop.)	... / ...	7.7 / 14.3	... / ...
Intentional homicide rate (per 100 000 pop.)	...	14.9 i	...
Seats held by women in the National Parliament (%)	...	26.5	28.5 j

Environment and infrastructure indicators	2010	2015	2020
Individuals using the Internet (per 100 inhabitants)	...	5.5	8.0 a
Threatened species (number)	...	42	61
CO2 emission estimates (million tons/tons per capita)	... / ...	2.0 / 0.2	1.5 / 0.1 a
Energy production, primary (Petajoules)	...	321	238 a
Energy supply per capita (Gigajoules)	...	3	3 a
Important sites for terrestrial biodiversity protected (%)	33.6	33.6	33.6 c
Net Official Development Assist. received (% of GNI)	...	14.77	60.53 k

2017. **b** South Sudanese Pound. **c** 2019. **d** 2018. **e** Data classified according to ISIC Rev. 4. **f** Estimate. **g** Data refers to a 5-year period preceding the reference year. **h** Including refugees. **i** 2012. **j** Data are as at 1 January of reporting year. **k** 2016.

Spain

Region	Southern Europe	UN membership date	14 December 1955	
Population (000, 2020)	46 755[a]	Surface area (km2)	505 944[b]	
Pop. density (per km2, 2020)	93.7[a]	Sex ratio (m per 100 f)	96.6[a]	
Capital city	Madrid	National currency	Euro (EUR)	
Capital city pop. (000, 2020)	6 559.0[c]	Exchange rate (per US$)	0.9[c]	

Economic indicators

	2010	2015	2020
GDP: Gross domestic product (million current US$)	1 420 722	1 195 119	1 419 735[d]
GDP growth rate (annual %, const. 2015 prices)	0.2	3.8	2.4[d]
GDP per capita (current US$)	30 272.6	25 606.8	30 405.8[d]
Economy: Agriculture (% of Gross Value Added)[e]	2.6	3.0	3.1[d]
Economy: Industry (% of Gross Value Added)[e,f]	25.2	22.1	22.1[d]
Economy: Services and other activity (% of GVA)[e,g,h]	71.7	74.8	73.9[d]
Employment in agriculture (% of employed)	4.2	4.1	4.0[i]
Employment in industry (% of employed)	23.0	19.9	20.2[i]
Employment in services & other sectors (% employed)	72.8	76.0	75.8[i]
Unemployment rate (% of labour force)[i]	19.9	22.1	13.0
Labour force participation rate (female/male pop. %)[i]	51.7 / 67.2	52.6 / 64.7	51.6 / 63.0
CPI: Consumer Price Index (2010=100)[j]	100	107	111[c]
Agricultural production index (2004-2006=100)	103	105	104[k]
International trade: exports (million current US$)	246 265	276 959	337 215[c]
International trade: imports (million current US$)	315 547	304 708	375 485[c]
International trade: balance (million current US$)	- 69 282	- 27 750	- 38 270[c]
Balance of payments, current account (million US$)	- 52 250	24 108	27 724[c]

Major trading partners

						2019
Export partners (% of exports)	France	14.6	Germany	10.3	Italy	7.7
Import partners (% of imports)	Germany	11.9	France	10.0	China	8.7

Social indicators

	2010	2015	2020
Population growth rate (average annual %)[a,l]	1.3	- 0.1	~0.0
Urban population (% of total population)[a]	78.4	79.6	80.6[c]
Urban population growth rate (average annual %)[a,l]	1.5	0.1	...
Fertility rate, total (live births per woman)[a,l]	1.5	1.3	1.3
Life expectancy at birth (females/males, years)[a,l]	84.4 / 78.1	85.3 / 79.6	86.0 / 80.6
Population age distribution (0-14/60+ years old, %)[a]	14.8 / 22.2	14.9 / 24.0	14.4 / 26.3
International migrant stock (000/% of total pop.)[a]	6 280.1 / 13.4	5 891.2 / 12.6	6 104.2 / 13.1[c]
Refugees and others of concern to the UNHCR (000)	6.6[m]	17.3	149.1[c]
Infant mortality rate (per 1 000 live births)[a,l]	3.4	2.9	2.3
Health: Current expenditure (% of GDP)	9.0	9.1	8.9[b]
Health: Physicians (per 1 000 pop.)	3.0	3.2	3.9[b]
Education: Government expenditure (% of GDP)	4.8	4.3	4.2[k]
Education: Primary gross enrol. ratio (f/m per 100 pop.)	103.6 / 104.4	107.2 / 105.6	103.6 / 101.9[b]
Education: Secondary gross enrol. ratio (f/m per 100 pop.)	120.7 / 117.6	124.6 / 125.3	126.9 / 125.2[b]
Education: Tertiary gross enrol. ratio (f/m per 100 pop.)	84.2 / 68.1	93.2 / 78.3	97.0 / 81.1[b]
Intentional homicide rate (per 100 000 pop.)	0.9	0.6	0.6[d]
Seats held by women in the National Parliament (%)	36.6	41.1	44.0[n]

Environment and infrastructure indicators

	2010	2015	2020
Individuals using the Internet (per 100 inhabitants)	65.8[o]	78.7[p]	86.1[d]
Research & Development expenditure (% of GDP)	1.3	1.2	1.2[d]
Threatened species (number)	240	551	752
Forested area (% of land area)	36.5	36.9	36.9[i,b]
CO2 emission estimates (million tons/tons per capita)	262.1 / 5.6	247.1 / 5.3	253.4 / 5.4[b]
Energy production, primary (Petajoules)[q]	1 419	1 367	1 368[b]
Energy supply per capita (Gigajoules)[q]	114	106	113[b]
Tourist/visitor arrivals at national borders (000)	52 677	68 175	82 773[d]
Important sites for terrestrial biodiversity protected (%)	54.6	57.6	57.6[c]
Pop. using safely managed sanitation (urban/rural %)	95.8 / 95.3	96.5 / 96.6	96.6 / 96.7[b]
Net Official Development Assist. disbursed (% of GNI)[r]	0.43	0.12	0.19[b]

a Including Canary Islands, Ceuta and Melilla. b 2017. c 2019. d 2018. e Data classified according to ISIC Rev. 4. f Excludes publishing activities. Includes irrigation and canals. g Excludes repair of personal and household goods. h Excludes computer and related activities and radio/TV activities. i Estimate. j Calculated by the UN Statistics Division from national indices. k 2016. l Data refers to a 5-year period preceding the reference year. m Data as at the end of December. n Data are as at 1 January of reporting year. o Population aged 10 years and over. p Population aged 16 74 years. q Data include the Canary Islands. r Development Assistance Committee member (OECD).

Sri Lanka

Region	Southern Asia	UN membership date	14 December 1955
Population (000, 2020)	21 413	Surface area (km2)	65 610 [a]
Pop. density (per km2, 2020)	341.5	Sex ratio (m per 100 f)	92.1
Capital city	Colombo [b]	National currency	Sri Lanka Rupee (LKR)
Capital city pop. (000, 2020)	606.2 [c]	Exchange rate (per US$)	181.6 [c]

Economic indicators	2010	2015	2020
GDP: Gross domestic product (million current US$)	56 726	80 604	88 942 [d]
GDP growth rate (annual %, const. 2015 prices)	8.0	5.0	3.2 [d]
GDP per capita (current US$)	2 799.6	3 855.2	4 189.7 [d]
Economy: Agriculture (% of Gross Value Added) [e]	9.5	8.8	8.6 [d]
Economy: Industry (% of Gross Value Added) [e]	29.7 [f]	29.3 [f]	29.4 [d]
Economy: Services and other activity (% of GVA) [e,g,h]	64.8	63.5	64.6 [d]
Employment in agriculture (% of employed)	31.8	28.7	23.7 [i]
Employment in industry (% of employed)	25.5	25.8	30.4 [i]
Employment in services & other sectors (% employed)	42.6	45.6	45.9 [i]
Unemployment rate (% of labour force) [i]	4.8	4.5	4.2
Labour force participation rate (female/male pop. %) [i]	34.4 / 76.5	35.7 / 75.8	35.3 / 74.3
CPI: Consumer Price Index (2010=100)	100 [j,k]	110 [l]	130 [l,c]
Agricultural production index (2004-2006=100)	123	127	128 [m]
International trade: exports (million current US$)	8 304	10 440	12 589 [i,c]
International trade: imports (million current US$)	12 354	18 967	17 992 [i,c]
International trade: balance (million current US$)	- 4 050	- 8 528	- 5 403 [i,c]
Balance of payments, current account (million US$)	- 1 075	- 1 883	- 2 814 [d]

Major trading partners					2019
Export partners (% of exports) [i]	United States	24.9	United Kingdom	8.9	India	6.7
Import partners (% of imports) [i]	India	21.1	China	19.7	United Arab Emirates	7.3

Social indicators	2010	2015	2020
Population growth rate (average annual %) [n]	0.7	0.6	0.5
Urban population (% of total population)	18.2	18.3	18.6 [c]
Urban population growth rate (average annual %) [n]	0.6	0.5	...
Fertility rate, total (live births per woman) [n]	2.3	2.2	2.2
Life expectancy at birth (females/males, years) [n]	78.5 / 71.5	79.3 / 72.4	80.0 / 73.3
Population age distribution (0-14/60+ years old, %)	25.4 / 11.9	24.8 / 14.0	23.7 / 16.4
International migrant stock (000/% of total pop.) [o]	39.0 / 0.2	39.7 / 0.2	40.0 / 0.2 [c]
Refugees and others of concern to the UNHCR (000)	435.3 [p]	51.8	37.6 [c]
Infant mortality rate (per 1 000 live births) [n]	10.2	8.8	7.6
Health: Current expenditure (% of GDP)	3.9	3.9 [q]	3.8 [a]
Health: Physicians (per 1 000 pop.)	0.7	0.9	1.0 [d]
Education: Government expenditure (% of GDP)	1.7	2.2	2.8 [a]
Education: Primary gross enrol. ratio (f/m per 100 pop.)	98.2 / 100.7	100.6 / 102.7	99.6 / 100.7 [d]
Education: Secondary gross enrol. ratio (f/m per 100 pop.)	97.5 / 96.3	101.8 / 97.2 [r]	102.6 / 98.0 [d]
Education: Tertiary gross enrol. ratio (f/m per 100 pop.)	20.9 / 11.7	23.9 / 15.5	23.4 / 15.8 [d]
Intentional homicide rate (per 100 000 pop.)	3.8	2.3	2.4 [d]
Seats held by women in the National Parliament (%)	5.8	5.8	5.3 [s]

Environment and infrastructure indicators	2010	2015	2020
Individuals using the Internet (per 100 inhabitants)	12.0	12.1	34.1 [i,a]
Research & Development expenditure (% of GDP)	0.1	0.1	...
Threatened species (number)	552	580	641
Forested area (% of land area)	33.5	33.0	33.0 [i,a]
CO2 emission estimates (million tons/tons per capita)	12.4 / 0.6	19.5 / 0.9	23.1 / 1.1 [a]
Energy production, primary (Petajoules)	184	181	167 [a]
Energy supply per capita (Gigajoules)	18	21	22 [a]
Tourist/visitor arrivals at national borders (000) [t]	654	1 798	2 334 [d]
Important sites for terrestrial biodiversity protected (%)	41.1	43.7	43.7 [c]
Pop. using safely managed drinking water (urban/rural, %)	88.1 / ...	90.1 / ...	90.8 / ... [a]
Net Official Development Assist. received (% of GNI)	1.00	0.57	- 0.30 [d]

[a] 2017. [b] Colombo is the capital and Sri Jayewardenepura Kotte is the legislative capital. [c] 2019. [d] 2018. [e] Data classified according to ISIC Rev. 4. [f] Excludes publishing activities. Includes irrigation and canals. [g] Excludes repair of personal and household goods. [h] Excludes computer and related activities and radio/TV activities. [i] Estimate. [j] Colombo [k] Calculated by the UN Statistics Division from national indices. [l] Index base: 2013=100. [m] 2016. [n] Data refers to a 5-year period preceding the reference year. [o] Including refugees. [p] Data as at the end of December. [q] Break in the time series. [r] 2013. [s] Data are as at 1 January of reporting year. [t] Excluding nationals residing abroad.

State of Palestine

Region	Western Asia	Population (000, 2020)	5 101[a]
Surface area (km2)	6 020[b]	Pop. density (per km2, 2020)	847.4[a]
Sex ratio (m per 100 f)	102.9[a]	Capital city	East Jerusalem[c]
Capital city pop. (000, 2020)	275.1[c,d]		

Economic indicators	2010	2015	2020
GDP: Gross domestic product (million current US$)	9 682	13 972	16 277[d]
GDP growth rate (annual %, const. 2015 prices)	5.8	3.7	1.2[d]
GDP per capita (current US$)	2 387.2	3 085.0	3 347.0[d]
Economy: Agriculture (% of Gross Value Added)[e]	10.6	8.7	8.5[d]
Economy: Industry (% of Gross Value Added)[e,f]	21.8	19.2	22.3[d]
Economy: Services and other activity (% of GVA)[e,g,h]	66.0	71.9	72.9[d]
Employment in agriculture (% of employed)	11.8	8.7	5.9[i]
Employment in industry (% of employed)	24.7	28.7	31.7[i]
Employment in services & other sectors (% employed)	63.5	62.6	62.4[i]
Unemployment rate (% of labour force)[i]	21.4	23.0	26.1
Labour force participation rate (female/male pop. %)[i]	13.8 / 64.7	17.6 / 69.2	17.9 / 69.8
CPI: Consumer Price Index (2010=100)	100	111	113[i,k]
Agricultural production index (2004-2006=100)	75	87	87[l]
International trade: exports (million current US$)	576	958	1 124[i,k]
International trade: imports (million current US$)	3 959	5 225	6 608[i,k]
International trade: balance (million current US$)	- 3 383	- 4 268	- 5 484[i,k]
Balance of payments, current account (million US$)	- 1 307	- 2 066	- 1 659[d]

Major trading partners						2019
Export partners (% of exports)[i]	Israel	83.7	Jordan	6.4	United Arab Emirates	2.3
Import partners (% of imports)[i]	Israel	55.3	Turkey	10.1	China	6.5

Social indicators	2010	2015	2020
Population growth rate (average annual %)[a,m]	2.5	2.2	2.4
Urban population (% of total population)[a]	74.1	75.4	76.4[k]
Urban population growth rate (average annual %)[a,m]	2.9	3.1	...
Fertility rate, total (live births per woman)[a,m]	4.6	4.2	3.7
Life expectancy at birth (females/males, years)[a,m]	74.2 / 70.8	74.9 / 71.4	75.5 / 72.2
Population age distribution (0-14/60+ years old, %)[a]	42.3 / 4.4	39.9 / 4.6	38.4 / 4.9
International migrant stock (000/% of total pop.)[a]	258.0 / 6.4	255.5 / 5.6	253.7 / 5.1[k]
Refugees and others of concern to the UNHCR (000)	...	~0.0	...
Infant mortality rate (per 1 000 live births)[a,m]	21.0	19.3	17.5
Education: Government expenditure (% of GDP)	6.7	5.1	5.3[b]
Education: Primary gross enrol. ratio (f/m per 100 pop.)	90.4 / 92.2	97.5 / 97.5	98.7 / 98.5[d]
Education: Secondary gross enrol. ratio (f/m per 100 pop.)	89.1 / 82.5	89.9 / 81.9	93.9 / 85.2[d]
Education: Tertiary gross enrol. ratio (f/m per 100 pop.)	54.9 / 41.1	55.6 / 35.3	54.3 / 34.5[d]
Intentional homicide rate (per 100 000 pop.)	0.8	1.2	0.5[d]

Environment and infrastructure indicators	2010	2015	2020
Individuals using the Internet (per 100 inhabitants)	37.4[i]	57.4[i]	64.4[d]
Research & Development expenditure (% of GDP)[n]	0.4	0.5[o]	...
Threatened species (number)	18	24	39
Forested area (% of land area)[i]	1.5	1.5	1.5[b]
Energy production, primary (Petajoules)	9	9	10[b]
Energy supply per capita (Gigajoules)	13	16	16[b]
Tourist/visitor arrivals at national borders (000)	522	432[p]	606[p,d]
Important sites for terrestrial biodiversity protected (%)	16.8	23.1	24.4[k]
Pop. using safely managed sanitation (urban/rural %)	61.4 / ...	64.2 / ...	64.7 / ...[b]
Net Official Development Assist. received (% of GNI)	26.41	13.01	13.18[d]

a Including East Jerusalem. b 2017. c Designation and data provided by the State of Palestine. The position of the UN on Jerusalem is stated in A/RES/181 (II) and subsequent General Assembly and Security Council resolutions. d 2018. e Data classified according to ISIC Rev. 4. f Excludes publishing activities. Includes irrigation and canals. g Excludes computer and related activities and radio/TV activities. h Excludes repair of personal and household goods Estimate. j Calculated by the UN Statistics Division from national indices. k 2019. l 2016. m Data refers to a 5-yea period preceding the reference year. n Excluding business enterprise. o 2013. p West Bank only.

Sudan

Region	Northern Africa	
Population (000, 2020)	43 849	
Sex ratio (m per 100 f)	99.8	
National currency	Sudanese Pound (SDG)	
Exchange rate (per US$)	47.5[b]	

UN membership date	12 November 1956
Pop. density (per km2, 2020)	24.8
Capital city	Khartoum
Capital city pop. (000, 2020)	5 677.9[a]

Economic indicators

	2010	2015	2020
GDP: Gross domestic product (million current US$)	54 678	83 934	50 515[b]
GDP growth rate (annual %, const. 2015 prices)	8.5	3.7	- 2.3[b]
GDP per capita (current US$)	1 582.8	2 157.5	1 208.4[b]
Economy: Agriculture (% of Gross Value Added)	42.6	32.9	24.8[b]
Economy: Industry (% of Gross Value Added)	14.0	13.0	14.0[b]
Economy: Services and other activity (% of GVA)	40.3	23.0	23.9[b]
Employment in agriculture (% of employed)[c]	45.6	41.5	39.7
Employment in industry (% of employed)[c]	14.7	16.8	15.9
Employment in services & other sectors (% employed)[c]	39.8	41.7	44.4
Unemployment rate (% of labour force)[c]	15.2	17.3	16.6
Labour force participation rate (female/male pop. %)[c]	28.1 / 71.3	28.6 / 69.2	29.1 / 68.1
CPI: Consumer Price Index (2010=100)[c]	100	350	...
International trade: exports (million current US$)[d]	...	5 588	4 127[c,a]
International trade: imports (million current US$)[d]	...	8 413	12 286[c,a]
International trade: balance (million current US$)[d]	...	- 2 826	- 8 159[c,a]
Balance of payments, current account (million US$)	- 1 725	- 5 461	- 4 679[b]

Major trading partners

2019

Export partners (% of exports)[c]	United Arab Emirates 27.5	China	20.3	Saudi Arabia	16.3
Import partners (% of imports)[c]	China	17.4	Russian Federation	15.1	Saudi Arabia	10.2

Social indicators

	2010	2015	2020
Population growth rate (average annual %)[e]	2.2	2.4	2.4
Urban population (% of total population)	33.1	33.9	34.9[a]
Urban population growth rate (average annual %)[e]	2.3	2.8	...
Fertility rate, total (live births per woman)[e]	5.0	4.8	4.4
Life expectancy at birth (females/males, years)[e]	63.5 / 59.8	65.5 / 62.1	66.8 / 63.1
Population age distribution (0-14/60+ years old, %)	43.0 / 5.1	41.5 / 5.4	39.8 / 5.7
International migrant stock (000/% of total pop.)[f,g]	618.7 / 1.8	620.5 / 1.6	1 223.1 / 2.9[a]
Refugees and others of concern to the UNHCR (000)	1 951.5[h]	2 767.9	2 974.1[a]
Infant mortality rate (per 1 000 live births)[e]	53.2	47.8	42.9
Health: Current expenditure (% of GDP)[c]	5.1[g]	7.2	6.3[i]
Health: Physicians (per 1 000 pop.)	0.3[i]	0.4	0.3[i]
Education: Government expenditure (% of GDP)	2.2[k]	...	...
Education: Primary gross enrol. ratio (f/m per 100 pop.)	67.8 / 75.6	69.8 / 76.4	74.4 / 79.2[i]
Education: Secondary gross enrol. ratio (f/m per 100 pop.)	39.4 / 45.5	45.3 / 46.0	47.0 / 46.3[i]
Education: Tertiary gross enrol. ratio (f/m per 100 pop.)	17.2 / 14.7	17.1 / 16.8	... / ...
Intentional homicide rate (per 100 000 pop.)	5.1[j]	...	...
Seats held by women in the National Parliament (%)	...	24.3	27.7[a]

Environment and infrastructure indicators

	2010	2015	2020
Individuals using the Internet (per 100 inhabitants)[c]	16.7	26.6	30.9[i]
Research & Development expenditure (% of GDP)	0.3[l,m]	...	...
Threatened species (number)	112	123	158
CO2 emission estimates (million tons/tons per capita)	15.1 / 0.3	16.4 / 0.4	18.8 / 0.5[i]
Energy production, primary (Petajoules)	...	457	412[i]
Energy supply per capita (Gigajoules)	...	13	13[i]
Tourist/visitor arrivals at national borders (000)[n]	495	741	836[b]
Important sites for terrestrial biodiversity protected (%)	9.1	9.1	17.8[a]
Net Official Development Assist. received (% of GNI)	3.35	1.10	2.55[b]

[a] 2019. [b] 2018. [c] Estimate. [d] Data up to 2011 refer to former Sudan (including South Sudan) and data beginning 2012 is attributed to Sudan without South Sudan. [e] Data refers to a 5-year period preceding the reference year. [f] Including refugees. [g] Including South Sudan. [h] Data as at the end of December. [i] 2017. [j] 2008. [l] Overestimated or based on overestimated data. [m] 2005. [n] Including nationals residing abroad.

Suriname

Region	South America	UN membership date	04 December 1975		
Population (000, 2020)	587	Surface area (km2)	163 820 [a]		
Pop. density (per km2, 2020)	3.8	Sex ratio (m per 100 f)	101.0		
Capital city	Paramaribo	National currency	Surinam Dollar (SRD)		
Capital city pop. (000, 2020)	239.5 [b,c]	Exchange rate (per US$)	7.5 [d]		

Economic indicators

	2010	2015	2020
GDP: Gross domestic product (million current US$)	4 368	4 787	3 458 [c]
GDP growth rate (annual %, const. 2015 prices)	5.2	- 3.4	2.6 [c]
GDP per capita (current US$)	8 255.8	8 562.2	6 003.7 [c]
Economy: Agriculture (% of Gross Value Added) [e]	10.2	10.0	12.3 [c]
Economy: Industry (% of Gross Value Added)	37.9	28.0	34.5 [c]
Economy: Services and other activity (% of GVA)	46.9	50.9	51.8 [c]
Employment in agriculture (% of employed) [f]	7.6	7.4	7.4
Employment in industry (% of employed) [f]	24.3	23.9	23.5
Employment in services & other sectors (% employed) [f]	68.1	68.7	69.1
Unemployment rate (% of labour force) [f]	7.2	7.2	7.5
Labour force participation rate (female/male pop. %) [f]	38.9 / 64.2	39.3 / 64.0	38.8 / 63.4
CPI: Consumer Price Index (2010=100) [g]	100	139	295 [d]
Agricultural production index (2004-2006=100)	137	144	146 [h]
International trade: exports (million current US$)	2 026	1 814	1 461 [d]
International trade: imports (million current US$)	1 397	1 904	1 711 [d]
International trade: balance (million current US$)	628	- 90	- 250 [d]
Balance of payments, current account (million US$)	651	- 786	- 411 [d]

Major trading partners

						2019
Export partners (% of exports)	Areas nes [i]	39.5	United Arab Emirates	36.7	Belgium	8.2
Import partners (% of imports)	United States	21.7	Areas nes [i]	14.6	Netherlands	12.0

Social indicators

	2010	2015	2020
Population growth rate (average annual %) [j]	1.2	1.1	1.0
Urban population (% of total population)	66.3	66.1	66.1 [d]
Urban population growth rate (average annual %) [j]	1.0	0.9	...
Fertility rate, total (live births per woman) [j]	2.7	2.6	2.4
Life expectancy at birth (females/males, years) [j]	73.2 / 66.7	74.3 / 67.8	74.8 / 68.3
Population age distribution (0-14/60+ years old, %)	29.4 / 9.1	27.9 / 9.7	26.7 / 10.8
International migrant stock (000/% of total pop.) [k]	39.7 / 7.5	43.1 / 7.7	46.2 / 7.9 [d]
Refugees and others of concern to the UNHCR (000)	~0.0 [l]	~0.0	0.4 [d]
Infant mortality rate (per 1 000 live births) [j]	23.7	20.3	17.5
Health: Current expenditure (% of GDP)	5.0	6.2	6.2 [a]
Health: Physicians (per 1 000 pop.)	0.7 [m]	1.0	1.2 [c]
Education: Primary gross enrol. ratio (f/m per 100 pop.)	113.8 / 114.2	116.4 / 115.2	108.7 / 109.0 [c]
Education: Secondary gross enrol. ratio (f/m per 100 pop.)	80.7 / 62.6	88.6 / 67.1	... / ...
Intentional homicide rate (per 100 000 pop.)	8.3 [n]	6.1	5.4 [a]
Seats held by women in the National Parliament (%)	25.5	11.8	31.4 [o]

Environment and infrastructure indicators

	2010	2015	2020
Individuals using the Internet (per 100 inhabitants)	31.6	42.8 [f]	48.9 [f,a]
Threatened species (number)	65	76	88
Forested area (% of land area) [f]	98.4	98.3	98.3 [a]
CO2 emission estimates (million tons/tons per capita)	1.7 / 3.2	2.1 / 3.7	1.9 / 3.4 [a]
Energy production, primary (Petajoules)	43	40	39 [a]
Energy supply per capita (Gigajoules)	76	78	71 [a]
Tourist/visitor arrivals at national borders (000)	205	228	278 [a]
Important sites for terrestrial biodiversity protected (%)	51.2	51.2	51.2 [d]
Net Official Development Assist. received (% of GNI)	2.36	0.34	0.48 [c]

a 2017. **b** Refers to the total population of the District of Paramaribo. **c** 2018. **d** 2019. **e** At factor cost. **f** Estimate. **g** Calculated by the UN Statistics Division from national indices. **h** 2016. **i** Areas not elsewhere specified. **j** Data refers to a 5-year period preceding the reference year. **k** Refers to foreign citizens. **l** Data as at the end of December **m** 2009. **n** 2008. **o** Data are as at 1 January of reporting year.

Sweden

Region	Northern Europe	
Population (000, 2020)	10 099	
Pop. density (per km2, 2020)	24.6	
Capital city	Stockholm	
Capital city pop. (000, 2020)	1 608.0[b,c]	

UN membership date	19 November 1946	
Surface area (km2)	438 574[a]	
Sex ratio (m per 100 f)	100.4	
National currency	Swedish Krona (SEK)	
Exchange rate (per US$)	9.3[c]	

Economic indicators	2010	2015	2020
GDP: Gross domestic product (million current US$)	495 329	503 651	556 086[d]
GDP growth rate (annual %, const. 2015 prices)	6.2	4.4	2.2[d]
GDP per capita (current US$)	52 749.7	51 577.4	55 766.8[d]
Economy: Agriculture (% of Gross Value Added)[e]	1.9	1.6	1.6[d]
Economy: Industry (% of Gross Value Added)[e,f]	27.0	24.8	25.5[d]
Economy: Services and other activity (% of GVA)[e,g,h]	72.1	72.3	72.5[d]
Employment in agriculture (% of employed)	2.1	2.0	1.6[i]
Employment in industry (% of employed)	19.9	18.3	17.7[i]
Employment in services & other sectors (% employed)	78.0	79.7	80.7[i]
Unemployment rate (% of labour force)[i]	8.6	7.4	6.7
Labour force participation rate (female/male pop. %)[i]	59.0 / 67.4	60.7 / 67.4	61.4 / 67.7
CPI: Consumer Price Index (2010=100)	100	104	111[c]
Agricultural production index (2004-2006=100)	95	104	100[i]
International trade: exports (million current US$)	158 411	140 001	160 538[c]
International trade: imports (million current US$)	148 788	138 361	158 710[c]
International trade: balance (million current US$)	9 622	1 641	1 828[c]
Balance of payments, current account (million US$)	29 196	20 695	20 783[c]

Major trading partners						2019
Export partners (% of exports)	Norway	10.6	Germany	10.3	United States	7.6
Import partners (% of imports)	Germany	17.8	Netherlands	9.4	Norway	9.1

Social indicators	2010	2015	2020
Population growth rate (average annual %)[k]	0.8	0.8	0.7
Urban population (% of total population)	85.1	86.6	87.7[c]
Urban population growth rate (average annual %)[k]	0.9	1.1	...
Fertility rate, total (live births per woman)[k]	1.9	1.9	1.8
Life expectancy at birth (females/males, years)[k]	83.1 / 79.0	83.8 / 80.0	84.4 / 80.8
Population age distribution (0-14/60+ years old, %)	16.5 / 24.9	17.3 / 25.2	17.6 / 25.9
International migrant stock (000/% of total pop.)	1 384.9 / 14.7	1 676.3 / 17.2	2 005.7 / 20.0[c]
Refugees and others of concern to the UNHCR (000)	110.8[l]	225.5	310.4[c]
Infant mortality rate (per 1 000 live births)[k]	2.6	2.4	2.0
Health: Current expenditure (% of GDP)	8.5	11.0	11.0[a]
Health: Physicians (per 1 000 pop.)	3.9	4.3	4.0[j]
Education: Government expenditure (% of GDP)	6.6	7.5	7.7[i]
Education: Primary gross enrol. ratio (f/m per 100 pop.)	101.2 / 101.7	125.5 / 120.5	127.4 / 125.8[a]
Education: Secondary gross enrol. ratio (f/m per 100 pop.)	97.6 / 98.6	150.0 / 131.5	157.9 / 148.1[a]
Education: Tertiary gross enrol. ratio (f/m per 100 pop.)	89.6 / 58.5	75.6 / 49.6	82.1 / 52.7[a]
Intentional homicide rate (per 100 000 pop.)	1.0	1.1	1.1[d]
Seats held by women in the National Parliament (%)	46.4	43.6	47.0[m]

Environment and infrastructure indicators	2010	2015	2020
Individuals using the Internet (per 100 inhabitants)	90.0[n]	90.6[o]	92.1[d]
Research & Development expenditure (% of GDP)	3.2[i]	3.3[p]	3.3[i,d]
Threatened species (number)	29	36	98
Forested area (% of land area)	68.4	68.9	68.9[i,a]
CO2 emission estimates (million tons/tons per capita)	46.1 / 4.9	37.1 / 3.8	37.6 / 3.7[a]
Energy production, primary (Petajoules)	1 354	1 400	1 491[a]
Energy supply per capita (Gigajoules)	225	190	205[a]
Tourist/visitor arrivals at national borders (000)	5 183	6 482	7 440[d]
Important sites for terrestrial biodiversity protected (%)	57.2	58.0	59.0[c]
Pop. using safely managed sanitation (urban/rural %)	93.9 / 87.7	94.2 / 87.8	94.2 / 87.8[a]
Net Official Development Assist. disbursed (% of GNI)[q]	0.97	1.40	1.02[a]

[2]017. b Refers to "tätort" (according to the administrative divisions of 2005). c 2019. d 2018. e Data classified according to ISIC Rev. 4. f Excludes irrigation canals and landscaping care. g Excludes computer and related activities [and] radio/TV activities. h Excludes repair of personal and household goods. i Estimate. j 2016. k Data refers to a 5-[yea]r period preceding the reference year. l Data as at the end of December. m Data are as at 1 January of reporting [yea]r. n Population aged 16 to 75 years. o Population aged 16 to 74 years. p The sum of the breakdown does not add [to] the total. q Development Assistance Committee member (OECD).

Switzerland

Region	Western Europe	UN membership date	10 September 2002
Population (000, 2020)	8 655	Surface area (km2)	41 291 a
Pop. density (per km2, 2020)	219.0	Sex ratio (m per 100 f)	98.5
Capital city	Bern	National currency	Swiss Franc (CHF)
Capital city pop. (000, 2020)	426.0 b	Exchange rate (per US$)	1.0 b

Economic indicators

	2010	2015	2020
GDP: Gross domestic product (million current US$)	583 783	679 832	705 141 c
GDP growth rate (annual %, const. 2015 prices)	3.0	1.3	2.8 c
GDP per capita (current US$)	74 760.8	81 939.3	82 708.5 c
Economy: Agriculture (% of Gross Value Added) d	0.7	0.7	0.7 c
Economy: Industry (% of Gross Value Added) d,e	26.6	25.9	25.8 c
Economy: Services and other activity (% of GVA) d,f,g	78.6	80.8	80.9 c
Employment in agriculture (% of employed)	3.5	3.4	2.9 h
Employment in industry (% of employed)	22.4	20.8	20.0 h
Employment in services & other sectors (% employed)	74.1	75.8	77.2 h
Unemployment rate (% of labour force) h	4.8	4.8	4.8
Labour force participation rate (female/male pop. %) h	59.9 / 74.3	62.4 / 74.2	62.8 / 73.5
CPI: Consumer Price Index (2010=100) i	100	98	100 b
Agricultural production index (2004-2006=100)	103	103	101 i
International trade: exports (million current US$)	195 609	291 959	313 630 b
International trade: imports (million current US$)	176 281	253 152	276 292 b
International trade: balance (million current US$)	19 329	38 807	37 338 b
Balance of payments, current account (million US$)	85 822	76 602	86 167 b

Major trading partners

						2019
Export partners (% of exports)	Germany	15.3	United States	14.0	United Kingdom	9.0
Import partners (% of imports)	Germany	20.8	Italy	8.1	United States	6.8

Social indicators

	2010	2015	2020
Population growth rate (average annual %) k	1.1	1.2	0.8
Urban population (% of total population)	73.6	73.7	73.8 b
Urban population growth rate (average annual %) k	1.1	1.2	...
Fertility rate, total (live births per woman) k	1.5	1.5	1.5
Life expectancy at birth (females/males, years) k	84.1 / 79.3	84.8 / 80.5	85.4 / 81.6
Population age distribution (0-14/60+ years old, %)	15.1 / 22.8	14.8 / 23.5	15.0 / 25.3
International migrant stock (000/% of total pop.)	2 075.2 / 26.6	2 416.4 / 29.1	2 572.0 / 29.9 b
Refugees and others of concern to the UNHCR (000)	61.9 l	86.6	120.1 b
Infant mortality rate (per 1 000 live births) k	4.2	3.9	3.4
Health: Current expenditure (% of GDP)	10.7	11.9	12.3 a
Health: Physicians (per 1 000 pop.)	3.8	4.2	4.3 a
Education: Government expenditure (% of GDP)	4.9	5.1	5.1 i
Education: Primary gross enrol. ratio (f/m per 100 pop.)	102.6 / 103.1	104.0 / 104.3	104.8 / 105.5 a
Education: Secondary gross enrol. ratio (f/m per 100 pop.)	94.6 / 97.5	99.6 / 103.2	100.2 / 104.7 a
Education: Tertiary gross enrol. ratio (f/m per 100 pop.)	52.7 / 53.2	58.5 / 56.9	60.3 / 58.8 a
Intentional homicide rate (per 100 000 pop.)	0.7	0.7	0.6 c
Seats held by women in the National Parliament (%)	29.0	30.5	41.5 m

Environment and infrastructure indicators

	2010	2015	2020
Individuals using the Internet (per 100 inhabitants)	83.9 n,o	87.5 n,o	89.7 a
Research & Development expenditure (% of GDP)	2.7 p	3.4	3.4 a
Threatened species (number)	45	62	128
Forested area (% of land area)	31.3	31.7	31.7 h,a
CO2 emission estimates (million tons/tons per capita)	43.3 / 5.5	37.3 / 4.5	37.1 / 4.4 a
Energy production, primary (Petajoules) q	515	495	460 a
Energy supply per capita (Gigajoules) q	137	121	116 a
Tourist/visitor arrivals at national borders (000)	8 628	9 305	10 362 c
Important sites for terrestrial biodiversity protected (%)	35.3	35.3	35.5 b
Pop. using safely managed sanitation (urban/rural %)	99.3 / 98.5	99.9 / 98.5	99.9 / 98.5 a
Net Official Development Assist. disbursed (% of GNI) r	0.39	0.51	0.47 a

a 2017. b 2019. c 2018. d Data classified according to ISIC Rev. 4. e Excludes publishing activities. Includes irrigation and canals. f Excludes computer and related activities and radio/TV activities. g Excludes repair of person and household goods. h Estimate. i Calculated by the UN Statistics Division from national indices. j 2016. k Data refers to a 5-year period preceding the reference year. l Data as at the end of December. m Data are as at 1 Januar of reporting year. n Population aged 14 years and over. o Users in the last 6 months. p 2008. q Including Liechtenstein. r Development Assistance Committee member (OECD).

Syrian Arab Republic

Region	Western Asia	UN membership date	24 October 1945
Population (000, 2020)	17 501	Surface area (km2)	185 180 [a]
Pop. density (per km2, 2020)	95.3	Sex ratio (m per 100 f)	100.2
Capital city	Damascus	National currency	Syrian Pound (SYP)
Capital city pop. (000, 2020)	2 353.6 [b,c]	Exchange rate (per US$)	700.0 [d,c]

Economic indicators

	2010	2015	2020
GDP: Gross domestic product (million current US$)	60 465	19 090	16 628 [e]
GDP growth rate (annual %, const. 2015 prices)	3.4	- 6.1	2.4 [e]
GDP per capita (current US$)	2 830.4	1 060.7	981.3 [e]
Economy: Agriculture (% of Gross Value Added) [f]	19.7	20.7	20.6 [e]
Economy: Industry (% of Gross Value Added) [f]	30.7	30.0	30.1 [e]
Economy: Services and other activity (% of GVA) [f]	52.7	48.1	45.6 [e]
Employment in agriculture (% of employed) [g]	14.5	12.0	10.5
Employment in industry (% of employed) [g]	31.0	28.3	26.5
Employment in services & other sectors (% employed) [g]	54.4	59.7	63.0
Unemployment rate (% of labour force) [g]	8.6	8.5	8.4
Labour force participation rate (female/male pop. %) [g]	13.1 / 72.8	14.1 / 73.6	14.3 / 74.0
CPI: Consumer Price Index (2010=100)	100	449	663 [h]
Agricultural production index (2004-2006=100)	89	73	79 [h]
International trade: exports (million current US$)	11 353	1 688 [g]	534 [g,c]
International trade: imports (million current US$)	17 562	3 206 [g]	980 [g,c]
International trade: balance (million current US$)	- 6 209	- 1 518 [g]	- 447 [g,c]
Balance of payments, current account (million current US$)	- 367	...	...

Major trading partners

						2019
Export partners (% of exports) [g]	Turkey	15.6	Saudi Arabia	14.2	Egypt	12.5
Import partners (% of imports) [g]	Turkey	25.0	China	18.4	United Arab Emirates	18.3

Social indicators

	2010	2015	2020
Population growth rate (average annual %) [i]	3.0	- 3.4	- 0.6
Urban population (% of total population)	55.6	52.2	54.8 [c]
Urban population growth rate (average annual %) [i]	3.4	- 3.6	...
Fertility rate, total (live births per woman) [i]	3.7	3.1	2.8
Life expectancy at birth (females/males, years) [i]	77.3 / 72.0	76.3 / 64.4	77.7 / 65.9
Population age distribution (0-14/60+ years old, %)	37.4 / 5.0	33.1 / 6.3	30.8 / 7.5
International migrant stock (000/% of total pop.) [j,k]	1 787.6 / 8.4	871.2 / 4.8	867.8 / 5.1 [c]
Refugees and others of concern to the UNHCR (000)	1 308.1 [l]	7 946.5	6 386.7 [m,c]
Infant mortality rate (per 1 000 live births) [i]	15.0	17.9	15.5
Health: Current expenditure (% of GDP)	3.3	3.6 [n]	...
Health: Physicians (per 1 000 pop.)	1.5	1.6 [o]	1.3 [h]
Education: Government expenditure (% of GDP)	5.1 [p]	...	...
Education: Primary gross enrol. ratio (f/m per 100 pop.)	114.7 / 118.8	80.2 / 83.1 [q]	... / ...
Education: Secondary gross enrol. ratio (f/m per 100 pop.)	72.3 / 72.1	52.4 / 52.7 [q]	... / ...
Education: Tertiary gross enrol. ratio (f/m per 100 pop.)	23.9 / 27.7	44.8 / 40.7	42.8 / 37.5 [h]
Intentional homicide rate (per 100 000 pop.)	2.2	...	0.9 [e]
Seats held by women in the National Parliament (%)	12.4	12.4	12.4 [r]

Environment and infrastructure indicators

	2010	2015	2020
Individuals using the Internet (per 100 inhabitants)	20.7	30.0 [g]	34.3 [g,a]
Threatened species (number)	78	108	147
Forested area (% of land area) [g]	2.7	2.7	2.7 [a]
CO2 emission estimates (million tons/tons per capita)	57.3 / 2.7	23.9 / 1.3	23.0 / 1.3 [a]
Energy production, primary (Petajoules)	1 165	196	172 [a]
Energy supply per capita (Gigajoules)	43	22	20 [a]
Tourist/visitor arrivals at national borders (000) [s,t]	8 546	5 070 [u]	...
Important sites for terrestrial biodiversity protected (%)	0.0	0.0	0.0 [c]
Net Official Development Assist. received (% of GNI)	0.21 [v]	...	...

a 2017. b Estimates should be viewed with caution as these are derived from scarce data. c 2019. d UN operational exchange rate. e 2018. f Including taxes less subsidies on production and imports. g Estimate. h 2016. i Data refers to a 5-year period preceding the reference year. j Refers to foreign citizens. k Including refugees. l Data as at the end December. m Refugee figure for Iraqis was a government estimate; UNHCR has registered and was assisting 800 Iraqis at mid-2019. Figure for stateless persons was an estimate. n 2012. o 2014. p 2009. q 2013. r Data are at 1 January of reporting year. s Including Iraqi nationals. t Including nationals residing abroad. u 2011. v 2007.

Tajikistan

Region	Central Asia	UN membership date	02 March 1992
Population (000, 2020)	9 538	Surface area (km2)	142 600 a
Pop. density (per km2, 2020)	68.1	Sex ratio (m per 100 f)	101.6
Capital city	Dushanbe	National currency	Somoni (TJS)
Capital city pop. (000, 2020)	893.8 b	Exchange rate (per US$)	9.7 b

Economic indicators

	2010	2015	2020
GDP: Gross domestic product (million current US$)	5 642	7 855	7 523 c
GDP growth rate (annual %, const. 2015 prices)	6.5	6.0	7.1 c
GDP per capita (current US$)	749.6	929.1	826.6 c
Economy: Agriculture (% of Gross Value Added)	21.8	24.7	20.9 c
Economy: Industry (% of Gross Value Added)	27.9	27.5	30.1 c
Economy: Services and other activity (% of GVA)	39.9	43.8	50.8 c
Employment in agriculture (% of employed) d	52.4	48.3	44.2
Employment in industry (% of employed) d	15.6	15.6	16.0
Employment in services & other sectors (% employed) d	31.9	36.1	39.9
Unemployment rate (% of labour force) d	11.6	11.5	11.0
Labour force participation rate (female/male pop. %) d	29.9 / 56.2	31.4 / 52.9	31.3 / 52.9
CPI: Consumer Price Index (2010=100) e	100	140	179 b
Agricultural production index (2004-2006=100)	124	162	159 f
International trade: exports (million current US$) d	1 206	891	2 065 b
International trade: imports (million current US$) d	2 659	3 435	2 773 b
International trade: balance (million current US$) d	- 1 453	- 2 544	- 708 b
Balance of payments, current account (million US$)	- 581	- 477	- 185 b

Major trading partners

						2019
Export partners (% of exports) d	Turkey	19.2	Switzerland	16.9	Uzbekistan	14.0
Import partners (% of imports) d	China	35.7	Russian Federation	23.9	Kazakhstan	16.4

Social indicators

	2010	2015	2020
Population growth rate (average annual %) g	2.1	2.3	2.4
Urban population (% of total population)	26.5	26.7	27.3 b
Urban population growth rate (average annual %) g	2.2	2.4	...
Fertility rate, total (live births per woman) g	3.6	3.6	3.6
Life expectancy at birth (females/males, years) g	70.1 / 65.6	71.8 / 67.2	73.0 / 68.6
Population age distribution (0-14/60+ years old, %)	35.7 / 4.8	35.8 / 4.8	37.3 / 5.8
International migrant stock (000/% of total pop.)	279.8 / 3.7	275.1 / 3.3	274.1 / 2.9 b
Refugees and others of concern to the UNHCR (000)	7.1 h	11.9	11.3 b
Infant mortality rate (per 1 000 live births) g	39.0	34.1	29.3
Health: Current expenditure (% of GDP)	5.7	6.9	7.2 a
Health: Physicians (per 1 000 pop.)	1.7	2.1 i	...
Education: Government expenditure (% of GDP)	4.0	5.2	...
Education: Primary gross enrol. ratio (f/m per 100 pop.)	100.2 / 102.7	97.1 / 98.1	100.3 / 101.4 a
Education: Secondary gross enrol. ratio (f/m per 100 pop.)	78.9 / 90.4	83.8 / 93.0 j	... / ...
Education: Tertiary gross enrol. ratio (f/m per 100 pop.)	15.8 / 29.9	21.3 / 31.6	26.9 / 35.5 a
Intentional homicide rate (per 100 000 pop.)	2.4	1.6 k	...
Seats held by women in the National Parliament (%)	17.5	16.9	19.0 l

Environment and infrastructure indicators

	2010	2015	2020
Individuals using the Internet (per 100 inhabitants) d	11.6	19.0	22.0 a
Research & Development expenditure (% of GDP) m,n	0.1	0.1	0.1 c
Threatened species (number)	40	41	48
Forested area (% of land area) d	2.9	3.0	3.0 a
CO2 emission estimates (million tons/tons per capita)	2.3 / 0.3	4.2 / 0.5	5.8 / 0.7 a
Energy production, primary (Petajoules)	115	131 d	157 d,a
Energy supply per capita (Gigajoules)	19	19	21 a
Tourist/visitor arrivals at national borders (000)	160	414	1 035 c
Important sites for terrestrial biodiversity protected (%)	15.8	16.8	16.8 b
Net Official Development Assist. received (% of GNI)	5.57	4.61	4.52 c

a 2017. b 2019. c 2018. d Estimate. e Calculated by the UN Statistics Division from national indices. f 2016. g Data refers to a 5-year period preceding the reference year. h Data as at the end of December. i 2014. j 2013. k 2011. l Data are as at 1 January of reporting year. m Excluding private non-profit. n Excluding business enterprise.

Thailand

Region	South-eastern Asia	UN membership date	16 December 1946
Population (000, 2020)	69 800	Surface area (km2)	513 120 [a]
Pop. density (per km2, 2020)	136.6	Sex ratio (m per 100 f)	94.8
Capital city	Bangkok	National currency	Baht (THB)
Capital city pop. (000, 2020)	10 350.2 [b]	Exchange rate (per US$)	30.2 [b]

Economic indicators	2010	2015	2020
GDP: Gross domestic product (million current US$)	341 105	401 296	504 992 [c]
GDP growth rate (annual %, const. 2015 prices)	7.5	3.1	4.1 [c]
GDP per capita (current US$)	5 076.3	5 840.0	7 273.6 [c]
Economy: Agriculture (% of Gross Value Added) [d,e]	10.5	8.9	8.3 [c]
Economy: Industry (% of Gross Value Added) [d,e,f]	39.9	36.2	35.6 [c]
Economy: Services and other activity (% of GVA) [d,e,g,h]	31.0	38.9	38.9 [c]
Employment in agriculture (% of employed)	38.2	32.3	31.2 [i]
Employment in industry (% of employed)	20.6	23.7	22.5 [i]
Employment in services & other sectors (% employed)	41.1	44.0	46.3 [i]
Unemployment rate (% of labour force) [i]	0.6	0.6	0.8
Labour force participation rate (female/male pop. %) [i]	63.9 / 80.0	60.9 / 77.7	58.9 / 75.8
CPI: Consumer Price Index (2010=100) [j]	100	110	113 [b]
Agricultural production index (2004-2006=100)	114	122	118 [k]
International trade: exports (million current US$)	195 312	214 309	233 674 [b]
International trade: imports (million current US$)	182 393	202 642	216 805 [b]
International trade: balance (million current US$)	12 918	11 667	16 870 [b]
Balance of payments, current account (million US$)	11 486	27 753	37 911 [b]

Major trading partners						2019
Export partners (% of exports)	United States	12.7	China	12.0	Japan	9.9
Import partners (% of imports)	China	21.1	Japan	14.0	United States	7.4

Social indicators	2010	2015	2020
Population growth rate (average annual %) [i]	0.5	0.4	0.3
Urban population (% of total population)	43.9	47.7	50.7 [b]
Urban population growth rate (average annual %) [i]	3.7	2.1	...
Fertility rate, total (live births per woman) [i]	1.6	1.5	1.5
Life expectancy at birth (females/males, years) [i]	76.6 / 69.8	78.9 / 71.6	80.6 / 73.1
Population age distribution (0-14/60+ years old, %)	19.2 / 12.9	18.0 / 15.7	16.6 / 19.2
International migrant stock (000/% of total pop.) [m]	3 224.1 / 4.8	3 486.5 / 5.1	3 635.1 / 5.2 [b]
Refugees and others of concern to the UNHCR (000)	649.4 [n]	625.3	576.9 [b]
Infant mortality rate (per 1 000 live births) [i]	13.4	10.1	7.8
Health: Current expenditure (% of GDP) [o]	3.4	3.7	3.7 [a]
Health: Physicians (per 1 000 pop.)	0.4	0.5	0.8 [c]
Education: Government expenditure (% of GDP)	3.5	4.1 [p]	...
Education: Primary gross enrol. ratio (f/m per 100 pop.)	96.3 / 97.4	97.6 / 103.5	99.8 / 99.8 [c]
Education: Secondary gross enrol. ratio (f/m per 100 pop.)	85.3 / 79.6	118.2 / 123.0	116.5 / 118.9 [c]
Education: Tertiary gross enrol. ratio (f/m per 100 pop.)	56.6 / 44.3	57.8 / 42.7 [q]	57.8 / 41.0 [k]
Intentional homicide rate (per 100 000 pop.)	5.4	3.5	2.6 [a]
Seats held by women in the National Parliament (%)	13.3	6.1	16.2 [r]

Environment and infrastructure indicators	2010	2015	2020
Individuals using the Internet (per 100 inhabitants)	22.4	39.3 [s]	56.8 [c]
Research & Development expenditure (% of GDP)	0.2 [t]	0.6	1.0 [a]
Threatened species (number)	477	595	674
Forested area (% of land area) [i]	31.8	32.1	32.1 [a]
CO2 emission estimates (million tons/tons per capita)	223.4 / 3.3	248.0 / 3.6	244.3 / 3.5 [a]
Energy production, primary (Petajoules)	2 952	3 161	3 150 [a]
Energy supply per capita (Gigajoules)	74	82	84 [a]
Tourist/visitor arrivals at national borders (000)	15 936	29 923	38 178 [c]
Important sites for terrestrial biodiversity protected (%)	70.7	70.7	70.7 [b]
Net Official Development Assist. disbursed (% of GNI)	~0.00	0.02	0.03 [a]
Net Official Development Assist. received (% of GNI)	- 0.01	0.02	- 0.09 [c]

2017. **b** 2019. **c** 2018. **d** Data classified according to ISIC Rev. 4. **e** At producers' prices. **f** Excludes publishing activities. Includes irrigation and canals. **g** Excludes repair of personal and household goods. **h** Excludes computer related activities and radio/TV activities. **i** Estimate. **j** Calculated by the UN Statistics Division from national ...ces. **k** 2016. **l** Data refers to a 5-year period preceding the reference year. **m** Including refugees. **n** Data as at the ...of December. **o** Data refer to fiscal years ending 30 September. **p** 2013. **q** 2014. **r** Data are as at 1 January of ...orting year. **s** Population aged 6 years and over. **t** 2009.

Timor-Leste

Region	South-eastern Asia	UN membership date	27 September 2002
Population (000, 2020)	1 318	Surface area (km2)	14 919[a]
Pop. density (per km2, 2020)	88.7	Sex ratio (m per 100 f)	102.2
Capital city	Dili	National currency	US Dollar (USD)
Capital city pop. (000, 2020)	281.1[b]	Exchange rate (per US$)	1.0[c]

Economic indicators

	2010	2015	2020
GDP: Gross domestic product (million current US$)	3 999	3 093	2 581[b]
GDP growth rate (annual %, const. 2015 prices)	- 1.2	20.6	2.8[b]
GDP per capita (current US$)	3 657.0	2 585.2	2 035.5[b]
Economy: Agriculture (% of Gross Value Added)[d]	5.7	8.9	10.0[b]
Economy: Industry (% of Gross Value Added)[d,e]	79.1	57.9	49.6[b]
Economy: Services and other activity (% of GVA)[d,f,g]	33.6	43.6	47.9[b]
Employment in agriculture (% of employed)	50.8	47.4[h]	43.7[h]
Employment in industry (% of employed)	9.3	10.0[h]	9.8[h]
Employment in services & other sectors (% employed)	39.9	42.6[h]	46.4[h]
Unemployment rate (% of labour force)[h]	3.3	4.4	4.6
Labour force participation rate (female/male pop. %)[h]	60.6 / 70.7	61.2 / 71.9	61.9 / 72.7
CPI: Consumer Price Index (2010=100)[h]	100	143	145[b]
Agricultural production index (2004-2006=100)	124	113	111[i]
International trade: exports (million current US$)[h]	42	45	154[c]
International trade: imports (million current US$)[h]	246	578	536[c]
International trade: balance (million current US$)[h]	- 205	- 533	- 382[c]
Balance of payments, current account (million US$)	1 671	225	134[c]

Major trading partners

						2019
Export partners (% of exports)[h]	Indonesia	25.4	United States	22.3	Germany	13.6
Import partners (% of imports)[h]	Indonesia	31.9	China	15.1	Singapore	13.1

Social indicators

	2010	2015	2020
Population growth rate (average annual %)[j]	1.9	1.8	1.9
Urban population (% of total population)	27.7	29.5	30.9[c]
Urban population growth rate (average annual %)[j]	2.8	3.5	...
Fertility rate, total (live births per woman)[j]	5.3	4.4	4.1
Life expectancy at birth (females/males, years)[j]	67.6 / 64.7	69.5 / 65.9	71.3 / 67.2
Population age distribution (0-14/60+ years old, %)	42.5 / 6.3	39.5 / 6.3	36.8 / 6.6
International migrant stock (000/% of total pop.)	11.5 / 1.1	8.5 / 0.7	8.4 / 0.7[c]
Refugees and others of concern to the UNHCR (000)	~0.0[k]	~0.0	~0.0[c]
Infant mortality rate (per 1 000 live births)[j]	53.3	44.9	37.3
Health: Current expenditure (% of GDP)	1.4	3.5[l,m]	3.9[m,a]
Health: Physicians (per 1 000 pop.)	...	0.7	0.7[b]
Education: Government expenditure (% of GDP)	2.4	4.3	3.8[a]
Education: Primary gross enrol. ratio (f/m per 100 pop.)	119.2 / 126.1	126.6 / 129.8	113.2 / 117.3[b]
Education: Secondary gross enrol. ratio (f/m per 100 pop.)	62.1 / 62.6	74.4 / 70.5	87.0 / 80.3[b]
Education: Tertiary gross enrol. ratio (f/m per 100 pop.)	14.8 / 20.6	... / ...	... / ...
Intentional homicide rate (per 100 000 pop.)	3.6	4.1	...
Seats held by women in the National Parliament (%)	29.2	38.5	38.5[n]

Environment and infrastructure indicators

	2010	2015	2020
Individuals using the Internet (per 100 inhabitants)[h]	3.0	23.0	27.5[a]
Threatened species (number)	18	21	41
Forested area (% of land area)[h]	49.9	46.1	46.1[a]
Energy production, primary (Petajoules)	186	147[h]	54[a]
Energy supply per capita (Gigajoules)[h]	4	6	6[a]
Tourist/visitor arrivals at national borders (000)[o]	40	62	75[b]
Important sites for terrestrial biodiversity protected (%)	34.0	34.0	39.5[c]
Net Official Development Assist. received (% of GNI)	8.69	7.60	8.78[b]

a 2017. b 2018. c 2019. d Data classified according to ISIC Rev. 4. e Excludes publishing activities. Includes irrigation and canals. f Excludes repair of personal and household goods. g Excludes computer and related activities and radio/TV activities. h Estimate. i 2016. j Data refers to a 5-year period preceding the reference year. k Data as at the end of December. l Break in the time series. m Data revision. n Data are as at 1 January of reporting year. o Arrivals by air at Dili Airport.

Togo

Region	Western Africa	
Population (000, 2020)	8 279	
Pop. density (per km2, 2020)	152.2	
Capital city	Lomé	
Capital city pop. (000, 2020)	1 785.3 c	

UN membership date	20 September 1960
Surface area (km2)	56 785 a
Sex ratio (m per 100 f)	99.0
National currency	CFA Franc, BCEAO (XOF) b
Exchange rate (per US$)	583.9 c

Economic indicators

	2010	2015	2020
GDP: Gross domestic product (million current US$)	3 426	4 178	5 165 d
GDP growth rate (annual %, const. 2015 prices)	6.1	5.7	4.9 d
GDP per capita (current US$)	533.5	570.5	654.8 d
Economy: Agriculture (% of Gross Value Added)	33.8	28.2	27.7 d
Economy: Industry (% of Gross Value Added) e	16.0	18.0	18.4 d
Economy: Services and other activity (% of GVA) f	47.1	58.3	61.1 d
Employment in agriculture (% of employed) g	44.0	40.2	37.2
Employment in industry (% of employed) g	12.4	12.8	12.9
Employment in services & other sectors (% employed) g	43.6	47.0	49.9
Unemployment rate (% of labour force) g	2.4	2.2	2.0
Labour force participation rate (female/male pop. %) g	77.6 / 80.7	76.6 / 79.9	76.1 / 78.9
CPI: Consumer Price Index (2010=100)	100	111	113 d
Agricultural production index (2004-2006=100)	123	142	142 h
International trade: exports (million current US$)	741	792	917 c
International trade: imports (million current US$)	1 350	1 877	1 844 c
International trade: balance (million current US$)	- 609	- 1 085	- 927 c
Balance of payments, current account (million US$)	- 200	- 461	- 185 d

Major trading partners

							2019
Export partners (% of exports)	Burkina Faso	14.4	Benin	12.0	India	11.7
Import partners (% of imports)	China	21.8	France	8.1	United States	6.6

Social indicators

	2010	2015	2020
Population growth rate (average annual %) i	2.7	2.6	2.5
Urban population (% of total population)	37.5	40.1	42.2 c
Urban population growth rate (average annual %) i	4.0	4.0	...
Fertility rate, total (live births per woman) i	5.0	4.7	4.4
Life expectancy at birth (females/males, years) i	56.4 / 55.1	59.8 / 58.3	61.4 / 59.7
Population age distribution (0-14/60+ years old, %)	42.8 / 4.4	42.1 / 4.5	40.6 / 4.7
International migrant stock (000/% of total pop.) j,k	255.4 / 4.0	277.4 / 3.8	279.1 / 3.5 c
Refugees and others of concern to the UNHCR (000)	14.2 l	22.6	13.0 c
Infant mortality rate (per 1 000 live births) i	63.2	55.7	49.7
Health: Current expenditure (% of GDP)	5.9	6.2	6.2 a
Health: Physicians (per 1 000 pop.)	0.3	~0.0	0.1 d
Education: Government expenditure (% of GDP)	4.1	5.1	5.0 h
Education: Primary gross enrol. ratio (f/m per 100 pop.)	120.8 / 133.9	124.9 / 131.2	121.5 / 126.0 d
Education: Secondary gross enrol. ratio (f/m per 100 pop.)	31.4 / 59.4 g,m	... / ...	52.1 / 71.6 a
Education: Tertiary gross enrol. ratio (f/m per 100 pop.)	... / ...	6.6 / 15.4	9.8 / 19.2 d
Seats held by women in the National Parliament (%)	11.1	17.6	18.7 n

Environment and infrastructure indicators

	2010	2015	2020
Individuals using the Internet (per 100 inhabitants)	3.0 g	7.1 g	12.4 a
Research & Development expenditure (% of GDP)	0.2	0.3 o,p,q	...
Threatened species (number)	54	66	94
Forested area (% of land area) g	5.3	3.5	3.5 a
CO2 emission estimates (million tons/tons per capita)	2.1 / 0.3	1.9 / 0.3	2.1 / 0.3 a
Energy production, primary (Petajoules)	99	113	120 a
Energy supply per capita (Gigajoules)	20	19	20 a
Tourist/visitor arrivals at national borders (000)	202	273	573 d
Important sites for terrestrial biodiversity protected (%)	75.0	75.0	75.0 c
Net Official Development Assist. received (% of GNI)	11.85	4.62	5.61 d

a 2017. b African Financial Community (CFA) Franc, Central Bank of West African States (BCEAO). c 2019. d 2018. e Construction refers to buildings and public works. f Refers to trade only. g Estimate. h 2016. i Data refers to a 5-year period preceding the reference year. j Including refugees. k Refers to foreign citizens. l Data as at the end of December. m 2007. n Data are as at 1 January of reporting year. o Excluding business enterprise. p Excluding private non-profit. q 2014.

Tokelau

Region	Polynesia	Population (000, 2020)	1
Surface area (km2)	12 [a]	Pop. density (per km2, 2020)	135.7
Sex ratio (m per 100 f)	100.0 [b,c]	Capital city	Tokelau [d]
National currency	New Zealand Dollar (NZD)	Exchange rate (per US$)	1.5 [e]

Economic indicators	2010	2015	2020
Agricultural production index (2004-2006=100)	108	113	115 [c]
International trade: exports (million current US$) [f]	~0	~0	~0 [e]
International trade: imports (million current US$) [f]	1	1	1 [e]
International trade: balance (million current US$) [f]	- 1	- 1	- 1 [e]

Major trading partners						2019
Export partners (% of exports) [f]	Singapore	22.3	United States	10.0	Burkina Faso	7.9
Import partners (% of imports) [f]	Samoa	35.2	Ireland	16.5	Philippines	13.2

Social indicators	2010	2015	2020
Population growth rate (average annual %)	- 1.3 [g]	1.9 [g]	1.6
Urban population (% of total population)	0.0	0.0	0.0 [e]
Urban population growth rate (average annual %) [g]	0.0	0.0	...
Fertility rate, total (live births per woman)	...	2.1 [h]	...
Population age distribution (0-14/60+ years old, %)	36.6 / 11.3 [i]	29.9 / 11.5 [j]	28.3 / 12.2 [b,c]
International migrant stock (000/% of total pop.)	0.4 / 37.6	0.5 / 38.9	0.5 / 37.6 [e]
Education: Primary gross enrol. ratio (f/m per 100 pop.)	... / ...	... / ...	125.0 / 150.8 [c]
Education: Secondary gross enrol. ratio (f/m per 100 pop.)	... / ...	... / ...	77.8 / 85.5 [c]

Environment and infrastructure indicators	2010	2015	2020
Threatened species (number)	41	46	54
Forested area (% of land area) [f]	0.0	0.0	0.0 [a]
Important sites for terrestrial biodiversity protected (%)	0.0	0.0	0.0 [e]

a 2017. **b** Break in the time series. **c** 2016. **d** The "capital" rotates yearly between the three atolls of Atafu, Fakaofo and Nukunomu, each with fewer than 500 inhabitants in 2011. **e** 2019. **f** Estimate. **g** Data refers to a 5-year period preceding the reference year. **h** 2012. **i** 2006. **j** 2013.

Tonga

Region	Polynesia	UN membership date	14 September 1999
Population (000, 2020)	106	Surface area (km2)	747 [a]
Pop. density (per km2, 2020)	146.8	Sex ratio (m per 100 f)	100.2
Capital city	Nuku'alofa	National currency	Pa'anga (TOP)
Capital city pop. (000, 2020)	22.9 [b]	Exchange rate (per US$)	2.3 [c]

Economic indicators

	2010	2015	2020
GDP: Gross domestic product (million current US$)	374	400	504 [b]
GDP growth rate (annual %, const. 2015 prices)	3.6	- 2.9	- 0.4 [b]
GDP per capita (current US$)	3 595.4	3 973.3	4 885.8 [b]
Economy: Agriculture (% of Gross Value Added)	18.2	22.6	22.0 [b]
Economy: Industry (% of Gross Value Added)	19.9	20.9	21.0 [b]
Economy: Services and other activity (% of GVA)	65.6	62.6	57.8 [b]
Employment in agriculture (% of employed) [d]	27.9	26.3	23.7
Employment in industry (% of employed) [d]	29.7	28.9	29.2
Employment in services & other sectors (% employed) [d]	42.3	44.8	47.1
Unemployment rate (% of labour force) [d]	1.2	1.1	1.2
Labour force participation rate (female/male pop. %) [d]	45.4 / 75.2	45.8 / 74.8	45.8 / 74.3
CPI: Consumer Price Index (2010=100) [d]	100	110	113 [e]
Agricultural production index (2004-2006=100)	135	139	137 [e]
International trade: exports (million current US$)	8	15 [d]	15 [d,c]
International trade: imports (million current US$)	159	208 [d]	311 [d,c]
International trade: balance (million current US$)	- 151	- 193 [d]	- 296 [d,c]
Balance of payments, current account (million US$)	- 87	- 44	- 8 [c]

Major trading partners

						2019
Export partners (% of exports) [d]	United States	37.9	Rep. of Korea	17.3	Australia	13.7
Import partners (% of imports) [d]	Fiji	27.9	New Zealand	23.3	China	12.2

Social indicators

	2010	2015	2020
Population growth rate (average annual %) [f]	0.6	- 0.6	1.0
Urban population (% of total population)	23.4	23.3	23.1 [c]
Urban population growth rate (average annual %) [f]	0.8	0.3	...
Fertility rate, total (live births per woman) [f]	4.0	3.8	3.6
Life expectancy at birth (females/males, years) [f]	71.8 / 67.9	72.2 / 68.4	72.7 / 68.8
Population age distribution (0-14/60+ years old, %)	37.4 / 7.9	36.4 / 8.7	34.8 / 8.7
International migrant stock (000/% of total pop.)	4.6 / 4.4	4.0 / 3.9	3.8 / 3.6 [c]
Refugees and others of concern to the UNHCR (000)	~0.0 [g]	...	~0.0 [c]
Infant mortality rate (per 1 000 live births) [f]	14.4	14.7	12.5
Health: Current expenditure (% of GDP) [h]	4.7	4.7	5.3 [a]
Health: Physicians (per 1 000 pop.)	0.6	0.5 [i]	...
Education: Primary gross enrol. ratio (f/m per 100 pop.)	107.3 / 109.4	116.0 / 116.7	... / ...
Education: Secondary gross enrol. ratio (f/m per 100 pop.)	107.2 / 100.4	102.4 / 99.4	... / ...
Intentional homicide rate (per 100 000 pop.)	1.0	1.0 [j]	...
Seats held by women in the National Parliament (%)	3.1	0.0	7.4 [k]

Environment and infrastructure indicators

	2010	2015	2020
Individuals using the Internet (per 100 inhabitants) [d]	16.0	38.7	41.2 [a]
Threatened species (number)	58	74	90
Forested area (% of land area)	12.5	12.5	12.5 [d,a]
Energy production, primary (Petajoules)	0	0	0 [a]
Energy supply per capita (Gigajoules)	16	16	20 [a]
Tourist/visitor arrivals at national borders (000) [l]	47	54	54 [b]
Important sites for terrestrial biodiversity protected (%)	26.1	26.1	26.1 [c]
Net Official Development Assist. received (% of GNI)	17.41	15.54	19.15 [b]

2017. b 2018. c 2019. d Estimate. e 2016. f Data refers to a 5-year period preceding the reference year. g Data at the end of December. h Data refer to fiscal years beginning 1 July. i 2013. j 2012. k Data are as at 1 January of reporting year. l Arrivals by air.

Trinidad and Tobago

Region	Caribbean	UN membership date	18 September 1962
Population (000, 2020)	1 400	Surface area (km2)	5 127 a
Pop. density (per km2, 2020)	272.8	Sex ratio (m per 100 f)	97.5
Capital city	Port of Spain	National currency	TT Dollar (TTD) b
Capital city pop. (000, 2020)	544.3 c,d	Exchange rate (per US$)	6.8 d

Economic indicators

	2010	2015	2020
GDP: Gross domestic product (million current US$)	22 182	25 063	23 808 e
GDP growth rate (annual %, const. 2015 prices)	3.3	1.8	- 0.2 e
GDP per capita (current US$)	16 701.8	18 289.6	17 130.3 e
Economy: Agriculture (% of Gross Value Added) f	0.7	1.1	1.1 e
Economy: Industry (% of Gross Value Added) f,g	52.3	40.1	42.8 e
Economy: Services and other activity (% of GVA) f,h,i	50.0	53.2	54.0 e
Employment in agriculture (% of employed)	3.8 i	3.4	2.9 i
Employment in industry (% of employed)	29.8 i	27.9	26.6 i
Employment in services & other sectors (% employed)	66.5 i	68.6	70.5 i
Unemployment rate (% of labour force) i	3.8	2.2	2.8
Labour force participation rate (female/male pop. %) j	51.1 / 73.9	50.8 / 73.2	49.8 / 69.6
CPI: Consumer Price Index (2010=100) k	100	134	142 e
Agricultural production index (2004-2006=100)	96	97	96 i
International trade: exports (million current US$)	10 982	10 756	12 336 j,d
International trade: imports (million current US$)	6 480	9 298	1 951 j,d
International trade: balance (million current US$)	4 502	1 458	10 385 j,d
Balance of payments, current account (million US$)	4 172	1 744	1 386 e

Major trading partners

						2019
Export partners (% of exports) j	United States	34.1	Spain	6.5	Guyana	5.9
Import partners (% of imports) j	United States	49.5	China	6.1	Netherlands	4.4

Social indicators

	2010	2015	2020
Population growth rate (average annual %) m	0.5	0.6	0.4
Urban population (% of total population)	54.0	53.3	53.2 d
Urban population growth rate (average annual %) m	0.1	0.2	...
Fertility rate, total (live births per woman) m	1.8	1.8	1.7
Life expectancy at birth (females/males, years) m	74.2 / 68.6	75.2 / 69.8	76.0 / 70.7
Population age distribution (0-14/60+ years old, %)	20.7 / 12.4	20.7 / 14.5	20.1 / 16.9
International migrant stock (000/% of total pop.)	48.2 / 3.6	50.0 / 3.7	59.2 / 4.2 d
Refugees and others of concern to the UNHCR (000)	0.1 n	0.2	43.0 d
Infant mortality rate (per 1 000 live births) m	28.5	26.1	22.0
Health: Current expenditure (% of GDP)	5.1	6.0	7.0 a
Health: Physicians (per 1 000 pop.)	1.8	2.6	4.2 e
Education: Primary gross enrol. ratio (f/m per 100 pop.)	104.4 / 108.0	... / ...	... / ...
Intentional homicide rate (per 100 000 pop.)	35.6	30.6	...
Seats held by women in the National Parliament (%)	26.8	28.6	31.0 o

Environment and infrastructure indicators

	2010	2015	2020
Individuals using the Internet (per 100 inhabitants) j	48.5	69.2	77.3 a
Research & Development expenditure (% of GDP)	~0.0	0.1	0.1 a
Threatened species (number)	48	65	126
Forested area (% of land area)	44.1	45.7	45.7 j,a
CO2 emission estimates (million tons/tons per capita)	21.8 / 16.5	21.3 / 15.6	18.0 / 13.2 a
Energy production, primary (Petajoules)	1 786	1 557	1 367 a
Energy supply per capita (Gigajoules)	627	586	514 a
Tourist/visitor arrivals at national borders (000) p	388	440	375 e
Important sites for terrestrial biodiversity protected (%)	32.0	32.0	32.0 d
Net Official Development Assist. received (% of GNI)	0.02	...	...

a 2017. b Trinidad and Tobago Dollar. c Data refers to the urban agglomeration. d 2019. e 2018. f Data classified according to ISIC Rev. 4. g Excludes publishing activities. Includes irrigation and canals. h Excludes repair of personal and household goods. i Excludes computer and related activities and radio/TV activities. j Estimate. k Data refer to the Retail Price Index. l 2016. m Data refers to a 5-year period preceding the reference year. n Data as at the end of December. o Data are as at 1 January of reporting year. p Arrivals by air.

Tunisia

Region	Northern Africa	UN membership date	12 November 1956
Population (000, 2020)	11 819	Surface area (km2)	163 610[a]
Pop. density (per km2, 2020)	76.1	Sex ratio (m per 100 f)	98.4
Capital city	Tunis	National currency	Tunisian Dinar (TND)
Capital city pop. (000, 2020)	2 327.8[b,c]	Exchange rate (per US$)	2.8[c]

Economic indicators

	2010	2015	2020
GDP: Gross domestic product (million current US$)	44 051	43 173	39 895[d]
GDP growth rate (annual %, const. 2015 prices)	3.0	1.2	2.5[d]
GDP per capita (current US$)	4 142.0	3 861.6	3 449.6[d]
Economy: Agriculture (% of Gross Value Added)[e]	8.1	10.9	10.4[d]
Economy: Industry (% of Gross Value Added)[e]	31.1	26.6	25.7[d]
Economy: Services and other activity (% of GVA)[e]	59.8	64.3	66.4[d]
Employment in agriculture (% of employed)	17.9	14.5[f]	12.7[f]
Employment in industry (% of employed)	33.4	33.3[f]	32.5[f]
Employment in services & other sectors (% employed)	48.6	52.2[f]	54.8[f]
Unemployment rate (% of labour force)[f]	13.0	15.2	16.2
Labour force participation rate (female/male pop. %)[f]	24.5 / 69.6	24.6 / 70.1	23.6 / 69.2
CPI: Consumer Price Index (2010=100)[f]	100[g]	127	138[a]
Agricultural production index (2004-2006=100)	106	142	117[h]
International trade: exports (million current US$)	16 427	14 073	15 489[f,c]
International trade: imports (million current US$)	22 215	20 223	22 453[f,c]
International trade: balance (million current US$)	- 5 789	- 6 149	- 6 964[f,c]
Balance of payments, current account (million US$)	- 2 104	- 3 850	- 4 429[d]

Major trading partners

						2019
Export partners (% of exports)[f]	France	30.6	Italy	16.5	Germany	11.6
Import partners (% of imports)[f]	Italy	15.6	France	15.1	China	9.0

Social indicators

	2010	2015	2020
Population growth rate (average annual %)[i]	1.0	1.0	1.1
Urban population (% of total population)	66.7	68.1	69.3[c]
Urban population growth rate (average annual %)[i]	1.5	1.6	...
Fertility rate, total (live births per woman)[i]	2.0	2.3	2.2
Life expectancy at birth (females/males, years)[i]	77.2 / 72.3	77.6 / 73.4	78.5 / 74.4
Population age distribution (0-14/60+ years old, %)	23.3 / 10.4	23.8 / 11.8	24.3 / 13.4
International migrant stock (000/% of total pop.)[j]	43.2 / 0.4	56.5 / 0.5	57.5 / 0.5[c]
Refugees and others of concern to the UNHCR (000)	0.1[k]	1.0	2.0[c]
Infant mortality rate (per 1 000 live births)[i]	18.0	14.6	12.7
Health: Current expenditure (% of GDP)	5.9	7.0	7.2[a]
Health: Physicians (per 1 000 pop.)	1.2	1.3	1.3[a]
Education: Government expenditure (% of GDP)	6.3	6.6	...
Education: Primary gross enrol. ratio (f/m per 100 pop.)	107.0 / 107.4	114.6 / 114.5	114.9 / 115.9[d]
Education: Secondary gross enrol. ratio (f/m per 100 pop.)	94.5 / 86.2	95.3 / 88.6[l]	99.3 / 86.9[h]
Education: Tertiary gross enrol. ratio (f/m per 100 000 pop.)	43.2 / 27.8	44.1 / 26.6	41.2 / 22.8[d]
Intentional homicide rate (per 100 000 pop.)	2.7	3.1[m]	...
Seats held by women in the National Parliament (%)	27.6	31.3	24.9[n]

Environment and infrastructure indicators

	2010	2015	2020
Individuals using the Internet (per 100 inhabitants)	36.8	46.5	64.2[d]
Research & Development expenditure (% of GDP)	0.7	0.6	0.6[d]
Threatened species (number)	75	83	107
Forested area (% of land area)	6.4	6.7[f]	6.7[f,a]
CO2 emission estimates (million tons/tons per capita)	23.3 / 2.2	25.6 / 2.3	26.2 / 2.3[a]
Energy production, primary (Petajoules)	341	260	230[d]
Energy supply per capita (Gigajoules)	40	40	41[a]
Tourist/visitor arrivals at national borders (000)	7 828	5 359	8 299[d]
Important sites for terrestrial biodiversity protected (%)	24.8	40.1	40.1[c]
Pop. using safely managed sanitation (urban/rural %)	82.2 / ...	86.9 / ...	88.3 / ...[a]
Net Official Development Assist. received (% of GNI)	1.31	1.19	2.10[d]

[a] 2017. **b** Refers to Grand Tunis. **c** 2019. **d** 2018. **e** At factor cost. **f** Estimate. **g** Break in the time series. **h** 2016. **i** Data refers to a 5-year period preceding the reference year. **j** Refers to foreign citizens. **k** Data as at the end of December. **l** 2011. **m** 2012. **n** Data are as at 1 January of reporting year.

Turkey

Region	Western Asia	UN membership date	24 October 1945
Population (000, 2020)	84 339	Surface area (km2)	783 562 [a]
Pop. density (per km2, 2020)	109.6	Sex ratio (m per 100 f)	97.5
Capital city	Ankara	National currency	Turkish Lira (TRY)
Capital city pop. (000, 2020)	5 018.0 [b,c]	Exchange rate (per US$)	5.9 [c]

Economic indicators	2010	2015	2020
GDP: Gross domestic product (million current US$)	771 877	859 794	771 355 [d]
GDP growth rate (annual %, const. 2015 prices)	8.5	6.1	2.8 [d]
GDP per capita (current US$)	10 672.0	10 948.7	9 367.9 [d]
Economy: Agriculture (% of Gross Value Added) [e]	10.3	7.8	6.5 [d]
Economy: Industry (% of Gross Value Added) [e,f]	28.0	31.7	32.9 [d]
Economy: Services and other activity (% of GVA) [e,g,h]	43.3	42.3	41.0 [d]
Employment in agriculture (% of employed)	23.7	20.4	18.0 [i]
Employment in industry (% of employed)	26.2	27.2	26.1 [i]
Employment in services & other sectors (% employed)	50.1	52.4	55.9 [i]
Unemployment rate (% of labour force) [i]	10.7	10.2	12.9
Labour force participation rate (female/male pop. %) [i]	27.0 / 69.6	31.4 / 71.6	33.9 / 72.4
CPI: Consumer Price Index (2010=100)	100 [i]	146 [i]	233 [c]
Agricultural production index (2004-2006=100)	110	128	129 [i]
International trade: exports (million current US$)	113 883	143 850	180 839 [c]
International trade: imports (million current US$)	185 544	207 207	210 343 [c]
International trade: balance (million current US$)	- 71 661	- 63 356	- 29 505 [c]
Balance of payments, current account (million US$)	- 44 620	- 27 314	8 691 [c]

Major trading partners						2019
Export partners (% of exports)	Germany	9.2	United Kingdom	6.2	Iraq	5.7
Import partners (% of imports)	Russian Federation	11.0	Germany	9.2	China	9.1

Social indicators	2010	2015	2020
Population growth rate (average annual %) [k]	1.3	1.6	1.4
Urban population (% of total population)	70.8	73.6	75.6 [c]
Urban population growth rate (average annual %) [k]	2.1	2.4	...
Fertility rate, total (live births per woman) [k]	2.2	2.1	2.1
Life expectancy at birth (females/males, years) [k]	76.9 / 69.9	78.7 / 72.4	80.2 / 74.3
Population age distribution (0-14/60+ years old, %)	26.9 / 10.4	25.6 / 11.5	23.9 / 13.1
International migrant stock (000/% of total pop.) [l]	1 367.0 / 1.9	4 346.2 / 5.5	5 876.8 / 7.0 [c]
Refugees and others of concern to the UNHCR (000)	17.8 [m]	1 985.3	3 940.1 [n,c]
Infant mortality rate (per 1 000 live births) [k]	16.4	11.8	8.9
Health: Current expenditure (% of GDP) [i]	5.1	4.1	4.2 [a]
Health: Physicians (per 1 000 pop.)	1.7	1.8	1.8 [a]
Education: Government expenditure (% of GDP)	2.8 [o]	...	...
Education: Primary gross enrol. ratio (f/m per 100 pop.)	100.6 / 102.0	102.7 / 103.4	92.7 / 93.6 [a]
Education: Secondary gross enrol. ratio (f/m per 100 pop.)	80.5 / 87.9	101.5 / 104.2	103.4 / 108.5 [a]
Intentional homicide rate (per 100 000 pop.)	4.2	2.8	2.6 [d]
Seats held by women in the National Parliament (%)	9.1	14.4	17.3 [p]

Environment and infrastructure indicators	2010	2015	2020
Individuals using the Internet (per 100 inhabitants)	39.8 [q,r]	53.7 [q]	71.0 [d]
Research & Development expenditure (% of GDP)	0.8	0.9	1.0 [a]
Threatened species (number)	150	370	435
Forested area (% of land area)	14.6	15.2	15.2 [i,a]
CO2 emission estimates (million tons/tons per capita)	267.8 / 3.7	319.0 / 4.1	378.6 / 4.7 [a]
Energy production, primary (Petajoules)	1 355	1 317	1 527 [a]
Energy supply per capita (Gigajoules)	61	69	76 [a]
Tourist/visitor arrivals at national borders (000) [s]	31 364	39 478	45 768 [d]
Important sites for terrestrial biodiversity protected (%)	2.3	2.3	2.3 [c]
Pop. using safely managed sanitation (urban/rural %)	66.6 / ...	69.5 / ...	69.6 / ... [a]
Net Official Development Assist. disbursed (% of GNI)	0.13	0.50	0.95 [a]
Net Official Development Assist. received (% of GNI)	0.14	0.25	0.16 [d]

a 2017. b Refers to Altindag, Cankaya, Etimesgut, Golbasi, Keçioren, Mamak, Sincan and Yenimahalle. c 2019. d 2018. e Data classified according to ISIC Rev. 4. f Excludes publishing activities. Includes irrigation and canals. g Excludes supply of personal and household goods. h Excludes computer and related activities and radio/TV activities. Estimate. j 2016. k Data refers to a 5-year period preceding the reference year. l Including refugees. m Data as at the end of December. n Refugee figure is a Government estimate and pertains only to Syrian refugees. o 2006. p Data are as at 1 January of reporting year. q Population aged 16 to 74 years. r Users in the last 12 months. s Turkish citizens resident abroad are included.

Turkmenistan

Region	Central Asia	
Population (000, 2020)	6 031	
Pop. density (per km2, 2020)	12.8	
Capital city	Ashgabat	
Capital city pop. (000, 2020)	828.1 c	

UN membership date	02 March 1992	
Surface area (km2)	488 100 a	
Sex ratio (m per 100 f)	97.0	
National currency	Turkmen. Manat (TMT) b	
Exchange rate (per US$)	3.5 d,c	

Economic indicators	2010	2015	2020
GDP: Gross domestic product (million current US$)	22 583	36 052	40 749 e
GDP growth rate (annual %, const. 2015 prices)	9.2	6.5	6.2 e
GDP per capita (current US$)	4 439.2	6 477.9	6 964.6 e
Economy: Agriculture (% of Gross Value Added)	11.5	9.4	9.1 e
Economy: Industry (% of Gross Value Added)	60.0	57.8	59.8 e
Economy: Services and other activity (% of GVA)	65.1	76.0	73.5 e
Employment in agriculture (% of employed) f	24.8	21.9	19.5
Employment in industry (% of employed) f	39.2	41.2	42.6
Employment in services & other sectors (% employed) f	36.0	36.9	37.9
Unemployment rate (% of labour force) f	4.0	4.0	4.1
Labour force participation rate (female/male pop. %) f	51.1 / 76.2	51.7 / 78.2	51.2 / 78.2
Agricultural production index (2004-2006=100)	98	100	102 g
International trade: exports (million current US$) f	3 335	3 670	3 962 c
International trade: imports (million current US$) f	2 400	2 596	2 764 c
International trade: balance (million current US$) f	935	1 074	1 198 c

Major trading partners						2019
Export partners (% of exports) f	China	76.4	Afghanistan	4.2	Uzbekistan	3.9
Import partners (% of imports) f	Turkey	24.1	Russian Federation	17.5	China	10.2

Social indicators	2010	2015	2020
Population growth rate (average annual %) h	1.4	1.8	1.6
Urban population (% of total population)	48.5	50.3	52.0 c
Urban population growth rate (average annual %) h	2.0	2.5	...
Fertility rate, total (live births per woman) h	2.6	3.0	2.8
Life expectancy at birth (females/males, years) h	69.6 / 62.2	70.8 / 63.9	71.5 / 64.5
Population age distribution (0-14/60+ years old, %)	29.5 / 6.1	30.4 / 6.8	30.8 / 8.1
International migrant stock (000/% of total pop.)	198.0 / 3.9	196.4 / 3.5	195.1 / 3.3 c
Refugees and others of concern to the UNHCR (000)	20.1 i	7.2	5.2 c
Infant mortality rate (per 1 000 live births) h	54.1	46.9	43.3
Health: Current expenditure (% of GDP)	5.0	6.3	6.9 a
Health: Physicians (per 1 000 pop.)	2.3	2.2 j	...
Education: Government expenditure (% of GDP)	...	3.0 k	...
Education: Primary gross enrol. ratio (f/m per 100 pop.)	... / ...	87.5 / 89.2 j	... / ...
Education: Secondary gross enrol. ratio (f/m per 100 pop.)	... / ...	84.0 / 87.6 j	... / ...
Education: Tertiary gross enrol. ratio (f/m per 100 pop.)	... / ...	6.2 / 9.7 j	... / ...
Intentional homicide rate (per 100 000 pop.)	4.2 l	...	...
Seats held by women in the National Parliament (%)	16.8	25.8	25.0 m

Environment and infrastructure indicators	2010	2015	2020
Individuals using the Internet (per 100 inhabitants) f	3.0	15.0	21.3 a
Threatened species (number)	45	49	59
Forested area (% of land area) f	8.8	8.8	8.8 a
CO2 emission estimates (million tons/tons per capita)	56.9 / 11.2	69.1 / 12.4	69.0 / 12.0 a
Energy production, primary (Petajoules)	1 982	3 407	3 223 a
Energy supply per capita (Gigajoules)	187	208	201 a
Tourist/visitor arrivals at national borders (000)	8 n	...	...
Important sites for terrestrial biodiversity protected (%)	14.0	14.0	14.0 c
Pop. using safely managed drinking water (urban/rural, %)	92.2 / 73.5	96.7 / 86.7	96.9 / 90.7 a
Net Official Development Assist. received (% of GNI)	0.21	0.07	0.05 e

a 2017. b Turkmenistan New Manat. c 2019. d UN operational exchange rate. e 2018. f Estimate. g 2016. h Data refers to a 5-year period preceding the reference year. i Data as at the end of December. j 2014. k 2012. l 2006. m Data are as at 1 January of reporting year. n 2007.

Turks and Caicos Islands

Region	Caribbean	Population (000, 2020)	37
Surface area (km2)	948 [a,b]	Pop. density (per km2, 2020)	38.9
Sex ratio (m per 100 f)	104.1 [c,d,b]	Capital city	Cockburn Town
National currency	US Dollar (USD)	Capital city pop. (000, 2020)	0.1 [e]

Economic indicators	2010	2015	2020
GDP: Gross domestic product (million current US$)	687	894	1 022 [f]
GDP growth rate (annual %, const. 2015 prices)	1.0	5.9	5.3 [f]
GDP per capita (current US$)	21 028.4	24 832.6	27 142.2 [f]
Economy: Agriculture (% of Gross Value Added)	0.6	0.6	0.6 [f]
Economy: Industry (% of Gross Value Added)	12.4	10.5	11.4 [f]
Economy: Services and other activity (% of GVA)	57.5	50.7	52.0 [f]
Employment in agriculture (% of employed)	1.2 [g,h,i]	...	...
Employment in industry (% of employed)	23.1 [g,h,i]	...	...
Employment in services & other sectors (% employed)	74.0 [g,h,i]	...	...
Unemployment rate (% of labour force)	8.3 [g,i]	...	...
International trade: exports (million current US$) [j]	16	5	5 [k]
International trade: imports (million current US$) [j]	302	410	488 [k]
International trade: balance (million current US$) [j]	- 286	- 405	- 482 [k]
Balance of payments, current account (million US$)	...	154	173 [f]

Major trading partners								2019
Export partners (% of exports) [j]	United States	29.8	Sudan	20.8	Zambia	9.2
Import partners (% of imports) [j]	United States	82.0	Italy	2.6	Brazil	2.5

Social indicators	2010	2015	2020
Population growth rate (average annual %)	3.2 [l]	2.0 [l]	1.5
Urban population (% of total population)	90.2	92.2	93.4 [k]
Urban population growth rate (average annual %) [l]	3.7	2.5	...
Life expectancy at birth (females/males, years)	... / ...	77.8 / 75.8 [m]	... / ...
Population age distribution (0-14/60+ years old, %) [d,c]	... / ...	19.8 / 6.9	19.2 / 7.6 [b]
International migrant stock (000/% of total pop.)	17.2 / 52.7	22.7 / 63.1	24.5 / 64.2 [k]
Refugees and others of concern to the UNHCR (000)	...	~0.0	~0.0 [k]
Education: Government expenditure (% of GDP)	2.5 [n]	3.2	2.8 [f]
Intentional homicide rate (per 100 000 pop.)	6.3 [o]	5.7 [p]	...

Environment and infrastructure indicators	2010	2015	2020
Threatened species (number)	34	56	65
Forested area (% of land area) [j]	36.2	36.2	36.2 [b]
Energy production, primary (Petajoules)	0	0	0 [b]
Energy supply per capita (Gigajoules) [j]	84	84	91 [b]
Tourist/visitor arrivals at national borders (000)	281	386	441 [f]
Important sites for terrestrial biodiversity protected (%)	27.9	27.9	27.9 [k]

a Including low water level for all islands (area to shoreline). b 2017. c De jure population. d Estimates should be viewed with caution as these are derived from scarce data. e 2001. f 2018. g Break in the time series. h Data classified according to ISIC Rev. 3. i 2008. j Estimate. k 2019. l Data refers to a 5-year period preceding the reference year. m 2012. n 2005. o 2009. p 2014.

Tuvalu

Region	Polynesia	UN membership date	05 September 2000		
Population (000, 2020)	12	Surface area (km2)	26[a]		
Pop. density (per km2, 2020)	383.3	Sex ratio (m per 100 f)	102.0[b]		
Capital city	Funafuti	National currency	Australian Dollar (AUD)		
Capital city pop. (000, 2020)	7.0[c]	Exchange rate (per US$)	1.4[d]		

Economic indicators

	2010	2015	2020
GDP: Gross domestic product (million current US$)	31	35	46[c]
GDP growth rate (annual %, const. 2015 prices)	- 3.3	9.2	7.0[c]
GDP per capita (current US$)	2 981.5	3 156.9	4 000.6[c]
Economy: Agriculture (% of Gross Value Added)	27.3	21.4	21.9[c]
Economy: Industry (% of Gross Value Added)[e]	5.7	12.7	12.5[c]
Economy: Services and other activity (% of GVA)	75.5	72.8	69.9[c]
Unemployment rate (% of labour force)	6.5[f]	...	...
Labour force participation rate (female/male pop. %)	47.9 / 69.6[f]	... / ...	... / ...
Agricultural production index (2004-2006=100)	104	110	111[b]
International trade: exports (million current US$)[g]	~0	~0	~0[d]
International trade: imports (million current US$)[g]	12	12	12[d]
International trade: balance (million current US$)[g]	- 12	- 12	- 12[d]
Balance of payments, current account (million US$)	- 14	7[h]	...

Major trading partners
2019

Export partners (% of exports)[g]	Thailand	41.9	Indonesia	33.1	Ecuador	12.4
Import partners (% of imports)[g]	Fiji	26.7	Singapore	24.2	Japan	22.4

Social indicators

	2010	2015	2020
Population growth rate (average annual %)	1.0[i]	0.9[i]	0.9
Urban population (% of total population)	54.8	59.7	63.2[d]
Urban population growth rate (average annual %)[i]	2.9	2.6	...
Fertility rate, total (live births per woman)	...	3.6[i,k]	...
Life expectancy at birth (females/males, years)	71.9 / 67.4	... / ...	... / ...
Population age distribution (0-14/60+ years old, %)	... / ...	... / ...	31.1 / 9.9[b]
International migrant stock (000/% of total pop.)[l]	0.2 / 2.1	0.2 / 2.1	0.2 / 2.0[d]
Infant mortality rate (per 1 000 live births)	10.3	...	...
Health: Current expenditure (% of GDP)[m]	16.4	16.7	17.1[a]
Education: Primary gross enrol. ratio (f/m per 100 pop.)	108.4 / 112.6[n]	97.8 / 101.7	82.5 / 89.4[c]
Education: Secondary gross enrol. ratio (f/m per 100 pop.)	... / ...	90.9 / 75.2	71.2 / 62.5[c]
Intentional homicide rate (per 100 000 pop.)	9.5	18.6[k]	...
Seats held by women in the National Parliament (%)	0.0	6.7	6.2[o]

Environment and infrastructure indicators

	2010	2015	2020
Individuals using the Internet (per 100 inhabitants)[g]	25.0	42.7	49.3[a]
Threatened species (number)	85	93	99
Forested area (% of land area)[g]	33.3	33.3	33.3[a]
Energy production, primary (Petajoules)	...	0	0[g,a]
Energy supply per capita (Gigajoules)	12	13[g]	13[g,a]
Tourist/visitor arrivals at national borders (000)	2	2	3[c]
Pop. using safely managed drinking water (urban/rural, %)	49.5 / ...	49.8 / ...	49.8 / ...[a]
Pop. using safely managed sanitation (urban/rural %)	4.7 / 7.8	4.2 / 9.7	4.2 / 9.7[a]
Net Official Development Assist. received (% of GNI)	27.27	88.66	31.55[c]

2017. **b** 2016. **c** 2018. **d** 2019. **e** Includes electricity, gas and water. **f** 2005. **g** Estimate. **h** 2013. **i** Data refers to 5-year period preceding the reference year. **j** Break in the time series. **k** 2012. **l** Refers to foreign citizens. **m** General government expenditure (GGE) can be larger than the Gross domestic product (GDP) because government accounts for a very large part of domestic consumption and because a large part of domestic consumption in the country is accounted for by imports. **n** 2006. **o** Data are as at 1 January of reporting year.

Uganda

Region	Eastern Africa	UN membership date	25 October 1962
Population (000, 2020)	45 741	Surface area (km2)	241 550 [a]
Pop. density (per km2, 2020)	228.9	Sex ratio (m per 100 f)	97.2
Capital city	Kampala	National currency	Uganda Shilling (UGX)
Capital city pop. (000, 2020)	3 137.7 [b,c]	Exchange rate (per US$)	3 665.2 [c]

Economic indicators

	2010	2015	2020
GDP: Gross domestic product (million current US$)	19 683	25 098	30 098 [d]
GDP growth rate (annual %, const. 2015 prices)	8.2	5.7	8.9 [d]
GDP per capita (current US$)	607.0	656.6	704.4 [d]
Economy: Agriculture (% of Gross Value Added) [e]	26.3	25.8	23.6 [d]
Economy: Industry (% of Gross Value Added) [e,f]	20.5	22.2	22.9 [d]
Economy: Services and other activity (% of GVA) [e,g,h]	57.0	56.8	58.1 [d]
Employment in agriculture (% of employed) [i]	66.8	72.6	72.4
Employment in industry (% of employed) [i]	7.8	6.8	6.6
Employment in services & other sectors (% employed) [i]	25.4	20.6	20.9
Unemployment rate (% of labour force) [i]	3.6	1.9	1.9
Labour force participation rate (female/male pop. %) [i]	66.0 / 76.3	66.6 / 75.3	67.1 / 73.9
CPI: Consumer Price Index (2010=100) [i]	...	151	177 [c]
Agricultural production index (2004-2006=100)	89	94	92 [k]
International trade: exports (million current US$)	1 619	2 267	3 597 [i,c]
International trade: imports (million current US$)	4 664	5 528	7 686 [i,c]
International trade: balance (million current US$)	- 3 046	- 3 261	- 4 089 [i,c]
Balance of payments, current account (million US$)	- 1 610	- 1 671	- 2 333 [c]

Major trading partners

						2019
Export partners (% of exports) [i]	Kenya	18.8	United Arab Emirates	18.2	South Sudan	11.5
Import partners (% of imports) [i]	China	17.6	India	12.1	United Arab Emirates	11.7

Social indicators

	2010	2015	2020
Population growth rate (average annual %) [i]	3.2	3.3	3.6
Urban population (% of total population)	19.4	22.1	24.4 [c]
Urban population growth rate (average annual %) [i]	6.1	6.0	
Fertility rate, total (live births per woman) [i]	6.4	5.8	5.0
Life expectancy at birth (females/males, years) [i]	56.2 / 52.5	61.1 / 57.7	65.0 / 60.4
Population age distribution (0-14/60+ years old, %)	49.1 / 3.0	48.0 / 3.1	46.0 / 3.2
International migrant stock (000/% of total pop.) [m]	492.9 / 1.5	851.2 / 2.2	1 734.2 / 3.9 [c]
Refugees and others of concern to the UNHCR (000)	594.4 [n]	646.5	2 445.8 [c]
Infant mortality rate (per 1 000 live births) [i]	70.7	59.0	46.1
Health: Current expenditure (% of GDP) [o]	10.5	6.8	6.3 [a]
Health: Physicians (per 1 000 pop.)	...	0.1	0.2 [a]
Education: Government expenditure (% of GDP)	2.4	2.8 [i]	2.6 [i,a]
Education: Primary gross enrol. ratio (f/m per 100 pop.)	122.4 / 121.5	103.7 / 101.6	104.1 / 101.3 [a]
Education: Secondary gross enrol. ratio (f/m per 100 pop.)	21.8 / 27.5 [p]	... / ...	... / ...
Education: Tertiary gross enrol. ratio (f/m per 100 pop.)	3.5 / 4.7	4.1 / 5.6 [q]	... / ...
Intentional homicide rate (per 100 000 pop.)	9.7	12.1 [q]	10.5 [d]
Seats held by women in the National Parliament (%)	31.5	35.0	34.9 [r]

Environment and infrastructure indicators

	2010	2015	2020
Individuals using the Internet (per 100 inhabitants)	12.5	17.8 [i]	23.7 [i,a]
Research & Development expenditure (% of GDP)	0.5	0.2 [s,q]	...
Threatened species (number)	166	188	266
Forested area (% of land area)	13.7	10.4 [i]	10.4 [i,a]
Energy production, primary (Petajoules)	477	595	625 [i,a]
Energy supply per capita (Gigajoules)	15	16	16 [i,a]
Tourist/visitor arrivals at national borders (000)	946	1 303	1 402 [a]
Important sites for terrestrial biodiversity protected (%)	70.6	70.6	70.6 [c]
Pop. using safely managed drinking water (urban/rural, %)	19.9 / 2.9	16.9 / 4.0	15.7 / 4.5 [a]
Net Official Development Assist. received (% of GNI)	8.52	6.16	7.30 [d]

a. 2017. b. Data includes Kira, Makindye Ssabagabo and Nansana. c. 2019. d. 2018. e. Data classified according to ISIC Rev. 4. f. Excludes publishing activities. Includes irrigation and canals. g. Excludes computer and related activities and radio/TV activities. h. Excludes repair of personal and household goods. i. Estimate. j. Index base: 1 July 2009 - June 2010=100. k. 2016. l. Data refers to a 5-year period preceding the reference year. m. Including refugees. n. Data as at the end of December. o. Unlike other countries, in Uganda Fiscal Years starting on July 1 and ending in June 3 are converted to the previous year and that is a special request from the country. p. 2007. q. 2014. r. Data are as at January of reporting year. s. Break in the time series.

Ukraine

Region	Eastern Europe	
Population (000, 2020)	43 734 [a]	
Pop. density (per km2, 2020)	75.5 [a]	
Capital city	Kyiv	
Capital city pop. (000, 2020)	2 973.3 [c]	

UN membership date	24 October 1945	
Surface area (km2)	603 500 [b]	
Sex ratio (m per 100 f)	86.3 [a]	
National currency	Hryvnia (UAH)	
Exchange rate (per US$)	23.7 [d,c]	

Economic indicators	2010	2015	2020
GDP: Gross domestic product (million current US$) [d]	136 012	91 031	130 832 [e]
GDP growth rate (annual %, const. 2015 prices) [d]	0.3	- 9.8	3.3 [e]
GDP per capita (current US$) [d]	2 970.2	2 026.4	2 956.9 [e]
Economy: Agriculture (% of Gross Value Added) [f]	8.4	14.2	12.0 [e]
Economy: Industry (% of Gross Value Added) [d,f,g]	29.3	25.6	27.5 [e]
Economy: Services and other activity (% of GVA) [f,h,i]	55.4	55.4	53.9 [e]
Employment in agriculture (% of employed)	20.3	15.3	14.1 [j]
Employment in industry (% of employed)	25.7	24.7	24.8 [j]
Employment in services & other sectors (% employed)	54.0	60.0	61.1 [j]
Unemployment rate (% of labour force) [j]	8.1	9.1	8.9
Labour force participation rate (female/male pop. %) [j]	48.4 / 63.0	47.4 / 63.6	46.5 / 62.8
CPI: Consumer Price Index (2010=100)	100	180	282 [c]
Agricultural production index (2004-2006=100)	107	135	153 [k]
International trade: exports (million current US$) [d]	51 430	38 127	50 060 [j,c]
International trade: imports (million current US$) [d]	60 737	37 516	60 783 [j,c]
International trade: balance (million current US$) [d]	- 9 307	611	- 10 723 [j,c]
Balance of payments, current account (million US$)	- 3 016	1 616	- 1 322 [c]

Major trading partners						2019
Export partners (% of exports) [j,d]	Russian Federation	7.7	Poland	6.9	Italy	5.6
Import partners (% of imports) [j,d]	Russian Federation	14.1	China	13.3	Germany	10.5

Social indicators	2010	2015	2020
Population growth rate (average annual %) [a,l]	- 0.5	- 0.4	- 0.5
Urban population (% of total population) [a]	68.6	69.1	69.5 [c]
Urban population growth rate (average annual %) [a,l]	- 0.2	- 0.4	...
Fertility rate, total (live births per woman) [a,l]	1.4	1.5	1.4
Life expectancy at birth (females/males, years) [a,l]	73.8 / 62.2	75.8 / 65.8	76.6 / 66.8
Population age distribution (0-14/60+ years old, %) [a]	14.1 / 21.0	15.3 / 22.2	16.0 / 23.6
International migrant stock (000/% of total pop.) [a]	4 818.8 / 10.5	4 915.1 / 10.9	4 964.3 / 11.3 [c]
Refugees and others of concern to the UNHCR (000)	46.4 [m]	1 426.6	1 540.4 [n,c]
Infant mortality rate (per 1 000 live births) [a,l]	12.6	8.8	7.2
Health: Current expenditure (% of GDP)	6.8	6.9 [o]	7.0 [o,b]
Health: Physicians (per 1 000 pop.)	3.5	3.0 [p]	...
Education: Government expenditure (% of GDP)	7.3 [q]	5.9	5.4 [b]
Education: Primary gross enrol. ratio (f/m per 100 pop.)	99.1 / 98.5	100.1 / 98.0 [p]	... / ...
Education: Secondary gross enrol. ratio (f/m per 100 pop.)	94.4 / 96.7	95.0 / 96.9 [p]	... / ...
Education: Tertiary gross enrol. ratio (f/m per 100 pop.)	89.5 / 71.3	88.8 / 76.8 [p]	... / ...
Intentional homicide rate (per 100 000 pop.)	4.3	6.3 [p]	6.2 [b]
Seats held by women in the National Parliament (%)	8.0	11.8	20.8 [r]

Environment and infrastructure indicators	2010	2015	2020
Individuals using the Internet (per 100 inhabitants)	23.3	48.9	62.6 [e]
Research & Development expenditure (% of GDP)	0.8	0.6 [s]	0.5 [s,e]
Threatened species (number)	61	87	132
Forested area (% of land area)	16.5	16.7	16.7 [j,b]
CO2 emission estimates (million tons/tons per capita)	266.6 / 5.8	187.6 / 4.2 [d]	171.3 / 3.8 [d,b]
Energy production, primary (Petajoules)	3 238	2 552 [d]	2 431 [d,b]
Energy supply per capita (Gigajoules)	120	84 [d]	85 [d,b]
Tourist/visitor arrivals at national borders (000)	21 203	12 428	14 104 [e]
Important sites for terrestrial biodiversity protected (%)	21.3	21.7	21.7 [c]
Pop. using safely managed sanitation (urban/rural %)	45.9 / ...	60.5 / ...	65.8 / ... [b]
Net Official Development Assist. received (% of GNI) [d]	0.49	1.61	0.96 [e]

a Including Crimea. b 2017. c 2019. d The Government of Ukraine has informed the United Nations that it is not in a position to provide statistical data concerning the Autonomous Republic of Crimea and the city of Sevastopol. e 2018. f Data classified according to ISIC Rev. 4. g Excludes publishing activities. Includes irrigation and canals. h Excludes computer and related activities and radio/TV activities. i Excludes repair of personal and household goods. j Estimate. k 2016. l Data refers to a 5-year period preceding the reference year. m Data as at the end of December. n The figure in Ukraine includes 700,000 conflict-affected persons. o Since 2014 Ukraine data does not include the Luhansk People's Republic, the Autonomous Republic of Crimea and the Donetsk People's Republic data. p 2014. q 2009. r Data are as at 1 January of reporting year. s Excluding data from some regions, provinces or states.

United Arab Emirates

Region	Western Asia	UN membership date	09 December 1971
Population (000, 2020)	9 890	Surface area (km2)	83 600 a
Pop. density (per km2, 2020)	118.3	Sex ratio (m per 100 f)	223.8
Capital city	Abu Dhabi	National currency	UAE Dirham (AED) b
Capital city pop. (000, 2020)	1 452.1 c	Exchange rate (per US$)	3.7 c

Economic indicators	2010	2015	2020
GDP: Gross domestic product (million current US$)	289 787	358 135	414 179 d
GDP growth rate (annual %, const. 2015 prices)	1.6	5.1	1.7 d
GDP per capita (current US$)	33 893.3	38 663.4	43 005.0 d
Economy: Agriculture (% of Gross Value Added)	0.8	0.7	0.7 d
Economy: Industry (% of Gross Value Added)	52.5	43.9	46.8 d
Economy: Services and other activity (% of GVA)	48.3	54.8	55.2 d
Employment in agriculture (% of employed) e	3.4	2.0	1.4
Employment in industry (% of employed) e	37.2	35.7	34.2
Employment in services & other sectors (% employed) e	59.4	62.4	64.4
Unemployment rate (% of labour force) e	2.5	1.9	2.4
Labour force participation rate (female/male pop. %) e	44.2 / 94.7	50.6 / 94.6	52.5 / 93.6
CPI: Consumer Price Index (2010=100)	100 f	109	115 c
Agricultural production index (2004-2006=100)	108	98	101 g
International trade: exports (million current US$)	198 362	300 479	412 260 e,c
International trade: imports (million current US$)	187 001	287 025	244 712 e,c
International trade: balance (million current US$)	11 361	13 454	167 549 e,c

Major trading partners						2019
Export partners (% of exports) e	Areas nes h	55.2	Saudi Arabia	5.6	India	3.3
Import partners (% of imports) e	China	15.5	India	9.4	United States	8.6

Social indicators	2010	2015	2020
Population growth rate (average annual %) i	12.4	1.6	1.3
Urban population (% of total population)	84.1	85.7	86.8 c
Urban population growth rate (average annual %) i	12.3	2.4	...
Fertility rate, total (live births per woman) i	2.0	1.7	1.4
Life expectancy at birth (females/males, years) i	77.3 / 75.1	78.2 / 76.1	79.1 / 77.1
Population age distribution (0-14/60+ years old, %)	13.2 / 1.4	14.2 / 1.8	14.8 / 3.1
International migrant stock (000/% of total pop.) j,k	7 316.7 / 85.6	7 995.1 / 86.3	8 587.3 / 87.9 c
Refugees and others of concern to the UNHCR (000)	0.6 l	0.8	8.7 c
Infant mortality rate (per 1 000 live births) i	7.7	6.5	5.5
Health: Current expenditure (% of GDP)	3.9	3.6	3.3 a
Health: Physicians (per 1 000 pop.)	1.4	2.2	2.5 d
Education: Primary gross enrol. ratio (f/m per 100 pop.)	102.1 / 101.1 m	111.6 / 111.4	107.3 / 109.4 a
Education: Secondary gross enrol. ratio (f/m per 100 pop.)	... / ...	... / ...	100.4 / 109.3 a
Intentional homicide rate (per 100 000 pop.)	0.8	0.6	0.5 a
Seats held by women in the National Parliament (%)	22.5	17.5	50.0 n

Environment and infrastructure indicators	2010	2015	2020
Individuals using the Internet (per 100 inhabitants)	68.0	90.5 e	98.4 d
Research & Development expenditure (% of GDP)	...	0.9	1.3 f,d
Threatened species (number)	48	48	69
Forested area (% of land area) e	4.5	4.5	4.5 a
CO2 emission estimates (million tons/tons per capita)	154.6 / 18.7	186.6 / 20.4	196.5 / 20.9 a
Energy production, primary (Petajoules)	7 496	10 235	9 692 a
Energy supply per capita (Gigajoules)	319	435	324 a
Tourist/visitor arrivals at national borders (000) o	7 126 p	17 472	21 286 d
Net Official Development Assist. disbursed (% of GNI) q	0.14	1.18	1.03 a

a 2017. b United Arab Emirates Dirham. c 2019. d 2018. e Estimate. f Break in the time series. g 2016. h Areas not elsewhere specified. i Data refers to a 5-year period preceding the reference year. j Refers to foreign citizens. k Including refugees. l Data as at the end of December. m 2007. n Data are as at 1 January of reporting year. o Arrivals in hotels only. Including domestic tourism and nationals of the country residing abroad. p 2005. q Data reported at activity level, represent flows from all government agencies.

United Kingdom

Region	Northern Europe	
Population (000, 2020)	67 886	
Pop. density (per km2, 2020)	280.6	
Capital city	London	
Capital city pop. (000, 2020)	9 176.5[b,c]	

UN membership date	24 October 1945
Surface area (km2)	242 495[a]
Sex ratio (m per 100 f)	97.7
National currency	Pound Sterling (GBP)
Exchange rate (per US$)	0.8[c]

Economic indicators	2010	2015	2020
GDP: Gross domestic product (million current US$)	2 475 244	2 928 591	2 855 297[d]
GDP growth rate (annual %, const. 2015 prices)	1.9	2.4	1.4[d]
GDP per capita (current US$)	39 004.9	44 466.8	42 526.4[d]
Economy: Agriculture (% of Gross Value Added)[e]	0.7	0.7	0.7[d]
Economy: Industry (% of Gross Value Added)[e,f]	21.0	20.3	19.6[d]
Economy: Services and other activity (% of GVA)[e,g,h]	78.3	79.9	79.9[d]
Employment in agriculture (% of employed)	1.2	1.1	1.0[i]
Employment in industry (% of employed)	19.2	18.7	17.7[i]
Employment in services & other sectors (% employed)	79.6	80.2	81.3[i]
Unemployment rate (% of labour force)[i]	7.8	5.3	4.1
Labour force participation rate (female/male pop. %)[i]	55.5 / 68.6	56.7 / 68.3	57.7 / 68.0
CPI: Consumer Price Index (2010=100)[j]	100	112	121[c]
Agricultural production index (2004-2006=100)	102	108	103[k]
International trade: exports (million current US$)	422 014	466 296	468 160[c]
International trade: imports (million current US$)	627 618	630 251	692 580[c]
International trade: balance (million current US$)	- 205 603	- 163 955	- 224 421[c]
Balance of payments, current account (million US$)	- 78 779	- 143 589	- 106 886[c]

Major trading partners					2019
Export partners (% of exports)	United States	15.7	Germany	9.9	France 6.7
Import partners (% of imports)	Germany	12.4	United States	9.7	China 9.5

Social indicators	2010	2015	2020
Population growth rate (average annual %)[l]	1.0	0.7	0.6
Urban population (% of total population)	81.3	82.6	83.7[c]
Urban population growth rate (average annual %)[l]	1.3	1.0	...
Fertility rate, total (live births per woman)[l]	1.9	1.9	1.8
Life expectancy at birth (females/males, years)[l]	81.8 / 77.5	82.7 / 78.9	82.9 / 79.4
Population age distribution (0-14/60+ years old, %)	17.5 / 22.6	17.6 / 23.3	17.7 / 24.4
International migrant stock (000/% of total pop.)	7 119.7 / 11.2	8 411.6 / 12.8	9 552.1 / 14.1[c]
Refugees and others of concern to the UNHCR (000)	253.3[m]	155.1	176.7[c]
Infant mortality rate (per 1 000 live births)[l]	4.8	4.1	3.8
Health: Current expenditure (% of GDP)	8.4	9.7	9.6[a]
Health: Physicians (per 1 000 pop.)	2.6	2.7	2.8[d]
Education: Government expenditure (% of GDP)	5.8	5.6	5.5[k]
Education: Primary gross enrol. ratio (f/m per 100 pop.)	104.3 / 104.8	101.9 / 102.0	101.0 / 101.3[a]
Education: Secondary gross enrol. ratio (f/m per 100 pop.)	103.1 / 102.7	126.4 / 122.8	127.7 / 124.1[a]
Education: Tertiary gross enrol. ratio (f/m per 100 pop.)	67.5 / 50.5	64.7 / 48.6	69.4 / 51.0[a]
Intentional homicide rate (per 100 000 pop.)	1.2	1.0	1.2[d]
Seats held by women in the National Parliament (%)	19.5	22.8	33.8[n]

Environment and infrastructure indicators	2010	2015	2020
Individuals using the Internet (per 100 inhabitants)	85.0[o]	92.0[o]	94.9[d]
Research & Development expenditure (% of GDP)	1.7[i]	1.7	1.7[p,d]
Threatened species (number)	73	87	176
Forested area (% of land area)	12.6	13.0	13.0[i,a]
CO2 emission estimates (million tons/tons per capita)	476.6 / 7.6	394.1 / 6.1	358.7 / 5.4[a]
Energy production, primary (Petajoules)[q]	6 217	4 936	5 023[a]
Energy supply per capita (Gigajoules)[q]	134	116	111[a]
Tourist/visitor arrivals at national borders (000)	28 295	34 436	36 316[d]
Important sites for terrestrial biodiversity protected (%)	80.8	81.9	82.8[c]
Pop. using safely managed sanitation (urban/rural %)	99.0 / 91.8	99.0 / 91.8	99.0 / 91.8[a]
Net Official Development Assist. disbursed (% of GNI)[r]	0.57	0.70	0.70[a]

2017. **b** Data refer to "Urban area" (Greater London). **c** 2019. **d** 2018. **e** Data classified according to ISIC Rev. 4. **f** Includes publishing activities. Includes irrigation and canals. **g** Excludes computer and related activities and radio/TV activities. **h** Excludes repair of personal and household goods. **i** Estimate. **j** Calculated by the UN Statistics Division from national indices. **k** 2016. **l** Data refers to a 5-year period preceding the reference year. **m** Data as at the end of December. **n** Data are as at 1 January of reporting year. **o** Population aged 16 to 74 years. **p** Provisional data. **q** Shipments of coal and oil to Jersey, Guernsey and the Isle of Man from the United Kingdom are not classed as exports. Supplies of coal and oil to these islands are, therefore, included as part of UK supply. Exports of natural gas to the Isle of Man included with the exports to Ireland. **r** Development Assistance Committee member (OECD).

United Republic of Tanzania

Region	Eastern Africa	UN membership date	14 December 1961
Population (000, 2020)	59 734[a]	Surface area (km2)	947 303[b]
Pop. density (per km2, 2020)	67.4[a]	Sex ratio (m per 100 f)	99.9[a]
Capital city	Dodoma	National currency	Tanzanian Shilling (TZS)
Capital city pop. (000, 2020)	261.6[c]	Exchange rate (per US$)	2 287.9[d]

Economic indicators

	2010	2015	2020
GDP: Gross domestic product (million current US$)[e]	31 553	47 379	57 145[c]
GDP growth rate (annual %, const. 2015 prices)[e]	6.4	6.2	7.0[c]
GDP per capita (current US$)[e]	732.2	946.8	1 044.1[c]
Economy: Agriculture (% of Gross Value Added)[e,f]	27.6	29.2	30.7[c]
Economy: Services and other activity (% of GVA)[e,f,g]	48.3	46.8	44.1[c]
Employment in agriculture (% of employed)[h]	70.4	67.5	64.9
Employment in industry (% of employed)[h]	5.8	6.4	6.8
Employment in services & other sectors (% employed)[h]	23.8	26.1	28.3
Unemployment rate (% of labour force)[h]	3.0	2.1	2.0
Labour force participation rate (female/male pop. %)[h]	84.2 / 89.2	79.8 / 87.9	79.4 / 87.2
CPI: Consumer Price Index (2010=100)[i]	100	158[i]	187[d]
Agricultural production index (2004-2006=100)	128	188	165[k]
International trade: exports (million current US$)	4 051	5 854	4 414[h,d]
International trade: imports (million current US$)	8 013	14 706	9 434[h,d]
International trade: balance (million current US$)	- 3 962	- 8 852	- 5 020[h,d]
Balance of payments, current account (million US$)	- 2 211	- 3 978	- 1 890[c]

Major trading partners

							2019
Export partners (% of exports)[h]	Rwanda	18.7	Kenya	9.2	Dem. Rep. of Congo	8.5	
Import partners (% of imports)[h]	China	20.7	India	14.3	United Arab Emirates	10.2	

Social indicators

	2010	2015	2020
Population growth rate (average annual %)[a,l]	2.9	3.0	3.0
Urban population (% of total population)[a]	28.1	31.6	34.5[d]
Urban population growth rate (average annual %)[a,l]	5.6	5.5	...
Fertility rate, total (live births per woman)[a,l]	5.6	5.2	4.9
Life expectancy at birth (females/males, years)[a,l]	57.7 / 54.8	63.1 / 58.8	66.6 / 63.0
Population age distribution (0-14/60+ years old, %)[a]	44.9 / 4.0	44.7 / 4.0	43.6 / 4.2
International migrant stock (000/% of total pop.)[a,m]	309.8 / 0.7	384.6 / 0.7	509.2 / 0.9[d]
Refugees and others of concern to the UNHCR (000)	273.8[n]	328.2	320.3[d]
Infant mortality rate (per 1 000 live births)[a,l]	55.5	46.9	41.2
Health: Current expenditure (% of GDP)[e,o]	5.3	3.6	3.6[b]
Health: Physicians (per 1 000 pop.)	...	0.1[p]	~0.0[k]
Education: Government expenditure (% of GDP)	4.5	3.4[p]	...
Education: Primary gross enrol. ratio (f/m per 100 pop.)	103.8 / 101.9	87.0 / 82.5	95.4 / 93.0[c]
Education: Secondary gross enrol. ratio (f/m per 100 pop.)	28.5 / 34.8	27.0 / 27.3	30.1 / 28.8[c]
Education: Tertiary gross enrol. ratio (f/m per 100 pop.)	1.9 / 2.4	2.8 / 5.2	... / ...
Intentional homicide rate (per 100 000 pop.)	8.8	7.3	6.5[k]
Seats held by women in the National Parliament (%)	30.7	36.0	36.9[q]

Environment and infrastructure indicators

	2010	2015	2020
Individuals using the Internet (per 100 inhabitants)	2.9[h]	20.0[r]	25.0[r,b]
Research & Development expenditure (% of GDP)[s]	0.4[t]	0.5[u]	...
Threatened species (number)	691	1 077	1 259
Forested area (% of land area)[h]	54.1	52.0	52.0[b]
CO2 emission estimates (million tons/tons per capita)	6.2 / 0.1	10.5 / 0.2	10.1 / 0.2[b]
Energy production, primary (Petajoules)	654	725	755[b]
Energy supply per capita (Gigajoules)	16	15	15[b]
Tourist/visitor arrivals at national borders (000)	754	1 104	1 378[c]
Important sites for terrestrial biodiversity protected (%)	62.9	62.9	62.9[d]
Pop. using safely managed drinking water (urban/rural, %)	28.0 / ...	34.1 / ...	35.0 / ...[b]
Pop. using safely managed sanitation (urban/rural, %)	24.0 / 15.0	29.3 / 20.3	31.4 / 22.4[b]
Net Official Development Assist. received (% of GNI)	9.42	5.56	4.37[c]

a Including Zanzibar. b 2017. c 2018. d 2019. e Tanzania mainland only, excluding Zanzibar. f Data classified according to ISIC Rev. 4. g Excludes computer and related activities and radio/TV activities. h Estimate. i For Tanganyika only. j Break in the time series. k 2016. l Data refers to a 5-year period preceding the reference year. m Including refugees. n Data as at the end of December. o Data revision. p 2014. q Data are as at 1 January of reporting year. r Population aged 18 years and over. s Excluding business enterprise. t Partial data. u 2013.

United States of America

Region	Northern America	UN membership date	24 October 1945
Population (000, 2020)	331 003	Surface area (km2)	9 833 517 [a]
Pop. density (per km2, 2020)	36.2	Sex ratio (m per 100 f)	97.9
Capital city	Washington, D.C.	National currency	US Dollar (USD)
Capital city pop. (000, 2020)	5 264.5 [b]		

Economic indicators

	2010	2015	2020
GDP: Gross domestic product (million current US$)	14 992 052	18 224 780	20 580 223 [c]
GDP growth rate (annual %, const. 2015 prices)	2.6	2.9	2.9 [c]
GDP per capita (current US$)	48 516.2	56 796.5	62 917.9 [c]
Economy: Agriculture (% of Gross Value Added) [d,e]	1.0	1.0	0.8 [c]
Economy: Industry (% of Gross Value Added) [d,e,f]	19.7	18.8	18.9 [c]
Economy: Services and other activity (% of GVA) [d,e,g,h]	78.4	75.9	76.5 [c]
Employment in agriculture (% of employed)	1.4	1.4	1.3 [i]
Employment in industry (% of employed)	19.6	19.9	19.7 [i]
Employment in services & other sectors (% employed)	78.9	78.7	79.0 [i]
Unemployment rate (% of labour force) [i]	9.6	5.3	3.9
Labour force participation rate (female/male pop. %) [i]	57.5 / 69.9	55.8 / 68.4	55.9 / 67.9
CPI: Consumer Price Index (2010=100) [j]	100	109	117 [b]
Agricultural production index (2004-2006=100)	106	112	117 [k]
International trade: exports (million current US$)	1 278 100	1 501 850	1 644 280 [b]
International trade: imports (million current US$)	1 968 260	2 313 420	2 567 490 [b]
International trade: balance (million current US$)	- 690 161	- 811 579	- 923 216 [b]
Balance of payments, current account (million US$)	- 431 271	- 407 769	- 498 350 [b]

Major trading partners

						2019
Export partners (% of exports)	Canada	17.8	Mexico	15.6	China	6.5
Import partners (% of imports)	China	18.4	Mexico	14.1	Canada	12.7

Social indicators

	2010	2015	2020
Population growth rate (average annual %) [l]	0.9	0.8	0.6
Urban population (% of total population)	80.8	81.7	82.5 [b]
Urban population growth rate (average annual %) [l]	1.1	0.9	...
Fertility rate, total (live births per woman) [l]	2.1	1.9	1.8
Life expectancy at birth (females/males, years) [l]	80.7 / 75.7	81.3 / 76.5	81.3 / 76.3
Population age distribution (0-14/60+ years old, %)	20.2 / 18.4	19.2 / 20.5	18.4 / 22.9
International migrant stock (000/% of total pop.)	44 183.6 / 14.3	48 178.9 / 15.0	50 661.1 / 15.4 [b]
Refugees and others of concern to the UNHCR (000)	270.9 [m]	491.7	1 043.2 [n,b]
Infant mortality rate (per 1 000 live births) [l]	6.8	6.0	5.8
Health: Current expenditure (% of GDP)	16.4	16.8 [o]	17.1 [o,a]
Health: Physicians (per 1 000 pop.)	2.4	2.6	2.6 [a]
Education: Government expenditure (% of GDP)	...	5.0 [p]	...
Education: Primary gross enrol. ratio (f/m per 100 pop.) [i]	99.8 / 100.8	100.3 / 100.3	101.4 / 102.2 [a]
Education: Secondary gross enrol. ratio (f/m per 100 pop.) [i]	95.4 / 94.3	98.2 / 97.2	98.7 / 99.2 [a]
Education: Tertiary gross enrol. ratio (f/m per 100 pop.) [i]	108.3 / 77.7	102.7 / 75.8	102.0 / 75.0 [a]
Intentional homicide rate (per 100 000 pop.)	4.8	4.9	5.0 [c]
Seats held by women in the National Parliament (%)	16.8	19.4	23.4 [q,r]

Environment and infrastructure indicators

	2010	2015	2020
Individuals using the Internet (per 100 inhabitants)	71.7 [s]	74.6 [s]	87.3 [a]
Research & Development expenditure (% of GDP) [t]	2.7	2.7	2.8 [i,c]
Threatened species (number)	1 152	1 299	1 655
Forested area (% of land area)	33.7	33.9 [i]	33.9 [i,a]
CO2 emission estimates (million tons/tons per capita) [u]	5 352.1 / 17.3	4 928.6 / 15.3	4 761.3 / 14.6 [a]
Energy production, primary (Petajoules) [v]	72 292	84 453	83 352 [a]
Energy supply per capita (Gigajoules) [v]	301	286	278 [a]
Tourist/visitor arrivals at national borders (000)	60 010	77 774 [w]	79 746 [c]
Important sites for terrestrial biodiversity protected (%)	49.4	51.2	51.2 [b]
Pop. using safely managed drinking water (urban/rural, %)	99.7 / ...	99.7 / ...	99.7 / ... [a]
Pop. using safely managed sanitation (urban/rural, %)	95.2 / ...	95.5 / ...	95.5 / ... [a]
Net Official Development Assist. disbursed (% of GNI) [x]	0.20	0.17	0.18 [a]

2017. **b** 2019. **c** 2018. **d** Data classified according to ISIC Rev. 4. **e** Including taxes less subsidies on production and imports. **f** Excludes publishing activities. Includes irrigation and canals. **g** Excludes repair of personal and household goods. **h** Excludes computer and related activities and radio/TV activities. **i** Estimate. **j** Urban areas. **k** 2016. **l** Data refers to a 5-year period preceding the reference year. **m** Data as at the end of December. **n** Figures for asylum-seekers pertain to mid-2019 for claims by the Department of Homeland Security and end-2018 for claims by the Executive Office for Immigration Review. **o** Data revision. **p** 2014. **q** Total refers to all voting members of the House of Representatives. **r** Data are as at 1 January of reporting year. **s** Population aged 3 years and over. **t** Do not correspond exactly to Frascati Manual recommendations. **u** Including overseas territories. **v** Oil and coal trade statistics include overseas territories. **w** Break in the time series. **x** Development Assistance Committee member (OECD).

United States Virgin Islands

Region	Caribbean
Surface area (km2)	347 [a]
Sex ratio (m per 100 f)	90.5
National currency	US Dollar (USD)

Population (000, 2020)	104
Pop. density (per km2, 2020)	298.4
Capital city	Charlotte Amalie
Capital city pop. (000, 2020)	52.3 [b]

Economic indicators	2010	2015	2020
Employment in agriculture (% of employed) [c]	4.2	3.7	3.2
Employment in industry (% of employed) [c]	23.2	20.3	19.6
Employment in services & other sectors (% employed) [c]	72.6	76.0	77.2
Unemployment rate (% of labour force) [c]	10.0	9.5	8.8
Labour force participation rate (female/male pop. %) [c]	59.4 / 67.6	58.9 / 64.2	58.1 / 62.4
Agricultural production index (2004-2006=100)	107	107	107 [d]

Social indicators	2010	2015	2020
Population growth rate (average annual %) [e]	- 0.3	- 0.2	- 0.1
Urban population (% of total population)	94.6	95.4	95.8 [f]
Urban population growth rate (average annual %) [e]	- 0.1	- 0.1	...
Fertility rate, total (live births per woman) [e]	2.4	2.3	2.0
Life expectancy at birth (females/males, years) [e]	80.3 / 75.5	82.2 / 76.7	82.9 / 77.7
Population age distribution (0-14/60+ years old, %)	20.7 / 20.4	20.3 / 24.1	19.3 / 27.6
International migrant stock (000/% of total pop.)	56.7 / 53.4	56.7 / 54.0	56.7 / 54.3 [f]
Infant mortality rate (per 1 000 live births) [e]	10.7	9.0	8.2
Intentional homicide rate (per 100 000 pop.)	52.8	49.3 [g]	...

Environment and infrastructure indicators	2010	2015	2020
Individuals using the Internet (per 100 inhabitants) [c]	31.2	54.8	64.4 [a]
Research & Development expenditure (% of GDP)	~0.0 [h,i]	...	...
Threatened species (number)	33	53	74
Forested area (% of land area)	51.9	50.3	50.3 [c,a]
Energy production, primary (Petajoules) [c]	...	0	0 [a]
Energy supply per capita (Gigajoules) [c]	...	1	1 [a]
Tourist/visitor arrivals at national borders (000)	572	642	381 [b]
Important sites for terrestrial biodiversity protected (%)	39.9	39.9	39.9 [f]

a 2017. **b** 2018. **c** Estimate. **d** 2016. **e** Data refers to a 5-year period preceding the reference year. **f** 2019. **g** 2012. **h** Partial data. **i** 2007.

Uruguay

Region	South America
Population (000, 2020)	3 474
Pop. density (per km2, 2020)	19.8
Capital city	Montevideo
Capital city pop. (000, 2020)	1 744.7 [b,c]

UN membership date	18 December 1945
Surface area (km2)	173 626 [a]
Sex ratio (m per 100 f)	93.5
National currency	Peso Uruguayo (UYU)
Exchange rate (per US$)	37.3 [c]

Economic indicators	2010	2015	2020
GDP: Gross domestic product (million current US$)	40 285	53 274	59 597 [d]
GDP growth rate (annual %, const. 2015 prices)	7.8	0.4	1.6 [d]
GDP per capita (current US$)	11 992.0	15 613.8	17 278.1 [d]
Economy: Agriculture (% of Gross Value Added)	8.0	6.7	6.2 [d]
Economy: Industry (% of Gross Value Added)	27.3	28.0	26.9 [d]
Economy: Services and other activity (% of GVA)	41.7	44.8	45.9 [d]
Employment in agriculture (% of employed)	11.6	8.8	7.9 [e]
Employment in industry (% of employed)	21.4	20.5	18.7 [e]
Employment in services & other sectors (% employed)	67.0	70.7	73.4 [e]
Unemployment rate (% of labour force) [e]	7.2	7.5	8.8
Labour force participation rate (female/male pop. %) [e]	55.3 / 76.8	55.7 / 75.2	55.7 / 73.4
CPI: Consumer Price Index (2010=100) [f]	100	150	203 [c]
Agricultural production index (2004-2006=100)	119	128	118 [g]
International trade: exports (million current US$)	6 724	7 670	7 886 [e,c]
International trade: imports (million current US$)	8 622	9 489	8 226 [e,c]
International trade: balance (million current US$)	- 1 898	- 1 820	- 340 [e,c]
Balance of payments, current account (million US$)	- 731	- 491	419 [c]

Major trading partners						2019
Export partners (% of exports) [e]	China	20.0	Brazil	15.1	United States	6.1
Import partners (% of imports) [e]	China	18.9	Brazil	18.4	Argentina	12.4

Social indicators	2010	2015	2020
Population growth rate (average annual %) [h]	0.2	0.3	0.4
Urban population (% of total population)	94.4	95.0	95.4 [c]
Urban population growth rate (average annual %) [h]	0.5	0.5	...
Fertility rate, total (live births per woman) [h]	2.0	2.0	2.0
Life expectancy at birth (females/males, years) [h]	80.0 / 72.6	80.7 / 73.2	81.3 / 73.9
Population age distribution (0-14/60+ years old, %)	22.2 / 18.5	21.1 / 19.2	20.3 / 20.2
International migrant stock (000/% of total pop.)	76.3 / 2.3	78.8 / 2.3	81.5 / 2.4 [c]
Refugees and others of concern to the UNHCR (000)	0.2 [i]	0.4	21.5 [c]
Infant mortality rate (per 1 000 live births) [h]	11.3	10.0	8.7
Health: Current expenditure (% of GDP)	8.6	9.0	9.3 [a]
Health: Physicians (per 1 000 pop.)	4.0 [j]	...	5.1 [a]
Education: Government expenditure (% of GDP)	2.9 [k]	4.4 [l]	4.9 [a]
Education: Primary gross enrol. ratio (f/m per 100 pop.)	110.9 / 114.6	109.8 / 112.2	107.6 / 109.3 [a]
Education: Secondary gross enrol. ratio (f/m per 100 pop.)	109.5 / 93.2	... / ...	126.6 / 114.1 [a]
Education: Tertiary gross enrol. ratio (f/m per 100 pop.)	58.0 / 34.5 [k]	... / ...	... / ...
Intentional homicide rate (per 100 000 pop.)	6.1	8.6	12.1 [d]
Seats held by women in the National Parliament (%)	14.1	13.1	21.2 [m]

Environment and infrastructure indicators	2010	2015	2020
Individuals using the Internet (per 100 inhabitants)	46.4 [n]	64.6	74.8 [d]
Research & Development expenditure (% of GDP)	0.3	0.4	0.5 [a]
Threatened species (number)	80	103	116
Forested area (% of land area)	9.9	10.5	10.5 [e,a]
CO2 emission estimates (million tons/tons per capita)	6.0 / 1.8	6.4 / 1.9	5.9 / 1.7 [a]
Energy production, primary (Petajoules)	89	126	136 [a]
Energy supply per capita (Gigajoules)	51	62	63 [a]
Tourist/visitor arrivals at national borders (000)	2 353	2 773	3 469 [d]
Important sites for terrestrial biodiversity protected (%)	20.7	20.8	20.8 [c]
Pop. using safely managed drinking water (urban/rural, %)	94.2 / ...	94.5 / ...	94.6 / ... [a]
Net Official Development Assist. received (% of GNI)	0.12	0.05	0.08 [a]

a 2017. b Data refer to the department of Montevideo and localities of the departments of Canelones and San José (Ciudad de la Costa, Las Piedras, Pando, Cerámicas del Sur and Ciudad del Plata). c 2019. d 2018. e Estimate. f Calculated by the UN Statistics Division from national indices. g 2016. h Data refers to a 5-year period preceding the reference year. i Data as at the end of December. j 2008. k 2006. l 2011. m Data are as at 1 January of reporting year. n Population aged 6 years and over.

Uzbekistan

Region	Central Asia	UN membership date	02 March 1992
Population (000, 2020)	33 469	Surface area (km2)	448 969 a
Pop. density (per km2, 2020)	78.7	Sex ratio (m per 100 f)	99.6
Capital city	Tashkent	National currency	Uzbekistan Sum (UZS)
Capital city pop. (000, 2020)	2 490.3 b	Exchange rate (per US$)	9 502.0 c.b

Economic indicators

	2010	2015	2020
GDP: Gross domestic product (million current US$)	46 909	81 847	50 500 d
GDP growth rate (annual %, const. 2015 prices)	8.5	7.4	5.1 d
GDP per capita (current US$)	1 645.0	2 646.3	1 555.0 d
Economy: Agriculture (% of Gross Value Added)	32.9	33.6	31.7 d
Economy: Industry (% of Gross Value Added)e	25.9	25.9	31.3 d
Economy: Services and other activity (% of GVA)f,g	53.0	54.2	55.2 d
Employment in agriculture (% of employed)h	30.9	26.7	23.3
Employment in industry (% of employed)h	25.4	27.7	29.9
Employment in services & other sectors (% employed)h	43.6	45.6	46.8
Unemployment rate (% of labour force)h	5.4	5.2	6.1
Labour force participation rate (female/male pop. %)h	51.6 / 75.4	52.3 / 77.4	52.3 / 78.1
CPI: Consumer Price Index (2010=100)	...	...	153 i,j,b
Agricultural production index (2004-2006=100)	127	168	167 k
International trade: exports (million current US$)	11 688 h	12 871 h	14 930 b
International trade: imports (million current US$)	8 680 h	12 416 h	21 867 b
International trade: balance (million current US$)	3 008 h	455 h	- 6 938 b
Balance of payments, current account (million US$)	...	1 071	- 3 246 b

Major trading partners

					2019
Export partners (% of exports)	Areas nes l	44.0	Russian Federation	13.6	China 11.8
Import partners (% of imports)	China	23.1	Russian Federation	18.2	Rep. of Korea 11.5

Social indicators

	2010	2015	2020
Population growth rate (average annual %)m	1.5	1.6	1.6
Urban population (% of total population)	51.0	50.8	50.4 b
Urban population growth rate (average annual %)m	2.5	1.5	...
Fertility rate, total (live births per woman)m	2.5	2.4	2.4
Life expectancy at birth (females/males, years)m	72.2 / 66.1	72.7 / 67.8	73.6 / 69.4
Population age distribution (0-14/60+ years old, %)	29.1 / 6.2	28.4 / 6.9	28.8 / 8.3
International migrant stock (000/% of total pop.)	1 220.1 / 4.3	1 170.9 / 3.8	1 168.4 / 3.5 b
Refugees and others of concern to the UNHCR (000)	0.3 n	86.8	95.9 b
Infant mortality rate (per 1 000 live births)m	40.7	27.7	20.8
Health: Current expenditure (% of GDP)o	5.6	6.1	6.4 a
Health: Physicians (per 1 000 pop.)	2.5	2.4 p	...
Education: Government expenditure (% of GDP)h	...	7.1	6.3 a
Education: Primary gross enrol. ratio (f/m per 100 pop.)	93.1 / 94.7	99.2 / 100.6	103.4 / 105.0 d
Education: Secondary gross enrol. ratio (f/m per 100 pop.)	89.9 / 89.8	91.3 / 92.4	92.7 / 93.9 a
Education: Tertiary gross enrol. ratio (f/m per 100 pop.)	7.6 / 11.1	6.3 / 10.0	8.2 / 11.8 d
Intentional homicide rate (per 100 000 pop.)	3.0 q	1.6	1.1 a
Seats held by women in the National Parliament (%)	22.0	16.0	32.0 r

Environment and infrastructure indicators

	2010	2015	2020
Individuals using the Internet (per 100 inhabitants)	15.9 h	42.8 h	55.2 d
Research & Development expenditure (% of GDP)	0.2	0.2	0.1 d
Threatened species (number)	50	54	62
Forested area (% of land area)h	7.7	7.6	7.6 a
CO2 emission estimates (million tons/tons per capita)	100.6 / 3.5	92.2 / 2.9	81.2 / 2.5 a
Energy production, primary (Petajoules)	2 309	2 120	2 205 a
Energy supply per capita (Gigajoules)	63	56	59 a
Tourist/visitor arrivals at national borders (000)	975	1 918	5 346 d
Important sites for terrestrial biodiversity protected (%)	10.1	10.1	10.1 b
Pop. using safely managed drinking water (urban/rural, %)	85.4 / 30.2	85.9 / 30.9	86.1 / 31.1 a
Net Official Development Assist. received (% of GNI)	0.49	0.54	1.07 b

a 2017. b 2019. c UN operational exchange rate. d 2018. e Excludes publishing activities. Includes irrigation and canals. f Excludes computer and related activities and radio/TV activities. g Excludes repair of personal and household goods. h Estimate. i Base: 2016 = 100 j Calculated by the UN Statistics Division from national indices. k 2016. l Areas not elsewhere specified. m Data refers to a 5-year period preceding the reference year. n Data as at the end of December. o Data revision. p 2014. q 2008. r Data are as at 1 January of reporting year.

Vanuatu

Region	Melanesia	
Population (000, 2020)	307	
Pop. density (per km2, 2020)	25.2	
Capital city	Port Vila	
Capital city pop. (000, 2020)	52.7 [b]	

UN membership date	15 September 1981
Surface area (km2)	12 189 [a]
Sex ratio (m per 100 f)	102.8
National currency	Vatu (VUV)
Exchange rate (per US$)	114.3 [c]

Economic indicators	2010	2015	2020
GDP: Gross domestic product (million current US$)	701	760	889 [b]
GDP growth rate (annual %, const. 2015 prices)	1.6	0.2	3.2 [b]
GDP per capita (current US$)	2 966.9	2 801.9	3 037.2 [b]
Economy: Agriculture (% of Gross Value Added) [d]	21.9	23.1	22.8 [b]
Economy: Industry (% of Gross Value Added) [d,e]	13.0	11.5	11.2 [b]
Economy: Services and other activity (% of GVA) [d,f,g]	53.7	67.5	63.0 [b]
Employment in agriculture (% of employed) [h]	60.2	58.3	55.3
Employment in industry (% of employed) [h]	6.9	6.1	6.3
Employment in services & other sectors (% employed) [h]	32.9	35.6	38.4
Unemployment rate (% of labour force) [h]	4.6	4.6	4.4
Labour force participation rate (female/male pop. %) [h]	60.6 / 78.9	60.9 / 79.0	60.9 / 78.7
CPI: Consumer Price Index (2010=100)	100	107	117 [i,j,c]
Agricultural production index (2004-2006=100)	128	123	124 [k]
International trade: exports (million current US$)	46	39 [h]	51 [h,c]
International trade: imports (million current US$)	276	354 [h]	289 [h,c]
International trade: balance (million current US$)	- 230	- 316 [h]	- 238 [h,c]
Balance of payments, current account (million US$)	- 42	- 4	85 [b]

Major trading partners						2019
Export partners (% of exports) [h]	Mauritania	32.3	Japan	25.4	Thailand	10.6
Import partners (% of imports) [h]	China	21.3	Australia	19.3	Fiji	11.2

Social indicators	2010	2015	2020
Population growth rate (average annual %) [l]	2.4	2.8	2.5
Urban population (% of total population)	24.5	25.0	25.4 [c]
Urban population growth rate (average annual %) [l]	3.6	2.7	...
Fertility rate, total (live births per woman) [l]	4.2	4.0	3.8
Life expectancy at birth (females/males, years) [l]	70.4 / 67.3	71.2 / 68.0	71.9 / 68.8
Population age distribution (0-14/60+ years old, %)	38.2 / 5.7	39.1 / 5.7	38.4 / 5.8
International migrant stock (000/% of total pop.)	3.0 / 1.3	3.2 / 1.2	3.2 / 1.1 [c]
Refugees and others of concern to the UNHCR (000)	~0.0 [m]	~0.0	~0.0 [c]
Infant mortality rate (per 1 000 live births) [l]	24.0	24.3	22.4
Health: Current expenditure (% of GDP) [n]	3.4	4.2	3.3 [a]
Health: Physicians (per 1 000 pop.)	0.1 [o]	0.2 [p]	0.2 [k]
Education: Government expenditure (% of GDP)	5.0 [q]	5.5	4.7 [a]
Education: Primary gross enrol. ratio (f/m per 100 pop.)	121.9 / 123.0	107.8 / 110.7	... / ...
Education: Secondary gross enrol. ratio (f/m per 100 pop.)	59.5 / 59.6	54.9 / 53.5	... / ...
Seats held by women in the National Parliament (%)	3.8	0.0	0.0 [r]

Environment and infrastructure indicators	2010	2015	2020
Individuals using the Internet (per 100 inhabitants)	8.0	22.4 [h]	25.7 [h,a]
Threatened species (number)	121	137	144
Forested area (% of land area) [h]	36.1	36.1	36.1 [a]
Energy production, primary (Petajoules)	1	1	1 [a]
Energy supply per capita (Gigajoules)	11	11	11 [a]
Tourist/visitor arrivals at national borders (000)	97	90	116 [b]
Important sites for terrestrial biodiversity protected (%)	2.8	2.8	2.8 [c]
Net Official Development Assist. received (% of GNI)	16.19	25.84	14.90 [b]

2017. **b** 2018. **c** 2019. **d** Data classified according to ISIC Rev. 4. **e** Excludes publishing activities. Includes irrigation and canals. **f** Excludes computer and related activities and radio/TV activities. **g** Excludes repair of personal and household goods. **h** Estimate. **i** Monthly average for quarter or index for quarter. **j** Calculated by the UN Statistics Division from national indices. **k** 2016. **l** Data refers to a 5-year period preceding the reference year. **m** Data as at the end of December. **n** Government expenditures show fluctuations due to variations in capital investment. **o** 2008. **p** 2012. **q** 2009. **r** Data are as at 1 January of reporting year.

Venezuela (Bolivarian Republic of)

Region	South America	UN membership date	15 November 1945
Population (000, 2020)	28 436	Surface area (km2)	912 050 a
Pop. density (per km2, 2020)	32.2	Sex ratio (m per 100 f)	96.8
Capital city	Caracas	National currency	Bolívar (VEF)
Capital city pop. (000, 2020)	2 935.5 b,c	Exchange rate (per US$)	10.0 a

Economic indicators

	2010	2015	2020
GDP: Gross domestic product (million current US$)	393 806	344 417	208 338 d
GDP growth rate (annual %, const. 2015 prices)	- 1.5	- 6.2	- 18.0 d
GDP per capita (current US$)	13 846.9	11 449.3	7 212.2 d
Economy: Agriculture (% of Gross Value Added)	5.7	6.3	5.9 d
Economy: Industry (% of Gross Value Added)	51.0	30.5	35.4 d
Economy: Services and other activity (% of GVA)	39.8	48.3	48.4 d
Employment in agriculture (% of employed)e	8.3	7.4	8.4
Employment in industry (% of employed)e	21.8	20.3	16.1
Employment in services & other sectors (% employed)e	69.9	72.3	75.5
Unemployment rate (% of labour force)e	7.1	7.4	9.4
Labour force participation rate (female/male pop. %)e	49.5 / 78.4	49.2 / 76.8	45.2 / 74.3
CPI: Consumer Price Index (2010=100)f	100	772	1 932 g,c
Agricultural production index (2004-2006=100)	111	120	109 h
International trade: exports (million current US$)	66 963	37 236 e	3 783 e,c
International trade: imports (million current US$)	32 343	40 146 e	1 051 e,c
International trade: balance (million current US$)	34 620	- 2 910 e	2 732 e,c
Balance of payments, current account (million US$)	5 585	- 16 051	- 3 870 h

Major trading partners

						2019
Export partners (% of exports)e	China	34.3	India	27.4	United States	9.7
Import partners (% of imports)e	United States	23.5	China	21.2	Brazil	7.8

Social indicators

	2010	2015	2020
Population growth rate (average annual %)i	1.5	1.1	- 1.1
Urban population (% of total population)	88.1	88.2	88.2 c
Urban population growth rate (average annual %)i	1.6	1.4	...
Fertility rate, total (live births per woman)i	2.5	2.4	2.3
Life expectancy at birth (females/males, years)i	77.0 / 69.2	77.0 / 69.4	76.1 / 68.4
Population age distribution (0-14/60+ years old, %)	29.9 / 8.4	28.4 / 9.6	27.3 / 12.1
International migrant stock (000/% of total pop.)	1 347.3 / 4.7	1 404.4 / 4.7	1 375.7 / 4.8 c
Refugees and others of concern to the UNHCR (000)	217.4 j	174.9	452.6 c
Infant mortality rate (per 1 000 live births)i	14.8	15.0	25.7
Health: Current expenditure (% of GDP)	6.8	5.1 k	1.2 k,a
Education: Government expenditure (% of GDP)	6.9 l	...	...
Education: Primary gross enrol. ratio (f/m per 100 pop.)	101.3 / 104.2	99.8 / 102.0	96.0 / 98.3 a
Education: Secondary gross enrol. ratio (f/m per 100 pop.)	86.6 / 79.0	94.5 / 87.7	91.6 / 84.7 a
Education: Tertiary gross enrol. ratio (f/m per 100 pop.)	100.3 / 59.3 e,m	... / ...	... / ...
Intentional homicide rate (per 100 000 pop.)	46.0	52.0	36.7 d
Seats held by women in the National Parliament (%)	17.5	17.0	22.2 n

Environment and infrastructure indicators

	2010	2015	2020
Individuals using the Internet (per 100 inhabitants)	37.4 e	64.0 e	72.0 a
Research & Development expenditure (% of GDP)	0.2	0.3 o	...
Threatened species (number)	270	312	379
Forested area (% of land area)e	53.9	52.9	52.9 a
CO2 emission estimates (million tons/tons per capita)	171.5 / 5.9	140.5 / 4.5	113.7 / 3.6 a
Energy production, primary (Petajoules)	7 948	7 361	6 055 a
Energy supply per capita (Gigajoules)	106	79	65 a
Tourist/visitor arrivals at national borders (000)	526	789	427 a
Important sites for terrestrial biodiversity protected (%)	52.5	52.5	52.5 c
Net Official Development Assist. received (% of GNI)	0.01	0.01 o	...

a 2017. b Refers to multiple municipalities and parishes (see source). c 2019. d 2018. e Estimate. f Calculated by the UN Statistics Division from national indices. g Figures in millions. h 2016. i Data refers to a 5-year period preceding the reference year. j Data as at the end of December. k For 2015 - 2017, WHO is using the exchange rate United Nations to report health expenditrue indicators in USD. l 2009. m 2008. n Data are as at 1 January of reporting year. o 2014.

Viet Nam

Region	South-eastern Asia	UN membership date	20 September 1977
Population (000, 2020)	97 339	Surface area (km2)	330 967 [a]
Pop. density (per km2, 2020)	313.9	Sex ratio (m per 100 f)	99.7
Capital city	Hanoi	National currency	Dong (VND)
Capital city pop. (000, 2020)	4 479.6 [b,c]	Exchange rate (per US$)	23 155.0 [c]

Economic indicators

	2010	2015	2020
GDP: Gross domestic product (million current US$)	115 932	193 241	244 901 [d]
GDP growth rate (annual %, const. 2015 prices)	6.4	6.7	7.1 [d]
GDP per capita (current US$)	1 317.9	2 085.1	2 563.2 [d]
Economy: Agriculture (% of Gross Value Added) [e,f]	21.0	18.9	16.2 [d]
Economy: Industry (% of Gross Value Added) [f,g]	36.7	37.0	38.1 [d]
Economy: Services and other activity (% of GVA) [e,f,h,i]	55.3	57.8	61.6 [d]
Employment in agriculture (% of employed)	48.7	44.0	36.2 [j]
Employment in industry (% of employed)	21.7	22.7	28.4 [j]
Employment in services & other sectors (% employed)	29.6	33.2	35.4 [j]
Unemployment rate (% of labour force) [j]	1.1	2.1	2.0
Labour force participation rate (female/male pop. %) [j]	71.4 / 81.4	73.3 / 83.3	72.6 / 82.2
CPI: Consumer Price Index (2010=100)	100	145	164 [c]
Agricultural production index (2004-2006=100)	120	140	138 [k]
International trade: exports (million current US$)	72 237	162 017	264 610 [c]
International trade: imports (million current US$)	84 839	165 776	253 442 [c]
International trade: balance (million current US$)	- 12 602	- 3 759	11 168 [c]
Balance of payments, current account (million US$)	- 4 276	- 2 041	5 899 [d]

Major trading partners

						2019
Export partners (% of exports)	United States	23.2	China	15.7	Japan	7.7
Import partners (% of imports)	China	29.8	Rep. of Korea	18.5	Japan	7.7

Social indicators

	2010	2015	2020
Population growth rate (average annual %) [l]	1.0	1.0	1.0
Urban population (% of total population)	30.4	33.8	36.6 [c]
Urban population growth rate (average annual %) [l]	3.1	3.2	
Fertility rate, total (live births per woman) [l]	1.9	2.0	2.1
Life expectancy at birth (females/males, years) [l]	78.7 / 70.4	79.1 / 70.8	79.4 / 71.2
Population age distribution (0-14/60+ years old, %)	23.6 / 8.8	23.0 / 10.2	23.2 / 12.3
International migrant stock (000/% of total pop.) [m,n]	61.8 / 0.1	72.8 / 0.1	76.1 / 0.1 [c]
Refugees and others of concern to the UNHCR (000)	12.1 [o]	11.0	34.1 [c]
Infant mortality rate (per 1 000 live births) [l]	19.0	17.9	16.7
Health: Current expenditure (% of GDP)	6.0	5.7	5.5 [a]
Health: Physicians (per 1 000 pop.)	0.7	0.8	0.8 [k]
Education: Government expenditure (% of GDP)	5.1	5.7 [p]	4.3 [k]
Education: Primary gross enrol. ratio (f/m per 100 pop.)	103.2 / 108.1	110.1 / 109.7	111.9 / 109.5 [d]
Education: Tertiary gross enrol. ratio (f/m per 100 pop.)	23.0 / 22.6	29.2 / 29.0	31.7 / 25.5 [k]
Intentional homicide rate (per 100 000 pop.)	1.5	1.5 [q]	...
Seats held by women in the National Parliament (%)	25.8	24.3	26.7 [r]

Environment and infrastructure indicators

	2010	2015	2020
Individuals using the Internet (per 100 inhabitants)	30.6	45.0 [s]	70.3 [d]
Research & Development expenditure (% of GDP)	...	0.4	0.5 [a]
Threatened species (number)	424	565	738
Forested area (% of land area) [j]	45.6	47.6	47.6 [a]
CO2 emission estimates (million tons/tons per capita)	126.7 / 1.4	182.6 / 2.0	191.2 / 2.0 [a]
Energy production, primary (Petajoules)	2 747	3 082	2 812 [a]
Energy supply per capita (Gigajoules)	26	32	31 [a]
Tourist/visitor arrivals at national borders (000)	5 050	7 944	15 498 [d]
Important sites for terrestrial biodiversity protected (%)	30.3	39.2	39.2 [c]
Net Official Development Assist. received (% of GNI)	2.48	1.73	0.71 [d]

a 2017. b Refers to urban population in the city districts. c 2019. d 2018. e At producers' prices. f Data classified according to ISIC Rev. 4. g Excludes publishing activities. Includes irrigation and canals. h Excludes repair of personal and household goods. i Excludes computer and related activities and radio/TV activities. j Estimate. k 2016. l Data refers to a 5-year period preceding the reference year. m Including refugees. n Refers to foreign citizens. o Data as at end of December. p 2013. q 2011. r Data are as at 1 January of reporting year. s Population aged 18 years and over.

Wallis and Futuna Islands

Region	Polynesia	Population (000, 2020)	12	
Surface area (km2)	142 a	Pop. density (per km2, 2020)	82.5	
Sex ratio (m per 100 f)	93.4 b,c	Capital city	Matu-Utu	
National currency	CFP Franc (XPF) d	Capital city pop. (000, 2020)	1.0 e	
Exchange rate (per US$)	106.2 f			

Economic indicators		2010	2015	2020
Agricultural production index (2004-2006=100)		105	112	112 c
International trade: exports (million current US$) g		1	1	1 f
International trade: imports (million current US$) g		35	49	65 f
International trade: balance (million current US$) g		- 34	- 48	- 63 f

Major trading partners						2019
Export partners (% of exports) g	Singapore	45.8	France	33.7	Belgium	9.1
Import partners (% of imports) g	France	38.4	Fiji	22.3	Areas nes h	12.4

Social indicators	2010	2015	2020
Population growth rate (average annual %)	- 1.6 i	- 2.1 i	- 0.9
Urban population (% of total population)	0.0	0.0	0.0 f
Urban population growth rate (average annual %) i	0.0	0.0	...
Fertility rate, total (live births per woman)	...	2.1 j	...
Life expectancy at birth (females/males, years)	... / ...	78.7 / 72.8 b,j	... / ...
Population age distribution (0-14/60+ years old, %)	... / ...	... / ...	25.5 / 15.4 c
International migrant stock (000/% of total pop.)	1.6 / 12.8	1.1 / 8.6	1.0 / 8.9 f
Infant mortality rate (per 1 000 live births)	5.2 k,l	...	...

Environment and infrastructure indicators	2010	2015	2020
Individuals using the Internet (per 100 inhabitants)	8.2	9.0 g,m	...
Threatened species (number)	74	88	92
Forested area (% of land area)	41.6	41.6	41.6 g,a
Energy production, primary (Petajoules) g	0	0	0 a
Energy supply per capita (Gigajoules)	27	28	30 g,a

a 2017. b Break in the time series. c 2016. d Communauté financière du Pacifique (CFP) Franc. e 2018. f 2019. g Estimate. h Areas not elsewhere specified. i Data refers to a 5-year period preceding the reference year. j 2013. k Data refers to a 4-year period up to and including the reference year. l 2008. m 2012.

Western Sahara

Region	Northern Africa	
Surface area (km2)	266 000[a,b]	
Sex ratio (m per 100 f)	109.5	
National currency	Moroccan Dirham (MAD)	
Exchange rate (per US$)	9.6[d]	

Population (000, 2020)	597	
Pop. density (per km2, 2020)	2.2	
Capital city	El Aaiún	
Capital city pop. (000, 2020)	232.4[c]	

Economic indicators	2010	2015	2020
Employment in agriculture (% of employed)[e]	24.4	21.9	19.8
Employment in industry (% of employed)[e]	24.0	25.1	25.7
Employment in services & other sectors (% employed)[e]	51.5	53.0	54.5
Unemployment rate (% of labour force)[e]	9.7	9.6	9.4
Labour force participation rate (female/male pop. %)[e]	24.3 / 79.3	25.2 / 79.6	26.0 / 79.3
Agricultural production index (2004-2006=100)	102	107	107[f]

Social indicators	2010	2015	2020
Population growth rate (average annual %)[g]	1.9	1.8	2.5
Urban population (% of total population)	86.3	86.5	86.8[d]
Urban population growth rate (average annual %)[g]	1.9	1.9	...
Fertility rate, total (live births per woman)[g]	2.6	2.6	2.4
Life expectancy at birth (females/males, years)[g]	68.1 / 64.7	70.3 / 66.9	71.9 / 68.2
Population age distribution (0-14/60+ years old, %)	29.4 / 3.8	28.5 / 4.8	27.2 / 6.3
International migrant stock (000/% of total pop.)[e]	4.5 / 0.9	5.2 / 1.0	5.4 / 0.9[d]
Infant mortality rate (per 1 000 live births)[g]	43.0	34.1	28.8

Environment and infrastructure indicators	2010	2015	2020
Threatened species (number)	39	39	58
Forested area (% of land area)[e]	2.7	2.7	2.7[b]

a Comprising the Northern Region (former Saguia el Hamra) and Southern Region (former Rio de Oro). b 2017. c 2018. d 2019. e Estimate. f 2016. g Data refers to a 5-year period preceding the reference year.

Yemen

Region	Western Asia	UN membership date	30 September 1947
Population (000, 2020)	29 826	Surface area (km2)	527 968 [a]
Pop. density (per km2, 2020)	56.5	Sex ratio (m per 100 f)	101.5
Capital city	Sana'a	National currency	Yemeni Rial (YER)
Capital city pop. (000, 2020)	2 874.4 [b,c]		

Economic indicators	2010	2015	2020
GDP: Gross domestic product (million current US$)	30 907	26 660	26 672 [d]
GDP growth rate (annual %, const. 2015 prices)	3.3	- 30.5	- 1.3 [d]
GDP per capita (current US$)	1 334.8	1 006.1	935.9 [d]
Economy: Agriculture (% of Gross Value Added)	12.1	18.2	19.3 [d]
Economy: Industry (% of Gross Value Added)	38.7	20.1	20.6 [d]
Economy: Services and other activity (% of GVA)	18.5	28.9	24.3 [d]
Employment in agriculture (% of employed)	24.1	29.2 [e]	28.6 [e]
Employment in industry (% of employed)	19.0	12.8 [e]	10.0 [e]
Employment in services & other sectors (% employed)	56.9	58.0 [e]	61.4 [e]
Unemployment rate (% of labour force) [e]	12.9	13.4	12.8
Labour force participation rate (female/male pop. %) [e]	10.0 / 68.8	6.0 / 68.4	5.7 / 70.2
CPI: Consumer Price Index (2010=100) [e]	100	158 [f]	...
Agricultural production index (2004-2006=100)	136	133	141 [g]
International trade: exports (million current US$)	6 437	510	24 [c]
International trade: imports (million current US$)	9 255	6 573	4 716 [c]
International trade: balance (million current US$)	- 2 818	- 6 063	- 4 692 [c]
Balance of payments, current account (million US$)	- 1 054	- 3 026	- 2 419 [g]

Major trading partners							2019
Export partners (% of exports)	Egypt	49.6	Turkey	28.0	Oman	10.5
Import partners (% of imports)	United Arab Emirates	24.0	China	10.4	Saudi Arabia	6.5

Social indicators	2010	2015	2020
Population growth rate (average annual %) [h]	2.8	2.7	2.4
Urban population (% of total population)	31.8	34.8	37.3 [c]
Urban population growth rate (average annual %) [h]	4.6	4.4	...
Fertility rate, total (live births per woman) [h]	5.0	4.4	3.8
Life expectancy at birth (females/males, years) [h]	66.4 / 63.1	67.7 / 64.3	67.7 / 64.4
Population age distribution (0-14/60+ years old, %)	42.7 / 4.3	40.7 / 4.4	38.8 / 4.6
International migrant stock (000/% of total pop.) [i,j]	288.4 / 1.2	379.9 / 1.4	385.6 / 1.3 [c]
Refugees and others of concern to the UNHCR (000)	508.6 [k]	1 540.5	3 922.9 [c]
Infant mortality rate (per 1 000 live births) [h]	48.6	43.3	43.2
Health: Current expenditure (% of GDP) [e]	5.2	4.2	...
Health: Physicians (per 1 000 pop.)	0.3 [l]	0.5 [f]	...
Education: Government expenditure (% of GDP)	5.2 [m]	...	...
Education: Primary gross enrol. ratio (f/m per 100 pop.)	82.3 / 100.9	89.4 / 106.6 [n]	87.1 / 99.9 [g]
Education: Secondary gross enrol. ratio (f/m per 100 pop.)	33.6 / 54.2	40.0 / 58.2 [n]	43.3 / 59.6 [g]
Education: Tertiary gross enrol. ratio (f/m per 100 pop.)	6.5 / 14.9	6.2 / 14.0 [o]	... / ...
Intentional homicide rate (per 100 000 pop.)	4.7	6.8 [n]	...
Seats held by women in the National Parliament (%)	0.3	0.3	0.3 [p,q]

Environment and infrastructure indicators	2010	2015	2020
Individuals using the Internet (per 100 inhabitants)	12.4	24.1 [e]	26.7 [e,a]
Threatened species (number)	269	287	313
Forested area (% of land area) [e]	1.0	1.0	1.0 [a]
CO2 emission estimates (million tons/tons per capita)	22.4 / 0.9	11.7 / 0.4	8.9 / 0.3 [a]
Energy production, primary (Petajoules)	804	173	77 [a]
Energy supply per capita (Gigajoules)	14	7	5 [a]
Tourist/visitor arrivals at national borders (000) [r]	1 025	367	...
Important sites for terrestrial biodiversity protected (%)	19.4	19.4	19.4 [c]
Pop. using safely managed sanitation (urban/rural %)	67.4 / ...	67.0 / ...	67.0 / ... [e]
Net Official Development Assist. received (% of GNI)	2.29	4.31	29.67 [d]

a 2017. **b** Data refers to the urban agglomeration. **c** 2019. **d** 2018. **e** Estimate. **f** 2014. **g** 2016. **h** Data refers to a year period preceding the reference year. **i** Including refugees. **j** Refers to foreign citizens. **k** Data as at the end of December. **l** 2009. **m** 2008. **n** 2013. **o** 2011. **p** Data are as at 1 January of reporting year. **q** Data corresponds to the composition of the House of Representatives elected in 2003, and of the Consultative Council appointed in 2001. **r** Including nationals residing abroad.

Zambia

Region	Eastern Africa	UN membership date	01 December 1964
Population (000, 2020)	18 384	Surface area (km2)	752 612 [a]
Pop. density (per km2, 2020)	24.7	Sex ratio (m per 100 f)	98.1
Capital city	Lusaka	National currency	Zambian Kwacha (ZMW)
Capital city pop. (000, 2020)	2 646.6 [b]	Exchange rate (per US$)	14.1 [b]

Economic indicators

	2010	2015	2020
GDP: Gross domestic product (million current US$)	20 265	20 859	27 283 [c]
GDP growth rate (annual %, const. 2015 prices)	10.3	2.9	4.1 [c]
GDP per capita (current US$)	1 489.4	1 313.6	1 572.3 [c]
Economy: Agriculture (% of Gross Value Added) [d]	10.0	5.3	3.0 [c]
Economy: Industry (% of Gross Value Added) [d,e]	34.1	35.3	35.5 [c]
Economy: Services and other activity (% of GVA) [d,f,g]	59.4	56.9	56.3 [c]
Employment in agriculture (% of employed) [h]	64.3	51.7	48.5
Employment in industry (% of employed) [h]	8.8	10.7	10.8
Employment in services & other sectors (% employed) [h]	26.9	37.7	40.7
Unemployment rate (% of labour force) [h]	13.2	10.1	11.4
Labour force participation rate (female/male pop. %) [h]	71.1 / 82.5	70.2 / 80.3	70.4 / 79.0
CPI: Consumer Price Index (2010=100)	100 [i]	144	212 [b]
Agricultural production index (2004-2006=100)	164	183	183 [j]
International trade: exports (million current US$)	7 200	6 607	7 029 [b]
International trade: imports (million current US$)	5 321	7 934	7 221 [b]
International trade: balance (million current US$)	1 879	- 1 328	- 192 [b]
Balance of payments, current account (million US$)	1 525	- 768	242 [b]

Major trading partners

					2019
Export partners (% of exports)	Switzerland	41.3	China	21.4	Dem. Rep. of Congo 12.8
Import partners (% of imports)	South Africa	30.8	China	14.1	United Arab Emirates 10.3

Social indicators

	2010	2015	2020
Population growth rate (average annual %) [k]	2.8	3.1	2.9
Urban population (% of total population)	39.4	41.9	44.1 [b]
Urban population growth rate (average annual %) [k]	4.1	4.3	
Fertility rate, total (live births per woman) [k]	5.6	5.2	4.7
Life expectancy at birth (females/males, years) [k]	54.0 / 49.6	61.5 / 57.0	66.2 / 60.3
Population age distribution (0-14/60+ years old, %)	47.3 / 3.3	46.2 / 3.3	44.0 / 3.4
International migrant stock (000/% of total pop.) [l]	150.0 / 1.1	132.1 / 0.8	170.2 / 1.0 [b]
Refugees and others of concern to the UNHCR (000)	57.9 [m]	51.8	81.8 [b]
Infant mortality rate (per 1 000 live births) [k]	64.7	53.3	45.6
Health: Current expenditure (% of GDP) [n]	3.7	4.4	4.5 [a]
Health: Physicians (per 1 000 pop.)	0.1	0.2 [o]	1.2 [c]
Education: Government expenditure (% of GDP)	1.1 [p]	...	...
Education: Primary gross enrol. ratio (f/m per 100 pop.)	107.3 / 106.6	101.6 / 101.3	99.9 / 97.5 [a]
Education: Tertiary gross enrol. ratio (f/m per 100 pop.)	... / ...	3.5 / 4.8 [o]	... / ...
Intentional homicide rate (per 100 000 pop.)	6.0	5.4	...
Seats held by women in the National Parliament (%)	14.0	12.7	16.8 [q]

Environment and infrastructure indicators

	2010	2015	2020
Individuals using the Internet (per 100 inhabitants)	10.0	21.0 [h]	14.3 [c]
Research & Development expenditure (% of GDP)	0.3 [i,p]	...	...
Threatened species (number)	67	83	107
Forested area (% of land area) [h]	66.5	65.4	65.4 [a]
CO2 emission estimates (million tons/tons per capita)	1.6 / 0.1	3.5 / 0.2	6.0 / 0.4 [a]
Energy production, primary (Petajoules)	319	389	448 [a]
Energy supply per capita (Gigajoules)	25	27	29 [a]
Tourist/visitor arrivals at national borders (000)	815	932	1 072 [c]
Important sites for terrestrial biodiversity protected (%)	45.5	45.5	45.5 [b]
Pop. using safely managed drinking water (urban/rural, %)	47.1 / ...	46.3 / ...	46.2 / ... [a]
Net Official Development Assist. received (% of GNI)	4.86	3.83	3.84 [c]

2017. **b** 2019. **c** 2018. **d** Data classified according to ISIC Rev. 4. **e** Excludes publishing activities. Includes irrigation and canals. **f** Excludes repair of personal and household goods. **g** Excludes computer and related activities and radio/TV activities. **h** Estimate. **i** Break in the time series. **j** 2016. **k** Data refers to a 5-year period preceding the reference year. **l** Including refugees. **m** Data as at the end of December. **n** Data revision. **o** 2012. **p** 2008. **q** Data are at 1 January of reporting year.

Zimbabwe

Region	Eastern Africa	UN membership date	25 August 1980
Population (000, 2020)	14 863	Surface area (km2)	390 757 [a]
Pop. density (per km2, 2020)	38.4	Sex ratio (m per 100 f)	91.3
Capital city	Harare	National currency	Zimbabwe Dollar (ZWL)
Capital city pop. (000, 2020)	1 521.3 [b]	Exchange rate (per US$)	16.8 [b]

Economic indicators	2010	2015	2020
GDP: Gross domestic product (million current US$)	12 042	19 963	24 312 [c]
GDP growth rate (annual %, const. 2015 prices)	19.7	1.8	4.8 [c]
GDP per capita (current US$)	948.3	1 445.1	1 683.8 [c]
Economy: Agriculture (% of Gross Value Added)	10.9	9.3	9.2 [c]
Economy: Industry (% of Gross Value Added)	23.5	25.0	22.9 [c]
Economy: Services and other activity (% of GVA)	25.4	32.9	33.9 [c]
Employment in agriculture (% of employed) [d]	65.5	67.2	66.3
Employment in industry (% of employed) [d]	9.2	7.1	6.5
Employment in services & other sectors (% employed) [d]	25.2	25.7	27.2
Unemployment rate (% of labour force) [d]	5.2	5.3	5.0
Labour force participation rate (female/male pop. %) [d]	77.3 / 88.4	77.8 / 89.2	78.2 / 89.0
CPI: Consumer Price Index (2010=100)	100	106	106 [a]
Agricultural production index (2004-2006=100)	98	96	100 [e]
International trade: exports (million current US$)	3 199	3 411	4 279 [b]
International trade: imports (million current US$)	5 852	6 053	4 787 [b]
International trade: balance (million current US$)	- 2 653	- 2 642	- 508 [b]
Balance of payments, current account (million US$)	- 1 444	- 1 678	- 308 [a]

Major trading partners					2019
Export partners (% of exports)	South Africa	49.2	United Arab Emirates	19.5	Areas nes [f] 16.7
Import partners (% of imports)	South Africa	38.7	Singapore	25.2	China 8.6

Social indicators	2010	2015	2020
Population growth rate (average annual %) [g]	1.0	1.7	1.5
Urban population (% of total population)	33.2	32.4	32.2 [b]
Urban population growth rate (average annual %) [g]	1.2	1.8	...
Fertility rate, total (live births per woman) [g]	3.9	4.1	3.6
Life expectancy at birth (females/males, years) [g]	46.7 / 43.3	58.3 / 54.9	62.2 / 59.2
Population age distribution (0-14/60+ years old, %)	41.6 / 4.4	42.6 / 4.4	41.9 / 4.6
International migrant stock (000/% of total pop.) [h]	398.3 / 3.1	400.5 / 2.9	411.3 / 2.8 [b]
Refugees and others of concern to the UNHCR (000)	4.9 [i]	308.1	20.8 [j,b]
Infant mortality rate (per 1 000 live births) [g]	62.7	51.2	38.7
Health: Current expenditure (% of GDP)	10.7	7.5	6.6 [a]
Health: Physicians (per 1 000 pop.)	0.1	0.2	0.2 [c]
Education: Government expenditure (% of GDP)	1.5	6.1 [k]	...
Education: Primary gross enrol. ratio (f/m per 100 pop.)	... / ...	108.7 / 111.1 [l]	... / ...
Education: Secondary gross enrol. ratio (f/m per 100 pop.)	... / ...	51.3 / 53.5 [l]	... / ...
Education: Tertiary gross enrol. ratio (f/m per 100 pop.)	5.7 / 7.8	9.2 / 10.9	... / ...
Intentional homicide rate (per 100 000 pop.)	5.6	7.5 [m]	...
Seats held by women in the National Parliament (%)	15.0	31.5	31.8 [n]

Environment and infrastructure indicators	2010	2015	2020
Individuals using the Internet (per 100 inhabitants) [d]	6.4	22.7	27.1 [a]
Threatened species (number)	55	60	122
Forested area (% of land area) [d]	40.4	36.4	36.4 [a]
CO2 emission estimates (million tons/tons per capita)	9.5 / 0.7	11.8 / 0.7	9.7 / 0.6 [a]
Energy production, primary (Petajoules)	369	450	427 [a]
Energy supply per capita (Gigajoules)	31	34	33 [a]
Tourist/visitor arrivals at national borders (000)	2 239	2 057	2 580 [c]
Important sites for terrestrial biodiversity protected (%)	76.1	81.2	81.2 [b]
Pop. using safely managed sanitation (urban/rural %)	19.8 / ...	17.3 / ...	16.3 / ... [a]
Net Official Development Assist. received (% of GNI)	6.71	4.38	2.57 [c]

a 2017. **b** 2019. **c** 2018. **d** Estimate. **e** 2016. **f** Areas not elsewhere specified. **g** Data refers to a 5-year period preceding the reference year. **h** Including refugees. **i** Data as at the end of December. **j** A study is being pursued to provide a revised estimate of statelessness figure. **k** 2014. **l** 2013. **m** 2012. **n** Data are as at 1 January of reporting year.

Below are brief descriptions of the indicators presented in the world, regional and country profiles. The terms are arranged in alphabetical order.

Agricultural production index is calculated by the Laspeyres formula based on the sum of price-weighted quantities of different agricultural commodities produced. The commodities covered in the computation of indices of agricultural production are all crops and livestock products originating in each country. Practically all products are covered, with the main exception of fodder crops. Production quantities of each commodity are weighted by the average international commodity prices in the base period and summed for each year. To obtain the index, the aggregate for a given year is divided by the average aggregate for the base period 2004-2006. Indices are calculated without any deductions for feed and seed and are referred to as "gross" by the Food and Agriculture Organization of the United Nations (FAO).
Source of the data: Food and Agriculture Organization of the United Nations (FAO), Rome, FAOSTAT database, last accessed May 2018.

Balance of payments is a statement summarizing the economic transactions between the residents of a country and non-residents during a specific period, usually a year. It includes transactions in goods, services, income, transfers and financial assets and liabilities. Generally, the balance of payments is divided into two major components: the current account and the capital and financial account. The data on balance of payments correspond to the current account category. The current account is a record of all transactions in the balance of payments covering the exports and imports of goods and services, payments of income, and current transfers between residents of a country and non-residents.
Source of the data: International Monetary Fund (IMF), Washington, D.C., Balance of Payment (BOP) Statistics database, last accessed June 2020.

Capital city and capital city population is the designation of any specific city as a capital city as reported by the country or area. The city can be the seat of the government as determined by the country. Some countries designate more than one city to be a capital city with a specific title function (e.g., administrative and/or legislative capital). The data refer to the year 2020, unless otherwise stated in a footnote.
Source of the data: United Nations Population Division (UNPD), New York, "World Urbanization Prospects (WUP): The 2018 Revision", last accessed May 2018.

CO$_2$ emission estimates represent total CO2 emissions from fuel combustion. This includes CO2 emissions from fuel combustion in IPCC Source/Sink Category 1 A Fuel Combustion Activities and those which may be reallocated to IPCC Source/Sink Category 2 Industrial Processes and Product Use under the 2006 GLs.
Source of the data: International Energy Agency, CO2 Emissions from Fuel Combustion 2019 Highlights, last accessed June 2020.

Technical notes (*continued*)

CPI: Consumer price index measures the period-to-period proportional change in the prices of a fixed set of consumer goods and services of constant quantity and characteristics, acquired, used or paid for by the reference population. The index is constructed as a weighted average of a large number of elementary aggregate indices. Each of the elementary aggregate indices is estimated using a sample of prices for a defined set of goods and services obtained in, or by residents of, a specific region from a given set of outlets or other sources of consumption. The indices here generally refer to "all items" and to the country as a whole, unless otherwise stated in a footnote.
Source of the data: United Nations Statistics Division (UNSD), New York, Monthly Bulletin of Statistics (MBS), last accessed June 2020.

Economy: agriculture, industry and services and other activity presents the shares of the components of Gross Value Added (GVA) at current prices by kind of economic activity; agriculture (agriculture, hunting, forestry and fishing), industry (mining and quarrying, manufacturing, electricity, gas and water supply; and construction) and in services and other sectors based on the sections of the International Standard Industrial Classification of All Economic Activities (ISIC), Revision 3, unless a different revision is stated in a footnote.
Source of the data: United Nations Statistics Division (UNSD), New York, National Accounts Statistics: Analysis of Main Aggregates (AMA) database, last accessed June 2020.

Education: Government expenditure shows the trends in general government expenditures for educational affairs and services at pre-primary, primary, secondary and tertiary levels and subsidiary services to education, expressed as a percentage of the gross domestic product.
Source of the data: United Nations Educational, Scientific and Cultural Organization (UNESCO), Montreal, the UNESCO Institute for Statistics (UIS) statistics database, last accessed May 2020.

Education: Primary, secondary and tertiary gross enrolment ratio is the total enrolment in the primary, secondary and tertiary levels of education, regardless of age, expressed as a percentage of the eligible official school-age population corresponding to the same level of education in a given school year. Education at the primary level provides the basic elements of education (e.g. at elementary school or primary school). Education at the secondary level is provided at middle school, secondary school, high school, teacher-training school at this level and schools of vocational or technical nature. Education at the tertiary level is that which is provided at university, teachers' college, higher professional school, and which requires, as minimum condition of admission, the successful completion of education at the second level, or evidence of the attainment of an equivalent level of knowledge. Enrolment is measured at the beginning of the school or academic year. The gro

Technical notes (*continued*)

enrolment ratio at each level will include all pupils whatever their ages, whereas the population is limited to the range of official school ages. Therefore, for countries with almost universal education among the school-age population, the gross enrolment ratio can exceed 100 if the actual age distribution of pupils extends beyond the official school ages.

Source of the data: *United Nations Educational, Scientific and Cultural Organization (UNESCO), Montreal, the UNESCO Institute for Statistics (UIS) statistics database, last accessed May 2020.*

Employment in agricultural, industrial and services and other sectors: The "employed" comprise all persons above a specified age who, during a specified brief period, either one week or one day, were in "paid employment" or in "self-employment", see ILO's Current International Recommendations on Labour Statistics. The data refer to those 15 years and over, unless otherwise stated in a footnote, who perform any work at all in the reference period, for pay or profit in agriculture (agriculture, forestry and fishing), industry (mining and quarrying; manufacturing; electricity, gas, steam and air conditioning supply; water supply, sewerage, waste management and remediation activities; and construction) and in services and other sectors based on the sections of the International Standard Industrial Classification of All Economic Activities (ISIC), Revision 4, unless an earlier revision is stated in a footnote.

Source of the data: *International Labour Organization (ILO), Geneva, Key Indicators of the Labour Market (KILM 9th edition) and the ILOSTAT database, last accessed January 2020.*

Energy production, primary, is the capture or extraction of fuels or energy from natural energy flows, the biosphere and natural reserves of fossil fuels within the national territory in a form suitable for use. Inert matter removed from the extracted fuels and quantities reinjected, flared or vented are not included. The resulting products are referred to as "primary" products. It excludes secondary production, that is, the manufacture of energy products through the process of transforming primary and/or other secondary fuels or energy. Data are provided in a common energy unit (Petajoule) and refer to the following primary energy sources: hard coal, brown coal, peat, oil shale, conventional crude oil, natural gas liquids (NGL), other hydrocarbons, additives and oxygenates, natural gas, fuelwood, wood residues and by-products, bagasse, animal waste, black liquor, other vegetal material and residues, biogasoline, biodiesels, bio jet kerosene, other liquid biofuels, biogases, industrial waste, municipal waste, nuclear, solar photovoltaic, solar thermal, hydro, wind, geothermal, and tide, wave and other marine sources. Peat, biomass and wastes are included only when the production is for energy purposes. See International Recommendations for Energy Statistics (2011) and the UN publication Energy Balances for a complete description of the methodology.

Source of the data: *United Nations Statistics Division (UNSD), New York, Energy Statistics Yearbook 2017, last accessed February 2020.*

Technical notes (*continued*)

Energy supply per capita is defined as primary energy production plus imports minus exports minus international marine bunkers minus international aviation bunkers minus stock changes. For imports, exports, international bunkers and stock changes, it includes secondary energy products, in addition to primary products.

Source of the data: United Nations Statistics Division (UNSD), New York, Energy Statistics Yearbook 2017, last accessed January 2020.

Exchange rate in units of national currency per US dollar refers to end-of-period quotations. The exchange rates are classified into broad categories, reflecting both the role of the authorities in the determination of the exchange and/or the multiplicity of exchange rates in a country. The market rate is used to describe exchange rates determined largely by market forces; the official rate is an exchange rate determined by the authorities, sometimes in a flexible manner. For countries maintaining multiple exchange arrangements, the rates are labelled principal rate, secondary rate, and tertiary rate.

Source of the data: International Monetary Fund (IMF), Washington, D.C., the International Financial Statistics (IFS) database supplemented by United Nations Department of Management (DM), UN Treasury operational rates of exchange, last accessed June 2020.

Fertility rate is the total fertility rate, a widely used summary indicator of fertility. It refers to the number of children that would be born per woman, assuming no female mortality at child bearing ages and the age-specific fertility rates of a specified country and reference period. The data are an average over five-year ranges; 2005-2010 data are labelled "2010", 2010-2015 data are labelled "2015" and 2015-2020 data are labelled "2020", unless otherwise stated in a footnote.

Source of the data: United Nations Population Division (UNPD), New York, "World Population Prospects (WPP): The 2019 Revision"; supplemented by data from the United Nations Statistics Division (UNSD), New York, Demographic Yearbook 2015 and the Pacific Community (SPC) Statistics and Demography Programme for small countries or areas, last accessed June 2019.

Forested area refers to the percentage of land area occupied by forest. Forest is defined in the Food and Agriculture Organization's Global Forest Resources Assessment as land spanning more than 0.5 hectares with trees higher than 5 metres and a canopy cover of more than 10 percent, or trees able to reach these thresholds in situ. It does not include land that is predominantly under agricultural or urban land use. Data are calculated from the forest estimates divided by the land area.

Source of the data: Food and Agriculture Organization of the United Nations (FAO), Rome, FAOSTAT database, last accessed January 2020.

GDP: Gross domestic product is an aggregate measure of production equal to the sum of gross value added of all resident producer units plus that part (possibly the total) of taxes on products, less subsidies on products, that is not included in the valuation of output. It is also equal to the sum of the final uses of goods and services (all uses except intermediate consumption) measured at purchasers' prices, less the value of imports of goods and services, and equal to the sum of primary incomes distributed by resident producer units (see System of National Accounts 2008). The data are in current United States (US) dollars and are estimates of the total production of goods and services of the countries represented in economic terms, not as a measure of the standard of living of their inhabitants. To have comparable coverage for as many countries as possible, these US dollar estimates are based on official GDP data in national currency, supplemented by national currency estimates prepared by the Statistics Division using additional data from national and international sources. The estimates given here are in most cases those accepted by the United Nations General Assembly's Committee on Contributions for determining United Nations members' contributions to the United Nations regular budget. The exchange rates for the conversion of GDP national currency data into US dollars are the average market rates published by the International Monetary Fund, in International Financial Statistics (IFS). Official exchange rates are used only when free market rates are not available. For non-members of the Fund, the conversion rates used are the average of UN Treasury rates of exchange. It should be noted that the conversion from local currency into US dollars introduces deficiencies in comparability over time and among countries which should be considered when using the data. For example, comparability over time is distorted when exchange rate fluctuations differ substantially from domestic inflation rates.

Source of the data: United Nations Statistics Division (UNSD), New York, National Accounts Statistics: Analysis of Main Aggregates (AMA) database, last accessed January 2020.

GDP growth rate is derived on the basis of constant 2010 price series in national currency. The figures are computed as the geometric mean of annual rates of growth expressed in percentages.

Source of the data: United Nations Statistics Division (UNSD), New York, National Accounts Statistics: Analysis of Main Aggregates (AMA) database, last accessed January 2020.

GDP per capita estimates are the value of all goods and services produced in the economy divided by the population.

Source of the data: United Nations Statistics Division (UNSD), New York, National Accounts Statistics: Analysis of Main Aggregates (AMA) database, last accessed January 2020.

Health: Physicians includes generalist medical practitioners and specialist medical practitioners, expressed as the number of physicians per 1 000 population. The classification of health workers used is based on criteria for vocational education and training, regulation of health professions, and activities and tasks of jobs, i.e. a framework for categorizing key workforce variables according to shared characteristics.

Source of the data: World Health Organisation (WHO), Geneva, WHO Global Health Workforce statistics database, last accessed January 2020.

Health: Current expenditure refers to all health care goods and services used or consumed during a year excluding capital spending, or rather "gross capital formation", which is the purchase of new assets used repeatedly over several years. These estimates are in line with the 2011 System of Health Accounts (SHA). Current expenditure is expressed as a proportion of Gross Domestic Product (GDP).

Source of the data: World Health Organization (WHO), Geneva, WHO Global Health Expenditure database, last accessed January 2020.

Important sites for terrestrial biodiversity protected shows land which contributes significantly to the global persistence of biodiversity measured as a proportion of which is wholly covered by a designated protected area. Data are based on spatial overlap between polygons for Key Biodiversity Areas from the World Database of key Biodiversity Areas and polygons for protected areas from the World Database on Protected Areas. Figures for each region are calculated as the proportion of each Key Biodiversity Area covered by protected areas, averaged (i.e. calculated as the mean) across all Key Biodiversity Areas within the region.

Source of the data: United Nations Environment Programme (UNEP) World Conservation Monitoring Centre (WCMC), Cambridge, Sustainable Development Goals (SDGs) statistics database, last accessed March 2020.

Individuals using the Internet refer to the percentage of people who used the Internet from any location and for any purpose, irrespective of the device and network used. It can be via a computer (i.e. desktop or laptop computer, tablet or similar handheld computer), mobile phone, games machine, digital TV, etc. Access can be via a fixed or mobile network. There are certain data limits to this indicator, insofar as estimates have to be calculated for many developing countries which do not yet collect information and communications technology household statistics.

Source of the data: International Telecommunication Union (ITU), Geneva, the ITU database, last accessed January 2020.

Infant mortality rate is the ratio of infant deaths (the deaths of children under one year of age) in a given year to the total number of live births in the same year expressed as a rate per 1 000 live births. The data are an average over five-year ranges; 2005-2010 data are labelled "2010", 2010-2015 data are labelled "2015" and 2015-2020 data are labelled "2020", unless otherwise stated in footnote.

Source of the data: United Nations Population Division (UNPD), New York, "World Population Prospects (WPP): The 2019 Revision"; supplemented by data from the United Nations Statistics Division (UNSD), New York, Demographic Yearbook 2015 *and the Pacific Community (SPC) Statistics and Demography Programme for small countries or areas, last accessed June 2019.*

Intentional homicide rate: The rates are the annual number of unlawful deaths purposefully inflicted on a person by another person, reported for the year per 100 000. For most countries, country information on causes of death is not available for most causes. Estimates are therefore based on cause of death modelling and death registration data from other countries in the region. Further country-level information and data on specific causes was also used.

Source of the data: United Nations Office on Drugs and Crime (UNODC), Vienna, UNODC Statistics database, last accessed June 2020.

International migrant stock generally represents the number of persons born in a country other than that in which they live. When information on country of birth was not recorded, data on the number of persons having foreign citizenship was used instead. In the absence of any empirical data, estimates were imputed. Data refer to mid-year. Figures for international migrant stock as a percentage of the population are the outcome of dividing the estimated international migrant stock by the estimated total population and multiplying the result by 100.

Source of the data: United Nations Population Division (UNPD), New York, "International migrant stock: The 2019 Revision", last accessed January 2020.

International trade: Exports, imports and balance show the movement of goods out of and into a country. Goods simply being transported through a country (goods in transit) or temporarily admitted (except for goods for inward processing) do not add to the stock of material resources of a country and are not included in the international merchandise trade statistics. In the "general trade system", the definition of the statistical territory of a country coincides with its economic territory. In the "special trade system", the definition of the statistical territory comprises only a particular part of the economic territory, mainly that part which coincides with the free circulation area for goods. "The free circulation area" is a part of the economic territory of a country within which goods "may be disposed of without Customs restrictions". In the case of exports, the transaction value is the value at which the goods were sold by the exporter, including the cost of transportation and insurance, to bring the goods onto the transporting vehicle at the frontier of the exporting country (an FOB-type valuation). In the case of imports, the transaction value is the value at which the goods were purchased by the importer plus the cost of transportation and insurance to the frontier of the importing country (a CIF-type valuation). Both imports and exports are shown in United States dollars. Conversion from national currencies is made by means of currency conversion factors based on official exchange rates (par values or weighted averages). All regional aggregations are calculated as the sum of their components.

Source of the data: United Nations Statistics Division (UNSD), New York, Commodity Trade Statistics Database (UN COMTRADE), last accessed June 2020.

Technical notes (*continued*)

Labour force participation rate is calculated by expressing the number of persons in the labour force as a percentage of the working-age population. The labour force is the sum of the number of persons employed and the number of unemployed (see ILO's current International Recommendations on Labour Statistics). The working-age population is the population above a certain age, prescribed for the measurement of economic characteristics. The data refer to the age group of 15 years and over and are based on ILO's modelled estimates, unless otherwise stated in a footnote.

Source of the data: International Labour Organization (ILO), Geneva, Key Indicators of the Labour Market (KILM 9th edition) and the ILOSTAT database, last accessed January 2020.

Life expectancy at birth is the average number of years of life at birth (age 0) for males and females according to the expected mortality rates by age estimated for the reference year and population. The data are an average over five-year ranges; 2005-2010 data are labelled "2010", 2010-2015 data are labelled "2015" and 2015-2020 data are labelled "2020", unless otherwise stated in a footnote.

Source of the data: United Nations Population Division (UNPD), New York, "World Population Prospects (WPP): The 2019 Revision"; supplemented by data from the United Nations Statistics Division (UNSD), New York, Demographic Yearbook 2015 and the Pacific Community (SPC) Statistics and Demography Programme for small countries or areas, last accessed June 2019.

Major trading partners show the three largest trade partners (countries of last known destination and origin or consignment) in international merchandise trade transactions. In some cases a special partner is shown (i.e. Areas nes, bunkers, etc.) instead of a country and refers to one of the following special categories. Areas not elsewhere specified (i.e. Areas nes) is used (a) for low value trade, (b) if the partner designation was unknown to the country or if an error was made in the partner assignment and (c) for reasons of confidentiality. If a specific geographical location can be identified within Areas nes, then they are recorded accordingly (i.e. Asia nes). Bunkers are ship stores and aircraft supplies, which consists mostly of fuels and food. Free zones belong to the geographical and economic territory of a country but not to its customs territory. For the purposes of trade statistics, the transactions between the customs territory and the free zones are recorded, if the reporting country uses the Special Trade System. Free zones can be commercial free zones (duty free shops or industrial free zones. Data are expressed as percentages of total exports and of total imports of the country, area or special partner.

Source of the data: United Nations Statistics Division (UNSD), New York, Commodity Trade Statistics Database (UN COMTRADE), last accessed June 2020.

National currency refers to those notes and coins in circulation that are commonly used to make payments. The official currency names and the ISO currency codes are those officially in use, and may be subject to change.

Technical notes (*continued*)

Source of the data: International Organisation for Standardization (ISO), Geneva, Currency Code Services – ISO 4217 Maintenance Agency, last accessed May 2018.

Net Official Development Assistance received or disbursed is defined as those flows to developing countries and multilateral institutions provided by official agencies, including state and local governments, or by their executive agencies, each transaction of which meets the following tests: i) it is administered with the promotion of the economic development and welfare of developing countries as its main objective; and ii) it is concessional in character and conveys a grant element of at least 25 per cent. It is expressed as a percentage of Gross National Income of either the donor or recipient. The multilateral institutions include the World Bank Group, regional banks, financial institutions of the European Union and a number of United Nations institutions, programmes and trust funds.

Source of the data: Organisation for Economic Co-operation and Development (OECD), Paris, the OECD Development Assistance Committee (DAC) statistics database, last accessed June 2020.

Population refers to the medium fertility projected de facto population as of 1 July 2020, unless otherwise stated in a footnote. The total population of a country may comprise either all usual residents of the country (de jure population) or all persons present in the country (de facto population) at the time of the census; for purposes of international comparisons, the de facto definition is used, unless otherwise stated in a footnote.

Source of the data: United Nations Population Division (UNPD), New York, "World Population Prospects (WPP): The 2019 Revision", last accessed June 2019.

Population age distribution refers to the percentage of the population aged 0-14 years and aged 60 years and older at the mid-year unless otherwise stated in a footnote.

Source of the data: United Nations Population Division (UNPD), New York, "World Population Prospects (WPP): The 2019 Revision"; supplemented by data from the United Nations Statistics Division (UNSD), New York, Demographic Yearbook 2015 and the Pacific Community (SPC) Statistics and Demography Programme for small countries or areas, last accessed June 2019.

Population density refers to the medium fertility projected population as of 1 July 2020 per square kilometre of surface area, unless otherwise stated in a footnote.

Source of the data: United Nations Population Division (UNPD), New York, "World Population Prospects (WPP): The 2019 Revision", last accessed June 2019.

Population growth rate is the average annual percentage change in total population size. The data are an average over five-year ranges; 2010-2015 data are labelled "2010", 2010-2015 data are labelled "2015" and 2015-2020 data are labelled "2020", unless otherwise stated in a footnote.

Technical notes (*continued*)

Source of the data: United Nations Population Division (UNPD), New York, "World Population Prospects (WPP): The 2019 Revision", last accessed June 2019.

Refugees and others of concern to the UNHCR: The 1951 United Nations Convention relating to the Status of Refugees states that a refugee is someone who, owing to a well-founded fear of being persecuted for reasons of race, religion, nationality, political opinion or membership in a particular social group, is outside the country of his or her nationality and is unable to, or owing to such fear, is unwilling to avail himself or herself of the protection of that country; or who, not having a nationality and being outside the country of his or her former habitual residence, is unable or, owing to such fear, unwilling to return to it. In this series, refugees refer to persons granted a humanitarian status and/or those granted temporary protection. Included are persons who have been granted temporary protection on a group basis. The series also includes returned refugees, asylum-seekers, stateless persons and persons displaced internally within their own country and others of concern to UNHCR.

Source of the data: United Nations High Commissioner for Refugees (UNHCR), Geneva, UNHCR population statistics database, last accessed March 2020.

Region is based on macro geographical regions arranged according to continents and component geographical regions used for statistical purposes as at 31 July 2017.

Source of the data: United Nations Statistics Division (UNSD), New York, Statistical Yearbook 2017 edition (60th issue) Annex I - Country and area nomenclature, regional and other groupings (based on Series M49: Standard Country or Area codes and Geographical Regions for Statistical Use), last accessed October 2017.

Research & Development expenditure refers to expenditure on creative work undertaken on a systematic basis in order to increase the stock of knowledge, including knowledge of humanity, culture and society, and the use of this stock of knowledge to devise new applications, expressed as a percentage of Gross Domestic Product (GDP). It is the total intramural expenditure on R&D performed on the national territory during a given period. It includes R&D performed within a country and funded from abroad but excludes payments made abroad for R&D.

Source of the data: United Nations Educational, Scientific and Cultural Organization (UNESCO), Montreal, the UNESCO Institute for Statistics (UIS) statistics database, last accessed June 2020.

Safely managed water and sanitation: population using safely managed drinking water sources is currently being measured by the proportion of population in urban and rural areas, according to national definitions, meeting the criteria for using safely managed drinking water sources (SDG 6.1.1) by using an improved basic drinking water source which is located on premises, available when needed and free of faecal and priority chemical contamination. Improved drinking water sources are those that have the potential to deliver safe water by nature of their design and construction

Technical notes (*continued*)

and include: piped water, boreholes or tubewells, protected dug wells, protected springs, rainwater, and packaged or delivered water. Population using safely managed sanitation facilities is currently being measured by the proportion of the population in urban and rural areas, according to national definitions, meeting the criteria for having a safely managed sanitation service (SDG 6.2.1a) by using a basic sanitation facility which is not shared with other households and where excreta is safely disposed in situ or transported and treated off-site. Improved sanitation facilities are those designed to hygienically separate excreta from human contact, and include: flush/pour flush to piped sewer system, septic tanks or pit latrines; ventilated improved pit latrines, composting toilets or pit latrines with slabs.

Source of the data: World Health Organization (WHO) and the United Nations Children's Fund (UNICEF), Geneva and New York, the WHO/UNICEF Joint Monitoring Programme (JMP) for Water and Sanitation database, last accessed July 2019.

Seats held by women in the National Parliament refer to the number of women in the lower chamber of the National Parliament expressed as a percentage of total occupied seats in the lower or single House, situation as of 1 January 2020.

Source of the data: Inter-Parliamentary Union (IPU), Geneva, Women in National Parliament dataset and the Sustainable Development Goals (SDGs) statistics database, last accessed March 2020.

Sex ratio is calculated as the ratio of the medium fertility projected population of men to that of 100 women as of 1 July 2020, unless otherwise stated in a footnote.

Source of the data: United Nations Population Division (UNPD), New York, "World Population Prospects (WPP): The 2019 Revision"; supplemented by data from the United Nations Statistics Division (UNSD), New York, Demographic Yearbook 2015 and the Pacific Community (SPC) Statistics and Demography Programme for small countries or areas, last accessed June 2019.

Surface area refers to land area plus inland water, unless otherwise stated in a footnote.

Source of the data: United Nations Statistics Division (UNSD), New York, Demographic Yearbook 2017 and the demographic statistics database, last accessed June 2019.

Threatened species represents the number of plants and animals that are most in need of conservation attention and are compiled by the World Conservation Union IUCN/ Species Survival Commission (SSC).

Source of the data: International Union for Conservation of Nature (IUCN), Gland and Cambridge, IUCN Red List of Threatened Species publication, last accessed June 2020.

Technical notes (*continued*)

Tourist/visitor arrivals at national borders is any person who travels to a country other than that in which he or she has his or her usual residence but outside his/her usual environment for a period not exceeding 12 months and whose main purpose of visit is other than the exercise of an activity remunerated from with the country visited, and who stays at least one night in a collective or private accommodation in the country visited (see Recommendations on Tourism Statistics of the United Nations and the World Tourism Organization). The data refer to arrivals of non-resident tourists at national borders, unless otherwise stated in a footnote.
Source of the data: World Tourism Organization (UNWTO), Madrid, the UNWTO statistics database, last accessed January 2020.

UN membership date: The United Nations (UN) is an intergovernmental organization whose members are the countries of the world. Currently there are 193 Member States of the United Nations, some of which joined the UN by signing and ratifying the Charter of the United Nations in 1945; the other countries joined the UN later, through the adoption of a resolution admitting them to membership. The process usually follows these steps: first, the country applies for membership and makes a declaration accepting the obligations of the Charter; second, the Security Council adopts a resolution recommending that the General Assembly admit the country to membership and finally the General Assembly adopts a resolution admitting the country.
Source of the data: United Nations (UN), Department of Public Information (DPI), News and Media Division, New York, Member states and date of admission, last accessed May 2018.

Unemployment refers to persons above a specified age who during a specified reference period were: "without work", i.e. were not in paid employment or self-employment as defined under employment; "currently available for work", i.e. were available for paid employment or self-employment during the reference period; and "seeking work", i.e. had taken specific steps in a specified recent period to seek paid employment or self-employment (see ILO's current International Recommendations on Labour Statistics). The data refer to the 15 years and over age group and are based on ILO's modelled estimates, unless otherwise stated in a footnote.
Source of the data: International Labour Organization (ILO), Geneva, Key Indicators of the Labour Market (KILM 9th edition) and the ILOSTAT database, last accessed January 2020.

Urban population is based on the number of persons at the mid-year defined a urban according to national definitions of this concept. In most cases these definitions are those used in the most recent population census.
Source of the data: United Nations Population Division (UNPD), New York, "World Urbanization Prospects (WUP): The 2018 Revision", last accessed May 2018.

Urban population growth rate is based on the number of persons defined as urban according to national definitions of this concept. In most cases these definitions are those used in the most recent population census. The data are an average over five-year ranges; 2005-2010 data are labelled "2010", 2010-2015 data are labelled "2015" and 2015-2020 data are labelled "2020", unless otherwise stated in a footnote.

Source of the data: United Nations Population Division (UNPD), New York, "World Urbanization Prospects (WUP): The 2018 Revision", last accessed May 2018.

Statistical sources and references

Statistical sources

Food and Agriculture Organization of the United Nations (FAO), Rome, FAOSTAT database, available at http://www.fao.org/faostat/en/#home.

International Energy Agency (IEA), Paris, available at https://www.iea.org/data-and-statistics?country=WORLD&fuel=Energy supply&indicator=Total primary energy supply (TPES) by source

International Labour Organization (ILO), Geneva, the ILOSTAT database, available at http://www.ilo.org/ilostat.
_____, *Key Indicators of the Labour Market (KILM 9th edition), available at http://www.ilo.org/global/statistics-and-databases/research-and-databases/kilm/lang--en/index.htm.*

International Monetary Fund (IMF), Washington, D.C., Balance of Payment (BOP) Statistics database, available at http://data.imf.org/bop.
_____, *the International Financial Statistics (IFS) database, available at http://data.imf.org/ifs.*

International Organisation for Standardization (ISO), Geneva, Currency Code Services – ISO 4217 Maintenance Agency, available at https://www.iso.org/iso-4217-currency-codes.html.

International Telecommunication Union (ITU), Geneva, the ITU Database, available at http://www.itu.int/en/ITU-D/statistics/Pages/default.aspx.

International Union for Conservation of Nature (IUCN), Gland and Cambridge, IUCN Red List of Threatened Species publication, available at http://www.iucnredlist.org/about/summary-statistics.

Inter-Parliamentary Union (IPU), Geneva, Women in National Parliament dataset, available at https://data.ipu.org/women-ranking.

Organisation for Economic Co-operation and Development (OECD), Paris, the OECD Development Assistance Committee (DAC) statistics database, available at http://stats.oecd.org/.

Pacific Community (SPC) Statistics and Demography Programme, Nouméa, Population and demographic indicators, available at http://sdd.spc.int/en/.

United Nations (UN), Department of Economic and Social Affairs (DESA), Population Division (UNPD), New York, "International migrant stock: The 2019 Revision", available at http://www.un.org/en/development/desa/population/migration/data/index.shtml.
_____, *"World Population Prospects (WPP): The 2019 Revision", available at https://esa.un.org/unpd/wpp/.*
_____, *"World Urbanization Prospects (WUP): The 2018 Revision", available at https://esa.un.org/unpd/wup/.*

Statistical sources and references (*continued*)

United Nations (UN), Department of Economic and Social Affairs (DESA), Statistics Division (UNSD), New York, Commodity Trade statistics database (UN COMTRADE), available at https://comtrade.un.org/.

_____, Demographic Yearbook (Series R, United Nations publication), available at https://unstats.un.org/unsd/demographic-social/products/dyb/.

_____, Energy Statistics Yearbook (Series J, United Nations publication), available at http://unstats.un.org/unsd/energy/yearbook/default.htm.

_____, Monthly Bulletin of Statistics (Series Q, United Nations publication), available at http://unstats.un.org/unsd/mbs/.

_____, National Accounts Statistics: Analysis of Main Aggregates (AMA) database (Series X, United Nations publication), available at http://unstats.un.org/unsd/snaama/introduction.asp.

_____, Statistical Yearbook (Series S, United Nations publication), available at https://unstats.un.org/unsd/publications/statistical-yearbook/.

_____, Sustainable Development Goals (SDGs) statistics database, available at https://unstats.un.org/sdgs/indicators/database.

United Nations (UN), Department of Management (DM), Office of Programme Planning, Budget and Accounts (OPPBA), New York, UN Treasury operational rates of exchange, available at https://treasury.un.org/operationalrates/OperationalRates.php

United Nations (UN), Department of Public Information (DPI), News and Media Division, New York, Member states and date of admission, available at http://www.un.org/en/member-states/index.html.

United Nations Educational, Scientific and Cultural Organization (UNESCO), Montreal, the UNESCO Institute for Statistics (UIS) statistics database, available at http://data.uis.unesco.org/.

United Nations High Commissioner for Refugees (UNHCR), Geneva, UNHCR population statistics database, available at http://popstats.unhcr.org

United Nations Office on Drugs and Crime (UNODC), Vienna, UNODC Statistics database, available at https://data.unodc.org/.

World Health Organization (WHO) and the United Nations Children's Fund (UNICEF), Geneva and New York, the WHO/UNICEF Joint Monitoring Programme (JMP) for Water and Sanitation database, available at https://washdata.org/monitoring/sanitation.

World Health Organization (WHO), Geneva, WHO Global Health Expenditure database, available at http://apps.who.int/nha/database.

_____, WHO Global Health Workforce statistics database, available at http://www.who.int/hrh/statistics/hwfstats/en/.

World Tourism Organization (UNWTO), Madrid, the UNWTO statistics database, available at http://www.e-unwto.org/loi/unwtotfb.

References

Food and Agriculture Organization of the United Nations (2015). Global Forest Resources Assessment 2015, available at http://www.fao.org/forest-resources-assessment/en/.

International Labour Organization (2000). Current International Recommendations on Labour Statistics, 2000 Edition, available at http://www.ilo.org/global/publications/ilo-bookstore/order-online/books/WCMS_PUBL_9221108465_EN/lang--en/index.htm.

International Monetary Fund (2009). Balance of Payments and International Investment Position Manual, Sixth Edition, available at https://www.imf.org/external/pubs/ft/bop/2007/bopman6.htm.

United Nations (1951 and 1967). Convention relating to the Status of Refugees of 1951 (United Nations, Treaty Series, vol. 189 (1954), No. 2545, p. 137), art. 1) and Protocol relating to the Status of Refugees of 1967 (United Nations, Treaty Series, vol. 606 (1967), No. 8791, p. 267), available at https://treaties.un.org/doc/Publication/UNTS/Volume%20189/volume-189-I-2545-English.pdf and https://treaties.un.org/doc/Publication/UNTS/Volume%20606/volume-606-I-8791-English.pdf.

United Nations (1982). Concepts and Methods in Energy Statistics, with Special Reference to Energy Accounts and Balances: A Technical Report. Statistical Office, Series F, No. 29 and Corr. 1 (United Nations publication, Sales No. E.82.XVII.13 and corrigendum), available at http://unstats.un.org/unsd/publication/SeriesF/SeriesF_29E.pdf.

United Nations (2008). International Standard Industrial Classification of All Economic Activities (ISIC), Rev. 4. Statistics Division, Series M, No. 4, Rev.4 (United Nations publication, Sales No. E.08.XVII.25), available at http://unstats.un.org/unsd/publication/SeriesM/seriesm_4rev4e.pdf.

United Nations (2008). Principles and Recommendations for Population and Housing Censuses Rev. 2. Statistics Division, Series M, No. 67, Rev. 2 (United Nations publication, Sales No. E.07.XVII.8), available at http://unstats.un.org/unsd/publication/SeriesM/Seriesm_67rev2e.pdf.

United Nations (2010). International Merchandise Trade Statistics: Concepts and Definitions, Statistics Division, Series M, No.52, Rev.3, (United Nations publication, Sales No. E.10.XVII.13), available at http://unstats.un.org/unsd/publication/SeriesM/SeriesM_52rev3E.pdf.

United Nations (2011). International Recommendations for Energy Statistics (IRES), Statistics Division, available at http://unstats.un.org/unsd/statcom/doc11/BG-IRES.pdf.

Statistical sources and references (*continued*)

United Nations (2013). International Merchandise Trade Statistics: Compilers Manual Revision 1 (IMTS 2010-CM), Statistics Division , Series F, No. 87, Rev.1 (United Nations publication, Sales No. E.13.XVII.8), available at https://unstats.un.org/unsd/trade/publications/seriesf_87Rev1_e_cover.pdf.

United Nations (2018). Standard Country or Area Codes for Statistical Use, Statistics Division, Series M, No. 49, available at http://unstats.un.org/unsd/methods/m49/m49.htm

United Nations, European Commission, International Monetary Fund, Organisation for Economic Cooperation and Development and World Bank (2009). System of National Accounts 2008, Statistics Division, Series M, No. 2, Rev.5 (United Nations publication, Sales No. E.08.XVII.29), available at http://unstats.un.org/unsd/nationalaccount/sna2008.asp.

World Health Organization (2007). International Statistical Classification of Diseases and Related Health Problems, Tenth Revision (ICD-10), (Geneva) available at http://www.who.int/classifications/icd/en/.

United Nations and World Tourism Organization (2008). International Recommendations for Tourism Statistics 2008, Statistics Division, Series M, No. 83/Rev.1 (United Nations publication, Sales No. E.08.XVII.28), available at http://unstats.un.org/unsd/publication/SeriesM/SeriesM_83rev1e.pdf.

Related statistical products

The World Statistics Pocketbook can also be viewed online in PDF format as well as an app for Android and Apple devices at http://unstats.un.org/unsd/publications/pocketbook/ and in UNdata at http://data.un.org/en/index.html.

Other statistical publications offering a broad cross-section of information which may be of interest to users of the World Statistics Pocketbook include:
1. The Monthly Bulletin of Statistics (MBS) in print and the Monthly Bulletin of Statistics Online, available at http://unstats.un.org/unsd/mbs/.
2. The Statistical Yearbook (SYB) in print and online in PDF format, available at http://unstats.un.org/unsd/publications/statistical-yearbook/.

Both publications are available for sale in print format (see below for instructions on how to order). For more information about other publications and online databases prepared by the United Nations Statistics Division, please visit: https://unstats.un.org/unsd/publications/. For additional information about the work of the United Nations Statistics Division, please visit http://unstats.un.org/unsd. To order United Nations publications, please visit https://shop.un.org or contact:

United Nations Publications
300 East 42nd Street
New York, NY 10017
Tel: 1-888-254-4286 / Fax: 1-800-338-4550 / E-mail: publications@un.org

Please provide the Development Data Section – which is responsible for producing the World Statistics Pocketbook, the Monthly Bulletin of Statistics and the Statistical Yearbook – your feedback and suggestions regarding these statistical products, as well as the utility of the data, by contacting statistics@un.org.